DATE DUE

PRINTED IN U.S.A.

THE COMPLETE BOOK
OF EDIBLE LANDSCAPING

Sierra Club Books, San Francisco

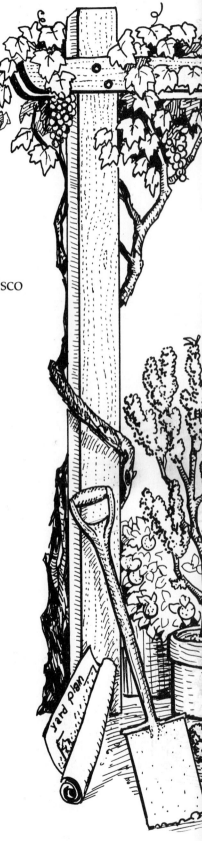

ROSALIND CREASY

THE COMPLETE BOOK OF EDIBLE LANDSCAPING

Illustrations by Marcia Kier-Hawthorne

83234

The Sierra Club, founded in 1892 by John Muir, has devoted itself to the study and protection of the earth's scenic and ecological resources—mountains, wetlands, woodlands, wild shores and rivers, deserts and plains. The publishing program of the Sierra Club offers books to the public as a nonprofit educational service in the hope that they may enlarge the public's understanding of the Club's basic concerns. The point of view expressed in each book, however, does not necessarily represent that of the Club. The Sierra Club has some fifty chapters coast to coast, in Canada, Hawaii, and Alaska. For information about how you may participate in its programs to preserve wilderness and the quality of life, please address inquiries to Sierra Club, 530 Bush Street, San Francisco, CA 94108.

Library of Congress Cataloging in Publication Data

Creasy, Rosalind.
  The complete book of edible landscaping.

  Bibliography: p. 365
  Includes index.
  1. Landscape gardening. 2. Plants, Edible.
3. Organic gardening. 4. Vegetable gardening.
5. Fruit-culture. I. Title.
SB473.C73   635   81-14465
ISBN 0-87156-249-9   AACR2
ISBN 0-87156-278-2 (pbk.)

All photographs not otherwise credited are by the author.

Cover design by Bill Wells
Book design by Anita Walker Scott
Layout by Donna Davis
Printed in the United States of America
10 9 8 7 6 5 4 3 2

To my father,
who gave me my first vegetable garden.

To my mother,
who never doubted that I could, and would, write this book.

CONTENTS

ACKNOWLEDGMENTS

THIS BOOK was five years in preparation, and a great many people had a share in bringing it into being. Bear with me, for I wish to acknowledge as many of their contributions as possible.

Much of the credit for making me aware of the need for such a book goes to the participants in my classes and lecture groups on landscaping with edibles, who responded enthusiastically to my ideas and complained about the lack of comprehensive source material on these unfamiliar plants and changing horticultural practices. With my mother, Alice Reeves, who on hearing these reactions suggested that I write a book, rests the credit for my taking the plunge into unfamiliar territory. Her contribution has been immense. A professional writer herself, she showed me how my ideas could be set down by the simple expedient of her typing as I talked. In addition to helping with the early chapters, she worked on the preliminary outline for the book and made a good start on the encyclopedia. And her support and encouragement through the difficult times have been unfailing.

The writing was not easy for me, and I needed help. Early in the project two friends, Donna Breed and Ann Clifton, assisted me in organizing the material and beginning to put it together. Sheldon Edelman and Jamie Jobb helped me contact a publisher, and James W. Wilson, executive director of the National Garden Bureau, gave pertinent advice on publishing. William Olkowski of the University of California at Berkeley encouraged my efforts and shared his knowledge of integrated pest management. A triumvirate of teachers from Foothill College, Charles Konigsberg, William Patterson, and Robert Will, were very helpful. They shared their considerable knowledge with me and played devil's advocate, honing my intelligence and preparing me for future questions.

Ken Arutunian of Arutunian, Kinney Associates in Palo Alto was generous in providing me with excellent standards for architectural design. Klaus Hertzer, a friend and colleague from Modern Landscaping of San Jose, California, shared his design and construction knowledge. Robert Kourik of the Farallones Institute of Berkeley, who is actually working at what this book is all about, and Craig Dremann, a seedsman who has researched many of the edible plants mentioned in this book, have both been most helpful in sharing their experience.

Throughout the course of the project it seemed that whenever I had a particular need, a person or persons with the particular talent appeared. I was very fortunate in finding Marcia Kier-Hawthorne, a botanical illustrator who could draw anything I asked for, from Grandma's kitchen garden to a sophisticated water garden of water chestnuts and lotus. Marcie gave of herself in many ways and has become a valued friend, as has her husband Daniel, who lent enthusiastic and continuing support. At around the same time I found Maggie Gage, a garden writer possessing strong environmental convictions, a good knowledge of plant materials, and a light touch in her prose that are in evidence throughout the text. Maggie was my mainstay. Day after day she produced fine copy from rough data, augmented my research, and gave me constant support. I am most appreciative of her many hours of rewriting and editing.

A number of special people shared their technical expertise along the way. Richard Turner's knowledge of landscape design was invaluable. Nate Gage helped tighten the prose and shared his extensive publishing experience. Garden writer Walter Doty shared his extensive knowledge and resources. Nancy Garrison, Santa Clara County Farm Advisor, gave me hours of her time. Robert Woolley of Dave Wilson's Nursery freely gave of his expert knowledge about the major fruit trees. Robert Raabe contributed to the plant disease section. Landscape designer Karla Patterson did some of the groundwork on the architectural drawings, and draftsman Raymond Ten rendered the drawings in ink. Timmie Gallagher's background in botany was put to the test in verifying the botanical names and facts in the encyclopedia. Dave Smith and Paul Hawken, specialists in hand tools, contributed their expertise. Ruth Troetschler, a biologist working in the field of basic and applied research in arthropod control, provided extensive input to the pest control section of Chapter 7. Larry Breed shared his love of the English language and devoted many hours to copyediting and proofreading.

Specialists in many fields from all over the country who took time from their busy schedules to help me include David Burmaster, formerly of the President's Council on Environmental Quality; Jeff Cox of *Organic Gardening* magazine; Marie Giasi of the Brooklyn Botanical Garden; Richard Goodwin and William Niering of Connecticut College; and Charles Gould of the Maine Extension Service.

The following nursery and seed people gave valuable help: Ed Carman, Los Gatos, California; Al Cieslak, Los Altos, California; Corwin Davis, Bellevue, Michigan; Henry Leuthart, East Moriches, New York; Louis Lipofsky, Brunswick, Maine; Frank Reid, Ft. Lauderdale, Florida; John Stephenson, San Jose, California; as well as representatives of the Burpee Seed Company, Park Seed Company, Tsang and Ma International, and the Vermont Hardy Bean Seed Company.

Plant lovers, as a group, are generous with their experience. I am particularly grateful to the following for their contributions: John Riley and Joe and Katherine Massidda of the California Rare Fruit Growers; Paul Jackson of the International Association for Education, Development, and Distribution of Lesser-Known Food Plants and Trees; Penney Logeman of the New England Wildflower Society; and herb specialist Adelma Simmons of Coventry, Connecticut; other members of the California Rare Fruit Growers Association and the Home Orchard Society; and my students and clients.

Working with the staff and freelance personnel of Sierra Club Books has been a pleasure. In addition to contributing their competence and conscientious attention to detail and quality, they have been enthusiastic, supportive, and cooperative. Special thanks go to copy editor Suzanne Lipsett, who so beautifully refined the prose; to designer Anita Walker Scott, who gave the book its visual style; to production director Eileen Max and the entire production staff, who demanded consistently high quality; and to my editor, Diana Landau, for her organizational ability and overall vision of the book's potential. Gene Coan, a neighbor and member of the Club's conservation staff, was a most obliging and uncomplaining courier.

Many friends and relatives have helped immeasurably in a variety of ways. They opened their gardens and kitchens to me, took me to visit local nurseries in many parts of the country, collected materials and researched information locally, and generally provided whatever support or help I needed. They include John and Joan Creasy, Nancy and Richard Olds, David and Jennifer Reeves, Gail and John Gallagher, Jeannette and Philip Valence, Ruth and Richard White, Don Hatfield, and Paul and Carolyn Kuckein. My neighbors Arvind and Bhadra Fancy offered support on almost a daily basis.

I have had two of the most dedicated typists any author could want. Margaret Creasy not only typed for hours at a time but took special initiatives such as checking my outrageous spelling; sharing her gardening experience; and organizing, arranging, and alphabetizing. My neighbor and friend Alberta Lee has been willing to stay up late and get up early to meet deadlines. My dearest thanks to them both.

Jane McKendall rates a paragraph to herself. A dear and long-time friend as well as my business partner and helpmate, she is a great holder of the nervous hand. She also provided factual information and writing and organizational assistance. The book would have been less without her.

Perhaps the people who deserve the most gratitude are my husband, Robert, and my two children, Bob and Laura. They have enthusiastically provided financial and emotional support and have tolerated the less-than-full attention of their spouse and mother for many months. I love, appreciate, and thank them.

Welcome to the Edible Landscape

IF JOHNNY APPLESEED were to visit present-day suburbia, he would weep. In most yards he would be likely to find not a fruit-laden apple tree, but a flowering crabapple, cherry, plum, or peach tree—none bearing fruit. Fifty years ago, he would have had more luck. Our grandmothers usually kept a fruiting apple, cherry, or peach tree in their front yards, and grew vegetables and herbs near the kitchen door. The trees not only were beautiful at blossom time, but they provided fruits to be eaten fresh and preserved for the months ahead. Some of the vegetables, too, provided pleasure to the eye as well as provender for the pantry. But Grandma's main interest was food. Beauty in a producing plant was a bonus, not a requirement.

Somewhere between Grandma's era and the present we have developed an "edible complex," that is, a resistance to including edible plants in our landscaping plans. A number of factors brought about this attitude. One of the most important was the massive shift in population from rural areas to urban centers and suburbs that began early in this century and accelerated dramatically after World War II. This trend was paralleled by the development of an efficient agricultural community, which produced inexpensive

foods we would have had to work hard to grow ourselves. A rapidly developing technology, a long period in which oil was cheap and readily available, and vast expanses of fertile land all combined to make the United States the number one food-producing nation in the world. Agribusiness became so efficient that currently 5 percent of our people can produce all the food we need. In that context, what difference could a backyard apple tree possibly make?

Despite the old saying that "you can take the person out of the country, but you can't take the country out of the person," the whole nation seemed to agree that we were well rid of the need to grow our own food. But even if we had wanted to grow some edibles—just for fun, perhaps—other developments constrained us. For example, as suburbs and subdivisions multiplied, individual families found themselves with less land and fewer opportunities to express their personal tastes through landscaping. Developers often dictated the landscaping tone for whole neighborhoods by cutting down trees and putting in lawns; "neighbor pressure" further contributed to conformity.

The impulse toward uniformity fit in well with the principles of landscaping we inherited, mainly from the formal

1

tradition perfected in seventeenth- and eighteenth-century Europe. This style, developed for the leisure class, concerned itself almost exclusively with ornamental plants. It was expressed in manicured lawns, shaped shrubbery, and flowering ornamentals. Later, in middle- and upper-class suburbs, where yards were assumed to have no function other than a recreational or aesthetic one, food-bearing plants were relegated to the inconspicuous hobby garden. A suburbanite or city dweller with a yen for dirt daubing usually wound up trying to develop more floriferous fuchsias or lusher lawns.

The result of these combined influences was a conventional style of American home landscaping that stressed large, pristine, and manicured lawns; formally trimmed ornamental shrubs and trees; and the decorative use of flowering annuals and perennials. The function of landscaping was seen as cosmetic, period! "Messlessness" became a primary objective. For example, the fruitless mulberry came into favor because, although mulberries were tasty, they were messy, and unless harvested regularly accumulated on the lawn. We even asked propagators to sacrifice fruits for the sake of bigger flowers. In response they made available numerous varieties of nonfruiting cherries, almonds, apples, plums, pears, and peaches, and even a nonproducing carob and olive.

But, you might ask, why tilt at this particular windmill? Those fruitless trees are not hurting anyone, lawns do set off our homes nicely, and flowers are among life's greatest pleasures. Will this book take a stand against beauty? Will it advocate that we spend all our free time "putting up" or drying peaches? To these questions, I reply that as a gardener I enjoy flowers and all growing things, as a landscape designer I am a seeker after beauty, and as a homemaker I do not need any more chores. Still, the fact that most Americans are totally dependent on commercial agriculture for their food supply concerns me greatly. I consider the average citizen's lack of involvement with the land, our most basic source of sustenance, to be one of the most destructive results of the escalating complexity and specialization of our society. Among my other concerns are skyrocketing food prices and the possible health hazards associated with the increasing number of chemicals used in commercial food production. Finally, I am alarmed at the waste of natural resources our present practices generate. In a world where fertile soil is an endangered resource, millions of acres of our nation's best agricultural soil are covered with ornamental shrubs and lawns. Soil can be brought into production for agriculture only at great economic and environmental cost. Why do we allow so much of what we have to remain unproductive? Furthermore, the water we use to irrigate our purely decorative landscape is finite, and the fossil fuels we use in maintaining them are nonrenewable. We are becoming aware that our wasteful ways may be having irreversible consequences.

Oil deserves special mention in this context. Few people need to be told that petroleum use is problematical in this day and age. For many, the energy shortage of 1974-75 was a dramatic warning that our extravagant use of petroleum products must be curbed. However, the pervasive use of petroleum in home landscaping is far less obvious to most people than a crisis at the gas pump. While we are aware of its use when filling the power mower's gas tank, it is not immediately apparent that many fertilizers are made from natural gas, and that the great majority of pesticides and herbicides are petroleum-based products. Power equipment—mowers, edgers, blowers and the like—not only use petroleum for fuel, their manufacture also utilizes great quantities of energy. The '74 crunch was the turning point for me. It made me suddenly aware of what keeping my lawn green and luxuriant cost in energy alone: the heavy fertilizing to keep the grass green; the fungicides, herbicides, and insecticides to keep it healthy and uniform; and the power equipment to keep it trim all represented prodigal use of a dwindling resource. Thus, for me, growing food at home became one aspect of a greater goal: making our landscaping practices more environmentally sound.

As a result of these concerns, for the better part of the last decade my work as a professional landscaping designer and teacher and my own home-gardening efforts have been aimed at finding ways to revise standard landscaping practices to meet certain primary goals. These are: to provide delicious, healthful food for the table; to curtail practices that waste water, soil, and energy; and—most important, since it provides incentive for the rest—to create beautiful, well-planned landscapes with the use of edible plants.

This book grew out of my experience in researching, developing, and practicing methods of realizing these goals. I have learned—despite resistance to the idea from some landscaping professionals and nursery personnel who still suffer from the "edible complex"—that it is possible to plan a yard that is both productive *and* beautiful. Not all food-bearing plants have been hybridized to serve commercial interests in facilitating harvesting, packing, storing, and transporting. Home growers can produce foods that are tastier, fresher, and less altered than commercially grown foods, and can preserve more of their vitamin content. Furthermore, home growers can choose to keep their land unpolluted, uncontaminated, and healthy.

Many people are already aware of the practical benefits of growing edibles, but it seemed to me that developing and promoting their decorative value was essential in order to bring them back into favor in landscaping. I don't want to leave the impression that you trade off on appearance for taste in shifting from pure ornamentals to edible ornamentals. Nor is it merely the fruits that are decorative; the flowers, the leaves, the very shape of many edible plants please the eye long before the fruits appear. In most cases the fruits or vegetables are a bonus to a plant's contribution to the garden's appearance or to the plan of a yard in general. For example, in the course of this book I will recommend specific fruiting varieties of plum, pear, peach, and apple trees that are particularly beautiful in bloom and provide sweet, juicy, sun-ripened fruit. I'll talk of combining flowers and selected vegetables in perennial borders; substituting edible, ornamental shrubs for barren ornamentals in foundation plantings; and using handsome nut trees for shade. In every case, both the landscaping and culinary uses of a plant are considered.

I cannot overemphasize the potential for beauty that landscaping with edibles holds, since many people still have difficulty accepting this notion. I came to understand this potential by experimenting in my own yard, in the process relearning the joys of eating fresh-picked peas, vine-ripened tomatoes, and sun-warmed apricots. I purchased dozens of different varieties of vegetables to plant in my food garden but also to interplant in my flower garden. Red cabbage with its colorful foliage, string beans with purple flowers, the many varieties of lettuce with their interesting leaf patterns, artichokes with their gray-green, fernlike foliage and magnificent blue thistles, and the heavenly purple globes of the eggplant were extremely effective in my standard flower bed. Since my first tentative experiments, I have developed and thoroughly researched a list of ornamental edible plants that can be grown in different areas of the United States. The plants selected range from the exotic water chestnut to the familiar apple. I have also discovered some unusually attractive varieties—string beans with large, showy, white flowers; bush cucumbers with compact vines; peaches with showy, pink, double blossoms; and plum trees with delicious fruit and red foliage. I found that some standard food-growing practices—for example, staking bean vines with an odd assortment of poles or "caging" tomatoes—could be replaced by less intrusive, more aesthetically pleasing techniques. I found, too, that some edible plants were hard to manage in a landscape situation. These have not been included in my list of ornamental edibles, which constitutes the encyclopedia section of this book.

A word now on how this book is organized. The first chapter makes a case for the personal benefits of landscaping with edible plants, suggesting ways in which it can have a positive effect on your family's food supply, eating pleasure, and household budget. Chapter 2 focuses on environmental concerns, with particular attention to agricultural chemicals. This chapter will also encourage you, I hope, to question the wisdom of allowing these substances to be used in commercial farming with the abandon that currently characterizes their use. Finally, these introductory chapters explain why the produce you grow will be tastier, more healthful, and cheaper than that available in the market.

Chapter 3 describes the basic functions and aesthetic principles of landscaping and offers a brief historical survey of this ancient art. In this context, I propose a new approach that eliminates some standard landscaping procedures and reintroduces many beautiful and utilitarian techniques of the past—an approach I'll call "landscaping for the twenty-first century."

Chapter 4 details the physical considerations—the nuts and bolts—that must be accounted for in your landscaping plans. Here you will learn how to block out your plans on paper before beginning and to incorporate such environmentally sound principles as climate control, and water, soil and energy conservation. Concluding sections describe the variety of living and structural elements used in landscaping.

Chapter 5 shows you how to combine the elements and techniques of landscaping to meet your particular needs. Here we'll see how to choose an effective design, how to adapt versatile landscaping styles to the use of edibles; and we'll see a variety of design options for different parts of the yard: entryways, sideyards, backyards, patios, and so on. The illustrations and architectural plans in this chapter should help you visualize some of these options.

For those with little space but lots of heart for gardening, Chapter 6 covers container growing and other small-garden techniques for raising edibles.

Though some yards take less work than others, no residential landscape is completely maintenance free, and many of the popular edible plants require considerable amounts of care. Chapter 7 provides the specific information you need to get your plantings off to a good start and to keep them in good shape. This chapter also discusses composting and pruning as well as environmentally healthful methods of watering, fertilizing, and pest control.

As noted earlier, Part Two of the text is an encyclopedia describing nearly 140 edible ornamental plants. Each entry describes a plant or related group of plants; identifies the zones in which it will grow; assesses the effort required to grow the plant; describes its uses both in the kitchen and in the landscape; and provides relevant information on growing, purchasing, and preserving.

Part Three, Resources and References, contains several appendices. The first is a list of 225 edible plants, many of which are not covered in the encyclopedia but which might be used in a yard; basic information about each plant is given in table form. Appendix B includes an annotated list of 75 nurseries from which the plants can be obtained, as well as sources of nonplant supplies such as hand tools. Appendix C lists sources of information: organizations, periodicals, and the like. Following the appendices are a glossary and an annotated bibliography.

This book cannot pretend to be the final word, the alpha and omega of gardening books. You won't learn basic botany here, or how to install a sprinkler system, or how to lay brick. Rather, it is intended to convey one person's vision of how we can use our land constructively for our own benefit and for the good of the planet generally. It is designed to give readers a comprehensive picture of what is possible. For guidance in solving specific problems, consult the sources listed in the bibliography. Three books that I particularly recommend to supplement the information in this book are *The Why and How of Home Horticulture* by Darrel Bienz; *Practical Guide to Home Landscaping* by the editors of

Reader's Digest; and, for gardeners in the West, Sunset's *New Western Garden Book.* I have used all the books listed in the bibliography and have found them helpful in different ways.

If you follow the landscaping guidelines in this book and search out supplemental information in solving individual problems, you will begin to feel the satisfaction of assuming responsibility for at least that portion of the environment that is solely under your control. In addition you will enjoy marvelous eating, give a boost to your budget, and have a beautiful yard. If only one out of every ten United States citizens planted just two fruiting trees, the world would be richer by nearly 6 billion pounds of fruit!* Nowhere is it written: Thou shalt landscape only with barren ornamentals. So—welcome to the edible landscape!

*By a conservative estimate, two mature, standard fruit trees—one apple and one pear—could produce 250 pounds of fruit a year. Multiplied by 23 million people (one-tenth the population of the United States), these trees would produce 5.75 billion pounds of fruits.

PART ONE

FOODSCAPING AND HOW TO DO IT

CHAPTER 1

The Joy of Edibles

THE REWARDS of landscaping with edible ornamentals are myriad. To me, however, three take precedence over the rest: producing healthful, flavorful food; the distinct financial benefit of growing your own food in this era of sky-rocketing prices; and the personal satisfaction you can derive from creating a yard that is both productive and beautiful.

The first two rewards are easy to grasp, but the third is best appreciated in relative terms. Compare the thankless job of digging dandelions out of the lawn with the work of picking blueberries for dessert. Imagine yourself cleaning up the inedible berries, seeds, and leaves under a Texas privet tree when you could be cleaning up under an almond tree and collecting the nuts for food. Or consider the satisfaction you could derive from contemplating both a nasturtium and a cucumber vine climbing up the same sunny fence. Think, too, of the admiration a handsome eggplant bush might elicit from your visitors. Every part of this plant is eye-pleasing, and if the product is not one of your favorites you will still have the pleasure of giving the handsome purple fruits to an eggplant aficionado. Finally, give thought to the simple satisfaction of bartering—for example, trading your extra stringbeans for some of your neighbor's plums.

Now think of the more palpable advantages. Compare to store-bought products some homegrown peaches, so full of juice that it runs down your chin. Or compare apples from the market with those from the sunny side of the tree, where fruits ripen extra sweetly. Taste first a commercially grown strawberry and then an Alpine strawberry, which tastes like a strawberry with the volume turned up. The result is irrefutable: most homegrown produce is tastier. The chief reason is that home growers can pick their produce at its prime whereas commercial growers usually pick the food unripe, since it often faces a long trip to market. Furthermore, many commercial varieties have been hybridized to tolerate mechanical picking. They have been bred for a high cellulose content, since this quality keeps them unbruised during picking, storing, and transporting. In contrast, the homegrown product can be chosen for different criteria—its juices, its texture, and its flavor.

The financial benefits of home growing are the simplest of all to state. An apple tree on your property can be made to pay for itself in fruits in its first year of full production.

1.1. Sun-warmed fruit straight from the tree is one of life's great pleasures.

Thereafter for many years, whatever fruits it produces will represent a profit. What else do you need to know?

Finally, there is the health benefit. I feel strongly that the apples you grow will be better for you than commercial ones, not only because they will be fresher and riper, with their nutrients intact, but also because they will be free of the numerous questionable chemicals currently being applied to commercially grown produce. It is this area of health and safety, fraught with complex commercial considerations and moral dilemmas, that I'll examine first.

Food Without Chemicals

The consumer movement has worked hard and long to achieve truth in labeling on cereals, cookies, and canned goods. Few consumers know, however, that if fresh vegetables and fruits were labeled, in some cases the lists of chemical additives would be longer than those on most so-called "junk foods." Most of us are aware that small amounts of pesticides and fungicides are applied to our produce but have little awareness of the true number of chemicals used routinely. Nor do most of us know that some chemical pesticides travel through the soil into the plants we eat, or that many of these substances are contaminating our water supply.

We Americans seem to want our apples to be the reddest, the biggest, and the cheapest in the world. We like blemish-free oranges with a bright orange color and seedless grapes the size of baby carrots. We also demand that a large variety of produce be available at any one time. Gone are the days when root vegetables, cabbage slaw, and home-canned fruit made up our winter fare. Now we expect varied and beautiful produce the year round. We seem willing to buy asparagus in January despite a price that could serve as a down payment on a baby's shoes, and yet at the same time we want our food to be inexpensive. Few people are aware, however, that the pristine, convenient, and inexpensive produce we have come to value is usually achieved by the use of many different agricultural chemicals.

In addition to the insecticides, fungicides, miticides, and herbicides commonly used on most kinds of fruits, for example, other chemicals known as plant growth regulators are often used. (See the accompanying sidebar.) To lessen the weight on the branches, to prevent alternate-year bearing, and to create those tremendous apples we are accustomed to finding in the market, growers spray their trees with a thinning chemical, such as Sevin, which causes fruit drop. The process is analogous to disbudding a camellia or a chrysanthemum to encourage the growth of show-size flowers. Fruit trees usually produce five to ten fruits per branch. If you remove, by spraying or by hand, all but two or three fruits, the remaining ones will grow much larger than they would have otherwise.

To get those big seedless grapes, to accelerate artichoke bud development, and to force early rhubarb shoots, growers spray with gibberelic acid, a commonly used plant hormone. To promote ripening of tomatoes and bananas, and to hasten hull splitting and nut drop in walnuts, they are

1.2 *If produce had to be labeled, the list of "ingredients" in some cases would be longer than on many processed foods.*

How Safe Are Pesticides?

The safety of a number of pesticides has come under consistent attack in the last few years. Much is being questioned and much has yet to be documented, but present evidence suggests that some of these chemicals are not as safe as once thought. Many of the chemicals being examined are commonly used on food crops. The following is a sampling of headlines and summaries from articles concerning pesticide safety.

"Chemicals Used on Raisins Worries EPA"

Captan, a commonly used fungicide, is being studied as a possible carcinogen by the Environmental Protection Agency. (Associated Press, February 1978)

"Pesticidal Produce"

A lawsuit questioning California Department of Food and Agriculture's criteria to set tolerance levels for pesticide residues was filed. An example used in the suit: 7½ ounces of avocado is all a person could eat in one year without exceeding chemical residue levels recommended by the government. (Levels of pesticide residues allowed in California agriculture affect people in all parts of the country, because California grows such a large proportion of the country's vegetables and fruits.) (*San Jose Mercury*, February 1980)

"Potentially Lethal Chemical Still Found on Shelves"

Dioxin, a lethal poisonous byproduct of many herbicides and pesticides, is still being found in products on shelves, even though the federal government knew it was a proven carcinogen in 1966. (*San Jose Mercury*, reprinted from *Newsday*, August 1979)

"Cancer Risk Studied"

The National Cancer Institute reported toxaphene, the largest-selling pesticide in the world, has caused liver cancer in mice. Over 100 million pounds of this pesticide were produced in 1976. (*New York Times*, May 1979)

sprayed with Ethephon. Another hormone, succinic acid hydrazide, is sprayed on peaches to extend storage life and to create those lovely rosy cheeks. 2, 4-D, notorious for its use as a defoliant in Vietnam, is used in smaller doses to prevent fruit drop and to increase the storage life of some citrus. Still another chemical, maleic hydrazide, is used to keep potatoes and onions from sprouting while in storage. It should be obvious that most of these agricultural chemicals, as well as a number of other herbicides and pesticides, cannot be washed or peeled off your produce. They are absorbed into the plants, and minute percentages are usually present in the fruits and vegetables.

The Problem of Testing

The law of averages suggests that some of the chemicals we ingest can be harmful. But on a more empirical level, many questions have been raised about the testing procedures employed on agricultural chemicals and the government regulations intended to control toxicity levels.

Testing chemicals for possible effects that might show up twenty years in the future is hard enough. But testing the effects of all available chemicals in all their possible combinations, to determine whether they are harmful together, is downright impossible. How could one ever determine the hazard of one growth regulator sprayed on an apple in combination with a particular pesticide and herbicide, *plus* the medication for high blood pressure in the body of someone, somewhere, who eats the apple for breakfast? There are too many variables; comprehensive testing is impossible.

Furthermore, some of the existing laws that set allowable levels of pesticides are absurd. For example, in some cases the federal government determines tolerance levels—that is, the amount of pesticide residue deemed acceptable by law—by dividing, say, the number of black-eyed peas eaten in the United States by the total population. That makes as much sense as dividing the combined weight of everyone in the United States by the total number of people and then making all blue jeans to fit the average size. If 7½ ounces of black-eyed peas annually is the amount deemed safe by the government, what happens to the person who eats them once a week?

I am not a doom predicter. I am willing to grant the probability that most of the chemicals used in commercial food production are harmless. But I think that the fewer of those chemicals I ingest the better off I will be. In the past, there have been cases of panaceas turning into tragedies, so let us act as if an *internal* environmental impact report had to be on file, at least when it comes to food from our own yards.* Let us learn to enjoy the tastier and cheaper, sometimes less perfect, produce from our own yards, and demand that the chemicals we are asked to consume on market produce be tested as fully as possible and the results interpreted with logic and common sense.

*The effects of chemicals on the external environment are covered in Chapter 2.

Growth Regulators

Plant growth regulators are naturally occuring or synthetically manufactured organic compounds that promote, inhibit, or alter physiological processes.

These chemicals can influence the growth of trees, shrubs, or herbaceous plants in many ways. Apples are one of the fruits most heavily treated with growth regulators; the following is a list of those which growers are legally permitted to use on apples, and their desired consequences.*

SADH (Succinic acid) 2,2-dimethyl hydrazide—influences flowering, increases fruit firmness, intensifies red color, lengthens storage life.

DNOC (Elgetol), 4,6-dinitro-o-cresol—promotes fruit thinning.

Ethephon, 2-chloroethyl phosphonic acid—promotes flowering on young trees, loosening of fruit, uniform ripening, and intensifying of color in red varieties.

NAA (Vitamin B-1), a-Naphthaleneacetic acid—promotes fruit thinning; prevents premature fruit drop.

2,4-D, 2,4-Dichlorophenoxyacetic acid—prevents premature fruit drop.

NAD, Naphthalenacetamide—promotes fruit thinning.

Sevin (Carbaryl), 1-Naphthyl Methylcarbamate—promotes fruit thinning.

TIBA, Triiodobenzoic acid—promotes branching and widening of branch angles; initiates flower bud formation on non-bearing trees.

GA_{47}, Gibberellin A_4/A_7—aids fruit set without fertilization in some apple cultivars; alters fruit shape.

NPA, Naphthylphthalamic acid—promotes post-bloom fruit thinning.

The Money Motive

In 1980, Gardens for All, a nonprofit gardening association, commissioned a Gallup survey to determine how much food could be produced by a home grower who made a $19-dollar annual investment and had 620 square

*Information in this section was derived from *Plant Growth Regulators— Study Guide for Agriculture Pest Control Advisors*, publication no. 4047 (Berkeley: Division of Agricultural Sciences, University of California, 1978).

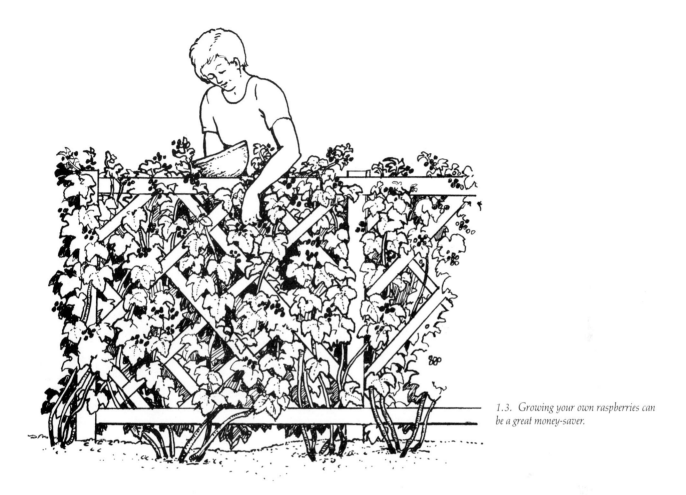

1.3. Growing your own raspberries can be a great money-saver.

feet of garden area available. On the average, gardeners in the survey estimated that they produced $460 worth of vegetables. Clearly, with food prices up 70 percent in the last ten years, the home vegetable garden is a sound investment. To estimate how much money you personally could save by growing some of your family's food, start by determining how much money you spend on food annually. Then compute how much time you can devote to gardening, how much space you have for growing, and how much money you'll spend on water and auxiliary costs such as soil amendments and fertilizers. Be aware that buying fancy gardening gadgets will eat into your potential savings considerably. Let's consider each factor separately.

How Much Time Do You Have?

Consider realistically the amount of time you have for gardening before deciding what to plant (and check the Effort Scale for each plant listed in the encyclopedia). Some crops need continuous care and others do not. Some plants need watering and intermittent care throughout the growing season; others require large blocks of time at harvest. For instance, peaches, apricots, berries (except blueberries), and figs just won't wait. They spoil in a few days once they

are ready for harvesting. If you are unable to make time for them, all your savings can rot away.

How Much Space Do You Have?

To maximize savings you must use the space you have creatively. Consider landscaping your front yard with food crops, for example, by substituting ornamental edible fruit trees for strictly ornamental varieties. Or consider planting artichokes instead of junipers. And stretch your planting area by starting vegetables such as lettuce, spinach, and scallions in flats and then interplanting them in a flower border.

Will You Preserve Your Produce?

You'll make a large savings if you can preserve the surplus from your garden for later use. But remember that the apparatus for preserving—canning jars and lids, a freezer, a good dryer or drying screens—requires an initial investment. And those beautiful jars of golden apricots need storage space. Also, running a freezer can exact a considerable amount in energy costs. These factors, plus the time required for preparing foods for preserving, could counteract the financial benefit of preserving. Again, compute the trade-offs before making the investment.

1.4. *Dried fruit is expensive to buy, but drying your own apricots is easy.*

Drying your food is by far the most economical means of preserving it. Purchasing or building a drying closet will pay for itself in a year. For information on how to dry fruits see APRICOT in the encyclopedia.

It is possible to minimize the initial investment you make on preserving. For example, save on jelly jars by collecting any suitable jars during the winter. (Narrow-mouth jars are not very satisfactory because they are hard to fill and the wax is often hard to remove.) Mason jars work well in the freezer, as do other glass jars, since freezer jars do not have to withstand the high temperatures and pressures of the canning process. Save used lids and those that failed to seal during canning and use them for freezer jar lids; used canning lids work well, as long as they aren't bent and have no holes in them. *Do not try to reuse lids for canning* unless they are designated as reusable.

Contrary to a certain folk myth, canning without sugar is safe. However, unsweetened products should be used within a few months, since their flavor fades quickly, but the lack of sugar does not make the food spoil faster. When you do can with sugar, use as little as possible. Light syrup is 3:1 (3 parts water to 1 part sugar), but 4:1 syrup is fine for most fruits. Also, you can freeze without sugar without risking a deterioration of flavor or quality. See the bibliography for references about preserving.

Will You Compost?

Once your garden is established, soil amendments such as manure, compost, peat moss, and fertilizers remain high-cost items—if you must purchase them. But by composting garden clippings and kitchen scraps, and thus essentially creating your own soil enrichers, you can reduce these costs substantially. (Other advantages to composting, particularly those relating to resource conservation and environmen-

tal protection, are covered in later chapters.) Sometimes nongardening neighbors can be persuaded to donate lawn clippings for your compost or shredded leaves for use as a mulch. (Mulch is any organic material spread on the ground around plants to prevent evaporation, the freezing of roots, and the growth of weeds.) In such cases make sure the material you are given is free of herbicides and pesticides. Also, if you live near a farm or stable, you can often pick up manure and used straw for free or for a nominal charge to use as soil amendments and mulch. Manure should be aged in hot compost piles (see Chapter 7) before use to ensure that weed seeds are killed. Finally, some municipalities compost leaves and prunings and make the organic matter available to citizens.

What Will Your Water Costs Be?

In many parts of the country, water represents one of the largest expenses in gardening, and water-conservation practices can save money. These practices include planting drought-resistant shrubs and trees; planting a winter vegetable garden in areas with arid summers; employing drip irrigation where necessary; measuring the depth of water penetration in your soil so you can avoid overwatering; avoiding overhead watering while the wind is blowing; and mulching in hot weather to minimize evaporation. (See Chapters 4 and 7 for further information on water conservation.)

Selecting Plants for Savings

Clearly, you will only save money by gardening if you eat what you grow, so choose heavy-bearing fruits and vegetables that are popular with your family. If your family likes supermarket avocados, you will really save money with a mature tree that yields a few hundred avocados annually. In some cases the money you save may well depend on how many nights in a row you can tolerate the cry, "What, zucchini again?" Does your family enjoy exotic fruits and vegetables such as mulberries and artichokes, or old favorites such as peaches and green beans? A careful assessment of your family's particular eating habits will enable you to plan for maximum consumption. Also, you won't save much if you plant foods that are usually cheap in markets (for example, winter squash).

Most people don't have unlimited space, so plant crops that yield a large amount of produce in proportion to the space they occupy. Homegrown asparagus and corn, for example, are wonderful but take up considerable space while yielding relatively small amounts of food. Likewise, winter squash vines can take over your whole garden and produce only two or three fruits. Economically speaking, you're almost always better off buying such vining squash and preserving it. On the other hand, tomatoes, strawberries, eggplant, peppers, and zucchinis are good producers. Dwarf fruit trees usually are a better choice than standard trees, since they bear more heavily for the space they occupy, and you can prolong the harvest season by planting early- and late-bearing trees.

Choose produce that can be used in a variety of ways in the kitchen. Consult individual entries in the encyclopedia under "In the Kitchen" to determine the versatility of particular species.

The most economical planting method is to start all your annual vegetables from seed, since bedding plants cost more than seeds do. Look for an organic gardening center that sells vegetable seeds in bulk or by the spoonful, which is much cheaper than by the packet and more realistic in terms of the number of seeds one gardener can use. Who needs a hundred tomato plants, after all? If you cannot purchase seed in small quantities locally, one mail-order source, the Pine Tree Seed Company, has a wide selection of vegetable seeds and sells in small quantities. Write for their catalog: P.O. Box 1399, Portland, ME 04104. Also, save some of your own seeds for planting the following year. Learn which plants and varieties can be saved. Avoid hybrids, as they will not usually come true from seed.

See Appendix B, *Sources of Plants and Other Materials,* for more detailed information on obtaining and saving seed.

The Pleasure Factor

Let us remember that, aside from the practical rewards home growing yields, gardening is a creative and satisfying activity. Nothing gives me more pleasure than the feeling of sun on my back and good soil in my hands. And when the garden chiefly consists not of ornamentals but of ornamental *edibles,* the pleasures are multiplied. I get a lift when I pass the grocery store produce department and see the ever-increasing cost of string beans, tomatoes, and artichokes, knowing that at home I have these foods for the picking. I can also have such luxuries as snow peas, asparagus, and sorrel, though I refuse to pay the high prices retailers ask for them. And in addition I produce delicacies that are not sold at all in most supermarkets—for instance, Alpine strawberries, purple string beans, Armenian cucumbers, and fresh herbs.

In the end, growing my own food gives me a real feeling of independence. The economy can go to rack and ruin, but my family will still eat. In this feeling alone my efforts are repaid. But the beauty of my yard gives me endless pleasure as well. Why settle for one or the other when you can have both practical advantages and aesthetic enjoyment? Foodscaping brings you the best of both worlds.

CHAPTER 2

Landscaping for a Small Planet

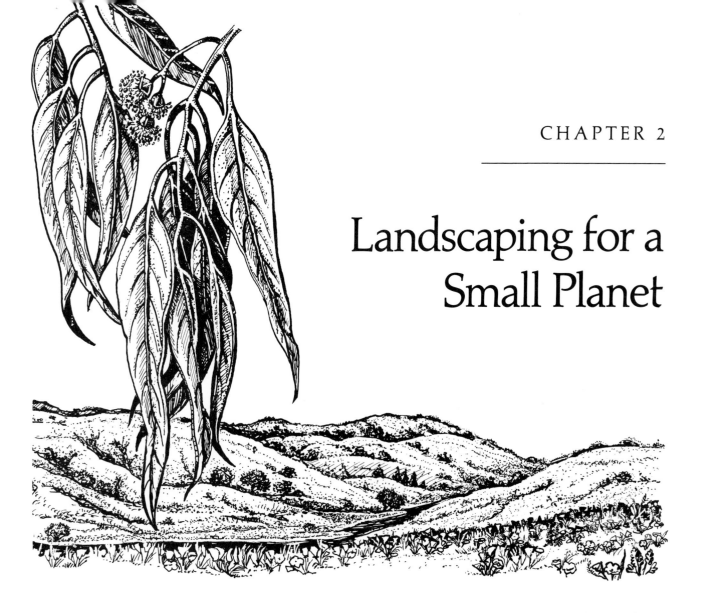

When the West was young, get-rich schemes abounded. One such notion was to import eucalyptus trees from Australia to California for use as building timber. The eucalyptus grew so quickly that you could plant the seeds and return in ten years to harvest the wood and make your million—or so went the sales pitch. But, alas, the entrepreneurs of the eucalyptus found that the wood split much too easily to serve as a good lumber.

In those days no one had to file an environmental impact report. If they had, they might have learned that the eucalyptus scheme would affect more than just a few bank accounts. Eucalyptus leaves hang vertically, instead of horizontally as most leaves do, so when the moisture of fog condenses on the leaves it drips to the ground. Enough eucalyptus trees had been planted in certain sections of the San Francisco Bay area to diminish the fog in those areas and thus deprive neighboring native vegetation of its moisture. Moreover, as we now know, eucalyptus trees are vigorous growers and have crowded out native plants in a number of places. Obviously this has not been the only threat to native vegetation in the region, but the pattern is classic: throughout the United States bountiful natural treasures have been

lost forever because the consequences of how land was used were never considered.

The landscaping profession bears as much responsibility as any other group for the misuse of America's precious resources. Like the car manufacturers of the 1960s, traditionalists in the industry have long stressed style, size, and performance, favoring the biggest redwood deck, the most floriferous fuchsia, and the most neatly trimmed lawn. Until recently, they gave little thought to the facts that virgin forests have been heavily logged to build those impressive decks; petroleum-based fertilizers have been consumed by the ton to produce the multiplicity of flowers; and water, fertilizers, and pesticides have been used in enormous quantities to keep our lawns lush and weed-free. In 1977, it was estimated, 200 million gallons of gasoline were used just for power equipment to mow American lawns.* It has been estimated that we annually use 3 million tons of fertilizer to keep our lawns green—15 percent of the nation's production and as much as India uses in a year for

*William Niering, "Put Your Mower in Mothballs," *Connecticut College Alumni Magazine* 54, no. 2 (1977).

2.1. Most lawns in the U.S. are mowed with power equipment.

food crops.* A disregard for the waste of natural resources characterizes all these practices. The same attitude is reflected in our use of some of the world's best agricultural soil for growing inedible ornamentals.

One of my chief aims in this book is to urge you to consider the environmental consequences of your landscaping practices, and to think of ways of saving water, energy, soil, and native plants, and of controlling pollution, before you make your choices. In this context, it is important to think in collective rather than individual terms; your lawn alone might not consume massive amounts of water, petroleum, and electricity, but 40 million lawns do. Your grass clippings alone won't cause the dump to overflow; your use of diazinon on those mealybugs won't pollute anything but your own space; and a little weed killer on that knotweed is going to stay right there. But vast numbers of us using these pollutants have a significant negative impact on the environment. Furthermore, landscaping strictly with ornamentals wastes more resources of many kinds, including potentially productive soil, than does home food growing. Again, it might not sound like a big deal for one family to

grow two fruit trees, three tomato plants, a patch of strawberries, and a hedge of blueberries—but if you multiply the land they would occupy (about .025 acre) by 20 million households, the result would be a half a million acres of producing soil and a tremendous amount of food. And if each person designing a yard began to incorporate conservation measures, professionals would inevitably respond with more responsible designs and products.

In this chapter I'll attempt to present an overview of environmental problems and concerns in home landscaping in three key areas: water, energy, and soil conservation. In Chapter 4, we'll look at each of these areas again in the context of planning your home landscape, to see how environmental principles can be incorporated at the planning stage. And Chapter 7 provides specifics on using environmentally sound practices in the planting and maintenance of your yard.

Water Conservation

Towing icebergs from Antarctica? Piping water from Alaska? These are but two of the dramatic ideas that have been suggested as to how we can expand our usable water supply. Many experts believe that a water crisis as severe as the energy crisis is inevitable by the end of this century. Such a development would disrupt society in ways as complex and financially interrelated as those caused by the oil shortage. In this country we tend to think of water supply as problematical only in sections of the arid Southwest, but this assumption is no longer correct. Wells in the north central states are going dry from overpumping, swamps in Florida are drying up, and there are conflicts between some New England communities over water sources. Among the more dramatic examples is the once-mighty Colorado River, which is diverted hundreds of times for agricultural and municipal water use, so that it becomes a mere trickle before it even reaches its destination, the Gulf of California. According to *U.S. News and World Report,* "so rapidly are the Americans using water . . . that virtually every section of the country will be confronted with serious shortages of drinking water in the coming decades."*

We have to remember that despite the fact that 70 percent of the earth's surface is water, 97 percent of that total contains salt, making it unusable for drinking or agriculture. Another approximately 2.6 percent lies deep inside the earth or is locked up in icebergs. Thus, only about four-tenths of a percent of the earth's total water is accessible to its growing population.**

Generally, when we think of water use on our property,

*William Niering and Richard H. Goodwin, "Energy Conservation on the Home Grounds," *Connecticut College Bulletin,* 21 (1975).

*"Is U.S. Running out of Water?" *U.S. News and World Report,* 18 July 1977.

**Richard Wenn and Eleanor Young, eds., *Resources for Appropriate Technology in Santa Clara County* (Santa Clara County, Calif.: County Environmental Management Agency, 1978).

we think of the water that comes out of the hose, some of which comes to us via above-ground reservoirs. But another source of fresh water is affected. Beneath most gardens lies a reservoir of groundwater, the upper limit of which is called the water table. Sometimes the water table is only 3 or 4 feet beneath the surface, sometimes a hundred or more feet. If it lies fairly near the surface, this water is accessible to the roots of trees and shrubs. When it lies deep underground we often pump it to the surface. Almost half of our domestic water and 40 percent of our agricultural water is obtained from groundwater.*

Like a bank account, if the underground water reserve is not replenished it disappears. Since the early 1900s the United States has been on a water-spending binge. What nature has stored drop by drop over a million years, we have used in a flood in the last forty to fifty years. And in many parts of the country, according to water scientists, we are mining—that is, taking it from the earth without replacing—water that has been building up since the Pleistocene epoch, more than 2 million years ago.**

The Ogallala Aquifer, an underground lake that provides water for parts of Nebraska and south to the Texas Panhandle, is a dramatic example of our misuse, or overuse, of water. Water from this source has long enabled this region to provide vast quantities of cotton, corn, soybeans, wheat, and sorghum for the rest of the country. But this underground lake has dropped 700 feet in some places since about 1950, and expensive pumping operations are now necessary to maintain the level of productivity expected of the area.***

Even the contours of the land and quality of the water can change as water-table levels drop. When the water gets too low in coastal areas, salt water can seep in to pollute vital fresh water supplies. And often, as this store diminishes, the earth loses some of its ability to hold water, so that restoring the underground reservoir to its original level can become impossible. Finally, losses in this volume can cause subsidence, that is, a sinking of the land. In San Jose, California, for example, some portions of the city have sunk 14 feet or more in the last 60 years.† Such land subsidence can cause damage to buildings and highways.

But how does your yard's landscaping affect the groundwater supply? Before your house was built your yard was probably a forest, a meadow, or a prairie, and considerable amounts of rainfall soaked into the earth instead of running off it. Today much of that rainfall is intercepted by roofs, gutters, and driveways, ending up in the sewer rather than

in the underground reservoir where it is needed. Even lawns can contribute to this problem, since poorly maintained lawns filled with thatch (see Glossary) absorb very little water in a heavy rain, often causing the water to sheet off into the street.

While homeowners are not the nation's primary water consumers—agriculture leads—landscaping often accounts for more than half the water used by a household in the arid parts of this country, and lawns use over half of that. Until recently, no one considered the water used on lawns to be wasted. A lawn, like the "gas guzzler" parked in the driveway, was a standard part of the American householder's dream. But we have begun to understand that growing lush lawns in arid climates is wasteful, as are other habitual practices. We overwater, allowing water to run down the gutters and into the sewers—lots of fun for children playing with leaf-sail boats but not good for conserving a dwindling resource. Also, we may water in the hottest part of the day, when evaporation is most rapid; plant lawns on slopes, where quick runoff is inevitable; and blithely hose down our patios, driveways, and sidewalks. We seem to have been lulled into insensitivity by the fact that traditionally water has been our cheapest household utility.

With some experts predicting local water rationing by the year 2000, we can no longer afford to think of our water supply as infinite. Nor can we consider it instantly and cheaply available, for water costs are necessarily linked to energy costs. The deeper the wells from which water is pumped, the greater the cost in fuel. Transporting water over long distances from water-rich to water-hungry areas, through aqueduct systems that usually must surmount hills, also involves high fuel costs.

Particularly in arid climates, we can reduce profligate water use by planting drought-resistant species. Instead of the hydrangea, which is native to countries that receive 60–100 inches of rain per year and so requires frequent watering in dry-summer areas, it would be more appropriate to plant manzanita, which comes from areas with only 10–30 inches of rainfall and usually needs no watering at all.* Another objective in arid areas should be to make the soil more water-retentive by increasing its organic content and using mulch to conserve the moisture within it. Finally, to get the best return on the water we invest, we can plant food plants rather than strictly ornamental ones.

It should be pointed out that raising food plants is not a conservation measure in itself, since food plants are often water-hungry. The return on the investment in the form of food, not a water savings per se, is the benefit. Within this context, one can choose plants in accordance with their water requirements and try to minimize the use of edibles that are heavy water users. (See individual entries in the en-

*The Tenth Annual Report of the Council on Environmental Quality (Washington, D.C.: U.S. Government Printing Office, 1979).

**Philip Nobile and John Deedy, The Complete Ecology Fact Book (New York: Anchor Press, 1972).

***"Is U.S. Running out of Water?"

†Wenn and Young, Resources for Appropriate Technology.

*Saratoga Horticultural Foundation, Selected California Native Plants with Commercial Sources (Saratoga, Calif.: Saratoga Horticultural Foundation, 1979).

2.2. *Nut trees such as this pecan provide welcome shade in summer as well as a valuable harvest.*

cyclopedia for information on water use.) Basically, good planning is the key to incorporating water-conservation principles into your landscape design.

Energy Conservation

In this country landscaping is usually not only a water-based but a fuel-based enterprise. Most insecticides and herbicides, as well as many fungicides, are made from petroleum; modern sprinkler pipes are made from poly-vinylchloride which is oil based; most lawn fertilizers are made from natural gas and other petroleum-based products; and power mowers, blowers, rototillers, trimmers, aerators, and hedge clippers all use gasoline or electricity. As in other cases of heavy consumption of a failing resource, the necessity for landscaping's dependence on these energy resources is now being called into question.

Our priorities are changing as our awareness of the problems grows. The most effective means of conserving energy in your residential landscape are (1) incorporating protective and cooling vegetation; (2) taking advantage of the principles of solar energy that affect household energy use; (3) educating yourself about hidden ways in which your landscaping practices use energy; and, once again, (4) growing your own food. This section covers these points in some detail, but for a comprehensive treatment of the whole subject of energy conservation and landscaping, I recommend *Landscaping That Saves Energy Dollars*, by Ruth Foster (see Bibliography). This book is a must for those about to build a new house or to start a major landscaping project.

Saving Household Energy

Remember the big shade trees that used to be found to the south and west of farmhouses in the past? Our forebears knew a lot of things we have chosen to forget—for example, that a strategically placed deciduous tree near a house can serve as a natural weather modifier. When such a tree loses its leaves in winter it allows the sun to warm the house; in the summer, having leafed out again, the same tree protects the house against the sun's blistering rays. Thus, if planted on the south or west side of the dwelling, a deciduous tree will save energy and money by helping to warm the house in winter and cool it in the summer. The United States Department of the Interior estimates that a beech tree, which releases 75–100 gallons of water on a summer day (in transpiration from its leaves), has the cooling effect of 10 room-size air conditioners running 20 hours a day.* Researchers in home-temperature control estimate that in most areas air conditioning bills can be cut by 20 percent by strategically placed deciduous trees. Another study, by the American Association of Nurserymen, reports, "On a sunny 80-degree day, shade trees can reduce the inside temperature of a house by as much as 8 degrees."** Well-placed trees that bear fruits or nuts yield an additional bonus.

Our grandparents also knew the value of planting evergreen windbreaks to slow down the winter winds. It has been shown that

it takes twice as much fuel to heat a house at an outside temperature of 32 degrees F with a wind of 12 miles per hour as it does for the same temperature with a wind at 3 miles per hour. So a windbreak of trees [and evergreen shrubs] which can diminish the impact of the winter wind is going to make a substantial difference in the amount of heating energy required. Reliable tests have shown this difference can be greater than 30 percent economy in the amount of heating fuel needed.***

Chapter 4 covers the subjects of how and where windbreaks and weather-conditioning trees should be placed for maximum value, and contains a list of the different plant materials that have proven most successful for this purpose.

Solar Energy

Continuing research on the use of solar energy is showing that this resource—infinite, if properly channeled—can be vitally helpful in our efforts to conserve other energy sources. If you are planning a new home, you are in the best position to incorporate solar principles to maximum advantage. If you are already settled, you can still consider adding a solar collector to supplement your existing system. Again, see the book by Foster cited earlier, as well as *Homeowner's Guide to Solar Heating* by the editors of Sunset Books, and *The Integral Urban House* by the Farallones Institute.

Agricultural Energy Use

To understand the energy-conserving value of growing your own food, you must have a sense of the amounts of fuel used in commercial food production. Fundamentally, food production in America is an oil-based industry. Often,

*American Association of Nurserymen, "Enjoying Cleaner, Filtered Air for Your Outdoor Rooms" (Washington, D.C., 1979).

**American Association of Nurserymen, "Grow Your Own Energy Savers: A Beautiful Investment" (Washington, D.C., 1979).

***American Association of Nurserymen, "Our Grandparents Had an Energy-Saving Secret" (Washington, D.C., 1979).

the food you buy in a market has never been touched by human hands: machines do everything from preparing the soil to packaging the product (see the accompanying sidebar).

We are presently spending over 20 percent of our national energy budget to produce food. In terms of British Thermal Units (BTUs), the standard unit of measure for energy, we now use 20 BTUs of fuel energy to produce 1 BTU of food energy. By comparison, in 1910 that ratio was 1 to 1.*

Particularly within the framework of these massive energy expenditures, the home growing of food is an energy-conserving practice. Homegrown food expands the nation's food supply at little extra energy cost.

Energy-Conserving Landscaping Practices

To me it is clear that radical reversals of our standard landscaping procedures are called for in two specific areas: the wholesale consumption of petroleum-based products and the unrestricted use of water for the growing of ornamentals. Though we might have to work hard to break old habits, environmentally sound solutions are close at hand, at least for home landscaping. Using more manure, compost, and organic-type soil amendments and fertilizers instead of relying heavily on commercial fertilizers; using thick mulches and hand weeding instead of herbicides to control weeds; and using mechanical and biological pest-control programs instead of synthetic products whenever possible represent the kinds of approaches that are appropriate. These approaches, as well as the use of plants that require less water, can also help reduce energy use in the area of water delivery. These practices, together with a renewed interest in the home growing of food, can begin to make a difference in the energy shortage we face.

*Sharon Ross, "Our Bill is Coming Due," *The Family Food Garden*, August–September 1980.

The Untouched-by-Human-Hands Tomato

Tractor discs the field.

Tractor plants the seed.

Herbicide, spread by machine, weeds the field.

Electric pumps irrigate the field.

Machines spread oil-based fertilizer.

Machines pick, sort, and pack the tomatoes.

Trucks transport tomatoes to wholesale outlets.

Trucks transport tomatoes to retail stores.

Soil Conservation

Before 1972, my lawn was as big as anyone's and my property was full of enchanting, floriferous, water-using shrubs, ground covers, and herbaceous perennials. In that year I went to Israel and saw the sad consequences of centuries of uncontrolled and unthinking use of the soil. During many of those centuries the Aleppo pine and oak forests had been logged, agricultural fields had been overfarmed, and grasslands had been overgrazed by goats. I was told that in its desert reclamation efforts, Israel spent around $15,000 to produce one new acre of tillable soil. Furthermore, bringing this one acre up to food-producing quality takes five to seven years.

At about the same time, I was helping with some research concerning the preservation of agricultural soils in California's Santa Clara Valley. There seemed to be no way to save the valley's farms from being squeezed out of existence by the encroaching subdivisions. The proximity of residential areas made the spraying of pesticides too dangerous. Smog was affecting some crops. And the cream of the jest was that as property values of the surrounding developed properties increased, the farmers' taxes soared. They were often forced to sell, leaving more and more of the "best soil in the world" to be covered by houses, yards, and shopping centers. While this particular use of the land may not be as irreversible as when the soil is eroded away through clear-cut logging, overgrazing, or overfarming, it nevertheless removes the land from production for many generations.

Or does it? Can't those of us who live on such land do our share to return some of this land to productivity? The end result in an individual yard might not alter the national economy, but it will improve the budget of the family living there. If you intend to embark on a soil-reclamation effort, your first step should be to educate yourself about your soil. Your responsibility in an environmentally sound yard will be to develop, maintain, and conserve a healthy patch of ground. You might find that it is in this area that your ideas will have to change the most. First, you will have to think of your soil as a friend, not just as dirt that gets tracked onto your carpet.

Organic Matter

The muddy plot on which your house sits contains billions and billions of tiny microorganisms and soil creatures, most of which are necessary to the growing cycle. Soil scientists estimate that a thimbleful of soil contains hundreds of thousands of bacteria, fungi, and protozoa. Your soil is not merely an inert mineral but a living entity, alive with hungry animals: protozoa, insects, and worms; and hungry plants: algae, bacteria, fungi, and actinomycetes. All these creatures turn the organic material they ingest (here "organic" is defined as anything once living, plant or animal, that will decompose into useful nutrients) into humus. Humus—which can be the duff that is found on the forest floor or material at the bottom of your own composting system—is the end product of decomposition and the food form useful to plants. It is a complex material that contains moderate amounts of plant nutrients including nitrogen, phosphorus, and sulfur. It is also endowed with many trace substances that may promote plant growth.

When you realize that soil has a living component, you can appreciate that it also has nutritive requirements. The organisms within the soil need to be fed properly in order to create humus. Simply put, the formula is this: organic materials make food for the microorganisms, which make humus, which provides nutrients for the plants.

Your humus might be the end product from a mulch. Or you might feed your soil with kitchen wastes, digging them into the soil in the fall and allowing the microorganisms to work on them for a season. Or maybe you leave fallen leaves in the ivy or short grass clippings on the lawn (clippings that are too long and heavy will retard growth of the lawn). All these methods provide food for the living part of our soil and thus for our plants, while decreasing our dependency on fossil-fuel-based fertilizers.

Besides making nutrients available to plants, organic matter in all stages of decay plays an equally important role in improving the soil's physical structure, whatever its type. (Soil types are discussed in detail in Chapter 4.) If the soil has too much clay, adding organic matter will lighten it so it does not become a gummy mass in the rain or a bricklike sheet in the sun. Sandy soil will become more absorbent, so that water doesn't run through it, leaching out the nutrients as it goes; and this increased water-retentiveness will make it less prone to erosion. The additional organic matter also will increase the air-holding capacity of the soil; plant roots breathe and need oxygen. And heavy soil will warm up faster in the spring because it will drain better.

Finally, maintaining organic matter in our soil provides a sound opportunity for making use of otherwise worthless waste products. It was estimated that in 1977 17 percent of the solid waste produced in this country from residential and post-consumer sources was food waste and another 17.5 percent was yard waste. The total of both was 5.1 million tons!* Counting other forms of organic waste, another source estimated in "the U.S. nearly one ton of domestic organic wastes are generated per person each year."**

Current composting technology and the economics of modern agriculture make it impossible for us to compost organic wastes on a massive scale for farming. But although commercial farmers in general still find it unfeasible, recycling organic household wastes into compost for your soil makes good sense for you as a gardener. Nor will your contribution to the total environment be inconsequential. If

*Tenth Annual Report of the Council on Environmental Quality.

**Nyle C. Brady, The Nature and Property of Soils, 8th ed. (New York: Macmillan Co., 1974).

2.3. A retaining wall planted on top is an effective way to control erosion.

you can think of your garden as part of a mighty collective farm, you will realize that you can have a positive effect on preserving the soil available to everyone. And while you are improving your soil by recycling your household's organic wastes, you will be diverting some of the material that is rapidly filling our local dumps.

Erosion

Erosion is the weathering of the soil or any component of the earth by wind and water, resulting in a gradual loss of the original material. The Dust Bowl of the 1930s was a dramatic and disastrous example of erosion's power to ruin the land. Thousands of acres of magnificent farmland were destroyed because of thoughtless farming practices that exposed the soil to strong winds and heavy rains. Since that time the federal government, in an effort to prevent other large erosion problems from forming, has invested over $20 billion to develop and institute new methods of soil conservation. Nevertheless, the erosion of agricultural lands continues to be one of the nation's most serious problems. The National Resource Inventory estimates that 4 billion tons of soil are lost to water erosion each year,* reducing the land's productivity and simultaneously polluting the rivers and streams.

Many agricultural practices contribute to erosion: the tilling of overly large acreages, which leaves the land open to winds before it can be planted; farming on slopes, which facilitates erosion by water; furrow irrigation, which scours away soil; and the failure to maintain necessary levels of organic material in the soil, which reduces absorbency and allows water to run off, carrying soil with it.

Erosion is usually not a serious problem in home land-

Tenth Annual Report of the Council on Environmental Quality.

scaping, but some general principles do apply for protecting the soil. They include:

1. Maintaining a high organic content in the soil to increase absorbency.
2. Applying mulches and planting windbreaks to protect against wind erosion.
3. Planting a winter crop or leaving stubble of the summer crop to reduce exposure of open areas.
4. Using retaining walls and erosion-resistant plants on slopes.
5. Where possible, using drip irrigation to prevent soil runoff.

Soil Contamination and the Chemical Question

Besides maintaining a high level of organic matter in the soil and controlling erosion, a third major consideration in soil conservation is protecting it from contamination. Soil contamination is a legacy of the 1950s, when many labor-saving chemicals were introduced to make gardening easier and gardens more lush. Commercial fertilizer in pellet form freed gardeners from the work of spreading piles of manure and turning compost. Used by the farmer, synthetic fertilizer made more food available at cheaper prices, and thus assured us that we would never have to grow our own. Herbicides allowed us to weed without stooping, and pesticides allowed us to grow a wider variety of pest-prone plants. Once blissfully unaware of the possible negative effects of these materials, we are now learning that our own health as well as our nonrenewable resources are directly threatened by some of them. Furthermore, the harm these chemicals do to our physical environment in general is beginning to appear inestimable. The latter consideration is the focus of this section.

In our country, the use of synthetic fertilizers in agriculture and most landscaping is standard. Approximately 13 million tons of synthetic nitrogen fertilizer is sold annually in the U.S.* Pesticides constitute the second major category of garden chemicals. These materials take the form of fungicides, herbicides, insecticides, nematocides, and rodenticides. Approximately 5 pounds of pesticides are used annually for every man, woman, and child in the U.S.** And, as with fertilizers, use of these pesticides is routine among home landscapers. In fact, "limited survey data of pesticide use in nonagricultural sectors show that they may account for one-third or more of the amount consumed in this country."* One study has even suggested that suburban lawns and gardens receive more pesticides per acre than any other kind of land in the nation.**

What, specifically, are the effects on the environment of applying massive amounts of these chemicals to our land? More and more we are finding that garden and agricultural chemicals are contributing to air pollution and to the contamination of our underground water supplies, which provide so much of the nation's agricultural and domestic

---

*Carolyn Haynes, "The High Cost of Nitrogen Fertilizer," *Horticulture,* March 1980.

**George W. Ware, *The Pesticide Book* (San Francisco: W. H. Freeman and Co., 1978).

*Dale R. Bottrell, *Integrated Pest Management* (Washington, D.C.: Council on Environmental Quality, 1979).

**R. von Rumker et al., "The Use of Pesticides in Suburban Homes and Gardens and their Impact on the Aquatic Environment," Pesticide Study Series 2 (Washington, D.C.: Environmental Protection Agency, Office of Water Programs, Applied Technology Division, 1972).

Lead Pollution

Of the heavy metals, lead is the most common pollutant of air and soil in residential areas. Lead is part of the particulate matter in most automotive exhaust, and in this form can settle on the fruit and leafy foliage of plants located close to roads. It is also present in the soil in many older neighborhoods, where lead-based paint has flaked off or been scraped off houses and allowed to remain on the soil. Since this occurs close to buildings, foundation plantings are most likely to be affected; the roots of some of them can take up the lead from the soil.

Young children are particularly vulnerable to lead poisoning, and its early symptoms are difficult to detect. You can help protect your family in several ways:

1. If you live on a heavily traveled road, avoid planting edibles adjacent to it. Ornamentals can often be located between your edibles and the road.

2. If you suspect that lead in your soil may be a problem, have the soil tested. If levels are high, a drastic but workable solution is to plant only in raised beds using imported soil.

3. Fruit and leafy vegetables from plants close to the road should be washed well in acidulated water before cooking or serving. The usual formula is 2–3 tablespoons of vinegar to a quart of water (you can keep a squeeze bottle handy under the sink). Then wash again with fresh water.

water. These underground water sources are much harder than rivers and streams to decontaminate. But soil contamination is the most serious effect of chemical use. The effect of pesticides as a soil pollutant has been a concern for a number of years, but we are only now becoming aware of their pervasiveness and persistence. Some agricultural materials (both pesticides and fertilizers) leave a residue in the soil of such inorganic elements as mercury, cadmium, lead, arsenic, nickel, copper, zinc, manganese, fluorine, and boron, all of which are toxic to human beings and other animals in varying degrees.[*] Many of these chemicals persist in the soil for decades, some indefinitely.

Despite our dawning understanding of the dangers of the chemicals we have been adding to the land that yields our food, old habits die hard. I would like to convince you to practice your landscaping with as few commercial additives as possible. To that end, the following sections describe each of the major categories of the chemical products available, the hazards they may pose to the soil and other parts of the environment, and the existing alternatives.

Fertilizers

Commercial fertilizer comes in many formulations. Those most closely associated with pollution and health problems are the synthetic nitrogen and phosphate types.

Air quality is affected by both of these types of fertilizers. The process of manufacturing phosphate fertilizers can result in the emission of particulates and fluorides into the air, thus contributing to air pollution.[**] Nitrate forms of nitrogen fertilizer also affect our air, as the nitrates in the material are not all absorbed by the plants and soil but are passed off as vapor into the air. According to one study, under normal agricultural conditions 15–20 percent of the nitrates can oxidize into the atmosphere.[***] There is concern that nitrates reaching the stratosphere, like propellants used in some aerosol spray cans, can damage the ozone layer. Ozone filters out potentially dangerous ultraviolet rays before they reach the surface of the earth.

Many commercial fertilizers (as well as manures) add salt to the soil. In arid climates, where rainwater does not flush such salts away and where irrigation water itself often has a high salt content, the soil can become so salty that most plants are unable to grow. In addition, impurities in synthetic fertilizers can add contaminants to the soil.

Some types of fertilizers can cause water pollution, especially where runoff is a problem. For example, much of the fertilizer applied to lawns on a slope never reaches the grass but runs off the soil into a nearby stream or bay, resulting in contamination of water sources far from the site of the original application. Runoff from fertilized land usually

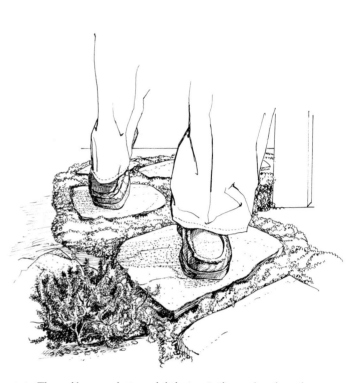

2.4. Thyme, like many plants, needs little or no fertilizer and can be used as a substitute for lawn in small areas with no foot traffic.

contains nitrates and phosphates, both of which are water soluble. These chemicals are the major cause of a pollution problem known as accelerated eutrophication. Eutrophication is the natural aging process that bodies of water undergo. Where large amounts of nutrients, namely nitrogen and phosphorus, are added to lakes—as in runoff—the aging process is speeded up. Often these excess nutrients cause the algae in the lake to multiply in dizzying amounts. When the overblown algae populations die, their decomposition utilizes the oxygen dissolved in the water, which, in turn, causes fish to suffocate.[*] Eutrophication also makes water much more difficult to treat for drinking. Given the fact that food and clean water are already scarce in many parts of the world, accelerated eutrophication is a serious problem, and fertilizer runoff is one of its major causes.

The contamination of underground sources of water is another serious problem caused by commercial fertilizers, particularly the highly soluble nitrogen types. Research shows that when these nitrogen fertilizers reach groundwater, they can be pumped up by well pumps, and when

*Brady, *Nature and Property of Soil.*

**Nobile and Deedy, *Ecology Fact Book.*

***Parker Pratt, *The Nitrate in Effluents from Irrigated Land,* (Riverside, Calif.: University of California, 1979).

*David F. Salisbury, "Cleansing Earth's Waters," *Christian Science Monitor,* 4 July 1977.

drunk by infants can cause "blue baby syndrome." Heavy irrigation can leach more than half of the excess fertilizer into local water tables. Of great concern in this regard is the fact that even if nitrate use was immediately stopped, it would take 10 to 50 years, or maybe even a hundred years, before the nitrates would move out of the surface water.*

Thus the heavy use of these commercial fertilizers is a hazard to human health and to the environment. The costs in terms of resources are also considerable, since the majority of these substances are made from nonrenewable resources, and their production uses energy as well. However, environmental issues are seldom cut and dried. Some of the organic fertilizers such as dried bloodmeal and steamed bonemeal also take petroleum energy to process. And commercial fertilizers clearly have provided more food for the world. Researchers estimate that U.S. food production would drop by a third without them. It is obvious that commercial agricultural enterprises would not find it easy to decrease their dependence on chemical fertilizers.

Fortunately, home gardeners are more easily able to use fertilizers that are protective of the environment. Many people feel that vegetables, fruits, and ornamentals grown in soil containing large amounts of organic matter are often healthier and have fewer pests than those fertilized chemically, and this view has brought about a renewed interest in organic soil additives and fertilizers. Chemical fertilizers are no longer being used as routinely in home gardens; rock phosphate, manures, bonemeal, and compost are often used instead. These alternatives are not as high in nitrogen and phosphorus as chemical fertilizers, but the utility of very large amounts of nitrogen is being questioned. It now seems probable that high nitrogen use causes lush vegetative growth that is more susceptible to injury by pests, diseases, and cold. Thus, synthetic fertilizers high in nitrogen might actually cause some plant-growth problems as well as environmental ones. Furthermore, organic fertilizers provide nutrition in a slower but steadier dosage than many processed fertilizers, improve soil structure, and supply many micronutrients that plants need. Maintaining soil quality over a long period, instead of applying nutrients to a particular plant for a season's quick return, has become the new goal.

One indirect advantage of using organic household waste such as vegetable parings and lawn clippings as a soil conditioner (see the section on composting in Chapter 7) is the control of accelerated eutrophication. Many dumps and garbage sites are located near bodies of water, and runoff from the decaying vegetative matter deposited there contributes to the eutrophication process. If the organic material in those piles were used for compost in gardens, it would help to fertilize the plants instead of the algae in the lake.

Pesticides

In 1962 Rachel Carson awakened the world to the hazards of indiscriminate pesticide use. Numerous studies since have shown the dangers of a number of specific pesticides. Nevertheless, the agricultural use of pesticides seems to be here to stay. Some experts estimate that crop yields would be reduced by at least 9 percent, others estimate a crop reduction by as much as 50 percent, were such use discontinued.* So it is not surprising that the search for new and more effective pesticides continues.

The full environmental impact of millions of pounds of pesticide in our air, water, and soil is incalculable. Insecticides, fungicides, and herbicides are introduced into the air by spraying and by volatilization (vaporizing into the air), into the water by leaching and runoff, and into the soil by direct application. Basically we can only measure their potential damage by identifying conditions they have caused and then generalizing.

Pesticides are damaging bee populations and contaminating commercial fisheries. One government report showed that commercial "chemical pesticides have seriously harmed many non-economic species of fishes, birds, and other wildlife. Harmful effects may involve direct kill of desirable species, interference with reproductive performance, or disruptions of food chains and resulting starvation of animals that depend on food chains. These effects have been documented many times."**

The heavy metals found in some pesticides—including lead, arsenic, copper, and mercury—are implicated in long-term inorganic soil contamination. Many of the persistent organochlorine pesticides, such as DDT, DDE, dieldrin, aldrin, BHC, endrin, heptachlor, and mirex, are incriminated in the phenomenon known as biomagnification,*** "the process by which poisons can be passed along the food chain and accumulate in toxic levels after several such passages."† Such chemicals are not readily broken down by microorganisms, enzymes, heat, or ultraviolet light, and are virtually insoluble in water. However, these same chemicals are soluble in fatty tissue, and thus are passed through the food chain, accumulating in the tissues of animals at the top. A study of Clear Lake, California, showed that DDD, a persistent pesticide, was found in the plankton to be 265 times the concentrate in the water. In the tissues of predatory fish and grebes, the levels of DDD exceeded those in the water by 75,000–80,000 times.††

*Pratt, Nitrite in Effluents.

*Bottrell, Integrated Pest Management

**Bottrell, Integrated Pest Management.

***Ware, Pesticide Book.

†Farallones Institute, The Integral Urban House (San Francisco: Sierra Club Books, 1979).

††M. L. Flint and R. Van den Bosch, A Source Book on Integrated Pest Management (Washington, D.C.: Dept. of Health, Education and Welfare, Grant No. G007500907).

Not only do insecticides, fungicides, and herbicides contribute to air, soil, and water pollution, their effectiveness against pests is coming into question.

Insecticides

Insecticides in particular may prove not to be the only solution to the pest problem, as was once thought. When these "weapons" were first developed, agricultural science invested huge sums in a massive offensive against the insect world, thinking they were facing an enemy they would eventually vanquish. What folly! The insects have been around for 250 million years, far longer than human beings. Most people now know we can hope only to control them, not to defeat them. Pest management should be the goal, not winning the war, and we should be relying less on purely chemical solutions.

Many factors and much new information have led to this new goal of pest management. One of these factors is the phenomenon known as resistance, which limits the effectiveness of pesticides. Resistance is an acceleration of the evolutionary process. It works in the following way. When a pesticide is sprayed on an area the insects susceptible to it die but the few that are resistant live on and breed with each other. The pesticide is used again, and the process is repeated. After a number of sprayings, the only pests left are the resistant ones. Since the pesticide doesn't work on them, the population builds up again. More than 300 species of insects, mites, and ticks are known to be resistant to at least one pesticide.*

Another important new area of research concerns the delicate balance between insect predators and prey. This ecological balance prevails throughout the animal kingdom. For example, gophers are preyed upon by coyotes; when coyotes are killed by farmers for killing lambs, the gophers overpopulate and themselves become a problem. The farmer then needs to trap and kill gophers. In another example, if a broad-spectrum insecticide (one that kills many species) is used to kill aphids, the ladybug larvae are killed along with the aphids they usually eat. The result is more aphids. Because aphids can reproduce faster than ladybugs, another application of pesticide is needed, and the whole process repeats itself.

We need to study resistance factors and predator-prey relationships further in order to learn of and practice natural methods of maintaining ecological balance. One means of pest control that incorporates new knowledge on this subject is called Integrated Pest Management (IPM). This and other new methods and their use for home landscaping are discussed in Chapter 7.

Herbicides

Herbicides, pesticides that kill plants, also need further

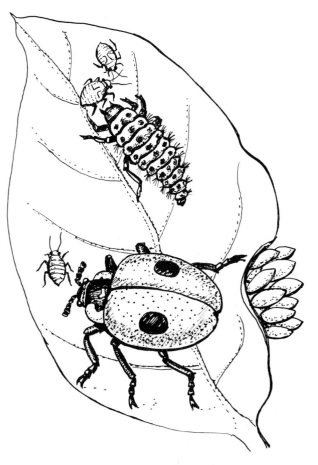

2.5. Ladybugs are probably the best-known insect predator.

scrutiny. These chemicals have been phenomenally popular and are now the most widely used of all the pesticides. According to a Department of Agriculture report, "Herbicides accounted for over 60% of all crop pesticides used in 1976 . . ."* Homeowners use them widely, particularly on lawns as part of a "weed and feed" program, and professional gardening services rely on them heavily.

Herbicides were once thought to be nontoxic to human beings because they only killed plants. That idea has been challenged by new information. Many pesticides, including herbicides, are being questioned regarding their eventual safety. According to a list compiled by the Rachel Carson Trust, a nonprofit research organization concerning itself with the hazards of pesticides, a number of commonly used herbicides are suspected of being either known carcinogens or mutagens. For example, two widely used herbicides, 2,4,5-T and silvex, were temporarily banned by the EPA in 1980 because they were suspected of causing miscarriages and birth defects.

---

*G. P. Georghiou and C. E. Taylor, "Pesticide Resistance as an Evolutionary Phenomenon," *Proceedings of the Fifteenth International Congress of Entomology* (1977).

*T. R. Eichers et al., "Farmers' Use of Pesticides in 1976," Agricultural Economics Report no. AER-418 (Washington, D.C.: Dept. of Agriculture, Economics, Statistics and Cooperative Services, 1978).

My own experience has led me to discourage the use of herbicides wherever possible. One personal encounter was particularly instructive. A number of years ago I decided to convert a parking strip in front of my house into a flower and vegetable border. With great enthusiasm I planted artichokes, lavender, Shasta daisies, and herbs. A week later they were all dead. Cautiously I put in a few more plants; they too turned brown and died. I was forced to do some detective work.

For a number of years I had contracted to have diesel oil sprayed on the strip in the spring and fall to kill the weeds. This type of oil was not supposed to persist in the soil—but what else would affect the plants so drastically? Finally, I called the gardener who had done the spraying. He had discovered a kind of spray that suppressed the weeds for a much longer time than diesel oil and had assumed I would prefer one shot to four. He had used a sterilizing dose of simazene, which was indeed effective against the recurring spurge, purslane, and knotweed; unfortunately, it was also effective against anything else that might be planted in that area!

It took a year of flushing with water, and many cubic yards of compost, to make that piece of soil compatible with plants—and even then it remained marginal for a long time. Now, after five years, plants grown there are healthy and robust. (I have since learned that activated charcoal added to the soil would have deactivated the chemical quickly and is an effective purifying agent for many herbicides.)

This is not an uncommon problem. Many of my students and clients who move into new homes have this same disappointing experience with their first efforts at gardening in the soil on their new property.

Pulling weeds is an onerous job that no one enjoys, which is probably why herbicides are becoming the fastest selling garden chemical in the United States. What are the alternatives? You can pull weeds or keep a number of them down by laying a thick organic mulch, or you can try to take the easy way out and apply an herbicide. As in all aspects of life, there is no free lunch, and the easy way often extracts a price.

Herbicides kill plants. If used in excessive amounts or too frequently, if carried by the wind, or if used too near a desirable plant, they will kill a favorite blueberry bush along with the crabgrass or dandelions. Water runoff carrying herbicides pollutes rivers and underground water supplies. Even if used correctly, herbicides can upset the microorganism balance of the soil, because many soil microorganisms are plants. Furthermore, where these herbicides have killed the weeds, they have left chemical residues in the soil. There is some evidence that repeated applications of an herbicide can change its chemical action. It has been speculated that the chemicals do not break down completely and that residues build up with repeated applications, rendering the recommended dosages incorrect. Further evidence has also shown that many of the herbicides slow root development of the desired plants.

In summary I cannot discourage the use of herbicides enough. Herbicide damage is now more prevalent in suburban areas than insect or disease damage. Not only can herbicides be an environmental problem, but when not properly applied they can become a plant-growth problem as well. Check Chapter 7 for specific techniques of controlling pests and weeds, but be forewarned that none of the alternative solutions proposed are as simple as applying a commercial chemical. Nevertheless, though some effort will be required, home gardens have fewer pest problems in general than commercially grown crops, and the average home gardener has less difficulty controlling pests without using chemicals than the farmer.

Gardening Without Chemicals

Gardening without chemicals is generally referred to as *organic gardening.* But the term *organic* has taken on some emotional connotations and for many people brings to mind a number of popular, although unproven, theories and misconceptions as well as many valid and useful gardening techniques. Since you are going to eat what you grow, I feel it is important to present a strong argument in favor of gardening without most pesticides and herbicides, and to use an integrated pest management approach. In order to do that, I must make an effort to clear up the confusion surrounding the term *organic.*

Too many "organic" approaches are really an overreliance on a single nonchemical solution—or a few solutions—to an array of gardening problems. This blanket approach is not unlike the dependence on potent chemicals for keeping a garden pest free. The key to true organic gardening is the careful matching of nonchemical solutions with accurately diagnosed problems. Above all, it entails "belly learning," that is, getting down on your knees and stomach, finding out what is crawling under your herbs or turning leaves over and looking for signs of, say, mummified aphids that have been attacked by parasitic wasps. The organic gardener has to go out at night with a flashlight to look for snails or cutworms. In short, to be organic, you have to be actively involved with your garden and its visitors.

I inspect my garden daily. When I water with a hose, I turn leaves over and look carefully for spider mites. When I weed, I lift leaves up and look under the perennials for snails. And when I cultivate under the tomatoes, I look for fresh tomato-hornworm excrement (often the only way of finding these well-camouflaged worms). Besides yielding chemical-free fruits and vegetables, this gardening method has opened up to me a whole mini-universe, a wildlife population I would have missed if I had automatically used the chemical-spray method of pest control.

If you have been a heavy user of the chemicals discussed in this chapter, all is not lost. Nature's recuperative powers will help you bring your soil back to life. Rainwater will help to flush out the possible salt build-up resulting from the use of commercial fertilizers and to leach away some of the contaminants. Time will help degrade some of the pesticides. You can aid immeasurably in the restoration of the soil by adding to it large amounts of organic matter. As you add more organic materials, the microorganisms will return, speeding up the breakdown of some of those unwanted chemicals while replenishing the soil with humus.

People concerned about the quality of the environment often feel helpless in the face of the damage they perceive. I myself used to feel frustrated sitting in on county zoning hearings, trying to save agricultural land from urban development, listening to farmers who would testify that urban pressures were driving them off some of the best farmland in the world. However, my research on modern agricultural methods has shown me that economic pressures have often forced farmers to use irrigation practices that waste water and to rely heavily on oil-based, polluting products and chemicals. I now question the ability of many farmers to be guardians of the soil. But suburban gardeners with a reverence for the land can reverse the pattern of wasted or contaminated soil on their own property by using techniques that enrich the land, not waste or contaminate it. Such a reversal, repeated a millionfold across the country, would represent a major contribution to the preservation of the earth and a turn toward healthful eating practices by the consumer of organically homegrown produce. Furthermore, as the world population continues to grow and more prime agricultural land is given over to development, the contribution to the world food output by millions of home growers using environmentally sound techniques could mean the difference between depending on a dwindling resource and self-sufficiency.

CHAPTER 3

The Evolution of Landscaping

LANDSCAPE DESIGN, like fashion design and architecture, is involved with beauty, but, also like those enterprises, it is an applied art. Landscape designers are not in the business of producing beauty for its own sake, as fine artists do; rather, they create a product that will serve a specific function as beautifully as possible. Even in landscaping's most resplendent era, the French and Italian Renaissance, royal gardens were not ends in themselves but rather expressions of wealth and power. Elaborate fountains, topiary (the shearing of evergreen plants into fanciful shapes), and statuary were embellishments to gardens that had to be suitable places for entertaining the court. The grounds contained large promenades to accommodate festive crowds and secluded places where political tête-à-têtes and romantic interludes could take place. The pathways were covered with gravel so milady's sweeping gown wouldn't get muddy, and were lined with rows of trees to shade the strollers. Magnificence went hand in hand with utility.

Concepts of beauty change with the ages: Gregorian chants and pensive Madonnas express beauty to one generation, symphonies and pastoral scenes to another, progressive jazz and abstract expressionist painting to yet another.

The applied arts are as changeable as the fine arts, but in the former shifts are often dictated by new functional requirements rather than by taste alone. Hoop skirts and pinched waists for example, were appropriate for Scarlett O'Hara in *Gone with the Wind*, fitting the image of the helpless, decorative woman. But a hoop skirt on today's fashionable woman would sweep newly typed contracts to the floor as she hurried through the office on her way to an executive meeting. As with fashion design, today's landscape design must be appropriate to modern needs.

But what kind of landscaping is appropriate in the last two decades of the twentieth century? Basically, we need beautiful gardens that shade our homes, protect them from winter winds, protect the soil, maximize the usable living space, are climatically suitable, and provide delicious, fresh produce. No longer appropriate is the use of large amounts of petroleum-based energy and products, water, or polluting chemicals. This concept of landscaping might seem new but it borrows much from styles of the past. In the short history of landscape design that follows, you will see that our current Western ideas of beauty and function in the garden have come down to us from far back in time.

A Brief History of Landscape Gardening

The first landscapes were probably natural grottoes or valleys. Our ancestors were particularly fond of these formations and probably used them for religious ceremonies or courtship. Whatever their function, however, they were enjoyed as they were, unaltered by human intervention. The first gardening, of course, was motivated by survival, not aesthetics.

In Ancient Times

The Egyptians of King Tut's time appear to have been one of the first peoples to design a landscape; that is, to deliberately plan the grounds around a dwelling for aesthetic and utilitarian reasons. Fascinating pictures from as early as 1400 B.C. show gardens of well-to-do Egyptians and give us an idea of what these people sought in their surroundings. Pools for fish; trees bearing figs, pomegranates, and dates; grapevine-covered trellises; and beds of flowers—these were the elements of such gardens. Areas were laid out in formal, rectangular shapes and surrounded by walls that offered both protection and a feeling of intimacy. The results were pleasure gardens that provided cool shade, aesthetic pleasure, and succulent fruit—true oases in the desert.

It was the Persians, however, who perfected the pleasure garden. They wove the elements of fragrance, pools of water, shade from the desert sun, beautiful imported flowers, fruiting trees, and geometrically arranged plants and walls into complex designs that invited outside entertaining, dining, and lovemaking. The Persians made the garden an extension of the indoor living space. Over the centuries (from around 400 B.C. through the 1700s), "paradise gardens," as they were called, became more and more elaborate, incorporating fountains and ever more intricate designs. But they consistently featured both ornamental and edible plants in a subtle intermingling of beauty and utility. Weavers copied the designs of many of these magnificent gardens and incorporated them into Persian carpets. Through these carpets we can still enjoy the beauty of the paradise gardens.

Whereas the Egyptians and Persians, and later the Indians and the Moors, constructed oasis gardens that modified their climates, enlarged their living spaces, and provided food, beauty, and pleasure, the Romans contributed a much more formal kind of garden art. The homes of wealthy Romans were extensive villas based to some extent on Greek gymnasia where scholars gathered to philosophize. The Romans furnished these gardens with elaborate fountains, impressive feats of engineering that utilized water brought from miles away. Roman gardens were filled with statuary and exotic plants from all parts of the empire. Although accounts of Rome's early gardens mention fruits and herbs, and much was written about agriculture, the use of edibles in ornamental gardens decreased in importance as time went on. Later gardens seemed to be devoted entirely to ornamentation. Pliny the Younger had 500 slaves on his property to maintain his garden—shaping the sculptured shrubs; caring for the many plants, each species needing different treatment; and doing the general picking up that such large areas require.

Villa gardens, elaborate fountains, and topiary became consuming interests of the Romans. Some of their topiary gardens depicted whole scenes of hunting parties or fleets of ships. Imagine my empathy when I read that in 1 A.D. the writer and agronomist Columella was seriously concerned because lavish gardens were increasingly usurping valuable agricultural lands.*

Many other great writers and thinkers of the day, such as Pliny, Horace, Varro, and Cato, condemned the large estates and the excesses of the Roman lifestyle. One historian comments: "The feeling was deep-rooted in the best of [the Romans] that the dislike of agricultural life was the beginning of the end for the Roman people."**

In addition to large, elaborate topiary gardens, Roman villas also had courtyard gardens, where many of the day's activities took place. The courtyard garden was the most prominent design concept to be carried over into monastery gardens, the next important development in the history of landscaping.

The Medieval Era

With the Dark Ages that followed the fall of Rome, the elaborate, ornamental, villa-style garden disappeared. In the medieval monastery garden and the few secular gardens that existed, function was again stressed. Enclosed herb gardens where fruits and vegetables were often interplanted were the norm. Grafting of fruit trees to produce better fruits, and planting in raised beds bordered with wooden planks, were widely practiced. Fish ponds provided food. A few flowers were grown for pleasure, and the lawn, that great usurper of human energy, was institutionalized.

Formerly grass had been used informally near modest homes and kept trim by domestic livestock. In the monastery gardens, lawns were planted for pleasure. They were usually to be found in the center of the cloister, contributing to a soothing environment conducive to study and meditation. The earliest practitioners of the lawn-growing art poured boiling water over an area to kill existing vegetation, then dug out the area and filled it in with pieces of turf from a nearby meadow. (No Kentucky bluegrass in seed or sod form existed in those days.) The turf was then beaten in place with wooden mallets.

*Anthony Huxley, *An Illustrated History of Gardening* (New York and London: Paddington Press, 1978).

**Marie Louise Gothein, *A History of Garden Art,* vol. I (New York: Hacker Art Books, 1966).

3.1. Formal gardens with clipped hedges and symmetrical plantings were common on the estates of European nobility.

The Renaissance

During the Renaissance, pleasure gardens for the nobility and the well-to-do again came to the fore in Europe. Much effort was devoted to copying and elaborating on famous villas of ancient Rome. During the fourteenth and fifteenth centuries, Renaissance pleasure gardens in France and Italy reached their zenith. Such gardens might contain acres of clipped hedges, mazes, topiaries, orangeries (for growing fruit out of season), exotic plants from all over the world, fountains, romantic grottoes, and statuary. During this time the "joke garden" came into being as well. In such a design, jets of water would be strategically placed to shoot off unexpectedly from benches, tables, or garden paths, presumably amusing the host no end. One wonders how the guests felt about serving as the butts of these elaborate jokes.

With the development of the Renaissance pleasure garden the notion grew that fruits and vegetables should be consigned exclusively to the kitchen garden. In the first written statement of this idea that I have found, Leon Battista Alberti, a famous and influential Florentine architect who laid down many ground rules for landscaping a property, dictated:

All the paths are to be bordered with box and other evergreens. Bright streams of water must run through the garden, and above all must start up unexpectedly, their source a grotto with colored shell work. Cypresses with climbing ivy must be in the pleasure garden, but fruited trees and even oaks are relegated to the kitchen garden.*

So fashions are made.

The Rise of the Pastoral Landscape

Between the Renaissance and the seventeenth century some nonhorticultural features of the pleasure gardens were eliminated, but the formalism—the controlling hand of human beings over nature—remained in vogue. The gardens at Versailles are an example. In reaction against this controlled look, and possibly owing to increased exposure

*Gothein, *History of Garden Art*, vol. II.

to the Orient, the English in the early 1700s developed a softer, more informal style of landscaping. Straight, geometric forms were superseded by free, natural forms. Clipped hedges became passé, considered rigid, pompous, and unnatural. The standard of beauty for that time was influenced by an acceptance of nature's own forms. Joseph Addison, a strong spokesman for this new movement, said:

> For my own part, I would rather look upon a tree in all its abundance and diffusions of boughs and branches, than when it is cut and trimmed into a mathematical figure; and cannot but fancy that an orchard in flower looks infinitely more delightful than all the little labyrinths of the most finished parterre.*

Eighteenth-century English landscapes were idealized reflections of the natural landscape. Actually they were characterized by a rather tightly controlled design contrasting open "meadow" with closed "wood." Careful attention to views and visual axes was evident throughout these landscapes, just as in earlier gardens on the Continent. These natural landscapes were developed in imitation of the landscape paintings of the period: "nature" imitating art.

The shift from formal to informal and from fenced to unfenced styles took place gradually until about 1730, when, as one writer puts it, "William Kent 'leaped the fence.' Suddenly there was no beginning, and no end to the garden. It was all 'landskip' (in the spelling of the day) to be idealized as an earthly paradise with classical overtones."**

Kent was an architect and painter who composed naturalistic pictures with sweeping lawns, water, trees, and architecture. He was succeeded by "Capability" Brown, the garden genius who perfected the so-called English style. Brown made the picturesque pastoral scene the ideal that the landed gentry strove to express in their estates. The grounds were to be composed of acres of rolling lawns and clumps of trees. No visual excitement was intended; rather the scene was to be soothing. The vast acreages were often unmarred by fence or wall, and lawns came right up to the residence. It was the era of the ha-ha, a ditch or moat, that served as a hidden barrier around the entire property. This ingenious device kept the sheep, cattle, and deer from coming too close to the house but was so well camouflaged that the grazing animals seemed to be a natural part of the bucolic scene.

Ornamental Edible Gardens

Both before and after these great, green scenes appeared in England, gardeners of a more practical sort in France and Scotland were developing decorative as well as functional vegetable gardens. These gardens were usually formal in design, utilizing clipped box hedges, walks, and rectilinear patterns. Vegetables were interplanted with flowers to fill the beds, and fruit trees were espaliered along walls and walks. Such gardens were cultivated not only by the wealthy but also by the developing middle class. Gardens of this type still exist in Europe but are seldom found in the United States. One wonders why this style did not carry over more pervasively into the nineteenth and twentieth centuries, when more middle-class people owned their own land and could work it to suit their own tastes.

The Victorian Period

In the nineteenth century the landscaping ideal changed again. The eighteenth-century style was called boring and insipid; and in reaction, it seems, a new school developed, often called the museum school. According to John Brookes, in his delightful book *Room Outside:*

> The nineteenth century produced a new gardening public, with smaller gardens. The essence of the eighteenth century park was scaled down and natural plantings were replaced by recently imported specimens. There was also a revival of interest in formal Italian garden layout. The result was a mess.*

The essence of the new style was eclecticism. Nineteenth-century Victorian gardeners borrowed from practically every previous landscaping style, embellishing their grounds with lawns, statuary, metal furniture, iron deer, urns, busts, pseudo-ruins, and some of the new plants available from China, India, and the western United States as a legacy of the great explorations. Edibles became in vogue if they were exotic or could be produced out of season in greenhouses—strawberries at Christmas or oranges in February, say.

Following the confusion of the Victorian gardens came a new trend: the appreciation of a plant for the form and texture of its foliage, the glorious color of its blooms, and the opportunities it offered as an element in an impressionistic picture that would live and grow. These ideas reached their peak in the horticultural practice and writings of William Robinson and the painter Gertrude Jekyll, both of whom are considered to be the developers of the mixed herbaceous border and the informal cottage-type landscapes containing lawns, paths, and large flower beds. Such beds were filled with perennial plants chosen for their forms, textures, and leaf shapes, and to provide a controlled show of color from spring to fall.

Twentieth-Century Styles

The last century has seen a growing exchange between the Orient and the West that has had an influence on some of our modern landscape design. Despite the fact that many aspects of Oriental garden designs are strongly rooted in the religions of China and Japan, we have been able to incorporate many Oriental ideas into our own yards. It is now common to use a single boulder or a group of rocks as

*Gothein, *History of Garden Art,* vol. II.

**Hugh Johnson, *The Principles of Gardening* (New York: Simon and Schuster, 1979).

*John Brookes, *Room Outside* (New York: Penguin Books, 1979).

3.2. Bamboo has many uses in landscaping.

the focal point in a landscape, whether as a lovely accent in its own right or as a background for plants. We have learned to appreciate the beauty of gravel raked to create the appearance of ripples on a pond, and have sharpened our sensitivity to the usefulness of varying leaf textures. Our taste in pruning has also been broadened by exposure to Oriental styles. We can see how the natural shape of a tree or shrub can be accentuated through pruning to make the plant a living, informal sculpture rather than a geometric, formal shape.

Another Oriental influence felt widely in this country is the recreation of nature in miniature within an extremely small space. Excitement is often created in such gardens by the use of hidden surprises. A sudden turn may bring you to a Tsukubai arrangement (a bamboo flume and stone basin, illustrated on page 43; a tiny bonsaied conifer may grow snugly against a mossy boulder; or a garden may be broken up by an intricate gate woven of branches and brush or split bamboo. The last is perhaps the most significant in terms of what we might call "appropriate" landscaping for our times. Indeed, the creative use and recycling of natural materials is one of the greatest enrichments we have gained from our cultural exchange with the Far East.

Other influences with origins closer to home have

shaped modern home landscaping styles. Early Colonial landscaping in America involved herb gardens, fruit trees, vegetables, and flowers, usually surrounded by picket fences to keep out livestock. American landscaping since the Civil War has been influenced most heavily by Andrew Downing and his disciples, who advocated large shade trees, lawns, and a few specimen trees and shrubs. Later came the informal, cottage-type English landscape and an interest in native plants. In the late 1800s and in the early 1900s the use of foundation plantings, to conceal exposed foundations and to soften the angles of a house, became a common feature in home landscape design. This style is limited in utility, as it gives no privacy, and in design potential as well, but nonetheless it soon became so widely used as to be abused. Homes with a mandatory "moustache" of a few shrubs around the front entry combined with a lawn and two street trees became a standard sight in American towns.

In the years since World War II many other influences have changed American landscaping. The rise of the suburb and subdivision combined with the growing cost of real estate has resulted in smaller yards in general. Driveways, pools, barbeques, and the West Coast phenomenon of hot tubs have created new uses for yards. And the ready availability of pesticides, fungicides, herbicides, and chemical fertilizers has encouraged us to strive for the perfect lawn or rose—which in turn has led to the county-fair, blue-ribbon syndrome—the relentless search for the *biggest* flower or fruit.

Other practical developments have made landscaping a less tedious pursuit than in the past. Power mowers, edgers, blowers, and trimmers have permitted us all to maintain manicured lawns and shrubs without a retinue of servants. Magazines, garden clubs, and how-to books have both disseminated information and dictated styles. And local nurseries have helped to provide a wide variety of plants and growing information.

Perhaps the most significant factor of all has been the progress made in agriculture, which has freed people from having to grow their own food. Many Americans who left the farm for the city came to consider food growing to be straight from "Hicksville"; that is, food growing was a low-status activity. For many years professional designers and style setters discouraged the use of food-producing plants in the garden. As a result, those who wished to buck the tide were given few design guidelines. What food-producing plants were used were generally planted in what I call the "plunk landscaping" style. That is, one went to the nursery, asked for a peach tree, and then went home to "plunk" it in the ground. No thought went into how the tree looked, only into what it would produce. "Plunk landscaping" has given the use of edibles a bad name among those concerned with aesthetics.

In summary, foundation planting, Japanese gardens, large lawns, English perennial borders, all have left their mark on our modern landscaping style. Like so many other elements in our culture, the American yard has been shaped by many different influences. The result is often an unsatisfactory mishmash, a yard that gives little pleasure or utility and is a chore to maintain. Many of our current standard landscaping practices are appropriate to other times, other classes, other conditions, and other places, but some factors have proven impervious to the whims of fashion. Before we can go on to discuss the appropriate functions of landscaping for our time, it will be valuable to identify the elements and aesthetic principles that are common to all effective landscape design, whatever the era.

Aesthetic Considerations

Throughout the centuries and despite the changes in landscape styles, certain aspects of landscape design have remained unchanged. Most experts will agree that all successful landscape designs include a number of design elements and observe certain aesthetic principles. All these essential aspects are explored in more detail in Chapters 5 and 6. For more comprehensive coverage of the fundamen-

tal principles of landscaping, see *Room Outside* by John Brookes, *How to Plan Your Own Home Landscape*, by Nelva Weber, *Creative Ideas in Garden Design*, Brooklyn Botanical Handbook, and *Landscaping Your Home* by William R. Nelson Jr. All are listed in the bibliography.

Design Elements

Think of the yard as an outdoor room (or rooms) in which the elements of design must be considered three-dimensionally, or in several planes. Vertical dividers to create enclosed spaces and privacy may be brick or stone walls, fences, hedges, or planting groups. The "floors" of the garden, whether made of concrete, lawn, or ground covers, provide surfaces for various activities and should form interesting and pleasing topographic patterns. The "ceiling," which can offer shade and privacy, can be formed by trees, trellises, and vines. Circulation patterns must be created in the outdoor rooms. Walks, steps, and ramps provide access for both people and equipment. All of these elements can be embellished for interest and utility by furniture, sculpture, water, and plantings.

The element of water contributes another dimension to a garden, and its soothing sparkle has deep emotional appeal. Water can be incorporated in many ways, for instance in ponds, in fountains, or as trickles over the side of a rock. In arid climates a small fountain can have the psychological cooling effect of a large lawn, while using much less water.

Once the structures in the landscape have been determined, the plant materials are chosen, and herein lies the true subtlety of the landscaper's art. Plants must be considered in terms of their overall form; the size, shape, and color of their foliage; and the flower show they provide (if any). Plant materials must be selected with care because of the strength of their effect on the garden's appearance. A few examples: too many shiny plants give a garden a plastic look; too many dark green or gray-foliaged plants lend a somber touch that must be lightened with brighter green foliage; large-foliaged plants are best for large areas or for a yard with a tropical theme. Wonderful effects can be achieved by mingling lacy and solid foliage or the many gray and green tones that exist in the plant world. These subtle variations can be used like a wash in an impressionist painting.

The living and structural elements of landscape design are examined in more detail in Chapter 4.

Levels of Formality

Modern landscape designs may be characterized as formal, informal, or naturalistic. These general categories reflect many of the historical developments in landscaping that we've just reviewed. Deciding on the level of formality is the first and most basic decision to be made in landscape planning.

A formal garden is characterized by at least some of the following elements: strong geometric lines, strong architectural features, symmetry, clipped hedges, topiary, neat borders, deep green foliage, uniformly shaped plants, and geometrically espaliered fruits. The heritage of Roman and Renaissance landscaping is seen most strongly here, and formal gardens generally demand a high level of maintenance.

Informal gardens can incorporate both geometric and free-flowing lines, asymmetry, and plants allowed to grow in their natural forms; they display the influence of Oriental gardens, and Robinson's and Jekyll's informal cottage-type gardens.

Naturalistic gardens, inspired by "wild" landscapes, are a variation of the informal style and are the legacy of the eighteenth-century pastoral landscapers. They are non-geometric, employ natural, flowing lines, and may emphasize appropriate plants. Quite often plants native to an area will be used in woodland or meadow gardens. Naturalistic gardens generally require the least maintenance.

3.3. The huge leaves of the banana tree provide a dramatic accent in the landscape, but such plants should be used with restraint.

Design Principles

A yard that is well designed is a pleasure to look upon because it is cohesive. It provides a sense of unity that is restful to the eye and to the spirit. Most artistic endeavors—a graceful cathedral, a gracious living room, or a painting—strive for this quality, and the design principles used to achieve unity in landscaping are similar to those used in any art form.

Any good design will consider relative *scale* as one principle that helps to achieve harmony. In the garden the factor of scale is particularly vital because living materials have different growth patterns and can change radically in appearance over the course of time. A young pine in a five-gallon can may seem just right for your small yard, but at its final, fifty-foot height it will overwhelm the yard. Gemlike Alpine plants stay small and need a jewel-box setting; they become insignificant in a border of other flowers that grow larger. A two-story blank wall is not enhanced by a single low-growing azalea, and a small cottage loses its intimate character if formal yews that grow to twenty feet are planted at its corners.

Scale has to be considered in your garden structures, too. Massive walls around small yards make that yard seem smaller, whereas a three-foot-high white picket fence around a stately French colonial house is inadequate and seems like an afterthought. The general principle is that garden components, whether plants or construction, should be in proportion to the space they occupy.

In choosing the components of a landscape, another factor to consider is the *balance* of the various parts. It is probably impossible to achieve a balanced appearance from every angle of your property, so concentrate on the areas most commonly viewed, such as the view from the street, from your living room window, or from your outdoor living area. As you look, imagine a vertical axis through the middle of the viewed area.

If yours is to be a formal yard it will be designed with a mirror-image symmetry around the vertical axis. For instance there might be a row of matching shrubs, trees, or planters on either side of the walk or entryway. (See Figure 5.18.) Formal balance, provided, for instance, by clipped hedges, espalier fruit trees against brick walls, and avenues of identical shade trees, gives a feeling of stateliness and stability, and considerable visual pleasure. However, when there is too much repetition of the same plants or structures, the yard can appear stiff and sometimes dull.

In less formal yards, plants and structures should be arranged to strike an asymmetrical but pleasing visual balance. A large tree might be balanced by a cluster of shrubs or a gazebo; a large section of patio can be balanced with a large area of ground cover. Informal balance gives a feeling of movement and interest. But don't overuse such juxtapositions; too much movement and interest can result in a yard that looks busy and agitated.

The warnings about doing too much in your garden bring

3.4. *Identical plantings flanking a doorway are an example of formal balance.*

us to the principle of *simplicity*—certainly an important factor in designing for unity. A landscape should have an overall framework in which a few plants of similar texture, form, foliage, and color dominate. Some of the plants forming the framework are used at regular intervals. Only a few construction materials should be used, and their textures should be complementary. Brick, gravel, and wood are pleasant together, but the further addition of tile or stucco would result in a jumble. The plants and structures that form the framework establish the tone of the whole, in the same way that the major decisions you make about your interior space—wall color, carpet, furnishings—determine your choice of lamps, area rugs, or artwork for the walls.

Within the larger framework, certain plants or small structures are made to stand out, and the limited use of such *accents* is part of another design principle, *variety.* Plants used as accents are known as *interest plants,* and they usually have some outstanding feature—the graceful, pendulous form of a weeping plum, the brilliant white flower show of an almond, the flame-colored skin of the persimmon fruit, or the huge leaves of a banana. But here, too, restraint is important: too many of these stunning plants competing for our attention can lead to chaos rather than comfort. We must learn to leave collections to the arboreta and let simplicity take precedence over variety.

When I was a child, my grandmother had a friend called Mrs. Johnson. Whenever Mrs. Johnson went out, she would wear a large hat with flowers, a colorful scarf, two or

three bracelets, three strings of beads, a polka-dot blouse, and, of course, lace gloves. When I was tempted to overdress, my grandmother would admonish me with, "You have too much Johnson!" The temptation to use too many interest plants and have a yard with "too much Johnson" should be resisted.

Themes

To help create a unified landscape most designers choose a *theme.* Themes may be cultural in origin, such as Japanese, Colonial, or Spanish styles; horticultural, such as those fea-

3.5. *A house with a strong period character, such as this Victorian, would not be well complemented by, for instance, a Spanish or Oriental theme garden.*

turing native plants, flowering plants, or collections of cacti or alpine flora; or functional, such as those oriented around a recreational swimming pool, an entertaining area, or a food production garden.

The choice of a horticultural theme often depends in large part on where you live. Gardens featuring exotic species have been popular at various times in the past, but most are high-maintenance and resource-hungry—for example, fuschia collections and hybrid tea-rose gardens. Again, better to leave the collecting of this type of exotica to the arboreta and public gardens. The recent trend toward using native-plant themes is an encouraging one; it will be discussed further in the last part of this chapter.

Functional themes span a wide range of possibilities, most of them limited only by your taste and budget. Not everyone can afford to plan his property around a swimming pool, and—despite my encouragement—not everyone wants to focus completely on food growing. We will look more closely at various landscaping styles and hobby gardening at the end of this chapter and in Chapter 5.

Some themes have a distinct and consistent motif, often derived from other cultures, eras, or architectural styles. Some examples are a Colonial theme, characterized by a white picket fence, rambling roses, and a kitchen garden of herbs; and a Spanish theme, in which terra-cotta tile, bright flowers, and strong accent plants complement the highly stylized Spanish architecture. Theme gardens can be created with great imagination and sensitivity, but are successful only when the theme serves to unify all the elements and not to distract the observer from them. The elements of the landscape must harmonize with the architecture of the house—a tropical garden would clash with a southern Colonial house, for example, and Japanese lanterns would not blend with a New England "salt box." The theme should also suit the style of the immediate neighborhood and the natural vegetation and contours of the area. A clipped box maze would be conspicuously out of place in a modern subdivision and an English perennial border would look strange indeed with a background of Florida scrub with its Spanish-bayonet and palmetto.

Surrounding Areas

All well-designed landscapes—not just theme landscapes—should display a harmony with the surrounding land as well as within their own boundaries. I have seen elaborate gardens in Palm Springs, California, complete with lawn and clipped hedges, that come to an abrupt end against desert scrub and sand, like a carpet sheared off in a straight edge. Such yards are as jarring as billboards would be in the midst of a flower bed. The transition between the landscaped property and its surroundings should always be subtle, regardless of the character of those surroundings.

In residential yards an effort should be made to blend with the tone of neighboring properties. For example, in a neighborhood where most houses have highly tailored

3.6. *Spanish tile-roofed architecture blends well with many edibles, including this pomegranate.*

yards, a completely untamed wildlife garden would be too sharp a contrast. And in a neighborhood of manicured, flat lawns and low ground covers, a yard full of trees and shrubs up to the property line would look out of place. Conversely, landscaped yards in relatively undeveloped surroundings should contain plants that blend in color and type with the native vegetation. Topiary and other formal styles should be avoided altogether or kept near the building. The area between the wild vegetation and the landscaping near the buildings should serve as a gradual transition from one type of environment to another. For example, if the surroundings of the property were a deciduous woodland with bright-green foliage, and if gray-foliaged plants or plants with deep-green needles were situated near the house, the plants approaching the woodland would be increasingly similar to the species growing wild. Or in a chaparral or desert area, where the natural tones were predominantly grays and the plants near the house mostly bright green, the color plants in between would lessen in intensity the closer they were to the surrounding area.

Borrowed Landscapes

The great Italian and Oriental landscape designers often took advantage of their surroundings by incorporating the views of neighboring property into their designs. If a nearby property contained a venerable old cherry tree, a gnarled cedar, or some other eye-catching tree that was visible from the property being designed, the designer would highlight this accent. A view of a church steeple or some smoky hills

3.4. Though they can be a nuisance if you grow many edibles, wild creatures add another dimension to a natural garden.

in the distance might also be featured as part of the design. Such "borrowing" of existing elements is sound practice in modern landscaping. The landscaper may incorporate the borrowed feature by leading the viewer's eye to it by means of a path, hedgerow, or an expanse of lawn. Borrowing objects from the surrounding areas draws the eye out of the immediate vicinity and can make a small garden appear larger.

The Total Effect

Although the visual appeal of an artistically landscaped yard usually receives the greatest emphasis, a good design should appeal to all the senses. The fragrance of orange blossoms or Alpine strawberries ripening in the sun, the pungency of herbs as we brush past them, and that special tomato-plant scent that hints at the flavor to come, are some of the olfactory pleasures we can enjoy. Those tomatoes ripening on the vine, a sun-drenched, juicy peach, or a crunchy walnut will gratify our sense of taste. Everyone appreciates the feel of dewy grass underfoot, of pussy willow or catkins in the hand, and the contrasting texture of rough bark and silky leaves. And auditory delights can include the splash of a fountain, the rustle of leaves, and the songs of the birds that nest in our shrubs and trees.

The total effect of a landscape is more than just the sum of its parts, and not all the factors are entirely under our control—but this is as it should be. A quail scurrying down a path or a flock of cedar waxwings eating berries that are rightfully ours, can bring as much pleasure as our carefully selected plants. The acrobatic antics of squirrels enchant us, even though we know the little monsters are decimating our almond crop. These are some of the unplanned pleasures that a good landscape design invites and enhances.

Landscaping Styles for a Resource-Conscious Age

In bygone days, when only a privileged few enjoyed landscaped gardens and most land was left more or less undisturbed, the owners of vast landscaped estates had the luxury of considering only their own needs. In our day, however, great numbers of families own their own plots of land, and their landscaping decisions affect not just their own households but, ultimately, all people sharing the earth's diminishing resources. I have discussed the cumulative effect of thousands of lawns and hundreds of water-hungry hydrangeas and fertilizer-hungry floriferous fuchsias on some of those resources. It is clear that now our gardens must function not only to fulfill our individual needs but to protect and preserve the environment as well.

What follows is a discussion of the ways in which landscaping should function for our particular era. The basic concepts identified here will benefit both the residential yard and the environment in general. Fortunately, in most cases, what is good for one is also good for the other.

For the Homeowner

In the landscaping philosophy promoted in this book, the most basic function of a landscaped yard is to provide both aesthetic enjoyment and fresh food for its residents. But a well-designed yard has more practical functions as well. It should provide privacy from the neighbors, keep small children and dogs safely contained, enable householders to keep mud and dirt out of the house, provide a utility area for storing wood, garbage cans, and compost heaps, and provide a place to dry clothes.

In a very real way, a good landscape design makes a living space more livable. Well-placed walls, high mounds of earth, hedges, and trees can temper noise, wind, and glare, and reduce the particulate matter in the air (foliage collects solid particles of pollution such as lead and dirt). As noted earlier, strategically placed trees can shade a living space in hot weather, and south-facing patios can focus warmth on cool days. By incorporating such practical considerations into our landscaping plans, we can make space more useful for relaxation and entertaining. The outside living space should be an integral part of any landscape design. However, in much of the country the importance of this concept is ignored or minimized.

Landscaping has even more specific uses in certain areas of the country. In the arid West, appropriate plantings can help to control erosion and mudslides, and serve as buffers in case of brushfire. In snowy areas, well-placed fences and hedges keep blowing snow from drifting over walks, driveways, and porches. Clearly, the practical functions of good landscaping are myriad, and landscaping solutions exist for a multitude of homeowners' problems. We'll see how to carry out a number of them in subsequent chapters.

For the Planet

The function of landscaping that is new to our age is environmental preservation. This concept is related to the unprecedented size of our population. The ultimate goal is to save energy and resources and protect the health of all species, but the key to conservation-minded landscaping is conscientious planning. One needs to perceive both a problem and a solution to use the sun's rays to warm that south wall in winter and still plant wisely to shade the same wall from summer sun. And one needs foresight and a good knowledge of available shrubs to provide windbreaks from winter gales. All aspects of a yard have to be thought out in order for the use of gasoline, fertilizer, pesticides, fungicides, and water to be minimized. And practices such as composting, mulching, and erosion control must be learned (or relearned) and incorporated to preserve and renew the soil. A natural development will be a shift to lawn-maintenance techniques that require less fuel and water, or the gradual replacement of the lawn as a routine landscaping feature by other elements that put less stress on world resource supplies. Finally, food production must be considered an integral aspect of our evolving landscaping style. This factor alone could change the face of American yards over the next fifty years.

It is important to note here that although foodscaping seems to me to be the ideal landscaping style of our time, others might not be in full agreement and might favor other landscaping modes. Alternatives in keeping with conservation principles do exist and are gaining favor across the country as the resource crunch becomes ever more palpable. Landscaping with native species to highlight the natural environment; landscaping to create woodland, meadow, and prairie gardens; landscaping to recreate or simulate the ecosystem around a dry creek bed—all these approaches represent new landscaping styles that preserve and protect the natural environment while enhancing the land being designed.

Natural Gardens

Informal, natural gardens are appropriate alternatives to the formality of manicured lawns and clipped hedges. Natural gardens are an option in all areas of the United States. Such gardens not only help to preserve native species of plants, but they preserve the wildlife that feeds on those plants as well. Furthermore, such gardens are among the most inviting settings for outdoor relaxation and activities.

The rationale behind natural gardens is not only to preserve a plant species or two, but to help preserve a habitat or an ecosystem, which are as varied as the different parts of the country. Thus, for example, a natural garden might recreate a grove of tulip trees carpeted with bloodroot, mayapple, and jack-in-the-pulpit; the native bluestem grasses interplanted with wildflowers of the prairie; prickly pear side by side with sagebrush; palmetto together with loblolly pine; or vine maple combined with mountain dogwood. North or south, east or west, the native plants can be used to form a soothing, comforting haven.

The native plant theme focuses on the use of native, or indigenous, plant species—those adapted to a particular climate, soil type, and set of growing conditions—to recreate a naturally occurring habitat or ecosystem. It should contain a representative variety of the species that might have been found on a property long before it was developed.

Interest in native plant gardens picked up noticeably during the 1970s. The West Coast drought of 1976–77, the oil crunch, revelations about the possible effects of garden chemicals on the environment, and the high cost of garden and park maintenance all contributed to this trend. Today information on native plants is readily available from government agencies, interested horticulturists, university programs, and many hobbyists. Native plant societies all over the continent are sources of informational and instructional material.

Large gains have been made, too, in the availability of the plants themselves. Nursery catalogs now contain long lists of native plants, and a number of local and mail-order nurseries carry native plants exclusively. Following are a few of the more popular and versatile styles of native gardens.

Woodland Gardens

Woodland gardens are landscapes carved out of natural wooded areas and enhanced by judicious planting and

3.5. Leaving part of a lawn in meadow can create a pleasant natural effect and saves mowing. The mowed and unmowed grass should meet in a graceful line. Mow the meadow part twice a year—in midsummer and midfall—for a neater appearance and to control the growth of woody plants. In fall or early spring, overseed with a wildflower mix.

pruning, and the addition of paths and patios. These natural settings are further improved, for example, by a walkway to a streamside area or rock outcropping. Other woodland gardening techniques include clearing the brush away from individual trees with beautiful flowers or branching patterns, and providing open spaces (glades) planted with indigenous wildflowers. Small lawn areas or patios can be added to the yard to permit people to sit down and enjoy the surroundings.

The character and existing vegetation of the site largely determine the result. For those who want to create a woodland garden from a bare lot, much study and time must be invested. A book titled *Landscaping with Native Plants in the Middle Atlantic Region* (see bibliography) will be very helpful to residents of the Northeast.

Meadow and Prairie Gardens

These styles, which primarily involve converting lawns into natural grassland, offer both beauty and low resource consumption. A meadow or prairie garden is not merely an untended lawn sporting dandelions and crabgrass, but rather a fairly stable plant community of perennial native grasses, forbs (broadleaf herbaceous plants), and some woody plants.

Meadows are usually open areas, though sometimes they are adjacent to woodlands. Meadow gardens are most suitable for large lots and informal settings. Once established, they are low-maintenance, but they do require mowing once or twice a year to prevent the sun-loving grasses from being taken over by shrubs and young trees.

Two publications are useful in planning a meadow garden: *Energy Conservation on the Home Grounds* and the aforementioned *Landscaping with Native Plants in the Middle Atlantic Region.*

A prairie is a specific type of meadow, a treeless expanse dominated by native grasses and forbs. Different prairie types cover a great part of the country, from Iowa west to Colorado, and from northern Texas to the Dakotas. Like the meadow garden, the prairie garden lends itself to large yards and informal designs. Ideally, they should surround low, unobtrusive sod-covered houses, nestled into hillsides. Modern cluster developments, in which houses are grouped together near a hillside and their common properties are joined together in open space, are also ideal for prairie landscaping. For most homes, however, a modified concept of the prairie garden is more suitable. This would incorporate windbreaks and shade trees to modify the climate and edible plants near the house.

Prairie gardens do not give instant rewards; most of these grasses require two to three years to become well established. Maintenance involves occasional mowing and weed control. For information on planting a prairie garden, write for the brochure titled *Prairie Propagation Handbook,* $1.75, to Boerner Botanical Gardens, 5879 S. 92nd St., Hales Corners, WI 53130.

Dry Creek Beds

Homeowners in arid parts of the West who are interested in landscaping their yards without lawns have an attractive option. In place of large expanses of plain ground cover a replica of a dry creek bed is created and native plants alone or in combination with drought-tolerant exotics are planted along the creek. Dry-creek landscaping can give design and a dramatic accent to an otherwise uninteresting yard.

Dry creeks are not limited to arid areas, however. They can be planned for any climate, with plants that grow easily there. I have seen one on a steep slope in western Washington that was planted with dwarf conifers. In that instance the dry creek was water-filled during the rainy season; the water that didn't go into the soil was drained away from the residence and into a vacant meadow by underground drainage tiles.

To fulfill their potential, dry creeks must be installed with artistry. One cannot replicate a dry creek bed simply by lining up a few boulders. The boulders must be placed to look as if they had come to be there naturally. This means they must be dug into the soil 6–7 inches, not just set on top. Study the boulders, and place them with much patience and artistry. They should look natural, as if they were there before the creek was.

The base of these boulders will serve as ideal growing places for your plant material. They offer wind protection and keep the soil moist so plants can be clumped around them, just as in nature.

The natural gardens described above are only some of the alternatives appropriate for our times. Every geographic region offers unique opportunities for imaginative and resource-conscious landscaping. While I encourage and employ all these approaches, I am still convinced that landscaping with edibles—what I call foodscaping—embodies the most benefits by incorporating the advantages of healthful food production. Radical though it may seem, foodscaping appears to be our only chance to effect a turnaround from environmental degradation to healthful food production. But for home landscapers, what a fine opportunity it is to derive a sense of satisfaction on both a practical and an aesthetic plane. Beauty plus bounty—watchwords for the future!

CHAPTER 4

Laying the Groundwork

Beautiful, productive yards are no happy accident. They are the results of good planning. Beauty, productivity, and ease of maintenance all depend on the extent to which a yard has been thought out in advance. Good planning can also help you to avoid some common pitfalls—for example, incurring unexpected expenses, provoking neighbors' objections leading to expensive alterations, and problems such as the flooding of basements owing to unforeseen drainage changes. Less drastic but more common are overcrowded plantings and disappointing yards. All such outcomes are preventable with foresight and a bit of research.

Whether you are starting from scratch with an undeveloped piece of property, contemplating a total makeover of an existing landscape, planning to add some edible plants to your yard, or attempting to incorporate conservation principles into your general landscaping approach, the steps outlined in this chapter will smooth your way. I have broken down the process of landscape planning into several stages. The first step is the analysis on paper of your property in terms of your specific needs, desires, potential problems, and time and budget constraints. The next step is to determine how environmentally sound, resource-saving

techniques can be effectively incorporated into your landscape plans. The final step in the planning stage is to assess and select from available construction and plant materials.

A couple of cautionary notes are in order before we plunge ahead. If you are considering a major landscaping project involving a lot of construction, or if steep slopes, soil, or drainage problems are involved, do hire a professional to help you. Most licensed landscape architects work with industrial and government clients, but a number work with homeowners. Landscape designers, as opposed to landscape architects, usually work exclusively for homeowners and often advertise in the telephone book yellow pages. Remember, though, that many landscaping professionals think in terms of spacious lawns, few edibles, and large expanses of concrete or redwood decking—that is, in the traditional ways unattuned to environmental concerns. You can make good use of their technical knowledge while still maintaining your own sense of the importance of conservation measures and the plants you consider appropriate.

Second, bear in mind that this book is not a complete guide to standard landscape planning, construction techniques, and materials. Many good books on the market cover the engineering and construction aspects of brick and concrete work, decking, carpentry, drainage, and sprinkler systems. These books also contain such specifics as turn-around space for parking cars, the optimum height of stair risers, the options available in patio covers, and ornamental plants to complete your plantings. Among the books listed in the bibliography, the following are particularly useful as guides to specific topics: *Reader's Digest Practical Guide to Home Landscaping; Western Home Landscaping;* the Ortho series of garden books, particularly *Garden Construction Know-How* and *How to Design and Build Decks and Patios;* and the Sunset Books garden series, which includes *How to Build Fences and Gates, Garden and Patio Building Book,* and *How to Build Walks, Walls and Patio Floors.*

Putting It on Paper

Step one in any landscape plan is to measure your yard and draw it on paper to scale. This is a time-consuming process but enormously valuable for several reasons. First, it helps you to see the whole picture in one place at one time. Second, it helps avoid costly and frustrating mistakes during the installation phase. Third, it allows you to communicate your ideas and desires to others in a clear and concise manner. And finally, it greatly facilitates completion if the project must be done piece by piece over a period of time.

If you can locate an architect's or developer's drawing of the house and property, your job will be easier, but make sure the drawing is accurate. If the plan has been photocopied, check to see whether it has been reduced. If it has been, you must recalculate your scale. Most yards of less than 80 × 60 feet can be laid out on a standard 8½ × 11-inch sheet of ⅛-inch graph paper, on which eight squares equal an inch. For large or complicated jobs, buy some sheets of vellum, a translucent paper. This material is available at drafting supply stores and is usually sold by the sheet. Vellum allows you to lay out plans of large yards, and it can be blueprinted, so you can provide copies to the contractors bidding on the work to be done, or have extra copies to make notes on for yourself. A particularly useful type of vellum has ⅛-inch squares already imprinted on it; these lines do not reproduce when the drawing is blueprinted, giving a clean-looking result. Vellum comes in many sizes. The most common is 17 × 22 inches, which will accommodate a drawing of the standard ¼-acre suburban lot, though larger sizes are available.

Whether you use graph paper or vellum, the eight-squares-to-the-inch scale is handiest. In this scale, each ⅛-inch mark on a ruler equals 1 foot, which allows you to use a ruler to measure distances instead of having to count squares. If your yard covers more than a quarter-acre, however, it is usually easier to scale the drawing to 1/16 inch (or less) to the foot, in order to fit the drawing on a standard sheet of vellum.

In addition to the vellum or graph paper, a notebook, ruler, pencil, and a 100-foot measuring tape will be sufficient to complete the task. The next step is to go outside and do some actual measuring. Measuring is easier and more efficient when done by two people rather than one. Besides the steps that are saved, two observers can doublecheck each other's readings for accuracy. Figures 4.1 and 4.2 will help you visualize how to get started, and demonstrate some commonly used symbols.

After locating the house in relation to the property lines, locate other major structures such as walks, driveways, walls, and telephone poles. At this point you should also locate all relevant utility lines such as sewer, water, and electrical lines so you will not disturb them or risk injury during construction; and downspouts, so you know where excess water will fall and perhaps gather. This is a good time, too, to become aware of all the major trees and shrubs on your property. Some might have to be removed because they have outgrown their space, are diseased, or simply don't fit in your new design, but those you want to retain should be noted in your plan.

Next, locate any overhanging structures such as eaves, porch roofs, and patio covers. These overhangs will shade plants and also help to keep walls cool in the summer, so they are important landscaping features. In the same vein, note all first-floor windows, doors, and porches, so you will avoid placing plants in front of them that would obstruct a view, breeze, or entry. If your yard has a slope, try to approximate on the plan where it begins and ends. Also estimate its angle. For most yards, these approximations are all that is necessary. But if you have a steep slope or are installing permanent structures on the slope such as retaining walls, stairs, or decking, more sophisticated measuring is needed.

Now step back and take a look at aspects of the adjoining properties and general vicinity that may be relevant to your design. Some features may be negative and need screening, such as a neighbor's windows or unsightly sideyard complete with garbage cans. Others might be positive, such as the sight of a distant steeple, a nearby row of elegant trees, or surrounding woods.

Finally, locate north somewhere in the margin of your drawing. This can be done with a compass, or by finding your house on a local street map. Determining your property's exposure to the sun's path is important when you intend to incorporate into your design energy-saving features such as windbreaks or the shading of a hot south wall. Your yard's exposure will also influence your choice of plants.

Measuring and locating to scale all the features of your yard on paper might seem like a chore, but the end product will prove to be invaluable as you proceed. Don't be intimidated. Making a paper model is one of those jobs that appears to be more difficult in the explaining than in the doing. Still, if you are planning any major construction, you might need professional help even at this stage, and you should not hesitate to ask for it.

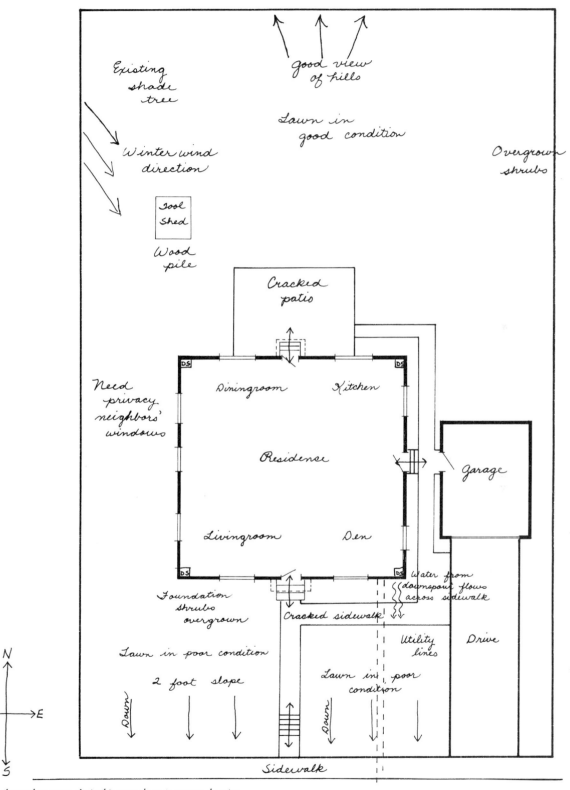

Existing shade tree

good view of hills

Lawn in good condition

Overgrown shrubs

Winter wind direction

Tool Shed

Wood pile

Cracked patio

DS

Diningroom   Kitchen

DS

Need privacy neighbors' windows

Residence

Garage

Livingroom   Den

DS

DS   Water from downspout flows across sidewalk

Foundation shrubs overgrown

Cracked sidewalk

Utility lines   Drive

Lawn in poor condition

2 foot slope

Down

Lawn in poor condition

Down

N
W ←→ E
S

Sidewalk

4.1. *Putting the yard on paper. As in this example, note on your drawing such items as building locations, driveway, overhangs, steps, slopes, and utility lines; also note any problems regarding drainage, view, and so on.*

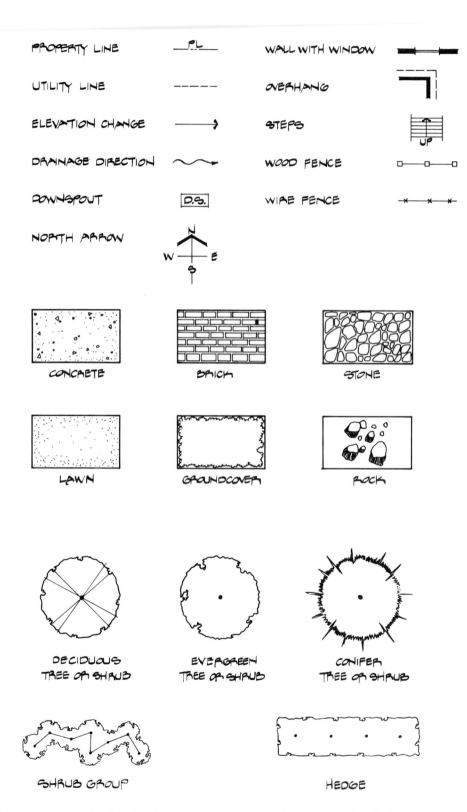

4.2. *Professional designers use symbols such as those shown here to represent landscaping features. Becoming familiar with the more common symbols—for types of plants, building materials, property lines, etc.—will help you to interpret architectural plans and to design your yard.*

Analysis and Troubleshooting

This stage of planning involves noting the basic characteristics of your property, which to a great extent will influence what you are able to do. At the same time, take note of its potential problems. After you have measured your yard and drawn it to scale, walk around the area, notebook in hand, and examine it carefully, making notes on your findings. Your first step should be identifying your soil type and determining any problems it might pose; other aspects to check and note are exposure and wind direction, unusual topographic features, drainage, the health of existing plants, and possible erosion problems.

Soil Types

Soil is composed of mineral particles of many sizes, organic matter in different stages of decay, water, and air. Soil is classified by the particle size of its mineral components into three major textural types: the designations are sand, silt, and clay. Sand is fairly large and the individual particles can be seen with the naked eye. Silt is smaller but can be seen with a microscope. Clay particles are so small they can only be seen through an electron microscope. Most garden soils are a combination of all these types.

Each soil type has its own specific characteristics.

1. *Sandy soils* are made up of a large proportion of relatively large, sometimes rough and sometimes rounded particles. These particles are primarily quartz which is generally inactive chemically. Sandy soils have many pores—spaces containing air that allow roots to receive oxygen—but don't retain water well and therefore dry out quickly. In addition, nutrients are easily leached out of sandy soils so plants growing in this soil type often do poorly. The advantages of sandy soils are their ability to drain well and to warm up quickly in the spring. Very sandy soils benefit greatly from the addition of organic matter.

2. *Silt soils* are fine-textured soils that combine some of the features of both sandy and clay soils.

3. *Clay soils* are made up of extremely small, flattened, usually scalelike mineral particles. They contain few air spaces and pack down very easily. They retain water for long periods of time, and sometimes roots in clay soil get waterlogged and die. Drainage is very important in clay soils. Fertility is less problematic with clay soils than with sandy soils because most clay soil holds nutrients well; the chemical nature and large surface area of the particles, as well as the slow drainage, prevent nutrients from leaching. (Surface area, an important factor in soil science, refers to the surface area of each particle. Because of the fineness and platelike structure of the particles, there is more total surface area in clay soil than in a like volume of sandy soil.)

Good garden soil contains optimum amounts of all three types of soil particles and is called loam. Loam is the best soil type for growing most plants, particularly many of the more demanding edibles.

Use this rough test to determine your soil type. When slightly damp, clay soils can be squeezed between the thumb and fingers to make a continuous ribbon. Sandy soils are gritty, and when dry will run through your fingers. Dry silt has a talcum-powder feel to it and will have some plasticity or stickiness when damp. For more sophisticated tests consult your local university extension service.

The structure of soil as well as its texture is important. Soil structure is the arrangement of the soil particles into aggregates or "crumbs." These aggregations prevent the formation of brick-hard soil that crusts over. Soils with good structure are easily worked, and allow rapid water and root penetration.

The addition of large amounts of humus rectifies most soil structure problems. Sandy soils do not form aggregates well, and the humus helps hold them together; it also improves water retention and adds fertility. In clay soils humus helps to create pore space and to prevent packing. Loams benefit in trace elements and improved structure from added organic matter.

Sometimes sharp contractors' sand (not smooth beach sand) is thoroughly incorporated to lighten clay soils. Perlite and vermiculite are also occasionally added, but if used for large areas they are quite expensive. None of these three additives are permanent. The sand tends to sift down into the subsoil, and the others gradually decompose. While humus also decomposes, annual applications of humus constitute the most effective and generally the most economical way to improve all types of soil.

In analyzing your soil situation, remember that plant roots breathe. Some need more air in the root zone than others. If your soil is a heavy clay and you choose not to modify it, your plant choices will be different from those for a sandy or loamy soil. See the encyclopedia for plants that tolerate heavy soil. If your soil is sandy and you choose not to add humus, you will need to fertilize and water more often.

Soil Problems

Few garden soils are perfect, but most problems can be identified and corrected without a major effort.

Acidity

Most plants grow well under slightly acidic conditions, but if the soil is too acidic, it will starve plants of vital nutrients and will have to be limed, or sweetened. Acid soil is a soil with a pH of less than 7.0 (see glossary), and is usually associated with areas of high rainfall, or sandy or very organic soils. If you suspect that your soil is too acidic, have it tested by your university extension service and follow their directions, or purchase a simple soil test-kit to confirm your suspicion. If the diagnosis proves correct, add lime-stone, following the directions on the bag for dosage. Some plants, such as blueberries and cranberries, require an acidic soil. See the encyclopedia entries for plants with special pH requirements.

Alkalinity

Soils with a pH of 7.0 or higher are considered alkaline. Some plants, particularly grasses, prefer a slightly alkaline soil. Alkaline soils are associated with areas of low rainfall and soils high in lime or sodium. For mildly alkaline soils, most organic matter helps, but the most helpful additives are powdered sulfur, peat moss, and pine needles. Applying a good amount of any of these materials is usually sufficient to alleviate an alkalinity problem. For highly alkaline soils, raised beds must be provided and supplemental chelated minerals added. (Chelated minerals are minerals in a special form that makes the nutrients available to the plants; they are available in nurseries.) Pomegranate and jujube are two edibles that can tolerate quite alkaline soils.

Salinity

Another common soil problem is salinity—a build-up of salts in the soil. This usually occurs in areas of the country that receive less than 30–40 inches of rain a year. Sometimes the salts occur in the soil itself, but often they come from the irrigation water or result from a build-up of chemical fertilizer or manure. Sometimes all three sources are present. The first signs of salt damage on plants is usually a browning on the leaf edges. Salt also causes a withering of the leaves, stunted growth, and poor seed germination.

If you have a salinity problem and your drainage is good, flood the soil thoroughly before planting and at regular intervals thereafter. If the problem is serious, drip irrigation, with the constant moisture it provides, is helpful; so are raised beds and planter boxes. Avoid using manure and chemical fertilizers with a high salt index, such as most nitrate types and urea (see the information on fertilizing in Chapter 7), and don't choose plants that are particularly sensitive to salt burn, such as apples, peas, plums, pears, cabbage, lemons, oranges, avocados, and peaches. If you have serious salt problems, see your university extension service and consult Ortho's *All About Fertilizers, Soils, and Water* (see bibliography).

Hardpan

Occasionally, soil is packed down hard within the first few feet of topsoil or deeper. The result is called hardpan. Sometimes hardpan is a natural condition of the soil, and other times it is man-made—often created when heavy equipment is driven over wet clay soil and compacts it. Hardpan prevents roots from penetrating the soil properly and prevents water from draining off. If the hardpan layer is thin, you can usually break it up with a tractor or punch holes in it with a power auger. In serious cases you will need professional help to install sumps, drain tiles, or raised beds.

Nutrient and Organic Matter Deficiencies

Plants need the major nutrients—nitrogen, potassium, and phosphorus—plus many trace minerals. Most soils are fairly fertile but are usually deficient in one or more of the nutrients needed by plants. Initial soil testing for nutrient levels can be helpful. In most parts of the country, most soils benefit from phosphorus added before new plants are planted, and some form of supplemental nitrogen must be added annually.

Organic matter deficiencies are prevalent throughout most of the country. Preplant applications of organic matter to improve the quality of the soil are usually needed. Manures, composts, and the majority of organic materials are quite low in the major nutrients, but they are used to improve soil structure, to add trace minerals, and to keep soil microbe activity high, which in turn makes nutrients more available to higher plants. See the heading "Plant Nutrients" in Chapter 7 for information on fertilizer and deficiency symptoms.

Erosion

Other problems you might have concern erosion. The severity of such problems will be related to the length and steepness of the slope. See the section headed "Saving Soil," later in this chapter.

Exposure and Wind Direction

Is your yard sunny or quite shady? Sun patterns change with seasons; see Chapter 6 for information on how to predict some of these changes. Few edibles grow in the shade, so it is critical to know where the shade is.

Where does the wind come from in summer? Where in winter? Local weather bureaus can give general information but your own observations will be more useful. You'll need wind-direction information in planning to protect your house from winter winds and to direct summer breezes.

Unusual Features

Are there any unusual features on your property that you'll have to plan around, such as a stream, marsh, or slope? Such features add interest to the landscape but can also pose potential problems, so now is the time to do some troubleshooting. Overlay your drawn plan with tracing paper and note the location of problem areas. Look for drainage problems. Are there places where water stands for a few days at a time? Where do the downspouts on the house empty? Will water collect there and keep the soil too wet? Or will the pipes empty out onto a patio and form puddles, making the surface mossy and slippery? If you do have standing water problems, your options are either to direct the water with underground drainpipes or to plant plants that can use great amounts of water continuously.

Health of Existing Plants

Do existing trees and shrubs look sick? Are they pale

overall, or are their leaves pale and darkly veined, or are their leaves edged with brown? Are there a number of dead or dying plants around the yard? Pale leaves usually indicate that the soil is lacking in nitrogen. Pale leaves with dark veins usually indicate chlorosis (see glossary), which can occur in soils that are too alkaline or are suffering from herbicide damage. And brown-edged leaves can mean that there is too much salt in the soil, that the soil has been overfertilized, or that the plant has been allowed to dry out. A number of dead or dying plants indicates a serious problem— either herbicide damage, bad drainage, or a soil disease. Find out which it is! Take *large* pieces of the problem plants to the nursery or university extension office and have their problem diagnosed.

Herbicide Contamination

Is there evidence that herbicides have been used improperly on the soil? Be particularly careful if you or the previous owner employed a professional gardener; most of them routinely use herbicides to control weeds. Herbicides are used in two distinct ways: (1) to sterilize the soil, thereby killing all vegetation, to make parking strips and utility areas; or (2) to kill weeds selectively, permitting favored plants to grow. The great majority of plants you try to grow in sterilized soil will probably die. If you suspect that an area has been sterilized, test it first by trying to germinate radish or nasturtium seeds in it. Do this at least twice. If the seeds do not grow, have the soil tested. If there is a problem, you'll either have to dig out the soil and replace it; apply large amounts of humus, combined with deep-watering, every few days to leach out the herbicide; or treat with activated charcoal. Under most circumstances extra organic material and leaching are the solution. In extreme cases removing the soil or treating with charcoal are called for. Both processes are expensive.

Not all herbicides are absorbed and deactivated by activated charcoal but most are. Among the most widely used herbicides that are absorbed by activated charcoal are 2,4-D, Amitrole, Benefin, Dicamba, Simazine, and Silvex.

The recommended rate of application is 300 pounds of charcoal per acre, applied following the directions on the package.* Activated charcoal is purchased in limited areas of the country, from charcoal suppliers listed in the Yellow Pages.

Adjacent Areas

As you analyze your yard for possible problem areas, don't forget to consider the areas adjacent to your property. For example, if you are surrounded by arid grasslands or chaparral, remember that they can become fire hazards and consider planting some fire-retardant plants as a buffer. *The New Western Garden Book* lists such plants.

*John A. Jagschitz, "Charcoal's Neutralizing Powers," *Golf Course Management,* November 1979.

Planning for Utility and Enjoyment

The exercise of measuring, drawing, and noting structures, large plants, significant features, and potential problems should make you comfortably familiar with your yard. Now you'll be able to consider how you can make the yard an enjoyable and functional extension of your living space. What precise functions do you and your family want your yard to serve? This section describes many of the common needs home landscaping should serve and limitations often encountered; in Chapter 5 we'll examine in detail how to meet these needs through effective design.

Functions

Every yard should have at least a small area set aside for a vegetable garden. Everyone has room and time for at least a few vegetable plants. But if you want your yard to provide a large amount of food, be realistic. Many major food plants require good soil, plenty of sun, and considerable attention. Can you meet their needs? Some of the less commonly grown food plants—for example, elderberry, pomegranates, figs, and many of the herbs—are more tolerant of soil type and demand less time; and a few food plants do well in the shade. Before you plan for big harvests, consider the time and energy you are willing to devote to your plants and check individual species in the encyclopedia for effort and growing conditions required.

If you will be using your yard for entertaining large groups, a large patio area—preferably near the kitchen— should be a part of your plan. Screened porches are necessary in areas of the country where mosquitoes and flies are a problem. Other possible elements are a barbecue, fire pit, hot tub, pool, or ball court. Most of these are large and expensive projects. If you intend to install any of the elaborate construction projects, plan on getting professional advice and making a large investment.

If your children are young and you want to provide them with a safe play area, remember to consider the cost of fencing and the amenities of any good play space—a sandbox, a swing, and a climbing apparatus. Be aware, too, that the children will outgrow this space in a few years and the area could become available for a hobby or vegetable garden. Plan the first use with an eye to the second.

All yards need a utility area. Its function can include storage (garbage cans, wood, tools, toys, perhaps even a boat); a composting area; a clothes-drying area; and a potting shed. The primary goals in locating the utility area are, of course, that it be unobtrusive but accessible; sideyards are often a good place.

Perhaps you have pets. Provide enough room for a run, a shelter, and some shade. Fencing may be a factor here too, depending on your neighborhood.

Maybe you are considering a hobby garden in which to grow old rose varieties; ingredients for gourmet cooking or wine or beer making; a collection of cacti; cutting flowers;

raw materials for dyes—the options are innumerable. Clearly, this space will have to be planned for in advance. (See Chapter 5 for some specific suggestions.)

Many people think of their garden as primarily a place where they can simply and unashamedly relax. If you feel this way, plan an informal garden with low maintenance requirements. Informal gardens don't give you the constant feeling that a weed should be pulled or a hedge should be trimmed. And they often attract creatures that actually help you relax—for example, a pair of brown towhees, pecking around in their inimitable way, or some squirrels that come to store their winter supplies. In general, keep in mind that a yard is for all seasons and all tastes. Try to make an environment that will suit the particular temperament of your family.

Time and Effort Requirements

How much time are you willing to spend on garden maintenance? Will you be willing to mow grass, pick cherries, or do both? Do you like tidy, manicured gardens or are you more inclined toward natural gardens where leaves blow around freely without causing consternation? The average manicured garden usually requires three to four hours a week during the growing season for raking, sweeping, weeding, and trimming. If you can afford the weekly services of a qualified gardener, it might help you to know that this is the kind of yard professionals are most comfortable with. Be aware, if this is the route you take, that you will have to pay more money to keep your garden chemical

free. Hand weeding is a lot more time consuming and takes more effort than spreading a weed killer, and for busy professionals time is at a premium. Also, professionals paid to keep a garden manicured don't like the looks of an occasional chewed leaf, so you'll have to be prepared to remind your gardener not to spray routinely for pests.

In contrast to manicured gardens, informal ones can require as little as an hour a week—for a little pruning, a little trimming, and a little weeding. But note that low-maintenance gardens don't really qualify for the name until after the first two years—about the time it takes for plants to become established and ground covers to fill in.

As noted earlier, many food plants, such as peaches, apples, and strawberries, need regular and constant care. Such plants can consume many hours a week in spraying, thinning, and harvesting. In August and September, I spend about twenty hours a week picking, drying, canning, and freezing the summer harvest from my ambitious garden. To me this work is justified by the satisfaction I derive from seeing my shelves filled with dried apricots, pickled beets, and applesauce made from homegrown produce free of any adulterations. But you might be unable to spare the time. I advise you to start with a small garden, adding what you can as you learn to assess the time involved.

Working Out Your Budget

Landscaping can cost anywhere from $1,000 to $100,000, depending on the elements you choose. Construction items far outprice plants in landscaping costs. For example, at this writing a patio can cost $2,500, whereas three trees might amount to only $100. In most landscaping jobs, plants represent only 10 percent of the total cost. Sidewalks, fences, patios, walls, earthmoving, rocks, extra soil, sprinkler systems—all these expenditures will add considerably to the cost of the job.

Although it's most economical to do as much of your own work as possible, concrete work represents the exception. There is a knack to finishing concrete so it looks smooth and even. If you don't have it, this knack is worth paying for.

If you are going to do the work yourself, work out your own estimate. Call around and try to find the best prices for lumber, plumbing, and plants. For tips on how to keep costs down, see the section later in this chapter headed "Using Recycled Materials."

Zoning Restrictions

Most Americans feel that the right to "life, liberty, and the pursuit of happiness" includes the right to do anything they please with their land. Actually, there are many legal restrictions on what we can do to our land. Be sure to check with the local building authorities before you start any major projects. Many cities and counties have fence laws, for instance. These laws refer to height restrictions and placement. Some cities outlaw fences; others require them. Most

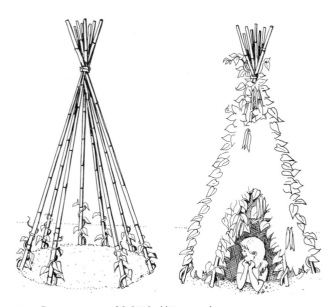

4.3. Bean teepees are a delightful addition to a play area.

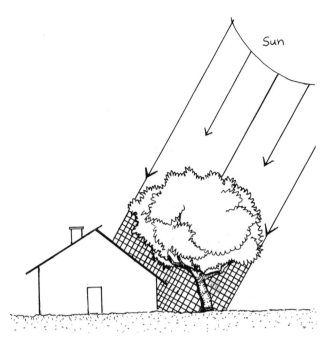

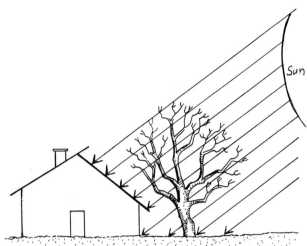

4.4. *Deciduous shade trees planted near a south wall can dramatically cool a house.*

4.5. *When bare in the winter, deciduous trees allow the sun's rays to warm the house.*

cities and towns also have laws governing the placement of patio covers, pools and pool equipment, and arbors. Usually, these features cannot be situated near a neighbor's property line. Municipal weed-abatement programs also affect new landscape design; fire departments in particular are interested in eradicating grassy weeds in arid-summer areas. Sometimes such programs place constraints on establishing informal meadow or prairie gardens.

Environmental Planning

All too often the effects of landscaping on the environment—both in modifying the microclimate that is your own yard and in conserving soil, water, and fossil-fuel energy—are slighted in current practice. As I have emphasized throughout, environmental protection is one of the most important functions of landscaping for the age we live in, so let's look at how to put it into practice.

Landscaping for Climate Control

As noted earlier, before the days of central heating and air conditioning our grandparents used trees, shrubs, and vines to help keep their houses warm in winter and cool in summer. On the Great Plains, rows of poplars protected homes from wind and sun. In other parts of the country, spreading trees such as elms cooled the front verandah and an arbor covered with grapevines often protected the passage to the ice house. Today incorporating climate-control techniques in our landscaping again makes sense. In some parts of the country thoughtful landscape planning can save 20 to 30 percent a year on heating and even more on air conditioning.[*]

Also, in recent years we've seen a trend toward designs in homes that specifically utilize passive solar and wind technology. This subject is outside the scope of this book. See the bibliography for selected references.

In the following sections, I present some general climate-control guidelines. If you make use of these techniques, I would estimate that you will achieve about two-thirds of the energy savings possible through the use of landscaping techniques. Should you want to explore these and other techniques more fully, consult *Landscaping that Saves Energy Dollars*, or *Landscape Planning for Energy Conservation*, both included in the bibliography.

Controlling sun and wind are the primary aims in climate control. Solar radiation can be desirable or undesirable, depending on where you live. Landscaping in Florida would aim to reduce that radiation; in Maine, a design would take full advantage of it. Wind, too, can be either a problem or an advantage, depending on where you live. You might be in an area of hot, drying winds, or of cool breezes off a nearby body of water. Obviously, such geographical factors will influence your landscaping decisions.

Your more immediate surroundings will also be a factor.

*American Association of Nurserymen, "Our Grandparents Had an Energy-Saving Secret" (Washington, D.C., 1979).

Perhaps your yard is surrounded by dark-colored masonry walls and paved surfaces that absorb the heat. Or maybe you live in a wooded area that doesn't get much sunshine.

However, since most homes in the United States are located in temperate regions that experience a large temperature range over the year, climate control rarely is just a simple matter of trying to keep cool or stay warm. You will probably be faced with solving one problem in the summer and another in the winter. The object in both cases is to maximize your blessings by planning your landscaping to serve this dual function. For example, in winter deciduous trees, having dropped their leaves, will let 75 percent of the sun's rays through to heat a south wall. In summer, when the trees have leafed out, not only do they create shade and prevent the house wall from heating, but also evaporation from the leaves actually cools the wall by creating a breeze under the tree. Using annual vines in combination with the trees—say, on an arbor over a patio—is even better than relying on the trees alone, since quick-growing vines such as runner beans or bitter melon will fill in the arbor for the first year or two while you wait for the trees to grow large enough to do the job. Another valuable design feature is a south-facing patio made of dark-colored masonry that absorbs heat. Combined with shading annual vines or some deciduous vines and trees, such a patio will serve both as a cool, shaded refuge in summer and a source of radiated heat in winter.

Some of the following tips and techniques for climate control with landscaping should be appropriate to your area.

Cooling Techniques

Provide shade for south- and west-facing house walls and windows. South walls are exposed to the sun most of the day. Walls facing west receive sun in the afternoon, usually when the sun is the hottest. The aim is to keep the hot summer sun from striking the south and west walls of a house and heating them, and to keep sunlight and its heat from windows in those walls. Deciduous trees, arbors with vines, patio covers, or awnings can all be used to shade the walls. It has been shown that a large tree shading a south or west window from direct sun rays can reduce the inside temperature by 15–20 degrees.

Do not install driveways, walks, or patios of dark-colored masonry near the house—or eliminate them where possible—unless they can be shaded in summer.

In tropical climates, provide at least a 3-foot overhang protection for windows and doors, either as part of the house construction or in the form of awnings. This feature will allow you to keep windows and doors open during cooling rains that often occur on hot days in the tropics.

Funnel summer breezes into the patio or house by using hedges and shrub borders. Living things do a better job of funneling cool air than masonry walls. In the hottest climates, plant evergreen trees to shade south walls and plan a cool, north-facing patio.

Warming Techniques

Expose as much of the south-facing house wall and window area to the winter sun as possible.

In cool climates, install asphalt or concrete driveways and patios near the south wall of the house. These materials will absorb heat and radiate it back to the house at night for added warmth.

Install a windbreak of evergreen trees and shrubs to redirect prevailing winds in winter. See Figure 4.7. Experiments have shown that when the outside temperature is 32 °F, twice as much fuel is necessary to heat a house to the comfort range when the wind measures 12 miles an hour as when it measures 3 miles an hour. Thus, a 30 percent saving in heating fuel can result from properly placed windbreaks.* Use evergreen shrubs and trees or earthen berms (large mounds of earth) on the north and west sides of your dwelling. Berms should be constructed with a slope ratio that does not exceed 3:2—that is, 3 feet in width to 2 feet high—and planted with a ground cover that has a strong root system.

*American Association of Nurserymen, "Our Grandparents Had an Energy Saving Secret."

4.6. A deciduous vine on an arbor is one of the most efficient means of shading a south wall.

Note: Winter winds come from the north and west in most parts of the country, but check your own yard because mountains, hills, large buildings, and bodies of water can alter wind patterns.

Create air pockets to insulate the north wall of the house by planting evergreen shrubs close to the wall or evergreen vines that cling to the masonry. Sun never strikes a north wall to heat it. The point of creating the air pocket is for insulation to prevent heat loss from the house.

Extend your spring and fall outdoor living by providing wind protection to south-facing patios.

In extremely cold climates, instead of deciduous trees you might want to use canvas patio covers that can be completely dismantled for winter. Thus you wouldn't lose even the 25 percent of the sun's radiation that dissipates through tree branches or vines.

Deciduous Trees to Shade South-Facing Walls

Food-bearing species included in the encyclopedia are designated by an asterisk here. See *How to Use the Encyclopedia* for information about growing zones and a map.

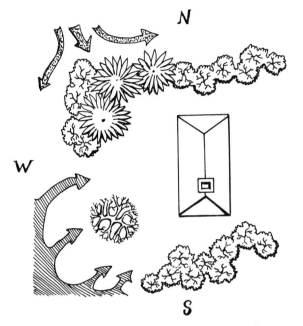

4.7. *Well-placed windbreaks can divert winter winds and, in summer, direct breezes to cool your house.*

LARGE TREES (40 FEET OR TALLER)
Chinese pistache, *Pistacia chinensis*—60 ft., zones 9-10
European beech, *Fagus sylvatica*—80 ft., zones 4-8
Ginkgo, *Ginkgo biloba*—100 ft., zones 4-10
*Hickory, *Carya* species—100 ft., zones 5-9
Little leaf linden, *Tilia cordata*—90 ft., zones 3-8
London plane, *Platanus acerifolia*—100 ft., zones 5-9
Norway maple, *Acer platanoides*—70 ft., zones 4-9
Oak, *Quercus* species—many different species for many zones
*Pecan, *Carya illinoinensis*—75 ft., zones 6-9
*Red maple, *Acer rubrum*—100 ft., zones 3-9
Sargent cherry, *Prunus Sargentii*—50 ft., zones 5-8
*Sugar maple, *Acer saccharum*—100 ft., zones 3-8
Sweet gum, *Liquidambar Styraciflua*—100 ft., zones 5-10
Thornless honey locust, *Gleditsia triacanthos inermis*—70 ft., zones 4-10
Tulip tree, *Liriodendron Tulipifera*—100 ft., zones 4-10
*Walnut, *Juglans* species—to 80 ft., zones 3-9

MEDIUM-SIZE DECIDUOUS TREES
Brazilian pepper, *Schinus terebinthifolius*—40 ft., zones 9-10
Bradford pear, *Pyrus calleryana 'Bradford'*—40 ft., zones 5-10
Eastern redbud, *Cercis canadensis*—35 ft., zones 4-8
Golden raintree, *Koelreuteria paniculata*—35 ft., zones 5-10
Serviceberry, *Amelanchier* species—40 ft., zones 3-8
Silk tree, *Albizia julibrisson*—40 ft., zones 5-10
*Sweet cherry, *Prunus avium*—35 ft., zones 5-9

SMALL DECIDUOUS TREES
*Almond, *Prunus dulcis* var. *dulcis*—30 ft., zones 6-9
*Apple, *Malus* species—30 ft., zones 3-9
*Apricot, *Prunus Armeniaca*—25 ft., zones 5-9
Crape myrtle, *Lagerstroemia indica*—25 ft., zones 7-9

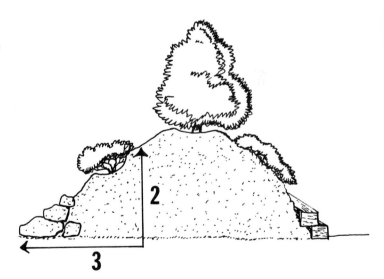

4.8. *An earthen berm, supported with rocks or railroad ties to control erosion, can be an effective windbreak. It can be as high as is practical but the slope ratio should not exceed 3:2, as indicated.*

Flowering dogwood, *Cornus florida*—30 ft., zones 5-9
*Nectarine, *Prunus Persica nucipersica*—20 ft., zones 5-9
 Orchid tree, *Bauhinia blakeana*—30 ft., zone 10
*Peach, *Prunus Persica*—20 ft., zones 5-9
*Persimmon, *Diospyros* species—30 ft., zones 6-10
*Plum, *Prunus* species—20 ft., zones 4-10
 Russian olive, *Elaeagnus augustifolia*—20 ft., zones 2-10
 Serviceberry, *Amelanchier grandiflora*—25 ft., zones 4-7

Resource Conservation

This section is concerned with practical ways of conserving key resources in our landscaping practices. Specifically, the resources at issue are fossil fuels (as used in ways other than heating and cooling), water, and soil.

Saving Petroleum Energy

We can relearn from the past how to care for lawns and shrubs without resorting to motorized equipment or chemicals. In the early 1900s, lawns didn't consume petroleum at all. White clover, with its nitrogen-fixing* abilities, was often interplanted with grass, or manure was applied to meet the latter's high demands for nitrogen. Weeding, mowing, trimming, and raking were all done by hand, and the fertilizers used were organic manures and compost. Petroleum-based herbicides and insecticides were not available, so grass was less pristine and lush than in modern lawns. Also, lawns were smaller and adjacent areas were often kept in meadows. Furthermore, most people didn't have as much time for nonproductive gardens in those days. The majority were busy chopping the wood, stoking the furnace, feeding the livestock, and tending the vegetable garden. We must now relearn some of the old ways and plan for yards that conserve energy. Here are some conservation techniques you might be able to incorporate in your own plans:

1. *Keep lawns small and use alternative ground covers*, and/or maintain it in the manner suggested in Chapter 7. Obviously, the smaller your lawn, the less fuel your power mower and trimmer will use. Weeding, so often accomplished with petroleum-based herbicides, will also be minimized. Hand-weeding is not out of the question, of course, particularly where lawn areas are small. Once established, most evergreen ground covers need little weeding, which makes them an attractive alternative to grass.
2. *Use fertilizers wisely.* Select plants that have low fertilizer needs or that provide a food dividend for the fertilizer used. Use organic fertilizers when appropriate.

3. *Choose plants that require minimal spraying for pest control.* Use biological pest control practices whenever possible.
4. *Use drought-resistant plants where appropriate.* As noted previously, transporting and pumping water can consume significant amounts of fuel.
5. *Use recycled construction materials where possible* (see "Recycled Materials" at the end of this chapter).
6. *Plant food-producing plants.* To summarize these points, the food you produce will not consume the energy that the farmer would use to grow it, that the trucker would use to bring it to market, or that the market would use to keep it looking fresh for days. You will have helped add to the world's food supply at no energy cost.

Saving Soil

Our specific soil-conservation concerns in the landscape planning stage are (1) to make sure the organic content of the soil is sufficient, and (2) to protect the soil from erosion.

The first step toward maintaining the level of organic material in the soil is to choose a site for a compost system. All yards should contain some sort of composting system; the two basic types and how to prepare them are discussed in Chapter 7. If you are planning an extensive vegetable garden, it is important that the system you incorporate be a high-production one. For convenience and to avoid possible odor problems, plan to place your compost system away from the residences and near the vegetable garden. See the bibliography for books that detail different methods of composting. (Chapter 6 covers the subject of composting for small-area and container gardening.)

If you have slopes in your yard, erosion could be a matter for concern. Installing retaining walls into the slope or planting the area with perennials that have strong root systems will help hold the soil. Plants and ground covers useful for erosion control are listed at the end of this section. Jute netting is helpful to hold the soil on steep slopes until the vegetation fills in. This material is available through nursery supply houses. It should be installed at planting time and secured by wire fasteners pushed into the ground. The new plants are planted through the netting spaces, and the jute remains in place until it decays, by which time the plants have become established.

Keeping the soil high in organic materials is especially important when planting on slopes. Humus-rich soil can absorb more water, thus preventing the rain from sheeting off and taking precious topsoil with it. Organic mulches are also helpful. They fight against erosion in three ways: by keeping rain from sheeting off, by holding soil down in the wind, and—when dug into the soil or allowed to decay naturally—by contributing organic material to the soil.

In arid climates watering technique is a factor in controlling erosion. Even on slopes of the slightest angle, irrigation water can carry off soil. To prevent runoff of this type, plan to use drip irrigation or careful overhead irrigation, methods that irrigate slowly enough to enable the water to

---

*Nitrogen-fixing refers to a process involving the interrelationship between certain plants, usually legumes, and various bacteria found in the soil. The process results in the release, for plant use, of nitrogen upon the death of the microorganisms.

soak into the soil. For overhead irrigation, automatic sprinkler systems that can cycle on and off at five-minute intervals work well, since they are least likely to wash away soil. (See the section on watering in Chapter 7.)

If your land contains steep slopes or if you plan considerable construction that involves cutting and filling, you should consult your county soil-conservation service or a landscape architect to help you determine the best methods of erosion control.

Erosion can sometimes be a problem even on level ground. Soil becomes vulnerable to heavy rain and wind when, for example, a large vegetable garden is left bare for periods of time between crops. Mulches are helpful here, as well as on a slope. Another precaution is to plant a green-manure crop in the winter months. Green-manure crops are herbaceous plants such as clover or winter rye or wheat that are plowed under in the spring. They hold the soil in winter and enrich it for planting time. Where winters are too harsh for cover crops, plan to leave the plant residues and stubble in place in the vegetable garden. In areas where wind is severe, your design might have to include a windbreak of hedges or trees. Another potential erosion problem is newly bulldozed land on construction sites. Instead of leaving the ground bare for the winter, plant a green-manure crop.

PLANTS FOR EROSION CONTROL

African daisy, *Osteospermum fruticosum*—zones 9 and 10
Boston ivy, *Parthenocissus tricuspidata*—zones 4-10
Ceanothus, *Ceanothus* species (low growing types)—zones 7-10
Cotoneaster species (low growing types)—zones vary
Dwarf coyote bush, *Baccharis pilularis*—'Twin Peaks' variety recommended, zones 9 and 10
Euonymus Fortunei—zones 5-10
Grasses, Gramineae family—many different species, zones vary
Japanese spurge, *Pachysandra terminalis*—zones 4-9
Juniperus species (low growing types)—zones vary
Periwinkle, *Vinca minor*—zones 4-10
Rockrose, *Cistus* species—zones 9 and 10
Rosemary, *Rosmarinus officinalis*—zones 8-10
St. John's Wort, *Hypericum calycinum*—zones 6-10

Saving Water

Until recently, we have practiced ostrichism regarding the state of our water supply—we buried our heads in the sand in the face of the facts. Now, with widespread water rationing a real possibility in the near future, we are beginning to realize that the era of unrestricted water use is coming to a close.

OASIS PLANTING

As noted earlier, in arid areas of the Southwest the water problem is the most pressing. It is inevitable that lawns and begonias in the desert will go the way of the dinosaurs. But this doesn't mean that, even in these areas, landscaping

must limit its materials to cacti and rocks. With wise landscaping and conservation practices, lovely gardens will continue to enchant desert dwellers.

When I design a yard in an arid climate I often follow the oasis principle, borrowed from the early Egyptians. That principle allows the use of water-using plants, but only in a small area close to the house where the blossoms, foliage, form, and fruits are certain to be seen and appreciated. The rest of the yard is planted in drought-resistant materials. Planting the oasis near the house makes watering easy and efficient. Hand-watering is possible or a sprinkler system can be designed to water only those plants that need irrigating.

JUSTIFYING EDIBLES

Many edible ornamentals use a considerable amount of water. For example, most edible annuals, such as the leafy greens—lettuce, spinach, and chard—as well as the cabbage family and the cucurbits, are very heavy water users. While I justify their use with the arguments that they return an edible product on my water investment, and that watering methods used at home can be much more efficient than commercial irrigation, the fact is that these plants still use considerable amounts of water. The watering techniques described in Chapter 7 minimize water use as much as possible where plants have high water requirements.

LAWNS AND ALTERNATIVES

Obviously, the same restrictions on lawn planting that relate to fuel conservation have relevance for water conservation. Since lawns are the heaviest water users in the landscape, minimize or eliminate unnecessary lawn areas from your landscape design. Ask yourself how much lawn you really need for croquet, badminton, football practice, frisbee throwing, somersaulting, and other such pleasures. If you come to the conclusion that no lawn is necessary at all, use drought-resistant ground covers.

If you must have some lawn, however, select the grass variety that is optimum for your area—the one that grows well and requires the least amount of water and fertilizer. Lawn-grass varieties and cultural conditions differ from region to region, but a few generalizations can be made. For instance, in all areas of the country avoid the velvet and creeping varieties of bentgrass; they are particularly heavy water users (and use much fertilizer and pesticides as well). For Midwest gardens, consider planting some of the native prairie grasses (see Chapter 3). Unfortunately, the most drought-resistant varieties of grass, such as Bermuda and zoysia, can become as pervasive as weeds and can be hard to keep out of shrub borders and other beds. They are also difficult to eradicate if you want to convert their space into food-growing or ground-cover areas. And Bermuda, despite its drought tolerance, requires large amounts of fertilizer, so it represents a trade-off with respect to its conservation value. Choosing the right grass species for your yard is a complex task. Consult James Beard's *Turfgrass*, or your university extension service so you can make an informed choice for your particular soil, climate, and needs.

When lawns are a necessary part of your landscape, try to restrict them to level ground. Again, watering and fertilizing on a slope mean water and nutrients down the drain unless the utmost care is taken. On slopes, substitute soil-holding ground covers for lawns whenever possible.

See the section titled "Maintaining a Lawn" in Chapter 7.

GROUND COVERS FOR LAWN SUBSTITUTES

All the plants covered under erosion control can be used as ground covers, plus the following:

Asparagus fern, *Asparagus Sprengeri*—18 in., zones 9 and 10
Bearberry, *Arctostaphylos Uva-ursi*—12 in., zones 2–10
Crown vetch, *Coronilla varia*—24 in., zones 3–10
English ivy, *Hedera Helix*—8 in., zones 5–10
Hottentot fig, *Carpobrotus edulis*—6 in., zone 10
Indian strawberry, *Duchesnea indica*—3 in., zone 2–10
Lantana, *Lantana montevidensis*—18 in., zone 10
Star jasmine, *Trachelospermum jasminoides*—24 in., zones 9 and 10
Woolly yarrow, *Achillea tomentosa*—2–4 in., zones 3–10

ABSORBENCY AND CONSTRUCTION MATERIALS

If your landscaping plan includes patios, driveways, and work areas, try to minimize wasteful runoff by using materials that facilitate absorption (see the section headed "Surfaces" later in this chapter). Absorbent surfaces allow a significant proportion of the rainwater that falls to sink in and recharge water resources rather than to run down the sewer.

DIRECTING RUNOFF

Another conservation measure is to direct rain runoff from house downspouts to an area of the yard that can absorb it. Well-placed drain tiles underground will deliver the water where it can be absorbed by the soil.

POOL COVERS

If you have a swimming pool, use a water-saving pool cover. It will prevent constant evaporation so you won't have to refill your pool as much to maintain the proper water level.

SPRINKLER SYSTEMS AND DRIP IRRIGATION

Today's sophisticated sprinkler systems can aid in saving water, but only if used properly. Drip irrigation, a relatively new method, is particularly useful in some situations. More information on both these watering techniques can be found in Chapter 7.

DROUGHT-TOLERANT PLANTS

Finally, use drought-tolerant plants, both natives and exotics. Consult references listed in the bibliography, including *Easy Gardening with Drought-Resistant Plants.* When using edibles where water conservation is critical, be sure to consult the encyclopedia, and choose those plants that are most drought resistant.

Elements of the Landscape: Structures

Now that your property is laid out on paper, your needs and limitations are carefully noted, and, I hope, the conservation measures relevant to your plans have been identified and incorporated, you are ready for the final stage of planning: choosing the structures and plants for your landscape. Your choices will depend on personal taste, considerations discussed in the preceding sections, and availability of materials locally (or by mail, for plants). The possibilities are almost limitless, which in itself can be bewildering, but the first step is to learn what those possibilities are. In this section I will describe the range of structural elements, both common and unusual, and how they will affect your planning; a section on plant materials concludes this chapter.

Garden structures—the man-made elements in a garden—are basic to any landscape plan; they can form the frame for the picture you want to create. Beyond this, these structures will enrich your outdoor living space. Patios and their sheltering covers will increase that space; planter boxes and walls will add interest by breaking up the space and introducing new heights, textures, and colors. Paths, retaining walls, and fences will lend visual interest in the same way, although their purpose is largely utilitarian.

From a large array of traditional and nontraditional structures and materials, I have concentrated on those that are best for the environment. They can help cool the house in summer but retain heat in winter, prevent erosion, make use of solar energy; and, in the case of paving surfaces, allow water to percolate into the soil. Where relevant, the use of recycled materials is stressed.

Many books are available on the subject of garden structures, and contractors are well-versed in traditional construction materials. The emphasis in this section, therefore, is on not only resource-conserving structures but also nontraditional garden structures and new ways of handling traditional situations involving landscape construction. Bricks in mortar, decking, and cement aggregate—some conventional solutions to construction problems—can be very handsome, but alternatives are needed.

Recycled Materials

Using recycled materials in construction saves energy and other resources; wherever such an item is incorporated, a new brick is saved for another use or a tree might live a bit longer. Some recycling helps to keep already full dump sites from getting fuller. Many recycled items, such as railroad ties and used grapestakes, can be useful and attractive elements of an informal garden. They can add individuality to a garden and provide a pleasant change from the standard concrete patio or regulation fence. Some even work in a formal garden—for example, antiques such as brass carriage lamps for entryways, salvaged wrought iron gates, or mossy-green copper tubing used as a free-form fountain sculpture.

Some recycled materials, such as broken-up concrete or old wood from structures being demolished, can be obtained free of charge. Keep your eyes open for demolition work in progress, and read the classified section of the newspaper. Note that most dumps do not allow scavenging, so you must get the materials before they end up there.

Many recycled materials must be purchased. Garden supply houses often carry railroad ties and used bricks, and occasionally they stock cobblestones. These items are not inexpensive; in most areas of the country used brick is more expensive than most kinds of new brick. Near large cities demolition and scavenging firms often sell materials from old houses and factories. Flea markets and garage sales are other possible sources.

Antique Garden Items

Treasures from the past can lend distinction to a landscaped garden. Their potential is limited only by the designer's imagination. Sources for these items vary according to their function. For instance, if you live near the water and would like to give a nautical feel to your yard, look for a marine salvage firm. Such places occasionally carry old oak hatch covers, a few of which could make a small screen. Old heavy rope suspended between posts makes a decorative fence, and brass lamps from a ship look nice in an entryway. House-wrecking services often sell old newel posts, painted tiles, and wrought iron fencing. In Connecticut, I visited a firm of this type that covered a full acre. I could have browsed for days. Imagine what you could do with some of these items! Victorian newel posts could be used for gate posts and 5-foot cable-spool tops for gates. Old stained glass windows could be covered with plexiglass and used in decorative screens. Pieces of copper gutter could be stacked and used as a spill fountain. Visit these places with an open mind.

Paving Materials

One of the most versatile recycling materials, particularly useful in informal gardens, is broken-up concrete. My clients sometimes balk at the idea of using broken concrete, but my answer is that you can't beat the price, since it is yours for the taking. It is no heavier than brick and comes in interesting shapes that can be set in sand and soil, with low ground covers planted between the pieces, to make a patio that is permeable to water. Or it can be set in mortar and used for paths to utility areas and to set garbage cans on. Potting shed floors, drying areas—any utility area can utilize this material. Finally, broken-up concrete can be arranged as a wall or divider (see Figure 4.9) with the aggregate side

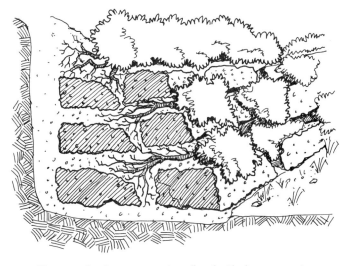

4.9. *Plantings soften the appearance of a wall made of broken concrete. As you build the wall, put soil mix between the layers, and when the wall is finished, plant the pockets with heat-loving, drought-tolerant herbs, such as thyme, sage, oregano, and marjoram.*

showing. The pockets between the pieces can be planted with herbs and succulents of many kinds.

This magic material of many uses is available wherever a concrete contractor is working. The concrete broken up on a job on occasion has to be carried away, and usually the contractor will be delighted to have someone pick up some of it. If you are close enough to the job, he may even have his truck deliver a load to you. Also, keep an eye out for demolition jobs. But when selecting your concrete, be a little choosy. Take material that is not stained, and, if you are going to use it for either a flat surface or a wall, try to take it all from the same batch, since the colors vary a great deal.

Old Lumber

Railroad ties are wonderful for paths, stairs, and retaining walls. They can be ordered from a nursery supply house, and the more battered they are, the cheaper they will be. Be careful when using old ties that they are not oozing creosote, an oily substance used as a wood preservative. Shoes will pick up this material and track it on carpeting, or people may sit on it and stain their clothing. And excessive creosote can damage plants. Also, railroad ties can be so full of grit that they are hard on drill bits and saws. Use old equipment on them when possible.

Telephone poles are another recycled garden material. They are pressure-treated with a preservative, and are thus useful for retaining walls, in decks, as arbor supports, and even for curbing. Sections of weathered telephone pole

4.10. A retaining wall can be constructed from sections of used telephone poles set on end. Beveling the top softens the appearance. Also, slices of the poles can be set in gravel for a paving surface.

with the tops beveled look informal and rustic placed on end near a deck or patio or next to a low set of stairs (see Figure 4.10). The poles can be sliced into rounds for use as a paving material for informal paths and patios. These pieces can be mortared or set in sand with low ground covers interplanted between them. The availability of used telephone poles varies throughout the country. Some utility companies invite the public to pick up used poles free for the asking; others won't allow it. Sometimes garden supply houses sell them.

Surface Areas

Before our houses were built on the land along with their driveways, sidewalks, roads, and patios, rain water landed on vegetation, forest duff, or bare dirt, and much of it soaked into the soil to replenish underground water tables. Today, much of the soil surface in residential areas is cov-ered with impermeable concrete, blacktop, or brick set in mortar, and the water is diverted away from the land into drains, gutters, and sewers. Suburban areas must have gutters and sewers so that runoff from the rain does not flood yards.

We needn't give up our driveways, walkways, or patios in order to stem this waste of water. Rather, in many cases we can make these surfaces more permeable, to enable water to percolate into the soil. Brick on sand with planting space between, for example, absorbs more water than mortared brick. Gravel walks absorb more water than concrete walks. Using such materials requires caution, however. In arid climates, planting in cracks with water-loving plants can be counterproductive; such plants may use more water than is saved. Also, patios should not be made of a permeable surface material where water would percolate under the house or into a basement. You must have good drainage *away* from the house to use this method.

Patios

Patios are areas near a house that are used for family recreation and dining. They are usually paved with a hard surface to accommodate chairs and tables, but nowadays the ideal patio is made from recycled or naturally occurring materials and installed in a way that allows water to permeate the soil. Traditional patios are made from concrete, brick, or slate, making the surface a considerable investment, but some recycled materials are cheaper. Railroad ties, used stone, broken concrete, and wood rounds can be used this way.

In most areas of the United States, a patio is best located on the south side of the house so that it will be warm in spring and fall and can help to heat a south wall with reflected heat in winter. The patio should be shaded by deciduous trees, arbors, lath with a vine covering, or a patio cover of awning canvas that is easily dismantled for the winter (see "Patio Covers," later in the chapter). The resulting shade will protect people and the facing walls from the hot southern summer rays; when the shade is removed in cold months the winter sun will warm humans and those same walls. In cool climates, providing wind protection for the patio is also important. And in areas of the country where mosquitoes are a major problem, patios must be screened. Screened patios and patios with solid roofs need solid concrete flooring.

Paths and Walks

Paved paths are necessary to keep people's feet dry as they walk from one part of the yard to another. Paths can be made from the traditional concrete, brick, and asphalt; from the materials mentioned in the preceding section on patios; or from rocks, wood chips, or gravel. Solid concrete or brick in mortar are recommended for heavily traveled front walks and those walks or paths where big equipment, such as wheelbarrows, mail carts, and mowers might occasionally roll.

Paths lead the eye, and are therefore strong elements in a design. Straight paths give a formal feeling, while curved paths lend a more casual mood. But don't plan to put an arbitrary curve in a front walk or in other heavily traveled paths, even in an informal garden; people will walk in the shortest line, ignoring the path. Paths leading from a patio through an area of ground cover to a secluded grove of trees with a bench can give much interest to an otherwise dull yard. When you plan a path, it is helpful to lay out a garden hose or string to mark its course. See Figure 4.11 for several path designs.

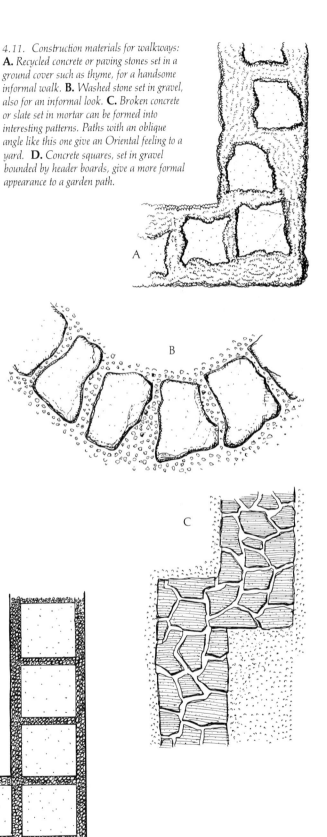

4.11. *Construction materials for walkways:* **A.** *Recycled concrete or paving stones set in a ground cover such as thyme, for a handsome informal walk.* **B.** *Washed stone set in gravel, also for an informal look.* **C.** *Broken concrete or slate set in mortar can be formed into interesting patterns. Paths with an oblique angle like this one give an Oriental feeling to a yard.* **D.** *Concrete squares, set in gravel bounded by header boards, give a more formal appearance to a garden path.*

4.12. *Hollow concrete blocks set on edge and filled with gravel make a permeable surface for parking strips.*

Larger Surfaces

Sometimes sizable areas need to be paved, such as fire-truck access roads, extra parking spaces for campers and boats, or turn-around areas for cars. Even these large areas can be permeable. Two possibilities for permeable paving materials are hollow concrete blocks—set with the hollow side up, filled with gravel or soil, and planted with a sturdy ground cover—and precast concrete forms with holes for grass or ground covers.

In some regions, blocks can be planted with zoysia or polygonum, an attractive way to break up the look of too much concrete or asphalt. Note, however, that in arid parts of the West, blocks used under the large native trees should be filled with gravel only. Any fill-in plants would require summer watering, which in turn would invite soil fungus that could kill the trees.

Paving with blocks and planting them can help cut down on reflected heat in hot climates, but perhaps the most valuable use for this technique is to save old, established trees. Sometimes paving is needed at the base of these trees, for parking or a fire lane, for instance. Standard paving materials smother the roots and don't allow the tree to receive water or oxygen, often causing the trees to die. Hollow blocks filled with gravel allow the free flow of air and water and give a firm surface for vehicles.

Hollow concrete blocks are readily available from concrete supply houses and building supply stores. Occasionally, a concrete supply house can provide preformed concrete honeycomb blocks just for this purpose. These special blocks are strong enough to take constant traffic, and can even be used for driveways. Sprinkler systems can be installed under these blocks so that ground covers planted in them can be watered easily. They are available from Bomanite Corp., 81 Encinas Ave., Palo Alto, CA 94301, and Interlock Paving Manufacturers Association, 6 Bond St., Great Neck, NY 11021.

Patio Covers

The optimum patio cover for most areas of the country provides shade in the summer but allows the sun to pour through in the winter. It is easy to achieve this ideal by using a wooden trellis covered by deciduous vines, such as grape or kiwi, or annual vines, such as bitter melon or scarlet runner beans. Another option is to erect a canvas covering on metal poles that can be completely dismantled in winter. This option, of course, doesn't give you the pleasure of picking fruit from your trellis.

Whatever you choose for a patio cover, to effectively shade a south wall it should overhang the building by at least 8 feet. Anything smaller will not keep your house wall cool. At the same time, in cold-winter areas you should avoid creating a dense, permanent cover of lath or plastic panels that cannot be removed. Such a patio cover will keep the winter sun from heating your walls and make winter living cold and dark. In Florida, Hawaii, and low deserts, however, permanent dense lath works well. Evergreen vines, such as passion fruit vines and bitter melon, which will stay perennial in those areas of the country, also function well in these warm-winter regions.

Arbors and Gazebos

Arbors and gazebos, delightful additions to a backyard, are usually made of wood. Gazebos are usually airy, free-standing, roofed structures that bring a touch of whimsy to a landscape; arbors are upright supports for climbing vines or shrubs. Arbors can be used to define an area or frame a view, and both are useful as accents in a landscape (see Chapter 5). Children love to play under arbors and play house in gazebos. Both kinds of structures provide support for grapes, kiwis, pole beans, and other, less productive vines. Arbored walks can help provide shade to south and west walls.

Containers and Planter Boxes

Plant containers and raised planter boxes are useful in yards with bad drainage. But even in yards with no drainage problems, a plant in a large container can add interest to a porch or a patio where the flatness of the surface might be dull and uninspired without different levels and a focal point. (See Chapter 6 for extensive information on growing edibles in containers.)

Recycled materials often make good plant containers. Wine or whiskey barrels, for example, are excellent containers for dwarf fruit trees. Drain tiles can serve as bottomless containers for use near a patio. Large packing crates painted to match the house trim make charming informal containers for squashes, marigolds, and cucumbers. Soy tubs—the containers used for fermenting soy sauce (see Figure 4.13)—or small wooden boxes are suitable for pepper and eggplant. I am not inclined toward using old automobile tires or bathtubs as planters; I have yet to see any that look attractive.

Planter boxes are often part of a permanent landscape design. They can be made of the traditional brick, stone, adobe, redwood, or railroad ties, stacked horizontally or vertically.

4.14. Rough-hewn grapestakes (used to support grapevines in vineyards) are made of redwood and make handsome informal fences for Western gardens.

4.13. Soy tubs make attractive containers for annual vegetables. They come in a number of sizes and are sometimes available in import stores.

Fences and Walls

Fences and walls are used as windbreaks and to provide privacy and protection from intruders. They also define spaces, exclude or contain animals, and provide limits for children. Fences and walls can be strictly utilitarian, for example, chain link fences used to form a dog run, or strictly decorative, as with a split rail fence used to define an area and add interest to the landscape. Most fences and walls, however, are used for both purposes. Hedges can be used for most of the same functions as fences. They are discussed later in this section.

Fences are usually made of wire or wood; walls are made of masonry. Both fences and walls add much to the usefulness and structure of a garden but they are expensive. A large portion of the total cost is for the materials alone. Obviously, using recycled materials would cut the cost considerably.

Fencing materials that can be recycled are bamboo, used house or barn lumber, and grapestakes (see Figure 4.14). A lovely idea borrowed from the Orient is the interweaving of gnarled branches for a rustic gate (see Figure 4.15). Recyclable wall materials are stone, used brick, sections of tele-

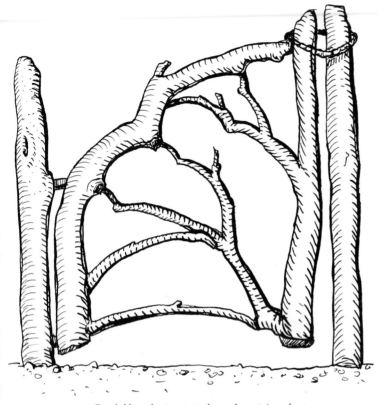

4.15. Gnarled branches intertwined to make an informal gate.

phone poles (on end), and railroad ties. Most fences and walls can be softened by vines and shrubs.

Personally, I find chain link unattractive in its bare state, but its cold appearance can be modified by a covering of sturdy vines, such as grapes, pole beans, hops, or kiwi. Because of this fence material's openness, fruiting vines grow well on it, where they receive more sun and better air circulation than they would on a solid fence.

Whatever material you choose for a fence or a wall, check with local zoning codes and consider the tastes of your neighbors. Property-line fences involve the families on both sides of that fence, and should be a joint venture.

Hedges

Clearly, hedges aren't man-made structural elements, but they are living fences and can be used in most of the same ways as structural fences. Also, they are considerably cheaper than constructed fences, won't absorb heat in warm climates, and often provide luscious food. Hedges require more upkeep than built fences, however, especially when they are to have a formal, clipped appearance. Hedges can be extremely informal and thorny, making them more effective as barriers to intruders than fences. No

one scales a barrier of prickly pear or rugosa roses. See the section on plant materials at the end of this chapter for ideas on individual species.

Retaining Walls

Retaining walls are used to hold soil on the side of a hill or on a slope. Walls higher than 2 ½ feet usually need to be professionally engineered and installed. Low retaining walls can be made of native stone, broken concrete, or sections of railroad ties installed on end or stacked and secured by metal pipes. Remember that retaining walls usually change the drainage of the area, and that you will need to provide drainage to carry water away from the bottom of the wall. The list of plants that grow at the top of a retaining wall is limitless, because of the good drainage, but only plants that tolerate waterlogged soil can grow at the base of the wall. Decorative drainage rock is also an option for the bottom of retaining walls.

Retaining walls can give exciting lines and add much interest to a yard. They are particularly attractive with plants spilling over them (see Figure 4.16).

Pools

Decorative Pools and Fountains

For the enjoyment they provide, small decorative pools and fountains use small amounts of water and energy. A tiny pump that will lift 135 gallons of water an hour to a height of 2 feet uses only 1/55 of 1 horsepower. Combine this minimal energy use with the fact that the water used is recirculated and you find that the resource consumption of a fountain is negligible.

Small pools and fountains are simple enough to install. The Sunset book *Garden Pools, Fountains, and Waterfalls* is a complete source of information on the subject, including how to recycle the water. But resist the temptation to put in large pumps with gushing waterfalls. They are not needed and often look pretentious. The drawing at the start of this chapter shows a very simple but effective use of water: the *tsukubai*, a bamboo flume and stone basin.

Small spill fountains can be constructed from an endless array of recycled materials: old copper plumbing equipment, stacked used flower pots, industrial antiques from old factories, or a collection of native fieldstones are all possibilities.

Edibles can be used imaginatively in and around small pools. Edible lotus or water chestnuts grow well in pools, and cranberries, natal plums, bananas, citrus fruits, clumping bamboo, sorrel, and most of the herbs do well around them. See especially the encyclopedia entries for lotus and water chestnut.

Swimming Pools

The installation of a swimming pool represents a large investment. Such pools must be installed professionally and are expensive to keep up. They need to be cleaned, treated

4.16. *Broken-up concrete makes a pleasant, serviceable retaining wall for informal yards. Set the pieces of concrete in a mix of sand and light soil to help the drainage, placing them so they slant back into the slope.*

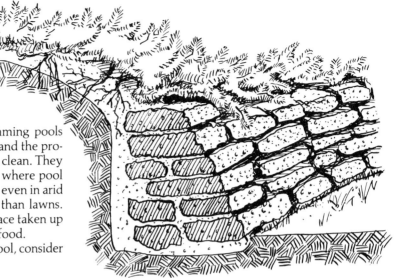

with chemicals, and refilled constantly. Swimming pools consume energy in the filtering of their water and the production of the chemicals required to keep them clean. They also utilize significant amounts of water, even where pool covers are used; still, it has been estimated that even in arid climates swimming pools use no more water than lawns. But surely by now you know my bias—the space taken up by a pool could be better used for producing food.

Nevertheless, if you do install a swimming pool, consider the following recommendations:

1. *Employ conservation measures.* Today, manufacturers of pools are more conscious of good water and energy use, so pools have become less wasteful. Pools presently being installed should be unheated or heated by solar energy.
2. *Use a pool cover.* Pools should be covered whenever they are not being used. The covers prevent water evaporation and heat loss, and help keep the water free of leaves and insects. Some covers on the market can also serve as solar collectors, and some serve as safety devices, keeping toddlers and adventurous children from falling into the water. Most covers are easiest to install and use on a rectangular pool; free-form pools are generally the hardest to cover.
3. *Select plants for safety and cleanliness.* When choosing the plants that will grow around your pool, avoid varieties that will drop slippery fruit on the decking or in the pool or that will drop leaves or small litter, such as pine needles or bottlebrush stamens, since these materials clog the filter. Many plants are sensitive to the chlorine used in pool water and should not be planted nearby. Nor will you want to use plants around the pool that attract bees. If you choose to have a swimming pool you must accept the fact that only a few kinds of plants, such as bamboo, natal plum, and some herbs, can be grown around it.

Elements of the Landscape: Plant Materials

Choosing plants is the last and, for many of us, the most enjoyable step in the planning of a landscape. At this stage, we can visit nurseries to see what is available locally and then go back to the nursery catalogs to study the possibilities of growing things the local nurseries don't carry. It can be an exciting, informational time, the frosting on the cake.

Before you start, remember that when you are growing food plants in your landscape and eating food straight from the plant, it is imperative that you become aware of the danger of some of the poisonous ornamentals. Never, never eat anything growing in your yard unless it has been properly identified. Teach children always to check with an adult before eating something from the yard. Also, when you are choosing plants for your yard, don't select plants that look similar to edibles—for example, sweet peas, whose pods look like those of edible peas. Be aware also that *parts* of some edible plants are poisonous—rhubarb and potato leaves, for instance. Check the encyclopedia for specific information on each plant, and *never eat anything you are unsure of.*

Some Common Poisonous Ornamentals

Autumn crocus, *Colchicum autumnale*
Black locust, *Robinia Pseudoacacia*
Bleeding heart, *Dicentra* species
Box, *Buxus sempervirens*
Buckeye, *Aesculus* species
Castor bean plant, *Ricinus communis*
Cherry laurel, *Prunus caroliniana*
Daffodil, *Narcissus jonquilla*
Daphne, *Daphne* species
English ivy, *Hedera Helix*
Foxglove, *Digitalis purpurea*
Golden chain tree, *Laburnum anagyroides*
Hydrangea, *Hydrangea macrophylla*
Lantana, *Lantana* species
Larkspur, *Delphinium* species
Lily of the valley, *Convallaria majalis*
Mountain laurel, *Kalmia latifolia*
Oleander, *Nerium oleander*
Privet, *Ligustrum vulgare*
Rhododendron, *Rhododendron* species
Sweet pea, *Lathyrus odoratus*
Wisteria, *Wisteria floribunda*
Yew, *Taxus baccata*

Criteria for Plant Selection

Your choice of plant materials will be determined to a certain extent by local growing conditions. Chief among these factors are climate, exposure, and soil requirements. These are discussed in each entry in the encyclopedia of edible plants; for other plants your best guides are specialized reference books, mail-order catalogs, or a well-informed nursery.

In making your final choices among the many plants suitable for your growing conditions, the basic questions to consider are: (1) Does the plant produce something I want? and (2) What does the plant look like? The former is a subjective matter. The latter can be broken down into the separate characteristics of plant size, form, leaf texture, and color. In considering these characteristics, and how your selections will work together in the landscape, bear in mind the general design principles discussed in Chapter 3. Choose a few basic plant forms, textures, and foliage colors, and use them throughout the design. Then choose those plants with unusual features as accents.

Size

Plant size is a practical as well as aesthetic consideration. All too often home landscapers base their choice on the size of the plant as it goes into the ground, giving little or no thought to the size that it will attain within five or six years. Outsized foundation plants are the most common example of this problem—such plants rather quickly cover windows, put stress on eaves or overhangs, or simply crowd entryways and look out of proportion. Conversely, a fully grown plant might prove too small to serve the purpose for which it was intended. Quinces, for example, rarely grow tall enough to shade the south wall of a two-story house. Therefore, it is important to investigate the probable growth habits—both height and width—of plants under consideration before you make your final selections.

Form

Shape, or form, is the most obvious characteristic of most plants. See Figure 4.18 for examples of different plant forms. The most common form among edible plants is a rounded shape such as that of the apple, almond, peach, persimmon, tea, or citrus. Another typical shape is the upright form, as of the currant, bamboo, ginger, and pear. Some plants, such as the pomegranate and elderberry, are somewhat fountain shaped, while others, such as thyme, chamomile, and cranberry, take the form of a mat. Some plants, both edible and not, come under the category of interest or accent plants (discussed in Chapter 3) on the basis of their striking form. In the edible category, these include the 'Weeping Santa Rosa' plum; pawpaw, with its pyramidal form; and banana, with its large, dramatic leaves and upright growth. The forms of these plants dominate the area where they are

placed, so you need to take special care to give them space where they can be used to their full advantage and not made to compete with other strong forms. Let such plants serve as focal points.

Texture

Plants have different textures as well as different forms. Texture is usually described in terms of the coarseness or fineness a plant suggests, basically through the size and shape of the leaves and the spacing between them. The most dominant aspect of texture is leaf size. The big, bold banana leaves, which are usually more than six feet long, and the tiny, narrow, half-inch-long leaves of asparagus, which give an almost wispy appearance, exemplify contrasting textures. The size of the space between the leaves and the length of the leaf stem (or petiole) also influences texture. The close spacing of the leaves on the short stems of an orange tree, for example, gives orange a coarser tex-

4.17. *Most varieties of jujube have a weeping form.*

4.18. *Some common plant forms, from left to right: the weeping form of the 'Weeping Santa Rosa' plum, the rounded form of most citrus, the fountain shape of elderberries, the ground-hugging mat form of thyme, and the upright form of the pear tree.*

ture than that of pear, whose leaves are farther apart and set on longer stems.

Color

Plants give color to the landscape in many ways. The most fundamental is through a variety of greens—from the rich, deep green of strawberry leaves, through the bright, light green of lettuce leaves, to the gray-green of olive foliage, for example. When considering color in the landscape, think in terms of the summer-foliage colors—greens of every hue and intensity. Since most plants produce flowers, showy fruits, or colorful foliage for only a very short period of the year, the green, summer-foliage colors should serve as the backbone of your color design.

After choosing the basic foliage colors, most people enjoy supplementing their garden with trees, shrubs, and herbaceous plants that bloom at different times of the year, adding interest. Be warned, however, that it is well to limit flower colors to two or three basic colors when choosing flowers that bloom simultaneously. For a more detailed treatment of flowers in the garden, see the discussion on perennial borders in Chapter 5.

Choosing Edibles

By now you know that edibles are my preference wherever a choice of plants is involved. Many edibles are as decorative as strictly ornamental plants and offer as well the incomparable bonus of food. Does a forsythia bear lovely fruit after the blossoms are gone? The equally attractive bush cherry does. Why plant a cup and saucer vine when a 'Dutch White' runner pole bean would serve the same landscape purpose? Does a lawn offer sweeter-than-sweet berries in the midst of that lush green? And what could be nicer than a shrub border of genetic dwarf fruit trees? As you can see, I discuss this subject with icy objectivity!

You can, of course, grow inedible rhododendrons with your blueberries and salal; you can have inedible red salvia along with your pomegranate. Many combinations of in-

edible ornamentals and edibles are possible. My aim is to convince you to plan for your edibles first and then find ornamentals that will thrive in similar conditions.

The sections that follow describe categories of plants based on their landscaping uses and provide lists of edibles suitable for each purpose. For specific information on each edible plant mentioned, see the encyclopedia. Each ency-

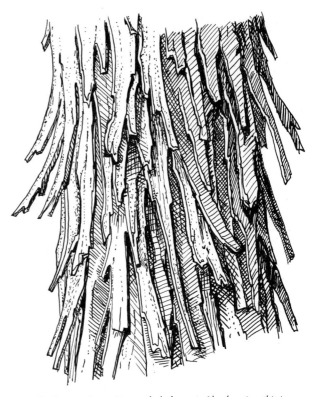

4.19. *Bark texture is an often-overlooked aspect of landscaping; this is a shagbark hickory.*

clopedia entry describes the plant, identifies the growing zone, and lists recommended varieties. In addition, it gives growing requirements and indicates whether more than one plant is required for pollination. Check the glossary for definitions of unfamiliar horticultural and landscaping terms.

Acquiring edibles can be easy or a challenge, depending on the varieties sought. General guidelines for buying edibles are given in the introduction to the encyclopedia and in Appendix B. If a plant listed in the encyclopedia is difficult to obtain, a source is given.

No strictly ornamental plants are discussed here; as I mentioned earlier, you'll probably want to include some in your plans, but there are multitudes of books that tell you what ornamentals to use in each category.

Ground Covers

Ground covers are low-growing plants that can cover large areas. They can substitute for part of a lawn area and are useful on slopes and under trees and shrubs. With the exception of chamomile, which takes light foot traffic, none of the edible ground covers are meant to be walked on.

4.20. Strawberries are a delicious "filler" for small areas of the garden.

Ground Cover Edibles

Chamomile	Peanut
Cranberry	Strawberry
Dwarf natal plum	Thyme
Dwarf rosemary	Sweet Potato
Mint (creeping type)	

Herbaceous Borders

Herbaceous border plants are those that can be used in a perennial or annual border and combined with flowering plants. Borders are beautiful next to walks, driveways, and patios, where they can be appreciated up close. They are also useful to break up large expanses of lawn or ground cover.

Herbaceous Border Edibles

Artichoke	Endive
Basil	Kale
Beans (bush)	Nasturtium
Borage	Okra
Cabbage	Parsley
Cantaloupe (bush)	Peanut
Chamomile (tall)	Pepper
Chard	Rhubarb
Chives	Sage
Cucumber (bush)	Sugar pea
Eggplant	Summer squash

Shrub Borders

These plants can be used in a shrub border next to a walk or driveway. They are also effective near groups of trees. Shrub borders are combined with ground covers or are used as foundation plantings. They are most effective when they contain a diversity of foliage types and colors.

Shrub Border Edibles

Almond (genetic dwarf)	Nectarine
Apple (dwarf and	(genetic dwarf)
genetic dwarf)	Peach (genetic dwarf)
Apricot (genetic dwarf)	Pear (genetic dwarf)
Artichoke	Pineapple guava
Blueberry	Pomegranate
Bush plum	Quince
Cherry (genetic dwarf)	Salal
Citrus (dwarf)	Sweet bay
Currant	Tea
Gooseberry	
Natal plum	

Hedges

Hedges can be either clipped or unclipped. (See section on hedges under "Fences and Walls" earlier in the chapter.) A clipped hedge is a formation of plants pruned to a definite geometrical shape and usually associated with a formal landscaping plan. Such hedges can be used as borders or

4.21. Many types of dwarf fruit trees can be trained as a hedge; these are dwarf apples.

barriers, but are often used as distinctly ornamental parts of a landscape plan. An edible hedge plant that is unclipped usually will yield fewer fruits than a lightly clipped plant.

An informal hedge is pruned lightly—only enough to keep it in bounds—so that it will develop its natural form. Unclipped hedges are generally used to define a boundary or as a screen for privacy.

Hedge Edibles (Clipped)

Apple (dwarf)	Pineapple guava
Bamboo	Rosemary
Carob	Salal
Citrus fruits	Surinam cherry
Natal plum	Sweet bay
Olive	Tea
Pear (dwarf)	

Hedge Edibles (Unclipped)

Almond (genetic dwarf)	Nectarine (dwarf and
Apple (dwarf and	genetic dwarf)
genetic dwarf)	Peach
Apricot (genetic dwarf)	Pear (dwarf and
Avocado (dwarf)	genetic dwarf)
Bamboo	Pineapple guava
Blueberry	Pomegranate
Bush plum	Quince
Citrus fruits (dwarf)	Rose (hips)
Currant	Rosemary
Elderberry	Salal
Gooseberry	Surinam cherry

Trees such as carob or full-size citrus can be used for large hedges.

Boundary or Barrier Plants

Boundary or barrier plants are shrubs that have dense, compact, and sometimes thorny growth. They are used to define boundary lines or to direct traffic away from an area. Once plantings with thorns are established, even dogs and children will be unable to penetrate them.

Shrub Edibles with Thorns

Brambleberries	Natal plum
Gooseberry	Prickly pear
Lemon (some varieties)	Rose (hips)

Thornless Shrub Edibles with Dense Growth

Bamboo	Pineapple guava
Carob	Rosemary (tall varieties)
Citrus fruit (dwarf)	Salal
Elderberry	

Foundation Plants

A foundation plant is a shrub, large perennial, or small tree used near the foundation to soften the right angles of a house or other structures. Many of the edibles listed below can be used together but they are most effective when mixed with a few evergreen plants to give the planting some form in winter, as most edible foundation plants are deciduous.

4.22. *Blueberries used as a foundation planting.*

Edible Foundation Plants

Almond (genetic dwarf)	Nectarine
Apple (genetic dwarf)	(genetic dwarf)
Apricot (genetic dwarf)	Peach (genetic dwarf)
Artichoke	Rhubarb
Blueberry	Rosemary
Bush cherry	Salal
Currant	Surinam cherry
Gooseberry	Tea
Natal plum	

Screens and Windbreaks

A tree or shrub with dense foliage and a relatively large growth habit is used as a screen to block a view, or as a windbreak situated to divert winter winds or to funnel summer breezes into windows or across a patio area. Both deciduous and evergreen plants are used in this way. For small screens, see "Hedges" above.

Screen and Windbreak Edibles

Bamboo	Pecan
Carob	Pine (some species)
Cherry	Pineapple guava
Chestnut	Pistachio
Elderberry	Sea grape
Hickory	Sweet bay
Loquat	Walnut
Mango	

Espaliers

Espalier is a pruning method in which a plant is trained to grow in a flat shape—usually against a building, trellis, or other structure, sometimes as a free-standing screen or hedge. The technique is most often used with woody plants such as trees and shrubs—most fruit trees can be trained in this way—but may be used with vines as well. The art of espalier creates living sculptures in the landscape: the branches may be trained to a formal geometric shape or left in an informal pattern. Espaliers are particularly valuable for small gardens and limited spaces, where they can serve as screens or focal points (see Chapter 6).

If you plan to espalier, be aware that it requires considerable work. See Chapter 5 for information on how to use espaliers and illustrations of possible shapes; see Chapter 7 for information about pruning.

Espalier Edibles

Almond	Olive
Apple	Peach
Apricot	Pear
Cherry	Persimmon
Citrus fruit	Pineapple guava
Currant	Plum
Fig	Pomegranate
Gooseberry	Quince
Grape	Surinam cherry
Loquat	Tea
Nectarine	

Climbers

Climbers are plants with vigorous, long, and usually thin branches that generally climb by twining or sending out tendrils or when they are supported on a structure. These plants are useful for covering fences, arbors, and trellises, where they can serve to filter the sun's rays and to provide privacy for outdoor living.

Perennial Climber Edibles

Bitter melon	Kiwi
Grape	Scarlet and 'Dutch
Hops	White' runner bean

4.23. *Bitter melon is a highly decorative climber; in warm-winter areas it will thoroughly cover an arbor.*

Annual Climber Edibles

Bitter melon
Cantaloupe
  (vining types)
Cucumber
  (vining types)

Nasturtium
  (vining types)
Pole bean ('Royalty',
  'Dutch White'
  runner)

Lawn Trees

A lawn tree is a tree tolerant of lawn irrigation levels and deep-rooted so it will not compete with a lawn for moisture and fertilizer. Lawn trees must have a clean habit of growth, so the grass is not smothered, and their shade should be light enough to enable grass to grow beneath them. Most fruit trees do not perform well in a lawn because they cannot compete for water and nutrients and are prone to diseases if nicked by a mower or trimmer.

Lawn Tree Edibles

Jujube

Maple

Street Trees

A street tree is a tree of restricted growth and clean appearance that is adapted to suburban conditions, such as sidewalks and pollution. It should branch high and have a deep root system so it will not damage concrete. Fruit trees with moist fruits should not be planted near streets or sidewalks, since such fruits stain concrete and make surfaces slick and thus hazardous.

Street Tree Edibles

Almond
  (smog sensitive)
Bay
Maple (smog sensitive)

Pine (piñon; some
  varieties are smog
  sensitive)

Large Trees

The definition of large here is a tree that grows to at least 30 feet. Such trees are excellent for giving summer shade and lend a stately feeling to large yards and woodland areas.

Large Tree Edibles

Avocado
Bay
Butternut
Cherry
Chestnut
Hickory

Mango
Pecan
Pine (most varieties)
Pistachio
Walnut

Interest Plants

An interest plant (sometimes called an accent plant) is a plant whose particularly striking form, foliage, flowers, or fruits make it an effective focal point.

Each entry below is followed by the element or elements of special interest on the plant.

Interest Edibles

Apricot (fruits and fall
  foliage)
Artichoke (form, gray
  foliage)

Nectarine, genetic
  dwarf (unusual
  form)
Olive (gray foliage,
  gnarled form)

Bamboo (form)
Banana (dramatic leaves, form)
Bush plum (fruits)
Cherry (bark)
Citrus (fruits)
Currant, some varieties (fruits)
Fig (dramatic leaves, gnarled form)
Grape (form)
Jujube (weeping form)
Kiwi (leaf pattern, form)
Loquat (dramatic leaves, form, fruits)
Lotus (leaves)
Mulberry, some varieties (weeping form)
Natal plum (fruits)
Peach, genetic dwarf (unusual form)
Persimmon (striking fall foliage, fruits, bark)
Pineapple guava (gray foliage, bark)
Plum, weeping or red leaf varieties (form, leaf color)
Pomegranate (fall foliage, fruits)
Prickly pear (sculptured form)
Rosemary (form, leaves)
Sea grape (dramatic leaves)
All espaliered plants (form)

Flowering Plants

Flowering plants, with their showy displays, are often used as interest plants. See Chapter 5 for a discussion of color in the landscape. Each entry below is followed by the most common color or colors of the particular plant.

Flowering Edibles

Almond (white, pink)
Apple (white)
Apricot, genetic dwarf (white, pink)
Artichoke (lavender)
Beans, some varieties (white, purple, red)
Blueberry (white, pink)
Borage (blue)
Bush plum (white, pink)
Capers (pink, blue)
Cherry (white)
Chestnut (white)
Chives (lavender, white)
Bush cherry (white, pink)
Eggplant (lavender)
Elderberry (white)
Jerusalem artichoke (yellow)
Kiwi (white)
Lotus (pink)
Nasturtium (red, yellow, orange)
Natal plum (white)
Nectarine, some varieties (pink)
Okra (white, yellow)
Peach, some varieties (pink)
Peanut (yellow)
Pineapple guava (deep red)
Plum (white, pink)
Pomegranate (red, orange)
Prickly pear (yellow, orange)
Quince (white, light pink)
Rose hips (white, rose, pink)
Rosemary (blue)
Saffron (mauve, white)
Sage (purple, red)
Sugar pea (purple, white)
Tea (white, pink)

Plants with Colored Foliage

Some varieties of the following edible plants have red veins or red to purple leaves.

Red-Foliage Edibles

Banana
Basil
Cabbage
Chard
Kale
Lettuce
Okra
Plums

Gray-Foliage Edibles

Artichoke
Marjoram
Olive
Oregano
Pineapple guava
Rosemary
Thyme

Fragrance Plants

Fragrance adds an extra dimension to any garden. A plant can produce fragrance from its flowers, fruits, or leaves.

Fragrant Edibles

Almond
Apple
Artichoke
Basil
Bay
Blueberry
Chamomile
Citrus
Crabapple
Fig
Hickory
Kiwi
Loquat
Maple
Mint
Natal plum
Oregano
Pine
Plum
Rose
Sage
Salal
Strawberry
Tomato

4.24. *Water chestnut, one of the most pleasant water-garden edibles.*

Water Plants

Water plants are plants whose roots must be submerged in water at all times. They are used in pools or beside streams.

Water Plant Edibles

Lotus	Wild rice
Water chestnut	

Oriental Garden Plants

Certain plants are appropriate to an Oriental garden specifically. See Chapter 5 for an illustrated example of an edible Oriental garden.

Oriental Garden Edibles

Bamboo	Lotus
Bitter melon	Persimmon
Cherry	Plum
Jujube	Tea
Loquat	Water chestnut

Container Plants

Container plants have restricted growth and will grow for many years in a tub or other container. They are usually shrubs, dwarf trees, annuals, or perennials. For specific types and varieties of edible plants particularly suited to containers and hanging baskets, see the table in Chapter 6.

Conclusion

From the above lists, it is clear that a large selection of edible ornamental plants exists to choose from. To increase the range of choices even more, see the encyclopedia and Appendix A.

Now that you have measured your yard, drawn a paper model, done your environmental planning, and considered the construction and plant possibilities, you are ready to combine all these elements in a cohesive design. The next chapter directs you in creating specific styles and solving particular design problems.

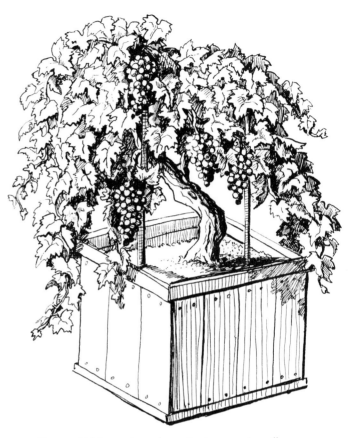

4.25. *Grapes, which have a strong, deep root system, are not usually grown in containers, but where the container effect is desired a bottomless container built over the soil works well for grapes and other such plants.*

Designing with Edibles

JOHNNY CASH sings a song, "One Piece at a Time," about a fellow who works on a car assembly line and steals car parts, one at a time each day, so he can make himself a free automobile. The final product featured, among other odd parts, '74 Cadillac bumpers and a '75 Chevrolet hood. The many elements of landscaping will appear thrown together in the same way if you don't coordinate the plan and see the yard as a whole.

The emphasis in this chapter is on putting your edible landscape together in an environmentally appropriate manner. The first part presents a detailed analysis of a sample case—a property in the Pacific Northwest—outlining a range of possible approaches to its landscaping problems and needs, and then describing how the chosen solution was executed. The second part covers a number of specific techniques and ornamental styles for using and enhancing the beauty of edibles. Finally, the third section discusses and illustrates regional examples of the ways edible plants can be used in various parts of the yard.

Choosing a Design—A Test Case

Begin by looking at your yard with new eyes. Now is the time to consider the color of the house—will you change it? Would you use a part of the yard off the den or master bedroom if there were a door there instead of a window? Would a small patio or deck increase your living space in a pleasant way? What fruits and vegetables do you like the best? Where can you put them? Which variety will taste the best and look the most attractive? Will it grow in your area?

An effective way to plan the best use of your property is to make several simple "bubble drawings"—sketches that demarcate the various activity areas. First you will need the scale drawing you have made of your yard on graph paper or vellum, as described and illustrated at the beginning of Chapter 4 (Figure 4.1 illustrates the same yard depicted below.) Lay a sheet of tracing paper over your scale drawing and circle potential activity areas as shown in Figures 5.1–5.4. Figure 5.1 depicts what currently exists, the other

"Bubble drawings" allow you to demarcate use areas in the yard and sketch out design possibilities. Here are four different approaches to our sample property:

5.1 (top left). The yard in its existing state, before remodeling.

5.2 (top right). Treatment featuring a public front yard, a remote patio, and a large play area.

5.3 (bottom left). Treatment featuring a public front yard, a play area close to the house, and large areas of screening.

5.4 (bottom right). Treatment featuring a private, sunny front-yard patio, and a large play area.

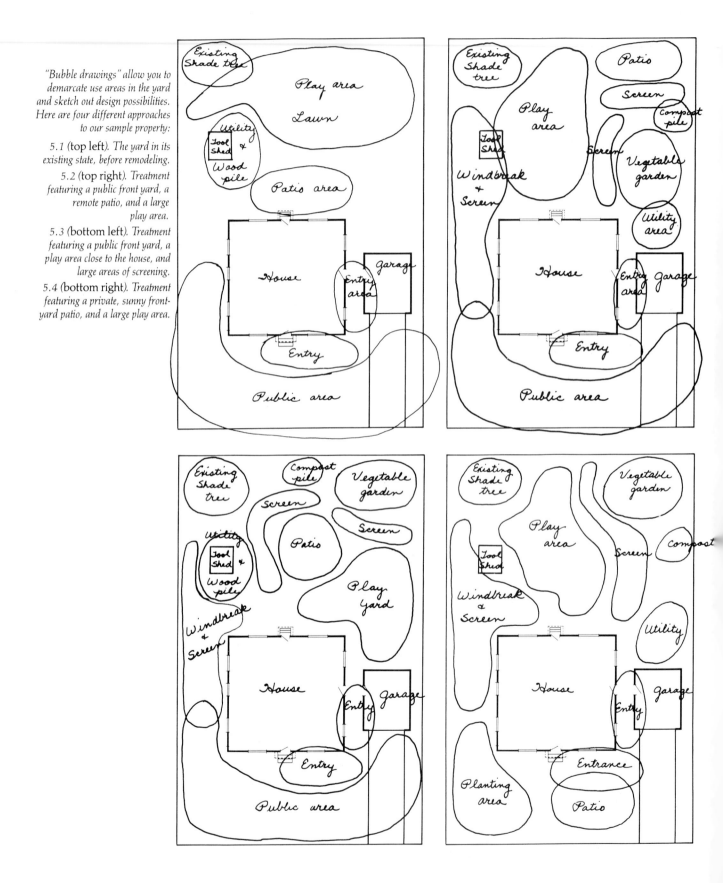

three show possible new treatments. Often a yard can be laid out in six or eight different ways. Experiment with different layouts, incorporating the needs and necessities of your particular family and circumstances.

In constructing the layouts in Figures 5.2–5.4, I worked on the assumption that I was balancing the needs and desires of a family of four: mother, father, and two children aged five and eight. This hypothetical family has no pets, enjoys adult entertaining, and plans to remain in this house indefinitely. The two-story house was built in the early 1900s and is located on a fairly quiet suburban street in a cool-summer, mild-winter area of the Pacific Northwest (zone 8).* The house and yard need refurbishing—the house needs new paint, for example, and the cracked concrete walks and back patio need to be replaced. As Figure 5.1 indicates, the traditionally styled existing yard contains a direct front walk, foundation shrubs, and lawns. While the backyard contains one lovely old tree and has a nice view of the nearby hills, the cracked concrete patio is chilly and damp during a good part of the year due to its northern exposure; also, it is uninviting for adult entertainment due to the proximity of the utility area and play yard. The front rooms are afforded no privacy from the street, and the frontyard lawn is on a slope, which makes mowing, watering and fertilizing hard.

Having noted these existing conditions and limitations, I considered the following family "wants" in constructing new possibilities as shown in Figures 5.2–5.4: a separate, sunny, and warm adult area for relaxation and entertaining; a defined play area for the children; a defined and unobtrusive utility area; a permanent vegetable garden and compost area that could be screened from view; winter-wind protection for the back of the house; privacy from the neighbor's windows and from the street; elimination of the sloped front lawn—all to be accomplished at a moderate price.

Figure 5.2 shows my first attempt at planning out alternative possibilities. The prominent features of this plan are a public frontyard, a remote patio, and a large play area. We can outline the advantages and disadvantages as follows:

	Pro	Con
PATIO	Sunny	Windy, and therefore cold much of year
Distant from kitchen
Little privacy and quiet for adults
FRONT ENTRY	Comparatively inexpensive	Slope wastes water
No privacy from street
Not very interesting

*See Introduction to the Encyclopedia for an explanation of zones and a zone map.

PLAY AREA	Can incorporate old toolshed as a playhouse
Has both sun and shade	None
UTILITY AREA	Convenient to house and garden	Needs to be screened from kitchen windows
VEGETABLE GARDEN	Convenient to kitchen	More shade than desirable
Needs screening from patio
COMPOST AREA	Near vegetable garden
Somewhat convenient to kitchen	Too near patio

Figure 5.3, the second approach, features a public front yard and a play area close to the house. It has the following assets and liabilities:

	Pro	Con
PATIO	Somewhat convenient to kitchen	Less sunny than desirable
Little privacy and quiet for adults
FRONT ENTRY	Comparatively inexpensive	Slope wastes water
No privacy from street
Not very interesting
PLAY AREA	None	Smaller than desired
Impractical to incorporate toolshed as playhouse
UTILITY AREA	Near toolshed	Inconvenient to house
Requires a visual screen
VEGETABLE GARDEN	Lies in full sun	Some wind exposure
Inconvenient to kitchen
Would require visual screen
COMPOST AREA	Near vegetable garden	Inconvenient to kitchen
Would require visual screen, spoiling view in distance from patio

The third possibility, Figure 5.4, is characterized by a private frontyard patio and a large play area. It can be analyzed thus:

	Pro	Con
PATIO	Warm and sunny Private for adults Allows for front foot-traffic needs Interesting approach Has modernizing effect Replaces part of undesirable lawn Provides sunny setting and reflected heat off paving for those edibles that need it	Inconvenient to kitchen Requires screening with a fence or hedge—if a hedge, then will be a wait for privacy while hedge grows Exposure to traffic and noise More expensive; requires retaining wall and dirt fill
FRONT ENTRY	See PATIO	See PATIO
PLAY AREA	Large; incorporates old toolshed as playhouse Has both sun and shade	None
UTILITY AREA	Convenient to house and garden Convenient to vegetable garden Convenient to compost area	Requires visual screen
VEGETABLE GARDEN	Lies in full sun	Inconvenient to kitchen Cooled by wind more than desirable Would require visual screening
COMPOST AREA	Convenient to vegetable garden Fairly convenient to kitchen Necessary screening could tie in with that of vegetable garden and utility area	None

Weighing all the advantages and disadvantages in each of the three experimental plans, I settled on the last treatment, Figure 5.4. This option offers the advantage of a warm, sunny patio for brunches, summer suppers, and sunbathing. The sunny, south-facing patio will also help reduce winter fuel bills and updates the entrance to the house. The backyard play areas are generous. Finally, the food-producing capabilities of the yard have been well utilized and at the same time make the yard more attractive.

Carrying Out the Design

Having arrived at a plan for our sample yard, we now need to provide the following features: foot access from the sidewalk and driveway to the front door; foot access to the vegetable garden and utility area; a children's play area; privacy for the patio; winter windbreaks; a means of screening off the view from the neighbor's windows; elimination of the front lawn; and elimination of the frontyard slope. It would also be nice to modernize the looks of the front of the property, if possible without major expense.

Construction materials are needed for some of these functions and plant materials for others. The owners of this property are most comfortable with an informal style, and this inclination will have an influence on the selection of both construction and plant materials.

Construction Materials

Because considerable amounts of broken concrete will be available following the demolition of the old patio and walks, this material was chosen for the garden paths and sideyard walks. Broken concrete was also selected as the paving surface for the utility area. Random chunks were set in sand and soil to allow for maximum percolation of water back into the soil.

In order to eliminate the undesirable frontyard slope, and to increase the level area desirable for the adult patio, a retaining wall was built of railroad ties. Topsoil was then imported to fill in behind the wall and build the area up to be level.

Finally, used brick, also set in sand, was selected for the adult patio flooring. Not only is it a recycled material, but it also added an informal feeling to the entry.

Plant Selection

The plants chosen were those that produced a high yield of the family's favorite fruits. The time that used to be spent mowing and trimming lawns is now used for keeping the hedge clipped, spraying the fruit trees, and harvesting the fruits. There will be more work to do but it will be more rewarding because most of the family's fruits and fresh vegetables will be homegrown. The evergreen ornamentals near the house were replaced by deciduous plants that allow the winter sun to warm the wall.

In the frontyard two large apple trees were chosen to give substance and balance to the yard. The varieties of 'Prima' and 'Priscilla' in standard size were selected, because of their resistance to scab, a disease common in the moist climate. Two varieties were needed for pollination. The trees' springtime blossom show is a bonus, and their large harvest can be enjoyed fresh, in applesauce, or dried. The apples were chosed for these areas because, unlike some fruits, they do not create juicy fruit drop over patios and sidewalks.

A dwarf almond was chosen for the same reasons—no mess, just beauty and production. The other dwarf trees chosen were the genetic dwarf apricot 'Garden Annie' and the dwarf 'Stanley' plum. Another dwarf tree, a kumquat, is sensitive to winter cold, so it was put in a large movable planter on the patio and can be moved into the house during the coldest part of the winter.

Blueberries, chosen for their lovely flowers, fall color, and, of course, tasty fruit, were placed near the entryway.

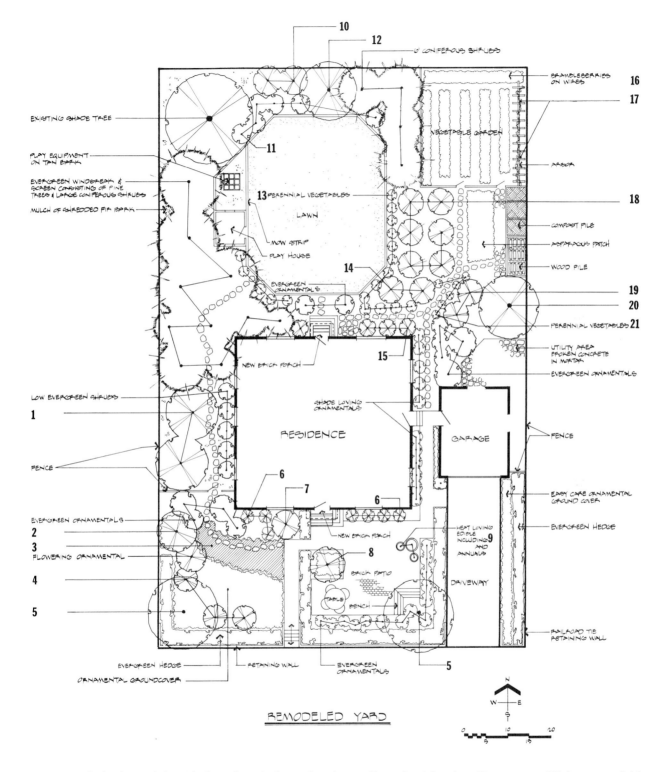

Labels on the drawing:

- EXISTING SHADE TREE
- PLAY EQUIPMENT ON TAN BARK
- EVERGREEN WINDBREAK & SCREEN CONSISTING OF PINE TREES & LARGE CONIFEROUS SHRUBS
- MULCH OF SHREDDED FIR BARK
- LOW EVERGREEN SHRUBS
- 1
- FENCE
- EVERGREEN ORNAMENTALS
- 2
- 3
- FLOWERING ORNAMENTAL
- 4
- 5
- EVERGREEN HEDGE
- ORNAMENTAL GROUNDCOVER
- RETAINING WALL
- EVERGREEN ORNAMENTALS
- 10
- 12
- 6' CONIFEROUS SHRUBS
- 11
- 13 PERENNIAL VEGETABLES
- LAWN
- MOW STRIP
- PLAY HOUSE
- EVERGREEN ORNAMENTALS
- 14
- NEW BRICK PORCH
- SHADE LOVING ORNAMENTALS
- RESIDENCE
- 15
- 6
- 7
- 6
- NEW BRICK PORCH
- 8
- BRICK PATIO
- TABLE
- BENCH
- VEGETABLE GARDEN
- BRAMBLEBERRIES ON WIRES — 16
- 17
- ARBOR
- 18
- COMPOST PILE
- ASPARAGUS PATCH
- WOOD PILE
- 19
- 20
- PERENNIAL VEGETABLES 21
- UTILITY AREA BROKEN CONCRETE IN MORTAR
- EVERGREEN ORNAMENTALS
- GARAGE
- FENCE
- EASY CARE ORNAMENTAL GROUND COVER
- EVERGREEN HEDGE
- HEAT LOVING EDIBLE INCLUDING AND ANNUALS 9
- DRIVEWAY
- RAILROAD TIE RETAINING WALL
- 5

N W E S

0 10 20
5 15

REMODELED YARD

5.5. *A completed architectural plan of the design chosen for the sample yard ("bubble drawing" 5.4). It includes the following edibles, keyed by number:*
1. Filbert 2. European semidwarf plum 3. Strawberries 4. Gooseberries 5. Apples 6. Blueberries 7. Genetic dwarf apricot 8. Genetic dwarf almond 9. Kumquat 10. Elderberries 11. Salal 12. Sour cherry 13. Artichokes 14. Genetic dwarf nectarines 15. Currants 16. Raspberries 17. Grapevines 18. Genetic dwarf peaches 19. Genetic dwarf pears 20. Japanese plum 21. Rhubarb

Gooseberries were planted in the shady section of the yard, behind the hedge, and under the apple tree. Two kinds of edible strawberries were used as part of the ground cover. Heat-loving annuals such as eggplant and tomatoes were placed in pots on the patio where they would get sun and reflected heat.

Some strictly ornamental plants were used to fill in some beds and to add interest to others. In shady areas, pachysandra was used for ground cover. Evergreen shrubs such as azaleas and junipers went into the planting beds to provide form in winter, and day lilies were planted among the strawberries to break up the flatness and give a pleasant contrast to form.

In the backyard, the emphasis in plant selection was on providing high food production, providing a winter windbreak, and screening off the the play yard, vegetable garden, and compost area. Screening was achieved through the careful placement of dwarf fruit trees. Surrounding the lawn are a number of shrub-sized edibles including elderberries, bush plums, artichokes, and a sour cherry. Raspberries, rhubarb, asparagus, dwarf pears, and a plum tree augment the vegetable garden area. Currants grow in the shade of the house. The edible plants were filled out by ornamental evergreens. Different sized conifers were strategically placed to temper winter winds and provide privacy. The lawn was reconditioned and provided with a concrete mow strip to cut down on maintenance.

Adaptability

While it was designed for a home in the Pacific Northwest, this plan is applicable to the other mild parts of the Northwest, Northern California, and the Northeast. And variations of this yard could be created in other parts of the country. The basic physical characteristics of the property—its size, shape, and existing features before the plan was executed—are similar to those of many American homes, the needs of the family were like those of many others, and the construction materials used are widely available.

The choice of plants, of course, is the element that will vary most according to geographical location. In choosing edible plants suitable for your area, consult the encyclopedia and the lists at the end of Chapter 4. Also look through the rest of this chapter to get a feel for how these plants can best be used.

After you have chosen the edible plants you want in your yard, fill in the gaps with ornamentals. When you choose ornamental plants, try to select those that are appropriate for your climate. In cold climates choose hardy plants that require little frost protection. In arid climates try to limit yourself as much as possible to drought-tolerant plants. If they fit in with the design of your yard, try to include native plants and plants that will feed birds and small mammals—particularly in the winter. Make sure that the ornamentals you choose to interplant with your edibles

need few pesticides and require the same cultural care.

Keep in mind that while the sample yard we've just analyzed offers many possibilities, countless others exist. The remainder of this chapter will describe a range of options.

Design Styles and Techniques

The effective use of edible plants in home landscaping involves discovering new and reviving time-honored techniques to gain flexibility. In addition, to give more design alternatives, variations on traditional edible gardens are needed. This section looks at some landscaping styles and techniques borrowed from ornamental horticulture, and expands on traditional food-garden formats.

Note: Most of the color illustrations found in the remainder of this chapter are accompanied by outline drawings, in which plants are numbered and labeled for convenient reference to the text descriptions.

The Espalier

The espalier technique has been in use for hundreds of years, especially with fruit trees. The art of espalier is not only useful as a training method per se but also is an efficient way to fit an edible plant into a small yard. Plants trained in this way can be flat against a wall or fence, or they can be used free-standing as a screen or a hedge. Several of the illustrations in this chapter show espaliered fruit trees in various uses (see Figure 5.6).

How to Buy an Espalier Plant

The easiest way to have espaliered fruits in your yard is to buy a plant already started in this way. Most local nurseries carry many types, and will show you how to prune to maintain the plant you buy. Espaliered trees are also available from Henry Leuthart Nursery (see Appendix B for the address). This nursery specializes in hardy espaliered fruit trees. The plants are sent parcel post with directions for continued pruning.

If you cannot find the tree you want already trained to the desired form, buy untrained young plants and train them yourself. Most varieties of standards, semidwarf, and dwarf fruit trees can be trained to espalier—see the list at the end of this section for some suggestions.

Where to Plant an Espalier

With the exception of gooseberries and currants, which like cool and shady areas, most fruit trees need lots of sun. South-facing walls are ideal; on such a wall the fruits get the most sun and heat. As a bonus, since most fruit trees are deciduous, they shade the south wall in the summer and let the winter sun heat the wall in the coldest part of the year.

Note: If your summer temperatures exceed 90°F by very

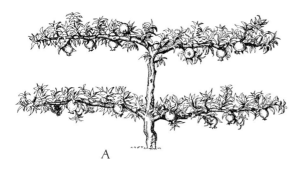

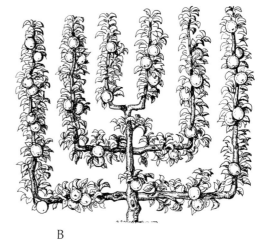

A

B

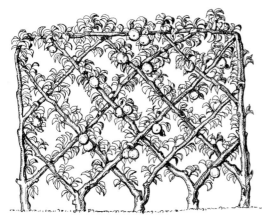

C

D

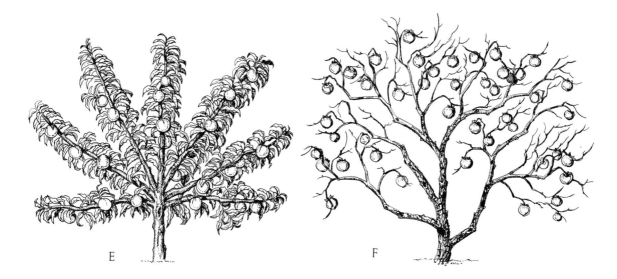

E

F

5.6. *Most of the popular fruit trees can be espaliered in a number of different forms.* **A.** *A pomegranate tree pruned to a four-armed horizontal form, or cordon.* **B.** *An apple trained to a six-armed palmette verrier. Pears as well as apple are often pruned to this form.* **C.** *The Belgian fence, one of the most decorative espalier patterns. This form requires as least five trees but can be done with many more. It is usually used with apples and pears.* **D.** *Fig trees trained in a large, dramatic horizontal espalier.* **E.** *A fan-shaped espalier, particularly suitable for peaches and nectarines.* **F.** *Most of the popular fruit trees can be trained in informal shapes, such as this persimmon. For more espalier drawings, see* CITRUS *and* PEAR *in the encyclopedia.*

much, your fruits will cook rather than ripen. Therefore, in hot-summer regions, plant your fruit trees against an east or southeast wall. Also, in hot-summer areas the trunks of most espaliered fruit trees will benefit from whitewash or a similar protecting substance. With the espalier form, the trunk is often exposed directly to the sun's rays and will sunburn.

Be aware of shadows. South walls with an overhang that are in full sun in April may be in total shade through June and half of July—and, although you may appreciate that shade from the overhang, your espaliered fruits will not. That is the time for most to be ripening and sweetening.

Pruning for Espalier

Training for espalier is sometimes the only way you can have fresh fruits from a small yard or narrow space, but it is also an excellent example of the old American adage that there is no free lunch. All espaliered fruit trees must be consistently pruned to maintain their shape. Although fruits often will be sweeter and larger than on nontrained trees owing to the fruit's greater access to sunshine resulting from the severe pruning and thinning, and although spraying and harvesting will be easier, the fact remains that the regular pruning is a price exacted for these plusses.

An espaliered fruit tree requires pruning at least two or three times every year, usually more often. How you prune depends on the shape of the espalier you want as well as the type of tree. Proper training can be an exciting challenge, but will take time and energy to get those delicious fruits. Loquats or figs, for example, can make a two-story espalier, but both require a major pruning effort involving a ladder. See the following list and the various illustrations for types of espalier shapes possible. Consult pruning books recommended in the bibliography, and seek the advice of local authorities on how to prune each fruit tree mentioned.

The following list indicates the styles most commonly used for popular espalier plants.

Apple—dwarf or semidwarf usually used; easily espaliered to many forms, including hedges, double cordon, candelabrum, palmetto, double lattice (Belgian espalier fence).

Apricot—dwarf or semidwarf usually used; can be pruned to hedges and fan shapes; needs fairly heavy pruning.

Citrus—dwarf usually used; calamondin, lemon, kumquat, limequat espalier the easiest; need supports, usually pruned to six- or eight-armed cordon.

Currant and gooseberry—best used as fan espaliers against cool walls.

Fig—large espaliers with natural form, or low, horizontal-armed, formal shape; particularly suited to hot south walls that protect them from the cold but give them summer sun.

Grape—trained to a four-armed Kniffen system along

wires; south walls are good where the sun will sweeten the fruit.

Loquat—very large espalier, can be a two-story plant; fairly slow growing in vertical cordon or informal shape.

Peach and nectarine—fruit on new wood only; require vigorous pruning to produce new fruiting branches and to maintain espalier form; best shapes are hedge or fan.

Persimmon—the Oriental persimmon is one of the best for a large, informal espalier.

Pineapple guava—marvelous, large, informal espalier; this treatment of the plant shows off the handsome bark to good advantage.

Pomegranate—best in informal shapes, or in four-, six-, or eight-armed cordons.

Decorative Techniques for Annual Vegetables

Harvesting some types of annual vegetables can result in aesthetic problems. When a root vegetable such as carrot, beet, kohlrabi, parsnip, radish, onion, or leek is pulled, it leaves a hole in the planting bed. A similar problem occurs with some of the greens, such as spinach, lettuce, or kale. The root vegetables must be harvested in one piece, and while some greens can be picked a leaf at a time over a period of several weeks, sooner or later—usually sooner—they must be pulled out entirely.

Solutions to this problem can be borrowed from the art of bulb culture. The foliage of many flowering bulbs, such as tulips, daffodils, and hyacinths, turns an unattractive yellow-brown after blooming and remains visible for a long period after the beautiful flower is just a memory. Two methods of dealing with this problem have been used in strictly ornamental gardens for years. The first is to plant these bulbs in containers, which can be moved out of sight when the display is no longer attractive. The second is to plant in the same vicinity a fast-growing floriferous plant that spreads rapidly and widely, and soon covers the unsightly foliage (or fills in the bare spots if the bulbs are removed from the area after blooming).

Both techniques can be applied beautifully to the culture of annual vegetables. Containers that were once filled with annual vegetables can be moved as easily as any others. And, while there are a number to choose from, I recommend four annual flowers for bulb covers that will hide bare spots quickly and colorfully. They are viola (*Viola cornuta*) in deep purple, blue, white, yellow, ruby red, and apricot; sweet alyssum (*Lobularia maritima*) in pink, white, and purple; lobelia (*Lobelia Erinus*) available in deep blue, light blue, plum and carmen reds, and white; and dwarf nasturtium (*Tropaeolum minus*) in cream, yellow, orange, mahogany, red, and rose. All these plants are easy to grow under most conditions and need no pesticides in most parts of the country; they grow quickly, take some shading by other plants, produce drifts of flowers, are easily obtained, and, most important, creep and spread along the ground to fill in

5.7. **Left:** *Beets planted without an annual flowering filler leave holes in the garden when harvested.* **Right:** *Sweet alyssum fills in between harvested red beets.*

empty areas in their vicinity. Because of the crowded growing conditions, special care is needed to make sure the soil is in good condition and that sufficient fertilizer and water are provided, but this effort is easily justified by the resulting efficiency and beauty.

To use the "bulb cover" technique, plant vegetable seed in a band 18 inches wide (rather than in narrow, inch-wide rows). Give the vegetables a 2–3 week head start, then plant flower seed around the edges and in the empty areas where vegetable seeds failed to germinate.

Shrub Borders Containing Edibles

Groupings of shrubs are often used along driveways, walks, and property lines, as screens, and near buildings, where they are usually referred to as foundation plants. The object of these groupings is to create a pleasing mixture of shapes, texture, and, to a lesser degree, color. Choose plants with a similar form, texture, and size, but vary these with a few plants of different textures, colors, and sizes to avoid monotony. It is pleasant to include a few flowering plants or fall-foliage plants for color and at least a few evergreens to give the design more substance in the winter. Edible plants can be included in shrub borders; see the list in Chapter 4.

A foundation planting is a specialized form of shrub border popular in the United States. The primary use of a foundation planting is to soften the right angles of the building foundation where it meets the ground, and to help the house blend into the surrounding garden. Figure 5.8 is an example of an informal foundation planting done with edibles. It is asymmetrical and planted with blueberries, gooseberries, and strawberries, supplemented with holly.

Perennial Borders Containing Edibles

The mixed herbaceous border, commonly called the perennial border, has been popular since the late nineteenth century. In the style based on this border, large beds of mostly herbaceous (as opposed to woody) plants are used in a

5.8. *The foundation plantings for this New England house are mainly edibles. To the left of the entrance are a gooseberry shrub, two low-bush and one high-bush blueberries. The porch is flanked by English holly; while not edible, this ornamental evergreen lends form and color to the landscape in winter. Alpine strawberries line the walk on both sides, and to the right of the entrance are more blueberries and gooseberries.*

subtle weaving of form, texture, and color. These beds can be sited along a driveway, fenceline, or path, or on shallow hillsides; or to define spaces and shapes in lawn areas. The scenes change with the season and are a delight to the eye. The basic plantings are perennial flowers with a sprinkling of annual flowers added for quick color. Popular flower choices for this type of ornamental border are lilies, irises, peonies, phlox, daisies, lavender, coreopsis, asters, chrysanthemums, poppies, and many more. A delightful variation on these borders is the addition of a number of vegetables and a few small fruits.

The following guidelines should prove helpful in the design of these mixed beds:

1. Keep the border less than 3 feet wide or provide a path or access of some sort on both sides of the beds to allow for picking of produce and flowers and other maintenance.
2. Combine plants that have similar soil, exposure, and water requirements.
3. When selecting the plant materials, choose one or two types of plants to use in large quantities to unify the entire border.
4. Use a basic foliage color and a basic plant shape as further unifying elements.
5. Limit the flower colors. Too many colors confuse the eye. Red, orange, and yellow with a dash of blue or white make a striking combination. Another pleasant mixture is made by combining blues, lavenders, and pinks. One helpful resource on this subject is *Gardening with Color—Ideas for Planning and Planting with Annuals, Perennials, and Bulbs,* by Margaret Brandstrom Pavel (see bibliography under Ortho Books).

Part of the author's front garden, planted with artichokes (at rear), California poppies, herbs, and annual vegetables in season.

This basket of bounty from the author's garden includes a number of unusual and beautiful annual vegetables: 'Royal Burgundy' beans, lemon and Armenian cucumbers, 'Gold Rush' zucchini, and 'Golden' beets.

6. Keep taller plants at the back of the border with low creepers at the front.
7. Do not use flowering plants that need pesticides among your edibles.
8. Avoid flowering plants that reseed themselves heavily, as they will need continual thinning.

Herbaceous borders can be adapted to all parts of the country. The one shown in Figure 5.9 will grow well in most of zones 5 through 9. Here, a rich, medium-green is used for the basic foliage color, and the flower-color range is limited to orange, yellow, and light blue, with a small amount of

5.9. *This backyard perennial border combines tall, blue stock, blackeyed susans, and marigolds with many beautiful vegetables. Red okra and asparagus form the background. In the middle of the border along the path are many herbs, peppers, tomatoes, bush melons, and rhubarb. The front of the border contains more herbs and many low, flowering annuals.*

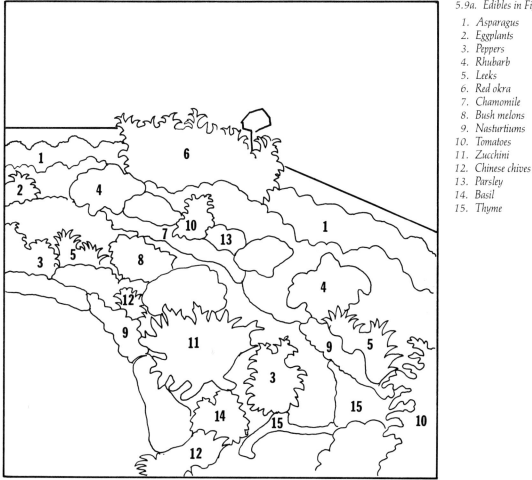

5.9a. Edibles in Figure 5.9:
1. Asparagus
2. Eggplants
3. Peppers
4. Rhubarb
5. Leeks
6. Red okra
7. Chamomile
8. Bush melons
9. Nasturtiums
10. Tomatoes
11. Zucchini
12. Chinese chives
13. Parsley
14. Basil
15. Thyme

red. Phlox, butterfly weed, black-eyed Susans, marigolds, and lobelia are used. They are easy to care for and bloom over an extended period. The numerous edibles include many types of peppers, with their rich, green foliage and red and yellow fruits; patio-size tomatoes; bush melons and cucumbers; leeks; zucchini; rhubarb; and the perennial asparagus, with its filmy foliage to contrast with the other, coarser-leaved plants. Placed in the background is red okra, with its bold leaves and tall form. Many herbs are interspersed throughout the border, including chamomile, basil, parsley, chives, and thyme.

In keeping with the informality of the border plantings, curving lines are used to give movement and rhythm to the bed. A stone path is added to allow the plants to be tended and harvested.

Hobby Gardens

Growing edible gardens combines well with many types of hobbies, with cooking being the most obvious. Culinary gardens can allow you the pleasure of growing foods for the table which are unobtainable from grocery stores. For a stunning end to a French meal, serve homegrown Alpine strawberries. For a Mexican meal entrée, try the pads of prickly pear cactus in dishes calling for *nopale* (see PRICKLY PEAR in the encyclopedia). In the following sections, two culinary gardens are described as examples: an herb garden and an Oriental garden.

Another time-honored hobby is growing plant materials for floral arrangements. The dried flowers or seed pods of okra, artichokes, hops, chives, lotus, and rose hips all look marvelous in dried arrangements. Many more edibles are beautiful in fresh-flower arrangements. See Chapter 4 for a list of flowering edibles.

An increasingly popular hobby is extracting vegetable and fruit juices and using them to dye yarn for weaving. A number of edibles, including onions, apples, cranberries, blueberries, sunflowers, elderberries, and saffron, can be used in this way. For further information see the recom-

*5.10. Herb gardens are one of the most rewarding hobby gardens to grow.
This one contains most of the commonly grown culinary herbs as well as some
decorative herbs, lavender and calendulas for cut flowers.*

mended titles in the bibliography under the listing of pamphlets from the Brooklyn Botanic Garden.

Herb Gardens

One of the most delightful and easily cared for of all hobby gardens is the herb garden. Such a garden is most effective when given a strong geometric pattern. Historically, this bold patterning is used to create form and unity from the diverse shapes of the many possible plants included. Designs based on a wagon-wheel or knot motif are traditional, but, of course, the opportunities for experimentation are almost limitless. Another natural unifying aspect to these assemblages is the predominance of gray or gray-green foliage color.

The herb garden pictured in Figure 5.10 contains a large variety of herbs, most of which can be grown successfully in zones 5 through 9 and the cooler sections of zone 10. The taller herbs are located in the back, and the herbs that take the most water are clustered around the birdbath.

The encyclopedia includes a number of herbs. For a more complete discussion, consult *Herbs and Their Ornamental Uses* and *Japanese Herbs and Their Uses*, both published by the Brooklyn Botanical Garden; see also, Adelma Simmons' *Herb Gardening in Five Seasons*. All are cited in the bibliography.

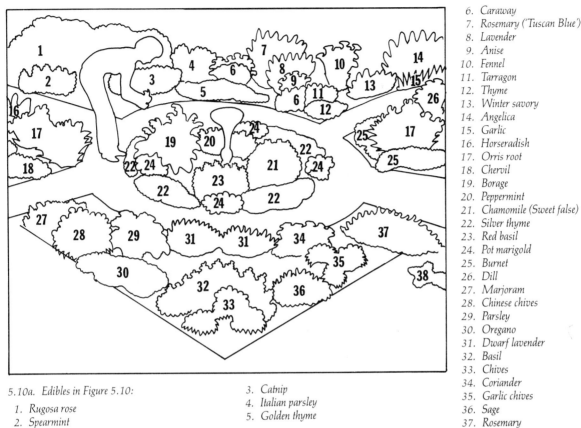

5.10a. Edibles in Figure 5.10:

1. Rugosa rose
2. Spearmint
3. Catnip
4. Italian parsley
5. Golden thyme
6. Caraway
7. Rosemary ('Tuscan Blue')
8. Lavender
9. Anise
10. Fennel
11. Tarragon
12. Thyme
13. Winter savory
14. Angelica
15. Garlic
16. Horseradish
17. Orris root
18. Chervil
19. Borage
20. Peppermint
21. Chamomile (Sweet false)
22. Silver thyme
23. Red basil
24. Pot marigold
25. Burnet
26. Dill
27. Marjoram
28. Chinese chives
29. Parsley
30. Oregano
31. Dwarf lavender
32. Basil
33. Chives
34. Coriander
35. Garlic chives
36. Sage
37. Rosemary
38. Corsican mint

The herbs in this New England garden include 'Dark Opal' and sweet basil, silver thyme, and Chinese chives.

A number of mail-order nurseries specialize in herbs and have catalogs available. Among them are: Caprilands Herb Farm, Silver Street, Coventry, CT 06238; The Yarb Patch, 3726 Thomasville Rd., Tallahassee, FL 32303 (catalog 50¢); McLaughlin's Seeds, P.O. Box 550, Mead, WA 99021 (catalog 50¢); and, with one of the largest selections, Taylor's Herb Garden, 1535 Lone Oak, Vista, CA 92083 (catalog 50¢). Other mail-order nurseries with large selections of herbs are: **9, 16, 17, 32, 35, 47, 48, 51, 54,** and **56.** (Names and addresses of these are found in Appendix B under the corresponding numbers.)

The Edible Oriental Garden

This hobby garden combines a love of Oriental gardens with an interest in Oriental cooking. The primary design

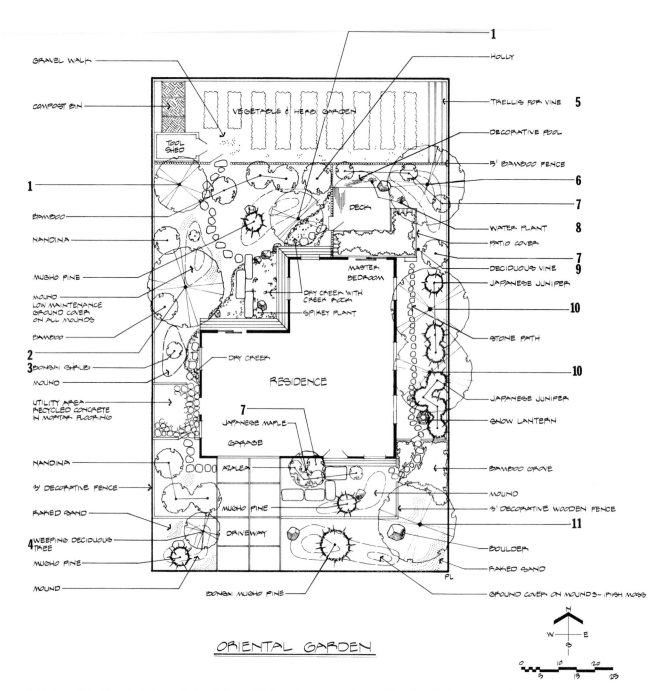

GRAVEL WALK

COMPOST BIN

1

HOLLY

TRELLIS FOR VINE 5

DECORATIVE POOL

5' BAMBOO FENCE

6

7

WATER PLANT 8

PATIO COVER

7

DECIDUOUS VINE 9

JAPANESE JUNIPER

10

STONE PATH

10

JAPANESE JUNIPER

SNOW LANTERN

VEGETABLE & HERB GARDEN

TOOL SHED

1

BAMBOO

NANDINA

MUGHO PINE

MOUND
LOW MAINTENANCE
GROUND COVER
ON ALL MOUNDS

BAMBOO

2

3 BONSAI SHRUB

MOUND

UTILITY AREA
RECYCLED CONCRETE
IN MORTAR FLOORING

NANDINA

3' DECORATIVE FENCE

RAKED SAND

4 WEEPING DECIDUOUS
TREE

MUGHO PINE

MOUND

DECK

MASTER
BEDROOM

DRY CREEK WITH
CREEK ROCK

SPIKEY PLANT

DRY CREEK

RESIDENCE

7

JAPANESE MAPLE

GARAGE

AZALEA

MUGHO PINE

DRIVEWAY

BONSAI MUGHO PINE

BAMBOO GROVE

MOUND

3' DECORATIVE WOODEN FENCE

11

BOULDER

RAKED SAND

PL

GROUND COVER ON MOUNDS- IRISH MOSS

ORIENTAL GARDEN

N
W   E
S

0   10   20
5   15   25

5.11. *This Oriental garden features raked sand, dry creek beds, and mounds. Foliage plants, including many edibles, predominate, and a large vegetable and herb bed provides vegetables for Oriental dishes. The main garden contains: 1. Jujube 2. Persimmon ('Fuyu') 3. Kumquat 4. Plum ('Weeping Santa Rosa') 5. Bitter melon 6. Plum 7. Tea 8. Water chestnuts 9. Kiwi 10. Oriental pears 11. Apricot*

The vegetable and herb bed contains: Adzuki beans (Adzuki); Amaranth (Chinese spinach, hinn choy); Asparagus pea (bin dow); Baseball-bat squash (poo gwa); Chinese cabbage (pe tsai); Chinese chives (gow choy); Chinese cucumbers (kee chi); Chinese eggplant (ai kwa); Chinese mustard (bok choy); Chinese radish (lobok); Garland chrysanthemum (shungiku); Hot peppers (la chiao); Sesame (chih ma); Soybeans (soy); Yard-long beans (dow gauk)

materials used in the example depicted in Figure 5.11 are natural woods, bamboo, rocks, and sand. Few of the plants bloom and the plant materials are chosen for their form and texture. Most of the plants are edible but have been supplemented with mugho pines, azaleas, spiky butterfly iris, and a Japanese maple. Most of the herbaceous plants are located in the vegetable/herb garden.

Both the exterior and the interior of the house display an Oriental style, which makes the house and yard harmonious. The exterior has natural wood siding, shoji screens at the windows, and a low, Oriental-style deck system running around the front and back of the house. A larger deck off the master bedroom allows for more private relaxation. This area is fenced and contains a small pool planted with water chestnuts. A low, decorative fence encloses the front entryway and gives a sense of privacy.

If you are interested in more extensive information on Oriental landscaping, the following three books should help: *Japanese Herbs and Their Uses,* published by the Brooklyn Botanical Gardens; Sunset's *Oriental Gardens;* and *Grow Your Own Chinese Vegetables* by Geri Harrington. All three are listed in the bibliography.

Orchards

An orchard is a grove or collection of fruit- or nut-bearing trees. It is an efficient food producer and has been used for centuries. The advantage of an orchard is that a number of plants that might need similar care are placed together. If you want to grow fruit trees that need dormant spraying or occasional fungicides, for example, putting them in one area will save you the work of walking around a yard with a sprayer. Pruning, fertilizing, and mulching, too, can be localized, and harvesting is often easier. Orchards can be planted in attractive ways that contribute to the landscape and please the eye—for example, as neat rows of fruit trees surrounded by a low boxwood hedge, as lines of trees along a driveway, or in raised planters with gravel walks between them to form an attractive area off the back patio. Even a mini-grouping of genetic dwarf fruit trees, lined up on either side of a front walk or patio, will give a large harvest.

An orchard can also be created in the manner of a natural woodland. In one example I have seen, three semidwarf apricot trees were planted in one close circle as a multi-stemmed tree; semidwarf almonds, apples, and pears were arranged in other groups; and the ground cover was formed of sweet woodruff, Alpine strawberries, and pachysandra. In a woodland orchard, more than usual care must be taken to avoid diseases and to provide adequate air circulation. Choose disease-resistant varieties and prune individual trees to open the centers for air passage. Choose ground covers than can take raking so that dead leaves from the fruit trees, which may harbor disease organisms, can be removed.

The handsome bitter melon vine produces small yellow flowers, large cut leaves, and useful fruits.

5.12. *This orchard provides both beauty and a highly efficient way to grow the major fruit trees. The bottomless boxes provide excellent drainage as well as visual interest.*

A Boxed Orchard

Figure 5.12 shows a boxed orchard designed for beauty and efficient fruit production. A similar combination of temperate-zone fruit trees can be grown in most sections of zones 6 through 9 and cooler sections of zone 10. The raised wooden boxes do not have bottoms, so roots can penetrate the native soil for extra nutrients and water. This elevation provides ideal drainage, but also makes the tree roots more susceptible to frost damage. For this reason, hardy root stocks should be used in zones 6 and 7.

The trees chosen for this boxed orchard are standard-size peach, nectarine, plum, almond, and semidwarf apple and pear. Cross-pollination of the different varieties was carefully provided for. Raspberries are planted along the fence. The raised planter along the back of the house contains 'Dwarf Grey' sugar peas, and the base of each fruit-tree planter is adorned with strawberries. A vegetable garden with neat rows of annual vegetables is fenced in its own area at the side of the orchard.

The trees in this orchard have many different colors and

5.12a. *Edibles in Figure 5.12:*

1. *Apples*
2. *Plums*
3. *Almonds*
4. *Apricots*
5. *Peaches*
6. *Pears*
7. *Nectarines*
8. *Prune*
9. *Snow peas ('Dwarf Gray Sugar')*
10. *Raspberries*
11. *Strawberries*
12. *Bibb lettuce*
13. *Red lettuce*

types of foliage, blossoms of different colors, and fruits of different shapes and colors. To unify this area, the designer kept the construction materials simple, choosing wood that was the same color as the house trim. Gravel was the only other material used. Strong geometric lines were also used to unify the space. Finally, the vegetable garden is surrounded by the same type of fencing used elsewhere.

A Frontyard Orchard of Genetic Dwarfs

Figure 5.13 shows a variation on the boxed orchard. This version occupies a much smaller area, since the trees selected are only 4 to 6 feet in height. See the encyclopedia entry PEACH for detailed information about genetic dwarf fruit trees.

Some of the genetic dwarf varieties available have unusual forms, and these must be artfully arranged to make an effective design. The trees used here are peach, plum, nectarine, apple, cherry, and apricot. All are self-pollinating, so pollination is not a problem. The three types of trees with

Unlike most standard peach trees, the genetic dwarf cultivars display myriad showy pink blossoms in spring.

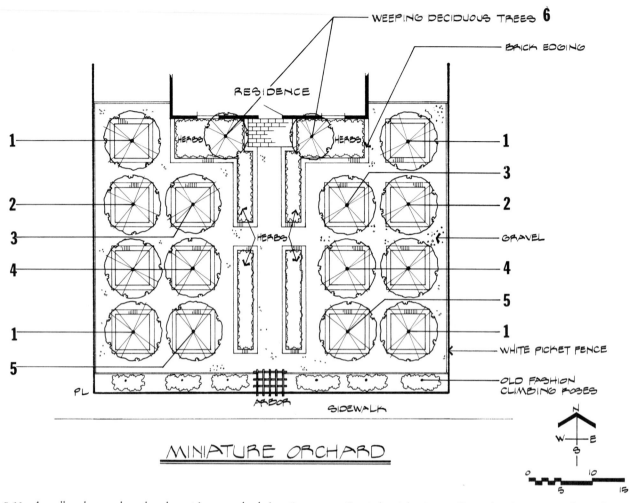

WEEPING DECIDUOUS TREES **6**

BRICK EDGING

RESIDENCE

HERBS   HERBS

1   1

2   3

3   2

4   GRAVEL

1   4

5   5

HERBS   1

PL   WHITE PICKET FENCE

ARBOR   OLD FASHION CLIMBING ROSES

SIDEWALK

N
W—E
S

0   5   10   15

MINIATURE ORCHARD

5.13. *A small yard can produce a large harvest from an orchard of genetic dwarf fruit trees. Here an informal frontyard miniature orchard is surrounded by old roses and a white picket fence—an inviting entrance throughout much of the year. This design includes the following trees:*

1. Genetic dwarf cherries 2. Genetic dwarf apricots 3. Genetic dwarf peaches 4. Genetic dwarf apples 5. Genetic dwarf nectarines 6. Plums ('Weeping Santa Rosa')

the strongest and most unusual forms—the weeping plum, peach, and nectarine—are placed with an eye to unifying the design. The weeping plums go on either side of the front door; the peaches and nectarines, which are identical in form, go along the walk. Four cherry trees, which have a fairly strong upright form, occupy the four corners; and the apples and apricots are used to fill in the other areas.

A white picket fence with old-fashioned climbing roses and a border of herbs give a feeling of informality and interest to the Cape Cod-type house. The fence also discourages peach pilferage. Finally, brick is used as a border around the walks and fruit-tree areas. The brick unifies and gives form to the area while at the same time holding the gravel in the paths.

An Informal Frontyard Orchard

Figure 5.14 shows standard fruit trees being used in an informal frontyard orchard. Such a grouping can be grown successfully in most of zones 6 through 9 and cool parts of zone 10. The example shown here stands in front of a two-story New England-type farmhouse.

The large size of these fruit trees helps to soften the imposing facade of the house. The trees are planted primarily in groups of two to facilitate cross-pollination and to unify the design. A meadow adjoins the property and is allowed to grow under the trees. In the spring it is seeded with wildflowers. This area is mowed twice, once in midsummer and again in the fall, for a neater appearance and to control shrubby weeds. The first mowing is after the wildflowers

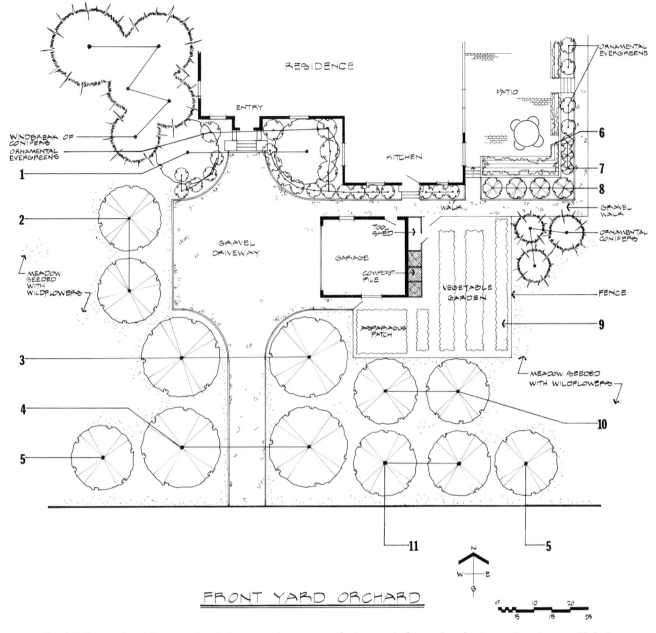

RESIDENCE

ENTRY

KITCHEN

WINDBREAK OF
CONIFERS
ORNAMENTAL
EVERGREENS

1

2

MEADOW
SEEDED
WITH
WILDFLOWERS

GRAVEL
DRIVEWAY

3

4

5

GARAGE

TOOL
SHED

COMPOST
PILE

ASPARAGUS
PATCH

VEGETABLE
GARDEN

WALK

PATIO

ORNAMENTAL
EVERGREENS

6

7

8

GRAVEL
WALK

ORNAMENTAL
CONIFERS

FENCE

9

MEADOW SEEDED
WITH WILDFLOWERS

10

11

5

N
W E
S

FRONT YARD ORCHARD

0   10   20
5   15   25

5.14. *Stately full-size apple and cherry trees line the driveway to this farmhouse-style dwelling. The large yard planted in edibles can produce enough fruits and vegetables for the average family's annual needs. The design includes the following edibles: 1. Pears 2. European plums 3. Sweet cherries 4. Apples 5. Sour cherries 6. Grapevines 7. Rhubarb 8. Blueberries 9. Brambleberries 10. Hardy peaches 11. Hardy almonds*

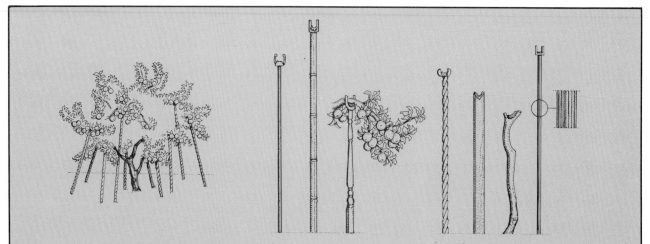

5.15.   *For close-up viewing and formal yards, decorative branch supports can add to the pleasure of growing fruit trees. Materials that can be used for such supports include, from left to right, a painted metal pole, bamboo, two turned wooden poles, a painted two-by-four, a gnarled branch, and a fluted curtain rod.*

Decorative Branch Supports

Sometimes fruit trees bear such heavy loads that the branches need extra support so as not to break. Usually, scrap lumber is wedged under the branch to provide the necessary support. But this solution is not very attractive and is out of place in a formal yard. A number of alternatives are possible. If you do use scrap lumber, you can make the scraps less obtrusive and more attractive by painting them all one color—a rich brown or black, perhaps, or, if your house has an earth-tone trim, paint the supports the same color.

Another possibility is to make the supports themselves decorative. See Figure 5.15 for some less traditional supports. To enrich a patio area where the sup-

ports will be seen up close, try recycling or buying turned or fluted wood curtain rods, or, if you are handy, do your own woodworking. Recycled metal pipes are another alternative; they should be painted black or brown and their tops padded so the trees' bark will not be scraped. Or borrow an idea from Oriental gardens, where fruit trees are sometimes given a supporting trellis, usually made from bamboo, that becomes a decorative part of the landscape.

There are many options; use your imagination freely. Make sure the materials are strong and weather-resistant, and provide some sort of padding or notch to help hold the branch without damaging it.

have set seed and the nesting birds have left. The trees are heavily mulched in an area 6 to 8 feet out from the trunk. The mulch helps to supply nutrients continuously to the roots and keeps the mower away from the trunks, where accidental bumping could cause damage. Bricks line the gravel driveway, giving a strong design line and a neat border to retain the gravel. The evergreen shrubs planted on either side of the entry give interest in winter.

Edibles in Containers

Edibles lend themselves beautifully to container gardening. While containers often are virtually the only alternative for small apartment patios, as we'll see in the next chapter, they also have advantages for people with large yards. They allow for the enjoyment of beautiful plants at close range while permitting a design flexibility impossible with plants in the ground. Plants in containers can be moved

around and rearranged when an edible is ready for harvest, or just to change a decorative pattern. Plants in containers give visual interest to a design by creating different levels on flat areas.

They also provide climatic flexibility: plants can be started early in a cold frame, solar greenhouse, or sunny kitchen window and brought out when the weather warms up. Dwarf trees in containers can be moved into a garage during the coldest part of the winter in severe climates. Finally, container gardening allows people with physical handicaps to enjoy their gardens without having to stoop and bend to plant, weed, and harvest.

The guidelines for designing with container plants are the same whether the project involves edibles or ornamentals. Figure 5.16 illustrates a warm-weather container garden planted primarily with edibles; this garden could be grown in warm-summer sections of zones 3 through 10. The pre-

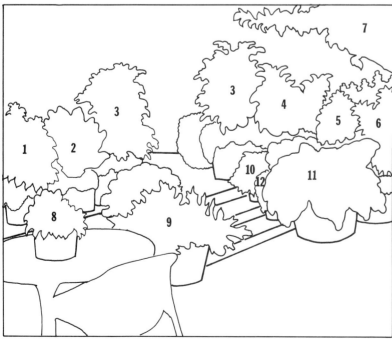

5.16. Container gardens have great flexibility. Pots filled with annual vegetables and flowers can be moved around when they are spent, and others can take their place.

5.16a. Edibles in Figure 5.16:

1. Pepper ('Gypsy')
2. Chard ('Ruby')
3. Tomato ('Patio')
4. Eggplant
5. Pepper ('California Wonder')
6. Cherry ('Garden Bing')
7. Pear
8. Pepper ('Holiday')
9. Zucchini ('Gold Rush')
10. Bush cucumber ('Spacemaster')
11. Rhubarb
12. Thyme

dominant design theme is derived from the colors of the fruits and flowers. Bright reds, yellows, and blues are used freely. The edibles included—peppers, eggplant, ruby chard, tomatoes, and golden zucchini—are highly decorative up close, and all bear their harvest over a long season. The design is unified by limiting the color range and banding the flowers of the lobelia and marigold; for instance, the blue line of the lobelia flowers flows from one container to another. A pear tree provides summer shade.

Clusters of containerized edibles such as these can be used in entryways and on porches, patios, decks, and front steps. Large containers limit the need for frequent watering, and clustering them permits drip irrigation. Toward the end of the season, when the tomato, cucumber, and zucchini plants begin to look a bit unkempt, some may be replaced with chrysanthemums and others with cool-season leaf vegetables such as lettuce, kale, or spinach.

Not all containers need have bottoms. Bottomless containers can be used to accommodate plants with vigorous root systems, to vary height levels of plantings, or to avoid drainage problems in poorly drained sites. An example is the grape shown in Figure 4.25. Keep in mind, however, that bottomless containers are not portable.

Parts of the Property: Regional Treatments

This section covers the various distinct areas a given property can contain—frontyard and entryway, sideyard, backyard, and patio area—and describes some possible treatments for each area. The illustrations and accompanying text cover geographical regions all over the country, from southern California to New England; for many of the sample treatments alternative plant materials are suggested, making the plans adaptable to different climatic regions.

Entryways

I am amazed at the number of houses I visit whose interiors are dramatically beautiful, but whose frontyards and entryways are completely unimaginative. The frontyard and entryway should set the stage and welcome the visitor with grace. Rarely does a lawn with a few shrubs by the front door succeed.

Typically, the average house in a development has an uninspired concrete front walk and entryway. Contractors install fancy bathroom fixtures, kitchen tiles, and so on, but rarely offer any but the plainest of plain front entries. In such a house, the money spent to cover a dull concrete walk with brick pavers, slate, or tile is money well spent. Taking the plain walk out altogether and making a more interesting one, or adding steps, is often worth even more effort and money. Planter boxes, containers, small flowering trees, stonework, brick, and so on can also help to make the entry inviting. And make sure that the front door is clearly the main entrance. Don't hide it, forcing visitors to hesitate and guess where they should go. Make the door dramatic and obvious.

When planning your frontyard, remember that unless you provide privacy, you probably won't use the yard. Unenclosed lawns serve strictly as decoration. Maybe a yard such as the one discussed early in this chapter, which would provide a private patio and a considerable amount of food, would be more appealing. In most areas of the country and on most properties, the frontyard belongs to the public and the backyard to the family—even when the frontyard is the sunniest, most pleasant part of the lot or, in hot climates, the coolest. Frontyards can be made private and useful through good planning. Reclaiming the frontyard for family use can enhance outdoor living.

Before erecting any fences or walls, check with your building department to determine local restrictions. Some municipalities do not allow fences above 2.5 feet in the frontyard; others say 4 feet is the limit. Corner lots are the most restricted because people in cars need to see around the corner.

An Informal Entryway for Southern California

Figure 5.17 shows a dramatic and colorful entrance for a two-story home. This entryway was planned for a yard where the objective was to provide as much livable space as possible for an active family with teenagers still at home. The backyard has a large patio off the family room for teenage parties and the courtyard has an adult patio off the living room. The design provides a large number of edible plants and maintenance is relatively easy. The planting is planned for zone 10.

The stunning blossom of the 'Gold Rush' zucchini is itself a culinary treat, deep-fried Italian style or chopped and folded into an omelet.

5.17. This inviting entry, designed for a southern California home, is fairly drought-tolerant, has relatively low maintenance requirements, and provides both pleasure and bounty.

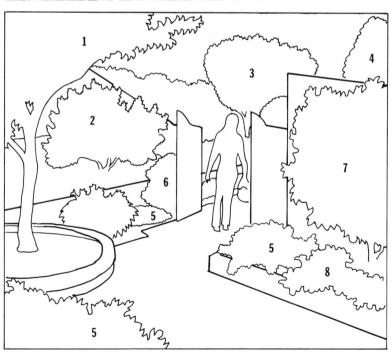

5.17a. Edibles in Figure 5.17:

1. *Apple (low chill)*
2. *Pomegranate*
3. *Plum (low chill)*
4. *Avocado*
5. *Natal plums*
6. *Lime*
7. *Oranges*
8. *Strawberries*

Pomegranates provide a long show of brilliant red flowers, replaced in fall by decorative red fruits and yellow foliage.

In this design, the front gate is obvious and inviting. The walled frontyard gives privacy to a small patio around the corner. The 5-foot wall also hides part of the yard, inviting one to turn the corner to see what is waiting to be revealed.

The entryway makes use of recycled railroad ties set into gravel, which permit whatever water is received in this low-rainfall area to percolate down into the soil. The planter boxes are also made of railroad ties. They make an attractive background for all sorts of plants, and convey the informal feeling of the whole yard.

With the exception of the citrus, apple, and plum trees, which can be drip irrigated, and the strawberry bed, which is small enough to be hand-watered, this landscape is drought tolerant. In the areas of this entryway that are not covered with edibles, one could plant a low baccharis (dwarf coyote bush) or a carpet juniper. These plants are also drought resistant.

Finally, with the intention of controlling air-conditioning costs, we have planted an evergreen avocado to protect the south wall from the summer heat and fruit trees to shade the west wall.

As you look at the drawing of this entryway you will see to the far left of the property a standard-size apple, 'Beverly Hills'. Apples usually require more winter chilling than the Los Angeles area offers, but a few varieties will grow in this mild climate. Close by is a pomegranate, 'Wonderful', which offers its beautiful fruit, often in combination with glorious red flowers (see photo at left). The leaves of the pomegranate also provide a true yellow in the fall landscape. Next to the pomegranate is a 'Bearrs' lime, a lovely rounded small tree when mature.

Between the lime and the 'Santa Rosa' plum is a bougainvillea, 'San Diego Orange'. It adds a splash of color behind the wall (the color of this variety will not clash with the other plants as some of the magenta shades do).

In the foreground as you enter this yard are low-growing 'Tuttle' natal plums. Handsome all year with their dark-green, shiny leaves, these plums are used in three different areas to pull the parts of the design together. The orange trees in the front bed are of different varieties, 'Washington' and 'Valencia'. These trees don't require cross-pollination, but having two varieties prolongs the harvest season. Another orange tree could be planted on the other side of the driveway (not illustrated) to balance the frontyard.

The avocado tree, 'Bacon', is barely visible behind the oranges on the other side of the wall. Its primary use, beside fruiting, is to shade the patio and the front rooms of the house. Other than the bougainvillea and the ground covers, the only ornamentals are heat-loving annuals, planted along the hot western walk.

A Formal Entryway for the Southeast

This entryway (Figure 5.18) was planned for a home in Virginia (zone 7), and is generally applicable to zones 6 to 9. This is a formal entry to match the formality of the architecture of the two-story house.

In keeping with the style, the plants are placed in symmetrical patterns. The lines of the walk are straight, and the planting beds on either side emphasize the geometric design. Two potted sweet bays, clipped in a rounded topiary form, stand at either side of the door. A small amount of topiary goes a long way in lending formality to a plan.

One aspect of the design that adds grace is the framing of the front door with the walls and the branches of the trees. A framed view is often more appealing than a completely revealed view. In addition, the deciduous trees cool the south wall in summer, and the bare branches allow the sun in during the winter. In spring the lacy foliage of the almond trees adds even more interest to the picture. The same can be said of the pecan tree behind the house.

A formal yard design permits fewer options in choosing edible plant materials. Your choice of plants is limited to those that have a formal form and foliage and you need to consider the double harvest, that is, the yield from double or symmetrical plantings of the fruits from some plants. Rather than a varied yield from several different fruit trees, you may get an unmanageably large harvest of just one or two fruits.

The plants chosen for this yard are pecan, sweet bay, almond, grape, peach, blueberry, and plum. The stately pecan tree gives shade to the backyard in summer. It also softens the two-story building. The two potted sweet bay shrubs can be brought in during the coldest part of the winter. In-

5.18. This elegant formal entry offers almonds, blueberries, plums, peaches, and grapes, as well as a gracious welcome.

5.18a. Edibles in Figure 5.18:

1. Pecan
2. Plums ('Allred')
3. Almonds
4. Blueberries
5. Grapes
6. Sweet bay
7. Genetic dwarf peaches

A 'Nonpareil' almond in the full glory of its spring bloom.

side the fence on either side of the walk are two almond trees, 'Texas' and 'Nonpareil' (try to imagine their springtime show of white blossoms, as the illustration shows the house later in the season). On the fence are both 'Concord' and 'Himrod' grapevines. Blueberry bushes, two genetic dwarf peaches, and two 'Allred' plums flank the entry on either side. The deep red foliage of the plums is striking in the summer season.

The ornamentals used to complete this landscape are tulips in the planting beds next to the front walk (replaced by annuals in summer) and, under the almonds, low evergreen junipers, which provide interest in winter.

The edible plants, you will notice, are all planted in even numbers. The purpose of this design technique, common in formal yards, is to achieve a symmetrical effect. Consider the implications of this approach in an edible yard. For example, two grape vines provide a nice amount of fruit—the 'Himrod' is a white, seedless grape, good for eating fresh; the 'Concord' gives marvelous fruits for juice and jelly—and the vines look the same, except for fruit color. Blueberries are no problem. Six bushes supply a nice amount of fruit, and since a cross-pollinator is needed there have to be at least two plants, so a hedge or border of blueberries makes good sense.

The use of standard nut and fruit trees becomes more complex in a formal, symmetrical landscape design. Instead of 'Texas', we could have chosen for the cross-pollinator of the 'Nonpareil' almond the variety 'Hall's Hardy', but the latter has pink rather than white blooms, and using one pink-blossoming and one white-blossoming tree on either side of the walk would have defeated the symmetrical style. The problem came up again with the selection of plums; I wanted the trees to be alike, and no other plum tree beside 'Allred' has the rosy blooms and the deep-red foliage.

In choosing the 'Allred' I also had to consider questions of pollination and size of harvest. My catalogs did not have pollination information, so I consulted Henry Field's nursery, which carries this variety. (Most nurseries are pleased to supply information about their stock; be sure to enclose a stamped, self-addressed envelope.) Field's replied that the 'Allred' would self-pollinate but would probably not provide as large a harvest as one of their better pollinators, such as 'Ozark Premier'. This was actually welcome news, since two full-size, heavily bearing trees would yield an excessive amount of fruit for one family.

Another solution would have been to choose alternative plants that had more manageable harvests and less complicated pollination needs. For example, instead of the plums two apples or pears of similar flowering and growth patterns could have been used.

In colder parts of the country, such as zones 5 and 6, you could adapt this basic design by substituting semidwarf apples for the almonds and using hardy pears as the street trees. On the warm end of the spectrum, in zones 9 and 10, citrus or loquats could be used instead of plums.

Midwest Entryway

Figure 5.19 illustrates the use of many popular edibles in a design for a west-facing frontyard in colder parts of the country. In these locations, which include the Midwest, New England, and other areas in zones 4 through 6, winters are severe and summers fairly warm. Among the primary considerations of the landscaping here are modifying winter temperatures in the house and selecting cold-hardy plant materials that will survive and thrive from year to year.

Large pines are planted along the north and east sides of the house for wind control. Their size also helps frame and soften the large mass of this two-story house, while smaller trees are selected for the front. Deciduous trees—quince, apple, and pear—are sited along the south wall to allow the winter sun to warm the house.

Again, for balance, this large house is softened in front by a commensurately large shrub border. The small lawn gives form to the design and creates an informal line for the shrub border. The edibles include marjoram, bush plum, apple, gooseberry, elderberry, blueberry, pear, chives, strawberry, and quince.

The quinces are a risk in some parts of zone 4, so they have been placed against a south wall for extra warmth and

5.19. The large shrub border in this front yard produces a sizeable harvest as well as softening the façade of the two-story house.

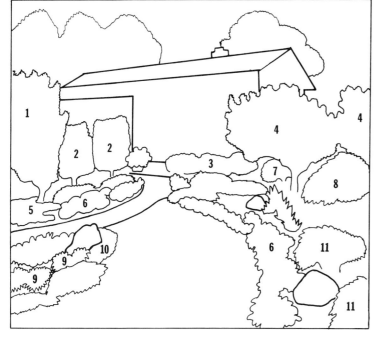

5.19a. Edibles in Figure 5.19:

1. Pear
2. Quinces (espaliered)
3. Bush plums
4. Apple
5. Wintergreen
6. Strawberries
7. Gooseberries
8. Elderberry
9. Chives
10. Marjoram
11. Blueberries

5.20. *Tropical gardens offer many edible options.
Most of the tropical edibles are outstanding
ornamentals as well as providing a luscious harvest.*

5.20a. *Edibles in Figure 5.20:*

1. *Coconut palms*
2. *Mango*
3. *Surinam cherry*
4. *Banana ('Dwarf Cavendish')*
5. *Natal plums*
6. *Strawberry guava*
7. *Loquat*
8. *Orange*
9. *Lime*

5.21. *Narrow sideyards can become ornamental and food-production areas.* *beans, and red geraniums are planted at the bottom for summer color.*
Here, scarlet runner beans alternate on trellises with 'Dutch White' runner

protection. The gooseberries are in the shade of the apple trees, and the marjoram is slightly elevated on the side of a mound for good drainage.

A number of evergreen junipers are planted near the walk and in the shrub border to give substance to the area when the other plants are out of leaf. To give extra color and cohesiveness to the design, red petunias, strawberries, and the junipers are repeated in different beds. It would be best to extend the shrub border to the side property line and out to the street; it then could include many more blueberries, and currants and pawpaw might be added as well.

A Mediterranean Entryway in a Tropical Climate

Figure 5.20 shows an inviting entryway for the frost-free areas of the United States—southern Florida, the coastal regions of Southern California, and sections of Hawaii. To complement the slightly Spanish architecture and tropical environment, plants with large foliage and bold forms and colors are used.

In the backyard, the house is framed with palms and a large mango. In the atrium, bananas are protected from the wind and kept warm. Among the plantings in front of the house are a number of food-producing shrubs, including Surinam cherry, natal plum, strawberry guava, dwarf orange, and dwarf lime. The shrub grouping is accented by a dramatic multistemmed loquat. To give variety to the

plantings and to vary the plant heights in a basically flat area, assorted herbs and ginger in containers are included. A low ground cover of fragrant star jasmine is used to tie all the different planting areas together. Finally, adding height and color to a predominantly rounded, dark-green plant combination, are red hibiscus, which blooms for a large part of the year, and the exotically shaped and colored bird-of-paradise.

Most temperate-zone stone fruits cannot be grown in tropical gardens, but a large selection of tropically adapted plants is available in those regions. An avocado or a bread-fruit tree would be as appropriate as the mango. And instead of the dwarf orange and dwarf lime, one might use any one of a number of other dwarf citrus trees, including lemon, tangelo, tangerine, limequat, and kumquat. The dramatic form of the loquat could be achieved somewhat differently but equally successfully by substituting a cherimoya.

Sideyards

Sideyards and back entryways are the areas of a yard most often neglected. Frequently they are narrow spaces, and their transformation into beautiful, food-productive places takes imagination. Figure 5.21 features a southern exposure with two kinds of pole beans, used to soften a narrow vertical space. The types selected are 'Dutch White'

5.22. *Patio areas are a natural for edible plants. This one provides fresh fruit as well as herbs for salads and soups. The varying forms of the plants lend interest to this small area.*

5.22a. *Edibles in Figure 5.22:*

1. *Plum ('Weeping Santa Rosa')*
2. *Chilean guavas*
3. *Rosemary (prostrate)*
4. *Kiwi (female with a male branch grafted on)*
5. *Tea*
6. *Mixed herbs*
7. *Chamomile*
8. *Dwarf tangelo*
9. *Strawberries*

runner and scarlet runner. Both have showy flowers and bear throughout a long, warm summer, so they need not be removed halfway through a growing season. Inedible geraniums are used for bright color. This planting is applicable to most of zones 4 through 10.

Many alternate plantings could have been used, depending upon food preference and locale. In cool, foggy-summer areas in zones 2 through 7 in coastal zones, and in locations with mild winters, you might select the vining 'Sugar Snap' peas and alternate them with tall vining nasturtiums. You might then fill the bottom planting bed with orange or yellow calendulas and oakleaf lettuce. For areas with short summer growing seasons, you might want to use 'Royalty Burgundy' pole beans and underplant them with purple-leafed basil and pink or purple petunias. A totally different approach for an area of this size and shape would be the use of espaliered fruit trees, discussed earlier in this chapter, or trellises covered with vines such as grapes, bitter melon, or kiwi.

Note: This area has only a slight roof overhang. If the area you are considering has an overhang of more than a foot or so, the sun will not shine on that area for most of June and part of July; thus the location will not be suitable for the plants mentioned in this section.

Patio Areas

Few yards can fail to be enhanced by a private patio area, such as that shown in Figure 5.22. (Other ideas for patios are discussed in Chapter 6.) This patio is located off the kitchen-family room of a home in Northern California. The plants are appropriate to the warmest parts of zone 8, most of zone 9, and the coolest sections of zone 10. All are edible.

The design emphasis here lies in the contrast of foliage colors with plant forms. Most of the flowers are white, making a pleasant contrast to the dark-colored house. The primary foliage color is the dark green of the 'Weeping Santa Rosa' plum, Chilean guava, tea, kiwi, strawberry, and citrus. For contrast, a large area of yellow-green chamomile was added, along with the gray-green foliage of several herbs. For further variety, plants with different forms are used—note the weeping habit of the plum, the vining kiwi, and the mat form of the chamomile. Finally, to break up the flatness a large expanse of chamomile would otherwise have, the herb is planted on a slight mound.

This patio is located in a part of the country where summer evenings are cool. To make the area more comfortable for evening entertaining, a fire pit might be added. In warm, sultry summer climates where mosquitos can be a problem, the kiwi might be trained over a screened area that could connect to the house roof. For additional fruit production, dwarf fruit trees in containers could be added. In zone 8 and the colder parts of zone 9, the Chilean guava will need frost protection.

Backyards

Backyards usually have many functions, including entertaining, a play area for children, a utility area, and, not least, growing food. The first of our examples here is a multiuse yard; the second is designed for intensive food production.

A Backyard in Fall Color

The design illustrated in Figure 5.23 is suited for the warmer sections of the Carolinas, but it is also applicable in many areas of zones 7 through 9. The yard was designed for entertaining, strolling, food production, and the enjoyment of local wildlife.

The edibles incorporated include apples with low chilling requirements. Other food plants used are pecan, walnut, fig, muscadine grape, rabbiteye blueberry, pomegranate, Oriental 'Fuyu' persimmon, rhubarb, strawberry, herbs,

and saffron crocus. Enough plants of each species were included to permit the harvest to be shared with the neighboring wildlife.

The design of this yard incorporates two interesting techniques. The first is the framing of a view—in this case by means of the simple arbor. The second is the introduction of a hidden view implied at the end of the lawn. The long narrow lawn, small but large enough for croquet or children's games, disappearing out of sight invites a stroll to see what is around the corner—perhaps a birdbath, pool, or gazebo. Try visualizing the scene without the arbor and with a straight horizontal wall of shrubs and trees across the back of the lawn. You will probably find that version not nearly so interesting and inviting as the yard shown.

This design showcases the beauty of fall foliage. The pomegranate, persimmon, nut trees, and blueberries all give vibrant color in most areas of the country. They are supplemented by the ornamental barberries and liquidambar. Fall color is at its most dramatic when set off by rich

The delicious fruit of the 'Hachiya' persimmon enlivens the fall landscape long after its leaves are gone.

5.23. Many edibles have vibrant fall foliage. This colorful backyard leads the eye and invites strolling.

5.23a. Edibles in Figure 5.23:

1. Walnuts
2. Fig
3. Pecans
4. Persimmon ('Fuyu')
5. Apples
6. Muscadine grapes
7. Blueberries
8. Pomegranate
9. Rhubarb
10. Saffron crocuses
11. Thyme
12. Rosemary
13. Marjoram
14. Red basil
15. Strawberries

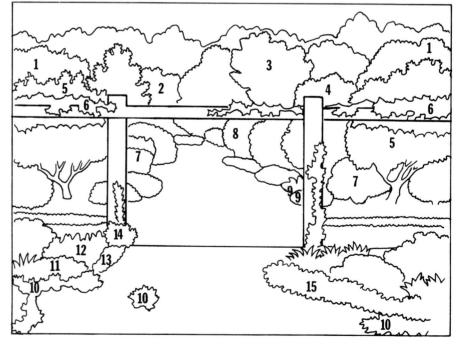

green foliage, provided here by pines in the backyard and holly interspersed among the border shrubs. These evergreens also give form to the garden in winter. In the spring the apples and blueberries put on a visual show that could be heightened even further by low-maintenance daffodils clustered in drifts near the lawn.

The patio area is planted with small, jewel-like plants best seen up close, such as saffron crocus, strawberries, and herbs. The herbs are convenient to the kitchen and the strawberries close at hand for a breakfast on the patio.

The informality of the yard is achieved by the asymmetry of the planting and by allowing the plants to grow to their natural shape, which also results in a minimum of maintenance. Neither the flower borders nor the hedging and trees need clipping. Harvest effort is minimized too, since only the apples and the figs ripen all at once in a quantity sufficient to require attention.

A Backyard with Raised Beds

An ideal way to maximize food production in a relatively limited space is to place the edibles in raised beds. Raised beds provide excellent drainage, do not become compacted by constant foot and equipment traffic, and require less stooping and leaning from the gardener during planting, weeding, and harvesting. Raised beds are also a solution to extreme soil problems such as hardpan, very high or low soil pH, and poor drainage. These advantages are augmented further by the aesthetic possibilities inherent in the use of raised beds. Strong design lines created by the beds, either on one level or a variety of levels, with plants spilling over the sides, can make for a very interesting and appealing yard. The epitome of the raised-bed edible garden is shown in Figure 5.24, in this case the backyard of a property in zone 8.

The entire area is planted in raised beds or containers laid out in a geometrical pattern, giving substance and shape to the area. The nonsymmetrical pattern allows for more planting flexibility. Had they been laid out symmetrically, the plants selected would have had to be more frequently repeated to reinforce the symmetry, and therefore could not have been so varied. The lines created by the shapes and placement of the beds are strong; thus, they dominate and unify the area. The long beds are broken in a number of places to allow better access to the plants. Gravel between the beds ensures dry footing and keeps weeds at a minimum. Railroad ties provide a stable deck area to support patio furniture.

For maximum food production, the beds are filled with a light soil mix containing large amounts of organic matter and are planted primarily with dwarf fruit trees and annual vegetables, which have a large potential harvest. Included are apricot, apple, plum, almond, citrus, grape, asparagus, rhubarb, strawberries, and herbs. The annual vegetables are beans, beets, eggplants, carrots, peppers, tomatoes, sorrel,

Heat-loving peanuts and salvia make a colorful summer combination in a raised bed or perennial border.

Cool springtime conditions actually intensify the colors of ornamental kale, planted here with daffodils.

5.24. *Gardening in raised beds has many advantages, including excellent drainage, ease of weeding and harvesting, and aesthetic appeal.*

1. *Dwarf oranges*
2. *Semidwarf apples*
3. *Sweet bay*
4. *Genetic dwarf apricots*
5. *Grapes*
6. *Genetic dwarf almond*
7. *Rhubarb*
8. *Chard*
9. *Sorrel*
10. *Strawberries*
11. *Chives*
12. *Marjoram*
13. *Oregano*
14. *Tarragon*
15. *Tomatoes*
16. *Cucumbers*
17. *Pole beans ('Dutch White' runner)*
18. *Bush beans ('Royalty')*
19. *Peppers*
20. *Onions*
21. *Beets*
22. *Basil*
23. *Asparagus*
24. *Carrots*
25. *Asparagus peas*
26. *Eggplants*
27. *New Zealand spinach*
28. *Nasturtiums*
29. *Peanuts*
30. *Sweet potatoes*
31. *Sage ('Tricolor')*
32. *Genetic dwarf peach*

chard, cucumbers, onions, sweet potatoes, peanuts, asparagus peas, and New Zealand spinach.

Bands of single colors are used, as they were on the container patio, to unify the whole. In this case, they are provided by annual flowers, including lavender sweet alyssum, yellow marigolds in clusters, and orange nasturtiums. The colors are limited to yellow, orange, and lavender, but could as easily have been other combinations, say, red, blue, and white, or pink, blue, and lavender. In addition, many substitutions for this selection of annual flowers are possible. I might have used red geraniums, white baby's breath, and deep blue and white lobelia.

Care was taken to soften the edges of the beds with cas-

cading plants. Here the plants used for this purpose are sweet alyssum, nasturtiums, thyme, sweet potato, asparagus peas, and New Zealand spinach. Other cascading edibles from which you might choose are compact varieties of cherry tomatoes, bush cucumbers, dwarf snow peas, and strawberries. Cascading petunias, many of the campanulas, and portulaca make good substitution possibilities for the annual flowers.

Instead of being placed randomly, the vegetables are planted in rows that run parallel to the lines of the beds. The root and leaf vegetables that will leave holes when harvested are surrounded by sweet alyssum, which will spread into the areas left by the harvested vegetables.

CHAPTER 6

Small-Area Landscaping

THE DELICIOUS BEAUTY plus bounty aimed for in this book can be achieved successfully on apartment balconies, on condominium patios, in townhouse atriums, or in the small yards characteristic of city properties and subdivision lots. In addition to suggesting design techniques for enhancing small gardens, this chapter will identify some of the problems specific to small-area landscape design, and suggest ways of dealing with them. Special attention is paid to container gardening and to what might be called container composting: small compost systems specially designed to yield enough humus for small plots, pots, and boxes. Finally, for those who want to reap the most benefit from limited spaces, a modified version of intensive gardening is described. This gardening method yields a large, beautiful harvest even in a cramped space. The chapter ends with an extensive table of plants for small areas and their suggested uses. This chapter covers the fundamentals of small-area gardening. For a highly detailed, book-length approach to the subject, see *Growing Midget Vegetables at Home, Dwarf Fruit Trees,* and *How To Grow More Vegetables* (all cited in the bibliography).

An increasingly popular alternative for gardening enthu-

siasts with limited personal space is the community garden. These marvelous group projects are springing up everywhere, from inner-city neighborhoods to suburbs, to retirement communities. Check around to see if one already exists in your area—or start one!—and consult *The Complete Book of Community Gardening* by Jamie Jobb, listed in the bibliography.

Designing the Small Garden

The Illusion of Space

In the design of a small garden planted with edibles, most of the same aesthetic principles apply as in any other design. In addition, certain design principles are used to make a small area more pleasing and less cramped looking. Just as we use lines in clothes design—vertical to draw the eye away from the short and stubby figure, horizontal to deemphasize the tall or thin figure—so we use lines to create the illusion of spaciousness in a small garden. As noted, the lines of patios, planter boxes, fences, walls, and paths all guide the eye of the observer. A long diagonal line for the

6.1. The angled patio gives a feeling of spaciousness to this small yard. The small pool is soothing and adds much interest to the area.

6.1a. Edibles in Figure 6.1:

1. Filbert
2. Blueberries
3. Herb basket
4. Red currants
5. Lowbush blueberries
6. Gooseberries
7. Sorrel
8. Alpine strawberries
9. Cranberries
10. Water chestnuts
11. Lotus

eye to follow, as opposed to a direct, short line leading to a close-in fence, will make a space appear larger.

Another means of creating the illusion of spaciousness is a technique borrowed from Oriental landscapes. The idea is to provide so much of interest in the space available that the viewer's eye stops and savors one visual treat after another—for example, a ripening peach, the gnarled limbs of a grapevine on an arbor, a planter box laden with cherry tomatoes, or a small fountain. As the eye rests on these different elements a feeling of space is engendered. The visual stop-and-go makes the observer forget the smallness of the space.

Figure 6.1 represents the shallow backyard of a subdivision in zone 8 of the Northwest. This design is also applicable to cool-summer areas of zones 5–7. Its strongest design feature is the angled deck. By building the deck across the longest diagonal of the yard, the viewer's eye is drawn along this length, conveying a sense of distance. The small, bubbling fountain and water garden contribute both visual and auditory interest.

The edibles incorporated in this suburban woodland oasis include filbert, blueberry, cranberry, currant, gooseberry, Alpine strawberry, sorrel, herbs, and the water plants lotus and water chestnut, both of which must be brought inside for winter frost protection. The woodland feeling is conveyed by the predominance of foliage plants and their informal shapes. Color is provided by the addition of the day lily, water lily, and lotus flowers. Fall foliage colors are supplied by the birch and blueberry, and winter interest is provided by the low evergreen shrubs and the pachysandra. For practicality, native stone stepping-stone paths are added so the nuts and berries can be harvested and an occasional weed pulled.

One of the loveliest aspects of this yard is its natural look. The house and deck appear to have been built around an existing woodland setting. In fact, though, the property was barren, flat, and dry when the homeowner moved in, and this "pre-existing" naturalism was created from scratch. To make it look as if the water pre-dated the deck, the pool was constructed to extend a few inches under the structure. The placement of the boulders, actually planned carefully but intended to suggest nature's randomness (including one around which the deck appears to have been built), and the addition of soil to create gentle mounds, complete the illusion.

In addition to the design techniques mentioned above, creating a little mystery can go a long way in distracting the observer from space limitations. A visitor will wonder what lies behind an espaliered apple or around a woven screen, and probably will not give much thought to the size of the space. My backyard is shallow, but a decorative fence with a path leading around it hides part of the yard as well as the compost heap. People visiting my yard for the first time always want to see what is beyond that fence. The compost heap is anticlimactic—I must do something about that—but

Many edibles can be grown beautifully on a small deck or porch. From left to right: red chard, cabbage, a second red chard, and eggplant. (Photo courtesy of Burpee Seeds.)

the effectiveness of the fence and a path as distractions from the shallowness of the yard is proven.

A third way to increase the apparent size of a yard is to use fine-textured plant materials predominantly. Since objects in the distance—in a painting or a landscape—always seem smaller than those in the foreground, psychologically we associate small items with distance. Thus, small-leaved plants convey a feeling of expanse, whereas plants with large, broad leaves, such as banana plants, stop and fill the eye. The foliage size of edible plants for small gardens is noted in the table at the end of this chapter.

Small-Garden Problems

Shadows

Small gardens, particularly city gardens, usually receive less sun than larger gardens, since shadows are cast from surrounding surfaces such as upper balconies, neighbors' houses, apartment buildings, and trees. In planning a garden for a courtyard, patio, or deck of an apartment, study your sun patterns carefully. If you have a choice of exposures in selecting your site, choose one that faces south. This will offer the most options, edibly speaking, as the majority of edible plants need at least six hours of sun daily. A small yard might receive full sun in the winter and all shade in the summer, or the opposite might be true. Clearly, then, it's imperative to know what your particular shadow patterns will be.

Once, the tomatoes I had planted against the south wall of my house in full sun during April ended up in full shade by June because of the roof overhang. My husband taught me a helpful trick for predicting the sun's pattern. Go out-

An espaliered tree, such as this pear, is a marvelous space-saving technique for small areas.

side at midnight on the night of the full moon, he said, and note where the moon's shadows are cast. This is approximately where the sun's shadows will fall at noon, six months later. For example, if you check the full moon's shadow in December, you will have a very good idea of where the noontime sun will shine in June.

Pollination

In small areas you might only have room for one vine of a particular variety. Since many plants need at least two individuals of different genders or varieties, to cross-pollinate and so to produce fruits, pollination problems can arise in small-area gardens. There are several ways of preventing such problems: (1) planting more than one tree in the same hole; (2) grafting a branch of a male tree onto a female tree or vine; or (3) grafting a branch of a cross-pollinating variety onto your favorite variety of fruit tree. Regarding the latter

option, often trees can be purchased from nurseries with the grafting already done.

Training Techniques

Two techniques that are particularly useful in small spaces are training plants on fences, and the espalier, the latter described in Chapter 5. Training on fences is used most often with vines, espaliering for woody plants such as stone fruits and citrus. The table at the end of this chapter suggests which plants are appropriate for each treatment.

Energy-Saving Techniques

Despite their size, gardens in small areas can help to conserve household energy by reducing air-conditioning and heating bills. Though a large nut tree might be inappropriate, a south wall might nevertheless be shaded with vines. Deciduous vines, such as kiwis and grapes, and annuals, such as beans or bitter melon, work best trellised against a wall or trained over arbors and patio covers. Espaliered fruit trees can help too. The leaves of the trees shade the wall in summer, and the bare limbs let the sun shine through in winter.

Subdivision Yards

This section provides two architectural plans for a small subdivision yard designed for edible plants. Figure 6.2 depicts a yard created for zone 9, and the cooler parts of zone 10. Figure 6.3 shows the same yard designed for zones 5 through 8.

In both cases the frontyard is primarily covered with an ornamental ground cover. In Figure 6.2 the primary ground cover could be sand strawberry (*Fragaria chiloensis*) or chamomile (*Anthemis nobilis*). In Figure 6.3 the primary frontyard ground cover could be English ivy (*Hedera helix*), bishop's hat (*Epimedium youngianum* 'Niveum'), or chamomile.

The backyard includes a small lawn, but the patio could be enlarged and a few more shrubs and ground cover could be substituted for the lawn. The strawberry ground cover under the fruit trees will be appropriate in the frontyard for the first three or four years until the fruit trees fill in. After that, a shade-loving ground cover, such as pachysandra or an attractive mulch, will be needed.

Climate control includes a deciduous vine over the front porch and deciduous trees on the south and west sides of the house. Evergreen windbreak trees are included in the northeast corner of the lot, and evergreen shrubs are planned against the north wall of the house for insulation.

Many of the shrubs, vines, and trees included in the yard are edible ornamentals. A considerable portion of the backyard is taken up with a combination flower and vegetable bed. The vegetables that require less sun are planted on the eastern side of the house. If high production is wanted the beds could be dug by the intensive method (see Chapter 6).

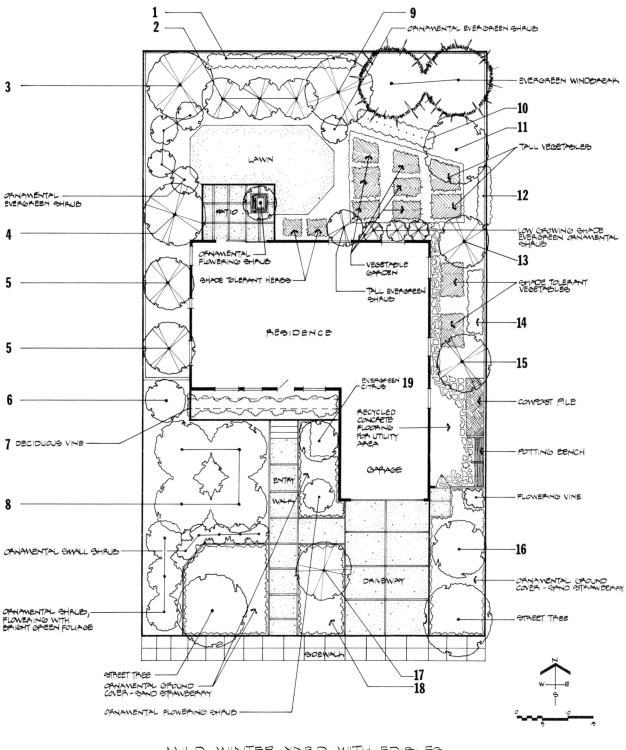

1 Dessert grapes
2 Genetic dwarf peaches
3
9 ORNAMENTAL EVERGREEN SHRUB
EVERGREEN WINDBREAK
10
11
TALL VEGETABLES
12
LOW GROWING SHADE EVERGREEN ORNAMENTAL SHRUB
13
SHADE TOLERANT VEGETABLES
14
15
COMPOST PILE
POTTING BENCH
19 EVERGREEN CITRUS
RECYCLED CONCRETE FLOORING FOR UTILITY AREA
GARAGE
FLOWERING VINE
16
ORNAMENTAL GROUND COVER - SAND STRAWBERRY
STREET TREE
ORNAMENTAL EVERGREEN SHRUB
4
5
5
6
7 DECIDUOUS VINE
8
ORNAMENTAL SMALL SHRUB
ORNAMENTAL SHRUB, FLOWERING WITH BRIGHT GREEN FOLIAGE
LAWN
PATIO
ORNAMENTAL FLOWERING SHRUB
SHADE TOLERANT HERBS
VEGETABLE GARDEN
TALL EVERGREEN SHRUB
RESIDENCE
ENTRY WALK
DRIVEWAY
STREET TREE
ORNAMENTAL GROUND COVER - SAND STRAWBERRY
ORNAMENTAL FLOWERING SHRUB
SIDEWALK
17
18
N
W E
S
0 5 10 15

MILD WINTER YARD WITH EDIBLES

6.2. Many edible options exist for small yards in mild-winter areas. The following are included in this design: 1. Dessert grapes 2. Genetic dwarf peaches 3. Semidwarf pear 4. Semidwarf self-pollinating apple 5. Semidwarf sweet cherry 6. Pineapple guava 7. Kiwi (male and female) 8. Dwarf oranges (two navel and two juice oranges) 9. Plum 10. Raspberries 11. Dwarf lemon 12. Wine grapes 13. Pomegranate 14. Jerusalem artichokes 15. Genetic dwarf apricot 16. Dwarf tangelo 17. Plum ('Weeping Santa Rosa') 18. Garden strawberries 19. Dwarf kumquat

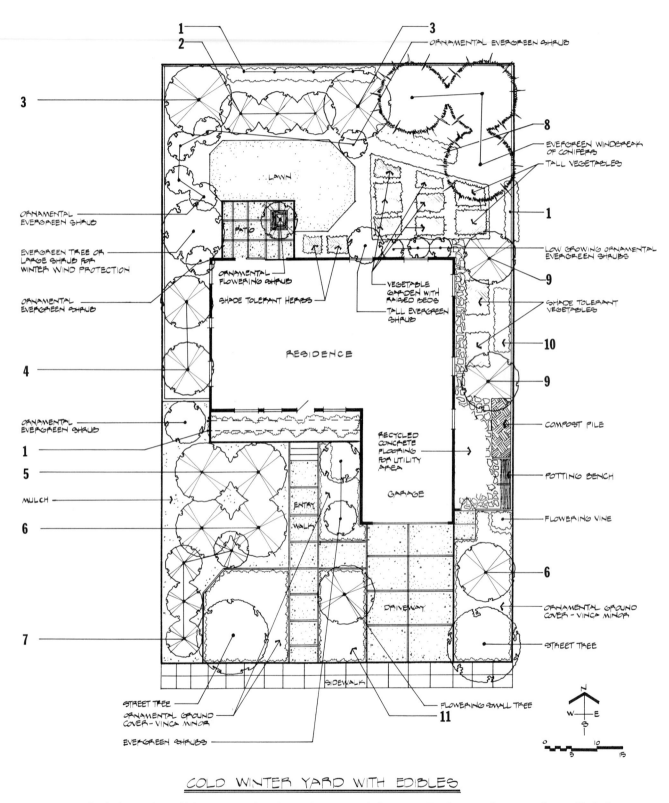

1 ... ORNAMENTAL EVERGREEN SHRUB
2 ... **3**
3
8 ... EVERGREEN WINDBREAK OF CONIFERS
TALL VEGETABLES
ORNAMENTAL EVERGREEN SHRUB
EVERGREEN TREE OR LARGE SHRUB FOR WINTER WIND PROTECTION
LAWN
1
ORNAMENTAL EVERGREEN SHRUB
PATIO
LOW GROWING ORNAMENTAL EVERGREEN SHRUBS
9
ORNAMENTAL FLOWERING SHRUB
VEGETABLE GARDEN WITH RAISED BEDS
SHADE TOLERANT HERBS
TALL EVERGREEN SHRUB
SHADE TOLERANT VEGETABLES
RESIDENCE
10
4
9
ORNAMENTAL EVERGREEN SHRUB
RECYCLED CONCRETE FLOORING FOR UTILITY AREA
COMPOST PILE
1
5
POTTING BENCH
MULCH
GARAGE
ENTRY WALK
FLOWERING VINE
6
6
DRIVEWAY
ORNAMENTAL GROUND COVER - VINCA MINOR
STREET TREE
7
STREET TREE
ORNAMENTAL GROUND COVER - VINCA MINOR
SIDEWALK
FLOWERING SMALL TREE
11
EVERGREEN SHRUBS

N
W E
S
0   5   10   15

COLD WINTER YARD WITH EDIBLES

6.3. *Even small suburban yards in cold climates can produce a bountiful harvest. The following are included here: 1. Grapevines 2. Bush plums 3. Sour cherry 4. Semidwarf pears 5. Dwarf plums 6. Dwarf apples 7. Blueberries 8. Raspberries on decorative trellis 9. Hardy dwarf apricot 10. Jerusalem artichokes 11. Strawberries*

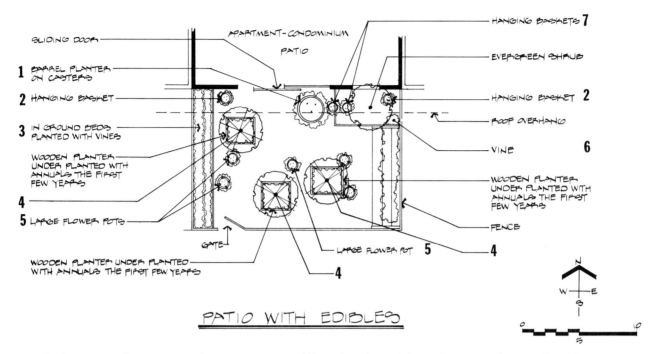

PATIO WITH EDIBLES

6.4. *This design for a small apartment or condominium patio features edibles in moveable containers for convenience and flexibility. The edibles are:*
1. Tomatoes and petunias (summer); broccoli, spinach, and violas
(winter) 2. Herbs 3. Peas or runner beans 4. Dwarf fruit trees
5. Annual vegetables 6. Grapevine 7. Cherry tomatoes

Container Gardening

Many people have no open garden space at all but garden nonetheless—on decks, tiny patios, even the edges of carports, if the sun reaches there. The new emphasis on container gardening is a response to the needs of condominium and apartment dwellers and city-garden enthusiasts, for whom this technique might literally be the only means of gardening in a limited space. Even gardeners with plenty of space can add to their close-in enjoyment by keeping some container plants on the back steps, the front walk, or around the outdoor living-room.

Many plants grow well in containers. (See the table at the end of this chapter for suggested container edibles.) And plant breeders have developed a whole new array of midget vegetables and dwarf fruit trees that thrive in containers. These plant materials have lost none of their ornamental value in the transition. Even the sprawling watermelon with its handsome cut foliage, which formerly took up to 12 feet of garden space, is now available in a midget variety that can be grown in a container.

Nor do containers themselves limit the visual interest such efforts can create. Planters, tubs, and barrels are varied enough to fit any style of landscape design. Elegant Italian urns can be planted with dwarf citrus, or an informal orange crate can be filled with marigolds and miniature melons. A favorite container of mine is a soy tub, available from most

import stores. Hanging baskets planted with cherry tomatoes will produce fruits for three to four months of the year, bringing to your living space both beauty and the special aroma that may take you back to your childhood. A trellis covered by lush, light green, Armenian cucumbers, pretty as any ivy, plus a planter full of herbs (chives, basil, parsley, and marjoram) and a tub of leaf lettuce will provide you with fresh salad for at least two months of the year.

Fragrance is a special bonus derived from living so close to your garden. The blossoms of citrus, loquat, and dwarf fruit trees, and the foliage of mint and tomatoes, will sweeten your space and glorify the landscape. And, of course, the fruits that follow will provide good eating.

All these advantages make container growing a true landscaping option for city growers, especially where the growing space faces south or receives at least six hours of full sun a day.

A Condominium Container Garden

Figure 6.4 illustrates a fairly standard first-floor condominium or apartment patio. In this case, it faces south. The concept, planter arrangement, and most of the plant materials are applicable anywhere in the country.

Containerized plants have the advantage of allowing you to move them at will, for maximum amounts of sun or to throw shade when desirable, as against the south wall during hot weather. They can even be moved to another home

Plants for Hanging Baskets

Try combining edible plants with flowers that spill over the sides of the containers. Flowering plants that can be used in combination with the edibles listed are named in parentheses.

Cherry tomato ('Red Cascade' petunia)

Cucumbers (cascading petunia)

Dwarf snow pea, in a large container (pink or purple sweet alyssum)

Mint (Italian bellflower or impatiens)

Oregano (purple or pink alyssum)

'Royalty' bush bean, in a large container (purple alyssum, or pink or white cascading petunia)

Parsley (yellow or orange viola)

Peppers (dwarf nasturtium)

Strawberry (white lobelia)

Thyme (purple basil and pink alyssum)

6.5 *The dwarf varieties of cherry tomatoes are best for hanging baskets.*

if the need should arise. The large wooden planters such as those labeled 1, 4, 6, and 7 would need special moving equipment, however. Planter number 1 is planted with small- to medium-sized tomatoes, in this case 'Patio' and 'Sweet 100'. The barrel should be placed on a platform with casters so it can be moved out from under the eaves during June. In the cool season, the tomatoes are replaced with lettuce and spinach. Numbers 2, 12, and 14 are herb-filled hanging baskets; they must be placed on plant stands for most of June when the overhanging roof blocks too much of the sun, which is directly overhead at that time of the year. At other times, they get plenty of sun from their hanging location. The in-ground planting bed, number 3, faces east and can be best utilized by planting with a vine that tolerates cool morning sun—peas in this instance. Cucumbers and pole beans would be borderline in this location but perhaps worth a try. The bed is lined in the front with masses of dwarf nasturtiums. Planters 4, 6, and 8 are all planted with genetic dwarf stone fruit trees. In warm-winter areas, they could as easily be planted with dwarf citrus. For the first several years, the fruit trees can be interplanted with annual vegetables, and later, when the trees throw too much shade, these can be replaced with shade-loving ground covers, such as Alpine strawberries or sweet woodruff.

The small planters, labeled 5 and 7, are filled with annual vegetables including, in the cool season, carrots, beets, and leeks; in the warm season they are replanted with peppers and eggplant. They are interplanted with flowers, and the pots can be moved out of view when they are no longer attractive. The two strawberry jars (number 9), with their many pockets, are planted with strawberries and herbs. A grapevine (number 10) is planted in the ground and trained on a trellis. The remaining in-ground space is given here to a sweet bay, underplanted with annual flowers and vegetables. While sweet bay is not appropriate in many zones, any small evergreen shrub that can take full shade in June, when the overhang blocks the sun, but full hot sun in later summer, would work just as well.

Clearly, space is limited in this kind of gardening situation, but 40 or 50 pounds of produce can easily be grown here and is well worth the time and effort. For more design ideas see the patio and raised bed sections of Chapter 5.

Special Requirements

Soil and Drainage

Besides a fairly sunny spot, edible container gardening requires quick-draining soil in fast-draining pots. For plants on roofs or decks it is important to use a lightweight mix—

not only for the safety of the deck but also for the mobility of the pot, in case it has to be moved into the sun. These light mixes are available in many nurseries and usually contain high proportions of organic matter, perlite, or vermiculite. Most of these mixes require regular fertilizing; I suggest a fish emulsion in a light proportion. Often, it is wise to fertilize at half strength twice as often as the manufacturer recommends. The drainage holes in the containers should be covered with stones, pieces of broken clay pots, or screens to enable the water to get out while the soil stays in.

Watering

Even in rainy climates, plants in containers usually need regular watering, since their roots cannot seek water in the depths of the earth. Also, containers get heated by the sun, causing water to evaporate rapidly from the soil. To make up for the water loss due to evaporation, it is best to use the largest containers feasible for your space. Use plants that require little water, such as herbs, in your smaller containers.

To help retain moisture and to keep the soil from being disturbed by hose water, mulch the soil with stones, compost, wood chips, or shredded bark, or plant a ground cover of strawberries. In arid climates, even where a mulch is applied, plants in small containers may need daily watering in the summer—on the hottest days, perhaps even twice a day. But remember, since your containers are likely to be near the house, you can water with excess *clean* household waste water.

Containers should be watered with an appliance that will not wash away or splatter the soil. One possibility is a standard nursery-supply bubbler, which has a gentle water flow. Drip systems are the simplest and most efficient way to irrigate containers. They soak the soil thoroughly, save water, and prevent the build-up of salts, which can damage plants. (For more information on the use of drip systems with container plants, see the section on watering in Chapter 7.) If you are unable to rig up a drip system and must water by hand, fill each container to the top with water, allow it to drain, and then refill. Avoid the bad habit of light sprinkling. It will cause the roots to grow toward the sides and the top of the container, forming drainage channels through which water will be lost.

If you do not use a drip system, extra-deep watering before fertilizing is recommended to flush out accumulated salts from past watering and fertilizing. The sign that such a treatment is called for is the formation of a white deposit along the bottom and the sides of the pot.

The care necessary in watering is easily balanced by the advantages of container growing. Plants in containers are easy to prune, easy to fertilize, are easy to harvest and require little weeding.

Composting in Small Areas

When a gardening book mentions composting, readers with small gardens usually sigh and say, "Nice, but. . . ." Though they know that composting material not only saves money but enriches the soil, they consider the space a compost pile occupies better used for plants. In addition, they argue, it is difficult to make a compost pile attractive, and, worse, if the pile is not properly managed it will attract flies and other varmints unacceptable in an urban environment.

Small properties often have sideyards or an out-of-the-way corner that can be hidden by a fence, covered, of course, by cucumber, squash, pole beans, or grape vines. Even if no such space is available to house a conventional system, there are other ways to develop a supply of rich compost. One is to use an oil drum with holes made in the

6.6. *Containerized 'Gypsy' pepper plants. (Illustration courtesy of All-America Selections.)*

bottom by an electric drill or a cold chisel. Another is to use an old plastic garbage can with its entire bottom removed by means of a coping saw; the bottom is then screened with chicken wire or concrete reinforcing wire to keep the contents in place. Both such containers must be topped with an old window screen or other device to keep out the flies and raised on bricks or blocks to permit adequate drainage and air circulation. Placing a drip pan (from an auto supply store) under the container is advisable if they are over concrete, as in a corner of a garage, or over aggregate, as on a patio. There won't be much drainage, but what there is will stain.

To make compost in such containers, alternate layers of kitchen waste with a layer of fine soil, plus a source of nitrogen, such as bloodmeal, cottonseed meal, or well-rotted poultry manure. The resulting mixture should be kept moist but not wet. Too much moisture will make the bacterial action anaerobic rather than aerobic, and it is the anaerobic bacteria that make a gooey, odoriferous compost.

Another way of producing compost in a small space is with the help of the Bardmatic Garbage Eliminator. This is a cone-shaped device, 3 ½ feet tall. It fits over an 18-inch deep hole (see the accompanying illustration), sealing off hovering flies as well as odors. Your kitchen wastes and a compost activator included in the kit are put through a trap door in

6.7. Devices such as this garbage eliminator by Bardmatic make it convenient to compost in small areas.

the cone. After the hole is filled and you have used the compost, you move the cone to another hole. The old hole can be filled in and planted with a tree, a shrub, or a vine—producing edibles, of course. Lots of organic matter leached from the compost material will remain in that space; thus, if the spot receives enough sun, the plant you put there will have an auspicious start.

Admittedly, the cone is no great aesthetic addition to a garden, but it can be camouflaged by basil, tarragon, or chard, all of which grow prolifically under those circumstances. The Bardmatic is available from Bardmatic Company, P.O. Box 1081, Chicago, IL 60690. The company sends complete directions with each purchase.

Intensive Gardening

It is only recently that Americans have been faced with making vegetable gardens in small areas. We have always had space over the next hill, but this hasn't been true in other countries. Particularly where the land has been cultivated for centuries, gardens are small but extremely productive. Many European cities still have areas on their outskirts that are filled with tiny gardens, assigned to individuals, which continue to produce after many generations.

Techniques for growing highly productive gardens have come to us from many sources. From the cultivators of ancient Greece we learned that plants grow better in the aerated soil produced by landslides than in compacted soil. The Chinese, who have comparatively little arable land, developed and passed down efficient methods of succession planting and manuring. Parisians in the days of the horse-drawn carriage had manure for the taking, and they learned the advantages of adding to the soil great quantities of organic material. These separate strands of information have been gathered together under the rubric of intensive gardening and conveyed to interested gardeners by a number of people, among them Alan Chadwick, Peter Chan, John Jeavons, and Rudolph Steiner. All approach the subject from somewhat different viewpoints. Thus you may hear of the Chinese method, the Biodynamic/French Intensive method, or simply, "The Method."

The various approaches differ in some particulars but share some basic elements: deep-digging of the soil, usually referred to as "double-digging"; the addition of large amounts of organic matter to the soil; the making of raised beds (a natural result of all that added material); and the elimination of chemical fertilizers and pesticides. Corollaries to this fundamental approach are close planting and succession planting—the former to give a living mulch, the latter to use space continuously. Finally, the soil is never walked on, so it does not get compacted.

The intensive method enables air to reach the plants' roots, and provides humus or organic matter to both soil bacteria and the plants themselves. The end result is a healthful environment for plants. A garden grown by this system will also pay off in three or four times as much produce as a garden grown in the conventional way. Whether you want that much zucchini is your decision. My family would leave home if I produced zucchini intensively, but I can never serve too many snow peas or tomatoes.

As you may have guessed, the key to intensive gardening is soil preparation. The following method of preparing a bed for intensive gardening has worked for me and my friends. It does not contain certain techniques that some people swear by, simply because those techniques have not worked for me.

Choose the area of your yard that receives the most sun. Mark out a bed no wider than 5 feet. Such a bed is narrow enough to permit weeding and harvesting from either side with no footfall to mar the soft, aerated earth. The bed can be as long as you want it to be, or as you have space for, and the shape is also up to you. You might have one curving 5 × 20-foot bed, two rectangular 5 × 10-foot beds, or a 5-foot L-shaped bed. The shape can be whatever fits well in your design. Most descriptions refer to plots of 100 square feet for convenience. This size is workable, especially for a first effort, and is used in the following description.

Preparing the Bed

Start by removing the weeds. If you are taking up a lawn—*Hurray for you!*—remove the top 3–4 inches of sod. If you have been using many herbicides or pesticides on your lawn, you would do well to dig the beds by "The Method" as described below, and then plant them with a temporary cover crop of green manure, such as alfalfa, clover, or rye. Postpone your vegetable garden for one year to allow much of the herbicides and pesticides to degrade or leach away. Another, more expensive, way of purifying the soil is to apply activated charcoal (see Chapter 7).

The next step after weeding the area is to loosen the top foot of the soil. If you live in an arid climate where rains have not watered your soil, deep-water the area first and wait three or four days, until the top 12 inches of the soil is just damp, not wet. Clay soil is ready for digging if, when you squeeze it, it does not stay in a tight ball. Light, sandy soils will not pack down, so they can be worked unless sopping wet.

Before you double-dig the bed, use a spading fork to turn over the top 12 inches of soil. Spread 2–3 cubic yards— that's right, cubic *yards*, not feet—of compost or manure over every 100 square feet you dig. If your soil is heavy clay or very sandy, use the more generous figure. Mix these additives into the top 12 inches of soil. Let the soil rest for a day. The next day dig the whole plot. (See the accompanying diagrams.)

Spread another one-half to one cubic yard of compost over the entire bed (see Figure 6.8.A). Next dig a trench 1 foot deep by 1 foot wide and the length of the area to be dug (see Figure 6.8.B). Transport the soil from this trench in a wheelbarrow to the far side of the total area to be dug and dump it there for use later. Then take your spading fork and

loosen the soil in the bottom of the trench, to a depth of 8–12 inches (see Figure 6.8.C). This may be difficult, but do the best you can—whatever you accomplish will almost certainly be an improvement over previous soil preparation in that area.

Next, dig a second trench the same size as the first and parallel to it. But instead of putting the soil from this trench into the wheelbarrow, throw it into the first trench, filling it in as you dig. Again, loosen the soil in the bottom of the second trench. Repeat this process until you have removed the top 12 inches from the last trench and loosened the soil underneath. Finally, fill in this trench with the soil you previously transported from the first trench you dug (see Figure 6.8.D).

Level off the bed and shape it. Over the top of the bed sprinkle 2–4 pounds of bonemeal, 2–4 pounds of fresh hardwood ashes, and 2–4 cubic feet of manure. Lightly rake these amendments into the top 3–4 inches of soil and re-shape the bed. No matter what the shape of your bed, that built-up mound is going to look as if it should be marked "Here lies Fido." In the small-area garden, I suggest, for aesthetic reasons, that you confine your planting with two 2 × 6-inch boards or railroad ties. Such borders cut down on some of the air circulation but they make the beds more attractive and less gravelike.

As you can see, this method does indeed involve a significant amount of hard work and lots of organic material in the preparation stage, but the product is worth the extra effort. Double-digging is usually performed for three or four years in a row to thoroughly loosen the subsoil and to build up organic material to a sufficiently high level. After the first year, add only 1 cubic yard of new compost per 100 square feet, plus the same amount of ashes and bonemeal that were added the first year, as you prepare your soil for planting each spring.

Planting the Double-Dug Bed

Vegetables and fruits grown in double-dug beds are planted more closely together than in a standard garden bed because of the extra root room and nutrients available. The seeds or young plants are planted in a triangular pattern over the entire bed. The plants will be closer than usually recommended on the package or by a nursery, and they should be close enough so they will touch at maturity, thus shading and cooling the soil and providing a kind of "living mulch" (see Figure 6.8.E). For detailed information on spacing plants in double-dug beds, see *How to Grow More Vegetables* by John Jeavons. The following are a few of the recommended planting distances in his list: artichokes, 72 inches apart; asparagus, 12 inches; bush beans, 4 inches; pole beans, 6 inches; cabbage, 12–15 inches; carrots, 1–2 inches; eggplant, 18 inches; kale, 15 inches; bush peas, 3 inches; pole peas, 4 inches; peppers, 12 inches; spinach, 2 inches; and tomatoes, 24 inches.

For maximum use of the double-dug bed, practice succession planting, which involves keeping young transplants

6.8. Double-digging. **A.** *Spread one-half to one cubic yard of compost over the bed to be prepared.* **B.** *Dig a trench 1 foot deep by 1 foot wide the length of the area to be dug.* **C.** *After depositing the soil from this trench at the other end of the bed, loosen the soil in the bottom of the trench.* **D.** *Dig a second trench parallel to the first, placing the soil from this trench into the first trench. Loosen the soil in the bottom of the second trench. Repeat this process until the entire area is dug.* **E.** *Plants grown in double-dug beds have extra root room and can be planted more closely than normal.*

coming along to fill in the spaces left by harvested vegetables. This can be done by starting seeds in wooden nursery flats, flower pots, or in the ground. The most suitable plants for succession planting are lettuce, spinach, and scallions because they grow quickly and transplant well. Plants such as beets, carrots, radishes and turnips, because of their long taproots, do not transplant well.

The maintenance of double-dug beds requires keeping them continually damp but not too soggy. This will necessitate daily watering during the dry season in arid climates, as the beds dry out more quickly than conventional gardens due to the lightness and elevation of the soil. A few weeds will have to be pulled as they appear, but supplemental fertilizing will not be needed.

Edible Plants for the Small Garden

Hybridizers and nursery people have become aware of a large new market—people who want to grow edible plants in small yards or in containers—and have responded by developing many new varieties of midget vegetables and dwarf fruit trees. Some mail-order catalogs now have sections specifically devoted to these smaller edibles. New varieties are introduced every year.

The following table covers the edible plants listed in the encyclopedia that can be grown in containers and small yards. The varieties and types mentioned are those that, at this writing, are the smallest and most compact.

Edible Plants for Small Areas

NAME	FORM	EXPOSURE	FOLIAGE SIZE	CAN ESPALIER OR TRAIN ON FENCE	SIZE RECOMMENDED	PATIO TREE	SUITABLE FOR CONTAINER (SIZE)	VARIETIES OR SPECIES RECOMMENDED
Almond	Tree	Full sun	Small	Impractical to espalier	Dwarf, semi-dwarf, genetic dwarf	Yes	Yes (large)	'All-in-One' (semidwarf); 'Hall's Hardy' Dwarf; 'Garden Prince' (genetic dwarf)
Apple	Tree	Full sun	Medium	Espalier	Dwarf semidwarf, genetic dwarf	Yes	Yes (large)	Most major varieties available in semidwarf and dwarf sizes; genetic dwarfs available
Apricot	Tree	Full sun	Medium	Espalier	Dwarf, semi-dwarf, genetic dwarf	Yes (if fruit is picked before 100 percent ripe)	Yes (large)	Some major varieties available in semidwarf and dwarf sizes; genetic dwarfs available
Artichoke	Large herbaceous perennial	Sun or partial shade	Large	No	Standard	No	Yes (large)	All varieties
Avocado	Tree	Full sun	Medium-large	No	Dwarf	No	Yes (large)	'Littlecado'
Bamboo	Large grass	Full sun or shade	Small	No	Non-running short types	No	Yes (large)	*Bambusa glaucescens*
Banana	Large herbaceous perennial	Full sun	Very large	No	Dwarf	Yes	Yes (large)	'Dwarf Cavendish'
Basil	Herb	Full sun or partial shade	Small	No	All	No	Yes	All varieties

NAME	FORM	EXPOSURE	FOLIAGE SIZE	CAN ESPALIER OR TRAIN ON FENCE	SIZE RECOMMENDED	PATIO TREE	SUITABLE FOR CONTAINER (SIZE)	VARIETIES OR SPECIES RECOMMENDED
Bay (sweet)	Tree	Full sun or partial shade	Small	Espalier	Standard	Yes	Yes (medium to large)	All varieties
Beans	Annual vegetable	Full sun	Medium	Train (some varieties)	All	No	Yes (large)	All varieties, particularly those mentioned under BEANS in the encyclopedia
Bitter melon	Vine	Full sun	Large	Train	Standard	No	Yes (large)	All varieties
Blueberry	Shrub	Full sun or partial shade	Small	No	All	No	Yes (large)	All varieties; 'Tophat' is miniature variety best for small containers
Borage	Herb	Full sun	Medium	No	All	No	Yes	All varieties
Cabbage	Annual vegetable	Full sun or partial shade	Large	No	All	No	Yes	All varieties good; midget varieties particularly good in containers are 'Pee Wee', 'Little Leaguer', 'Baby Head', 'Junior', miniature Japanese
Capers	Shrublet	Full sun	Small	No	All	No	Yes (medium)	All varieties
Chamomile	Herb	Full sun or partial shade	Small	No	All	No	Yes	All types
Chard	Annual vegetable	Full sun	Large	No	All	No	Yes	All varieties
Cherry	Tree	Full sun	Medium	Impractical to espalier	Dwarf, semi-dwarf, genetic dwarf	No	Yes (large)	'Garden Bing' (sweet cherry, genetic dwarf); 'North Star' (sour cherry dwarf); alternatively, grow bush plums
Chives	Herb	Sun	Small	No	All	No	Yes	All types
Citrus	Tree, shrub	Sun or part shade	Medium	Yes	Dwarf	Yes	Yes (large)	Most citrus varieties available in dwarf sizes
Cucumber	Annual vegetable	Sun	Medium	Train (some varieties)	All	No	Yes	All vining varieties good on a fence; 'Bush Whopper', 'Pot Luck', 'Spacemaster', and 'Tiny Dill' best for containers or limited areas
Currant and gooseberry	Shrub	Sun or shade	Small	Yes	All	No	Yes	All varieties (medium to large)
Eggplant	Annual vegetable	Sun	Medium	No	All	No	Yes	'Morden Midget' and 'Early Beauty Hybrid' are particularly good for small spaces
Endive	Annual vegetable	Sun or part shade	Large	No	All	No	Yes	All varieties
Fig	Tree	Sun	Large	Yes	Semidwarf	No	Yes (large)	'Black Jack' genetic dwarf and 'Dwarf Everbearing' ('Texas Everbearing')

NAME	FORM	EXPOSURE	FOLIAGE SIZE	CAN ESPALIER OR TRAIN ON FENCE	SIZE RECOMMENDED	PATIO TREE	SUITABLE FOR CONTAINER (SIZE)	VARIETIES OR SPECIES RECOMMENDED
Filbert	Tree, shrub	Sun	Large	No	All	Yes	No	All varieties; dwarf not usually available
Ginger	Herbaceous perennial	Partial shade	Small	No	All	No	Yes	Only one edible species available
Grape	Vine	Full sun	Large	Espalier or train	All	No	No	All varieties
Kale	Annual vegetable	Full sun or partial shade	Large	No	All	No	Yes	All varieties; for very small areas try 'Miniature Flowering'
Kiwi	Vine	Sun or partial shade	Large	Train on high fence	All	No	No	Need male and female plants
Leek	Annual vegetable	Sun or partial shade	Medium	No	All	No	Yes	All varieties
Lettuce	Annual vegetable	Full sun or partial shade	Large	No	All	No	Yes	All varieties good; for very small areas try 'Ruby', 'Bibb', 'Tom Thumb', 'Deer Tongue', and 'Oak Leaf'
Marjoram	Herb	Full sun	Small	No	All	No	Yes	All types
Melons	Annual fruit	Full sun	Medium	Train (some varieties)	Midget varieties	No	Yes	Cantaloupe ('Bush Whopper', 'Mini', 'Midget', 'Minnesota Midget', 'Short 'n Sweet'); Watermelon ('New Hampshire Midget', 'Golden Midget', 'Kengarden'); Honeydew ('Oliver's Pearl Cluster')
Mint	Herb	Shade or partial sun	Small	No	All	No	Yes	All types
Mulberry	Tree	Full sun	Large	No	Semidwarf	No	No	'Black Beauty' (semidwarf)
Nasturtium	Annual	Full sun or partial shade	Medium	Train (vining species)	All	No	Yes	All varieties; dwarf varieties best for small areas and containers
Natal plum	Shrub	Full sun or partial shade	Small	Yes	Dwarf	No	Yes (medium)	'Fancy' and 'Tuttle' (dwarf)
Nectarine	Tree	Full sun	Medium	Yes	Dwarf, semidwarf, genetic dwarf	No	Yes (large)	Most major varieties available as dwarf or semidwarf tree; genetic dwarfs available
New Zealand spinach	Annual vegetable	Full sun or partial shade	Small	No	All	No	Yes	All varieties
Okra	Annual vegetable	Full sun	Large	No	Dwarf	No	Yes (medium)	'Dwarf Long Pod'
Oregano	Herb	Full sun	Small	No	All	No	Yes	All types

NAME	FORM	EXPOSURE	FOLIAGE SIZE	CAN ESPALIER OR TRAIN ON FENCE	SIZE RECOMMENDED	PATIO TREE	SUITABLE FOR CONTAINER (SIZE)	VARIETIES OR SPECIES RECOMMENDED
Parsley	Herb	Full sun or partial shade	Small	No	All	No	Yes	All species
Peach	Tree	Full sun	Medium	Yes	Dwarf, semidwarf, genetic dwarf	No	Yes (large)	Most major varieties available in dwarf or semidwarf sizes; genetic dwarfs available
Peanut	Annual vegetable	Full sun	Small	No	All	No	Yes	All types
Pear	Tree	Full sun	Medium	Yes	Dwarf, semidwarf, genetic dwarf	Yes	Yes (large)	Most major varieties available in dwarf or semidwarf sizes; a genetic dwarf exists
Pepper	Annual vegetable	Full sun or partial shade	Medium	No	All	No	Yes	All varieties; for very limited areas try 'Park's Pot', 'Hot 'n Sweet', 'Pinocchio', 'Holiday Cheer', 'Tequila Sunrise'
Persimmon	Tree	Full sun	Medium	Yes	Small	Yes	No	'Fuyu' (smaller variety than most)
Pineapple guava	Shrub	Full sun or partial shade	Small	Yes	All	Yes	Yes	All available
Plum	Tree	Full sun	Medium	Yes	Dwarf, semidwarf, genetic dwarf	No	Yes	Many varieties of plums available in dwarf size; 'Weeping Santa Rosa' is semidwarf
Plums, bush	Shrub	Full sun	Small	No	All	No	Yes (medium to large)	All varieties
Pomegranate	Shrub	Full sun	Small	Yes	All	Yes	Yes (large)	All varieties
Prickly pear	Cactus	Full sun	Large	No	Small species	No	Yes (medium)	Small species
Quince	Tree	Full sun	Medium	Yes	All	Yes	Yes (large)	All types
Rhubarb	Large herb	Full sun or partial shade	Large	No	All	No	Yes (medium)	All varieties
Rosemary	Shrub	Full sun	Small	No	All	No	Yes	All varieties
Saffron	Herbaceous corm	Full sun	Small	No	All	No	Yes	All varieties
Sage	Herb	Full sun	Small	No	All	No	Yes	All varieties
Salal	Shrub	Full sun to full shade	Small	No	All	No	Yes (medium)	All varieties
Snow pea	Annual vegetable	Full sun or partial shade	Small	Train, some varieties	All	No	Yes (large)	'Dwarf Grey Sugar'; Sugar Snap

NAME	FORM	EXPOSURE	FOLIAGE SIZE	CAN ESPALIER OR TRAIN ON FENCE	SIZE RECOMMENDED	PATIO TREE	SUITABLE FOR CONTAINER SIZE	VARIETIES OR SPECIES RECOMMENDED
Sorrel	Herb	Full sun or partial shade	Medium	No	All	No	Yes	All types
Spinach	Annual vegetable	Full sun or partial shade	Medium	No	All	No	Yes	All varieties
Strawberry	Herba-ceous	Full sun or partial shade	Small	No	All	No	Yes	All types
Surinam cherry	Shrub	Full sun or partial shade	Small	Espalier	All	No	Yes	All varieties
Sweet potato	Annual vegetable	Full sun	Medium	No	Small varieties	No	Yes (large)	'Bush Porto Rico'
Tea	Shrub	Full sun or partial shade	Medium	Espalier	All	No	Yes (large)	All varieties
Thyme	Shrub	Full sun	Small	No	All	No	Yes	All types
Tomato	Annual vegetable	Full sun	Medium	Train	Small varieties	No	Yes (medium)	Most varieties suitable, but for very small areas and in containers the best are 'Patio', 'Sweet 100', 'Cherry', 'Tiny Tim', 'Toy Boy', 'Bitsy', 'City Best'
Water chestnut	Herba-ceous corm	Full sun	Small	No	All	No	Yes	Only one species available

CHAPTER 7

Planting and Maintenance

REGARDLESS OF your landscaping style, the planting and maintenance of your garden are as important as the original plan. This chapter covers the basics of establishing and caring for a landscape, including soil preparation, seeding and planting, mulching, fertilizing, watering, pruning, composting, selecting and caring for tools, weed and pest control, and coping with plant diseases. For more detailed information on this vast subject I recommend *The Why and How of Home Horticulture* and many other books listed in the bibliography.

Seeding and Planting

Preparing the Soil

Assuming that in designing your landscape you have located your plants properly and installed structural elements, you are now ready to execute your plan by planting. But to grow healthy plants, one more preliminary step is vital: proper soil preparation. Poorly prepared soil is difficult to improve after a plant is established.

In Chapter 4, I covered means of analyzing soil for nutri-

ent deficiencies; excess acidity, alkalinity, and salinity; and hardpan. If you have taken measures to correct any such problems in your soil, you are now ready to prepare the ground for planting.

The first step is to remove large rocks and weeds from planting sites. Where large, established trees and shrubs are growing near a planting bed—plants that are deep rooted, not surface rooted like azaleas, blueberries, and camellias—prune off some of the large roots that intrude into the area; large shrubs and trees can usually tolerate the removal of some roots with no ill effects. Next, spade the areas over and, if you have not already done so, supplement your soil with organic matter, as most soils are deficient in humus, and lime if needed. Distribute the supplements evenly and incorporate them thoroughly into the soil by turning the soil over with a tiller or spade.

Finally, grade and rake the area. You are now ready to seed or dig planting holes. At this time, regardless of your soil type, it is particularly important to add phosphorus at the rate recommended on the package and mix it in. For food-producing perennials, trees, and shrubs, add phosphorus in the form of rock phosphate and manure, bonemeal or super-phosphate (at recommended rates) to the planting holes so it will be near the root zone where it is needed. Mix it into the material, called backfill, that will be put back into the holes.

Starting from Seed

Seeds can be started indoors in flats or other containers that have good drainage. Consider employing this method when you are concerned about giving your seedlings an early or safe start, since most young plants, especially warm-weather annuals, are susceptible to frost damage. Other reasons for starting plants indoors are to extend the growing season, to protect plants from pests, or to start vegetables and fruit production as soon as possible. When all danger of frost is past, the seedlings can be planted into the garden.

Propagation from seed is a complex subject because the cultural needs of seeds vary widely among species. Still, some basic rules apply to most seeding procedures. First, whether starting seed in the ground or in a container, make sure you have a loose, water-retentive soil that drains well. Good drainage is important, because seeds can get waterlogged and too much water can lead to the damping off of your seedlings. ("Damping off" is a disease caused by several fungi that kill seedlings at the soil line.)

Smooth the soil surface and plant the seeds according to the directions on the package or information obtained from a book, such as *Plant Propagation—Principles and Practices* (see bibliography). Pat down the seeds, and water carefully to make the seedbed moist but not waterlogged.

If you have started your seedlings in containers do not transplant them until they have their second set of true leaves and, if they are tender, until all danger of frost is past. Young plants started indoors or in a greenhouse should be "hardened off" before planting in the garden; that is they should be put outside in a sheltered place for a few days to let them get used to the differences in temperature, humidity, and air movement. Transplanted seedlings should be protected by shading them with a shingle or other protective device for a day or two if it is windy or the sun is hot.

If your garden is small or if you are planting in containers only, buying a whole packet of some types of seed is often a waste. When you intend to grow only a few tomato, cabbage, or squash plants for example, it is less work and cheaper to buy young plants from a reputable nursery. However, root crops such as carrots, beets, or parsnips and unusual varieties such as yellow tomatoes or red okra are not generally sold as transplants and must be bought as seeds.

Planting Annuals

Most varieties of annuals may be started from seed in place in the garden, or in containers and transplanted out into the garden. In both cases, the garden soil should be prepared as described above. In addition, large amounts of organic matter should be incorporated into the top 4–6

inches of the soil. Alternatively, you might choose to double-dig the bed, as described in Chapter 6. Extra organic matter and double-digging are particularly helpful for annuals, because most have shallow root systems, are heavy feeders, and need soil that is both light and high in organic matter.

Plant seeds according to the directions on the package, or set out transplants. When setting out transplants, if a mat of roots has formed at the bottom of the root ball it is important to remove it. In most cases, set the plant in the ground at the same height as it was in the container. Pat it in place with gentle hand pressure, and water it well. Tomatoes and members of the cabbage family should be planted deeper into the ground than they were in the container so that they will root more strongly.

Planting Trees and Shrubs

For years homeowners have been advised by experts to place soil amended with large amounts of light organic matter in planting holes for trees and shrubs to promote good growth. New evidence suggests that where the soil of the planting bed is heavy in density, this practice often causes the roots of trees and shrubs to remain confined in the original planting hole because they have trouble moving into the heavier surrounding soil after rapidly penetrating the fluffy amended soil.

In most medium to heavy soil, the following method is recommended: dig a hole two or three times the size of the root ball, add amendments to the back fill, and make a transition zone of half-amended and half-original soil, which will ease the roots' passage into the heavier soil of the planting bed.

In light to medium soils, this transition zone is usually not needed: just dig a fairly large hole, incorporate some organic matter and supplemental phosphorus, and plant the tree or shrub as shown in the accompanying diagrams.

If your soil is very heavy, consider using the following method with plants that will tolerate such soil. Dig a large hole to loosen the soil; place any needed fertilizer in the bottom of the hole and cover it with a small amount of soil, then place the plant in the hole and backfill with the loosened but unamended native soil. Use mulches around the plant to add organic matter to the soil.

Bare-Root Shrubs and Trees

Bare-root plants are deciduous shrubs and trees (and an occasional perennial) that are dug up while dormant and sold without soil on the roots. Many fruit-bearing shrubs and trees are best planted bare root (see Figure 7.1).

To plant bare-root plants, soak the roots overnight and, before planting, cut off any broken or withered roots. Dig a hole in the planting bed and make a cone of soil in the bottom. Set the tree or shrub so it rests a little high in the hole and carefully straighten and position the roots over the cone. The object is to plant the tree or shrub so that the

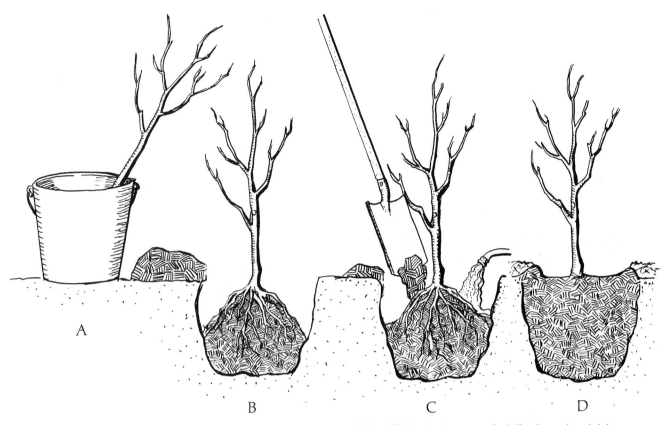

7.1. *Planting bare-root plants.* **A.** *Soak plants in water overnight before planting. (Do not let them dry out while waiting to be planted.)* **B.** *Spread out the roots over a cone of soil.* **C.** *Cover the roots lightly with backfill and water* well. **D.** *Fill the hole with remaining backfill and tamp down lightly to eliminate large air pockets. Make a watering basin around the plant and water in well. Apply mulch.*

original soil line usually visible on the trunk is visible above the new soil level. The tree will settle a little (about 10 percent) when it is watered and firmed into place; by placing the plant a little high you will give it room to settle. Do not cover the graft (a bump or onionlike bulge on the lower trunk).

Cover half the root zone with backfill and firmly press it into place, then water. Add more soil to fill the hole completely; then make a watering basin around the plant and soak it thoroughly. The trunks of young fruit trees should be painted with tree paint or whitewash, or temporarily covered with burlap or other material, to protect them from sun. If rodent damage is a potential problem wrap with chicken wire or trunk wrap, a material manufactured specifically for protecting tree trunks. If you are planting some of the weak-rooted dwarf trees, or if you live in a windy location, stake the trees with sturdy supports and a flexible tying material that will not choke or bind the trunks. As a final step, mulch the plant.

Balled and Burlapped Shrubs and Trees

The term balled and burlapped, or B and B, refers to a method of preparing plants for sale whose roots cannot be exposed to air for any period of time. The technique is used most often for conifers and evergreen ornamentals. Burlap

is wrapped around the root zone to hold the soil in place after the plant is dug out of the ground.

See Figure 7.2 for the method of planting B and B. The root zone is fragile, so handle the plant gently. Dig a hole twice the width of the root ball and 6 inches deeper than the root ball is long. If the root zone contains heavy soil around it, create a transition area of soil with backfill, adding one shovelful of organic matter to every three of your garden soil. If the B and B contains soil of the same type as your garden, add no soil amendments.

Plant as shown as in the illustration. Do not remove the burlap covering unless it has been especially treated to resist decay; ask your nurseryman if this has been done. Fill the hole partially with soil. Adjust the plant so that the top of the ball will be 2 inches above the soil line. (It will settle to be even with the soil line.) Fill the hole three-quarters of the way up with soil. Untie the top of the burlap and loosen it. Water the root zone in well, and fill up the rest of the hole, tamping the soil in place with your foot. Make a watering basin around the plant and water deeply. Stake if necessary. Mulch to within a few inches of the trunk.

Container Plants

Evergreen plants and some deciduous plants are often sold in nursery containers, where they are usually planted in a light, porous planting mix. If such plants are planted in heavy soils, a transition zone must be created between the light soil mix and the heavy soil. In addition, rough up the sides of the hole, since smooth, straight-sided holes in clay soil act like containers and prevent roots from penetrating.

See Figure 7.3 for the planting method for container plants. Dig a hole at least twice as wide and 6 inches deeper than the container. Fill the first 6 inches of the hole with the mixture of garden soil and organic matter. Slip the plant carefully out of the can or use can cutters to split the can. Before planting, examine the root zone. Often there will be a mass of roots on the outside and bottom; use a knife or sharp spade to cut through these masses. Straighten the roots out onto the backfill in the hole. Never turn or twist the root ball in the hole; this will encourage the roots to grow in a circle. If you want to turn the plant around when it's in the hole, lift it up gently and reposition it. Fill the hole three-quarters of the way up with soil, water it well, and fill the rest of the hole. Tamp the soil in place with your foot. Make a watering basin and water the plant deeply. Stake if necessary and mulch.

Maintaining the Edible Landscape

A good plan and proper planting set the stage for good garden maintenance. Some of the plants mentioned in this book require a minimum of maintenance. But peaches, strawberries, Oriental plums, and a number of other favorite fruits need some tender, loving care in the form of mulching, fertilizing, pruning, pest control, and, in some instances, regular watering. Consult the encyclopedia for the

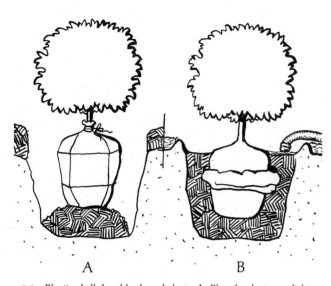

7.2. *Planting balled-and-burlapped plants.* **A.** *Place the plant on a slight mound of backfill in the bottom of the planting hole.* **B.** *Partially fill in soil around the root ball. Loosen and peel back the top of the burlap, then finish filling the hole. Make a watering basin, water in well, and mulch.*

7.3. *Planting container plants.* **A.** *Remove plant from the container.*
B. *Rough up the root ball and cut off large tangled masses, if present.*
C. *Place the plant on a mound of backfill in the bottom of the hole. Partially fill the hole, and water.* **D.** *Finish filling the hole, make a watering basin, water well, and mulch.*

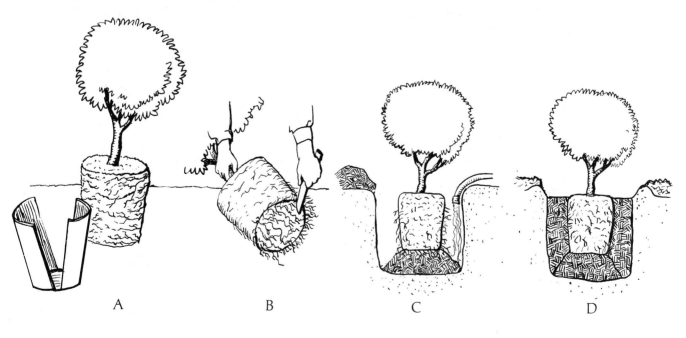

A   B   C   D

effort required to maintain individual species. Knowing what is required ahead of time, plus using superior hand tools, will help to keep maintenance chores manageable.

Horticultural consultants, nursery people, and landscape designers are often asked: How often do I water? What fertilizer should I buy? What spray can I use to kill all my pests? Most homeowners live busy lives and don't feel they have the time or inclination to learn the complexities of plant care. To simplify plant care, horticulturists and producers of garden products have tried to make all-purpose products and to specify unvarying application amounts. But there are many variables in plant care, and too often the all-purpose approach leads to wasting water and fertilizer and to the overuse of potentially harmful chemicals. Automatic watering systems have been devised that will water a yard once or twice a week whether the plants need it or not. Following the directions on an "all-purpose" fertilizer sometimes provides unneeded nutrients to plants in the yard. And pesticides formulated to kill numerous pests with a single spray will often kill useful predator species as well.

Because of our growing awareness of dwindling resources and the hazards and ineffectiveness of many pest controls, new products are being marketed and new methods developed. Water-saving systems such as drip irrigation are available; organic gardeners have renewed interest in natural fertilizers; and biological pest control practices have been devised. These systems and methods require more involve-

ment on the gardener's part, as well as some knowledge of soil chemistry and plant and insect physiology. The backbone of appropriate maintenance is your knowledge of your soil and weather, your ability to recognize basic water and nutrient deficiency symptoms, and as much information as you can amass about the plants you grow.

The goal of the following sections covering garden maintenance and pest control is to aid you in providing optimum conditions for plant growth in a manner which does as little damage as possible to the environment and its natural resources.

Plant Nutrients

Plant nutrition is a complex subject, and to maintain their gardens well, serious gardeners should understand basic soil chemistry and botany. The goal of fertilizing is to provide your plants with the nutrients that they may not be getting naturally, when they need them and in appropriate quantities. Obviously, in order to do this you must be familiar with both plant nutritional needs and with your own soil and its contents. If possible, get your soil tested for the primary nutrients and for pH. Some university extension offices will do this at no charge. Soil kits are also available to do a rough job yourself.

To live and be healthy, all garden plants need a number of nutrients. The three major nutrients and the chemical symbols are nitrogen (N), phosphorus (P), and potassium (K). In addition, ten minor nutrients are necessary for plant growth. These nutrients are discussed in detail in the following sections. Some of the plants listed in the encyclopedia have special nutritional needs; in such instances, the nutrients required are noted under the subhead "Fertilizing."

Nitrogen

Nitrogen stimulates shoot and leaf growth. It is important to supply the correct amount. Nitrogen deficiency is usually signalled by pale green or yellowish leaves. This symptom first appears on the lower or older leaves, which might start to drop. Too much nitrogen can be as harmful as too little. Excess nitrogen can cause the leaves to become too succulent and thus more prone to disease and frost damage, and sometimes stimulates leaf production at the expense of fruit production.

Nitrogen renewal in the soil is accomplished via the decomposition of animal and plant wastes, the deposition of ammonium and nitrate salts from rain water, the action of the nitrogen-fixing bacteria that live on the roots of some plants, and the application of organic or synthetic fertilizers that contain nitrogen.

Nitrogen from organic sources is slowly made available to plants by means of bacterial action. That action is further slowed in cold, very acid, or poorly drained soils. Organic fertilizers are made from animal or plant residues, and most are quite low in nitrogen. While organic sources of nitrogen are extremely variable, some approximate percentages can

7.4. As noted in Chapter 6, grouping two or three container plants in one hole can solve a small-space problem.

be given: bloodmeal, 10–14 percent nitrogen; dried fish, 8 percent; cottonseed meal, 7 percent; and castor pomace, 4 percent. The rest of the organic fertilizers, such as most manures, bonemeal, leaf mold, pine needles, seaweed, and most compost, are quite low in nitrogen, containing only 3 percent at most.

Inorganic or synthesized organic sources of nitrogen, fertilizers such as sulfate and calcium nitrate, make high amounts of nitrogen readily available to plants. Many of these fertilizers contain as much as 30 percent nitrogen. Synthetic nitrogen is available in fast acting forms, usually labeled nitrate or nitric, or in a more slow and controlled release form, labeled ammonic or slow-release. The fast-acting forms are directly available to plants and do not depend on bacterial action to make the nitrogen available.

Phosphorus

Phosphorus contributes to root growth, fruit development, and disease resistance. It is present in soil solutions (the microscopic film around the soil particles) in different forms, most of which are not available to plants. Microorganisms present in soils with sufficient organic matter help make phosphorus available to plants. Very acidic soils tie up phosphorus in a form unusable to plants.

The symptom of phosphorus deficiency in some plants, such as corn, tomatoes, and cabbage (not red cabbage), is a red-purple discoloration of the stems, leaf veins, and leaves.

Natural sources of phosphorus are finely ground phosphate rock, bonemeal, and fish meal. Small amounts of phosphorus can be found in cottonseed meal, bloodmeal, wood ash, and most manures. The most commonly used synthetic forms of phosphorus are superphosphate and ammonium phosphate. If you are growing high-yield vegetable or fruit crops, in addition to manure or compost you should add some form of supplemental phosphorus to the soil every year or two. Because phosphorus moves very little in the soil, it should be worked well into the soil to make it available to the roots or applied to the bottom of planting holes.

Potassium

Potassium, or potash, is the third major plant nutrient. Sufficient amounts of potash promote resistance to disease, cold, and drought. Potash deficiences result in poor crop yields, uneven ripening, poor root systems, leaves streaked or spotted with yellow, and dried or burned leaf edges. Potash deficiency is usually hard to diagnose, and potash is usually added for safety because deficiencies often show up too late to be rectified.

More potash is available to plants in arid climates than in other climates. Natural sources of potash are manures, compost, plant residues, granite dust, and green sand. Commercial sources of potash are muriate of potash and sulfate of potash. In eastern sections of the country it is customary to add some form of potash in the spring.

The Minor Nutrients

Certain micronutrients are necessary in varying amounts for healthy plant growth. These are calcium, magnesium, sulfur, and the trace elements zinc, manganese, iron, boron, chlorine, copper, molybdenum, and in some plants cobalt. Most soils containing a sufficient amount of organic matter can supply enough micronutrients. The major exceptions are acid soils with calcium deficiencies and alkaline soils with iron deficiencies. Regular applications of some form of lime to renew calcium are necessary in acid-soil areas. Iron can be supplied by applications of chelated iron. Other micronutrients are sometimes lacking in a few areas of the country. If you notice discoloration, stunted growth, chlorosis, or a die-back of the leaves and branches in your plants, it would be wise to have your soil tested for nutrient levels and pH. Local authorities can alert you to nutrient deficiencies prevalent in your area.

Fertilizing

Fertilizers are available in many forms. So-called "organic" types may be powders, liquids, or fibrous materials such as manures. Synthetic fertilizers can be liquid, granules, or powder. Some are combination formulas and others contain only a single nutrient.

By law, synthetic fertilizers must be labeled to indicate the percentage of each of the three major nutrients they contain. This labeling consists of numbers which express these percentages, always designated in the following order: nitrogen, phosphorus, and potassium (N, P, and K). Thus the labeled formulation might read 16-20-0, meaning that the product contains 16 percent nitrogen, 20 percent phosphorus, and 0 percent potassium. Labeling also includes information about the sources of these primary nutrients, and the presence of other micronutrients in the product. The nitrogen may be in the form of ammonium sulfate or urea, for instance, and the product may also contain other nutrients such as iron or zinc.

The contents of organic fertilizers often are not labeled in the same manner because it is too difficult to determine and standardize the exact amounts of nutrients in most of these materials.

In the last few years, much has been written about organic, or natural, fertilizers versus synthetic fertilizers. There are advantages and disadvantages to each. The advantages of organics such as manures, bonemeal, bloodmeal, and fish emulsion include the following:

1. Many improve the structure of the soil and provide optimum conditions for soil microbes.
2. They recycle valuable materials.
3. They release their nutrients slowly and evenly.
4. Their nitrogen content is less likely to be leached from the soil (thereby wasting the nutrient and possibly polluting water sources).
5. They usually contain fewer soil contaminants.

6. Most are less likely to burn or overfertilize plants.
7. Some forms can be very inexpensive or free.

The disadvantages include:

1. Bulk and weight make some hard to store, handle, and apply.
2. Many are expensive and limited in quantity.
3. They are variable in nutrient content.
4. Most are slow to act.
5. Some of the nutrients are unavailable when the soil temperature is under 50°F.

The advantages of synthetic fertilizers are:

1. Most are less bulky and easier to apply and store.
2. Often less expensive.
3. Amounts of nutrients are quantifiable.
4. Generally fast acting.
5. Some can be used effectively under cool soil conditions.

The disadvantages include:

1. In general, more petroleum is used in their manufacture than for organic types.
2. Many of the nitrogen forms leach from the soil relatively quickly.
3. Some contain soil contaminants and many are high in salt.
4. Provide little or no benefit to soil structure, microbes, or earthworms; some may be detrimental to soil inhabitants.

Organic-Type Fertilizers

BLOODMEAL

A powdered substance made from the blood from slaughterhouses; high in nitrogen, approximately 10–14 percent; can burn plants if applied too heavily; is expensive; uses petroleum energy in the drying process.

BONEMEAL

The steamed and ground-up bones from slaughterhouses; high in phosphorus, 15–25 percent; some nitrogen, 2–4 percent; releases its nutrients slowly; is expensive; reduces soil acidity.

COTTONSEED MEAL

Ground-up cottonseed; 6–7 percent nitrogen; 2–3 percent phosphorus; expensive; acidifying.

FISH MEAL AND FISH EMULSION

Ground-up fish by-products; fairly high in nitrogen and phosphorus; good for container plants; intense odor; expensive.

GREEN MANURES

Growing plants, usually legumes, are planted as cover crops and then tilled back into the soil to provide nutrients to subsequent crops and to increase the soil's content of organic matter. Types of plants generally used are rye grass (not a legume), clover, vetch, and alfalfa. Green manures are valuable providers of plant nutrients and can be used on vegetable garden areas, orchards, and for soil improvement on newly developed properties before lawns and gardens are installed.

MANURES

Animal excrement; varies widely in nutrient content from batch to batch; approximate percentages are given. Poultry manure: (N) 2–4½ percent, (P) 4–6 percent, (K) 1–2½ percent; steer manure, (N) 1–2½ percent, (P) 1–1½ percent, (K) 2–3½ percent. Generally inexpensive or free; must be weed free; generally should not be used fresh; some forms high in salts; valuable as soil conditioners as well as for nutrients provided.

PHOSPHATE ROCK

Finely ground rock; high in phosphorus as well as many micronutrients. This substance is nearly insoluble in water and is made available by microbial action. The nutrient release is slow and steady. To encourage microbial action phosphate rock must be applied in conjunction with an organic substance such as manure. Incorporate the manure a few months before applying the phosphate rock.

SEWER SLUDGE

Granulated or fibrous wastes from municipal sewage treatment plants. Comes in two forms, activated and composted. Activated has a higher nutrient content: (N) 5–6 percent, (P) 3 percent, and (K) 5 percent. Potentially a valuable fertilizer, but contaminants from sources such as industrial processes and pesticide usage currently make it unsafe for use on edible plants. At some future time it may be possible to monitor for harmful contaminants.

Synthetic-Type Fertilizers

AMMONIUM-BASED FERTILIZERS

These include ammonium sulfate and urea; they are high-nitrogen fertilizers that are fairly stable in the soil and not as prone to leaching as the nitrate forms of nitrogen. These fertilizers have an acidifying effect on the soil and leave salt residues. Some ammonium sulfate is the by-product of coke manufacturing, but most ammonium-based fertilizers are made directly from petroleum products.

MURIATE OF POTASH (POTASSIUM CHLORIDE)

Leaves a fair amount of salt in the soil but produces no soil pH reaction; is easily dissolved in water; has a high percentage of potash.

NITRATES

These include ammonium nitrate, calcium nitrate, potassium nitrate. They are fast-acting nitrogen fertilizers that work in cold or sterile soils but should generally be avoided because they are easily leached by rain water or irrigation. Nitrates consume much energy in the manufacturing process.

SLOW-RELEASE NITROGEN FERTILIZERS

These fertilizers have special formulations or coatings designed to release some fast-acting forms of nitrogen in a more controlled way. They include IBDU, Ureaform, Mag-Amp, as well as some wax- or paraffin-covered fertilizers in granule form. These fertilizers are quite expensive initially, but less fertilizer is wasted and the dosages are more even.

SUPERPHOSPHATE

This is a rock phosphate treated with sulfuric acid, and is more quickly available to the plants than the parent material. In addition to providing phosphorus, it also provides sulfur and calcium.

Fertilizing Schedules for Major Fruits

All stone and pome fruit trees, as well as most young nut trees, gooseberries, blueberries, strawberries, and bramble-berries, usually need supplemental fertilizing annually. A slow-release form of nitrogen plus phosphorus and potassium should be applied in the spring. These nutrients can be utilized best if applied in conjunction with some form of compost or manure mulch. In cold-winter areas, apply the mulch in late fall. In warm-winter areas, apply in late spring after the ground has warmed up. In many areas of the West, potassium is not needed for mature trees; have the soil tested to be sure. Watch for deficiency symptoms and consult local authorities to determine what is considered a normal amount of growth per year for your climate and the particular variety you are growing. In acid-soil areas, add lime every two years on normal soils and annually on light sandy soils.

Other Fruiting Perennials

On average soils, the following plants, once established, usually need little or no supplementary fertilizer: borage, caper, chamomile, chives, fig, jujube, Jerusalem artichoke, maple, marjoram, olive, oregano, pine, pomegranate, prickly pear, rosemary, sage, sweet bay, and thyme.

Annual Vegetables and Fruits

Annual fruits and vegetables have high nutrient needs. In vegetable gardens, cover crops such as winter wheat or rye are a valuable source of nutrients. In areas where cover cropping is not feasible, supplement the soil with large amounts of organic matter. In either case, incorporate phosphorus in the root zone. Supplemental nitrogen is usually needed, particularly for leafy vegetables. Tomatoes often need extra phosphorus, and root and tuber vegetables often need extra potassium.

The Environmental Impact of Fertilizers

Pollution problems concerning fertilizers, and their consumption of nonrenewable resources, have been discussed in Chapter 2. Edible plants, as a group, use large amounts of fertilizer. Therefore it is important to be familiar with fertilizers and their proper use in order to minimize their environmental impact. The following guidelines should prove helpful.

1. Whenever feasible, use a recycled material such as compost or manure.
2. As a rule, avoid nitrate or nitric forms of nitrogen fertilizers unless they are treated to release slowly, as they are easily leached into underground water supplies. In addition to polluting the water, many nutrients are wasted.
3. Have your soil tested to determine what nutrients are needed.
4. For most plants, keep the soil pH between 6 and 7 so that soil nutrients can be utilized properly.
5. Keep the soil high in organic matter to encourage microbial action; this makes indigenous nutrients more available and enables added nutrients to be better utilized.
6. Cut down on lawn areas, as most lawn grasses are heavy feeders, and maintain them as advised in a subsequent section in this chapter.
7. Don't plant heavy fertilizer users on a slope, as the fertilizer often washes off.
8. Incorporate the fertilizer into the top few inches of soil, so that it will not blow away or volatilize into the air.
9. Apply fertilizers where they will be used. Trees feed from "feeder roots." These are concentrated in an area from the drip line to within about 18 inches of the trunk. (The drip line is the perimeter on the ground directly under a tree's outermost branches.) Fertilizer placed much beyond the drip line or too near the trunk will be wasted.
10. Fertilizer should be watered in well, but don't flood the area and wash it away.
11. When the soil is cold, do not apply nitrogen fertilizers that depend on microbial action to break them down.

Fertilizer-related pollution problems are quite well-known, but the energy implications of fertilizer use are just beginning to be explored, and some of the issues are quite complex. While it would be ideal if we could use only organic recycled materials to fertilize our gardens, the fact is that there is not enough to go around. In addition, given the reality that the United States will not become a nation of vegetarians in the near future, many experts feel that some of the high-nitrogen organic fertilizers such as bloodmeal, cottonseed meal, and fish meal, might be better used as animal feed. Furthermore, some of the organic fertilizers are not as energy efficient as one might think. Manures, for example, come primarily from midwestern feedlots and are bulky and energy-consuming to transport across the country. Others such as steamed bonemeal require heat in their processing and so do their share of energy consuming. However, as a group the organic natural fertilizers use less energy, have fewer contaminants, and improve the health of the soil. While considerable study will undoubtedly result in future guidelines, for the time being use your best judgment based on what we now know.

Composting

Compost is the humus-rich result of the decomposition of organic matter, whether it be leafy kitchen waste, oak leaves, or lawn clippings. Organic materials will decompose whether or not they are in a compost pile—the breakdown of organic material takes place continually under every tree, shrub, and flower growing on the earth. The objective in maintaining a composting system is to speed up decomposition and centralize the material so you can gather it up and spread it where it will do the most good.

There need be no great mystique about composting. Basically, microbial action converts a pile of organic matter into the most beneficial soil amendment you can find. This section covers two different systems of composting: a very simple, cool, low-production method for dry wastes such as lawn clippings, leaves, and corn husks; and a more sophisticated high-production system for processing most kitchen waste.

Low-Production Systems

I have in my yard a very serviceable example of a low-production composting system. It is not a fast or high-production method, but it is simplicity itself. The materials it uses are dry and do not attract pests. All disease-free garden clippings are piled in a screened-off part of the yard. Excluded are weeds that have gone to seed, ivy clippings, or Bermuda grass clippings, because they do not always completely decompose and can lead to the growth of weeds, ivy, and Bermuda grass in the garden. Dry kitchen wastes, such as pea pods, egg shells, carrot tops, and apple peels, go in when I have them.

This system is a cool, slow-acting means of recycling needed organic matter; in its own small way it also helps to alleviate the pressure on our already full dumps. Because I do not often turn or water the pile, microbial action is slow and does not produce enough heat to kill weed seeds or diseased material. Also, many of the nutrients are leached out before they reach the garden. But much organic matter that would have ended up wasted at the dump ends up in my yard instead, in the form of soil-building humus.

If you choose a low-production compost system and you feel ambitious, you can speed production by occasionally turning the pile, adding some form of nitrogen, and, in arid climates, watering it once in awhile. The point to remember is that composting does not have to be a big production. Every yard should incorporate some method of developing this valuable material.

High-Production Systems

A well-designed high-production compost heap creates an environment in which decay-causing bacteria can live and reproduce at the highest possible rate. There are three requirements for providing this kind of environment: to keep a suitable amount of air in the pile; to keep the pile moist but not wringing wet; and to maintain a good balance of compatible material so that the microbes have sufficient nourishment. Much technical information has been circulated among experts regarding the optimum ratio between the available carbon and nitrogen. It is usually sufficient to know that if you build the pile with layers of fresh green material, alternating with layers of dried material and thin layers of soil, and occasionally add nitrogen in some form, you will have a successful compost pile. In warm weather the composting action will be much faster than in the winter. Omit or cut up large pieces of compost material, because they decompose very slowly.

An organized approach is necessary to maintain such a system. Two techniques exist: a series of bins (Figure 7.5) or the layered heap (Figure 7.6). The most efficient structure for composting in most yards is a wire bin 4–6 feet high. The wire siding can be supported on the sides by wooden posts. For ease in aerating and turning the compost, you might want to have two bins. Material can be transferred from one bin to the other once a week or more frequently, to speed up the composting process. Or you can use three bins: one for new material, a second for material being actively composted and frequently turned, and a third in which to store the finished product.

7.5. A three-bin system is one of the most efficient ways of producing large amounts of compost. The first bin contains raw materials, the second contains partially decomposed organic matter, the last contains finished compost.

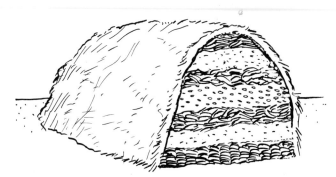

7.6. *Compost piles are most efficient when layers of dry and green material are alternated.*

Once the organic matter is composted, apply it to the garden or cover it with a tarp to prevent valuable nutrients being leached out of the pile by rain water.

Use whatever method you want, but do compost. It's the best possible thing you can do for the health of your plants. For further composting information, I recommend *The Gardener's Guide to Better Soil*, by Gene Logsdon, and *Let It Rot*, by Stu Campbell, both listed in the bibliography.

Mulching

A mulch is any material laid on the soil to reduce evaporation and control weeds. Usually it is a material that will improve soil structure and fertility. Besides these primary functions, mulching can have a number of secondary roles in garden maintenance. Mulch helps keep soil from becoming packed down by foot traffic and rain. A mulch at least 3–4 inches deep helps smother many weed seeds. Mulch acts as insulation and helps keep weather extremes from affecting plants. The soil stays cooler in summer and stays warmer in winter. And organic mulches decompose and help improve the structure of the soil. Clearly, mulching is an important part of garden maintenance. Mulched plants are healthier, and weed control around them is much easier. In addition, mulches can be an attractive addition to the landscape.

How to Use Mulches

In mild-winter areas, apply mulches after the ground has warmed up in the spring. Dig the mulch in lightly in the late fall. In cold-winter areas where the ground alternately freezes and thaws, causing plants to heave out of the soil, apply a thick, 4–6-inch layer of mulch before the first heavy frost.

Near trees, mulches can cause some problems, so they should be kept at least 6 inches away from trunks. Mice make homes in the mulch, and when they venture out the tree trunks are handy for nibbling. Also, mulch too near trunks can cause fungus problems by keeping a constantly moist condition there. Finally, if the mulch covers the scion—the fruiting wood above the bud union—of a grafted

tree, that tree may root above the graft. In such a case, a dwarf tree, for example, would become full size. In a very cold climate, however, the bud union should be mulched to protect it from hard freezing, but the mulch should be removed when the coldest part of the winter is past.

Mulching Materials

Mulches can be made from organic materials, such as compost, pine needles, or grass clippings, or from other substances, such as sheet plastic, rock, or gravel.

Where vegetable gardens are a good distance from the house and screened from view, the odor and appearance of a mulch are not particularly significant considerations; the best mulch there would be the one that promotes maximum production. But for landscaped areas of the yard, a foul-smelling or unattractive mulch is unacceptable. Manure near a front walk or black plastic near the patio just won't do, but many mulches actually enhance the appearance of the landscape. For example, earth-tone rock, peat moss, and well-rotted and screened compost are all attractive. The following are recommended mulches for landscaping situations. Availability varies from region to region.

BARK

Many different kinds of tree bark are available regionally. Bark is usually packaged and sold in garden supply houses, and comes in small-, medium-, and large-size chips. Large-size bark chips look coarser than the others, but they decompose more slowly and need to be replaced less often.

7.7. *Mulches of organic matter help conserve water, add nutrients to the soil, keep roots cool, and help keep down weeds.*

BUCKWHEAT HULLS

These hulls make a soft, beige-colored mulch, but they are lightweight so should not be used in windy locations.

COCOA BEAN HULLS

This attractive mulch breaks down fairly quickly. Furthermore, it is a disaster for "chocoholics"—the delicious aroma of chocolate pervades the yard for weeks after application and inspires weak souls like me to sneak downtown for a chocolate bar. It is fairly expensive unless you can pick it up in quantity from a chocolate factory.

COMPOST

Well-aged compost, screened and spread around landscape areas, is both pleasing to the eye and valuable as a soil conditioner. The major problem is production. Most families do not produce enough compost to fill all their mulching needs, so I strongly suggest that you give priority to your new fruit trees and your vegetable garden when applying this valuable material.

GRAVEL OR ROCK CHIPS

Many different types and sizes of rock mulch are available. These mulches do not break down and improve soil structure. Rock mulches are attractive but are hard to rake. This is a particular problem under the most popular fruit trees, because decaying fruit and diseased leaves need to be removed. White, "sparkly" rock should generally be avoided, as it often looks dirty.

PEAT MOSS

Peat moss is one of the most expensive mulches. It is useful for acid-loving plants, such as blueberries and camellias. It has a good appearance but is hard to remoisten if it dries out, so it should be kept moist at all times.

PINE NEEDLES

These needles are attractive, lightweight, and add acidity to the soil. Use them for acid-loving plants, but do not use them if you have a soil-acidity problem. They work well on strawberry plants to keep the berries from rotting on the ground.

SAWDUST

Sawdust can be used raw, well-aged, or treated. When treated, it is often called soil conditioner. If you use raw, fresh sawdust, treat it with ammonium sulfate or an organic, nitrogen-rich fertilizer, such as bloodmeal or cottonseed meal. The decomposition of the sawdust by soil microbes takes available nitrogen from the soil that has to be replaced. (This aspect is valuable if you want to prevent plant growth. Raw sawdust applied 3 or 4 inches deep on garden paths is a valuable weed deterrent.) Well-rotted or treated soil conditioner can be used without supplemental nitrogen.

Watering

No easy formula exists for the correct amount or frequency of watering. Proper watering takes experience and observation. The needs of a particular plant usually depend on soil type, wind conditions, and air temperature, as well as what kind of plant it is. To water properly you must learn to recognize water stress symptoms (often a dulling of foliage color as well as the better-known symptoms of drooping leaves and wilting); how much to water (too much is as bad as too little); and how to water.

Some general rules are:

1. Water deeply. Most plants need infrequent deep watering rather than frequent light sprinkling. Shallow rooted plants such as blueberries and azaleas are exceptions.
2. To ensure proper absorption, apply water at a rate slow enough to prevent runoff.
3. Do not use overhead watering systems when the wind is blowing.
4. Try to water early in the morning so that foliage will have time to dry out before nightfall, thus preventing some disease problems. In addition, because of the cooler temperature, less water is lost to evaporation.
5. Test your watering system occasionally to make sure it is covering the area evenly.
6. Use methods and tools that conserve water. When using a hose, a pistol-grip nozzle will shut the water off while you move from one container or planting bed to another (Figure 7.8). Canvas soaker hoses apply water slowly to shrub borders and vegetable gardens. Also see the following sections on sprinkler and drip irrigation systems.

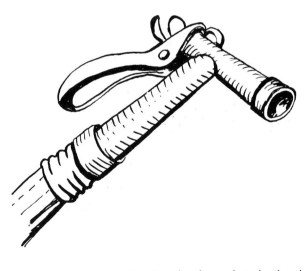

7.8. A nozzle with a pistol grip that shuts the water off when not in use saves water.

Sprinkler Systems

In general, sprinkler systems have been responsible for wasting a good deal of water. Formerly, they were designed and used in accordance with the rule of the highest common denominator: the plants needing the most water got their share and everything nearby got the same amount, regardless. The plants that could not tolerate overwatering were eliminated and were often labeled "hard to grow" by homeowners. More sophisticated, modern sprinkler designs irrigate heavy water users on one system and more moderate water users on another system. Sophisticated automatic timers also enable the apparatus to water, say, one area once a week and another area twice a week.

Some systems, the digital type in particular, are sophisticated enough to water an area for five minutes at a time, shut off and allow the water to soak in, and then go on again for five minutes, repeating the cycle until the proper amount of water has been applied. The system prevents the runoff that twenty minutes of straight watering could produce, particularly on a slope. Automatic systems can also be programmed to water in the early morning when evaporation is at a minimum, since temperatures are lower and wind is less strong than later in the day.

Basically, the proper use of automatic sprinklers is consistent with the principles of water conservation. Still, the emphasis here is on the words *proper use*. One warning to be carefully heeded, particularly with specialized systems, is, *Remember to turn the sprinklers off during the rainy season.* If the automatic system is not adjusted for seasonal changes, the amount of water wasted can be enormous. My partner and I learned this the hard way. We installed an automatic system and new plants on a hot September day, gave the client instructions on how the system worked and how it was to be reset to water less often during late fall and turned off during the winter rainy season, and then we left. Six months later I ran into our client in the theater and asked how his yard was. He said, "Terrible! Everything is covered with gray slime." We went to check, and sure enough, it was. The client had forgotten to reset the system, and it had been pouring out the amount of water needed for a hot summer day all winter long, rain or shine!

To summarize, automatic systems must be set and reset to match water-saving schedules that do not overwater plants. They are not meant to set and forget! Most plants require less water than we want to give them. Set your system with that in mind and adjust it for seasonal conditions. And be sure to turn it off during the rainy season!

Drip Irrigation

Drip, or trickle, irrigation systems (Figure 7.9) are advisable wherever such systems are feasible. Many vegetable gardens, orchards, and perennial and shrub areas are often well suited to these systems. Drip irrigation systems deliver water a drop at a time through spaghetti-like emitter tubes or plastic pipe with nozzles that drip water right onto the root zone of the plant. Drip irrigation is the only watering system devised for containerized plants (Figure 7.11). Another similar type of system called a porous-wall or ooze system (Figure 7.10) delivers water through porous plastic hoses along the whole length of a garden row. All of these systems are more efficient than furrow or overhead watering in delivering water to its precise destination. They deliver water slowly so it doesn't run off and they also water deeply, which encourages deep rooting.

However, though these methods often work well, I hesitate to recommend drip irrigation fully since it still has some problems. Drip irrigation can be frustrating because the tubes and emitters clog easily. Without a good filter system, often every emitter must be checked each time the system is used, especially if the water source has occasional grit in it. Obviously, this can be a chore in a system with 20 or 30 emitters. The porous wall or ooze systems, while not as versatile, have fewer clogging problems and are ideal for vegetable gardens and orchards. All these systems are, however, vulnerable to vandalism problems.

The future of drip irrigation looks promising, so examine

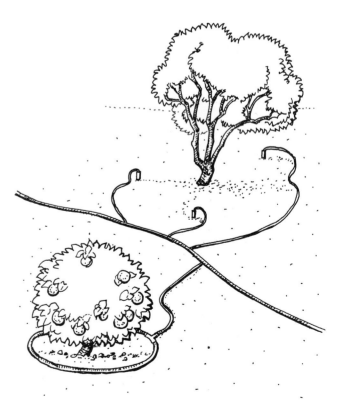

7.9. *Some drip irrigation systems have emitters on pegs that are pushed into the ground; others have porous tubing that oozes water in controlled areas. Both kinds of systems are prone to vandalism, but mulching sometimes can help camouflage the emitters.*

7.11. *A drip system with tubes leading to each pot is an extremely efficient way to water containerized plants.*

all new systems and see if one comes along that is right for you. Check agricultural supply outlets for the best selection of systems. *Western Home Landscaping* (see bibliography) gives detailed instructions on how to install all these drip or ooze systems.

Household Water Sources

Plan to plant heavy water users near the house so that all extra *clean* water can be used on them. By clean water I mean perfectly clean water that would otherwise go down the drain—for instance, cold water that precedes the hot water out of the shower or the water you rinse the teakettle with before you add fresh water. Such water has no foreign matter in it. Make sure, however, that no water softener containing harmful chemicals is added to your domestic supply. The waste water known as gray water—for example, dish water, rinse water, bath water, and so on—is usually produced in great quantities by most households, but gray water presents complicated health and soil problems and often needs processing before it is usable in the garden. For a thorough discussion of gray water, see *The Integral Urban House,* by the Farallones Institute.

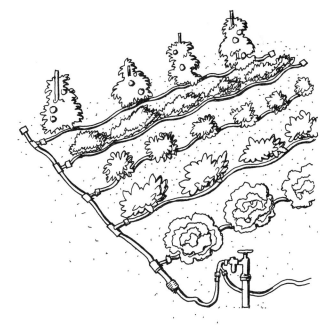

7.10. *Some ooze systems are particularly effective for the straight rows of a vegetable garden. Make sure that all the plants watered by one system have similar water requirements.*

Maintaining a Lawn

The lawn is the largest user of fertilizer and water in the average yard. A book entitled *Lawn Beauty the Organic Way,* by the editors of *Organic Gardening,* is a recommended source of information on maintaining a lawn with a minimum of nonrenewable resources. Maintained in this manner, lawn grass can be a valuable guardian of the soil. I recommend the book with one reservation, however: I disagree with the editors' reliance on sewer sludge as a basic lawn fertilizer. Lawn areas may eventually be sites of edible plantings, sewer sludge leaves many persistent soil contaminants that would make conversion questionable.

Information on grass varieties that are relatively easy on the environment can be obtained from the 15 December 1980 issue of *The Avant Gardener* (see Appendix C).

The following are basic considerations for preparing and maintaining an appropriate lawn:

1. Choose a level, sunny area without large trees that compete for nutrients.

2. Avoid areas that will be heavily traveled, or add a paved path through the lawn area. Constant foot traffic compacts the soil.

3. Plan lawn areas for ease of maintenance. Avoid long narrow areas where mowers are hard to manage. And as much as possible avoid spotting trees and shrubs in the lawn area. Plant them in ground-cover areas so that mowers won't nick the trunks and to avoid the need for hand clipping around the plants. Install a mow strip of brick, stone, concrete, or wood so that mechanized or hand edging can be avoided.

4. Choose a type of grass that is well suited to your geographical area. Avoid bentgrasses, which are heavy feeders and need much water and care.

5. Most people mow their lawn too short for optimum growth. Mow most bluegrass and rye varieties to 1½–2 inches long. This prevents them from drying out too fast. On the other hand do not let them get longer than 2½–3 inches tall. Mow regularly. Keep the mower sharp so that the grass blades are not ripped; clean cutting leaves them less prone to diseases. If the clippings are short and not diseased, leave them on the grass so that nutrients are not removed.

6. Top dress the lawn area with fine-screened organic matter at least once and preferably twice a year.

7. Apply a slow-release nitrogen fertilizer on a schedule that will vary with variety, climate, and soil type. Inquire locally for timing.

8. If supplemental watering is needed in your climate, water deeply when needed. Avoid frequent shallow watering. To acquire a good working knowledge of your lawn's water needs, learn to recognize physiological signs that indicate water stress. Most lawn grasses change color under water stress, from bright green to a slightly bluish green. In addition, the grass will not spring back rapidly when stepped on. Water until the soil is wet 3–4 inches down; dig around to check.

9. To prevent weeds, maintain a healthy, close-knit turf. Hand weed when necessary. Avoid lawn herbicides.

10. On heavy soils most lawns benefit from aeration. Schedule aeration when annual weeds are least active and when the grass is growing vigorously and is not under stresses such as drought or extreme heat. Use a tool that removes plugs of sod rather than a spiker that just pushes in holes. Aerating equipment can be purchased or rented, or the whole job can be done by professionals. Top dress and irrigate after aerating.

11. Do not use growth-inhibiting hormones.

12. Do not remove grass clippings unless they are over an inch long. Recent studies at Michigan State University and the Connecticut Agricultural Experiment Station showed that grass clippings are a valuable source of nutrients—the equivalent of a 4–1–3 fertilizer. Research showed that up to two extra pounds of nitrogen per 1,000 square feet could be saved if clippings were retained. In addition to the fertilizer saved, the tested turf was healthier and greener. And, contrary to what most people had thought, grass clippings do not contribute to the build up of thatch.*

*Dr. Richard Miller, article in *Bug Dope* 18 (September 1980), University of Ohio.

Pruning

Plants are pruned to shape them for aesthetic reasons, to control size, to repair damage, to promote good air circulation, to provide light to the interior of the plant, and to control or promote fruit production in some species.

The best way to learn to prune properly is to watch someone do it. If you have many plants that need to be pruned, it would be worthwhile to take a course or to ask a knowledgeable friend to show you how to train and prune them. Most university extension services supply pruning information and can suggest courses offered locally. See the bibliography for books on pruning. What follows here are only the basics of pruning techniques and tools.

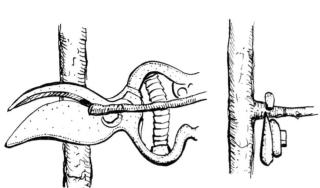

7.12. *An improper pruning cut leaves a stub that can become diseased.*

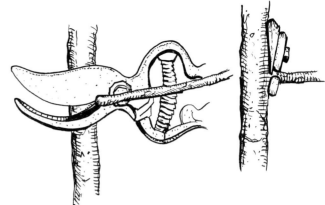

7.13. *A proper cut with a pruning shear is made cleanly, leaving no stub.*

Your climate and the type of plant determine when and how to prune. In most areas, deciduous trees and shrubs should be pruned while still dormant. Set aside a few days for pruning plants and cleaning up your yard. Food-bearing evergreens should be pruned in spring after frosts are no longer expected.

When pruning, remove all dead wood. Do not leave stubs that can rot and invite disease organisms to enter. Do not use pruning paint; recent studies have shown that wounds heal better if left unpainted.

For tools, use hand clippers for twigs, lopping shears for small branches, and pruning saws for long heavy branches. Keep your tools sharp and make clean cuts close to the branch (Figure 7.13). If you are cutting off diseased tissue, be sure to sterilize your tools between cuts with denatured alcohol, mercuric chloride, or a 10 percent solution of household bleach to prevent the transfer of disease from one part of the plant to another.

When cutting a large branch, remember to make the first cut on the underside of the branch. Otherwise, as you saw through the top, the weight of the branch will pull it downward, tearing the bark on the trunk of the tree.

Some types of trees produce suckers from their roots or, if grafted, from below the root graft. These should be removed. Upright-growing branches called water sprouts occasionally emerge from the main branches of a tree; these too should be removed. Some varieties of citrus are particularly prone to producing water sprouts.

Pruning Fruit and Nut Trees

Most deciduous fruit and nut trees are purchased as bare-root plants called "whips." When the young trees are planted, they are usually "headed back," or shortened to between 24 to 30 inches. Most mail-order nurseries will have done the critical first pruning before they send the tree to you. They usually include with your order detailed drawings that show you how to continue training the tree. Local nurseries will usually prune the tree when you buy it. Watch closely and ask specifically what to do the next spring.

For the next two to three years, your aim will be to form

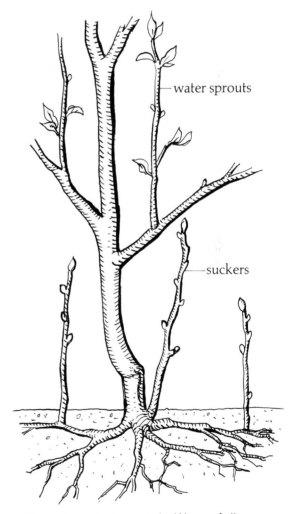

7.14. *These suckers and water sprouts should be pruned off.*

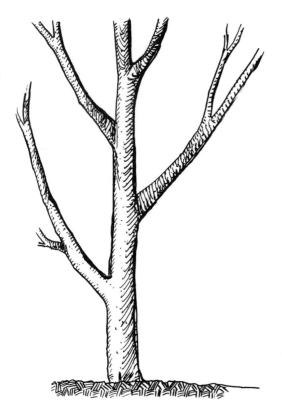

7.15. *Diagram of a grafted fruit tree, indicating terms used in pruning.*

the permanent framework of the tree. Three to five main branches that are evenly distributed radially are selected. Then you will choose among three major tree forms used by most fruit and nut growers. The first, called the *central leader* form, or system, is shown in Figure 7.16. This form is the strongest and is used for many nut trees, such as hickory, pecan, most walnuts, and occasionally for apples when they will be subjected to strong winds. The second form is a variation of the first and is called the *modified leader* or *delayed vase* shape. It is used with some fruit trees—most often apples and pears. The modified leader system has a short central trunk or leader that is headed back three or four years after planting when a strong system had developed. The modified leader system combines the strength of the central leader system with the advantages of more light and air circulation in the interior of the tree.

The third and most common training system for most fruit trees is called the *open center* or *vase* system. It is commonly used for peaches, nectarines, filberts, almonds, plums, apricots, and sour cherries. Figure 7.17 shows the basic shape of this system. The center of the tree is open for good air circulation, ease of spraying, and to increase fruit production. The tree is shorter overall and easier to harvest than those produced by the other two systems.

After the first three to five years, depending on the

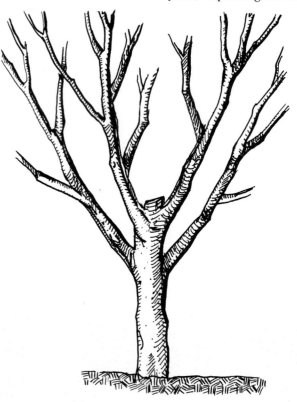

7.16. *A few fruit trees and most nut trees are trained to the central leader system.*

7.17. *Most fruit trees, including peaches, plums, apricots, and nectarines, as well as nut trees such as almonds and filberts, are generally trained to the vase, or open-center, system.*

species, fruit and nut trees have developed a permanent framework and will begin to bear their crops. Bearing trees of most species are pruned annually to shape them and to encourage fruit and nut production. Apples, pears, cherries, and most nut trees require little annual pruning to encourage fruiting. Peaches and nectarines need severe pruning yearly to encourage fruiting and to control fruit size and quantity. Apricots, sour cherries, Japanese plums, and filberts are intermediate between apples and peaches in the amount of pruning needed. See the individual entries in the encyclopedia.

Pruning Fruiting Shrubs

Some of the popular berries and fruits such as blueberries, elderberries, gooseberries, currants, and pomegranates, grow on deciduous shrubs. For the first few years, these shrubs should be pruned lightly only to shape them. Once established they should be thinned annually, as shown in Figure 7.18. Old, diseased, or dead wood is removed and some of the healthy branches thinned to promote more fruiting, improve air circulation, and give a more pleasing shape. If fruits on blueberries and elderberries seem particularly small, tip pruning may be helpful. See the individual entries in the encyclopedia for more information.

Hand Tools

Our emphasis on machine tools has denied a whole generation exposure to the advantages of superior hand tools. It's time we relearned the old lessons: these tools obviously save petroleum energy and they are safer to use than machines. (I recently read that an estimated 70,000 fingers and toes are lost to power mowers each year in the United States.) Furthermore, hand tools are also infinitely quieter, and they provide healthy exercise to a nation of under-exercised people.

Not many tools are necessary for home landscaping. A good shovel, spading fork, hoe, small trowel, rake, wheelbarrow (or child's wagon), hand weeder, hand pruning shears, pruning saw, and a pistol-grip hose nozzle are enough to start with. A good hand mower is necessary if you have a lawn. Check newspaper ads for used mowers. Often a well-made used mower will be easier to push and maintain, for the price, than a new bargain model. Always keep mower blades well sharpened.

Even low-maintenance yards need trimming occasionally. A few well-pruned trees that show an interesting branching structure, or a small piece of well-trimmed lawn or shrubbery, make a yard look cared for. One of the few motorized tools I recommend is a weed-eater type of trimmer that uses nylon fishing line to cut grass and weeds. Hand trimming is one of the most tedious jobs in landscape maintenance, but it makes a big difference in the appearance of a yard. Even a small well-trimmed lawn next to a large informal meadow can make the landscape look cared for. These small trimmers use little energy to manufacture or to use, and give a large return in the appearance of a yard.

No one ever said that hand mowing, shoveling, and weeding weren't hard work. The perspiration still trickles down our noses when my partner and I turn over a portion

7.18. *Pruning a fruiting shrub.*

of our vegetable garden. But good hand tools that feel comfortable in your hands and keep a sharp edge make a big difference. The following is a checklist of things to look for when you buy good hand tools.

1. Cutting tools should keep a sharp edge; you should be able to resharpen them for the life of the tool.
2. All tools should be lightweight but strong enough to do the job without bending or breaking.
3. Wheelbarrow wheels should have ball bearings for ease of pushing.
4. While hard to find these days, it's preferable to have pruning shears with replaceable blades.
5. Tool handles should be made from ash or hickory if possible.
6. Hoses should be made of rubber. Plastic hoses kink and are a constant source of frustration.
7. Nozzles should have a pistol grip and, to save water, should remain closed when not in use.
8. The tool should feel comfortable in your hand or hands.
9. Stress points should be reinforced.

The accompanying sidebar shows recommended brand-name tools and suppliers. To request catalogs, see Appendix B for the addresses of the suppliers. The tools recommended are not mass market commodities. This list represents a year's research by Dave Smith and Paul Hawken of Smith & Hawken tool company, who set out to find the best hand tools worldwide. The tools named are by and large more expensive initially than the mass market tools (though not usually over the life of the tool), and are expressly chosen for people who appreciate superior tools and expect to use them for many years.

Proper tool maintenance is as important as purchasing good tools. Always use the right tool for the job. Hand clippers are meant for small-diameter branches; if you try to use them instead of lopping shears on large branches you will bend the blades or ruin the alignment. When using a spade if you get overambitious with your digging and meet resistance, back off and take "half a bite" instead. Bring tools indoors when you are finished using them. Clean the blades with a wire brush or wooden scraper, oil the blades if possible with an oily rag, or insert the blades of tools in a bucket of sand that has oil in it.

Tool sharpening can't be learned from a book. Watch a professional, and then do it yourself. It is very important to sharpen the blades of your tools correctly and frequently. Clippers, mowers, spading shovels, and scythes should all be sharpened.

Weeds, Pests, and Other Problems

Your garden may appear to be a quiet place, but in reality it is an arena where hundreds of life-and-death dramas are played out every day. Birth and death, killing and nurturing, even intrigue and cunning are all part of the complex community of life waiting to be discovered—and sometimes struggled with—in your garden.

This hidden world can add a new dimension to your gardening pleasure. For example, on an April day, I can turn flower pots over to find startled earwig mothers that wave their pincers at me, protecting their broods. And every June the baby katydids hatch and start chewing on the new leaves of my grapevine. Within a week, three different species of spiders have divided up the territory around the grapes, and all day long they stalk the katydids. While not all pest problems are so easily solved, there are many ways in which you can use predator-prey relationships in garden maintenance. Knowledge of how plants and animals interact in the garden is at the heart of organic, or natural, gardening, and your chief tool for pest control will be your powers of observation of this miniworld around you.

Potential garden problems come in many forms: weeds, fungi, snails, slugs, insects, diseases, and even such wildlife as rabbits, deer, and birds. The list may seem overwhelming at first but most gardeners are actually faced with only a few pests. Everyone has to contend with weeds, however, so we'll consider weed control first.

Weed Control

As I emphasized in Chapter 2, I feel that herbicides are being overused. Because they often cause environmental problems, and some may cause health problems as well, only the most serious weed problems should require herbicide use. In fact, routine use often backfires by damaging valuable plants and allowing free rein to resistant weeds. Remember that even though herbicides are labeled weed killers, when improperly used they kill most plants.

There are two major types of herbicides: selective herbicides, which are formulated to kill only a target weed without harming the crop or plant being weeded; and nonselective herbicides which are designed to kill all vegetation. Read the package carefully to be sure that you are buying the type you want. If herbicides are to be used at all, selective herbicides are generally the better choice. Usually they kill fewer types of plants so the chance for harm is less. Some of the most serious problems I have seen in landscape work are due to herbicide damage. Sometimes the damage results from applying too much of the chemical, but plants are sometimes damaged even when directions are carefully followed. This may be due to an improper choice of herbicide or to residue buildup from previous applications.

My recommendation is to use herbicides only sparingly, for example, when establishing ground covers and when trying to control very persistent weeds, such as Bermuda grass, wild brambleberries, multiflora roses, and poison ivy. Do not use chemicals suspected of causing cancer or mutations, such as aminotriazole, atrazine, dicamba, 2,4,-D, and 2,4,5-T. And never use any herbicide near food plants.

Recommended Garden Tools and Equipment*

ITEM	BRAND RECOMMENDED	WHERE AVAILABLE	ITEM	BRAND RECOMMENDED	WHERE AVAILABLE
Wheelbarrows	John Houchins & Sons	Write John Houchins & Sons for outlets	Bow saws	Sandvik	A. M. Leonard and local hardware stores
	Kelly	Local hardware stores		Spear & Jackson	Smith & Hawken
	Yeoman	Local hardware stores and A. M. Leonard	Hoes	Scovil	Local nurseries
				Austrian	Smith & Hawken
Pruning shears (Secaeteurs)	Felco	Local professional nurseries, hardware stores, Smith & Hawken	Scythes	Swan	Smith & Hawken, Cumberland General Store, A. M. Leonard
Thinning shears	Corona	Local nurseries and hardware stores		V. I. C.	Smith & Hawken, Cumberland General Store, A. M. Leonard
Lopping shears	Seymour Smith ("snap-cut")	Local hardware stores			
	Wallace	Local hardware stores	Watering cans	Haws	Smith & Hawken, A. M. Leonard, Walter Nicke
	Wilkinson	A. M. Leonard, Walter Nicke			
	Smith & Hawken	Smith & Hawken	Lawn mowers	Yardman	Garden supply stores and mower shops
Pruning saw	Sandvik	A. M. Leonard, local hardware stores	Rakes	Smith & Hawken	Smith & Hawken
	Fanno	Local nurseries, A. M. Leonard, Smith & Hawken	Children's tools	Smith & Hawken	Smith & Hawken
			Root feeders (for watering)	Ross	Local nurseries
			Foggers	Fogg-it	Local nurseries
			Soil test kit	LaMotte	LaMotte Chemical Co., Smith & Hawken

*This table was compiled with the help of Dave Smith and Paul Hawken of the Smith & Hawken Tool Company.

There are a number of ways to control weeds without chemicals. If you don't like to weed very much, plan an informal yard with a minimum of garden-bed space that requires weeding. Woodland paths can be kept natural and should need only two or three weedings a year. Keeping small areas near the house weeded and trim will give a feeling of design and care to a yard left largely in woodland or meadow. A deep mulch, 4–5 inches, not only controls many weeds, but it also makes what weeds do grow easier to pull.

Of course, the most basic weed control uses hoe or hand. Hand-weeding can be tedious, and some people mind it more than others. I personally find working outside at a repetitive chore more enjoyable than working at an inside one such as dishwashing. I use weeding time to find out what is happening in my yard: I check for plant damage or new insect populations, and to see if plants are getting too crowded or dry. (Also, I find it more enjoyable to weed an edible planting such as Alpine strawberries, where I can help myself to an occasional berry, than to weed ornamentals.)

Take advantage of the best weeding tools available. Two of the tools I find most helpful are the scuffle hoe and the weeder. The scuffle hoe has a flat cutting blade that moves back and forth and a hoe-length handle. This tool is excellent for cutting young weeds off at the base. The weeder has a metal prong on the end of a 2-foot handle. It gets the long taproots of perennial weeds and can efficiently loosen the soil around more fibrous rooted weeds so whole root systems can be removed. Both of these tools are usually available at the nursery.

Pest Control

The application of synthetic chemicals to control pest populations has been routine for the last thirty or forty years. This reliance on chemical controls has many shortcomings, as outlined in Chapter 2. While big agriculture, because of economic constraints and its emphasis on monocrops is still heavily dependent on chemical pesticides, home gardeners are free to look for more environmentally satisfactory methods. Armed with information and techniques rather than synthetic chemicals, most gardeners can maintain a productive, beautiful yard. Proper plant selection, proper plant and soil care, and minimal interference with natural systems will take care of most pest problems. In the event that a major pest problem surfaces, information at the end of this section on specific pesticides should prove useful.

Though a few insects and mites, sow bugs, snails, and slugs are potential garden pests, most insects are either neutral or are beneficial to your purposes. Given the chance, the beneficials will do most of your pest control for you. The insect world is a miniature version of the animal world. Instead of predatory lions stalking zebra, predatory ladybugs or lacewing larvae hunt and eat aphids. Many gardeners are not aware of predator-prey relationships and are not able to recognize beneficial insects. My students, who can quickly identify the adult ladybug as an ally, have been amazed when I bring ladybug larvae to class, because they realize that they have often killed them. The illustrated information about beneficial and pest insects later in this section will help you to identify and classify individual groups. Once you can identify the insects in your yard, you can help preserve the ones that are beneficial to you by knowing a few basic facts and definitions.

Predators and Parasitoids

Insects that feed on other insects are divided into two types, the predators and the parasitoids. Predators are mobile. They stalk the plants looking for such plant feeders as aphids, mites, and caterpillars. Many predators, the preying mantids, for example, consume any smaller insect they find. Others, such as ladybugs, consume aphids or mealybugs only.

Though predators are valuable insect enemies, they are usually less effective than parasitoids, which are insects that develop in the bodies of other, host, insects. Most parasitoids are minute wasps or flies, whose larvae (young stages) eat other insects from within. Some of these wasps are small enough to live within an aphid or an insect egg. In another case, one egg will divide into thousands of identical cells, which in turn develop into thousands of identical miniwasps, which then can consume an entire caterpillar. Most of the fly parasitoids are larger; a single bombex-fly maggot grows up within one caterpillar. In any case, the parasitoids are the most specific and effective means of insect control.

It should be obvious that indiscriminate use of broad-spectrum pesticides to kill pest insects will usually kill the beneficial parasitoids as well. In my opinion, many so-called organic gardeners who use organic broad-spectrum insecticides have missed this point. While using an "organic" pesticide, they may actually be eliminating a truly organic means of pest control.

Here is an example of predator pest control. Every spring, like clockwork, aphids appear on the growing tips of my ivy. Soon I begin to see syrphid flies (flower flies), whose larvae eat aphids, hovering around the ivy. They've come to lay eggs. Within a month there is none but an occasional aphid around. The hatched syrphid maggots have eaten most of them. In a case like this, patience is the key to pest control. If I had sprayed with a broad-spectrum insecticide to kill the aphids, I would have killed the syrphid flies as well as the target pest; the aphid population would have built up again, more quickly than the syrphid fly population; and I would have had to spray again. This is often referred to as the pesticide merry-go-round.

The point is, you don't have to purchase a ticket for the pesticide merry-go-round to begin with. In my example, nature has the system arranged so that the hatching time for syrphid flies, and for most other predators, does not occur until a steady food supply is available. Furthermore, more prey organisms are provided than the predator can eat; thus, in this case, some aphids survive the predation of the flies. The system has to stay in balance, and the predator would not survive if all the prey were destroyed. Therefore, if you are committed to the idea of nonchemical pest control, you must be prepared to tolerate *some* insects on your plants.

Sometimes the natural system breaks down. For example, a number of imported pests have taken hold in this country. Unfortunately, when such organisms were brought here their natural predators did not accompany them. Two notorious examples are the European brown snail and the Japanese beetle; neither organism has natural enemies in this country that provide sufficient controls. Where such organisms occur, it is sometimes necessary to use selective pesticides that kill only the problem insect and do not upset the balance of the other insects in a yard.

Another problem is that sometimes, for whatever reason, predator-prey relationships become extremely unbalanced. When this happens, you may want to spray with a selective insecticide or purchase live predators from insectaries. (Since the latter must usually be purchased in quantities too large for one household to use, it's a good idea to try to collaborate with neighbors on the purchase.) Appendix B lists names of suppliers of live insects. Available predators are Aphytis wasps (for scale); Cryptolaemus beetles (for mealybugs); Encarsia wasps (for white flies); lacewings (for aphids, cabbage worms, mites, and mealybugs); and *Trichogramma* wasps (for cabbage worms and some other caterpillars). However, unless your problem is severe or you have a large acreage, it is doubtful if purchase of natural enemies is necessary or economical.

Making It Work

Here are some guidelines that will help to make a system of biological pest controls work effectively in your garden.

1. *Diversify plant materials*

The chances are that this system will be more effective if you have a diverse assortment of plant material in your yard. This statement should be qualified, however, by the warning that not just any assortment will work. By analogy, in a random grouping of species—such as a deer, a porpoise and a robin—the animals would have little relationship to each other. But where a grouping consisted of, say, a wolf, a deer, and wild oats, the deer would eat the oats and the wolf would eat the deer. The same type of interrelationships exists in the insect world. The only problem is that we're just learning about this system. Who feeds on what or whom? For example, there is some evidence that syrphid flies, whose larvae feed on aphids, are attracted by members of the Composite family, such as daisies (the adults probably eat the daisy nectar), so it wouldn't hurt to grow daisies. It is probable that although you might not know about such in-

tricate relationships, you will enable at least a few to flourish if you grow many different types of plants. Two plant groups that seem to be particularly good for this purpose are the *Umbelliferae* family, which includes many herbs such as anise, dill, fennel, and angelica; and members of the *Compositae* family, such as asters, yarrow, artemesia, chrysanthemums, cosmos, blackeyed Susans, marigolds, and zinnias. *Umbelliferae* and *Compositae* flowers appear to provide shelter and food for some stages of the insect-feeding insects.

2. *Remove all rotten fruits and diseased leaves and plants.*

Good sanitation is important! Diseased leaves and fruits left under a fruit tree in the fall harbor disease organisms and eggs of pests, as do leftover annual plants. Compost these items in a hot compost heap or, to be extra safe, discard them.

3. *Spray deciduous fruit trees with a dormant spray in the early spring if necessary.*

This spraying helps smother the eggs of young stages of some common pests. For many years gardeners have been routinely advised to spray all fruit trees with a dormant spray "to rid the garden of overwintering pests." Advice about timing or checking for pests was often not given. The value of dormant oil for pest, as distinct from disease, control is questionable in many situations. If your tree has a history of pear psyllid, scale, mite, or aphid infestations, it may be of value to apply a *light* oil just as the buds begin to swell in the spring. This oil will mechanically lower the populations of these soft-bodied insects or young scale crawlers by smothering them before their natural enemies are out in numbers. Again, remember that the predators usually don't hatch until their prey are present in numbers. If there is not a history of such pests, an oil spray for insect control is probably not appropriate. If you are spraying for fungus disease at the same season, most fungicides can be combined with the *light* oil; check the label to be sure.

4. *Determine specific treatments for the pests in your yard.*

If plant-feeding insects are present in intolerable numbers, you may need to resort to chemical pesticides. But select those that are as specific as possible to the problem at hand. Carefully follow the guidelines in the section titled "Pesticides and How to Use Them" and in the encyclopedia.

Natural Control Agents

This and the following sections will help you to identify both helpful organisms and those that may give you problems. A more detailed aid in identifying both types of insects is *Rodale's Color Handbook of Garden Insects* by Anna Carr. It contains full-color pictures of the insects, both predator and prey, in all stages of development.

Most of the beneficials listed below are either predators or parasitoids of plant-feeding insects. Their preservation and protection should be a major goal of your gardening strategy. Sometimes waiting for insects to control pests may

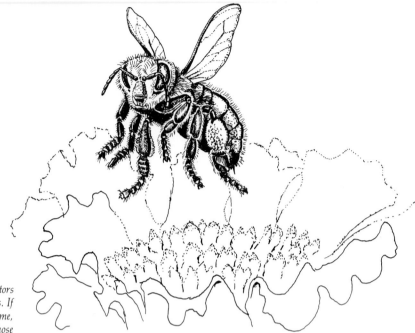

7.19. *Bees are the primary insect pollinators of most fruits and many vegetables. If insecticides must be used during blossom time, choose your materials carefully, avoiding those that are particularly toxic to bees, and apply such materials after dusk when most bees are in the hive.*

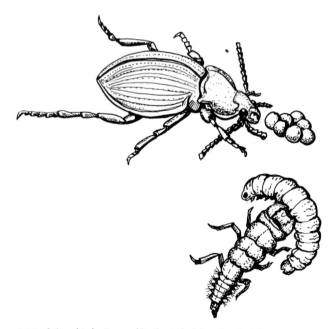

7.20. *Many kinds of ground beetles, in both larval and adult stages, are helpful predators in the garden. Depending on the species, they eat snail and slug eggs, the larvae of tent caterpillars, gypsy moth larvae, cankerworms, and cutworms.*

try your patience—like waiting for the cavalry to come to the rescue. In most cases, however, home gardeners will find their help invaluable.

BEES

While bees are not directly involved in pest control, as the major pollinators of fruits and vegetables they are probably the most valuable insect in the edible garden. Without them, our nation's food production would be severely affected. Attract bees to your garden by planting flowering plants, avoid spraying broad-spectrum insecticides at blooming time, and never use insecticides, such as Sevin, that are lethal to bees. If you have a number of fruit trees and live on a fairly good-sized piece of ground, and if no one in the vicinity is allergic to bees, a bee colony can increase your fruit crop and provide a bonus of honey. Many good books are available on the subject.

GROUND BEETLES

Ground beetles, members of the *Carabidae* family, are all predators. Some are small, but most are fairly large black beetles that scurry away when you uncover them. You will probably not see them the first year or two after planting a new garden. To encourage them, plant low-growing herbs under which they can hide, and keep an active compost pile, as these beetles thrive near them.

LACEWINGS

Lacewings are small green or brown gossamer-winged insects that in their adult stage eat nectar and pollen as well as aphids and mealybugs. In the larval stage they are fierce predators of aphids, psyllids, mealybugs, and moth eggs and larvae. They are one of the most effective insect predators for the home garden. Unlike ladybugs, which often fly away when released, purchased lacewings stay in your garden. When purchased and put out at the appropriate time, the lacewing larvae can be expected to continue their development in the area in which they are released.

LADYBUGS

Ladybugs are small beetles. There are about 400 types besides the familiar red one with black spots. Most people are familiar with ladybugs and know they are beneficial. Few people recognize the larvae of these beetles, on the the other hand: they are fierce and ugly looking. Learn to identify them. Ladybugs and their larvae eat aphids, mealybugs, scale, and other small insects. I do not recommend buying ladybugs for garden pest control, because most studies have shown that they usually fly away and often don't eat more than a few pests before leaving. Use in greenhouses would be the exception.

SPIDERS

Spiders are close relatives of the insects. I don't know how they got such a bad name, since, with the exception of the black widow and brown recluse, they are harmless, and these ever-present critters go about the business of eating up garden pests. We would be overrun with pests if it were not for their diligence.

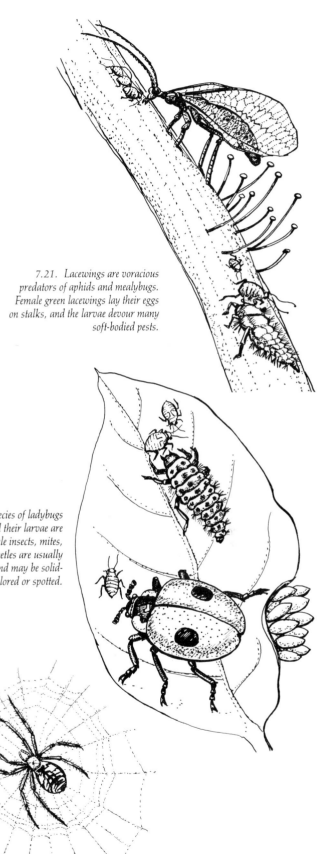

7.21. Lacewings are voracious predators of aphids and mealybugs. Female green lacewings lay their eggs on stalks, and the larvae devour many soft-bodied pests.

7.22. Many species of ladybugs (ladybird beetles) and their larvae are predators of aphids, scale insects, mites, and mealybugs. These beetles are usually red, black, or white, and may be solid-colored or spotted.

7.23. Spiders, which come in many forms, are among the most common predators in the garden. On the left is a familiar daddy-long-legs, on the right is a webbed spider.

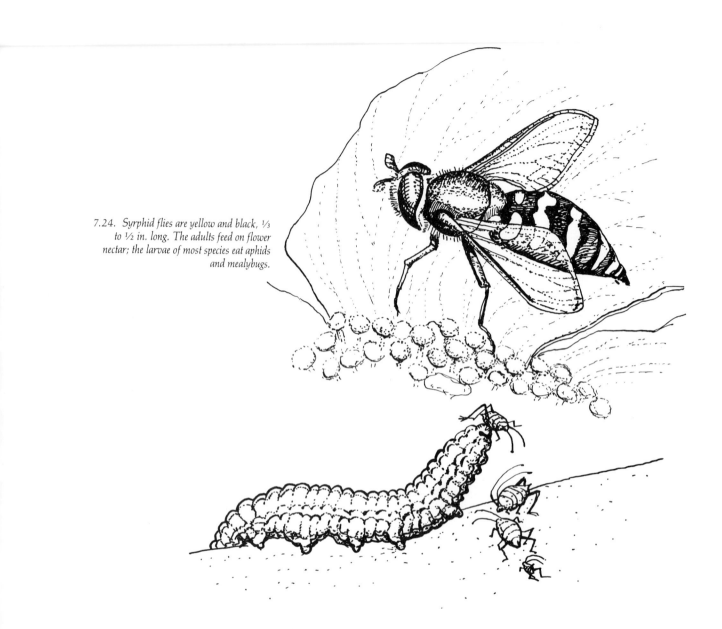

7.24. Syrphid flies are yellow and black, 1/3 to 1/2 in. long. The adults feed on flower nectar; the larvae of most species eat aphids and mealybugs.

SYRPHID FLIES

Syrphid flies (flower flies or hover flies) are members of the *Syrphidae* family. They may look like small bees hovering over flowers, but they have only two wings, like other flies. Most have yellow and black stripes on the body. Learn to identify them. They are found all over the United States and Canada. Their larvae are small green maggots which live on leaves, eating aphids, mealybugs, other small insects, and mites.

WASPS

Wasps are a large family of insects with transparent wings. Unfortunately, the few that sting have given wasps a bad name. In fact, all wasps are either insect predators or parasitoids. The parasitoid adult female lays her eggs in such insects as aphids and caterpillars, and the developing larvae devour the host. The predatory wasps feed on caterpillars, crickets, flies, and leafhoppers, among others. Encourage wasps whenever possible, and do not destroy caterpillars with brown cocoons attached, since these contain baby wasps or fly parasitoids.

OTHER BENEFICIAL INSECTS

Tiger, soldier and rove beetles feed on insects and their eggs, or on snails and slugs. They may be found on foliage or on the ground. The color and appearance of the several species is varied but all three groups are large (1/2–1 inch)

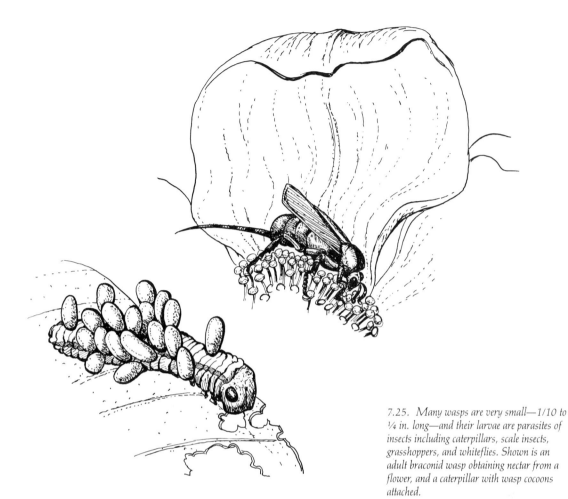

7.25. Many wasps are very small—1/10 to ¼ in. long—and their larvae are parasites of insects including caterpillars, scale insects, grasshoppers, and whiteflies. Shown is an adult braconid wasp obtaining nectar from a flower, and a caterpillar with wasp cocoons attached.

and generally rectangular in shape. The last six segments of the adult rove beetle's abdomen are exposed, giving it a nonbeetlelike appearance. All are valuable in insect control and should be protected.

Big-eyed and minute pirate bugs are valuable predators of soft-bodied destructive insects and mites. Both are small and blackish, oval to squarish in shape. Adult big-eyed bugs hibernate in garden litter—a good reason why the swept garden should sometimes be avoided.

Most assassin bugs and all damsel and ambush bugs are predators of plant-feeding insects. All are vase-shaped with small heads. Assassin and damsel bugs are large; ambush bugs are small. All may be found stalking insects on plants. Their colors are subdued; brownish, blackish, or greenish.

Snipe and robber flies are rapidly flying, predaceous flies of moderate to large size. The large head and thorax and the long curved abdomen of these flies give them a distinctive airplanelike appearance. The adults consume other flies, beetles, butterflies, and moths; the larvae prey on wood-dwelling, soil-dwelling, or aquatic insects.

Beefly adults are rounded, hairy, beelike flies, brownish in color, that often visit flowers. Their larvae are all insect-feeding, some being predators and others parasitoids.

Tachinid flies look like large, bristly houseflies. The maggots are parasitoids of moths, butterflies, beetles, grasshoppers, and wasps. Usually only a single fly develops in each host.

Spider mite populations (like their close relatives, spiders, mites are arachnids rather than insects) are generally controlled by predatory thrips (an insect), predatory mites, and syrphid fly maggots. Most of these natural enemies are more readily destroyed by insecticides than are the plant-feeding target mites. Pest mite outbreaks often follow the use of broad-spectrum insecticides.

AMPHIBIANS

Encourage toads and frogs to stay in your garden. When you know you have a resident toad, be careful you don't step on it. It takes steady nerves to weed the vegetable garden with a toad in it. When you least expect it, out jumps the toad from the beans or strawberries. But remember all the insects it eats, and go back to your weeding.

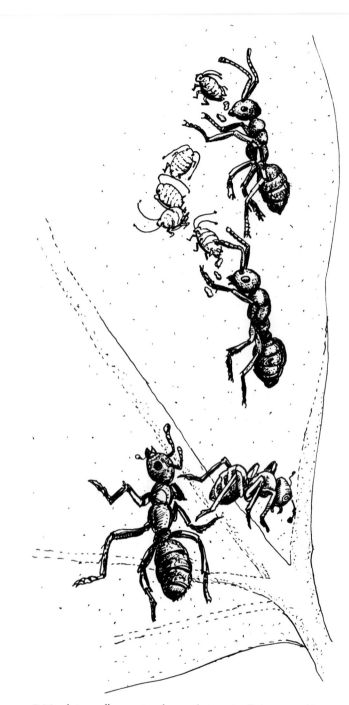

7.26. *Ants usually are not garden pests but occasionally become troublesome when feeding on the honeydew excreted by aphids, because they are reputed to protect the aphids from their natural enemies.*

Mixed Blessings

Most of the world's insects are neither economic pests nor the pests' biological control agents. Thus they are usually of little concern to most of us. Unfortunately, a few such creatures that are usually beneficial may cause an occasional problem when they appear in the wrong place or in large numbers. I include ants, earwigs, and sowbugs (crustaceans) in this category.

ANTS

Ants are general scavengers that remove dead insects and fallen fruit in the garden. Some species prey on such insects as small caterpillars, fruit flies, and fly larvae, and are natural enemies of termites. Other groups harvest weed seeds. Their nest-building activities may help to aerate the soil. However, many ants also feed on the honeydew exuded by aphids and mealybugs. The ants are believed to transport aphids and mealybugs from plant to plant. Their honeydew collecting activities interfere with the natural enemies of aphids and mealybugs, preventing adequate control of these pests.

If ants are contributing to your aphid or mealybug problem, use the commercial sticky substances that are available, such as Tanglefoot or Stickem. Apply these substances around tree trunks and places where the ants are traveling to prevent them from reaching the pests.

EARWIGS

Earwigs are fierce-looking brown insects with large pincers in the back. They are harmless to humans; they don't pinch. Earwigs prey on many bothersome pests, but they are occasionally a problem on young vegetable seedlings and ripe fruits. Observe them at night with a flashlight. If you have determined that they are eating your vegetables or fruits, trap them by laying rolled-up newspaper, bales of bamboo stakes, or corrugated cardboard around the garden. Earwigs will hide in these materials and you can destroy them in the daytime by shaking the collectors over soapy water.

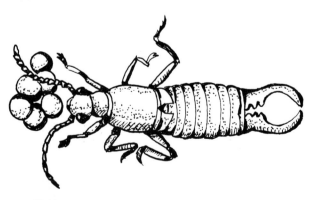

7.27. *Unlike most insects, earwigs protect their eggs and young from predators. While usually not a problem, sometimes they eat the foliage and ripe fruits of edible plants.*

SOWBUGS

Sowbugs (pillbugs) are not insects but crustaceans. They often roll up into a ball when they are disturbed. They prefer to eat decaying material, and if you mulch your garden you may see thousands. On occasion I have seen sowbugs eating young lettuce, bean seedlings, and tomato or strawberry fruits. Sufficient dry mulch under vulnerable crops helps prevent damage. There is also good evidence that sowbugs are secondary feeders. The initial damage to the fruits is likely caused by insects, snails, or slugs. Control of these other pests is the primary key to control of sowbugs.

Major Plant Pests

APHIDS

Aphids are soft-bodied, small, green, black, pink, or gray insects. They can produce many generations in one season. They suck plant juices and exude honeydew. If the leaves under the aphids turn black, a secondary mold is growing on the nutrient-rich honeydew. This unsightly mold will not directly harm the plant, though it does block sunlight coming to the leaves. The mold can be removed with a soapy spray (2 tablespoons of dishwashing liquid per gallon of water).

Aphids are a major food source for syrphid flies, lady beetles, lacewings, and wasp parasitoids. Among mammals, mice are analogous since they are a fast-reproducing food source for coyotes, owls, hawks, and the like. An aphid population can increase rapidly. If this happens, look for aphid mummies and other natural enemies mentioned above. Mummies are swollen, brown or metallic-looking aphids. They are valuable, so keep them. Inside the mummy a larval wasp parasitoid is growing. These aphids will never feed or reproduce again, and the wasp inside will hatch out and lay eggs in more aphids.

If natural enemies are not present, or if the growth of the plant is impaired or the leaf tips are curling (as often happens in citrus), you may need to intervene. Since aphids suck plant juices, large numbers of them can weaken a plant. In addition, some aphids spread viral or fungus diseases to vulnerable plants.

As in all control efforts, the simplest remedy should be tried first. Wash the affected plant with a strong stream of water. Some kinds of aphids will leave the plant under these conditions. If the aphids stick tightly, apply the soapy spray described above. The surfactant in the soap dehydrates aphids. Be sure to spray thoroughly the top and bottom of all leaves as well as the growing tips. Woolly and other especially waxy aphids may need to be treated twice at 24-hour intervals. Wash the plant with clean water 24 hours after the soap application. Usually, if the above steps are carefully followed, conventional pesticides are not needed for aphid control. When all else fails, use malathion.

BORERS

Borers are the larval stage of a number of different insects. These larvae damage plants by boring through stems

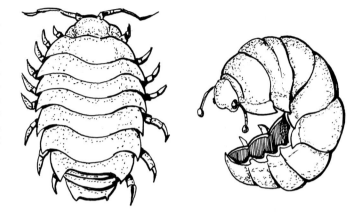

7.28. The sowbug, a grey crustacean whose outer covering resembles armor plate, often rolls up into a ball when disturbed. It is an occasional pest on strawberries and young seedlings.

7.29. Aphids, which are plant-sucking insects, produce many generations a year and are the major food source for many predatory and parasitic insects.

CODLING MOTHS

The "worms" in wormy apples are often codling moth larvae. They usually develop in apples and pears, but sometimes attack quinces and walnuts. This European insect is now common worldwide. Because most growers want perfect fruit, codling moths are the "key pests" in many fruit-tree pest control programs.

First-generation adult females lay eggs on leaves or twigs near the blossoms; later generation females lay eggs near the fruit. The young larvae enter and complete their development in the fruit. In spring, mature larvae pupate in crevices of bark and in hiding places on and near the ground. In fall, mature larvae spin cocoons in similar places and pass the winter there. They pupate only as the weather warms in spring. Overwintering larvae are preyed on by woodpeckers and other birds, as well as ants and other insect predators. Generally, none of these natural enemies provide enough control. Adult moths emerge from pupation over a 2–3 week period called a flight. Since optimum control of codling moths depends on strict timing of pesticide sprays, pheromone traps should be used (see the accompanying sidebar). These release the female codling moth's sex attractant. Male moths attracted to this fragrance, as to a female, are caught in the traps. Weekly counts of the trapped males help determine timing of sprays so that young larvae are killed just before they enter the fruit. If moth counts are

7.31. The lesser peach-tree borer burrows into the injured trunks and branches of apricots, cherry, and peach trees. Often this pest can be discovered by the gummy sawdust deposits it leaves on the bark.

7.30. Small parasitoid wasps lay eggs within aphids. The wasp larvae hatch out and parasitize other aphids.

and trunks. The first sign of damage is usually wilted foliage or sawdust around a hole on the trunk. Control borers by cutting the damaged branch or leaf off. When the borer is in the main trunk, straighten a wire hanger and push up into the tunnels to crush the borers. Even one or two borers can be fatal to a young fruit tree. Inspect the young trunks often in summer and early fall, particularly near the crown of the tree (where the bark meets the root zone).

Borers are a problem on apple, apricot, cherry, currant, peach, pear, pecan, plum, and raspberry. In addition, there are squash-vine stem borers. Cut off stems that have been affected below the entry hole.

A Pheromone Trap for Codling Moths

These guidelines for controlling codling moths with a pheromone trap should enable you to keep your wormy apple count below 15 percent.

1. At blossom time place 1 pheromone moth trap about 6 feet up on the south side of each mature tree. Change pheromone caps and trap liners every 6 weeks.

2. Once a week, count and remove trapped moths. Record count. Rake up and destroy fallen apples.

3. When apples are the size of ping-pong balls, thin to 2 apples per cluster. Destroy wormy fruit.

4. When moth count on a particular week is lower than the previous week, add up total moths counted for the entire moth flight. If moth total is less than 20, no spray is needed. If catch is greater than 20, and daytime temperatures exceeded 65° F on the previous 3 days, spray immediately. If daytime temperatures were lower than 65° F and the moth count still above 20, spray in 7 days (cool air slows egg hatch).

5. During a second or third flight, repeat steps 2–4. Between flights, the weekly count will drop to near zero. In step 4, add only moths caught in the most recent flight.

7.32. The codling moth is a major pest of apples throughout the U.S. The female deposits eggs that develop into larvae that burrow into the fruit.

7.33. Cutworms usually attack young annual vegetables and fruits. Look for them rolled up in the soil as you prepare the planting bed for seedlings. The seedlings can be protected with cardboard collars.

low, no spraying is needed. The most selective codling moth spray is ryania. The next best alternate is phosmet (Imitlan). Neither of these pesticides kills all the natural enemies of aphids and mites. These pests tend to increase if broad spectrum pesticides such as diazinon, methoxychlor, or carbaryl (Sevin) are applied. Because of the agricultural importance of codling moths, other control strategies are actively being studied. These include use of a viral disease and release of sterile male moths.

CUTWORMS

Cutworms are small chewing insects of the caterpillar family. They are usually found in the soil and will curl up into a ball when disturbed. Cutworms are a particular problem on annual vegetables when the seedlings first appear or when young transplants are set out. The cutworm often chews the stem off right at the soil line, killing the plant. Control cutworms by using cardboard collars or bottomless

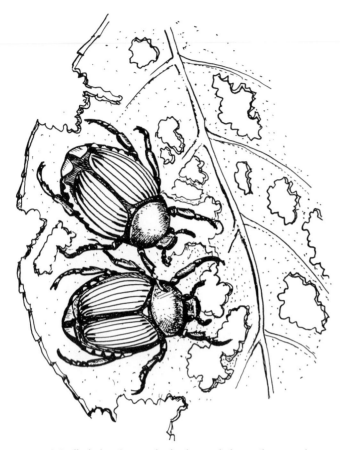

7.34. *Metallic-looking Japanese beetles chew on the leaves, flowers, and fruit of many plants.*

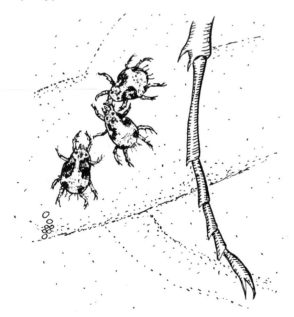

7.35. *Mites are minute members of the spider family. (They are dwarfed by an ant's leg.) Most mite infestations result from applications of broad-spectrum insecticides that kill the mites' natural enemies. Mite damage makes foliage look dirty and parched.*

tin cans around the plant; be sure to sink these collars 1 inch into the ground. Severe infestations can be controlled with *Bacillus thuringiensis. Trichogramma* miniwasps and black ground beetles are among cutworms' natural enemies.

JAPANESE BEETLES

Japanese beetles were accidentally introduced into the United States early in this century and are now a serious problem in the eastern part of the country. This metallic blue or green beetle with coppery wings chews its way through the leaves and flowers of apple, cherry, grape, peach, plum, quince, raspberry, rhubarb, and many other edible plants. The larval stage lives on the roots of grasses. In Japan a naturally occurring disease present in the soil controls these beetles in the larval stage. This disease, called milky-spore, has been produced for sale in this country and can be purchased at nurseries under the trade name Doom. The disease is slow to cut down the population, often taking three or four years to take hold. If serious infestations are a problem and you can't wait that long, hand-pick the beetles, knock them off into soapy water, or buy Japanese beetle bug traps that contain a pheromone (insect hormone) that attracts them. (See Appendix B for a source of the traps.) These traps seem to work most effectively if they are located at some distance from the plant to be protected, thus drawing the beetles away from the area.

MITES

Mites are among the few arachnids (spiders and their relatives) that pose a problem in the garden. Mites are so small that a hand lens usually is needed to see them. They become a problem when they reproduce in great numbers and suck on the leaves of such plants as citrus, apples, beans, and strawberries. The symptoms of serious mite damage can be dried-looking silvery or yellow leaves, sometimes accompanied by tiny webs. The major natural predators of mites are predatory mites. Mite-eating thrips and minute syrphids also help in mite control.

Mites are most likely to thrive on dusty leaves and in dry warm weather, thus plants near a dusty road, say, are likely to be mite-infested. The dust mechanically dehydrates delicate mite predators. A routine foliage wash and misting of sensitive plants helps mite control. I use a tool called a fogger which produces a strong blast of misted water (see Figure 7.36). In spring, when mite population on citrus may increase to large numbers, biweekly fogging is appropriate, if fungus diseases are not a problem. Mites are sometimes seen on beans and other vegetables but are seldom a serious problem, because large quantities of vegetables can still be harvested. If appearance is important, restrict these plants to the vegetable garden. Mites are sometimes described as serious fruit tree pests. Usually, mite damage on such trees is caused by previous spraying with broad-spectrum pesticides. Sometimes such a problem can take several years to rectify after such spraying ceases.

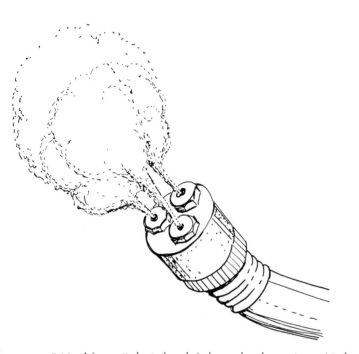

7.36. A fogger attaches to the end of a hose and produces a strong mist when the water is turned on.

7.37. Scale insects attach themselves permanently to the bark or leaves of a plant.

SCALES

Scales are plant-sucking insects that usually are covered with a shell or waxy coating. Adult females shed their legs and antennae and permanently attach themselves to a leaf or branch. The eggs are laid and the live young are born beneath the protective shell of the adult female. Generally, ladybugs and/or chalcid miniwasps keep scales in check, but since crawlers are especially susceptible to light oil sprays, you can use these in the dormant season if you have a problem. (See the section titled "Making It Work" for timing details.)

SNAILS AND SLUGS

My husband warns me teasingly that if snails are one of the Almighty's favorite creatures, then I'm in big trouble. I have killed thousands and thousands by hand. Gardeners on the East Coast battle Japanese beetles in the summer; gardeners on the West Coast battle snails all year round. It's said that a French gourmet brought the brown garden snail to this country for eating. He should have been baked in butter and garlic just like his beloved escargot!

Snails and slugs are not insects, of course, but mollusks. They eat most commonly grown fruits and vegetables.

7.38. Snails and slugs will eat most edible plants. Look for their damage after irrigation or rain. The slime trails they often leave can help you identify them as the pest.

7.39. *Weevils occasionally feed on the fruits and nuts of a number of popular edibles.*

They feed at night and can go dormant for months in times of drought or low food supply.

In the absence of effective natural enemies (a few snail eggs are consumed by predatory beetles and earwigs), several snail control strategies can be recommended. Since snails are most active after rain or irrigation, go out to hand-collect them on such nights. It is obviously impossible to find and collect all the snails, and only repeated forays will provide adequate control. In the more common situation where you do not have time for such sustained collection, you may occasionally need to use metaldehyde bait in pellet form as well. For best effect the bait should be applied to dampened soil in the area around young seedlings. In addition, it is appropriate to bait the entire garden once or twice a year. Never apply baits on a regular schedule such as weekly or even monthly. This practice has in some areas resulted in new generations of snails that are resistant to metaldehyde. A good time would be in the early spring, when they are most active (February or March in California), and again in early summer when the majority of young hatch. Again, pelleted baits should only be applied to damp ground. If you wish to prevent buildup of large snail populations, consider removing (or avoid planting) such well-known snail harborages as ivy or vinca (periwinkle) ground covers, and sheltering strap-leafed plants such as agapanthus or iris.

WEEVILS AND CURCULIOS

Weevils and curculios are beetles with long snouts. The ones with particularly long snouts are called curculios. In both larval and adult stages, they can be serious pests. They feed on fruits, nuts, and roots, and are a particular problem on chestnuts, plums, apples, beans, cabbages, blueberries, cherries, and pecans. A few of these insects around are not a problem but large numbers should be controlled. Control includes the scrupulous cleaning up of old leaves, dropped fruits, and nuts. Throughout the growing season, whenever you see weevils or curculios around, place sheets under fruit or nut trees, and shake the trees to dislodge the adults. Dispose of them. Control moderate infestations by dusting the foliage with diatomaceous earth, the pulverized skeletons of small fossilized algae. The sharp surfaces abrade the insects' covering and cause death by dehydration. It is sold under the trade name Perma-guard.

WHITE FLIES

White flies are sometimes a problem in mild winter areas of the country as well as in greenhouses nationwide. In the garden, *Encarsia* wasps and other parasitoids usually provide adequate white fly control. Occasionally, especially in cool weather, white fly populations may begin to cause serious plant damage (wilting and slowing of growth, flowering, or fruiting). Look under the leaves to determine whether the scalelike, immobile larvae and pupae are present in large numbers. Adults can easily be trapped using the following method. Apply Stickem or Tanglefoot to a mustard-yellow file folder. (No one knows why this color attracts white flies, but it does!) Hold the folder open near the affected plant, and give the plant an occasional shake. The adult white flies will fly to the folder and adhere to the sticky surface. Further development of the hard-to-control larvae can be stopped by any of several "houseplant sprays" containing methoprene, an insect-growth regulator appropriate for controlling several plant-sucking insects—but only on ornamental plants, not edibles. Since this compound readily degrades in sunlight, apply the spray at dusk. For edible plants, use a fogger often if fungus diseases are not a problem.

GRASSHOPPERS

Grasshoppers occasionally are a garden problem, particularly in grassland areas in dry years. Try controlling them with a bait containing a grasshopper disease, *Nosema locustae.* It is available from Reuter Laboratories, 2400 James Madison Highway, Haymarket, VA 22069.

NEMATODES

Nematodes are microscopic worms, sometimes called threadworms or eelworms. These organisms inhabit the soil in most of the United States, particularly in the Southeast. Most nematode species live on decaying matter or are predatory on other nematodes, algae, and bacteria. A few types are parasitic, attaching themselves to the roots of plants. Edible plants particularly susceptible to nematode damage include many annual crops such as beans, cantaloupe, eggplant, lettuce, okra, pepper, squash, tomatoes, and watermelon, as well as the perennial fig and brambleberries. The symptoms of nematode damage are stunted-looking plants and small swellings or lesions on the roots.

If nematodes are a problem in your area, prevent nematode damage by planting trees that are grafted onto nematode-resistant root stock, if available. Rotate annual vegetables with less susceptible varieties, keep your soil high in organic matter (this encourages fungi and predatory nematodes that help keep them under control), and, before planting, try the soil solarization procedure outlined later in this chapter.

Marigolds are sometimes planted to control nematodes. The limited documentation available has shown that some species of the plant do contribute to nematode control, but further documentation is needed. There are many species of both marigolds and nematodes, and a number of the combinations are not effective.

Pesticides and How to Use Them

Weather, good cultural techniques, and natural enemies are the most important elements in controlling pests. As you gradually learn how these natural controls operate,

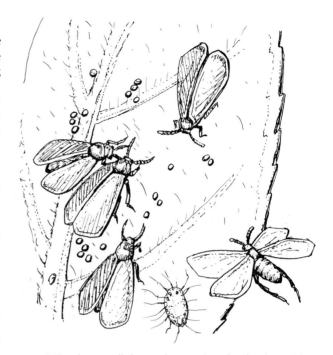

7.40. *White flies generally live in colonies on the underside of leaves. They usually fly around only when disturbed.*

you will find that chemicals are seldom required. If additional help is needed, try a nonchemical control method such as water, soapy water sprays, or traps, if available. If all these attempts fail and pests are doing substantial damage, you may have to resort to a chemical pesticide.

Because of the toxicological and other tests required before registration, pesticides are enormously expensive to produce. So pesticide manufacturers usually choose to market only those chemicals that will kill a great variety of organisms, or, in the case of selective pesticides, those that offer enormous sales potential. Such choices give them a chance to recover developmental costs and make a profit. Pesticides which kill many kinds of organisms have been dubbed "broad-spectrum." Broad-spectrum pesticides include some of the so-called "organic" pesticides such as nicotine and rotenone and sabodilla as well as the synthetic organophosphates such as malathion, chlorinated hydrocarbons such as DDT, and carbamate pesticides such as Sevin (carbaryl).

Your pest control strategy should differ from that of the pesticide manufacturer. If chemical aids are needed, use them as selectively as possible. For example, never spray the entire yard or treat for insects on a calendar basis. You should seek techniques and chemicals which affect only the target pest, allowing its natural enemies to survive. Sometimes you will use a truly selective pesticide. At other times you can apply a broad-spectrum material at an optimum time when it will kill the pest but preserve the most natural enemies. To give your strategy the best chance for success, you should learn as much as possible about the life cycles of the insects, mites, and mollusks in your garden. In addition you will need to know something about the pesticides themselves so you can choose those with the least potential to harm you and the environment.

Since most insecticides are designed to kill living insects quickly, few are truly nontoxic to humans. Though the compounds I have recommended are among those that are the least toxic to humans, you should always carefully follow the directions for use. Some people believe a little more is always better. Not so! When you use a little extra pesticide, you not only increase your personal risk, you may also injure your plants and unnecessarily kill natural enemies. While in a few situations it may be appropriate to use less, it is never appropriate to increase the dose.

Wear protective clothing when spraying pesticides. A long-sleeved shirt, pants, closed shoes, gloves, and even goggles and a face mask are often appropriate. Pesticides can penetrate your skin or enter your lungs. To avoid drift, spray when the air is still.

Pesticides are usually classified under two major categories: inorganic and organic. Until the 1940s, the majority of pesticides were inorganic. Examples of inorganic pesticides still in use are sulfur, Bordeaux solution, copper oxide, and boric acid. Many of these inorganics do not kill insects on contact. Those being used today function mainly as fungicides and stomach poisons.

Beginning with DDT in the 1940s, a variety of synthetic organic pesticides have been introduced. (Chemicals are called organic when they contain carbon, the element which is basic to life.) Most of the new synthetic organic insecticides kill insects on contact. Some organic insecticides are based on natural plant products. However, the fact that they are plant extracts does not necessarily make them any more "organic" or safer in use than the synthetic carbon-based insecticides. Some well-known plant-based organic pesticides are ryania, nicotine, sabodilla, pyrethrins and rotenone. Nicotine is extremely toxic to humans.

Many of the synthetic organic insecticides can be classified according to their chemical structures. These are the chlorinated hydrocarbons, the organophosphates, the carbamates, and the synthetic pyrethroids. Some of the newer organic materials should not be considered insecticides in the normal sense, since they do not kill insects directly. Instead they change insect behavior or development in such a way that the insect dies, primarily from starvation or exposure. Most of these compounds are classified as either behavior modifiers or as insect growth regulators. Many of the behavior modifiers are anti-feedants (chemicals which stop insects from eating). The insect growth regulators include cuticle synthesis inhibitors (which stop development of insect skin), juvenile hormone analogues (which resemble a normal insect hormone), and perhaps in the future, anti-juvenile hormones (which would remove a normal in-

sect hormone). Finally, specific insect-disease-causing organisms—bacteria, fungi, viruses, and nematodes—are now formulated as sprays to aid in insect control.

In addition to differences in structure and in activity, pesticides differ in stability. If they are readily changed to simpler compounds by microorganisms or animal enzymes, they are said to be nonpersistent or biodegradable. If they remain unchanged or little changed by natural processes, they are called persistent. In general, persistent pesticides have been proven to cause environmental problems. The persistent, inorganic, heavy-metal pesticides containing lead, arsenic, or mercury tend to build up in the soil, poisoning plants growing there and animals that eat the plants. The persistent chlorinated hydrocarbons are readily stored in the fatty tissues of fish, mammals, and birds; they may later cause death or reduce reproduction in these animals. In addition, several of these, including DDT, chlordane, aldrin, dieldren, and heptachlor, have been partially or totally banned because they are suspected carcinogens (cancer-causing compounds). You should avoid all persistent pesticides whose limited use is still permitted—these include the chlorinated hydrocarbons, lindane and toxaphene—as well as those that include arsenic, lead, or mercury.

RECOMMENDED INSECTICIDES

No pesticide can be recommended unequivocally. Environmental effects and eventual toxicity sometimes take years to surface. The following substances have the least potential for harm as of this writing. Your best defense is to stay informed.

If a pesticide is called for, your first choice should be a selective pesticide, since these do not directly kill beneficial insects. Of the available materials, the most selective are not chemicals but microorganisms. *Bacillus thuringiensis* (BT) contains bacterial particles that cause a caterpillar disease. It kills no other group of insects. BT is sold under the trade names Dipel, Thuricide, and Orcon Caterpillar Control. Milky spore disease (*Bacillus popilliac*) is a soil-borne bacterial disease that helps control Japanese beetle grubs. And grasshoppers are being controlled by a bait containing a grasshopper disease called *Nosema locustae*. Currently no other diseases are available for home garden use, but this may change in the near future. Remember that even these very selective disease-causing materials should be used sparingly. It has been experimentally demonstrated that repeated use can disrupt garden ecology by destroying the prey (food source) of the beneficial insects and causing them to starve.

Among the most selective and biodegradable materials are the juvenile hormone analogues (JHAs). They are suitable for use on homopteran insects (scales, white flies, aphids, and mealybugs) and on insects that are a problem as adults (some flies, fleas, and mosquitoes). Though they potentially affect all kinds of insects, in practice they tend to be very specific. To control adult pests JHAs must be applied to *late larval* stages. Further development stops at the beginning of the pupal stage. Currently two products containing methoprene (Altosid) are available for home use (though not, as mentioned previously, on edible plants): Dexol Whitefly and Mealybug Spray and Chacon House Plant Mist. Methoprene and other JHAs do not kill immediately, so wait a few days for the results. Another useful JHA, kinoprene (Enster) is currently registered for commercial greenhouse use to control some of the same pests. It probably will be available in the future for home use. Both of these JHAs are nontoxic to birds and mammals.

The proper timing of sprays is a useful way to increase pesticide selectivity. For example, light oil sprays are not intrinsically selective. However, when applied as a dormant spray just as buds begin to swell in the spring, they give good control of thrips, scale crawlers, and pear psylla, all of which begin to be mobile then. But they do not affect most natural enemies of these pests, since the beneficials, which hatch later, will still be protected in bark crevices and under bud scales. Conversely, a dormant oil spray to control insects in winter will actually control nothing, and a spray in late fall might kill important natural enemies that are still around. Dormant oil spray is available at nurseries. Generally this product cannot be used while plants are in foliage, but scale infestations on citrus or on some house plants can be controlled with a light oil formulated for this purpose. Follow directions carefully.

The use of pheromone traps to determine the need for and the proper timing of sprays is another way of minimizing pesticide use. In addition to the codling moth traps mentioned earlier, traps are available for apple and other fruit-feeding maggots, and for several scales. Pheromone traps are available from Zoecon Corporation, 975 California Ave., Palo Alto, CA 94304. They generally come in three-station kits, so it's a good idea to cooperate with neighbors when ordering.

Spraying in the evening allows you to use some broad-spectrum insecticides (those that biodegrade rapidly) while still protecting many beneficials. Resmethrin, a synthetic pyrethroid, disappears in a few hours, leaving day-active beneficials such as bees, wasps, and parasitic flies unaffected; other natural enemies will come back rapidly. Naturally, this technique should be used sparingly. Malathion, too, is less damaging (especially at low concentrations) when used this way, though its residues may still kill for about two days.

Because they function primarily as stomach poisons, the effects of some pesticides are limited mainly to plant-feeding insects. This is the case with ryania, the material recommended for codling moth control. Ryania degrades within a few days, so if you follow the directions on the container, residues on your fruit will not be a problem. The other codling moth insecticide, Imidan (phosmet) is neither as selective, nor as nontoxic as ryania. However, experiments have demonstrated that it does not lead to major pest outbreaks when used on apples. Pesticide residues are likewise not a problem with Imidan, since it is used a month or more before harvest. Do not graze animals under your trees after treatment.

A broad-spectrum pesticide can become selective when it is formulated to attract the pest. For example, the short-lived organophosphate metaldehyde is marketed in a bran bait that attracts snails and slugs. These baits should be used with care, however, since they can kill animals or children that eat them (see the section on snails and slugs for application directions).

Soap solutions are valuable in insect control because they remove some of the insect's waxy coating, causing dehydration and death, or they break the surface tension of water so that insects drown. Hold a jar of soapy water (1 tablespoon dishwashing liquid per quart of water) under plants laden with plant-feeding beetles or bugs, flip them into the solution, and they drown immediately. This is a good technique to rid your yard of earwigs, adult *Diabrotica* (cucumber) beetles, Japanese beetles, asparagus and harlequin bugs, and other hard-to-control, mobile pests. If aphids cause severe curling of leaves, as can occur on citrus or cherries (a few curled leaves on fruit trees are not important), do not wait for natural controls. Spray your tree with 2 tablespoons of dishwashing soap in a gallon of water, and the aphids will be gone in a day. The next day, wash the plant with clear water to remove the soap. Plants infested with woolly aphids should be drenched with two soapy water applications at 24-hour intervals; be sure to wash the soap off a day after the last treatment.

A number of widely available and popular insecticides should be avoided. These include: carbaryl (Sevin) which is relatively persistent, extremely toxic to bees and wasps, and can sometimes lead to aphid and mite outbreaks; two plant extracts, nicotine and rotenone, because they are broad-spectrum contact insecticides toxic to humans; and methoxychlor, which is the least persistent of the chlorinated hydrocarbons but which also can cause pest problems.

A word about homemade insecticides. They are not necessarily safer or more effective than commercial products. Remember that they have not undergone long-term toxicology tests, have not been formulated to protect you and your plants (the wrong formulation can be irritating to your skin or kill your plants), and have not been tested for effectiveness. The fact that no pests are seen after their application may be coincidence rather than cause and effect.

Disease Control

Plant diseases are potentially far more damaging to your crops than are most insects. Diseases are also more difficult to control because they usually grow inside the plant, and plants do not respond with immune mechanisms comparable to those that protect animals. Consequently, most plant disease control strategies feature prevention rather than control.

Plant Resistance

Research on plant diseases that have plagued commercial agriculture has resulted in the widespread availability of disease-resistant cultivars of several important vegetables and fruits. Certain varieties of wilt-resistant tomatoes and blight-resistant pears are examples of plants that resist diseases by genetic means. Always choose disease-resistant varieties whenever they are available.

In other instances—raspberries are an example—strict inspection and quarantine help to ensure that most commercially available plants are disease free. You should avail yourself of these products whenever possible. In addition, it is advisable to plant two or three different varieties of a particular vegetable in your garden to help prevent total crop wipeout from an invading disease.

Cultural Techniques

Changing the location in your garden of some disease-prone plants on a regular basis is helpful, as pests and diseases often build up in the soil. This is called crop rotation. Light, exposure, temperature, fertilizing, and moisture are also important factors in disease control. The entries for individual plants in the encyclopedia give specific cultural information.

Seriously diseased plants should be discarded. Diseased fruits should be picked up from the ground or pulled off the plant itself, and placed in a hot compost pile (risky) or in the garbage. In the fall, rake up all leaves and fruit from around disease-prone varieties. Apply dormant sprays when appropriate.

How to Use Soil Solarization

This complete process takes one month during the warmest season of the year.

1. Obtain sufficient clear polyethelene plastic film (4 mil thickness) to cover the treatment area.

2. Irrigate the plot 1 week before laying down the plastic tarping.

3. After 1 week, cultivate and level the treatment area. Install drip emitters or ditches on 3-foot centers for irrigation during treatment.

4. Place plastic film tightly over treatment area. Do not leave air spaces. Weight edges of plastic with soil.

5. Thoroughly irrigate area under plastic once a week.

6. One month later, remove plastic and plant as desired.

Soil Solarization

It has recently been discovered that a variety of soil-borne fungi, nematodes, and weeds can be controlled by a plastic mulch technique called soil solarization.* If you have problems with any of the serious soil-borne plant diseases such as *Verticillium* or *Fusarium* wilt, or if you have a serious nematode infestation, soil solarization is appropriate. (A significant reduction in weed growth can also be expected.)

Plant Diseases

The most common diseases of edible plants are described below. Conditions related to deficiencies and their symptoms are covered earlier in this chapter under "Plant Nutrients" and under "Soil Problems" in Chapter 4. Symptoms and cures, if any, are suggested. (Recommended fungicides are listed in a table at the end of this section.) For fruit trees, supplement this information with a regular pruning program.

BROWN ROT

There are two types of brown rot fungi. Once causes blossom blight and the dieback of shoots; the other causes spoilage of such stone fruits as apricots, peaches, cherries, and plums. Just as the fruit ripens, round brown spots appear which eventually affect the entire fruit. Unless removed from the tree, these fruits often stick tightly to the branches; the dried-up diseased fruits are known as "mummies." Prevention is helpful in some situations. Avoid planting these trees in lawns, where conditions are usually moist.

If the disease develops, remove and destroy all spoiled fruit. Do not leave it on the tree or the ground. If the spoilage level is intolerable fungal sprays may be required. For apricots and cherries spray with benomyl or bordeaux at pink-bud stage and full bloom. Use benomyl again two or three weeks before harvest. For peaches, nectarines, and plums, if blossom blight has been a problem, spray with bordeaux or wettable sulfur at pink-bud stage and full bloom. Preharvest treatment for fruit rot is usually needed for peaches and nectarines; use sulfur three weeks, and again one week, before harvest. (Never use sulfur compounds in hot weather or on apricots, since they damage the trees.)

FIREBLIGHT

Fireblight is a serious bacterial disease of fruit trees. In fact, in some warm, humid areas, some species should not be grown at all because of the fireblight risk. Such members of the rose family as pears, quinces, loquats, and apples are particularly prone to this disease. During the blooming period you must remain constantly vigilant for fireblight symptoms. At this time check weekly for blossoms, twigs, leaves, or branches that look burned and blackened. Act immediately; the disease spreads rapidly. Trim the diseased tissue off, cutting at least one foot into healthy tissue, and sterilizing your tools between cuts with a 10 percent solu-

---

*Katan, J. "Solar Pasteurization of Soils for Disease Control: Status and Prospects." Plant Disease Journal 64, 1980.

tion of bleach in water. Choose blight-resistant varieties, if you live in an area where fireblight is a serious problem. See the encyclopedia for fireblight-resistant varieties of individual species.

LEAF-SPOT FUNGI

A number of fungus plant diseases are associated with warm, wet weather: among them are anthracnose, scab, and shot-hole fungus. Plant resistant varieties, clean up all diseased leaves, and apply dormant sprays if possible. (See table for recommended fungicides.)

MILDEWS

Mildews are fungus diseases that affect plants under certain conditions. There are two types of mildews: powdery mildew and downy mildew. Powdery mildew appears as a white powdery dust; downy mildrew makes a velvety or fuzzy patch. Both affect leaves, buds, and tender stems. The poorer the air circulation and the more humid the weather, the more apt your plants are to have mildew. Make sure your plant has plenty of sun and is not crowded by other vegetation. Train your fruit trees to a vase shape, as described in the pruning section earlier in this chapter. If you must use overhead watering, do it in the morning so the water will evaporate by nighttime. Use sulfur and dormant sprays to control mildew on grapes, currants, and fruit trees.

PEACH LEAF CURL

Peach leaf curl is a serious fungus disease of peaches, nectarines, and sometimes almonds. It causes unnatural swelling, discoloration, and curling of the foliage. The injured leaves fall prematurely and are replaced with new healthy leaves. The need to replace the leaves twice annually seriously weakens the tree, and few fruits are produced. What fruits that are produced often become sunburned. The fungus overwinters in the bark, twigs, and fallen leaves. All leaves should be raked from the ground and prunings destroyed. All peaches and nectarines should be sprayed annually with a dormant lime sulfur spray, as described below under "Scab." Almonds do not require treatment unless the disease is seen.

SCAB

Scab is a serious disease of apples, crabapples, and sometimes pears in rainy climates. It results in deformed leaves and blotched and cracked fruit. Whenever possible, plant scab-immune apple varieties such as 'Priscilla' or 'Prima.' If you already have an established apple tree that suffers from scab, spray with lime sulfur just before the flower buds open in the spring. After the blossoms have started to turn pink and after three-fourths of the blossoms have fallen, spray with wettable sulfur. In summer and fall, clean up all leaves and fruits from the ground and destroy them. If it is a very rainy season and more control is needed, spray with one of the recommended fungicides.

VERTICILLIUM WILT

Verticillium wilt is a soil-borne fungus that is destructive in many parts of the country. The symptom of this disease may be a sudden wilting of one part of the plant. There is no cure, but the soil solarization procedure described earlier should help prevent it. Plant resistant species or varieties if this disease is in your soil. In general, apples, asparagus, bamboo, beans, citrus fruits, figs, mulberries, pears, walnuts, and certain varieties of tomatoes and strawberries are naturally resistant to verticillium wilt.

VIRUSES

A number of viruses attack plants. There is no cure for viral conditions, so most affected plants must be destroyed. Deformed or mottled leaves or stunted plants are symptoms of virus diseases. Grapes, raspberries, figs, tomatoes, strawberries, and beans are particularly susceptible. Buy virus-resistant plants, and order certified virus-free plants by mail whenever possible.

Some gardening books recommend using tobacco or cigarette extracts as a source of nicotine for use in controlling insects. This is a poor idea, since tobacco itself is susceptible to many viral diseases that will readily spread to such plants as peppers, tomatoes, and potatoes.

SOIL-BORNE FUNGI

Certain fungi become active and attack plants when drainage is poor. This problem is particularly severe in warm weather. One destructive disease associated with warm and wet soils in the West is *Armillaria*, or oak-root fungus. If oak-root fungus is a problem, choose resistant species of plants. Edibles known to be resistant include avocado, carob, chestnut (Spanish), fig ('Kadota' and 'Mission'), pear, pecan, persimmon, plum (Japanese), and walnut (California black). The extension service of the University of California can supply a list of resistant plants, ornamentals as well as edibles.

Selected Fungicides and Their Use

The following fungicides are available as of this writing. New materials are continually introduced, others are discontinued, and research sometimes uncovers new problems with old standbys. Keep up with current information as much as is possible.

Some varieties of fruiting plants cannot be grown without spraying for disease control. However, all fungicides are potentially toxic to natural insect enemies and some pose other environmental hazards; they should be used only when a need is proven. The following table of recommended fungicides is offered with some qualifications; take special note of the hazards, precautions, and toxicity level listed for each material.

Recommended Fungicides

NAME[1]	TYPE	LEVEL OF TOXICITY[2]	USE[3]	DISEASE CONTROLLED	HAZARDS AND PRECAUTIONS[4]
Benomyl (Benlate)	Carbamate	Low	D and G	Apple scab, brown rot, anthracnose	Birth defects; toxic to fish; do not graze animals below trees
Bordeaux	Inorganic (copper sulfate and lime)	Very low	D and G	D: brown rot, peach leaf curl, apple scab; G: fireblight, anthracnose, leaf spot	Corrosive to iron or steel—do not mix with other materials except oil
Copper oxide	Inorganic	Moderate	G	Apple scab, brown rot	Toxic to apricots, raspberries, and other copper-sensitive plants; do not graze animals under trees
Copper oxychloride	Inorganic	Low	G	Mildews, brown rot, leaf spot	Corrosive to iron; toxic to fish; apply only to wet foliage
Copper sulfate monohydrate	Inorganic	Very low	G	Fireblight at blossom time, leaf spot	Apply to damp foliage; toxic to fish
(Dikar)	Mixture of maneb, dinocap, and zinc	Very low	G	Apple scab, brown rot, mildews	Birth defects; toxic to fish and grazing animals
Ferbam	Carbamate	Low	G	Apple scab, brown rot, shot hole, anthracnose, mildews	Birth defects, black foliage residue
Folpet (Phaltan)	Phthalimide	Very low	G	Apple scab, mildews, anthracnose, leaf spot, rust	Fetal toxicity, birth defects; injures D'Anjou pears
Lime sulfur	Inorganic	Medium (protect skin)	D	Peach leaf curl, apple scab, mildews, anthracnose	Same as sulfur
Maneb (Dithane M-22 Manzate)	Carbamate	Very low	G	Brown rot, leaf spot, mildews, shot hole, rust	Birth defects
Sulfur	Inorganic	Very low (protect eyes)	G	Brown rot, mildews, apple scab, peach scab; also mites, scales, and thrips	Harmful to apricots, D'Anjou pears, raspberries, and cucurbits; do not apply in hot weather
Zineb (Dithane Z-78)	Carbamate	Low (protect face and skin)	G	Apple scab, mildews, anthracnose, leaf spots	Birth defects

[1]Names in parentheses are trademark names; all others are common names.

[2]Acute oral toxicity

[3]D = Dormant   G = Growing season

[4]Among these fungicides only benomyl has been found teratogenic (causing birth defects) in animal tests. However, I have noted this as a possible hazard with other recommended fungicides since these structurally resemble other teratogenic fungicides or are believed to degrade in cooking to known teratogens. Caution suggests that they not be applied by pregnant women. Careful washing should remove residue to below harmful levels.

Problems with Wildlife

Rabbits and mice can be problems for gardeners. If you suspect these animals of disturbing your young fruit trees, wrap the trunks with the plastic guards made for the purpose or use aluminum foil or chicken wire. With the latter, keep the wire at least 6 inches from the bark.

Gophers and moles are problems in some areas. Plant trees and shrubs in chicken-wire baskets. Make sure the wire sticks out of the ground at least a foot to keep the critters from reaching over the wire. Trapping usually is needed as well. Cats help with all the rodent problems but seldom provide adequate control.

Because of their omnivorous eating habits, squirrels are a serious problem for many gardeners. Nets over the fruit trees sometimes help, but trapping—which could result in squirrel stew—might be the only solution.

In rural areas, deer can cause such severe problems that edible plants cannot be grown without 9-foot fences or a trained dog. You can somewhat control summer deer prob-lems by getting lion manure from a zoo or spreading dried blood or mothballs. In winter, however, the odors of such substances are ineffective, and it is in winter that the deer problems are the most severe.

Such birds as starlings and finches can be major pests of berries and cherries. Dwarf trees and bushes can be effectively covered with black nylon bird netting. Radios playing, aluminum pie pans hung in trees, and scarecrows are somewhat effective, but they should not be used until just before harvest so the birds do not become desensitized to them.

This last section, by necessity, has covered a large number of pests, diseases, and other garden problems. An individual gardener, however, will encounter few such problems in a lifetime of gardening. Good garden planning, good hygiene, and an awareness of major symptoms will keep problems to a minimum and give you many hours to enjoy your garden and feast on its bounty!

7.41. *Children are fascinated by the insect world, and can learn to recognize useful predators such as this mantis.*

PART TWO

AN ENCYCLOPEDIA
OF EDIBLES

EUELL GIBBONS went into the wilds to discover edible plants. I went into my well-stocked pantry to discover which foods I could grow. It is possible that my pantry includes more edible exotica than most, owing to my lifelong interest in cooking, my family's adventurous collective palate, and my inability to resist the blandishments of seed catalogues. Still, with few exceptions, the foods I am concerned with and describe here could be called "domesticated." That is, they have been long used in the cuisine of many cultures. They are not wild edibles such as milkweed, cattails, or acorns.

In this section of the book I have described species of edible or food-bearing plants that both provide delicious food and beautify the home landscape. Selecting plants for aesthetic qualities took some doing, since edible species often come in many varieties, some more decorative than others— they may have showier blossoms, more attractive foliage, or more interesting forms. Few reference books emphasize the beauty inherent in edible plants or direct you to these varieties. Of course, beauty was not the only criterion for my final selection of edibles to be covered here. Flavor and disease resistance are also stressed. With a few exceptions,

sources are noted for most of the varieties mentioned in the encyclopedia.

In compiling this reference section, I systematically examined domesticated edibles with an eye to their place in the landscape. The entries in the encyclopedia were gleaned from a more extensive list of edibles documented in Appendix A. All plants covered in the encyclopedia fall into one of the following categories:

1. Popular, familiar edibles such as apples, oranges, and plums. These were chosen because they are the most loved. People know what they look like and how they taste, but often do not know how to use them in a landscaping situation. As noted earlier, farmers grow food and landscape designers tend to plan for ornamentation only; to combine these functions long seemed forbidden.
2. Common edibles from particular cuisines, often available in foreign food markets or in large suburban produce markets but otherwise difficult to find. Such items as sugar peas, water chestnuts, and Alpine strawberries were largely unknown to our parents, but we have

traveled more and our tastes have grown more sophisticated. We have learned to enjoy these delights from other lands.

3. Newly popular edibles such as kiwi, sugar snap peas, and carob.

4. Edibles that are local favorites—for example, pawpaw in the Midwest, beach plum on the East Coast, and sea grape in Florida. These attractive plants produce foods that have never been commercially grown but are appreciated by local residents. Their territories can and should be expanded for more peoples' pleasure. They are tasty, beautiful, and generally easy to grow. With encroaching subdivisions, lawns, and streets, some of these plants have become endangered, so it is important that they be grown purposefully in peoples' yards.

5. Edibles that are widely grown in some areas but whose bounty often goes unrecognized. Pine trees that develop pine nuts and bamboos that have edible shoots make up this final category. There is much confusion about which species of these plants provide the best food. This confusion can lead to the absurd situation of a gourmet cook going to the store to buy a pound of pine nuts for $20, and then coming home to park under a pine-nut-producing tree. In the case of bamboo, it's common to try to control its traveling ways with poisonous herbicides, but we would do better to control bamboo by harvesting it for our own eating pleasure. Generally, I do not recommend these plants for their edible product: pine trees take too many years to bear; bamboo is usually hard to find, and its rapid growth can present problems. But if these producers are already in your yard, it seems absurd not to eat the delicious, free harvest.

All the encyclopedia entries contain information on how hard a plant is to grow, its growing zones, its uses in the kitchen and the landscape, information on buying and growing it, and usually one or more recipes or suggested methods of preserving it. See the outline of a typical entry, below, for a more detailed explanation.

For uncommon plant materials, I have done some sleuthing work to turn up as much information as possible. For example, some of the data on bamboo had to be translated from a book from the People's Republic of China. Much of the information on bitter melon and ginger comes from a book brought to me by an Indian friend who combed bookstores in Bombay for pertinent material. The material on unusual fruits results from my long-standing interest in rare fruit trees; my membership in societies interested in their culture aided me greatly in obtaining information.

With more common plants, I have chosen not to present the available information in toto. If you can't find here your favorite apple variety, or the worst pest you have on your tomatoes, or a recipe for grape jam, it is because I feel that ample material already exists on these topics. If you need or wish to pursue such matters in detail, consult the books in the bibliography. Also, I encourage you to talk to your neighbors, join local garden societies, get to know your local agricultural agent, and seek assistance from university extension services. They provide much information that is both up-to-date and specific to your area, and it is usually free.

Guidelines for Buying Edibles

Late winter and early spring are the times to buy most edible plants. This is when nurseries offer the greatest variety of deciduous trees and shrubs, bare-root fruit trees, shrubs, vines, and herbaceous perennials. The largest selection of vegetable seed is also available in spring, as are the tender evergreens for mild-winter regions, such as citrus fruits, avocado, and guava.

It is still uncommon for local nurseries to carry a large selection of edible plants, other than the standard vegetable seeds and fruit trees, and when you go looking for more unusual edibles you are likely to encounter some common pitfalls. First, beware of nonfruiting varieties: there are peach trees that don't bear edible peaches and flowering almond trees that don't produce almonds. I once had a student who had moved into a new house. Her neighbor had told her there was a peach tree in her frontyard, so for two years my student watched her tree bloom and waited for the juicy peaches—but none appeared. When she brought a flowering branch to class, I had to give her the sad news that her peach tree was only a flowering peach and would never bear fruit. She looked at me wide-eyed and said, "Why would anyone plant a peach tree that doesn't bear fruit?" Why, indeed! There are flowering plums, crabapples, quince, pomegranates, pears, currants, gooseberries—all flowers, no fruit. As my father would say, "Big noise at the head of the stairs, but no one comes down." Thus, when you shop for edibles, stress the word *edible* and *fruiting*.

Flower-only varieties will not be the only pitfall you will encounter. In the case of carob trees, for example, a tree bought as a seedling may be a male and not bear pods. The usual mulberry tree you find in the nursery is the fruitless form. Again, make sure you are buying a fruiting plant.

To get a predictable product most people buy selected named varieties of fruit trees instead of growing them from seed: 'Concord' grape, say, or an 'Allred' plum. Most of the fruit trees you can buy are grafted varieties (or budded ones, the results of a similar method). These plants are the result of joining together two plants. The bottom of the plant is called the rootstock, and the top is called the scion. (See Figure 7.15.) Grafted or budded fruit trees are used for a number of reasons.

E.1. *Old, spreading apple tree at Sturbridge Village, Massachusetts.*

1. The scion contains genetic material that will guarantee a similar product for every tree, shrub, or vine onto which it is grafted—in other words, a clone. For example, all 'Concord' grapes will be deep purple and have a similar taste; every 'Allred' plum will have red foliage and red plums.
2. Fruits are generally produced a year or two earlier than on nongrafted varieties.
3. Rootstocks can be developed for specific soil conditions, such as heavy clay or sand, or for disease or pest resistance.
4. Grafted plants are usually more economical for nurseries to produce.
5. Grafting certain scions onto known rootstocks can produce a dwarfing effect on the plant. The resultant dwarf trees have a number of advantages over full-size trees (see the sidebar titled "What Size Fruit Tree" under APPLE in the encyclopedia for more on dwarf trees).
6. Grafting is necessary to reproduce members of the plant world that produce no seed, such as some grape, fig, or orange varieties.
7. Some plants are grafted to improve resistance to specific diseases.

Although the use of named, usually grafted, varieties has been emphasized in this book,*for the reasons just enumer-

*Or, in the case of annual fruits and vegetables, hybrids have been stressed. For more on the subject of hybrids, see Appendix B.

ated, growing fruit trees from seed is a viable alternative with most species. The results are fairly reliable; depending on the species, the chance of a seed you plant producing a tree and fruit similar to the parent could be 75–80 percent. (Among the notable exceptions are two well-known edibles, apple and almond; neither produces reliable products from seed.) However, growing fruit trees from seed has some advantages of its own. To summarize:

1. The initial investment for seed is low.
2. Most viruses are not transmitted by seed, so you are less apt to lose a fruit tree to these diseases than with a grafted variety.
3. Often seedling trees adapt better to their environment.
4. A number of species of unusual fruits are available only as seed.
5. If the resultant seedling-grown tree does not have good fruits, you can always graft onto it scion wood that does.
6. One of the strongest reasons for planting fruit trees from seed is to keep the genetic pool strong. The continued production of cloned fruit trees can produce large numbers of trees susceptible to the same diseases, and in addition gives us fewer naturally occurring variations to choose from for breeding material.

Growing your own fruit trees from seed can be a rewarding alternative to using commercially produced plant materials. For more information on the subject join the fruit- and nut-growing societies mentioned in Appendix C.

Further information on acquiring edibles is given in Appendix B and in the individual encyclopedia entries.

A Typical Encyclopedia Entry

Entry Title

Plants are listed alphabetically, generally under their most often used common name. In some cases, alternate common names are given in parentheses. Sometimes, too, the heading is for a compound entry, such as PEACH AND NECTARINE, or for a group of closely related plants, such as the cucurbits (cucumber, squash, and melon). All plants grouped together have similar landscaping uses and growing conditions.

The common names of plants can be confusing: blueberry to you may be huckleberry to me, my okra may be your gumbo, and papaya is often called pawpaw. Because common names can vary regionally, I have included the botanical, or Latin, name in each entry, so there will be no question as to the plant's identity. It is found after the entry title. If the entry title comprises more than one species, the common and botanical names of most or all of them are included.

Botanical names are not always agreed upon, however. I have used the third edition of *Hortus*, the major reference of many American horticulturalists, as the authority for names and spellings. In a few cases, based on other resource material, I have disagreed and used a different botanical name.

The botanical name includes genus, species (and sometimes subspecies), variety or horticultural variety (also known as a clone or cultivar).

A genus is a definable group of plants that are related and share certain characteristics. The genus name is always the first of the Latin names commonly given that constitute a plant's botanical name. The genus name for all pears, for example, is *Pyrus*. As you use the encyclopedia, you will notice that often several seemingly distinct groups of plants will share the same genus name, *e.g.* almonds, peaches, and plums all belong to the genus *Prunus*. Other examples are the genus *Brassica*, which includes mustard, kale, and cabbage; and *Vaccinium*, which includes cranberries and blueberries. Knowing a plant's genus helps you know more about a plant. For example, almonds, peaches, and plums are often bothered by the same pests. Cranberries and blueberries need similar soil acidity and moisture.

The second word in the botanical name indicates its species. Put simply, the species indicates an even closer relationship between plants in the same genus. A particular species of pear, then, would be *Pyrus communis*.

Further differentiation is indicated by the name of a particular variety, horticultural variety, hybrid, or strain. The form most often encountered in this book is the horticultural variety. These are usually choice varieties selected by horticulturists for special qualities, and are designated by single quotation marks, *e.g.* the 'Bartlett' pear. Thus the full botanical name of this pear is *Pyrus communis* 'Bartlett'.

Effort Scale

The degree of effort involved in growing and using edibles varies widely. To keep you from overburdening yourself and to help you have a successful gardening experience, the effort scale has been devised. My experience with students and clients has shown that newcomers to edible gardening sometimes get carried away. Overextension often leads to discouragement, and that is why I have tried to quantify the size of the project you are taking on. The effort scale is designed to eliminate unpleasant surprises—it tells you ahead of time what each plant will require from you in effort, time, and skill.

The effort scale is a simple 1–5 ranking. The ranking assigned to each plant represents the sum of a combination of factors: obtaining the plant; planting, growing, harvesting, and handling it; and processing the product. A ranking of No. 1 indicates that the plant requires minimal effort— perhaps as little as picking the fruit; while a No. 5 was assigned to plants that require both high maintenance and considerable effort to process the product.

Here are a few examples of the variables that affect a plant's effort ranking. If you live where olive trees grow well, you will find them easy to take care of. They have few pests and provide beauty with a minimum of effort. Of course, if you want the tree to develop a certain form, or if you want the wonderfully gnarled trunk to show, some pruning will be required, but basically the olive is simple to grow. The processing of its fruits, on the other hand, is difficult: it requires much harvesting time, usually the use of lye, fermenting the fruits, and canning, or else the pressing and clarifying of olive oil—so the effort for the olive becomes high, and consequently it was assigned a ranking of No. 4. On the other hand, citrus fruit trees take some work in pruning, mulching, fertilizing, watering, and disease control; but the fruits are easy to pick, most varieties do not have to be picked immediately, and are generally eaten fresh. Thus, citrus trees were ranked No. 3 on the effort scale. The ranking for bamboo is mainly determined by yet another tactic: it grows easily—almost too well—and is not bothered by many diseases or pests; however, it is often difficult to find in local nurseries. Its ranking is No. 2. Finally, the pomegranate, which is easy to grow, needs little watering, can be eaten fresh, has no major pests or diseases, and is easy to obtain in the areas where it grows. Hence it was ranked on the scale as No. 1.

The effort scale ranking assumes that you have selected a plant variety appropriate for your area. For example, a quince planted in the warm, humid Southeast will have more diseases than if it were grown in a cool, dry climate. Combating those troubles would obviously result in an increase in effort.

In some entries I have supplied two effort scale rankings for the same plant, indicating that growing requirements differ significantly from region to region or that different types of the same plant are easier to grow than others. However, I have supplied a dual reference only where a discrepancy can be quantified. Two examples will suffice for these dual rankings. Avocados are easier to grow in California (where they are ranked No. 2 on the effort scale) than in Florida (No. 3), where the moist climate leads to diseases not present in the drier heat of California. And *genetic* dwarf peaches (No. 3) are generally easier to grow everywhere than are standard-size peach trees (No. 5).

Finally, it is important to note that the effort scale is approximate and is meant to serve as a guide only. Different households, yards, and climates add to the variables involved.

Zones

The ratings in individual entries correspond to the climatic zone map on page 176, adapted from one compiled by the United States Department of Agriculture. Any map of this kind is only an approximation, since many factors that cannot be represented will influence the microclimate of a particular property.

Each zone on the map corresponds to a temperature range in increments of 10 °F. These 10 ° ranges represent the lowest temperature to which a plant is hardy. For example, a plant designated for zone 4 is hardy above –30 ° to –20 °F, and a zone 7 plant is hardy above 0 ° to 10 °F. Most of the plants in the encyclopedia are designated as growable within a range of several zones. The lowest-numbered zone in the range is a simple measure of the plant's hardiness, but the top end of the range may be determined by any of a number of factors: that the plant needs winter chilling, for instance, or that it does poorly in too much summer heat. The range assigned to gooseberries, for example, is zones 3–8, indicating that they are hardy to zone 3 temperatures but do not do well in zones 9 and 10 because they need winter chilling and dislike long, hot summers.

Again, zone numbers are meant only as rough guides, and further investigation on your part is required to assess a plant's needs. For that reason I urge you to study your yard, talk to your neighbors, question the nurseries of your choice, and check with your local university extension service. The information and experience you can glean in this way can help you decide which plant materials will be successful in your gardening space. In general I have been conservative when assigning zone numbers.

The following list describes some of the factors not reflected in the zone designation that will make a difference in the choice of plants that you can grow:

1. *Wind.* Cold winds are chilling; hot winds are drying. So even though a plant is designated zone 8, if you live in a part of zone 8 where desert conditions prevail—as opposed to a part of zone 8 in the humid Southeast—a plant adapted to humid conditions will need special protection from drying winds or may not grow at all.
2. *Hillsides.* Cold air drains off hillsides and collects at the bottom of a hill. A tree planted at the bottom of a hill in zone 5 could actually be exposed to colder temperatures than a tree planted on the side of a hill in zone 4.
3. *Proximity of water.* Large bodies of water maintain heat in the winter, thereby bringing some warmer air to nearby areas. A garden near a lake or the ocean would be warmer than one farther south but located some distance from a body of water.
4. *Length of summer-heat conditions.* Certain plants need a great deal of heat. For particular areas, this is usually defined in terms of the numbers of hours the location receives temperatures of over 65 °F. The amount of heat required is pertinent to two groups of plants mentioned in the encyclopedia: warm-season annuals, such as peanuts and most melons, and heat-requiring perennials, such as jujube, most citrus, and pistachio. These plants might grow adequately in less than optimum zones but will produce few or inferior fruits and nuts.
5. *Humidity.* The olive exemplifies the effect of humidity. Where the humidity is too high, the tree will grow well but the fruit will not form. Avocados will bear

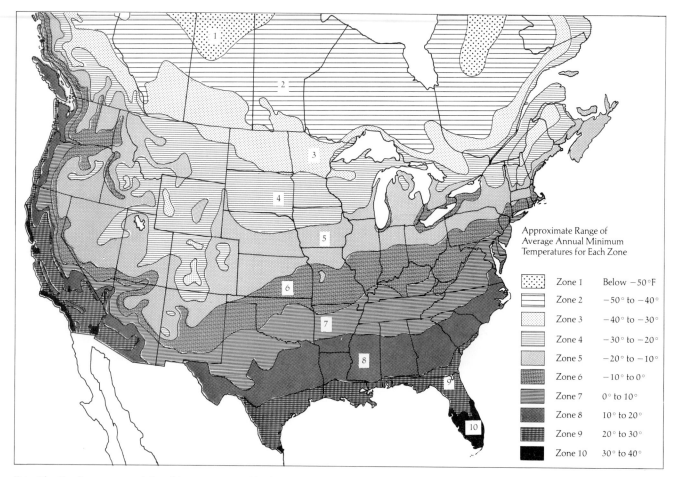

E.2. *Plant hardiness zone map (adapted from map prepared by the U.S. Department of Agriculture).*

Approximate Range of
Average Annual Minimum
Temperatures for Each Zone

	Zone 1	Below −50 °F
	Zone 2	−50° to −40°
	Zone 3	−40° to −30°
	Zone 4	−30° to −20°
	Zone 5	−20° to −10°
	Zone 6	−10° to 0°
	Zone 7	0° to 10°
	Zone 8	10° to 20°
	Zone 9	20° to 30°
	Zone 10	30° to 40°

good fruit but develop many diseases in climates that are moist, while many plants, such as ginger, flourish in humidity.

6. *Length of winter-cold conditions.* Plants that need many hours of winter cold do not do well in many warm, mild-winter southern climates. For example, pears, peaches, and apples require a certain number of hours of temperatures under approximately 45 °F (known as "chilling requirement" or "winter chill factor") before their dormancy will be broken. Mother Nature has some sophisticated survival mechanisms and this is one of them. If an apple tree started blooming or leafed out after a few freakish warm days in December, at the very least it would lose its chance to fruit, and the tree would probably die when winter weather returned. The chilling requirement combats this problem.

Many temperate-zone plants do not grow well in

Southern Florida, Southern California, the Gulf Coast, and the lower elevations of Hawaii. Plant breeders have tried to modify this situation by breeding plants with low chilling requirements for the areas with warmer winters. Varieties of many species now exist that have been developed for different climates—for example, a peach that will grow well in parts of Florida, and another particularly suited to Connecticut. Each has a different chilling requirement. It is imperative that you choose a variety suited for your climate.

7. *High summer-heat conditions.* A different problem involves the intensity of summer heat. Peas, spinach, and plants in the cabbage family, for example, are called cool-season annuals and cannot take high temperatures. Also, certain perennial plants, such as gooseberries, currants, and artichokes, will not thrive in the heat of the most southern latitudes.

Careful study of your property could increase your options. Even though you are in zone 4 on the map, you might have a warm, sheltered spot that would be perfect for a peach tree that is designated hardy only to zone 5. Conversely, you may be in zone 5 on the map but get so much winter wind that a peach tree could not survive. Also, find out the exact composition of your seasons. If you don't have 110 days of summer heat, don't plan to grow peanuts.

Note that only perennial plants have been given a zone number. Annuals are more flexible—their growing season can be extended if they are started indoors and protected from frost—so no zone number is supplied for them. Most can be grown throughout most of the United States. Check with your local weather service to find out the average dates of first and last frosts. In selecting annuals, you need only distinguish between cool-season and warm-season annuals. This information is given under "How to Grow" in each entry.

Thumbnail Sketch

Each entry begins with a brief sketch to allow you to see quickly the pertinent landscaping features and possibilities of each plant. This sketch will prove particularly useful when you are selecting your plant materials.

How to Use

In the Kitchen

A number of the plants included in the encyclopedia are somewhat unusual, so a brief description of each plant's edible portion has been given as well as suggestions for serving. For common edibles, a wide range of uses is indicated.

In the Landscape

In this section the plant or plants are briefly described and their landscaping uses detailed. These suggested uses are based on the landscaping principles, definitions, and techniques discussed in Chapters 3–6.

Caution: In many cases, I have suggested ways of combining plants, including inedible species. If a plant is not on the list in Appendix A, consider it inedible until you have given it much extra study.

How to Grow

Here I have supplemented material found in Chapter 7. Pertinent facts are supplied that will enable you to grow relatively simple annual food crops and perennial herbs. The more complicated work of growing demanding annuals and perennials, including woody shrubs and trees, is covered in an outline format, in which information on climate, exposure, soil, fertilizing, watering, pruning, pests and diseases, and harvesting can be quickly researched. Sometimes special material is featured, such as the planting techniques for asparagus, a list of the souces for "antique" varieties of apples, or discussions of dwarf trees under the entries for Apple and Peach and Nectarine.

Climate

The broad subject of climate is discussed in the zones section. Under "Climate" appears specific information on the weather limitations of individual plants, as well as information on where they grow best.

Exposure

Most edible plants require full sun. Some plants can grow in filtered sun, though, and an occasional plant requires shade. All instances are noted.

Soil

Under the "Soil" heading, soil pH and salinity are covered wherever they are factors that need to be considered for the successful growing of a particular plant. Special drainage needs are also noted here. A more general discussion of soil is found in Chapter 7.

Fertilizing

The fertilizing requirements of individual plants are briefly described. Where mulching is especially helpful, this fact is noted. A general discussion of fertilizing is found in Chapter 7.

Watering

Watering needs specific to each entry are handled in this section. These needs are more critical in arid and hot parts of the country, but during drought years this information is relevant nationwide. I recommend using plants with the lowest water requirements wherever possible. Chapter 4 gives general information on watering wisely and Chapter 7 covers principles and techniques of water conservation.

Pruning

To supplement the basic pruning information in Chapter 7, specific pruning needs of particular plants are noted here and diagrams are supplied where necessary. Pruning is a complicated subject; for pruning most of the major fruit trees I urge you to use one of the books on the subject listed in the bibliography.

Pests and Diseases

Specific pests affecting particular plants as well as suggested solutions, if not included in Chapter 7, are covered here. Drawings of the common pests, along with suggestions for their control, are provided in Chapter 7.

Harvesting

This subject is self-explanatory. Where possible, estimated yield ranges for mature standard-size trees or shrubs are given.

How to Purchase

Edible plants can be purchased as seeds, in containers, as bare-root plants, or balled and burlapped. Under the subheading "Forms and Sources" I have listed the most common forms for each entry as well as sources where the plant is available. The sources noted here—indicated by a bold-face number—are usually mail-order houses, whose full names and addresses are listed in Appendix B. In the "How to Purchase" section, the source number usually appears by the plant name or the plant description under the subheading "Varieties." Certain sources sell only one edible mentioned in this book.

Whenever possible, buy your edible plants locally. Your local nurseries know what grows best in your area. When mail-ordering fruit trees it is particularly important that you choose a source as close as possible to where you live. Fruit trees are bred and grafted onto rootstocks that are appropriate for certain soil types, weather, and disease and pest resistance. Only if you cannot find what you want from a local source should you consider ordering from distant sources. Do your homework well.

Before ordering plants from a mail-order nursery or the recommended sources, read the information these places supply on how to order, what they promise from their materials, their shipping dates, and their guarantees. These specifications are discussed further in Appendix B.

Pollinators

To bear fruits, many plants must be cross-pollinated (see glossary). Other plants will bear only a small crop unless they are cross-pollinated. And some plants need no cross-pollination at all. The latter are referred to as self-pollinating, self-fertile, or self-fruitful. When fruit is not involved, as when the leaves or the stalk are the edible parts, pollination is not a factor.

"Pollinators" falls within the "How to Purchase" section because at the time of purchase you need to know the pollination limitations. Where cross-pollination is required, you'll want to purchase a companion pollinating tree or shrub along with your original selection. In entries where pollination is not required, it usually is not mentioned.

Occasionally you will be fortunate enough to find an appropriate pollinator in a neighbor's yard. As a general rule, it is safe to assume that if you can see this potential pollinator from the proposed location of your new tree or shrub, it is close enough for effective pollination to occur.

Preserving and Preparing

In all encyclopedia entries, methods of preservation are recommended and described, with special emphasis on edibles that yield plentiful harvests. Basically, these are ways to put away some summer sun for winter pleasure. Food drying in particular is a preserving method that should be practiced more. The APRICOT entry contains basic information on food drying. The CRANBERRY entry contains information on making fruit leather. In the KIWI entry you'll find information on how to make jelly without added pectin. And the BASIL entry describes how to dry herbs.

One of the problems with growing edibles is that you often wind up with an overabundance of one particular food. Preserving is one answer, but other solutions exist as well. One of the best is instituting a barter system among friends and neighbors. I use this system extensively. In fact, I once had a marvelous mailman who streamlined the process and acted as an efficient distributor. While he completed his route he kept an eye on what was available. After work he would gather and redistribute the bounty. One day it would be young tomato plants, another day guava jelly or pears. Bartering works well and can be very enjoyable. Another solution for large harvests is creative cooking. In some encyclopedia entries I have included my favorite recipes for large harvests.

Beyond the Encyclopedia

The plants detailed in the encyclopedia are, of course, not the only edible plants that can be used in a landscape. Appendix A is a list of more than two hundred edible plants. Some of those listed can be used in a landscape, though others are best grown in a vegetable garden. This comprehensive list includes, where applicable, zones, sources, and part eaten, and briefly notes on the plant's landscaping value, if any. To aid you in selecting plants for your yard, the items in the encyclopedia are included in the appendix, marked with asterisks.

Almond

Prunus dulcis var. *dulcis*

Effort Scale

NO. 2
Vulnerable to some pests, including squirrels and blue jays
Large harvest on standard size trees

Zones

6–9

Thumbnail Sketch

Deciduous tree
Standard, 20–30 ft. tall; semidwarf varieties, 8–20 ft. tall;
   dwarf variety to 8 ft. tall
Propagated by grafting or budding
Needs full sun
Leaves are bright green, narrow, to 3 in. long
Blooms in early spring
Flowers are profuse, white or pink
Nuts are edible; harvested in summer
Used as street tree, accent plant, interest plant, screen, patio
   tree; dwarf variety used in containers and as large shrub

How to Use

In the Kitchen

The almond is a versatile nut, popular with most people. It's delicious for eating out of hand, roasted or raw. Roasted almonds, either slivered or chopped, make a great addition to casseroles, vegetables, and meats, and almonds in many forms give flavor and texture to candies and pastries. Amandine is haute cuisine!

In the Landscape

This deciduous tree is 20–30 feet tall, and its spread can be as wide. The dwarf and semidwarf varieties are 8–20 feet tall. The almond's bloom is white or pink, 1½ inches wide, grows in large clusters, and appears before the narrow, shiny, bright-green leaves develop. The tree has many uses in the landscape. An almond tree in bloom is one of the showiest flowering trees for early spring and makes an excellent accent or interest plant. One variety, 'Hall's Hardy', has fragrant, pink blossoms and comes in both a standard and a dwarf size. The almond tree in leaf has a lacy appearance since the narrow leaves do not form a solid mass. Mature trees can be used as street trees, small shade trees, or patio trees. They line a driveway handsomely and of course can always be used in a backyard orchard. The dwarf varieties do well in containers and can be used as shrubs.

How to Grow

Climate

Most varieties grow best where there are no spring frosts in March or April. The trees are quite hardy, but their blossoms come early and thus can be nipped by a frost. Almonds do not like cool summers or high humidity. 'Hall's Hardy' is as hardy as most peaches.

Exposure

Almond trees need full sun.

Soil

Trees will tolerate a variety of soils if they are well drained.

Fertilizing

Almonds respond well to compost mulches added annually. See Chapter 7 for information on fertilizing common fruit and nut trees.

Watering

Trees are drought resistant once they are established. In rainy climates they need no extra watering. In arid climates they respond well to an occasional deep watering.

E.3. *Almond tree in bloom. A floating deck has been constructed around the base to use for relaxation.*

Pruning

Prune only enough to shape and remove dead wood.

Pests and Diseases

Almonds are susceptible to some of the problems that affect peaches, but not as often or as seriously. (see PEACHES). Spider mites are the most serious problem in the West, but squirrels and jays are the biggest pests nationwide.

Harvesting

Beat the squirrels! Harvest the nuts off the tree when the shells split. A mature standard-size tree will yield about 20–25 pounds of nuts annually.

How to Purchase

Forms and Sources

Named varieties are available at local nurseries and from many mail-order firms in bare-root form in late winter or early spring and often in 5-gallon containers in summer.

Pollinators

Most standard almond trees need cross-pollination. Plant more than one variety, and be careful to choose those that pollinate each other well. If space is too limited for two full-size trees planted separately, plant more than one variety in the same hole, choose a self-fertile variety, use a dwarf variety for the pollinator, or plant dwarf trees.

Varieties

'All-in-One'—sweet nut; very large, showy white flowers; self-fertile; semidwarf; quite hardy; will pollinate 'Texas' and 'Nonpareil.' (**71**)

'Garden Prince'—medium-sized nut, showy pink flowers; self-fertile; genetic dwarf to 8 ft.; new variety, so pollinating capabilities not yet known. (**71**)

'Hall's Hardy'—hard-shell nut; pink flowers; blooms late; partially self-fertile, better yield with 'Texas'. 'Hall's' is the hardiest almond variety (**Readily Available**). Dwarf 'Hall's Hardy' occasionally available.

'Ne Plus Ultra'—large nuts; white flowers; needs pollinator, is often planted as pollinator for 'Nonpareil' and is pollinated by 'Nonpareil'. (**Readily Available**)

'Nonpareil'—best nut available; widely grown; white flowers; needs pollinator, usually 'Ne Plus Ultra'; 'Jordanolo' will also do. (**Readily Available**)

'Texas' ('Mission')—small nut; white flowers; good for cold winter areas; needs a pollinator: 'Nonpareil' or 'Hall's'. (**10, 24, 71**)

Preserving and Preparing

Almonds, like pistachios, filberts, and other nuts, have both a fleshy outside hull and an inside shell that contains the kernel. Nuts piled together with the hulls on tend to rot, so when you do the primary drying, spread the nuts out in a single layer. Dry almonds in hulls for a day or two, then after removing the hulls, dry in the sun for another week. Store in a dry, cool place.

Praline Dip

½ cup sugar   ½ teaspoon almond extract
2 tablespoons water   ½ cup toasted almonds

Caramelize the sugar with the water and almond extract. Boil until the mixture is deep brown, approximately 3 or 4 minutes. When sugar is caramelized, add ½ cup toasted almonds and bring mixture back to boil. Remove from heat and pour onto an oiled cookie sheet. When cold, break into pieces and pulverize in the blender.

This exciting confection can be used as a dip for home-grown fruits, as a lining for ice cream and pudding molds, and as a topping for cakes and cookies.

ALPINE STRAWBERRY. See *Strawberry*.

AMERICAN ELDERBERRY. See *Elderberry*.

AMERICAN GOOSEBERRY. See *Currant* and *Gooseberry*.

AMERICAN GRAPE. See *Grape*.

Apple and Crabapple

Malus species

Effort Scale

NO. 4 for most varieties
Pests and diseases are major problems, particularly in wet-summer areas (some varieties are more resistant than others)
Fertilizing and mulching necessary
Picking up fruits necessary
Standard-size tree yields large harvest

NO. 3 for disease-resistant varieties and dwarf varieties of apple

Zones

3–9

E.4. 'Gravenstein' apples, a popular variety for cooking.

E.5. *Like many fruit trees, apples can be pruned to create a hedge.*

Thumbnail Sketch

Deciduous tree
Standard, 20–30 ft. tall; semidwarf varieties, 12–18 ft. tall;
    dwarf varieties, 6–12 ft. tall
Propagated by grafting, budding, or from cuttings
Needs full sun
Leaves are soft green, 2–3 in. long; new growth is woolly
Blooms in spring
Flowers are white or pink
Fruits are edible; harvest in summer or fall
Used as interest tree, patio tree, small shade tree, espalier,
    hedge; dwarf varieties used in containers

How to Use

In the Kitchen

The familiar apple is a fruit to eat out of hand in lunches or as that famous snack that keeps the doctor away. Cooked apples can become a sauce that, when canned, provides a touch of freshness in winter. Baked apples with hard sauce (butter, sugar, and brandy) are sublime treats to the initiated, and dried apples are popular among campers and backpackers. The many varieties of apple butter make delicious spreads, and a layer of clear, subtly colored apple jelly is equally delectable on bread. Fermented cider kept our forebears happy, and, of course, apple pie is the great American dish. The apple is one of our true blessings.

The crabapple is used less as a raw fruit, although its tangy flavor is appealing, and it makes an even more beautiful jelly than the apple. When the whole fruit is pickled it becomes an attractive garnish for any plate. Crabapples and apples are often used as a pectin source.

Note: Not all crabapples produce usable fruits. Be sure you have chosen a tasty variety such as 'Transcendent'.

In the Landscape

The apple, a deciduous tree, is not only productive but also provides a dazzling show in the spring. The profuse pink buds develop into white flowers up to 1½ inches wide. One variety, 'Stark Red Bouquet Delicious' (**58**), has pink blossoms. The leaves of most apples are a soft medium green, and a gray fuzz on the back side of the leaves gives the new growth a gray tone. As the apples develop they become a decorative asset, whether they stay green or turn yellow or red.

Crabapples are even showier in the spring. Their buds are pinker than those of apples, their blossoms rosier, and their fruits are usually more colorful. In other respects crabapple trees are similar to apples.

Apple trees come in more different sizes than any other fruit tree. Standard trees grow as high as 30 feet, whereas dwarf or semidwarf varieties reach 6–18 feet. The smaller forms are usable in decorative containers, as espaliers, and as fruitful hedges.

Full-size crabapple trees are usually shorter than apples but standard-size trees are excellent shade trees. Both species form stately yet informal lines along a driveway, and because of their consistent beauty they are useful as interest plants. As with other fruit trees, neither type should be planted in a lawn, because both will compete for the lawn nutrients and water. Also, mowers are likely to nick trees so placed, giving problem diseases and insects a foothold. Finally, in the arid West, lawns stay moist near the crowns of trees, enabling the fungus causing crownrot to develop.

Note: Do not use apple trees near windows if apple scab and codling moth are severe problems. The sprays for controlling these conditions are usually difficult to clean off the glass.

How to Grow

Climate

Apples and crabapples are the hardiest of our popular fruits. A few varieties survive −40 °F, but most are not that stout hearted.

Both trees grow throughout most of the country except in areas with the warmest winters, where there is little or no winter frost.

E.6. *Dwarf and semidwarf apple trees will grow well in large containers.*

All varieties have some chilling requirements; that is, they require a certain number of hours under 45 °F before dormancy is broken and good fruit can be produced. In mild-winter areas choose varieties with low chilling requirements.

Exposure

To grow the sweetest fruit and to prevent diseases both trees should be planted in full sun.

Soil

Both apple and crabapple trees grow best in well-drained garden loam supplemented with an organic mulch.

Fertilizing

Nutrients need to be renewed annually. See Chapter 7 for details. Both trees benefit from annual applications of compost or manure.

Watering

In climates that have summer rain, well-established trees do not need watering. In dry-summer areas, deep watering is generally needed.

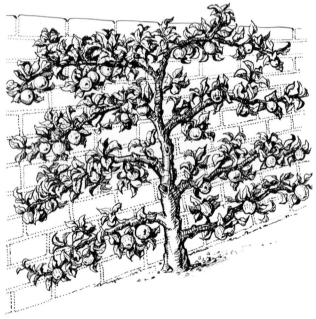

E.7. Apple trees can be espaliered in many different forms. (See Chapter 5.)

Pruning

For young trees, see Chapter 7, PRUNING. An established apple or crabapple tree needs only light pruning. Both species fruit on long-lived fruiting spurs. Prune when dormant to cut out weak growth and dead or crossing branches and to control the height for easy fruit picking. If you are having a mildew problem, thin out some of the branches to improve air circulation. Drooping branches on older trees should be cut back to prevent them from shading too much of the lower foliage.

Pests and Diseases

Apples and crabapples are prone to many pests and diseases. The most serious are codling moth, apple maggot, San Jose scale, apple scab, mildew, and fire blight. Dormant spraying is needed in most parts of the country. See Chapter 7.

Harvesting

Pick apples and crabapples carefully to prevent bruising. The fruits of a few winter storage types should be picked slightly underripe, but all other varieties should be harvested when fruits are fully ripe. Quality of ripe fruits left on the tree declines quickly.

A mature standard apple tree yields about 15–20 bushels; a mature dwarf tree yields about 1–2 bushels.

How to Purchase

Forms and Sources

Purchase trees bare root or in containers from local nurseries and mail-order houses. Some nurseries have large selections of unusual, "antique" or new apple varieties. You may want to send to the following for catalogues:

New York State Fruit
  Testing Cooperative
  Association
Geneva, NY 14456

Lawson's Nursery
Route 1, Box 294
Ball Ground, GA 30107

Suter's Apple Nursery
(sells scion wood only)
3220 Silverado Trail
St. Helena, CA 94574

C. D. Schwartze Nursery
2302 Tacoma Road
Puyallup, WA 98731

Pollinators

Most varieties of apples need a pollinator; most crabapples are self-pollinating. Self-pollinating types bear more heavily if other varieties are around.

Varieties

Only a few varieties of crabapples are grown for fruit, but hundreds of types of apples exist, all of them long-lived. Choosing one kind is often like playing roulette. There are apples suitable for severe or warm winters, apples that fruit early or ripen late, and apples resistant to some of the major diseases. Dwarf, middle-, and full-sized trees are available. Hybridizers have made many improvements to help the orchardist. Home growers can take advantage of these improvements in seeking the perfect tree for local conditions.

Before making your choice, gather as much information as possible. Consult your local university extension service and do research at your library. Organizations exist that are interested in sharing their fruit-growing experiences, particularly when it comes to apples. Often these groups also can provide budwood for some of the "antique" apple varieties. Members of such organizations are interested in preserving living wood of hundreds of old-time varieties whose valuable genes would otherwise be lost. Examples of these organizations are the North American Fruit Explorers, the Home Orchard Society, and the Worcester County Horticultural Society.

BEST APPLE VARIETIES

The trees in this list have been selected because the quality of their fruit and the strength of their disease resistance are high and because they are available in different sizes. Varieties are included that will grow in each of the geographical areas.

'Anna'—superior apple for low-chill parts of California and Florida; light green, crisp, and sweet; needs a pollinizer. (**58, 71**)

'Baldwin'—red fruits; older variety; short harvest season; good winter keeper; one of the varieties most resistant to apple scab and fire blight. (**6, 46, 57**)

'Delicious'—popular red apple with characteristic knobs at base; many offspring; midseason fruiting; susceptible to apple scab but some of its offspring more resistant. (**Readily Available**)

'Garden Delicious'—gold fruits with red blush; genetic dwarf 4–6 feet tall; late-summer fruiting; new variety. (**24, 60, 71**)

'Golden Delicious'—yellow fruits; great eating and cooking; self-fruitful in many areas; good pollinator; very adaptable; fall fruiting; somewhat resistant to apple scab. (**Readily Available**)

'Granny Smith'—yellow and green fruits; low chilling requirement; for southern California and Florida. (**1, 6, 57, 71**)

'Gravenstein'—green to yellow or light green and red striped fruits; very vigorous tree; widely grown; summer fruiting; world's best applesauce and pie. (**Readily Available**)

'Haralson'—red fruits; good flavor; late fall fruiting; stores well; grows in coldest Midwest areas. (**Readily Available**)

What Size Fruit Tree?

Just think of the glories of growing dwarf and semi-dwarf fruit trees in your yard. First, you'll have the sheer beauty of the blossoms to enjoy in the spring. Then, in summer and fall, you'll have the full-size, tree-ripened, easy-to-pick fruits. You might have a dwarf apricot, a dwarf peach, and a dwarf apple in place of one standard-size tree. The three would make for good and varied eating over a long period.

The harvest of most dwarf or semidwarf trees is plentiful but not overwhelming. You would have fruit for preserving, but not in such a quantity that you would be forced to give over much time to canning, freezing, or drying, as with the yield of a standard-size tree. Furthermore, dwarf or semidwarf trees are easier to spray, prune, and harvest than standard trees, and on the average they bear fruit two to three years earlier. Finally, their size makes them feasible for even the smallest yards.

The practice of dwarfing fruit trees has been going on for a long time, but it wasn't until 1900 that two horticultural research stations in England, in Malling and Merton, put some order into the process. Apple-tree root stock was sorted, identified, and classified at these stations, and a Malling-Merton (M or MM) number came to have a definite meaning. For example, an M #9 is a tree that grows to 6–9 feet; an M #7 is a semidwarf that grows to 12–15 feet. The M or MM number is still part of the name on many of these small apple trees. (There is no correlation between the M number and height.) Other dwarf fruit trees use different root stocks. Pear is sometimes grafted onto quince root stock. Peaches, plums, and apricots are usually grafted onto other species such as *Prunus Besseyi, P. cerasifera,* or *P. armeniaca.*

Using dwarfing root stock simply makes the tree smaller; the fruits will be the same as on a standard-size tree. If there is a disadvantage to dwarf trees it is that they are reputed to be somewhat shorter-lived than the standard trees. Also, the M #9 and #26 root stocks, both in common use, have shallow root systems, so the trees should be staked.

Genetic dwarf fruit trees are different from regular dwarf trees. They are naturally dwarfed but are still grafted for propagation purposes. See PEACHES for more information on genetic dwarf trees.

E.8. Four sizes of apple trees. From left to right: an 8-foot tree on M#9 root stock; a 12-foot tree on M#26; a 15-foot tree on M#7; and a full-grown standard-size apple tree, 25 feet tall.

'Jonathan'—red fruits; sprightly flavor; fall fruiting; best in cold climates; somewhat resistant to apple scab but quite prone to fire blight. (**Readily Available**)

'Liberty'—red fruits, sweet, one of the most disease-resistant apples available. Resists apple scab, fire blight, and mildew. (**6, 37, 46**)

'McIntosh'—red and green fruits; snappy flavor; tender flesh; stores poorly; late summer fruiting; quite susceptible to apple scab; has many improved offspring; grows well on East Coast and in cold areas. (**Readily Available**)

'Newtown Pippin'—green fruits; good eating; excellent cooking; late-season fruiting; grows over wide range. (**Readily Available**)

'Northern Spy'—red fruits; good for pies; slow to bear; quite susceptible to apple scab but resistant to fire blight; short harvest season; favorite on East Coast in cold areas. (**Readily Available**)

'Prima'—red and yellow fruits; good eating and cooking; mildew and fire blight resistant and scab immune; new variety. (**6, 30, 58**)

'Priscilla'—red and yellow fruits; dessert type; good pollinator for 'Prima'; new variety; scab and fire blight resistant. (**6, 30, 58**)

'Winter Banana'—yellow fruits; midseason fruiting; susceptible to apple scab; for mildest areas; all right for arid West since scab not a problem in dry areas. (**6, 46, 71**)

BEST CRABAPPLE VARIETIES

'Dolgo'—red, tart fruits; delicious for spiced jelly; extremely hardy to zone 3 and disease-resistant; beautiful white flowers; good pollinator for apples; heavy bearer. (**43, 46**)

'Transcendent'—yellow fruits with red cheeks; good for most areas. (**24, 62, 71**)

Preserving

Apple varieties differ as to ripening time. The summer apples do not usually store well and must be dried or made into applesauce. Some varieties are just for eating raw and are not good when preserved.

An old New England method is to wrap apples individually in newspaper, pack in barrels, and store in a cool place. Use only varieties designated as "winter apples" or good "keepers" for this purpose; late fall varieties are usually the best. The so-called winter apples are picked when not quite ripe and are allowed to ripen slowly in a dark, cool place.

Apples can be canned, frozen, dried, made into apple butter, cider, hard cider, vinegar, chutney, apple leather, or apple jelly.

Apricot

Prunus Armeniaca

Effort Scale

NO. 4
Mulching necessary
Susceptible to diseases and pests
Soft fruit ripens all at once
Large harvest
Pruning necessary

Zones

5–9, for most varieties

Thumbnail Sketch

Deciduous tree
Standard, 20–25 ft. tall; semidwarf varieties, 12–15 ft. tall; dwarf varieties, 4–8 ft. tall
Propagated by grafting, budding, or from cuttings
Needs full sun
Leaves are rich green, oval, 2–3 in. long; new growth is bronzy
Blooms in early spring
Flowers are white or pink, 1 in. across
Fruits are edible; usually harvested in July
Used as interest tree, small shade tree, espalier; dwarf varieties used as foundation shrub, and in containers

How to Use

In the Kitchen

Apricots are 2–3 inch long peachlike fruits, though they are smaller and smoother than peaches and have their own glorious, yellow-orange color, often tinged with red. Tree-ripened apricots are delicious raw, stewed, canned, dried, in preserves and jams, or made into nectar.

In the Landscape

This small- to medium-sized deciduous tree can grow as wide as it is tall, 20–25 feet. Most varieties have popcorn-white blossoms which contrast sharply with its almost black bark, making it an excellent interest plant. As they develop, the leaves are bronzy; as they mature they become deep green, and in the fall most varieties turn brilliant yellow. The fruits themselves are decorative. The apricot tree is, indeed, interesting in all seasons. Older trees tend to develop gnarled shapes, and even without foliage or flowers make a definite impact on the landscape.

To produce the best fruit, the tree must be heavily pruned. Unpruned trees produce many blossoms and numerous very small fruits. Many of the flowers are removed in such pruning; thus, one of the ornamental qualities of the tree is sacrificed for good production. Hand-thinning fruits reduces the need for severe pruning.

Full-size apricot trees are useful as small shade trees and are handsome when espaliered. Resist the temptation to plant them in a lawn. Like most fruit trees, they never live up to their potential in a lawn. Dwarf varieties are excellent in containers, as hedges, and as foundation plants. The hardy pink-flowered Manchurian varieties (**29, 39**) make useful shrubs in the coldest climates.

E.9. With age, apricot trees often take on gnarled shapes. A mulch is used to keep the roots cool in summer.

The luscious fruits are an extra bonus when you consider the beauty of the tree itself, but fruit dropping can be a nuisance over a patio or near a sidewalk. Therefore it is best to plant full-size apricot trees away from those areas.

How to Grow

Climate

Apricots are as hardy as peaches, but they bloom early so they do not fruit well where there are late frosts. New varieties that bloom later are being introduced. These would be worth a try in protected parts of zone 4; also a possibility in those regions is the hardy Manchurian apricot. Also in zones 4 and 5 try the dwarf varieties in movable containers, sheltering them during the coldest part of the winter and during late frosts. All apricots have a chilling requirement, but those with low chilling requirements are suitable in mild-winter areas. No apricots grow in the warmest winter areas.

Exposure

Apricot trees require full sun.

Soil

Apricots tolerate a variety of soils as long as they are well drained.

Fertilizing

Compost is beneficial in the spring and fall. Avoid overfeeding; it causes weak growth susceptible to splitting and diseases.

Watering

Occasional deep watering is needed in dry summer areas. Be particularly careful not to overwater on heavy soils.

Pruning

Apricots bear on fruiting spurs that live for three or four years. Annual pruning is needed to force new growth. The genetic dwarf apricots need less severe pruning. Follow the same procedure as with peaches, but prune less radically. Thin fruit if the fruit-set is very heavy.

Pests and Diseases

Apricot trees are susceptible to many pests and diseases. A dormant spray of oil or Bordeaux in spring is usually necessary to prevent scale, brown rot, and bacterial leaf spot. Good fall sanitation is a must. Destroy all old fruit and leaves in which disease organisms winter over. See Chapter 7 for details.

Harvesting

Mature standard trees yield about 3–4 bushels annually; dwarf varieties about 1–2 bushels. Fruit is ready to be picked when slightly soft and fully colored. Try not to leave town during the short harvest season or you will return to find 50 pounds of fruit rotting on the ground!

How to Purchase

Forms and Sources

Apricots are purchased bare root in late winter or early spring or in containers through summer. They are readily available from mail-order firms and local nurseries in favorable climates.

Pollinators

Most varieties bear heaviest with cross-pollination.

Varieties

Taste differs less among apricot varieties than with most fruits. The major differences lie in levels of hardiness, blooming time, and winter-chilling requirements. New varieties are being tested for resistance to brown rot and bacterial leaf spot but are not readily available. 'Harcot' and 'Harogem' are two possibilities from the New York State Fruit Testing Station. Research is being done continually to improve the genetic dwarfs, so keep an eye out for the newest introductions. Check with your local university extension service to see which varieties grow best in your area.

The following varieties are recommended:

'Blenheim' ('Royal')—most popular variety on the West Coast. (**Readily Available**)
'Curtis'—quite hardy; dwarf or standard available. (**18**)
'Early Golden'—good for mild winters; needs little chilling. (Dwarf, **28**; standard, **6, 62**)
'Garden Annie'—genetic dwarf, 8–10 ft. tall; ornamental plant. (**71**)
'Goldcot'—dwarf or standard; quite hardy. (**Readily Available**)
'Moongold'—one of the hardiest; should be planted with 'Sungold' for pollination. (**Readily Available**)
'Moorpark'—well suited for the West Coast; one of the most successful varieties for the Southeast. (Dwarf, **28**; standard, **Readily Available**)
'Newcastle'—good for mild climates; needs little winter chilling. (**14**)
'Stark Sweetheart'—the only variety with edible kernels; all other varieties have poisonous kernels. (**58**)

Drying Fruit

The easiest, and the most environmentally sound, way to preserve fruits is to dry them. Drying uses much less fossil fuel than does canning or freezing; it's a solar method. The sun is there and it's free, so let's use it. Other advantages of drying over alternative methods are its relative cheapness and the comparatively small storage space required by the finished product. I suggest preparing small packets of dried fruits. These can be flattened out for storage and can serve as a single meal's offering. Once large packets are opened, air and moisture can enter, causing fruits to become moldy. Small packets are excellent for schoolchildren, backpackers, campers, and bicyclists, since the dried fruit is lightweight, rich in vitamins, and full of goodness.

If you live in a damp, cool climate where hot sun is not readily or consistently available, a food dehydrator is a good investment. It uses less energy than an oven, is compact, and can be used for all your food drying needs, not just for fruits. You can dry fruits in an oven, but not in a microwave oven. The latter takes too long and is too small for any kind of a decent-size harvest.

The drying instructions below apply to apricots as well as most other fruits—apples, nectarines, peaches, and pears. Apricots don't need peeling, but apples, peaches, and pears usually do. Remember that apples and pears must be cored before they are dried and pears are usually picked when they are underripe and allowed to ripen in the house.

All the fruits mentioned turn brown when exposed to the air. If the discoloration doesn't bother you, it is a simple matter to dry the fruits after sectioning, pitting, or coring. However, if you prefer orange apricots, nectarines, and peaches and white apples and pears, methods exist for maintaining fresh-fruit color: blanching fruits for 3 minutes in boiling water; soaking fruit in a sodium metabisulfite solution for 1 minute; or sulfuring the fruit with sulfur smoke. The last two methods preserve more of the color and more of the vitamins than the first. They also kill any insects that might still be on the fruit. Ultimately, the choice of method is a personal one. Despite my prejudices against most chemicals, I find that fruits treated with sulfur taste and look better than blanched or untreated fruits, so I offer these methods as alternatives.

Sodium metabisulfate is available in crystalline form at some local canning supply stores, or from AMBIT Enterprises, P.O. Box 1790, Chula Vista, CA 92012. Directions for drying come with the crystals.

The process involves making a solution and dipping the fruits.

To sulfur apricots, place them cup side up in trays made from plywood or recycle the 17 x 13 inch size fruit lugs. You may also use small, wooden, nursery flats. (See Figure E.9) Elevate one tray with stacked bricks so it is 10 inches above the ground, then stack two or three trays on top, with blocks between them so there is good air circulation. Place a cup of sulfur (available from a drugstore or a nursery supply house) in a tin pie plate under the bottom tray. The 10-inch space will keep it from catching fire. Light the sulfur with a rolled-up paper wick. Cover the trays with a large cardboard box, at least 2 x 3 feet, and let the apricots sulfur for at least four hours or overnight.

Caution: Sulfur fumes are poisonous! Do the sulfuring a safe distance from the house, and keep children away.

After at least four hours, remove the trays and place them in the sun. Drying takes between six and ten days, depending on the weather. If rain is imminent, take the trays inside. Sulfured fruits may also be dried in a food dryer.

Store thoroughly dry fruits in an airtight container. I use plastic bags with self-closing tops. Squeeze out all the air before closing.

When you are ready to use the dried apricots, pour boiling water over them. This washes them and plumps them up so they are ready to use in cookies, pies, and meat stuffings—money in the cupboard, again.

E.10. When drying apricots, place them close together with the cup side up to preserve the juices.

'Sungold'—one of the hardiest; should be planted with 'Moongold' for pollination; has pink blossoms. (**20, 28, 33, 43**)

Preserving and Preparing

My home is situated in what was once a magnificent apricot orchard, and three venerable trees are left in my yard. My friends and neighbors know this versatile fruit intimately and have collected many wonderful ways to use it.

If you have an apricot tree, I highly recommend the booklet *A Harvest of Apricot Recipes,* obtainable from The Los Altos Quota Club, P.O. Box 731, Los Altos, CA 94022. Include $2.25 for tax and handling. The booklet contains 130 apricot recipes for nectar, cookies, cakes, candy, pies, and instructions for drying, canning, and freezing apricots.

Apricot Brandy

1¼ pounds rock candy   ½ gallon inexpensive vodka
1¼ pounds dried apricots

Place all ingredients in a glass gallon jar (obtainable from a local restaurant; maraschino cherries and mayonnaise come in this type of jar). Close lid tightly; if the lid is metal place plastic wrap on top of the jar before closing to prevent the metal from coming in contact with the brandy. Brandy will keep well for a year.

Wait at least two months before using, though three months would be better. Decant brandy into bottles with lids. Remove candy strings from the mixture.

Store the brandied apricots in a wide-mouth jar. Seal well.

Use these brandied apricots for fruit cake, nut bread, or in the following recipe.

Maureen's Apricot Trifle

½ cup stewed brandied apricots, cut into pieces
1 envelope boiled-custard mix such as Bird's Dessert Powder (or 1 recipe of boiled custard)
2 tablespoons sugar

1 3-ounce package of lady-fingers
½ cup apricot brandy
½ pint heavy cream
1 tablespoon sugar
1 teaspoon vanilla

Cover brandied apricots with boiling water. Add the 2 tablespoons of sugar and stew until soft.

Make custard according to directions.

Sprinkle ladyfingers with the apricot brandy and place half of them in the bottom of a trifle bowl or clear glass 2-quart bowl. Cover with half the apricot mixture and half of the custard. Make a second layer of ladyfingers; cover with the rest of the apricots and custard mixture. Put plastic wrap on the surface to prevent a skin from forming. Refrigerate.

Before serving, whip the cream with 1 tablespoon of sugar and 1 teaspoon of vanilla until stiff. Cover the top of the trifle with the cream and serve.

Serves 8 to 10.

Artichoke

Globe artichoke, *Cynara Scolymus*

Effort Scale

NO. 3
Spent fronds need cutting
Plant needs renewing every three or four years
Must be kept constantly moist
Mulching and fertilizing needed
Occasional pests
Winter protection required in some areas

Zones

8–9, more if given winter protection

Thumbnail Sketch

Herbaceous perennial sometimes planted as annual
3–5 ft. tall
Propagated by seed, from offshoots, or from divisions
Needs full sun; will tolerate partial shade in hot climates
Leaves are gray-green fronds, 4 ft. long
Blooming time varies
Flowers are lavender thistles, 4–6 in. across
Flower buds are edible; harvest season variable
Used in herbaceous borders, as interest plants, in containers

How to Use

In the Kitchen

The artichoke is a giant thistle whose flower buds, when cooked, are deliciously—and expensively, for those who must buy them—edible. The bud is served whole as a vegetable, or, with the "choke" removed, as an edible serving dish for seafood and chicken. When eating a whole artichoke you pull off the outside leaves and use your teeth to scrape the flesh off the bottom of the leaf. Tender young hearts of artichokes are canned, marinated or not. The hearts are used as an hors d'oeuvre or as an addition to salads or casseroles.

In the Landscape

Artichokes have a dramatic, sculptured look when placed in the back of a herbaceous border. Their handsome, silvery-gray, deeply lobed leaves are quite different from anything else in the garden.

The artichoke is fountain-shaped. Under average conditions they grow to about 4 feet and spread as wide. Six to eight plants should be ample for the average family and allow you to let some of the buds flower. When not picked for eating, they develop into massive blue-purple thistles that are extremely showy and fragrant. They make spectacular dried flowers.

Artichokes can be used as shrubs, in containers on a roof garden or patio, as interest plants, or as accent plants to line a walk or driveway. In areas with warm, arid summers, artichokes tend to die back in the summer. Try interplanting them with a few large pink and white cosmos. The cosmos grow up and hide the thinning foliage. The delightful cosmos reseed themselves yearly after providing cutting flowers all summer and shading the tender new artichoke fronds.

E.11. *Artichokes can line a fence beautifully. Allow a few of the chokes to bloom; the flowers are magnificent.*

How to Grow

Climate

Artichoke plants need cool, moist summers and mild winters. In cold winters they need protection, for example, by way of an over-turned basket filled with leaves or straw and placed above the roots. In coldest winter areas they are usually not successful unless the roots are brought inside during winter and kept moist and cool. In hot, early summers the artichoke buds open too soon and are tough.

Artichokes need to be dug up and thinned out every three or four years or they will slowly decline from overcrowding.

Exposure

Artichokes prefer full sun in cool summer areas and partial shade in hot summer areas.

Soil

Artichokes require rich, well-drained soil with plenty of organic matter. They respond well to deep mulches.

Fertilizing

Compost and manure are beneficial. Extra nitrogen should be added halfway through the growing season and after harvest.

Watering

Keep these moisture-loving plants well watered; deep mulches help.

Pests and Diseases

Aphids and snails are sometimes a problem. To knock aphids off, use a strong jet of water. Handpick snails.

Botrytis, a fungus disease, is serious but not common. It forms gray mold on leaves in warm, muggy summers. Since there is no known cure, affected plants must be destroyed. Send them to the dump or burn them.

Harvesting

Pick the young artichoke buds before they start to open. The younger the bud, the more tender it is and the more of it is edible.

How to Purchase

Forms and Sources

Rooted cuttings are sometimes available at nurseries. Seeds are available from the following mail-order firms: (**9, 28, 32, 48, 51, 63**).

Varieties

Only two varieties of artichokes are generally available: 'Green Globe' (**Readily Available**) and 'Grande Beurre' (**63**).

Preserving

Freeze or pickle artichoke hearts, or pickle whole small artichokes less than 3 inches in diameter.

Asparagus

Asparagus officinalis

Effort Scale

NO. 3
Initial soil preparation is heavy work
Vulnerable to some pests
Weeding necessary
Constant mulching necessary

Zones

4–9

Thumbnail Sketch

Herbaceous perennial
3–5 ft. tall
Propagated from seeds
Needs full sun
Leaves are tiny and fernlike
Blooms in summer
Flowers are white to green, insignificant
Female plant has red berries
Young shoots are edible; harvested in spring
Used as a background for a herbaceous border, or to line
 a walk

How to Use

In the Kitchen

Asparagus means spring to most of us. Despite the cost, those first bunches in the market are irresistible to asparagus lovers. Think of the pleasures you could have every spring from a bed of your own. Young, tender shoots are delicious raw in salads or served with flavorful dips. Most aficionados favor the simple approach to cooking asparagus; they like the stalks steamed or boiled until just tender and served with salt, pepper, and a touch of butter. Leftovers can be served vinaigrette the next night. Asparagus can be frozen or canned successfully. These processes alter the taste of the vegetable, but they do bring green to the winter table.

In the Landscape

Asparagus is a herbaceous perennial, dormant in the winter, whose edible spears show themselves early, heralding an end to winter. The shoots that are not cut for eating develop into airy, ferny foliage plants 3–5 feet high that can line a walkway or a split-rail fence, or serve as a billowy background in a flower bed. A row of large red salvia in front of them makes a beautiful combination. An added feature of asparagus are the bright red berries that develop on the female plants. As the plants often bear for 15 years you must plan a permanent place for them in the yard.

How to Grow

Climate

Asparagus grows in most areas of the United States except for the very coldest sections and southern Florida, the Gulf Coast, and Hawaii. The humid, warm winters in those areas do not allow the plant to become dormant and renew itself.

Exposure

Asparagus plants need full sun.

Planting

Start asparagus from seed or year-old rooted crowns (the base of the plant). The average family will need about 30–40 plants.

Because asparagus plants remain in one place for many years, the soil must be prepared very well. You will need about 200 square feet for two rows 20 feet long and 4–6 feet apart. Spade generous amounts of manure and compost into the top two feet of soil. In this spaded area dig two trenches 8–10 inches deep, 12 inches wide, and 20 feet long; then place the crowns in the bottom, about 12 inches apart, with their roots well spread out. Cover with 3–4 inches of soil. As the shoots emerge, continue to fill the trench with soil. The trench dimensions above are for a standard vegetable bed. If you are lining a walk or planting in the back of a flower border, you would vary the length of the trenches according to your design.

Soil

Asparagus needs a deep organic soil with good drainage. The pH of the soil should be 6.0–8.0.

Fertilizing

Use organic mulches 4–6 inches deep to provide nutrients and to help control weeds. Supplement with a balanced fertilizer in the spring.

E.12. Asparagus foliage provides a soft, fernlike background to a perennial border.

Watering

Only moderate amounts of water are needed during the growing season. In the arid Southwest, do not irrigate in the winter.

Harvesting

Do not harvest until the second year. The first harvest year should be very light; in subsequent years harvest until the spears begin to thin to less than ½ inch in diameter. Cut the spears carefully to avoid injuring the crowns. An asparagus knife is available just for this purpose.

Pruning

In mild climates cut down plants when they turn brown; in cold climates wait until spring.

Pests and Diseases

Asparagus beetles are generally the most serious pest. Fall clean-up helps remove some of the breeding adults. Keeping all the spears cut in the spring for a few weeks seems to help also.

The chalcid wasp is the asparagus beetle's natural predator. If you see the wasps around and do not find beetles in great numbers, do nothing. If the beetles are taking over, knock them off into a bucket of soapy water. Spray the larvae with pyrethrin.

Snails and a fungus disease called asparagus rust are occasional problems. The latter is associated with very damp weather. Plant resistant varieties, such as 'Waltham Washington', where asparagus rust might be a problem.

Where gophers are numerous they can be a serious problem. Plant the crowns in wire baskets to protect them.

How to Purchase

Forms and Sources

Asparagus is purchased as seeds or one-year-old rooted crowns. The plants are readily available bare root in early spring and occasionally through early summer in containers from local nurseries or mail-order firms.

Varieties

'Mary Washington'—fairly rust resistant.
'Waltham Washington'—fairly rust resistant.

Preserving

Asparagus may be frozen or canned.

Avocado

Persea americana

Effort Scale

NO. 2 in California
Some watering and fertilizing needed
NO. 3 in Florida and Hawaii
Watering and fertilizing needed
Susceptible to disease problems
Large harvest of perishable fruit

Zones

10 and Hawaii

E.13. *A 'Hass' avocado, showing the pebbly skin characteristic of this variety.*

Thumbnail Sketch

Evergreen tree
Standard, 20–40 ft. tall; dwarf variety available, 8–10 ft. tall
Propagated by grafting or budding
Needs full sun
Leaves are dark green, 4–8 in. long; new growth is bronzy
Blooms at different times, depending on variety
Flowers are insignificant
Fruits are edible; harvest season varies
Used as shade tree and screen; dwarf variety used as large
   shrub and in containers

How to Use

In the Kitchen

Avocados are 3–6 inches long and pear shaped. For those who love them, their buttery, yellow-green flesh is one of the world's more toothsome pleasures. Others can get along without them very well. Avocados are usually eaten raw, combined in salads with citrus, tomatoes, and sweet onions. They make a marvelous dip, guacamole, and can be used in hot and cold soups. Halved avocados can be filled with jellied consommé.

In the Landscape

This large evergreen tree is 20–40 feet tall. Since its spread can grow as wide, the tree gives marvelous shade. In an area where it grows well it is a beautiful specimen. The flowers are not important, nor do the green or black fruits offer ornamental accents. The tree is the thing. It has big, lush, green leaves that are bronzy in new growth.

The avocado tree can be controlled by judicious pruning, but it is better, if you have the space, to let it spread—you will have an enviable plant.

Leaf drop is constant, so the tree is a nuisance over a patio, though the shade might make frequent sweeping worthwhile. The fruit does not drop readily. It is usually harvested when mature but hard, and then ripened in a cool dark place.

The dwarf variety is handsome in a tub. It can also be grown as a large accent shrub or as a small screen.

How to Grow

Climate

The avocado is a semihardy tree. It freezes at 18–30 °F depending on the variety. Winter flowers and small fruits are damaged by significant frost and the tree needs protection from wind. Avocados are limited to the warmest climates of California, Florida, and Hawaii.

Tubbed dwarf and young trees benefit from covering during the winter in borderline climates.

Exposure

This tree requires full sun.

Soil

Avocados need deep, rich, very well drained soil. Roots will rot where the water table is high. Avocados have a very low tolerance to salt in the soil.

Fertilizing

On most soils in California, the avocado needs only light amounts of fertilizer supplemented with chelated iron. In Florida fertilize avocados in a manner similar to citrus. Avocados should be thickly mulched with avocado leaves or compost. The avocado is very shallow rooted.

Watering

Keep soil moist but not wet for healthiest growth. Never let water sit around the base of the plant.

Pruning

Prune only to control size and shape. Be careful to protect any exposed branches from sunburn. Paint the trunk and any exposed branches with whitewash.

Pests and Diseases

In Florida the main pest nuisance is scale. Diseases of the plant there are cercospora fruit spot, avocado scab, and anthracnose. The trees should be given three or four sprayings with neutral copper. Ask local authorities about the proper timing.

Very few pests and diseases beset California avocados. However, Southern California farmers are struggling with a root rot, *Pytophthora cinnamomi*, so in this region avoid planting avocados where they have been grown commercially.

Chlorosis can be a problem in avocados but can be treated with iron chelate. Salt burn can show up as a problem by stunted growth of the tree, or by brown edges of the leaves. If these symptoms appear, deep water the surrounding soil every third or fourth watering. Avoid manures and commercial fertilizers high in salts. If the problem continues, consult local authorities.

Many avocados, particularly the Guatemalan group, will bear heavily one year but poorly or not at all the next. This is the tree's pattern and has nothing to do with the health of the plant.

Harvesting

The fruits are harvested when they are mature but still hard. Fruits are ripe when they give slightly to pressure. Yields are generally higher in California than in Florida; for the varieties given in the table below, a ten-year-old healthy tree will produce about 2–3 bushels of fruit in California, 1–2 bushels in Florida.

How to Purchase

Forms and Sources

Avocados are sold in containers from local nurseries and from a few mail-order sources.

Pollinators

Most avocado varieties are somewhat self-fruitful, but for most varieties growers recommend cross-pollination for heavier crops. 'Mexicola' seems to do well by itself.

Varieties

Three main types of avocados are grown in the United States: Mexican, Guatemalan, and hybridized varieties. The Mexican varieties are the hardiest.

Preparing

Guacamole

Peel and mash 3 or 4 medium-size avocados. Add 1 diced tomato, ¼ teaspoon garlic powder, 1 tablespoon lime juice, and tabasco or taco sauce to taste. Mix well. Serve with corn chips or on sandwiches with cheese or bacon.

Guacamole can be frozen.

For a useful recipe booklet, send $1.00 to The Avocado Bravo, California Avocados, 4533 MacArthur Blvd., Suite B, Newport Beach, CA 92660.

Varieties of Avocado

NAME	TYPE	CHARACTERISTICS OF FRUIT	FRUITING SEASON	FORM OF TREE	NOTES
'Bacon'	Mexican	Good; medium size; green	Winter	Upright growth	Consistent annual crop; fairly hardy; (**10**)
'Choquette'	Hybrid	Excellent; large size; green	Winter	Spreading	Freezes about 26°F; available in Florida
'Duke'	Mexican	Good; medium size; green	Summer or fall	Moderately spreading	Freezes at about 20°F
'Fuerte'	Hybrid	Very good; medium size; green	Winter	Large	Grown primarily in California; (**10**)
'Hall'	Hybrid	Excellent; large; dark green	Winter	Spreading	Primarily grown in Florida; freezes about 29°F
'Hass'	Guatemalan	Excellent; medium to large size; black, pebbly skin	Spring and summer	Spreading	Grown primarily in California; (**10**)
'Littlecado' ('Wurtz')	Guatemalan	Fair; medium size; green	Summer	Dwarf, 10–25 ft.; weeping branches	Expensive; hard to find locally; alternate bearing; (**4**)
'Mexicola'	Mexican	Excellent; small size; black, smooth, thin skin	Summer or fall	Tall	One of the hardiest; to 18°F; often hard to find

E.14. *Avocado trees form large, spreading canopies useful for shade.*

E.15 Bamboo comes in many forms. In the foreground is golden bamboo. In the background is the giant timber bamboo.

Bamboo

Bambusa species
Phyllostachys species

Effort Scale

NO. 2 in mild climates
Easy to grow

NO. 3 in cold climates
Winter protection necessary

Preparing edible shoots time-consuming

Zones

7–10 and Hawaii

Thumbnail Sketch

Perennial evergreen grasses
Edible types are 8–60 ft. tall
Propagated by divisions
Needs full sun in mild climates, some shade in hottest areas
Leaves are bright green, 2–3 in. long
Woody ridged canes are very decorative
Flowers bloom infrequently and are insignificant
Shoots are edible; harvested in spring or summer
Used as hedge, container plant, interest plant, screen, windbreak

How to Use

In the Kitchen

Young shoots of these plants are cooked in many dishes. The familiar canned product does not compare in succulence with fresh bamboo. The young shoots taste something like sweet, young corn. They can be used as a boiled vegetable seasoned with butter and salt and pepper or as an addition to stir-fried Oriental dishes.

Caution: Powerful herbicides are used to control and eradicate bamboo. Do not accept friendly offers of young shoots unless you know their history!

In the Landscape

Bamboo is the most useful and beloved plant in the Orient. A clump, windbreak, hedge, or screen of bamboo will give an Oriental feeling to any garden. Planted in containers, these plants accent an informal pool, a patio, or an entryway. The woody, ringed canes can grow from 8 to 60 feet tall, depending on the species. These canes are graceful and have a special quality that is softened by the narrow, exquisitely airy, light-green leaves. It is important to remember that there are two kinds of bamboo: running (the *Phyllostachys* species) and clumping (the *Bambusa* species). Running bamboo does run—it can come up in your neighbor's rose garden, in the middle of your compost heap, or even up through asphalt. Its underground stolons (runners) know no boundaries, so it is wisest to confine them by a concrete header at least 2 feet deep or to plant them in large underground containers. In coldest climates their growth is not as invasive. The clumping type stays confined, sending up only basal stems.

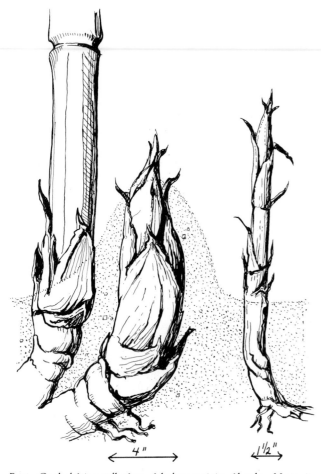

E.16.   *On the left is a stalk of one of the large varieties of bamboo. Next to it is a shoot covered with soil to keep it tender as it enlarges. The plant at right is a shoot of one of the small-diameter varieties. Both shoots depicted are ready to be harvested.*

How to Grow

Climate

Most kinds of bamboo are semihardy, but a few are hardy below 0°F. Several species, for instance, are currently thriving at the Arnold Arboretum in Boston, Massachusetts. To protect new shoots in winter, mulch well or, if bamboo is in a container, bring it into a well-lit room.

Exposure

In hot-summer areas bamboo needs some shade. In cool coastal areas the plants prefer full sun. In the coldest climates, plant bamboo against a protected south wall.

Soil

All species prefer well-drained, rich loam with a high organic content.

Fertilizing

During the first year, fertilize with a balanced fertilizer. Thereafter, the dropped leaves and an occasional application of nitrogen

will provide sufficient nutrients to maintain moderate growth. For more vigorous plants and numerous shoots, fertilize more heavily.

Watering

Most types are drought tolerant, but all do best and produce the most shoots when watered well. Newly established plants must not be allowed to dry out in the first year. Bamboo litter sometimes prevents water from penetrating the root area during irrigation, so watch for water penetration.

Pruning

For beauty, trim lower leaves to expose the canes. Thin out three-year-old canes.

Pests and Diseases

Bamboo plants have no major pests or diseases. Sometimes a leaf-spot fungus or rust might appear in warm, humid climates, and occasionally aphids or cottony bamboo scale might occur. Water in a hard spray is usually an effective cure.

To prevent the bamboo itself from becoming a pest, make sure the roots of the running types are contained within a concrete or metal barrier at least 2 feet deep, or plant in containers.

Harvesting

See the accompanying diagrams for harvesting information. Cut the shoots of the thick, heavy species as they emerge from the ground in early spring. (If you make 6-inch mounds of soil around the base of the plant before the shoots emerge, they will be longer and more tender.) Do not harvest all shoots; the plants need some to renew themselves. The more slender species, 1–2 inches in diameter, can be allowed to grow to a height of 12 inches before being harvested.

New shoots of the clumping bamboos usually appear in summer

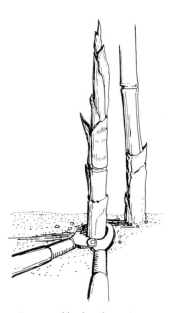

E.17.   *Small-diameter bamboos are cut off at ground level as shown; lopping shears work well. Large-diameter shoots are cut off below ground level with a knife. (Be careful not to slice into the other rhizomes.)*

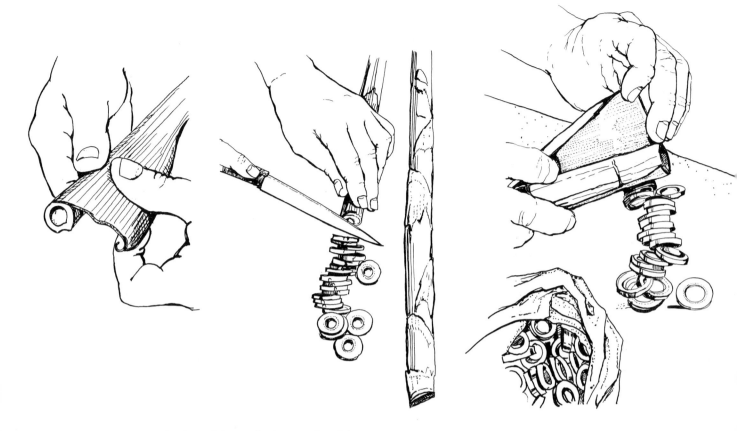

E.18. *Preparing bamboo.* **Left:** *The small-diameter bamboos must be peeled in sections.* **Center:** *Cut the shoot into slices and discard the woody joints.* **Right:** *Peel and slice the next section, continuing until entire shoot is done. After parboiling, slices can be frozen in plastic bags.*

or fall. The running bamboos generally send up their shoots in spring.

How to Purchase

Forms and Sources

Many types of bamboo plants are available from local nurseries or mail-order sources. Rhizomes may also be obtained from a friend's plant. When you dig up part of a friend's rhizome, however, be sure that the section is large enough to include growing buds. (As with any gift plant, make sure it is not carrying any pests or diseases.)

Mail-order sources of bamboo are: (**3, 39, 65**), and the Bamboo Collection of Robert Lester, 280 West 4th St., New York, NY 10014.

Varieties

In this case the title refers to the *species* described in the table below; there are few named varieties of bamboo.

All species of bamboo are edible, but some taste better than others. Most have a bitter taste that must be removed by parboiling. The table on page 196 shows those that are best for eating and most readily available.

Preserving and Preparing

Raw or Boiled Bamboo Shoots

For all types of bamboo peel the outer layer to expose the white flesh. Cut small-diameter shoots into rings one node at a time (see Figure E.18); cut large shoots into slices. If the shoots are sweet they are edible raw in salads or with dips as an appetizer. However, most shoots are bitter until parboiled for 15 to 20 minutes. Change the water after the first 10 minutes, and drain shoots when you are done parboiling them. To serve immediately, cook until tender, or preserve for later use. The raw shoots deteriorate very quickly, so process or serve them on the day they are harvested.

Preserve bamboo shoots by parboiling them and then freezing them in plastic bags. The frozen shoots remain crisp. Another preserving method is the Japanese drying technique. Boil shoots for 20 minutes, salt them, and put them in a food dryer. Process until they rattle.

Use bamboo shoots as you would any boiled vegetable. Serve alone with butter, salt, and pepper, use in stir-fried Oriental dishes, or add to tuna-noodle casserole for crispness. The texture and sweetness of the shoots make them an exotic addition to soups and stews. And of course they can be used in any recipe calling for canned shoots.

Species of Bamboo

BOTANICAL NAME	COMMON NAME	HEIGHT	ZONES (LOWER TOLERANCE LIMIT)	STEM DIAMETER	NOTES
Phyllostachys aurea	Golden	15–20 ft.	7	2 in.	Running
P. aureosulcata	Yellow Groove	12–25 ft.	5; hardiest species	1 ½ in.	Running
P. bambusoides	Giant Timber Bamboo (Madake)	15–45 ft.	7	6 in.	Running
P. dulcis	Sweet Shoot	20–40 ft.	8	2 ½ in.	Running; considered sweetest
P. pubescens [P. edulis]	Moso	20–60 ft.	7	8 in.	Running; does poorly in heat and humidity
P. viridis	Green Sulfur Bamboo	30–45 ft.	8	3 in.	Running
Bambusa beecheyana	Beechey	12–40 ft.	10	4–5 in.	Clumping; graceful
B. glaucescens	Hedge	8–25 ft.	8	1 ½ in.	Clumping; dense growth
B. Oldhamii	Oldham	15–40 ft.	8	3 in.	Clumping

Elinor's Bamboo Shoots

2 ½ cups raw, sliced bamboo shoots
3 tablespoons salad oil
½ cup water
2–3 tablespoons soy sauce

Parboil shoots for 20 minutes if bitter (see method above). Drain. In a frying pan put salad oil and bamboo shoots. Cook over medium heat for 3–5 minutes. Add water and soy sauce. Cover and simmer for 20–30 minutes or until tender.

Serve as a hot vegetable or refrigerate and add to salads. Or freeze the cooked shoots and use them to enhance string beans, pea pods, zucchini, and stir-fried Oriental dishes.

E.19. Banana trees lend a tropical accent to pool plantings and cause few litter problems.

Banana and Plantain

Musa species

Effort Scale

NO. 3
Constant fertilizing necessary
Mulches and watering needed
Large crop ripens all at once
Winter protection needed in borderline areas

Zones

10 and Hawaii

Thumbnail Sketch

Herbaceous perennials
6–25 ft. tall
Propagated from offsets (rhizomes) or suckers
Need full sun
Leaves are dramatic, 5–9 ft. long
Flowers are large, podlike, interesting
Fruits are edible; harvest season varies
Used as interest plants, near a pool, on a patio, or in atriums;
dwarf varieties used in containers and greenhouses

How to Use

In the Kitchen

Bananas are long, narrow, and sweet. They are an admirable food for traveling and for snacks because they are easy to peel and eat. They are also healthful without being too high in calories. However, such delicacies as banana fritters and flaming bananas cancel out the low-calorie advantage. For the days when you throw discretion to the wind, banana splits and chocolate-covered bananas are luscious indulgences. On a more sane level, dried banana chips have the advantage of being light-weight and extremely tasty, two characteristics of a good food for campers and backpackers.

Plantains (not to be confused with other plants of the same name) are a very close relative of bananas but are starchy and less sweet. They are a staple vegetable in most tropical regions and in this country are found chiefly in cities with sizable Latin American or Filipino populations. Like potatoes, they are very versatile and are served boiled, fried, or diced and added to omelets or stews.

Both banana and plantain leaves can be used like aluminum foil to wrap around food that is to be steamed. The natural wrapping imparts a perfumed flavor to the food inside.

In the Landscape

Bananas and plantains grow tall, 6–25 feet, but stay narrow. They lend a bold accent to a yard because of their tremendous leaves, which can grow to 9 feet long and 2 feet wide. Banana and plantain plants look alike and give a tropical appearance to courtyards and sunny atriums and are attractive near pools. The dwarf banana can be grown in a greenhouse.

How to Grow

Climate

Bananas are tender. They freeze at around 28°F and need two years of frostless winters to produce fruit. Plantains are slightly hardier. Best growing areas for both are southern Florida and Hawaii; they are grown in southern California with mixed results. For winter protection, cover plants to protect them from frost. For borderline climate areas, plant against a hot south wall.

Exposure

Bananas and plantains require full sun and protection from wind.

Planting

Bananas and plantains need a long, warm growing season to become established before winter. Plant them during March and April. Dig holes 3 x 1½ feet for each rhizome, 10 feet apart for the dwarf variety and 15 feet apart for large plants. Compost generously. If you are getting your plant from a neighbor's plant, select a rooted sucker with a strong stem and let it dry out for a day before planting it.

Soil

Both plants need rich, well-drained garden loam, and a deep organic mulch. They prefer a soil pH of 5.5–6.5.

Fertilizing

Bananas and plantains are extremely heavy feeders; keep well fertilized at all times. Few plants are fertilized well enough.

Watering

The large leaves of both plants permit evaporation of great quantities of water. Water copiously. In hot or windy weather, they may need water daily. Do not let the plants dry out.

Pruning

Banana plants sucker profusely and must be cut back regularly. Allow only one stalk to grow the first year; thereafter limit the plant to three or four stalks. Prune off all other suckers. Fruiting occurs only once on each stalk. The fruit is borne in bunches. After bearing, the stalk dies and is cut down. Keep others growing to take its place. It usually takes 12–18 months for a stalk to start flowering. After fruits have set, remove useless male flower from the end of the bunch to lessen weight on the stalk.

Caution: Sap stains clothing. In India banana sap once was used to make ink.

Pests and Diseases

Bananas and plantains have very few pests and diseases. A fungus, Panama disease, is sometimes a problem in Florida. If this is the case in your area, plant 'Lacatan', a fungus-resistant variety.

Harvesting

Cut down the entire fruit stalk when the bottom "hand" has fully formed but the fruit is still green. Bananas ripen in succession from the top down. Hang bunch for two weeks to develop full flavor. You get a large harvest at one time, so be prepared to make banana bread and to preserve.

How to Purchase

Forms and Sources

Bananas are available in containers from local nurseries or from the following mail-order sources: (**28, 39**). Better yet, if your neighbors have a plant, ask them to give you a rooted sucker from it.

Varieties

BANANAS

'Apple'—18 ft. tall; best flavor, short fat bananas.
'Dwarf Cavendish'—5–7 ft. tall; hardiest; most readily available.
'Lacatan'—good fruits; grown where Panama disease is a problem.
'Lady-Finger'—small, delicate banana.
'Red Jamaica'—most striking plant; reddish bronzy-green leaves; least hardy.

PLANTAINS

'Orinoco'—usually the only variety available; more hardy than most banana plants.

Preserving

Banana pulp may be frozen. It can also be made into banana bread and frozen or into banana butter and canned. My favorite ways of preparing bananas are to make dried banana chips or to freeze chocolate-dipped bananas on sticks.

Basil

Bush basil, *Ocimum minimum*
Sweet basil, *O. Basilicum*

Effort Scale

NO. 2
Must be planted annually
Watering and light fertilizing usually needed
Pinching and harvesting can be time-consuming

Zones

Annual

Thumbnail Sketch

Annual herb
1½–2 ft. tall
Propagated from seeds
Needs full sun; will tolerate partial shade
Leaves are bright green or purple, 2–3 in. long
Blooms in summer
Flowers are white or pink, small
Leaves are edible; used for seasoning; harvested in summer
Used in flower beds, herb gardens, containers

How to Use

In the Kitchen

The aromatic leaves are used fresh or dried in many dishes—soups, salads, stews, and spaghetti sauce, to name a few. To many people basil is best known as the base for pesto, an Italian herb sauce. To others it is the "only" accompaniment to fresh, ripe tomatoes. In any case, basil is an herb of many uses.

In the Landscape

This warm-season herbaceous annual can grow to 2 feet in height. The leaves of the common variety are 3 inches long and a glossy, bright green. They give a fresh touch to herb gardens, which often are mostly gray. Basil leaves also offer contrast in a mixed-flower bed and make a shining edge to a vegetable border. Planted among carrots, basil adds solidity; planted among lettuces it often brings another shade of green. Basil combines well with dwarf marigolds and nasturtiums. The purple-leaved variety looks gorgeous with dwarf pink zinnias, or alyssum. All varieties of basil do well in containers.

E.20. Basil is versatile in the kitchen, attractive and fragrant in the landscape.

How to Grow

Basil grows well in all areas of the country as long as it is planted in well-drained, fairly rich soil, receives full sun, and is watered regularly. Leaves stay large and succulent if the plants are fed once during the season with a fish-emulsion-type fertilizer. Pinch young plants to keep them bushy, and remove the flower spikes for better leaf production.

Pick as needed for use as a fresh herb.

How to Purchase

Basil is obtained as seed or in small containers from nurseries. Sweet (sometimes called common) basil is the kind most widely available; the three named varieties below belong to the same species, *Ocimum basilicum*. Bush basil is a different species.

Varieties

Bush—small plant, 6–12 in.; spicy lemon odor, somewhat bitter taste. (**32, 47, 51**)
Sweet basil—green; to 2 ft. high. (**Readily Available**)
'Dark opal'—Deep purple leaves, pink flowers. (**25, 32, 47, 48, 51, 54, 56**)
'Lettuce-leaved'—leaves green, broad, to 4 in. long. (**32, 47, 51**)
'Persian anise-scented'—large plant with purple-tinged foliage; strong, anise-like aroma. (**51**)

Preserving and Preparing

To preserve, follow the accompanying direction for drying herbs. Or make pesto, a wonderfully versatile sauce that freezes well.

Pesto

3 cloves of garlic
3 ounces freshly grated
  Parmesan cheese,
  or 2 ounces Parmesan
  and 1 ounce Romano
2 cups fresh basil leaves

¼ cup pine nuts
  (or walnuts)
1½ teaspoons salt
¼ teaspoon pepper
½ to 1 cup olive oil

In a blender jar or food processor, combine the garlic, basil leaves, nuts, salt, pepper, and half the oil. Puree, slowly adding the remaining oil. Transfer to a bowl and add the grated cheese, mixing thoroughly. Use immediately or cover with plastic wrap, since pesto turns brown if exposed to air. If you're a garlic fan, increase the quantity to taste.

Serve as a sauce for tagliarini or fettuccine noodles. Try combining cooked French-cut string beans with the noodles, or use pesto to flavor soups, spaghetti, grilled fish, or stews.

Pesto may be frozen and kept for four to six months. When freezing, leave the cheese out and add it before serving.

Drying Herbs

These directions may be followed for drying basil, borage, marjoram, mint, parsley, rosemary, sage, thyme, and other leafy herbs not included in the encyclopedia.

Pick the leaves in the driest part of the day. Wash quickly, if necessary, and pat dry. Place the leaves in a single layer on a screen. For quick drying, put the leaves in an oven at a very low temperature (140°F) for a few hours. If you have more time, place the screen in a warm, dry indoor place, such as a garage or attic, and dry for five to seven days. Stir the leaves once a day. When they are dry, store in airtight containers in a cool, dark place.

BAY. See *Sweet Bay*.

BEACH PLUM. See *Plums, Bush*.

Beans

Bush bean, *Phaseolus vulgaris humilis*
Hyacinth bean, *Dolichos Lablab*
Pole bean, *Phaseolus vulgaris*
Scarlet runner bean, *P. coccineus*

Effort Scale

NO. 3
Must be planted annually
Watering and light fertilizing needed
Vulnerable to some pests
Harvesting is time consuming

Zones

Annual

E.21. Pole beans have tendrils and will climb a trellis or latticework fence. The flowers of some varieties attract hummingbirds.

Thumbnail Sketch

Annuals or perennials treated as annuals
Vines, 6–8 ft. long; bushes, to 2 ft. tall
Propagated from seeds
Need full sun
Flower in summer
Flowers are white, purple, or red
Seeds and pods are edible; harvested in summer and fall
Bush types used in flower beds, raised beds, and in containers;
   vine types used to decorate arbors, trellises, and fences

How to Use

In the Kitchen

Green beans, cooked until they are just tender, are one of life's better gustatory experiences. All they need is a little salt and pepper and a dab of butter; a touch of grated fresh ginger is nice. Marinated whole beans are an attractive addition to a relish tray. Beans can be dressed up with water chestnuts or cheese sauce for gala occasions. 'Royalty' and 'Royal Burgundy' are purple beans that turn green when they are cooked; children call them magic beans.

In the Landscape

Whether bush or pole, beans are grown as annuals, and they have not been considered particularly useful in landscaping. However, well-grown plants have attractive leaves and handsome, long pods and are not unattractive. Most varieties of beans do not have showy flowers. If you want color try combining the bush types with nasturtiums or petunias. The pole varieties can be combined with morning glories. Some beans are attractive ornamentals in their own right. For example, the bush form of 'Royalty', with its deep-purple flowers, purple-tinged foliage, and purple beans, is a worthy background for a flower bed. The brilliant, red flowers of the scarlet runner bean, the large, white flowers of 'Thomas' Famous White Dutch' runner bean, and the purple flowers of 'Royal Burgundy' all look decorative on a trellis, arbor or fence. Hummingbirds are attracted to the scarlet runner and 'Thomas' Dutch' vines.

Help remove the stigma from this family of ornamentals: Remove overmature vines before they become yellow and shriveled, and save the hodgepodge of poles and wire cages for the vegetable garden.

How to Grow

Beans grow in most areas of the country. They are planted after all danger of frost is past; the purple varieties can tolerate colder soil than the standard green string bean. All beans need full sun and a good, loose garden loam with plenty of added humus. They are best watered deeply and infrequently at the base of the plants to prevent mildew from getting a start.

Beans have their share of pests—beanloopers, whiteflies, aphids, and cucumber beetles. Small numbers of these organisms are no problem. For large numbers, use water sprays to remove. See chapter 7 for a discussion of these pests

Harvesting

Beans, whether you call them green, string, or snap, are most delicious when the seeds are still immature. To enjoy as many of them as possible, keep those immature pods picked. With most varieties, if too many pods are allowed to mature the plants will stop producing. I speak of this with some passion, because as a fledgling gardener I planted my pole beans on a fence. After a few good meals of delicious, tender beans, the plants stopped producing enough

E.22. Bean teepees are a delightful addition to a play area. Wooden or bamboo poles can be used. The interior should be at least 4 feet in diameter. 'Royalty' pole or scarlet runner beans are a good choice; in cool conditions 'Sugar Snap' peas also work well. Plant seeds outside the circle of poles, and use a deep mulch so that foot traffic does not compact the soil.

for a decent family serving. The vines had grown over the fence and produced beans I could not see; when all the pods on the other side became overripe, the plants stopped producing.

How to Purchase

Forms and Sources

Beans are grown from seeds, most of which are readily available in local nurseries and from mail-order sources. Most of the specific varieties mentioned below are usually available only by mail order (see table under Varieties). One nursery (**67**) specializes in beans and peas and has a large selection of both.

Preserving

String-type beans can be frozen, dried in a food dryer, canned, and pickled.

Shelled beans can be blanched for 2 minutes and frozen, or blanched for 5 minutes (to prevent insect damage during storage) and dried. Store dried beans in airtight containers.

Types of Beans

NAME	GROWTH	FLOWER	POD	NOTES
Hyacinth bean	Vine	Fragrant; purple or white	Scimitar shape; green or purple	Perennial in warm-winter areas; can grow to 10–20 ft.; young pods and shelled beans eaten; (**51**)
'Royal Burgundy'	Bush	Purple	Purple	Tolerates fairly cold soil; an improved 'Royalty'; **Readily Available**
'Royalty' (Bush)	Bush	Purple	Purple	Tolerates fairly cool soil; delicious; **Readily Available**
'Royalty' (Pole)	Vine	Purple	Purple	Tolerates fairly cool soil; delicious; **Readily Available**
Scarlet runner	Vine	Red	Green	Perennial; lives through winter in mild-winter areas; pick beans when immature for tender string beans or eat fully mature as shelled beans; **Readily Available**
'Thomas' Famous White Dutch' runner bean	Vine	Large; white	Green	Perennial; lives through winter in mild-winter areas; strong grower; attracts hummingbirds; pods and seeds delicious, sweet; pest and disease resistant; (**25, 67**)
Wax beans	Vine or bush	White	Yellow	Many good varieties; look for disease-resistant types; **Readily Available**

BELL PEPPER. See *Peppers.*

Bitter Melon *(FOO GWA, BALSAM PEAR, KARELI)*

Momordica Charantia

Effort Scale

NO. 2
Must be planted annually in most climates
Large amounts of water and fertilizer necessary
Vines need training

Zones

5–10

Thumbnail Sketch

Perennial tropical vine; treated as an annual in zones 5–8
Tall, to 20 ft.
Propagated from seeds
Needs full sun
Leaves are palmate, 4–5 in. across

Blooms and fruits in summer and early fall
Flowers are yellow, 1–1½ in. across
Immature fruits are edible; harvested in summer
Fruits are green when edible, 6–8 in. long
Fruits are yellow with red arils when ripe
Use on arbors, trellises, pergolas, fences, and in large containers

How to Use

In the Kitchen

Bitter melon is a classic Chinese and East Indian vegetable. It is rarely seen in grocery stores but can be grown beautifully in most yards. The melon is 6–8 inches long, green, pointed, and warty—most unusual looking. The flesh is soft when cooked, somewhat like that of summer squash, and has a definite bitter taste due to the presence of quinine. If you like quinine water or strong beer, you probably will like bitter melon and will enjoy eating it in many Chinese stir-fry or East Indian dishes. If you are inventive, you will also find ways to use it in American cooking—steamed, deep fried, sauteed with onions and spices, or stuffed and baked. It also does well as a substitute for zucchini or in omelets. The young leaves may be used as greens.

Caution: Do not eat the *ripe* seeds; they are reputed to be a purgative.

In the Landscape

Bitter melon has been widely planted as an ornamental in much of the world. Its lobed, deeply veined leaves and small, yellow flowers look striking cascading over a retaining wall or large oak barrel. Try combining the bitter melon with a black-eyed Susan vine, *Thunbergia alata.* The unusual-looking green fruit of the bitter melon is decorative and lightweight enough to be trained against a fence, or, in long, warm-summer areas where it grows taller, on an arbor, trellis, or porch. Only the immature fruits are harvested, so if some get too ripe to eat, leave them to turn yellow and burst open to reveal their scarlet-coated seeds. The burst fruit looks beautiful hanging down through the rafters of a patio cover.

How to Grow

Climate

Bitter melon is a perennial treated as an annual in most areas of the country. It will survive as a perennial only in the warmest winter areas. In some areas of the Southeast it has even gone wild.

Exposure

The plants need full sun.

Soil

Bitter melon requires a rich, well-drained soil.

Fertilizing

Large amounts of high-nitrogen fertilizer are needed throughout the growing season. Wood ashes have been recommended by some growers.

Watering

The soil around bitter melons should not be allowed to dry out for any length of time. Water frequently if the weather is hot or windy.

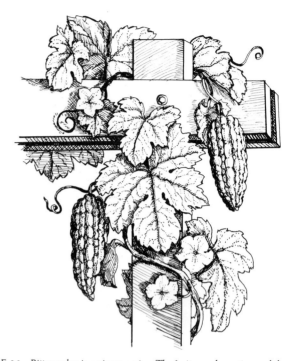

E.23. *Bitter melon is a vigorous vine. The fruits are decorative, and the foliage is handsome throughout the summer.*

Pruning

The vines need to be trained and tied up, with the growth directed to where you want it on the fence or trellis. If you are growing bitter melon in a container, you can provide stakes, or let the runners cascade over the side.

Pests and Diseases

Bitter melon has few pests and diseases as a rule. Occasionally, though, it is bothered by the same problems as cucumbers.

Harvesting

The younger the melon the less bitter it is. Start harvesting before the fruits are fully grown, when the green fruits are 3–4 inches long. Try larger ones if you want more bitterness. Most people consider the fruits inedible once they start to turn yellow. Leave them on the vine for next year's seed and for ornamentation.

How to Purchase

Bitter melons are grown from seeds that can occasionally be obtained from a local nursery but usually must be obtained through the following mail-order firms: (**25, 38, 64**). There are no named varieties.

Preserving and Preparing

Bitter melon may be sliced and dried or marinated with vinegar as a condiment. The following recipe may be frozen.

Bhadra's Fancy Bitter Melon

3 cups bitter melon, thinly
  sliced (as you would a
  cucumber)
1½ teaspoons salt
1½ cups diced potatoes
  with skins
⅓ to ½ cup vegetable oil
4 teaspoons ground
  coriander seed
2 teaspoons ground cumin

¼ to ½ teaspoon ground
  cayenne pepper, to taste
1 clove garlic, minced
1 tablespoon sugar
1 tablespoon raisins
2 tablespoons shredded
  coconut
2 tablespoons cashews
1 teaspoon lemon juice

Put sliced bitter melon in a dish. Sprinkle salt over it and let sit for 15–20 minutes. Squeeze the water out. (If you like your melon more bitter, leave some of the water in it.)

In a medium-size skillet, heat the oil over a medium flame. Add potatoes, and cook for about 5 minutes, stirring occasionally. Add the bitter melon and garlic, and cook until tender—about 10 minutes more. Add the coriander, cumin, and pepper, and stir for a few minutes. Just before removing from the heat, add the sugar, raisins, coconut, and cashews. Sprinkle lemon juice over the mixture just before serving.

For an authentic Indian meal, serve the bitter melon with split pea soup and Indian bread. (Tortillas, while less authentic, can be substituted.)

BLACKBERRY. See *Brambleberries.*

BLACK MULBERRY. See *Mulberry.*

BLACK WALNUT. See *Walnut.*

Blueberry

Highbush blueberry, *Vaccinium corymbosum*
Lowbush blueberry, *V. angustifolium*
Rabbiteye blueberry, *V. Ashei*

Effort Scale

NO. 3 in acid soil
Constant mulching necessary
Must be kept moist
Susceptible to some diseases
Vulnerable to some pests, including birds

NO. 4 in neutral soil
The same problems plus maintaining soil acidity

Zones

3–9

Thumbnail Sketch

Deciduous shrubs

1–18 ft. tall, depending on variety
Propagated by seed or from cuttings
Need full sun; will tolerate partial shade in hot climates
Leaves are dark green in growing season and yellow or scarlet
  in fall, ¾–3 in. long
Blooms in spring
Flowers are pinkish white, small, bell-like, grow in clusters
Fruits are edible; harvested in summer
Used for hedges, screens, interest plants, ground cover, in
  shrub borders, and in containers

How to Use

In the Kitchen

Blueberries are soft, blue berries that are wonderful fresh, with or without cream. Cereal topped with blueberries or pancakes with blueberry syrup make breakfast a banquet. Blueberry muffins right out of the oven are irresistible, and blueberry pie or cobbler (especially à la mode) is food for the gods.

E.24. *Blueberries are handsome in containers, and since they need acid soil, this is the only way you can grow them if your garden soil is alkaline.*

In the Landscape

The three species named have many assets in common. They are deciduous shrubs with dark-green leaves in spring and summer, often turning brilliant yellow or red in the fall. Early spring growth, which is bronze in color, is quickly followed by clusters of pinkish-white flowers resembling lily of the valley (blueberries are all members of the heath family, *Ericaceae*). As summer progresses, the flowers become berries that change from green to red to the typically gray-blue fruit we enjoy. At all times the plants are decorative. In winter some even have red twigs that contrast beautifully with the snow.

Because they differ in size, these plants have varying uses in your garden. Highbush usually grow to 5–6 feet tall, and rabbiteye plants can grow 15 to 18 feet, and make excellent hedges and screens. They can be combined with other acid lovers, such as rhododendrons, laurel, and azaleas, to form mixed shrub borders. The lowbush blueberries are not commonly cultivated but grow at the edge of woods or in wild gardens. Occasionally they are used as a ground cover or to line a woodland walk. All the cultivated blueberries make good container subjects because their appearance varies continuously.

How to Grow

Climate

The cultivated varieties commonly grown in the northern parts of this country are the improved offspring of the native highbush blueberry. They grow best in zones 5–8 and selected parts of zone 9. Some varieties are hardy to −20°F.

Lowbush blueberries, which are usually wild, are hardier and are grown in the northern parts of New England, Minnesota, and parts of Canada.

Rabbiteye blueberries are adapted to the southeastern United States. They are less hardy and more tolerant of warm weather than the other two species, and need less winter chill to produce good fruit. Blueberries generally prefer cool, moist conditions.

Exposure

Highbush and rabbiteye plants require full sun in most climates, though they take some shade in very hot climates.

Lowbush plants take full sun or some shade. Most blueberry authorities recommend growing lowbush plants in full sun only, but I remember as a child, on eastern Long Island, New York, picking lowbush blueberries in the dappled shade of an oak woods.

Soil

The most important considerations for blueberry culture are a light, well-draining soil and high soil acidity. Blueberries must grow in a very acid soil, pH 4.0–5.2. (See pH in the glossary.) This factor limits growth in many areas of the country. If azalea, mountain laurel, and rhododendron grow in your yard, blueberries probably will too. If in doubt test the soil. If your soil is neutral or only slightly acid, you can try to incorporate large amounts of acidic organic matter into the soil and apply constant acid mulches, sulfur, and fertilizers to maintain the high acidity. Acidic organic materials include pine needles, peat moss, composted oak leaves, and cottonseed meal. However, the added acidity will be constantly threatened by the surrounding soil, so it must be vigilantly maintained.

Planting blueberries in almost pure peat moss, in a large container, is a satisfactory solution if your soil is strongly alkaline. Do not let the peat moss dry out, as it is difficult to remoisten. Rabbiteye berries can tolerate a less acidic soil than the other types of blueberries

If drainage is questionable plant blueberries in raised beds or in containers.

Blueberries are shallow rooted. Do not disturb the roots with deep cultivation.

Fertilizing

Adding compost and cottonseed meal to the mulches is beneficial, as are light applications of the acid fertilizer ammonium sulfate, or azalea and blueberry fertilizer available in some areas. On soils with a high pH, chelated iron and magnesium are often needed to alleviate chlorosis.

Watering

Blueberries should be kept slightly moist at all times. Rabbiteye berries do not require as much water as the other species. For all the blueberries, mulches help to keep the moisture in.

Pruning

Blueberries should not be pruned, except to remove broken or weak branches, until the bushes are four years old. Then prune lightly, thinning out some of the oldest branches and spindly, weak growth each year. (See Figure E.25) Prune in late fall or early spring. If your fruit is undersized, cut back the tips of the canes so only four or five flower buds are left on each twig. That way the plant will not set as much fruit, and the remaining fruit will be larger. Most authorities recommend that you remove all the flowers the first year so that the plant will put its energy into vigorous growth.

Pests and Diseases

Birds are the biggest blueberry pest. Netting is often needed to keep your crop. The blueberry fruit fly, or maggot, can also be a problem. Use malathion if they get out of hand. Dormant sprays help control scale if that is a problem in your area.

The major disease problem is a nutritional one. If acidity cannot

E.25. Before pruning, a mature blueberry bush usually has too many old, weak, or crossing branches. To prune a mature bush, remove about a quarter of the oldest and weakest growth. If fruits have been small, remove some of the top growth.

be maintained, the plants are unable to take up enough nourishment and become chlorotic. The solution is to keep the acidity level below a pH of 5.2 by using acid mulches and fertilizers constantly. Chelated iron will help, too. Another disease is mummy berry, which causes berries to rot. Control this condition by removing rotten berries and destroying them. Canker can sometimes be a problem; plant resistant varieties.

Harvesting

To become completely ripe, blueberries usually need to stay on the plant for a week after they turn blue. Berries are ripe when they will fall off easily into your hand and they are sweet. Taste one to be sure. Most mature plants will yield about 5–6 pints of fruit annually.

How to Purchase

Forms and Sources

Blueberries are available bare-root and in containers from local nurseries or from mail-order firms (see individual varieties below). One nursery (**2**) specializes in cultivated highbush blueberries.

Pollinators

For good crops blueberries need cross-pollination from at least one other variety. Three or even more will usually give still better pollination.

Varieties

'Berkeley'—large berries; ripens midseason; tall, spreading plant; for northern California, the Northwest, and the Northeast into Maine. (**Readily Available**)

'Bluebelle'—large berries; grown in Florida and the Gulf Coast. (**23**)

'Bluecrop'—excellent flavor; erect, tall, attractive plant; hardier and more drought-resistant than most. (**6, 50, 58, 62**)

'Blueray'—large, flavorful berries; ripens midseason; upright, spreading, attractive plant; for New England and the West Coast. (**Readily Available**)

'Collins'—large, excellent berries; ripens midseason; erect, attractive plant; good for Northwest. (**50**)

'Coville'—large berries; ripens late season; tall, open, attractive shrub; very large leaves; for the Northwest. (**Readily Available**)

'Earliblue'—earliest large berries; tall, upright growth; large leaves; readily available in the Northwest, Michigan, and Northeast. (**2, 6, 50, 62**)

'Florablue'—for Florida and Gulf Coast. (**Locally Available**)

'Jersey'—mediocre berries; ripens late season; erect, tall plant; yellow fall color; widely grown in blueberry areas. (**Readily Available**)

'Northland'—early, medium-size berries with good flavor; short, to 4 ft., spreading; for coldest berry areas, even northern Michigan. (**2, 36**)

'Southland'—medium-size rabbiteye berries; ripens late; compact bush; good companion for 'Tifblue' in Southeast. (**23, 62**)

'Stanley'—large berries with excellent spicy flavor; ripens midseason; erect, medium-tall shrub; beautiful foliage; good for Northwest. (**6**)

'Tifblue'—excellent rabbiteye-type berries; ripens late; upright growth; for the Southeast. (**2, 23, 58, 62**)

'Tophat'—excellent berries; new, miniature bonsai-type shrub, particularly good for containers; for Michigan. (**28**)

'Wolcott'—midseason berries; resistant to canker; good for mid-Atlantic and Southeast. (**2**)

For more information on varieties for your area, contact your local university extension service or nursery concerning your particular climate.

Preserving and Preparing

To freeze, wash and pat dry 4 or 5 pounds of berries, then mix together with 1 pound of sugar. Place in airtight containers. Use for jam and syrup.

To dry, use firm but not overripe berries. Wash and pat dry. Carefully spread the berries on a plastic screen stapled to a wood frame. Place in a warm, dry place but not in direct sun. If you are drying berries outside, make sure the birds do not get a feast! Stir occasionally to insure even drying. Berries should be dry in four to five days unless the weather is damp. Dry berries rattle when stirred and exude no moisture when squeezed.

To reconstitute dried berries, cover the berries with water and refrigerate for several hours. Use in pies, pancakes, corn bread, or any recipe that calls for canned berries.

My favorite use of frozen or reconstituted dried blueberries is in cornbread. Blueberry cornbread makes a pleasant morning coffee cake. Make up your best cornbread recipe and add 1 cup of blueberries. Sprinkle the top with 1½ tablespoons of sugar. Bake a few minutes longer than usual.

For a dozen good blueberry recipes (and many others) I recommend the *Blueberry Hill Cook Book* by Elsie Masterton (New York: Thomas Y. Crowell Co., 1959).

Borage

Borago officinalis

Effort Scale

NO. 2
Easy to grow
Needs to be planted each year

Zones

Annual

Thumbnail Sketch

Annual herb
1½–2 ft. tall
Propagated from seeds
Needs full sun, will tolerate light shade
Leaves are gray-green and woolly, 3–6 in. long
Blooms in summer

E.26. *Borage is a perennial plant with gray-green foliage and stunning cobalt blue flowers.*

Flowers are cobalt-blue shooting stars, small, grow in clusters
Leaves and flowers are edible; harvested in summer
Used in flower beds, herb gardens, containers

How to Use

In the Kitchen

Both the leaves and flowers of borage are edible. The leaves, which taste something like cucumber, can be used raw to season salads, iced drinks, and wine. Claret cup, for example, is made with borage leaves. The raw leaves are hairy (the name *borage* is presumed to come from the Latin *barra*, meaning hairy garment). When cooked like spinach, the leaves lose this characteristic.

The raw flowers are added to salads. They can also be candied for eating or for use as decorations on pastries.

In the Landscape

Borage is a herbaceous annual that grows to 1½–2 feet. Its gray-green, hairy leaves are 3–6 inches long. The flowers are a stunning electric blue, small but growing in hanging clusters. They are a great favorite of bees, which are good to attract to the garden because of their generous pollinating activities. Borage plants are a valuable addition to any bed, be it flower, herb, or vegetable. They make an admirable container plant, and form an eye-catching array when grown with eggplant and purple alyssum.

How to Grow, Purchase and Preserve

Borage is readily available in seed from local and mail-order sources in all parts of the country. Plant when the soil warms up in the spring. It will grow in any soil but prefers soil that is somewhat dry. It withstands some shade. On occasion it will reseed itself.

Pull leaves off before flowers form so they will be young, tender, and flavorful. Pick the flowers just as they are opening.

The leaves may be dried according to the directions found under BASIL or frozen for use as a vegetable.

Use flowers candied or as a flavor-enhancing addition to a salad, lemonade or white wine.

BOSTON LETTUCE. See *Lettuce.*

BOYSENBERRY. See *Brambleberries.*

Brambleberries

Black raspberry, *Rubus occidentalis*
Boysenberry, *R. ursinus* var. *loganobaccus*
Himalaya berry, *R. procerus*
Red raspberry, *R. idaeus*
Thornless blackberry, *R. ulmifolius*
Hybrids

Effort Scale

NO. 4
Heavy pruning necessary
Mulching necessary
Vulnerable to diseases, and some pests, including birds
Most types need some vine training
Harvesting is time consuming
Provide winter protection in the coldest areas

Zones

3–9 for raspberry
5–8 for blackberry
8–9 for boysenberry, Himalaya berry, loganberry

Thumbnail Sketch

Deciduous, bushy plants with biennial canes
5–26 ft. tall, depending on species
Propagated by cuttings, from suckers, or by layering
Need full sun; will tolerate light shade
Leaves are compound, dark green; stems are prickly
Flowers are white or pinkish, 1 inch across
Fruits are edible; harvested in summer and fall
Used as barrier plants, hedges, and some types on trellises and arbors

How to Use

In the Kitchen

Red or black raspberries heaped on cereal, crushed and spooned over ice cream and meringues, or dripped over peaches in peach Melba—what elegant fare! Just as superb are boysenberries sun-warm and straight off the vine, in jam, or in hand-cranked ice cream on the Fourth of July. Aficionados can never get enough berries, but at today's prices, who can afford to have them often? Grow a hedge of these berries, and you will have enough for jam, wine, and pie, as well as your cereal bowl.

In the Landscape

Life has few guarantees, but you *can* be sure that no neighborhood children or dogs will push their way through your brambleberry hedge. A few thornless varieties do exist, but most of these hedges can be used to form impenetrable barriers.

Most types of brambleberries have deep-green leaves with light-colored undersides. They have prickly stems; open, five-petaled white flowers that grow in clusters; and red or black berries. Varieties with yellow and white fruit exist.

Brambleberry plants come in two different forms—erect, shrubby types and trailing, vinelike types. The former can be used as hedges or along fence rows. The latter must be trained on wires or trellises. To use brambleberries in a landscape successfully, you must keep them properly pruned and trained. Laxity will create a nightmare of sprawling, rampant vines.

A particularly attractive variety of brambleberry is the 'Thornless Evergreen' blackberry. It has beautiful, unusual foliage that turns purple in the fall.

How to Grow

The two major types of brambleberries are raspberries and blackberries. The raspberry-type fruits come off the vine without

E.27. Raspberries don't necessarily need to be trained on wires and relegated to the back of the vegetable garden. Try training the compact types on an attractive lattice fence.

the core, while blackberry types come off core and all. Confusingly, both types of berries can be either red or black. Red raspberries are the most hardy of the brambleberries, and grow on upright canes—narrow woody stems that arise from the ground—or on somewhat trailing vines. Both black raspberries and most blackberries are slightly more tender than the red raspberries and grow either on upright canes or on trailing vines. Some of the trailing blackberries such as boysenberries are quite tender and grow only in Zones 8 and 9. Most of the upright blackberries only do well in the Midwest and in the East. Red raspberries and most of the upright blackberries are propagated by suckers, shoots from the base of the plant. Most black raspberries are propagated by tip layering.

Climate

Red raspberries are very hardy. Some varieties are able to survive in milder sections of zone 3. Most black raspberries are hardy only to zone 5. Neither do well in hot summer areas, and only a few varieties are grown south of the Mason-Dixon line or in the Southwest.

Blackberries have a wide range of climate. There is a kind for most climates except the coldest winter areas, the Deep South, and desert areas.

To provide winter protection, in coldest areas mulch canes before the weather gets severe with 6–8 inches of straw. Where mice are a problem, or where canes are long, trench the soil and bury canes in 3–4 inches of soil, uncovering the canes as soon as possible in the spring.

Exposure

Brambleberries require full sun; in hot-summer areas they take light shade.

Planting

Prepare the planting bed with generous amounts of manure. For hedges, plant red raspberries 2–3 feet apart, black raspberries 3–4 feet apart. Plant erect types of blackberries 2–3 feet apart and trailing types 4–6 feet apart. Large, vigorous types such as 'Thornless Evergreen' and Himalaya berries should be planted no closer together than 10 feet apart.

Soil

All brambleberries prefer soil with considerable organic matter and good drainage.

Fertilizing

Too much fertilizer on brambleberries gives lush growth and few berries. Fertilize with manure in the spring. Keep the plants well mulched with compost or leaves.

Watering

Brambleberries need to be kept fairly moist, but not wet. Do not let them dry out.

Pruning

Some varieties of brambleberries are upright or can be pruned short enough to stand erect by themselves. Most brambleberries, however, are easier to control if they are trained and tied to a wire or fence.

Most brambleberries bear fruit on biennial canes. The canes emerge from the ground and produce foliage the first year, go dor-

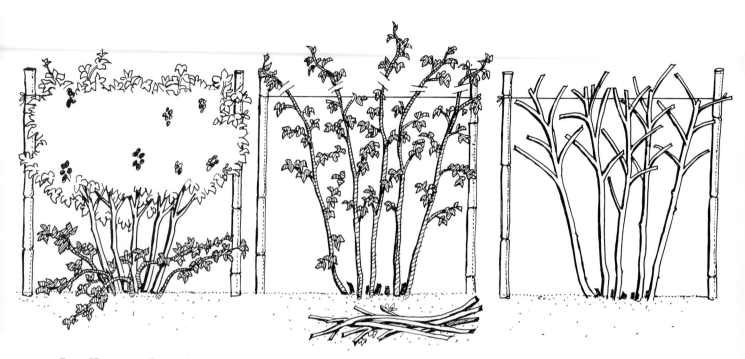

E.28. *This sequence illustrates how to prune single-crop raspberries, black raspberries, and upright blackberries.* **Left:** *Two-year-old bearing canes are tied to the wire. (New shoots—identified with stripes—are shown emerging from the ground.)* **Center:** *Second-year canes that are finished bearing are cut off; 5 or 6 robust new canes are selected and tied to the wire.* **Right:** *In spring, the two-year-old canes are tip pruned.*

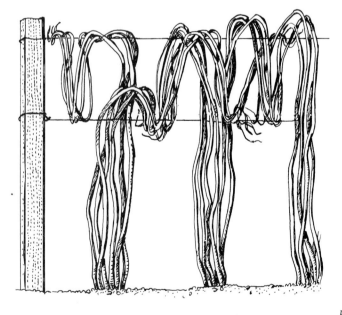

E.29. *Trailing types of brambleberries can be woven along a wire trellis.*

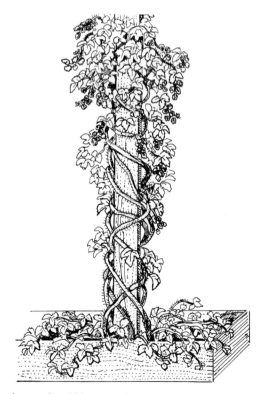

E.30. *Long, trailing-type brambleberries can be trained on posts. (Note next year's canes, the striped ones, at the bottom.)*

mant in winter, and flower and fruit the next summer. The canes then die. Depending on the variety, brambleberries may also sucker or root at the tips of branches, and if not pruned back will create impenetrable thickets. All these factors determine the pruning methods.

Single-crop raspberries, black raspberries, and upright blackberries can be pruned in the following way. Figure E. 28 shows the bush as it will appear the first year it bears fruit, with the two-year-old fruit-bearing canes tied to the wire. Next year's fruiting canes (identified by the striping) sprawl on the ground below.

After the fruit is harvested in summer, cut the two-year-old canes down to the ground. (See Figure E. 28) Select five or six of the healthiest new canes and tie them to the wire. To encourage new lateral growth along the wire, cut them back to within a few inches of the height of the wire, and cut the rest of the canes off at ground level. In winter prune the canes back to 4 or 5 feet high and prune the lateral branches back to about 18 inches long. All through the year remove all suckers that come up away from the crown of the plant.

With everbearing red raspberries, pruning is slightly different. The canes bear twice: in fall and again in the spring. After the fall crop, remove the tops of the canes that have borne fruit. The lower part of the cane will have lateral branches that will bear in the spring. Remove these canes completely after they have fruited in spring.

Trailing blackberries, boysenberries and loganberries are rampant growers and have trailing vines that need support. Train on wires as shown in Figure E. 29 or on a trellis or post as in Figure E. 30. Like raspberries, these trailing berries bear on biennial canes. The training is similar to that described for one-crop raspberries, but the canes are longer. After the summer harvest cut old canes down completely. Select five or six vigorous canes from those that have been growing along the ground and cut them to 4 feet long. Train them as shown along the wire or tie to a post.

Pests and Diseases

Brambleberries are not usually bothered by insects. Mites are an occasional problem and can be controlled by dormant sprays. Wilting foliage means borers may have invaded the canes. Where borers are a problem, cut the cane off below the damage. Examine the canes for borers to confirm your diagnosis. If no borers are found look for disease symptoms described below.

Diseases, rather than pests, are the most serious problem for brambleberries. You can avoid many troublesome conditions by only buying plants that are certified to be virus-free. Furthermore, choose resistant varieties, and when you detect symptoms—such as wilted, mottled, stunted, or deformed-looking growth—remove the plants. Virus diseases are common with black raspberries, and verticillium wilt is a serious problem with red raspberries. Blackberries are prone to more diseases in general than other species and have a particular problem with orange rust, which shows up as red-orange spores on the undersides of the leaf. None of the diseases mentioned has a cure. Remove the diseased plants as soon as you diagnose the problem. Do not compost the plants; burn them or take them to the dump.

Harvesting

Harvest brambleberries when they are fully colored and sweet. You will need to pick them every two or three days. Handle them very gently, as they are easily bruised. The large, trailing plants will yield about 1 quart of berries per foot of row; the erect, shrubby types about 1 quart per 2 feet of row.

How to Purchase

Forms and Sources

Purchase brambleberries bare root in early spring or in containers through early summer. Planting occurs in late fall in milder areas of the country. Buy your plants only from nurseries that carry certified virus-free plants. Combine early-, mid-, and late-season varieties to lengthen the harvesting season. Local nurseries and mail-order firms carry brambleberries. Two mail-order nurseries (**5, 50**) specialize in berries.

Pollinators

Most brambleberries are self-fertile.

Varieties

RED RASPBERRIES
'Citadel'—large berries; ripens midseason; vigorous and resistant to leaf spot. (**6**)
'Heritage'—medium-size red berries; everbearing type, bears July and September; bush is erect and quite hardy. (**Readily Available**)
'Newburgh'—large red berries; ripens midseason; tolerates heavy soil fairly well; short plants need little support; resistant to mosaic. (**18, 22, 37, 43, 46, 50**)
'Reveille'—large berries; ripens early; one of the hardiest for zone 3. (**Locally Available**)
'September'—medium-size berries; everbearing, major crop in the fall; hardy. (**5, 62**)
'Southland'—medium-size berries with an early spring and late summer crop; disease-resistant; best for southernmost berry gardens. (**5, 58**)

BLACK RASPBERRIES
'Cumberland'—large berries, big crops; ripens midseason. (**Readily Available**)
'Logan'—medium- to large-size berries; drought-resistant; resists mosaic virus and many other diseases. (**20**)

ERECT AND HARDY BLACKBERRIES
'Darrow'—large berries; long harvest season; erect plants; one of the hardier blackberries. (**Readily Available**)
'Ebony King'—purplish berries; early season; resists orange rust; hardy to −20°F. (**29, 62**)
'Ranger'—large berries; ripens midseason; good for wine. (**6**)
'Thornfree'—medium-size berries; ripens midseason; semiupright growth; does not sucker. (**6, 62**)

TENDER TRAILING BLACKBERRIES
'Boysen', or 'Thornless Boysen'—large wine-red berry; fairly hardy; long canes. (**Readily Available**)
'Evergreen', or 'Evergreen Thornless'—large, firm black berries; vigorous; semierect; long canes; handsome foliage. (**5, 60**)
'Himalaya'—black, medium-size berries with large seed; long season; vigorous, long vines; can spread and become a pest. (**Locally Available**)
'Olallie'—shiny, black berries; one of the best for California. (**24, 60**)

Preserving

Blackberries can be frozen, canned, dried, and made into wine or jam.

BUSH BASIL. See *Basil.*

BUSH BEAN. See *Beans.*

BUSH CHERRY. See *Plums, Bush.*

BUSH PLUM. See *Plums, Bush.*

BUTTER LETTUCE. See *Lettuce.*

BUTTERNUT. See *Walnut.*

Cabbage

Brassica oleracea, Capitata Group

Effort Scale

NO. 4
Must be planted annually
Constant moisture and fertilizing needed
Susceptible to many pests and diseases

Zones

Annual

Thumbnail Sketch

Annual or biennial planted as annual
12–18 in. tall
Propagated from seeds
Needs full sun; prefers light shade in hot climates
Leaves are ornamental, curled, ruffled, green, blue-green, red, purple, or blue
Blooms in warm weather
Flowers are yellow, usually not seen
Leaves are edible; harvested in spring, summer, and fall
Used in herbaceous borders, flower beds, containers

How to Use

In the Kitchen

Cabbage is a succulent vegetable used in salads, soups, and such main dishes as New England boiled dinner, corned beef and cabbage, and stuffed cabbage. It is a great favorite served pickled, as sauerkraut or kimchee (Korean pickled cabbage). In fact, nearly every country in the temperate zone has a favorite cabbage recipe. Red cabbage and flowering cabbage are both colorful and tasty in salads. The cabbage is a truly versatile vegetable.

In the Landscape

The puckery Savoy cabbage or the flowering cabbages, which look like giant peonies, are spectacular in raised beds, containers, and flower borders. The foliage of the flowering type, fringed or crinkled, comes in shades of pink, lavender, purple, blue, white or marbled cream. Together all varieties form a kaleidoscope of color and texture.

I like to plant the round-headed red variety up to its ruffled collar in a soy tub; it makes an elegant composition in color, texture, and form. All the cabbages perform beautifully in containers.

How to Grow

Climate

Cabbage is grown as a cool-season annual; it will bolt and go to seed in hot weather. In cold climates cabbage is grown in early spring or late summer; in the South and warm winter parts of the West, it is grown in fall, winter, and spring. The colorful flowering cabbages must have a frost to turn deep red or purple.

Exposure

Cabbage takes full sun, though in hot climates it takes light shade.

Soil

Cabbages need moist, rich soil.

Fertilizing

Fertilize with extra nitrogen. Keep well mulched.

Watering

Keep plants well watered.

Pests and Diseases

The biggest problem in growing cabbage is keeping ahead of the pests. The white cabbage butterfly has flitted her way across the

E.31. Try combining different colored cabbages in one pot, here a soy tub.

entire country, and her cabbage worm offspring happily chew on cabbage all season long. I have never grown a cabbage without a cabbage worm. If you get a severe infestation, the pesticide *Baccillus thuringiensis* controls the worm very effectively at very little cost to the environment. I usually control cabbage worms by picking the eggs off the undersides of the foliage where the butterfly deposits them every few days. These eggs are cream colored and about the size of a large pinhead.

Cabbage root fly is another pest that bothers cabbage. You can prevent the larvae from entering the soil by placing a 12-inch square of tar paper or black plastic directly over the roots of the plant. To do this, cut a slit about 6 inches long directly to the middle of the square and slip it around the plant.

Cutworms often attack young cabbage plants. A good preventive measure is to place a collar of cardboard around each seedling.

Aphids sometimes are a problem too. Try a heavy spray of water or consult chapter 7.

Clubroot is a serious fungus disease of the cabbage family. Good plant hygiene is your best preventive here. Buy disease-free plants and do not accept plants from friends who have had the problem. Rotate members of the cabbage family with other vegetable families to discourage the fungus. And pull up all cabbage-family weeds: mustard and shepherd's purse are the most common.

Harvesting

Harvest head cabbages any time after they have started to head up well and before they become so large they split. Mature cabbages can take temperatures as low as 20°F, so do not rush to harvest all of them before a frost. The Savoy types are the most hardy. If a hard freeze is expected, harvest all the cabbages and store them in a cool place, stacking them in straw if possible.

Most cabbages will yield about 3 pounds per 1½ feet of row.

How to Purchase

There are many different types of cabbages: red-leaved ones, Savoy types with their crinkly leaves, miniature ones for small areas, and the multicolored flowering cabbages. Some types are better for winter storage; some grow better in different times of the year; others are resistant to some of the cabbage diseases. Consult seed catalogs and packages to choose the varieties best suited to your needs and conditions. Cabbage seed is readily available from local nurseries and the following mail-order sources: (**9, 16, 20, 22, 25, 28, 32, 35, 47, 48, 51, 59**—a particularly large selection, **62, 63**). Flowering cabbages are available from: (**16, 28, 47, 59**).

Preserving and Preparing

The best way to preserve large amounts of cabbage is to make sauerkraut or kimchee.

Spicy Stuffed Cabbage

I created this recipe as a way to use an oversupply of wild-boar sausage. I am aware that not too many people have this problem, but the recipe works equally well with any good sausage. It also makes a good filling for peppers.

1 large cabbage	¼ teaspoon allspice
1 pound sausage meat	¼ teaspoon cinnamon
1 cup chopped onion	¼ teaspoon black pepper
1 clove of garlic, mashed	salt to taste
2 cups of cooked rice	1 cup beef bouillon

¼ cup raisins	1 cup tomato sauce
¼ cup pistachio nuts or pine nuts	

Prepare the cabbage for stuffing by pulling off the tough outer leaves and washing and coring the head. To separate the leaves, boil the cabbage head in a very large pot of water for about 5 minutes. Check after a few minutes to see if the outer leaves are getting soft and will pull away from the core easily. I usually end up taking the cabbage out and removing half the outside leaves and then boiling the remaining head for a few minutes more until the last of the leaves loosen.

Score the inside midribs of the very large leaves to allow for easy folding.

Brown and then crumble the sausage meat. Drain off all but 3 tablespoons of the fat, and cook the onions and garlic until translucent.

In a large bowl, combine the sausage, onions, garlic, rice, raisins, nuts, and spices. Mix well. Stuff each cabbage leaf with 1–2 tablespoons of the meat mixture, depending on the size of the leaf. Fold the leaf around the mixture and place packets, folded side down, in a large roasting pan. If you have extra leaves, lay them over the top of the stuffed leaves before you add the sauce. (If you have extra filling, freeze it and use it for stuffing peppers.)

Combine the bouillon and tomato sauce, and pour over the stuffed cabbage leaves.

Cover the pan, and bake for one hour at 350°. Add more sauce if necessary.

CALAMONDIN. See *Citrus Fruits.*

CALIFORNIA BAY. See *Sweet Bay.*

CALIFORNIA BLACK WALNUT. See *Walnut.*

Capers

Capparis spinosa

Effort Scale

NO. 2
Seeds are difficult to buy
Easy to grow
Must be pickled to be edible

Zones

Warmest parts of 9 and 10, as perennial
6–8 as annual

Thumbnail Sketch

Shrubby perennial, often grown as annual
3–5 ft. tall
Propagated from seeds or cuttings

Needs full sun
Leaves are fleshy, green, round, 2 in. across
Flowers in summer
Flowers are cream-colored with long pink or violet stamens,
     2–3 in. long
Flower buds are edible; harvested in summer
Used on hillsides, in large rock gardens, containers

How to Use

In the Kitchen

The flower buds of capers are pickled and used to add a touch of class to *hors d'oeuvres*, stuffings, sauces, salads, and even pickled shrimp. Capers are expensive to buy, so by growing them you are producing a real glamor item.

In the Landscape

In mild-winter areas, these evergreen, woody plants are perennials that can achieve both a height and width of 5 feet. In less salubrious climates, they are annuals and smaller. Their green, fleshy leaves are roundish and are carried on arching, wiry branches. Their lovely flowers have 2–3-inch petals and long pinkish or violet stamens. Capers are used in informal places such as large rock gardens, on dry rocky banks, as a background in an herb garden, or in containers.

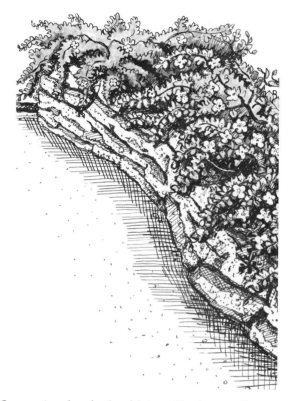

E.33. *Capers prefer rocky soil and good drainage. Here they are spilling over an informal wall made of recycled concrete.*

How to Grow

Capers are native to the Mediterranean region, so they like a mild, dry climate. Because they have a long growing season, when grown as an annual in zones 6–8 the seeds must be planted early in the spring or can be started inside in early spring. Keep the seedbed between 60–70°F. Set young plants out when all danger of frost has passed. Plant in a warm, sunny place.

Whether grown as perennials or annuals, capers like full sun and rocky or sandy soil. They will thrive in poor soil, but it must be well drained. They are drought resistant, and too much water will rot the plants. They need no fertilizing. Prune occasionally to prevent the plant from becoming straggly.

When harvesting for pickling, pick flower buds just before they open. The buds should be left in the dark for a few hours before they are given the pickling treatment. In India the fruits of the caper as well as the flower buds are pickled; you might want to try this.

How to Purchase

Seeds are available from: (**32, 48, 51**).

Preserving

Pickled Capers

1 quart caper buds
1 ½ cups wine vinegar

1 teaspoon mustard seed
1 teaspoon dill seed

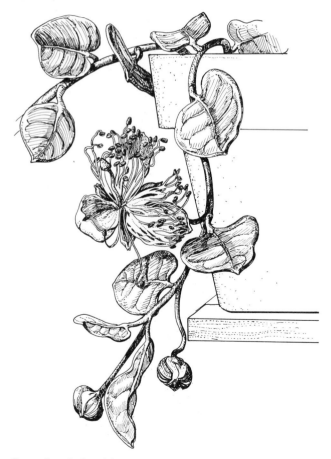

E.32. *Caper buds and flowers. The flowers have violet or rose stamens.*

½ cup water
⅓ cup brown sugar
1 teaspoon salt

1 teaspoon celery seed
1 clove garlic, crushed

Put the washed capers in sterilized canning jars. In a saucepan (avoid aluminum, which discolors the buds) combine all the ingredients except capers. Bring to a rolling boil, and boil rapidly for 10 minutes. Strain the vinegar mixture and bring to a boil again. Pour over the capers. Seal the jars tightly, and store them for at least two weeks before using.

CARAWAY-SCENTED THYME. See *Thyme*.

Carob *(ST. JOHN'S BREAD)*

Ceratonia Siliqua

Effort Scale

NO. 4
Easy to grow
Locating plants is difficult
Some raking required
Processing for powder is messy

Zones

9, 10

Thumbnail Sketch

Evergreen tree or shrub
20–40 ft. tall
Propagated from seeds and by budding
Needs full sun, will tolerate light shade
Leaves are glossy green, round, 4 in. across; new growth is bronzy
Blooms in summer
Flowers are insignificant
Pods are edible; harvested in fall
Used as interest tree or shrub, sheared formal tree or shrub, windbreak, and screen

How to Use

In the Kitchen

The big, handsome, brown pods of the carob tree can be eaten fresh and unprocessed out of hand. They are sweet and chewy, something like hard dates. Generally the pods are roasted and ground into a powder that is used in place of chocolate in ice cream, cakes, cookies, and even brownies. Unlike chocolate, carob powder contains no caffeine. It is a highly nutritious food, and very useful if its taste appeals to you. Processing the fruits—cooking and grinding them—is a sticky chore, so before you plant, process some to see if you think they are worth the effort. If you are among

E.34. *Carob pods are dark brown. The new foliage has a bronzy tint.*

those who enjoy unprocessed carob pods, you will reap an abundance of the pods with very little effort.

In the Landscape

In climates where carob trees will grow, no question arises as to their landscaping uses. These round-headed, evergreen plants, which can be multistemmed shrubs or single-stemmed trees, are extremely handsome. They can be kept to 20 feet, but will grow to 40 feet, attaining an equal width. Their foliage is dense, composed of shiny, dark, blue-green leaves made up of many round leaflets. New growth is a lovely reddish-bronze that appears to grow in star-shaped whorls.

Its dense foliage makes the carob an excellent shade tree or, when kept as a shrub, an effective windbreak or privacy screen. Carob trees are often used in California as street trees, but they must be root-pruned and deep-watered occasionally to prevent the sidewalk from buckling. Where this limitation can be solved, the trees make stunning driveway liners.

The carob's long, flat, brown, beanlike pods can grow to 10 inches in length and are an interesting contrast to the green foliage. If you do not plan to use them, however, picking them up can be a nuisance.

Because of their minimal water needs, carobs can be grown in desert conditions, where their shade is a blessing.

How to Grow

Climate

Carobs are native to the eastern Mediterranean and will take

E.35. *Carob trees have a naturally formal shape. Little shearing is needed to keep them looking trim and symmetrical.*

temperatures only as low as 20°F, so they are not usable in areas with harsh winters. They tolerate dry conditions very well but have a low tolerance for rainy climates. In this country, their culture is confined to the dry, mild-winter areas of the Southwest away from the ocean. The pods are prone to worms and mold if there is much rain when they are ripening in October and November.

Exposure

Carob trees require full sun or light shade.

Soil

The trees will grow in any well-drained garden soil, sandy or clay.

Fertilizing

Fertilizing is not needed under most conditions.

Watering

Regular watering is not needed once the tree is established, but supplemental watering will increase production.

Pruning

Prune mature trees only to shape, and to remove dead or weak branches.

Pests and Diseases

Worms that destroy the pods are a problem in warm, moist climates. Pick up and destroy all spoiled pods at the end of the season.

Harvesting

Pick pods when they have become dark brown. Taste them to see if they are sweet and have developed their sugar. A ten- to twelve-year-old tree can bear 100 pounds of pods.

How to Purchase

Forms and Sources

Carob trees with predictable fruit are hard to obtain. Although trees are sometimes sold at local nurseries, such trees are grown only for ornamentation and are seedlings with unknown fruit quality and unknown gender. Plant at least five trees if you are growing carob trees from seed. This will assure at least one male and one female tree for fruit production. Under good growing conditions gender will be apparent in 3–5 years. Seed is available from: (51) and plants from the International Tree Crops Institute.

Pollinators

Both male and female trees are needed for pollination, although a few varieties are self-fruitful.

Varieties

Named varieties are very hard to find, but the following have been available in the past:

'Amele'—female; worm free; best in deserts.
'Clifford'—self-fruitful; some worm problems; best in foothills.
'Santa Fe'—self-fruitful; worm resistant; good in California foothills but not desert.
'Sfay'—female; worm problems; best in California foothills.
'Tylliria'—female; wormy near coast; best in desert.

The International Tree Crops Institute (California branch; see Appendix B for address) carries five varieties, including 'Santa Fe' and 'Tylliria'.

Preparing

Processing Carob Powder

Carob pods have small, black seeds that must be removed before processing. If they are not removed, the seeds will clog up your grinding mechanism.

Wash the pods and place in a pressure cooker with water (instruction for use of cooker should indicate about how much is needed). Cook for 20 minutes at 15 pounds pressure.

Cooking softens the pods, making splitting them open fairly easy. Remove seeds, cut pods into small pieces, and dry.

Put the pieces in a blender and grind into a powder. Process only small amounts at a time.

This powder can be used as a substitute for cocoa powder.

Chamomile

Garden (or Roman) chamomile, *Chamaemelum nobile*
[*Anthemis nobilis*]
Sweet false (or German) chamomile, *Matricaria recutita*
[*M. chamomilla*]

Effort Scale

NO. 2
Perennial (garden) chamomile needs trimming and some
weeding
Sweet false chamomile must be planted annually

Zones

4–10 for the perennial
All for annual

Thumbnail Sketch

Garden Chamomile

Perennial herb
3–12 in. tall
Propagate from seed or divisions
Needs sun; will tolerate partial shade
Leaves are small, bright green, fernlike
Blooms in spring and summer
Flowers are usually small, white, daisylike; some forms have
yellow, buttonlike flowers
Flowers are edible; used as tea; harvested in summer
Used as walk-on ground cover and in herb gardens, herbal tea
gardens, rock gardens, and between stepping stones

Sweet False Chamomile

Summer annual
2–2½ ft. tall
Propagated from seed
Needs full sun
Leaves are small, bright green, fernlike
Flowers in summer
Flowers are usually white and yellow, daisylike, 1 in. across
Flowers are edible; used as tea; harvested in summer
Used in flower beds, herb gardens, containers

How to Use

In the Kitchen

The flowerheads of these plants, dried and steeped, make a
lovely, refreshing drink, and, as all readers of *Peter Rabbit* know,
chamomile tea has soothing qualities. The flavor of the garden
chamomile is stronger and more medicinal than that of the sweet
false. The latter has a slight flavor of pineapple. Either plant offers
refreshing, noncaffeinated beverages.

In the Landscape

Garden chamomile is an evergreen perennial. It forms a carpet
of fine, ferny foliage that can be mowed. It can be used as a lawn
substitute if it does not get too much foot traffic, and it stays lush if
mowed a few times during the summer. It is also useful as a filler
between stepping stones and as a specimen in rock gardens. The

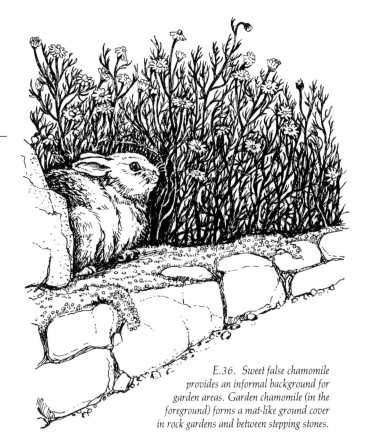

E.36. *Sweet false chamomile
provides an informal background for
garden areas. Garden chamomile (in the
foreground) forms a mat-like ground cover
in rock gardens and between stepping stones.*

most commonly grown variety has flowers that are usually yellow,
rounded buttons.

Sweet false chamomile is an annual, and has small ferny leaves.
It grows taller than garden chamomile, and is used in flower
borders, herb gardens, and containers. The flowers of this plant
resemble tiny Shasta daisies. It is delightful combined with small
yellow marigolds, blackeyed Susans, and 'Dutch Treat' peppers.

How to Grow, Purchase, and Preserve

Both plants thrive in most areas. They prefer full sun but will
grow in light shade. They have no particular soil or pollination
requirements, nor do they need to be fertilized.

The part of chamomile used for brewing tea is the flowerhead.
To pick the flowers, wait until the yellow center is conelike and the
petals bend downward.

Garden chamomile can be bought in nurseries as small plants,
usually in flats of 48 or 81 plants, or it can be grown from seed.
Sweet false chamomile is usually planted from seed that is readily
available from nurseries and seed catalogues.

Place the flowers on a cookie sheet in a very low oven or a very
warm place until they are completely dry. Store them in an airtight
container.

For a good cup of tea, you need 1–1½ teaspoons dried flowers
to 1 cup boiling water. Let the mixture steep for 5–10 minutes,
depending on the strength that pleases you.

CHARD. See *Greens.*

Cherry

Sweet cherry, *Prunus avium*
Sour cherry, *P. Cerasus*

Effort Scale

NO. 3
Vulnerable to some pests, particularly birds
Harvesting is time-consuming

Zones

4–9

Thumbnail Sketch

Deciduous trees
Sweet cherry, standard, 25–35 ft. tall; semidwarf varieties,
   10–15 ft. tall; dwarf varieties, 6–8 ft. tall
Sour cherry, 15–20 ft. tall; genetic dwarf, 8–10 ft. tall
Propagated by grafting and budding
Need full sun
Leaves are deep green, serrated, 2–6 in. long
Bloom in early spring
Flowers are white in large clusters, showy
Fruits are edible; harvested in summer
Used as shade tree, interest plant, large screen; dwarf used as
   hedge and foundation shrub, and in containers

How to Use

In the Kitchen

Cherries, glorious cherries! If you have ever lived near a cherry tree, you know the pleasure of picking and eating your fill, and beyond. The luscious red, yellow, or black globes of the sweet cherry tree can be canned, used in jams, in a chilled cherry soup, and of course flamed in cherries jubilee.

Sour cherries are eaten raw too, but their main use is in that great American favorite, cherry pie. Many people prefer the tartness of sour-cherry jam to jam made from sweet cherries.

In the Landscape

The cherry is among the most beautiful of trees. Even without its fruit it is a handsome addition to a yard. In the winter, the dark, rich, reddish-brown or silver dotted bark lends color and texture, and in the spring both species of this deciduous tree burst forth with masses of showy white flowers. Later, the colorful fruits themselves are decorative among the rich-green, serrated leaves. The leaves are plentiful, and, since the standard-size trees can grow to 35 feet, they make excellent shade trees and tall screens. However, if cherry trees are used to shade a house, a screen should cover the gutters, because fruit that collects there will ferment and smell rank. Also, a tree that needs a lot of spraying is best not planted near a window.

Sour cherry trees are the smaller of the two, growing to only 20 feet. They look fine along a driveway, make an excellent specimen tree that can be admired up close, and are useful as a medium-high screen. Recently, semidwarf and dwarf cherry trees have been developed; these grow to only 8–15 feet in height. They can be grown in containers, as informal hedges or screens, and as small accent plants. The fruits on these small varieties are more easily accessible.

How to Grow

Climate

Both sweet and sour cherries require some winter chilling and cannot tolerate very hot summers. Heavy rains just before harvest cause the fruit to split. Sweet cherries require about the same climatic conditions as peaches. The most successful sweet cherries are grown in the Hudson River Valley in New York, around the Great Lakes, and on the West Coast. Because they are more hardy, bloom later, and can tolerate more heat, sour cherries have a much broader range. They are grown along the Atlantic coast, in the colder sections of the West Coast, in the Mississippi Valley, and commercially in Wisconsin, Michigan, and New York.

Exposure

Sweet and sour cherries need full sun.

Soil

Cherries prefer light, well drained, sandy soil. Some varieties of sour cherries can take a heavier soil. All cherries respond well to mulches of compost or manure.

Fertilizing

If the soil is fertile the trees may not need any fertilizer. Light amounts of a nitrogen-type fertilizer should be used if the foliage is pale. But beware: too much nitrogen increases the trees' susceptibility to disease.

Watering

Cherry trees have shallow root systems and thus need to be kept fairly moist. Sour cherry trees are more drought tolerant.

Pruning

Cherries bear on long-lived fruiting spurs. Except for routine maintenance, regular pruning of sweet cherries is not necessary; however, as sour cherries grow older their branches need to be thinned occasionally. Young trees of both types should be trained to have wide crotches, since in untrained trees the crotches are often too narrow, and therefore too weak. Young sweet cherry trees are usually trained to a leader system; sour cherries are generally pruned to a modified leader system.

Pests and Diseases

The specific name for sweet cherries is *avium*, which means, loosely, "for the birds." Birds are the biggest problem. Covering the tree with netting provides protection, and of course the dwarf varieties are easier to net. Growing a fruiting mulberry tree also is some protection, because the birds prefer the mulberries to the cherries, but mulberries do have a very messy fruit drop. During the very wet years, brown rot and cracking fruit are the worst problems affecting cherries. Cherries are prone to most of the diseases that plums get (see Chapter 7).

Tent caterpillars, black aphids, curculio, and cherry maggots are sometimes troublesome.

Harvesting

Pick cherries with their stems on to delay deterioration of the

E.37. The silvery, textured bark of cherry trees is a year-round decorative bonus. Their serrated, dark green foliage and bright red fruits complete the tree's visual appeal.

fruits. Be sure to leave the fruit spurs on the tree when you pull the cherries off, since the spurs bear the next year's fruits. Most mature trees yield about 1–2 bushels of fruit annually.

How to Purchase

Forms and Sources

Buy sweet and sour cherry trees bare root in late winter or in containers through summer from your local nurseries and mail-order houses. (For availability of specific varieties, see below.)

Pollinators

Most varieties of sweet cherries need a pollinator. Be careful to choose the right varieties; not all varieties pollinate all other varieties.

Sour cherries are not reliable pollinators of sweet cherries except in California. Most varieties of sour cherries are self-pollinating.

Varieties

SWEET CHERRIES

'Bing'—the most popular sweet cherry; dark red fruits, prone to cracking in wet climates; excellent flavor; ripens midseason; needs a pollinator, usually 'Van', 'Sam', or 'Black Tartarian'; spreading tree and heavy bearer. (Standard, **Readily Available;** semidwarf, **6**)

'Black Republican'—medium-size black cherry; hardier than most sweet cherries; ripens late; good in borderline areas; can be pollinated by any sweet cherry. (**11**)

'Black Tartarian'—medium-size black cherry; excellent fruits; one of the earliest bearers; a good pollinator for 'Bing'; tree very erect. (**Readily Available**)

'Emperor Francis'—red, medium-size cherry; ripens late; easier to grow than many sweet cherries; more tolerant of soil type and good disease-resister. (Standard, **1, 6, 30, 40;** semidwarf, **6**)

'Garden Bing'—self-fertile genetic dwarf sweet cherry; 'Bing' type; does well in containers; not a heavy bearer, so try planting more than one. (**71**)

'Rainier'—excellent yellow cherry; ripens early to midseason; quite hardy; trees spread more than most. (**11, 12, 46**)

'Royal Anne' ('Napoleon')—an old favorite; prone to cracking; yellow blushed red; ripens midseason; good fresh or canned; tree large and somewhat spreading; not very hardy. (**Readily Available**)

'Stella'—the only self-fertile sweet cherry; ripens midseason; a good pollinator for other varieties; a shorter, more compact 'Stella'—a genetic dwarf—just introduced. (**11, 28, 46, 71**)

'Van'—dark fruit; quite hardy; good in borderline areas; bears as a fairly young tree; pollinators, most cherries including 'Bing' and 'Royal Anne'. (**1, 6, 10, 11, 71**)

'Windsor'—dark cherry; ripens late; quite hardy and disease resistant. (**6, 30**)

SOUR CHERRIES

'Early Richmond'—red fruits; old-time pie cherry for cold climates; not good in hot areas. (**22, 43**)

'English Morello'—dark red fruits; ripens late; good for cooking and preserving. (**46, 57, 60**)

'Meteor'—red fruits; extra-hardy dwarf; very good for northern gardens. (**Readily Available**)

'Montmorency'—red fruits; most popular sour cherry; medium- to large-size spreading tree. (**Readily Available**)

'North Star'—red fruits; genetic dwarf 8–10 ft.; attractive and hardy; resistant to brown rot. (**Readily Available**)

Preserving

Sweet-cherry jam is good. Sweet cherries can be frozen or canned for use in cherries jubilee. Sour cherries can be made into excellent jams and jellies, canned, frozen, dried, or used to make wine. To dry cherries, wash fruits, remove stems and pits, and drain on paper towels for an hour. Use a food dryer, following the manufacturer's directions, or use your oven, placing fruits on cookie sheets and baking cherries at a very low heat until they are not sticky anymore. Start drying at 120°F; then raise temperature to 150° until the cherries are dry. Dried cherries can be used in fruit cakes, cookies, and in any recipe calling for raisins.

Chestnut

Chinese chestnut, *Castanea mollissima*

Effort Scale

NO. 2
Raking is often needed
Occasional pest problems
Easy to grow
Harvesting large yields is time-consuming

Zones

5–9

E.38. *The serrated leaves of the chestnut are attractive, and the burrs guard the nuts from squirrels and bluejays.*

Thumbnail Sketch

Deciduous tree
60 ft. tall, 40 ft. spread
Propagated from seed or by grafting
Needs full sun
Leaves are deep green, coarsely toothed, 3–7 in. long
Blooms in summer
Flowers are small and white on large catkins, showy
Nuts are edible; harvested in fall
Used as shade trees, street trees, large interest trees

How to Use

In the Kitchen

Roasted chestnuts are a cold-winter treat. City people associate them with street vendors, picturesquely warming their hands over the hot coals on which they roast their wares. Other images are traditionally American: "chestnuts roasting on an open fire," and that luscious holiday specialty, chestnut turkey stuffing. These savory memories are associated with the native American *C. dentata* or imported European chestnut *C. sativa*, tragically decimated by blight early in this century. Happily, its Oriental cousin, *C. mollisima*, which is relatively blight resistant, is being introduced in many places; and in an even more encouraging development, healthy second-generation American chestnuts are now being propagated from a genetically resistant specimen (see "How to Purchase").

Chestnuts are among the sweetest of the nuts and are delightful both by themselves and used in cooked vegetable dishes. They lend their sweetness to red cabbage, mushrooms, onions, carrots, and sweet potatoes. Chestnuts are at their best as stuffing for or accompaniment to roast turkey, goose, venison, or pheasant. And, of course, with a supply of *marrons glacés* (glazed chestnuts) in your pantry, you will be prepared for the most honored guest. Even an instant pudding becomes an elegant presentation when topped with this delicacy.

Chestnuts are very expensive to buy in the store. Thus, it is only when you are fortunate enough to have your own tree that you can relish them with abandon.

In the Landscape

Chestnuts are magnificent spreading trees that lend stature to any spacious yard. A large chestnut tree cannot help but inspire the thought, "Now, there's a *real* tree!" Chestnut trees are what trees are all about—stateliness, grace, and permanence.

Chestnut trees can shade a hot south house wall and, with their long sweeping branches, make a dramatic addition to a yard. They are not only a decorative asset, but, with their edible nuts, a practical one as well. In the eastern part of the country, chestnuts grow well on lawns, unlike most fruit-producing trees. And, wherever these trees grow, their sturdy trunks and branching structures provide firm support for the most ambitious of tree houses.

How to Grow

Climate

With a tolerance to temperatures from −20° to −15°F, chestnut trees are slightly more hardy than peach trees and have the added advantage of blooming in early summer, which means their flow-ers escape damage from late frosts. However, these trees do not grow well in humid, tropical conditions, such as Florida and Hawaii.

Exposure

Chestnut trees require full sun.

Soil

Chestnuts do well in average soils and can tolerate gravelly soils, but they must have good drainage. They grow best in somewhat sandy soils that are slightly acid. Better soils result in bigger nuts and a larger harvest. These trees are intolerant of alkaline soil conditions.

Fertilizer

Chestnuts benefit from annual applications of manure and compost as well as leaf mulches.

Watering

In areas with rainy summers, supplemental watering is unnecessary. In arid-summer areas, occasional deep watering is needed.

Pruning

For pruning young trees, see HICKORY. Mature trees need pruning only to shape the tree and to remove dead or crossing branches.

Pests and Diseases

Chinese chestnuts are quite resistant to the blight fungus *Endothia parasitica*, which killed the American chestnut tree in the early 1900s.

E.39. Mature chestnut trees are magnificent giants that need plenty of room to spread.

Most of the pests and diseases that bother chestnuts are troublesome in the eastern part of the country. Oak wilt causes the leaves to wilt and then to look waterlogged. There is no control, and infected trees die.

The major pest is the chestnut weevil, an insect whose length varies according to the species from ¼ to ¾ inch long. The weevils are brown, have long snouts, and lay their eggs in the nuts. When they hatch, the larvae feast on the meat. To control, place a bedsheet under the tree and shake the tree. The adults will fall into the sheet. Destroy them. Also, pick nuts up off the ground daily and keep them in airtight containers to prevent the weevils from escaping and reinfecting next year's crop. For moderate infestations, diatomaceous earth dusted on the foliage is effective. Insecticides applied to the soil are sometimes needed if there are significant numbers of native chestnut or chinquapin shrubs around, since these species can harbor large numbers of weevils. Soil-applied insecticides are used to kill weevils as they emerge from the ground in the spring.

Harvesting

Chestnuts are ripe just as they fall and the burrs start to open. Pick the nuts off the tree or collect nuts from under the tree every few days. This way you will beat the squirrels, who must wait for the burrs to open more widely before they can get to the nuts. Nuts that are left in the sun too long quickly dry out and deteriorate.

A mature tree will yield about 50–75 pounds of nuts annually.

Weevil-affected nuts might still be edible if the larvae are killed in the egg stage before the harvest is stored. To kill the eggs, soak the nuts in 122°F water for 45 minutes. Dry and store.

How to Purchase

Forms and Sources

Buy chestnuts bare root or in containers from local nurseries or from these mail-order sources: (6, 7, 9, 22, 26, 61, 68, 72).

For information about the blight-resistant American chestnut mentioned above, contact Chestnut Hill Nursery, Rt. 2, Box 157P, Trenton, FL 32693.

Pollinators

Chestnut trees need cross-pollination. Plant more than one. If space is limited, plant two or three in one hole to form a multi-stemmed tree.

Varieties

'Crane'—good flavor and keeping qualities; good for southern and middle chestnut-growing areas. (26)
'Nanking'—most widely grown; heavy producer. (26)
'Orrin'—large nuts with good keeping quality. (26)

Preserving and Preparing

Chestnuts have a high water content and must not be allowed to dry out. They are best stored in the refrigerator, in a sealed plastic bag containing some peat moss; optimum temperature is 32–40°F.

Chestnuts can be roasted in an oven. Before roasting, pierce each nut with a sharp knife; a criss-cross pattern works well. Place nuts in a shallow pan with a small amount of oil. Roast at 450° for 10–15 minutes.

Peeled chestnuts may be braised for use as a vegetable. Place chestnuts in a heavy casserole and cover with beef broth. Bake covered, in the oven at 325° until tender, about 1 hour.

CHINESE CHESTNUT. See *Chestnut.*

CHINESE CHIVE. See *Chive.*

CHINESE DATE. See *Jujube.*

CHINESE GOOSEBERRY. See *Kiwi.*

CHINESE LOTUS. See *Lotus.*

CHINESE PEA POD. See *Snow Pea.*

CHINESE WATER CHESTNUT. See *Water Chestnut.*

Chives

Chinese or garlic chives, *Allium tuberosum* [*odorum*]
Garden chives, *A. Schoenoprasum*

Effort Scale

NO. 1
Dead foliage and flowers must be trimmed off in the fall

Zones

All; grow as annual in very coldest areas

Thumbnail Sketch

Chinese Chives

Perennial herb
16–20 in. tall
Propagated from seed or divisions
Needs full sun
Leaves are grayish green, flat, and grasslike, to 12 in. tall
Blooms in spring and summer
Flowers are white, flat-headed cluster, 1½–2 in. across, fragrant
Leaves and flowers are edible; used as seasoning; harvested throughout the growing season
Used in flower beds, rock gardens, herb gardens, containers

Garden Chives

Perennial herb
1–2 ft. tall
Propagate from seed or divisions
Needs full sun
Leaves are blue-green, tubular, grasslike, to 9 in. tall
Blooms in spring and summer
Flowers are lavender to purple, cloverlike
Leaves are edible; used as seasoning; harvested throughout growing season
Used in flower beds, rock gardens, herb gardens, containers

How to Use

In the Kitchen

These herbs have a mild onion or garlic flavor. They are used to flavor and garnish salads, cottage cheese, and cream sauce. A sprinkling of either one on a soup or a stew adds a fresh fillip. Pots of chives are a decorative asset to a sunny kitchen windowsill in in winter; garden chives are preferable for this purpose, as Chinese chives go dormant.

In the Landscape

These herbaceous perennials are delightful in herb gardens, rock gardens, flower gardens, or containers. The plants are attractive enough to be used as a border and add variety to any bed, herb or flower. Both species are similar in height but there their similarity ends. Garden chives have bright, blue-green tubular leaves (the specific name comes from *schoinos,* "reedlike"). Their purple clover-like blossoms come in the early spring, often blooming off and on again all summer.

Chinese or garlic chives have grayish, straplike leaves with white flowers in flat clusters in the summer. Some people think the flowers smell like roses, others, like violets—take your pick. Both chives combine well with frothy pink alyssum or ageratum, variegated sage, and thyme.

E.40. Chives are a natural for containers. You can stretch the fresh-chive season by growing some on a windowsill.

How to Grow, Purchase, and Preserve

Both kinds of chives are successful in all parts of the United States. They both prefer full sun, fairly rich soil, and moisture throughout the growing season. The old flower heads and dead leaves should be removed from both species, and both plants should be divided and replanted every two or three years.

Harvest chives as needed, cutting off the tops with scissors.

Garden chives are readily available as seeds or bedding plants. They are also available from friends who are dividing their plants. Chinese chives are available from: (**32, 35, 48, 64**).

To preserve, freeze harvested chives or bring a growing plant of garden chives indoors for winter use.

Citrus Fruits

Calamondin, *Citrus reticulata* x *Fortunella* sp. *mitis*
Grapefruit, *Citrus* x *paradisi*
Kumquat, *Fortunella margarita*
Lemon, *Citrus Limon*
Lime, *C. aurantiifolia*
Limequat, *C. aurantiifolia* 'Eustis' x *Fortunella margarita*
Mandarin (Tangerine), *C. reticulata*
Orange, *C. sinensis*
Pomelo (Shaddock), *C. maxima*
Tangelo, *C. paradisi* x *C. reticulata*

Effort Scale

NO. 3
Fertilizer and mineral supplements usually needed
Deep watering required, particularly in arid climates
Susceptible to some pests and diseases, particularly in humid climates
Mulching necessary
Some pruning needed

Zones

9, 10, and Hawaii

Thumbnail Sketch

Evergreen trees or shrubs
4–30 ft. tall, depending on type
Propagated by budding or grafting
Need full sun; some species tolerate light shade
Leaves are bright green, 2–7½ in. long
Bloom at different times of the year, depending on type
Flowers are small, white, fragrant, not showy
Fruits are edible; harvest season varies with type
Used as interest tree or shrub, screen, formal or informal hedge, foundation plant, espalier, and in containers

E.41. Citrus fruits are versatile landscape plants. Dwarf varieties planted around the front of this house include from left to right: orange, lemon, kumquat (in front), orange, limequat, lime, calamondin, a second kumquat, and orange. The large tree is a full-size tangerine.

How to Use

In the Kitchen

For breakfast, you might squeeze lime juice on melon and spread lemon marmalade on toast. Oranges, sliced and arranged with thin onion rings, might be your luncheon salad, and half a grapefruit, broiled with a little sherry, could serve as dessert for your evening meal. Such might be your citrus scenario for one day. On another day you might use these same fruits and flavors in a cream or chiffon pie or in mixed-fruit salads, or blend their juices into various sauces and dressings.

The less common citrus types lend an exotic touch. Calamondin makes magnificent marmalade. Small kumquats and limequats, their sweet rind and sour pulp eaten together, make a definite taste sensation, though whether or not a pleasant one is a personal matter. Both these small citrus preserved make handsome garnishes for meats. Mandarin oranges, and tangerines, are enjoyable just as they come from the tree owing to their ease of peeling. Canned, they make a delectable addition to fruit compotes and custards. Pomelos, one of the parents of the grapefruit, resemble their offspring but are larger. They are eaten raw and in sections as grapefruits are, but each section has to be peeled of its heavy membrane.

In the Landscape

Citrus fruit trees are as useful in the landscape as they are in the kitchen. These evergreens, whose foliage is bright green and very dense, can be either trees or shrubs. In both forms they are usually rounded, although kumquats and mandarins have a more upright growth than the others. The fragrance of numerous small, waxy, white citrus flowers is famous, and their orange, yellow, or green fruits are decorative in the winter when few other plants have color.

The fresh foliage, the pleasing shape, the fragrance, the color—all these features make citrus plants a fine addition to any yard in a suitable climate. I rarely design a yard that does not include at least one citrus fruit tree. They fit in with any design and, with prices rising apace, the grower's efforts are soon repaid.

Hybridizers have created a citrus for every niche, large and small. Most citrus trees come in standard and dwarf forms. The taller plants—lemon, orange, grapefruit, and tangerine—can shade a hot south wall. They can line a driveway or be used as single specimens, formal or informal depending on how they are pruned.

Take advantage of the famous citrus fragrance by planting a citrus fruit tree or shrub near your front entry—it will welcome your guests most pleasantly. And for your family's enjoyment, plant one on a patio or near a bedroom window, where the heavenly scent can waft inside.

The taller citrus trees can be espaliered against warm, two-story

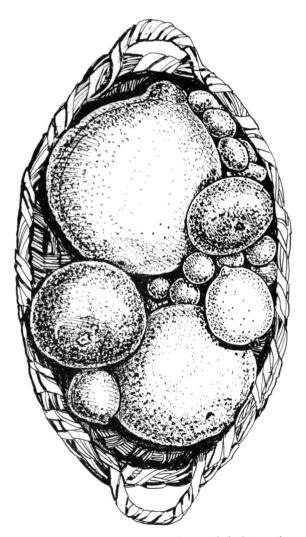

E.42. *Citrus fruits, counterclockwise from the top of the basket: pomelo, navel orange, lime, grapefruit, lemon, calamondin, tangerine, and kumquat.*

walls, while the smaller and dwarf kinds are useful as espaliers on low walls and fences. The dwarfs are also used as clipped or unclipped hedges, screens, as large shrubs in a border, and in foundation planting. The thorny kinds make excellent barrier plants. All the dwarfs are good in containers that can be moved to a protected corner on frosty nights.

The dwarf calamondins, kumquats, and mandarins lend themselves to pruning that leads to a gnarled and sculptured shape. The result is an exotic, semibonsai effect that is effective on patios and apartment balconies.

Citrus will not grow well in a lawn. They require a considerable amount of water that should go deep into the root zone, about 4 feet. At the same time, air must circulate all around their roots. These needs are not met with the frequent shallow watering that lawns receive. The constant wetness of lawns makes an ideal environment for the development of the fungus that causes root rot, though in sandy soils the problem is not as severe as in other soils. Finally, since lawns and citrus trees are both heavy feeders and compete for the soil's nutrients, neither will do well in conjunction with the other.

How to Grow

Space doesn't permit a more detailed discussion of citrus growing, so I recommend two books: *Florida Fruit,* by Albert Will, Eric Golby, and Lewis Maxwell, for residents of that state (listed in the bibliography); and a definitive book on citrus primarily for westerners but of interest to all citrus growers: *Citrus—How to Select, Grow and Enjoy,* by Richard Ray and Lance Walheim (also listed in the bibliography).

Climate

The best climate for citrus is determined by two factors: the amount of possible frost and the amount of heat available. For example, San Francisco is frostfree enough for most citrus to grow and develop fruit but does not have enough heat to sweeten oranges and grapefruit, though limes and lemons do well there. In any case, a citrus climate is a mild climate, so the use of this particular ornamental edible is limited to those parts of the country where the temperature does not fall below 20°F—the mild winter areas of Arizona, California, Florida, Hawaii, and Texas, and the warmest areas of the Gulf Coast. In borderline areas, some dwarf citrus do well if they are moved to a sunporch or a greenhouse as long as the humidity can be kept high. The following list will help you decide which citrus trees, if any, are appropriate for your climate.

The following plants accept some frost. They are listed from most to least cold-hardy.

Kumquat	Sweet orange
Calamondin	Tangelo
'Meyer' lemon	Pomelo
Rangpur lime	Grapefruit
Mandarin	Lemon

The following plants need long periods of high heat:

Most sweet oranges	Mandarin orange
Grapefruit	

The following plants need moderate heat:

Lemon	Calamondin
Lime	Kumquat

Exposure

Except in the hottest climates, all citrus prefer full sun. Lemons, kumquats, and Mandarin oranges will take some shade, if they have sufficient heat.

Soil

All citrus require well-drained loam. The plants all tolerate a pH of 5.5–8.0, and respond well to organic matter added to the soil before planting. Mulching with this same material throughout the year is a good practice.

Fertilizing

Citrus need high amounts of nitrogen as well as enough of the trace minerals iron, zinc, manganese, and magnesium. Use a citrus fertilizer, and keep well mulched with compost. To increase cold tolerance, do not apply nitrogen after midsummer.

Watering

Citrus need moist but not soggy soil. Do not let citrus dry out. After trees are three or four years old and well established, they usually need watering every two or three weeks in dry summer areas, more often if the soil is light or the weather windy or very hot. Container plants always need regular watering.

Pruning

Shape trees and remove dead or crossing branches. Keep suckers removed. Espaliered citrus must be pruned regularly to maintain shape. In extremely hot areas, a citrus trunk that has been exposed by pruning should be painted with whitewash or a light-brown water-based paint to prevent bark sunburn.

Pests and Diseases

Citrus is prone to a number of diseases. Consult your local university extension service or nursery to familiarize yourself with diseases that might be a problem in your area. Poor drainage and too much water will lead to root rot.

Some pests can be a nuisance. Aphids, scale, mealy bugs, and spider mites are not foreign to citrus plants. To control these pests, try a water spray first; if that is not effective, try a light oil spray formulated for evergreens. Do not use oil sprays if the weather is very hot or if freezing temperatures are expected.

Harvesting

Use clippers to cut fruit off the trees. Handle fruit carefully so it does not bruise.

How to Purchase

Forms and Sources

It's best to buy citrus locally where possible, as the plants are grafted onto root stocks that are adapted to specific areas. Citrus plants are available in containers from local nurseries, and your nursery can special order from the following wholesale growers (Four Winds will only sell wholesale):

Four Winds Growers
P.O. Box 616
Mission San Jose, CA 94538

Pacific Tree Farms
4301 Lynwood Drive
Chula Vista, CA 92010

The following mail-order sources also supply citrus; varieties are limited: (**4, 28, 39, 60, 71**)

Pollinators

Most citrus plants are self-pollinating.

Kinds and Varieties

CALAMONDIN
Very small, sour fruit; hardiest of the citrus; handsome, upright plant; no varieties.

GRAPEFRUIT
All varieties—large yellow fruits; sweet if given enough heat; handsome, full, large tree or dense shrub.
'Marsh'—seedless, white-fleshed fruits; fruits take 12–18 months to ripen; handsome tree; good in desert heat, the West, Hawaii, and Florida.
'Red Seedless'—red-fleshed fruits; ripens in winter; for Florida.
'Ruby'—red-fleshed fruits; good in desert, for the West.
'Thompson Pink'—pink-fleshed, nearly seedless fruits; for Florida.

POMELO (SHADDOCK)
Relative of grapefruit; very large yellow-fleshed, tender fruits; needs less heat than grapefruit; not eaten like grapefruit, individual sections must be peeled because of heavy membrane.
'Kao'—the variety commonly available.

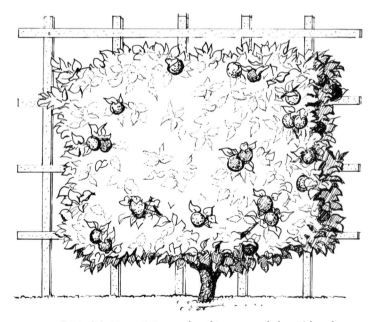

E.43. *Most types of citrus, such as this orange, make beautiful espalier plants. This is a particularly effective way to grow them in borderline climate areas because they can be nestled up against a south wall for extra warmth.*

E.44. *Dwarf kumquats are easily trained to a bonsai form.*

KUMQUAT

All varieties—fruits have very sweet rind and very sour flesh, are eaten all in one bite; handsome plant does very well in containers, can be trained in interesting shapes; full-size plant varies in size from 6 to 25 ft.; dwarf grows to 4 ft.

Meiwa Kumquat—grown mostly in Florida.

Nagami Kumquat—grown in the West and Florida; quite hardy.

LEMON

All varieties—yellow fruits; oval-shaped, medium-size tree to 20 ft. tall; when grown on dwarfing rootstock, small tree or large shrub.

'Eureka'—the grocery-store lemon; attractive shrub; few thorns; new growth purplish; grown commercially in California.

'Improved Meyer'—hardiest lemon; very perfumy taste (try one before deciding on it); grown in the West, Hawaii, and Florida.

'Lisbon'—full-size, handsome, small, thorny tree; can take more high heat and more cold than 'Eureka'; grown in Arizona and California.

'Villa Franca'—similar to 'Eureka' but larger and thorny; popular in Arizona, Hawaii, and Florida.

LIME

All varieties—small, 15–20 ft.; dense, rounded tree at maturity; some varieties quite thorny; dwarf limes available.

'Bears'—seedless juicy fruit; hardiest lime; tree quite thorny; grown in California.

Key Lime (Mexican)—fruits small, lemon-yellow color; grown extensively in southern Florida and southern California; seedling limes whose name refers to place of origin.

'Rangpur Lime'—not a true lime, but a sour Mandarin orange; much hardier than limes; has red-orange flesh.

'Tahiti'—tender; grown primarily in Hawaii and Florida.

LIMEQUAT

All varieties—cross between a lime and kumquat; tree shrublike, quite angular, and open; dwarf variety available.

'Eustis'—quite tender; tree shrublike and open; grown in West.

'Lakeland'—a little more hardy than lime; available in Florida.

MANDARIN ORANGE AND TANGERINE

All varieties—beautiful, upright-branching, small tree; handsome structure; dwarf available.

'Clementine'—must have a pollinator, 'Dancy' tangerine, 'Orlando' tangelo, or 'Valencia' orange will do; semi-open spreading growth; very ornamental tree; needs less heat then other tangerines to produce sweet fruits.

'Dancy'—fruits peel easily; seedy; upright tree, grown in Florida and the West.

'Kara'—seedy fruits; spreading tree; standard commercial fruit.

'King Mandarin'—seedy fruits peel easily; grown in Florida.

'Owari' (satsuma)—small tree; quite spreading; hardy plant grown to 20°F in Florida, the Gulf Coast, and the West.

SWEET ORANGE

All varieties—large, round, formal-looking tree; dense, dark-green foliage; large shrub on dwarfing rootstock.

Arizona Sweet—a group of varieties grown successfully in Arizona, comprises 'Diller', 'Hamlin', 'Marrs', and 'Pineapple'.

'Hamlin'—fruit nearly seedless; fall bearing; popular in Florida.

'Robertson' navel—winter and spring fruiting, two to three weeks earlier than 'Washington'; grows in the West.

'Tarocco'—blood orange with red pulp; excellent flavor; lower heating requirement than many oranges; late-spring fruiting; willowy branches and open growth make interesting landscaping tree; dwarf variety makes a very good espalier.

'Temple'—fruits deep reddish-orange color, strong flavor; winter bearing; popular Florida variety; not actually an orange but a cross between a sweet orange and a Mandarin, called a tangor.

'Valencia'—most commonly grown juice orange in California and Florida; not good in Arizona; can be harvested over a long period.

'Washington' navel—most commonly grown variety in the West, eating orange; winter and spring fruiting.

TANGELO

All varieties—cross between grapefruit and tangerine; trees similar to grapefruit but smaller.

'Minneola'—fruits bright orange, tangerine flavor, few seeds; ripens in spring; grown in Florida and the West; for highest fruit production; provide cross-pollination.

'Orlando'—fruits medium-size, flattened, peels easily; tree similar to 'Minneola' but leaves are cupped; grown in Florida and the West; for highest fruit production, provide cross-pollination.

Preserving and Preparing

Most varieties of citrus are self-preserving for a long time; that is, they remain good to eat when left hanging on the tree. In the event of a heavy frost warning, however, the whole crop should be picked or well-protected with plastic.

All citrus fruits make good marmalade. The rinds of all types can be candied, and mandarins and kumquats can be canned. Orange, lemon, lime, and grapefruit juices are easily frozen. Put the juice of lemons into ice cube trays. When they are frozen transfer them to plastic bags for frozen storage until needed. Two cubes, water, and sugar to taste, yields a lemonade that anyone can make.

Mandarin Almond Float

1 envelope unflavored
  gelatin
⅓ cup cold water
¾ cup boiling water
¼ cup sugar
1 cup milk
1 teaspoon almond extract

¼ cup chopped or pulverized
  almonds (optional)
1 pint jar of home-canned
  mandarin oranges
  (commercially canned fruit
  may be used)
1 kiwi, sliced

In an 8-inch cake pan, dissolve gelatin in cold water. Add the boiling water and sugar, and stir until mixture is completely dissolved. Add the milk and almond extract. Mix well. Refrigerate until hard.

Cut the gelatin mixture into 1-inch cubes, and combine with the fruit and its juice in small bowls.

Sprinkle almonds on top for a garnish.

Yields six to eight servings.

COMMON PEAR. See *Pear.*

COMMON SAGE. See *Sage.*

COMMON THYME. See *Thyme.*

CORSICAN MINT. See *Mint.*

CRABAPPLE. See *Apple* and *Crabapple.*

E.45. *Cranberries have small, delicate leaves with a bronzy tinge, an attractive foil to the bright red berries.*

Cranberry

Vaccinium macrocarpon

Effort Scale

NO. 4
Keeping plants sufficiently moist is hard
Weeding is usually a problem
Vulnerable to some pests
Harvesting is time consuming
Flooding or sprinkling sometimes needed for winter protection
  and pest control

Zones

3–8

Thumbnail Sketch

Evergreen vine
Low-growing mat 1 ft. tall, spreads to 3 ft.
Propagated by seed, from cuttings, or by layering
Needs full sun
Leaves are elliptical, deep green, ¾ in. long
Blooms in summer
Flowers are pink, small, grow in clusters
Fruits are red, edible; harvested in fall
Used as ground cover in boggy areas

How to Use

In the Kitchen

These small, tart, red berries are the source of the jelly and sauce that traditionally accompany Thanksgiving and Christmas feasts, whether they center around turkey, goose, or a lovely roast chicken. The cranberries seem to lend a balancing note to an otherwise overfull groaning board.

Cranberries are usually made into jelly or sauce, but these lovely berries can bring color and tartness to any meal as relishes, juices, sherbet, or additions to a salad mold. Cranberry leather is a delicious and light-weight food for campers and a good snack food for stay-at-homes as well. Cranberries are high in vitamin C, so they are a nutritional plus in any form.

In the Landscape

The cranberry vine is of limited use in the landscape. But if you have a bog area—that is, a patch of acid soil that is constantly moist—cranberries could be for you. The vine makes a lovely ground cover, with its small, bright-green leaves, clusters of pink, bell-shaped flowers, and red berries.

How to Grow

Commercial cranberries are grown in Maine, Massachusetts,

New Jersey, Michigan, Wisconsin, Minnesota, Oregon, and Washington. To determine if your particular conditions will permit you to grow cranberries successfully, consult local authorities. A soil pH of 3.2–4.5 and constant moisture are key requirements. These plants cannot stand hot summers and need protection—usually sprinkling or flooding—in severe winters.

If you think you have the spot for cranberries, be forewarned that flooding or irrigation is often necessary in the winter to protect the plants from cold damage. Flooding is also used to control the disease "false blossom" as well as the pests black-and-yellow-headed cranberry worm and cranberry fruit worm. Because of the mucky soil in which cranberries grow, weeding can be difficult.

How to Purchase

Cranberry plants are obtainable from local nurseries. One mail-order source of seeds is: (**51**).

Preserving and Preparing

If you have a good harvest, a delightful way to preserve them is to make fruit leather using cranberries for the fruit base.

Cranberry Fruit Leather

1 pound fresh cranberries	¾ cup corn syrup
½ cup sugar	¼ cup orange juice
rind of 2 large oranges, shredded (optional)	

Cook cranberries and orange juice in a saucepan over medium heat for 5–10 minutes, until berries get very juicy. Cover, but stir often.

Stir in corn syrup and sugar, cover pan, and simmer for 20 minutes. Strain or puree. Put strained mixture back into the saucepan, add the orange rind if you wish, and cook until mixture is very thick.

Line with plastic wrap two jelly-roll pans or two cookie sheets with raised rims. The plastic wrap should extend at least an inch beyond all the edges of each pan. Pour half the mixture into each pan, smoothing it into an even layer with a rubber spatula. It will spread out to about an inch from the edges.

Dry in a food dryer according to the manufacturer's directions, or dry in a gas oven using only the pilot light for heat, or dry in an electric oven at 100–150° for 1–2 days. Because most ovens can't be set at such a low temperature, you will have to turn the oven on low for a few minutes every hour or so. It can stay in a cold oven overnight. Sun drying works too, but only in warm, dry climates. With the latter method, cover the mixture with a screen to keep out insects.

When the mixture feels like leather, it is sufficiently dry. Peel leather off plastic wrap and rewrap it in a new sheet. Roll it up and store in the refrigerator or freezer; it can be kept in the refrigerator for three months or in the freezer for six months.

Fruit leather can be made from many other fruits, including peaches, plums, apples, grapes, cherries, apricots, loquats, strawberries, persimmons, pears, raspberries, and quinces.

CREEPING THYME. See *Thyme*.

Cucumber, Squash, and Melon

Cucumber, *Cucumis sativus*
Melon, *C. melo*
Summer squash, *Cucurbita Pepo* var. *melopepo*
Watermelon, *Citrullus lanatus*

Effort Scale

NO. 3
Annual planting
Vulnerable to some pests
Occasional watering necessary
Some weeding necessary
Training of vining types necessary
Fertilizing and mulches necessary

Zones

Annuals

Thumbnail Sketch

Annuals
Bush types, 2–3 ft. tall; vining types, to 6 ft. long
Propagated from seed
Need full sun
Leaves are light to dark green, large, vary with species
Flowers are bright yellow, 1–4 in. across
Fruits are edible; harvested summer and fall
Used in herbaceous borders, raised beds, containers

How to Use

In the Kitchen

Cucumbers, summer squashes, and melons, including water-

E.46. *Cranberries can be grown in boggy rock gardens.*

E.47. Bush cucumbers such as 'Spacemaster' have attractive foliage and can produce a respectable number of cucumbers in a small area.

melons, are all members of the *Cucurbitaceae* family, and are sometimes referred to as the cucurbits. These succulent fruits are associated with meals on warm summer days. Crispy cucumbers served with yogurt dressing are cooling and delicious; and as crispy dill pickles they are a classic. Try melons with ham slices, melons filled with vanilla ice cream or cottage cheese, or melons served in fruit salad—all great treats that aren't even fattening! Zucchini sautéed with garlic, basil, onions, and green pepper is a summer staple in some homes. The cucurbits are a truly versatile family.

In the Landscape

Most of the cucurbits have large, hairy, rough, ivy-like leaves. Some, like the Armenian cucumber, are 2–3 inches across and light green; others, like the zucchini, have 2-foot wide dark-green leaves. All have yellow, cup-shaped flowers. The flowers of cucumbers and melons are small, and those of many of the squashes are large and showy.

The bush-type cucumbers, squashes, and melons are useful in herbaceous beds near a patio or walk. They all do well in large containers on balconies, porches, or patios. The vining types can be used on low trellises, fences, over embankments, or spilling over the sides of a large hanging basket.

I have not included the long, running squashes and pumpkins as a choice for landscaping because I feel they belong they belong in a vegetable garden. These vines get very large, up to 12 feet long, and unruly. Often the leaves at the base of the plant get brown, mildewed, and unattractive before the fruits are ripe.

How to Grow

Cucumbers, melons, and summer squash are all warm-season annuals. In short-summer areas, seeds must be started indoors. These plants are usually grown in hills with two or three plants to a mound. In containers, they are planted singly. This group of plants needs rich humus soil and ample water during the growing season. Do not let the plants dry out. Keep young plants well weeded. Mature plants can usually crowd any weeds out.

Young plants in this family are susceptible to cutworms and snails. For cutworms, apply protective cardboard collars around the main stems. For snails, use traps or bait.

Striped or spotted cucumber beetles are sometimes a problem. Their larvae attack the roots of corn, and the adults attack cucurbit vines. As yet there are no biological controls for large numbers of cucumber beetles. See chapter 7 for control suggestions.

Mildew is sometimes a problem on the cucurbits, particularly late in the season. Mildew-resistant varieties are available, and you should choose from them if mildew is a problem in your area. I find that the mildew begins to show up just as the plants have almost finished producing, so I just pull the plants out. Resist the temptation to wait for that last cucumber or summer squash.

Other diseases affect the cucurbits, the most serious of which are mosaic virus on cucumbers and anthracnose on melons. The symptoms of mosaic disease are a mottling or shriveling of the leaves. Anthracnose symptoms are brown patches on the leaves and moldy fruit. Pull affected plants up, as no cure is known for either condition. Plant resistant varieties, and rotate your crops to prevent the problem from recurring.

Dwarf bush cucumbers yield about 3–4 fruits per plant; the larger vining types 8–12 per plant. Most types of melons produce about 2–4 melons per vine. Zucchinis produce about 1 fruit every day or two; the crookneck and pattypan types about 1 every two or three days.

How to Purchase

The cucurbits and melons are sold in seed form by most local and mail-order nurseries.

Types and Varieties

CUCUMBERS

There are many different types of cucumbers: round, yellow 'Lemon' cucumbers; long, light-green Armenian cucumbers; 'Burpless'; and pickling types. All of the above types are grown on long vines, and are attractive grown in large hanging baskets or tall planter boxes. In a landscape situation, these vines are more attractive trellised or grown against a fence or decorative support rather than on bean poles. A number of dwarf bush cucumbers are available; these are valuable for small areas and for herbaceous borders.

Cucumbers chosen for cooler areas should be resistant to mosaic virus and scab; in warm, humid areas, varieties should be resistant to mildew and anthracnose. Check the list that follows. Cucumbers are picked when they are immature. Do not let them ripen (turn yellow) on the vine, or the vine will stop producing.

The following varieties of cucumbers are recommended.

Armenian—delicious, long, grooved, light-green cucumbers, edible by those who cannot digest standard cucumbers; vines are long and need support. (**32, 51**)

'Burpee's M & M'—standard long, green cucumbers; vines are resistant to mosaic and mildew. (**9**)

'Bush Whopper'—standard cucumbers on compact bush; suitable for small gardens. (**48**)

'Liberty'—All American winner; dark green pickling cucumbers resistant to most cucumber diseases. (**Readily Available**)

'Marketmore'—standard cucumber; resistant to mosaic and scab. (**9, 48, 59**)

'Patio Pik'—standard cucumbers; can be picked young and used for pickling; disease resistant; small compact plants suitable for containers and hanging baskets. (**20, 22, 43, 48, 59**)

'Peppi Hybrid'—pickling cucumbers; resistant to mildew and scab; compact plant for small gardens. (**48, 59**)

'Poinsett'—standard cucumber; resistant to mildew and anthracnose. (**9, 59**)

'Pot Luck'—full-size 6-in. cucumbers on a very small 18-in. plant. (**8, 16, 22, 36, 43**)

'Spacemaster'—standard cucumbers on bush-type plant; mosaic resistant. (**9, 59**)

'Tenderfresh'—deep green long cucumbers; can cover trellis; long vines resistant to most cucumber diseases. (**36**)

MELONS

Numerous types of melons exist. Varieties of muskmelons (also known as cantaloupe in this country) and honeydew are available on compact, bushy plants used in a number of ways in the landscape. Most melons, however, grow on long vines suitable for growing on a fence or over an embankment.

To produce sweet fruit, melon plants need a long, hot growing season. If you plant them in a cool-summer climate, you can increase the heat around the plant by letting the vines run on concrete or by spreading black plastic under the vines in the vegetable garden. If you let the vines cascade over a rocky embankment, the rocks will hold the heat at night and achieve the same effect.

The following varieties of melons are recommended.

'Ambrosia'—standard-size fruit; one of the best eating cantaloupes; long vines, mildew resistant. (**9, 16, 59**)

'Bushwhopper'—cantaloupe, compact plant 2½ ft. wide. (**48**)

'Minnesota Midget'—small, sweet cantaloupe; ripens in 60 days; good in places with short growing season; 3-ft. vines, good for small planting areas. (**Readily Available**)

'Oval Chaca Hybrid'—cantaloupe; large vines, resistant to fusarium wilt and powdery mildew. (**48**)

'Short and Sweet'—cantaloupe; small plant with bushy growth, resistant to heat, drought, and powdery mildew. (**48**)

'Oliver's Pearl Cluster'—honeydew; 4–8 in. diameter, compact plant 2 ft. across, needs 110 days to ripen. (**48**)

SQUASHES

A number of squashes grow on bush plants. The large, deep-green leaves of the bushes are often up to 2 feet across. These plants are particularly attractive in large containers. Toward the end of the season, they tend to get mildewed and yellow. You can move them off the patio and out of sight at this time, and let them continue to produce for a few weeks more. One or two zucchini plants are usually sufficient for the average family, as this type is such a heavy producer, but three or four plants may be necessary for the yellow crookneck or pattypan types.

Choose from a large selection of zucchini, yellow summer squash, and pattypan types. All are bush-type squashes. The new All America hybrid 'Gold Rush' was particularly bred for small gardens and has a beautiful cut leaf and upright shape. The old standard 'Hybrid Zucchini' has been a prolific producer for years.

WATERMELON

Watermelon is a vining, hot-weather annual. The culture is similar to the other melons mentioned. The watermelon grows on very large vines with particularly beautiful crinkled leaves similar in shape to ivy leaves. Most varieties grow too rampantly to be used easily in a landscape situation, but a few small bush and vine varieties exist. Cucumber beetles can be a problem.

The following varieties of watermelon are recommended.

'Burpee's Sugar Bush'—6–8-pound melons, bush-type growth covers 6 square feet. (**9**)

'Golden Midget'—small yellow melons, small vines. (**16, 20, 43, 48**)

'Kengarden'—10–12-pound melons, bush-type growth, for small areas. (**22, 48**)

'New Hampshire Midget'—6-pound melons, good vines for short-summer areas; ripens in 70 days. (**9, 22, 62**)

Preserving and Preparing

Cucumbers, summer squash, underripe cantaloupe, and watermelon rind can all be pickled or made into relish. Cucumbers and

E.48. 'Gold Rush' zucchini has beautiful golden fruits and decorative split leaves. (Illustration by Hoppner, courtesy of All America selections.)

squashes can be dried. Melon balls can be frozen, but they tend to be quite mushy when defrosted. I have successfully used the following recipe (adapted from *The Better Homes and Gardens Home Canning Cookbook*) with both zucchini and Armenian cucumbers.

Bread and Butter Pickles

4 quarts unpeeled Armenian cucumbers, zucchini, or pickling cucumbers, sliced.

6 medium-size onions, sliced	5 cups sugar
	3 cups cider vinegar
2 green or red peppers, sliced	2 tablespoons mustard seed
	1½ teaspoons celery seed
3–4 cloves of garlic	1½ teaspoons turmeric
⅓ cup pickling salt	cracked ice

Combine the first 5 items, place in a large pot, and cover with cracked ice. Stir mixture well and let sit for at least 3 hours. Drain completely. Mix together the remaining ingredients and pour them over the cucumber mixture. Bring to a boil and pack immediately in hot, sterilized jars (½-pint or 1-pint), leaving ½ inch of headspace. Adjust the lids. Process in a canner in boiling water for 10 min. Makes 8 pints.

Currant and Gooseberry

Red currant, *Ribes sativum*
American gooseberry, *R. hirtellum*
European gooseberry, *R. uva-crispa*

Effort Scale

NO. 3
Some pruning necessary
Control of occasional pests and diseases necessary
Harvesting is time consuming
Mulching helpful

Zones

3–8

Thumbnail Sketch

Deciduous shrubs
3–5 ft. tall
Propagated from cuttings or by layering
Need full sun in cloudy-summer areas; grow well in filtered shade in hot-summer areas
Leaves are medium green, small to 3 in., palmate, decorative
Bloom in spring
Flowers are small, green to violet, not showy
Fruit is edible; harvested in summer
Used as foundation plants, interest plants, to cascade over retaining wall, and in shady borders and containers

How to Use

In the Kitchen

Currants are famous as a jelly. The color of currant jelly looks like something from a cathedral window, and the taste, to keep the imagery consistent, is heavenly. Currant jelly is superb on French toast or scones, or as a glaze to line a tart shell heaped with crème chantilly. Fully ripe currants are a real treat. Eaten out of hand, they are tartly sweet and juicy; in cooking they are used in sauces and sherbets and make an unusual spiced garnish.

To some, gooseberry pie is among life's greatest pleasures. Some people crave it to such an extent that they are driven to rush out in the middle of the night to buy a piece. I have a dear friend who has made this midnight run on numerous occasions. To be honest, gooseberry lovers baffle me, but I accept the fact that when it comes to gooseberries, to each his own.

The small green or pink berries of the gooseberry plant are extremely tart, tasting somewhat like juicy rhubarb. A few varieties are sweet enough to be eaten fresh, but these are generally European varieties that do poorly on the North American continent. The gooseberries grown here are usually served cooked. Some varieties of gooseberries have fruits with small spines.

Gooseberry lovers rave not only about gooseberry pie and gooseberry pie à la mode, but about gooseberry cobbler, gooseberry tarts, and gooseberry "fool," a traditional Scottish dish. Other favorites are gooseberry jams and jellies and spiced gooseberries.

In the Landscape

These medium-size deciduous shrubs fill a void in edible landscaping. Few plants will produce food without full sun, but these bushes do very well in partial shade. In addition, their size makes them ideal for foundation plants or for growing under spreading trees. Try alternating gooseberry bushes and plum trees down a driveway, planting the plums back far enough from the concrete to prevent dropping fruit from making a dangerous mess. Some of the gooseberry bushes are weeping in shape and cascade nicely over a retaining wall or down an embankment. Many varieties of gooseberries are quite thorny and can be effective barrier plantings; currants are thornless.

Both currants and gooseberries do well in large containers. The bright red clusters of currant fruits are a nice addition to a patio landscape.

How to Grow

Climate

Currants and gooseberries are extremely hardy; most varieties can be grown well up into Canada. Both plants prefer cool, humid summers and do poorly in hot, dry climates.

Exposure

These berries can take more shade than any of the other commonly grown fruit-bearing plants. Some varieties even do well on the north side of the house. In hot climates they are grown with only three or four hours of morning sun or under high-branching trees with filtered sun. In cloudy, cool summers they do better with full sun.

Soil

Currants and gooseberries prefer good garden loam but can take

E.49. *Some varieties of gooseberries, such as the plant on the left, have a graceful, draping form. On the right is an upright-growing currant.*

heavy or sandy soil quite well. A soil pH of 5.0–7.0 is optimum. Good drainage is necessary.

Fertilizing

These plants require mulching with generous amounts of manure or compost. Nitrogen should be kept to a minimum, as it stimulates succulent growth susceptible to mildew.

Watering

Only moderate watering is needed in arid climates; usually none is required in areas with rainy summers.

Pruning

Currants and gooseberries need annual pruning. The fruit is borne on new wood and on spurs—short twigs specialized for fruiting—of two- and three-year-old wood.

Thin out the canes—woody stems arising from the base of the plant—in early spring, keeping a balance between one-, two-, and three-year-old canes. Eight to ten canes are usually optimum on an established plant.

If you forget to prune for a year or two or move to a place where old bushes are growing, remove a third of the branches each spring, and in a few years the bushes will be back to full production.

Pests and Diseases

Currants and gooseberries are hosts to a serious disease known as white pine blister rust. This disease is fatal to pine trees but leaves the currants and gooseberries unscathed. Because the disease must live on both pine trees and currants or gooseberries to complete its life cycle, the fruits are banned in a number of states that

protect white pines. Before you order bushes, check with your local university extension service to be sure these plants are allowed in your area.

Currants and gooseberries are generally quite healthy, but occasionally a disease takes hold. The most serious disease affecting these plants is powdery mildew. The problem is particularly serious with regard to European varieties and is the main reason why they have not been widely grown in this country. If you have a problem with mildew, make sure the plant has good air circulation by pruning so that the middle is open.

Anthracnose is sometimes a problem. 'Welcome' is a gooseberry that is quite resistant to this disease.

Some unusual virus diseases affect currants and gooseberries, but you can avoid these by buying from a reputable nursery and by examining carefully any gift plants from friends.

Occasional pests affecting both plants are aphids, scale, saw flies, and fruit flies. Generally these pests are no problem, but if infestations get out of hand, try malathion. Dormant sprays help too.

Harvesting

Pick currants by the cluster. Choose underripe clusters for the best jams and jellies. Fully ripe berries are best eaten out of hand.

Pick gooseberries carefully one by one; they have thorns. Some varieties are more prickly than others.

The less ripe the gooseberry, the more sour it is. Some varieties become quite sweet and turn pink or light purple, a sign that they are fully ripe.

Currants yield about 2–3 quarts of fruit per plant annually; gooseberries about 3–4 quarts.

E.50. *Currants have interesting leaves, and most varieties have decorative red fruits.*

How to Purchase

Forms and Sources

Currants and gooseberries are available bare root in the spring and in containers throughout the growing season from local nurseries and the following mail-order firms: (**5, 6, 22, 28, 36, 43, 46, 57, 72**).

If you are interested in growing European gooseberries, which are superior in flavor and more versatile but harder to grow, contact (**57**). This source has the largest selection of gooseberries (nearly a dozen varieties) in the country.

Pollinators

Currants and gooseberries are self-pollinating.

Varieties

Be careful to choose varieties that produce good edible fruits. Some varieties are grown for their flowers only. The following are the most commonly available.

CURRANTS

'New Perfection'—red berries; heavy bearing. (**22, 43**)
'Red Lake'—red, medium to large berries; adaptable to all currant climates; late season. (**22, 28, 36, 43, 72**)

'White Imperial'—white berries, an improved 'White Grape'. (**46, 57**)
'Wilder'—large; red currants; very productive; ripen midseason. (**22, 28**)

GOOSEBERRIES

'Pixwell'—large, green berries, easy to pick because the fruit hangs away from the thorns. (**6, 22, 28, 36, 43, 72**)
'Poorman'—red berries, high quality; shrub vigorous and productive. (**46, 57**)
'Welcome'—pink to red berries, makes red jam; bush almost thornless; somewhat resistant to anthracnose. (**22, 28, 43**)

Preserving and Preparing

Currants and gooseberries can be made into jams, jellies, and sauces. They also can be preserved by canning, freezing, or pickling.

Fresh Gooseberry Fool

2 cups fresh gooseberries (or other berries)
sugar to taste, starting with ⅓ cup
1 recipe of boiled-custard mix (or 1 cup whipping cream and ¼ cup sugar)

Cook gooseberries with ¼ cup water and ⅓ cup sugar until tender. Puree gooseberries by forcing them through a sieve or blending in a blender. Chill. Make custard with custard mix, or whip cream and sugar. Just before serving, fold the gooseberry puree into the custard or whipped cream.

E.51. *Some varieties of gooseberries are quite thorny. This one is an unusual white gooseberry.*

DAMSON PLUM. See *Plums.*

DWARF NASTURTIUM. See *Nasturtium.*

Eggplant *(AUBERGINE)*

Solanum Melongena var. *esculentum*

Effort Scale

NO. 2
Must be planted annually
Watering and fertilizing necessary

Zones

Annual, 10 as perennial

Thumbnail Sketch

Herbaceous perennial cultivated as an annual
2–3 ft. tall
Propagated from seeds
Needs full sun
Leaves are gray and velvety, 4–5 in. long
Blooms in summer
Flowers are purple with yellow stamens, 1–2 in. across
Fruits are purple or white; edible; harvested in summer
Used in flower beds, herb gardens, raised beds, containers

How to Use

In the Kitchen

Ratatouille, moussaka, parmigiana—the names of eggplant dishes indicate the area of origin of this versatile plant. Although eggplant, a member of the potato family, is often used in combination with meats or other vegetables, it has a distinct life of its own when flavored with olive oil and garlic, soy sauce, or mixed herbs, and broiled. Eggplant caviar, in all its varieties, is a conversation piece when served with dark bread in a colorful pottery bowl or a shell made from a hollowed-out eggplant.

In the Landscape

Eggplant is a tender, herbaceous perennial that is usually grown as an annual in the United States. It grows to 3 feet, and because it is beautiful in all phases of its growth is an addition to any part of the garden. Its leaves are large and lobed, and have a definite purple overtone. The gracefully drooping blossoms are purple with contrasting yellow stamens. The dark-purple, shining fruits are either large and round or oval or, in the Japanese type, smaller and more slender. Some white, yellow, and striped eggplants exist too. All the fruits are decorative, usable in a border or alone in a decorative container. For a spectacle, try planting eggplants against a background of cleome and surrounding them with blue ageratum, purple basil, chives, and thyme.

E.52. All eggplants grow well in containers. This variety is 'Black Beauty'.

How to Grow

The eggplant's climate requirements are similar to that of its relative, the tomato. The plant is susceptible to any frost, so if you start your own from seed do not put the seedlings into the ground until all frost danger is past and the ground is warm. Eggplants grow best in a well-drained garden loam that is fertilized with blood meal and manure or fish emulsion about three times during the growing season. They need moderate watering and should never be allowed to dry out.

Flea beetles, spider mites, and white flies can be a nuisance, and mildew will develop in too humid climates. Treat flea beetles with diazinon.

How to Purchase

Many varieties of eggplant are available, and all are beautiful. 'Black Beauty' is a common standard-size fruit, 'Japanese' is a fruit of smaller size, and 'White Beauty' produces an unusual and decorative white-skinned fruit. 'Burpee Hybrid' is more resistant to drought and disease than other varieties. Eggplant seed is readily available from the major vegetable-seed catalog firms.

The fruit is ready to pick when it is full-colored but before it begins to lose any of its sheen. To help prevent fruits from deteriorating, they should be cut rather than pulled from the plant. Plants will produce more if fruits are picked regularly. Average annual yields are 6-8 fruits per plant.

Preserving and Preparing

Except when prepared as a luxury item such as pickled baby eggplant, this vegetable is used fresh.

Eggplant Caviar

1 large eggplant (about 1½ pounds)	1 tablespoon catsup
½ cup scallions including some green top, chopped fine	1 teaspoon salt dash of coarse ground pepper
3 tablespoons lemon juice	1 tablespoon olive oil

Prick skin of eggplant. Bake whole on cookie sheet in 400° oven until soft, about 45 minutes. Remove from oven and cool until eggplant can be handled. Cut in half and scoop out flesh. Discard skin. Mash flesh and beat smooth. Add other ingredients, mixing well. Let mixture stand overnight. Serve with black bread. The caviar can be garnished with black olives, fresh dill, parsley, or chives.

To make an eggplant serving dish, slice a thin piece lengthwise from a raw eggplant. Scoop out the pulp, leaving about a 2-inch rim. Brush the rim and the inside of the shell with lemon juice. Fill with eggplant caviar.

EGLANTINE, SWEETBRIAR. See *Rose Hip.*

Elderberry

American or sweet elderberry, *Sambucus canadensis*

Effort Scale

NO. 3
Suckers must be removed on some varieties
Pruning necessary in early spring
Protection from birds necessary
Harvesting and processing are time-consuming

Zones

2–9

E.53. *Elderberries have handsome cut leaves that partially hide clusters of deep purple berries.*

Thumbnail Sketch

Deciduous shrub or tree
6–10 ft. tall
Propagated from seeds, cuttings, or suckers
Needs full sun, will tolerate some shade
Leaves are divided into leaflets, usually seven to a leaf; medium green; 6 in. long
Blooms in spring
Flowers are large, white, grow in clusters, fragrant, 6–10 in. across
Fruits and flowers are edible; harvested in summer
Used for informal hedges, screens, shrub borders

How to Use

In the Kitchen

The small blue or purplish-black fruits of the elderberry are an excellent source of vitamin C. These berries are a great favorite of birds; humans usually enjoy them cooked in pies and jellies or fermented in wine. The dried berries are used to make a fruity, flavorful tea much sought after by herb-tea aficionados. In some households the flat-topped flower clusters are combined with pancake batter to make elder-blow fritters, described as a springtime treat by those who have eaten them.

Caution: The fruits of most red elderberries are not edible.

In the Landscape

Many types of elderberries grow wild in many areas of the country. Some species grow very tall, to 50 ft. These wild elderberries are usually rampant and sprawling, and are best reserved for wild gardens and backlot areas. Hybridizers have developed a number of varieties that are less unruly and make handsome additions to the yard. These hybrids of the American elderberry are hardy deciduous shrubs that can grow to 6–10 ft. and can be pruned to a clumping, somewhat fountain-shaped shrub.

Elderberries have magnificent clusters of white, fragrant flowers, decorative berries, and long compound leaves made up of leaflets up to 6 in. long. This combination of features makes them useful in many landscapes. Use them as you would spirea, lilacs, or other large deciduous shrubs. Elderberries are excellent as informal hedges, screens, and in shrub borders.

How to Grow

Climate

Elderberries are extremely hardy. Wild varieties grow from Florida to Nova Scotia and as far west as California. However, the new hybrid varieties are seldom grown except in cold winter climates. The new varieties are experimental in the colder parts of the West, but star in the Midwest and Northeast.

Exposure

They require full sun, but will tolerate some shade.

Soil

To fruit well, elderberries require a moist, fertile soil. Wet conditions are tolerated only with good drainage.

Fertilizing

These plants respond well to compost once a year.

Watering

They need average water but will accept much if drainage is good.

Pruning

In early spring, bushes should be cut back by one-half to encourage fruiting wood and to keep the size and shape under control. Prune off suckers extending more than 2 feet from the crown of the plant to keep the shrub under control.

Pests and Diseases

Birds are the chief pests. Pick berries as soon as they ripen. Net the bushes if possible. The birds can strip the bushes overnight.

Harvesting

Berries are ripe when they are slightly soft and deep colored. The birds will be your guide.

How to Purchase

Forms and Sources

Elderberries are available bare root or in containers from local nurseries and the following mail-order sources: (**6, 18, 22, 28, 37, 45, 46, 58, 69, 72**).

Pollinators

Cross-pollination is needed. Plant more than one variety unless wild ones are nearby.

Varieties

All of the following are hybrids and grow best in cold winter regions.

'Adams'—most often planted; large plant with large berries and clusters; early fruiting; good for early frost areas. (**6, 37, 72**)

'Johns Improved'—large berries; plant 5–6 ft. tall. (**22**)

'Kent'—plant 5–6 ft. tall; very productive; ¼-inch berries. (**22**)

'Nova'—large bush; heavy bearer; sweet, early ripening fruits. (**46, 58**)

'York'—large bush known for its large berries; ripens late. (**6, 46, 58, 72**)

E.54. *Cultivated elderberries have a graceful, informal shape and produce clusters of white flowers.*

Preserving and Preparing

Elderberries can be frozen, canned, dried, or made into jellies, jams, or wine.

Elderberry Jelly

3 pounds fully ripe elderberries	4½ cups sugar
¼ cup lemon juice	1¾-ounce package powdered pectin

Wash, stem, and crush berries. In a heavy pot, cook gently until juice starts flowing; then simmer for 15 minutes. Strain berries in a jelly bag or through cheesecloth. Combine 3 cups of berry juice with lemon juice in a large cook pot. Follow the standard procedure for making jelly with powdered pectin.

ENDIVE. See *Greens.*

ENGLISH WALNUT. See *Walnut.*

ESCAROLE. See *Greens.*

EUROPEAN FILBERT. See *Filbert.*

EUROPEAN GOOSEBERRY. See *Currant* and *Gooseberry.*

EUROPEAN GRAPE. See *Grape.*

EUROPEAN PEAR. See *Pear.*

EUROPEAN PLUM. See *Plums.*

Fig

Ficus carica

Effort Scale

NO. 2
Raking of spoiled fruits and dead leaves necessary
Sizeable harvest

Zones

8–10 and Hawaii

Thumbnail Sketch

Deciduous tree
Standard, 15–30 ft. tall; dwarf varieties, to 10 ft.
Propagated by grafting, air layering, or from cuttings
Needs full sun
Leaves are large, deeply lobed, palmate; 4–9 in. long
Usually "blooms" in summer
Flowers are insignificant
Fruits are edible; harvested in summer and fall
Used as shade tree, interest tree, espalier, large shrub, screen,
    and in containers

How to Use

In the Kitchen

A ripe, plump, soft fig—black, brown or green—is a real sweetmeat. Its sweetness makes it useful in pastry and cookie fillings. Fig newtons are almost a standard part of growing up, and dried figs are among everyone's favorite dried fruits.

The so-called "fruits" of the fig are not true fruits, but actually fleshy receptacles for the tiny flowers that grow inside.

In the Landscape

The fig tree is a beauty the year round. Its smooth gray bark, reminiscent of an elephant's hide, is dramatic against a sodden

E.55. *'Black Mission' figs hang from the branch, protected by dramatic palmate leaves.*

winter sky. In the spring and summer this bark contrasts sharply with the tree's rich green, deeply lobed leaves. In fall, in most climates, the leaves turn bright yellow. The trunk can become gnarled with age.

Although the fig tree can grow to 30 feet, it can be kept pruned to 15 feet. As a large tree the fig offers dense shade. As a small tree or shrub, in or out of a container, it makes a superb accent plant. Its interesting bark and sturdy branches lend themselves to training as a handsome espalier.

The softness of figs makes fruit drop a nuisance if the tree is planted too near a patio or deck, but the close-up beauty of the plant makes watchful picking worthwhile.

How to Grow

Climate

The mature fig tree is semihardy to about 15 °F. In colder areas figs should be planted near a south or west wall and given extra protection or planted in tubs. The tubs should be moved to a protected area during the coldest periods and watered once a

FIG 237

month. The harvest from container plants will be limited but worth the effort. In zone 8, where it often freezes, and in much of the Southeast, it is usually grown as a large shrub.

Exposure

Figs require full sun. The more heat they receive the sweeter the fruits become.

Soil

Figs fruit best in medium to poor soil but need good drainage. Sometimes they are planted in containers if the soil is too rich; this restrains their roots, forcing them to bear well. Add lime in acid areas.

Fertilizing

Use organic matter for fertilizer. Avoid adding nitrogen, however, because it leads to foliage rather than fruit production. Do not apply nitrogen fertilizers unless the tree is producing less than 1 foot of new growth a year.

Watering

Figs are drought tolerant once established, but optimum fruit production in arid climates will result from an occasional deep watering. Do not water once fruit has started to enlarge or the figs will split. In the Southeast, sandy soils and nematode problems often make regular supplemental watering necessary.

Pruning

Train young trees to branch 2–3 feet off the ground and to have three or four main branches. For mature trees, prune while dormant. Remove dead or crossed branches. To encourage fuller growth cut back some of the end growth slightly.

In temperate climates many varieties of figs, such as 'Mission', 'Osborn', and 'Kadota', bear two crops of figs a year. The first crop is called breba. Breba-crop figs are born on the ends of the previous year's growth. Therefore, when pruning these varieties, make sure you do not cut off all the end growth.

Different varieties are pruned in different ways, so it's advisable to consult local authorities about the optimum method for your particular plant.

Pests and Diseases

Figs are susceptible to very few pests and diseases. Mites are sometimes a problem. Do not plant where cotton has grown, since fig trees can contract cotton root rot. In Florida, fig rust can be a problem, requiring a spray of neutral copper when the leaves are half mature. Where nematodes might be a problem, try to find plants grafted onto resistant rootstock.

In some parts of the South the dry fruit beetle can enter the "eye" of the fig fruit and spoil it. Plant varieties such as 'Conadria', 'Celeste', and 'Texas Everbearing' that have closed eyes.

Harvesting

Pick fruits when they are soft and fall easily into your hand. If they exude white sap they are not ripe enough. If you plan to dry them, in arid climates you can let them wither on the tree and then pick them. A mature tree will yield about 25–35 pounds of fruit per year.

How to Purchase

Forms and Sources

Fig trees are available bare root in early spring from local nurseries and some mail-order firms, or in containers from nurseries and the following mail-order firms during the summer: (**4, 6, 10, 23, 28, 62, 71, 72**). The International Tree Crops Institute (California branch; see Appendix C for address) carries fifteen varieties.

Pollinators

Figs commonly used in the home garden are self-pollinating.

Varieties

'Black Jack'—black fruit; new variety; genetic dwarf, usually less than 6 ft. high; excellent for containers. (**4**)

'Black Mission' ('Mission')—black fruit; large tree; popular in California; resistant to oak-root fungus. (**Readily Available**)

'Brown Turkey' ('Black Spanish')—brownish-purple fruit, good for eating fresh; small tree; can be pruned back readily; grown in many areas. (**Readily Available**)

'Celeste' ('Blue Celeste', 'Sugar')—bronze-colored fruit; quite hardy; popular in Southeast. (**6, 23, 62**)

'Conadria'—white fruit, excellent flavor, large vigorous tree, fruit resistant to decay, small eye. (**71**)

'Magnolia' ('Brunswick', 'Madonna')—yellow fruit; one of the hardiest; good for borderline fig areas. (**6**)

'Texas Everbearing' ('Dwarf Everbearing', 'Eastern Brown Turkey')—dark brown fruit; quite hardy; good in containers. (**6, 62, 71, 72**)

E.56. Fig trees grown in western climates become large, spreading shade trees. In cold climates, they occasionally freeze back and regrow as large shrubs.

Preserving and Preparing

Figs can be dried, canned, pickled, frozen, candied, or made into jam.

Fig Filling for Cookies and Coffee Cake

Place 2 pounds fresh figs and sugar to taste (start with ¼ cup) in a saucepan. Cook on low heat, stirring occasionally, until thick. Freeze in containers. Makes approximately 1½ cups filling.

Fig Needhams

1 cup butter	2½ cups unbleached flour
1 cup brown sugar	2 teaspoons cream of tartar
2 egg yolks	1 teaspoon soda
3 tablespoons milk	½ teaspoon salt
2 teaspoons vanilla	½ cup fig filling (recipe above)

Cream shortening and sugar. Add egg yolks, milk, and vanilla, and beat well. Sift together the dry ingredients and add to mixture. Chill dough for 1 hour.

On a well-floured board, roll out the dough to ⅛ inch thick. Cut with round cookie cutter. Place ½ teaspoon fig filling on half the round surfaces. Cut small holes in center of other rounds and place these on top of the rounds holding the filling. Press edges together with a fork. Bake on ungreased sheet at 350° for 10–12 minutes.

E.57. Filbert leaves are showy, and the nuts are encased in decorative coverings.

Filbert *(Hazelnut)*

European filbert, *Corylus Avellana*

Effort Scale

NO. 3
Moderate amount of pruning needed
Mulching beneficial
Some raking required
Harvest must be processed
Vulnerable to some pests, including birds and squirrels

Zones

4–8

Thumbnail Sketch

Deciduous tree or shrub
Standard, 15–25 ft. tall; dwarf variety, 4 ft. tall
Propagated by layering and grafting
Needs full sun
Leaves are dark green, woolly underneath, 4 in. long
Blooms in winter or spring
Female flowers are inconspicuous; male flowers are catkins
Nuts are edible; harvested in fall
Used as large shrub, hedge, screen, small multistem tree,
   interest tree, screen, patio tree

How to Use

In the Kitchen

European filberts are tasty, round, hazel-colored nuts, closely related to the American hazelnut. They are a delectable and nutritious snack when roasted and salted, and are marvelous in stuffings for poultry, or as an addition to vegetable dishes. Filberts can also contribute to memorable desserts, as in filbert pie, filbert meringues, and fudge and brownies with filberts added. How decadent can you get!

In the Landscape

Filberts have large, dramatic leaves that stand out from each other clearly. The trunk is usually multistemmed and can be trained to sculptured shapes. Trained filberts look nice near a patio or entryway. The nut coverings add another ornamentation to this already beautiful tree. They are fringed and frilly, usually green, and sometimes have pink edges. The nuts grow in clusters of three to seven. In the winter the bare branches are decorated by the interesting male catkins, which hang on until spring.

Try using filbert trees as decorative screens or accent plants. In shrub form they serve admirably as informal hedges or screens.

How to Grow

Climate

European filberts are quite hardy, but they flower in late winter or early in the spring, exposing the delicate catkins to frosts. This factor limits nut production and consequently affects the tree's distribution. Filberts do poorly in areas with high summer heat, another limiting factor. They are grown most successfully in the inland areas of the Northwest; 95 percent of all filberts grown in this country come from Oregon and Washington. Scattered attempts at growing European filberts in the East have met with varying degrees of success. If you want to try them, choose a northern, cold exposure so a warm winter day will not inspire them to bloom prematurely.

Exposure

Filberts need full sun.

Soil

Filberts bear well in good, deep, well-drained garden loam mulched with 3 or 4 inches of organic matter.

Fertilizing

Organic mulches provide most of the nutrition filberts need. However, if the leaves are getting small or pale, apply nitrogen in moderate amounts. In cold winter areas too much nitrogen will produce succulent growth susceptible to winterkill.

Watering

Filberts need an occasional deep watering in arid summer areas. In the Northwest, where they are grown commercially, mature trees seldom need watering.

Pruning

Prune a young plant to a single trunk with four to six main branches if it is to be grown as a standard tree, or to three main trunks if grown as a multistemmed tree. Filberts bear on last year's wood, and need to be lightly thinned out every year to encourage new growth. Prune at the end of the blooming season. If you are growing filberts in a tree form, remove suckers throughout the year.

Pests and Diseases

The most serious problem for filberts is eastern filbert blight, a disease common in filberts grown on the East Coast. There is no cure, and affected plants eventually die.

Common pests of filberts are bluejays, crows, and squirrels.

Aphids and mites are sometimes a problem, though usually easily controlled. Try dormant sprays.

Harvesting

Gather nuts after they have fallen and before the birds discover them. A mature tree can yield 25 pounds of nuts to a crop. Filberts usually bear their crops in alternate years. This is normal.

How to Purchase

Forms and Sources

Buy filberts bare-root from local and mail-order nurseries in spring, or in containers from nurseries and the following mail-order firms into the fall: (**7, 9, 24, 26, 55, 60, 68, 69**). One nursery (**26**) has a large selection of grafted filberts.

Pollinators

Filberts need cross-pollination. Choose the varieties carefully, as all filbert varieties do not pollinate all others.

E.58. Filbert trees can be grown as large shrubs or trained as multistemmed trees like this one near an entryway.

Varieties

Be careful when choosing filbert varieties, since some are grown only as ornamentals and bear few or inferior nuts.

'Barcelona'—most popular filbert; commercial variety; large nuts of excellent quality; very susceptible to eastern filbert blight but high bud-mite resistance; 'Royal' is a good pollinator. (**Readily Available**)

'Du Chilly'—large nut; slow growing to 15 ft. (**7, 24**)

'Royal'—high-quality nuts; good pollinator for 'Barcelona'; low bud-mite resistance. (**7, 9, 10**)

Preserving and Preparing

Filberts stored at room temperature will soon become rancid. Store them in an outside building, such as a garage, where temperatures are in the fifties and the humidity is fairly high.

The foolproof way to preserve filberts is to shell and freeze them.

To toast filberts, place shelled nuts in a shallow pan and bake in a 350° oven until light golden brown, about 15 minutes. Watch carefully, as they can easily overbake.

Nutty Meringues

3 egg whites
¼ teaspoon cream of tartar
¼ teaspoon salt

1 teaspoon vanilla
¾ cup sugar
1¼ cups filberts (or almonds), chopped fine

Preheat oven to 250°. Make sure all the utensils are grease free. Place egg whites, cream of tartar, and salt in a clean bowl. Beat until soft peaks form. Add the vanilla, and gradually add the sugar, beating constantly, until peaks become very stiff. Fold in the chopped nuts. Cover a baking sheet with heavy brown paper. Drop meringue in 12 dollops onto the paper. Using the back of a large spoon or a rubber spatula, make a hollow in the center of each mound. Bake for 1 hour at 250°. Turn off heat and allow meringues to set in oven for 1½ hours. Serve meringues filled with ice cream or chocolate mousse (recipe below).

Chocolate Mousse

Make 1 small package of chocolate pudding (not the instant type), using ½ cup less milk than directions call for. Chill mixture for at least 3 hours. Remove from refrigerator and beat with a wire whip until creamy. Make whipped cream from 1 cup heavy cream, ½ teaspoon vanilla, and 2 tablespoons sugar. Fold whipped cream into pudding. Fill each meringue with a large spoonful of the chocolate mixture. Garnish with filberts.

FLOWERING KALE. See *Greens.*

FOO GWA. See *Bitter Melon.*

FRENCH SORREL. See *Sorrel.*

GARDEN CHAMOMILE. See *Chamomile.*

GARDEN CHIVE. See *Chive.*

GARDEN NASTURTIUM. See *Nasturtium.*

GARDEN RHUBARB. See *Rhubarb.*

GARDEN SORREL. See *Sorrel.*

GARDEN STRAWBERRY. See *Strawberry.*

GARLIC CHIVE. See *Chive.*

Ginger

Zingiber officinale

Effort Scale

NO. 3
Temperamental about growing conditions
Frequent fertilizing needed
Constant watering necessary
Winter protection necessary in most areas

Zones

6–10

Thumbnail Sketch

Herbaceous perennial with tuberous rhizomes
3–4 ft. tall
Propagated by division of rhizomes
Needs partial shade
Leaves are light green, straplike, 6–7 in. long
Blooms in spring
Flowers are yellow-green touched with purple, insignificant, seldom seen
Rhizomes and shoots are edible; harvested in fall
Used in shade borders, raised beds, containers, and as house plants

How to Use

In the Kitchen

The fleshy ginger rhizomes ("roots"), often available in produce departments or Oriental food stores, have a hot and pungent flavor and are used in many Oriental and Indian dishes. The fresh young shoots are used in stir-fry dishes. As ginger becomes more commonly available, we are learning to use it in American cookery. Try keeping a piece in the freezer, ready to be grated into vegetables, sliced into stir-fry dishes, or used in any recipe that calls for soy sauce and garlic. In the sweets department, candied or crystalized ginger is a delicious addition to divinity fudge. It also adds zest to puddings and dessert soufflés.

Fresh ginger is stronger in flavor than packaged ground ginger, which is made from the dried root, so it must be used cautiously. And, of course, ginger is a necessary ingredient in such traditional favorites as gingerbread and pumpkin pie.

In the Landscape

The stems of the ginger can grow to a height of 3 or 4 feet. Their leaves are narrow and a light, bright green, giving this species a more airy appearance than that of other ornamental gingers. The plants go well with begonias and camellias. When grown indoors they are a nice foil for larger-leaved house plants. The flower of this species is seldom seen and is insignificant.

How to Grow

These tender, deciduous perennials are tropical plants needing long, warm, humid summers. They are worth trying in cooler, drier climates, but tend to be temperamental and should be con-

E.59. *Ginger will thrive in a medium-size container.*

sidered an experiment. They prefer bright light to hot sun so plant them in a warm, fairly shady spot. They also need rich, moist soil with good drainage, since they will rot in cold, wet soil. Keep them well watered.

In Florida and similar regions, ginger is planted in early spring and harvested nine months later, in late fall. In cold-winter areas, start ginger in the house, planting outside when the weather warms up.

Ginger can be harvested after five months when it has plenty of full-grown leaves, but for the biggest harvest wait for eight or nine months. If the weather becomes too cold, either harvest the rhizomes or bring the entire plant into the house for the fall and let it grow in a well-lit room until fully mature. When harvesting, save a rhizome to replant, thus maintaining your own source of this delightful flavoring.

How to Purchase

Fresh rhizomes, called ginger roots, are available at produce stands or in Oriental markets. Choose rhizomes that show good growth buds (like "eyes" on a potato). Available by mail order from (**28**) and (**51**).

Preserving and Preparing

Crystallized Ginger

Scrape fresh, tender ginger roots to remove the skin. Slice very thinly. Cover with water and boil for 5 minutes; then drain. Repeat the boiling and draining procedure three more times. After the last boil, reserve the liquid. Measure the liquid, including the ginger, and add to it 1½ times as much sugar. Boil until the ginger becomes translucent. Drain the ginger, let it dry, and roll it in granulated sugar. Pack ginger in jars and seal.

GLOBE ARTICHOKE. See *Artichoke.*

GOOBER. See *Peanut.*

GOOSEBERRY. See *Currant* and *Gooseberry.*

Grape

American (fox) grape, *Vitis Labrusca*
European (wine) grape, *V. vinifera*
Muscadine grape, *V. rotundifolia*
Hybrids

Effort Scale

NO. 3
Susceptible to some pests and diseases
Yearly pruning needed
Harvesting and preserving are time consuming

Zones

4–10

Thumbnail Sketch

Deciduous climbing, woody vines
Can reach 50–100 ft.; usually kept at 12–20 ft.
Propagated from seeds and cuttings, and by layering, grafting, budding
Need full sun
Leaves are medium or blue green, palmately lobed, 4–8 in. long.
Bloom in spring
Flowers grow in clusters, are insignificant
Fruits and leaves are edible; fruits are harvested in early fall, leaves in summer
Used on pergolas, fences, arbors, patio covers; can be trained as a small weeping tree

How to Use

In the Kitchen

Grapes, wonderful grapes! These fruits are luscious and juicy

E.60. Grape arbors are a landscaping tradition.

when fresh. Just to have a bunch of, say, 'Concord' or 'Niagara' grapes in your hand can make you feel refreshed. A platter piled high with different kinds of grapes makes a lovely centerpiece—and an elegant dessert, along with cheese. Some grapes, such as the 'Concord', though eaten fresh are mainly used to make purple grape jelly. Grape juice is a nice change from other juices, grape leather is a favorite with youngsters, and of course wine grapes have a story all their own. The latter are not particularly palatable fresh, but where wine is concerned, the proof of the vintage is in the drinking, not the eating.

Table grapes can be frosted with egg whites and sugar for an unusual garnish; blue grapes make an excellent pie; white grapes add texture and flavor to chicken or meat salads; and all the grapes that do well out of hand belong in a seasonal fruit cup.

The fruit of the vine is not the grape's only gift. A supply of brined grape leaves in your pantry is like money in the bank when unexpected company arrives. You can simply fill the leaves with a meat or vegetable and rice mixture and roll them into dolmas, a Middle Eastern delicacy served hot or cold.

In the Landscape

Grapes grow on gnarled, woody, climbing vines with peeling bark. Grape leaves are palmately lobed, usually medium to blue green, lush, and dramatic, turning yellow in the fall.

The plants can be trained to climb on or cling to many different structures. They are beautiful on pergolas or pool houses, and the grapes themselves are eye-catching when they hang down through the lattice of a patio roof. (In the latter case, pick the grapes conscientiously as they ripen; otherwise fallen grapes will make the patio slippery.) Where grapes are espaliered against a wall, wires strung along the wall help to support the vine. The espalier treatment is particularly beautiful and advantageous in cool summer areas; if the wall faces south it absorbs extra heat to sweeten the grapes.

Many varieties of grapes can also be trained to be small weeping trees. See the sidebar on page 245 for details. Use weeping grape trees for a focal point near a patio or as beautiful accent plants. Lining a walk or arranged geometrically on the edges of an herb garden, they can supply grapes for the enthusiastic winemaker.

Grape arbors are traditional trysting places, and for children they are magical hideaways. To sit under an arbor and smell the ripening grapes, to reach up and pluck a few ripe ones, or to just lean back and enjoy a glass of homemade wine—that's fine living.

How to Grow

Four major classes of grapes are grown in the United States: the American grape, the European grape, the muscadine, and hybrids of the three named. All the members of this family differ somewhat in taste, use, climate adaptability, pruning requirements, and disease susceptibility.

American grapes—sometimes referred to as Fox or Concord type grapes—are native to the Northeast and are grown in bunches, have skins that slip off easily, and are generally eaten fresh or made into jelly, juice and occasionally wine.

European grapes have tight skins and a typically winey flavor. They separate into three main categories: those used for wine, the dessert grapes, and the raisin grapes.

Muscadine grapes, best characterized by the 'Scuppernong', are native to the Southeast. They grow in loose clusters, have a slight musky flavor, and are eaten fresh or made into jelly and occasionally into a fruity wine.

Many hybrids have been developed which combine many of the characteristics of the American, European, and muscadine grapes.

Climate

One or more types of grapes can be grown in almost every part of the country except for the high desert and the very coldest parts of the Midwest. All grapes are heat lovers. They grow strong and produce sweet fruits in the sun. Without heat grapes are sour and vines are prone to diseases. The American 'Concord' type is the hardiest and will grow in colder climates than its European relatives. It is the principal grape grown in the area east of the Rocky Mountains and north of Delaware. European grapes are less hardy, usually tolerating cold only to 5 °F, and they require many hours of heat to produce good grapes. These grapes are grown in milder sections of the East and Midwest but are best suited to California, Arizona, and Oregon. In the Southeast, muscadine grapes thrive. They take much heat and humidity, are fairly tender, and are seldom grown north of Delaware.

Many hybrids have been developed for specific areas of the country. Consult local authorities if you cannot find specific information about the climate adaptability of the variety you are interested in. It is very important to choose varieties suitable for your area.

Exposure

All grapes require full sun. In coldest grape areas, plant grapes on south walls and give them extra shelter during the coldest nights.

Soil

Grapes need deep, well-drained soil. They are not as fussy as most fruits about fertility but will produce more and better fruit on fertile soil.

Fertilizing

If your vines need fertilizer, apply compost, manure, and moderate amounts of a nitrogen-type fertilizer at the beginning of the growing season. Too much nitrogen at the end of the season produces lush foliage but few grapes. A nitrogen deficiency is characterized by pale foliage. In coldest areas, stop applying nitrogen fertilizer by midsummer so that vines can harden off before a heavy frost.

Muscadine grapes need more fertilizer than other species, since they are usually grown on sandy soils.

Watering

In arid climates, encourage grapevines to grow deep roots by occasional deep watering. The water should penetrate the soil to 3 feet. Apply water to the base of the plants, since many of the grapes grown in arid climates will develop fungus problems if watered from above. Grapes grown on sandy soils in the Southeast respond well to drip irrigation. Stop watering after August to allow the vines to harden off for winter.

Pruning

All grapes require heavy pruning for these reasons: (1) to maintain the vine at a manageable size, since an unpruned vine can reach 100 feet in length; (2) to encourage the continuous growth of new wood and fruiting buds, since grapes bear their fruit on the current year's growth; (3) to remove unproductive old canes (excess growth from the preceding or earlier seasons); and (4) to provide for the next year's growth by favoring one year-old wood that will be ready to take over the next year (the best fruiting wood for a current year is produced from the buds of the preceding year's wood).

Grape vines have branches only in what is called the renewal area, and all the branches in this area must be pruned every year. The renewal area can be 7–8 feet high up on an arbor, spread out on four arms such as shown in Figure E. 61, or 5–6 feet off the ground as shown in the diagrams accompanying the weeping grape.

It's important to know that different types of grapes are pruned in different ways. American grapes will not bear fruit on buds near the main stem, so leave longer canes when pruning them than you would for other types. Leave at least 10–12 buds on each vine cane. European wine-type grapes will bear too heavily if you leave that many buds; during the dormant period they should be cut back to two or three buds—to what is called a spur. Most of the previous year's growth is pruned off, and only these few spurs are left near the main trunk.

Muscadine grapes bear on spurs that produce for three or four years. They are extremely vigorous and need severe pruning to keep their canes from crowding each other out, as well as for aesthetic reasons. Muscadine grapes are generally trained on a single wire 5 feet off the ground or on arbors. They are cut back annually to spurs with 3 buds.

When purchasing grapevines, ask the nursery to point out the buds. Once you see the plant, this explanation will seem less confusing. But if you still need reassurance, many good books on pruning are available (see Bibliography).

Grapes that are to be trained up against a fence or on wires can be arranged in what is called the four-arm-Kniffen system. In this system, four canes, two in each direction, are trained along parallel wires or on arbors and trellises (see Figure E. 61). The support should be made of sturdy material, because grapevines are heavy and long-lived. This training system is the one most commonly used for most varieties of both spur- and cane-pruned grapes, and much information is available about it. The weeping grape method is less usual.

E.61. *American grapes and most wine grapes can be trained on wires in what is called the four-arm Kniffen system. Before pruning* (above), *there is much extra growth. After pruning* (below), *only the four "arms," each bearing 8–12 buds, remain.*

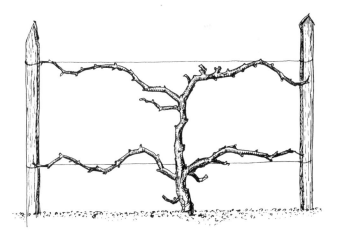

Pests and Diseases

Grapevines are often bothered, especially in humid climates, by fungal diseases, mildew (powdery white fungus on leaves and fruit), anthracnose (blotches of brown spots on leaves and fruits), and black rot (which turns fruit black and rotten). Selecting varieties of American or muscadine type, where appropriate, helps because they are more resistant to diseases than those of European-type grapes. Good pruning that provides good air circulation also helps. Choosing the right grape for a particular climate and avoiding susceptible varieties are the best solutions. Some varieties can

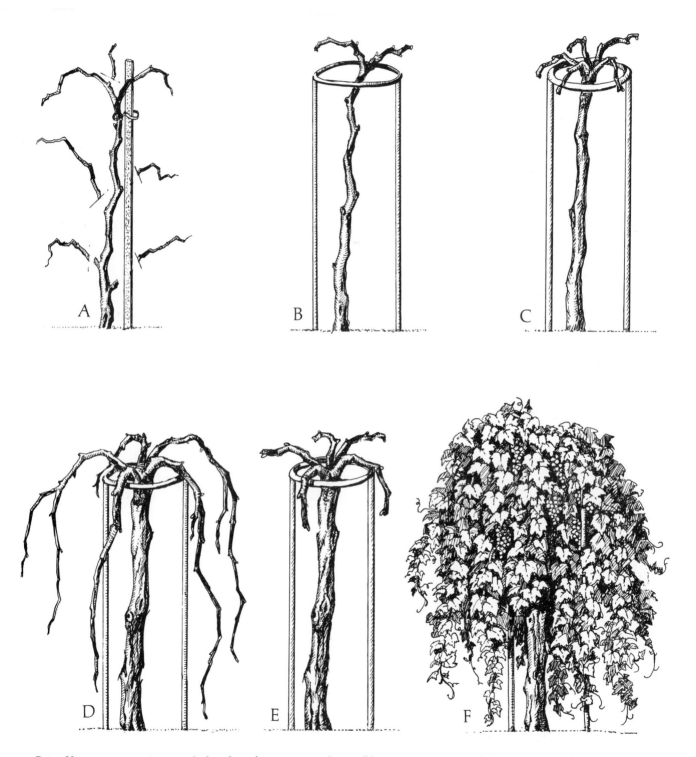

E.62. *How to prune a weeping grape.* **A.** *Second-year dormant pruning. Cut off all lateral growth and remove the central shoot, or leader, leaving only two or three lateral branches.* **B.** *Build a support of 2-inch metal or wooden posts. Attach a metal hoop 18–24 inches in diameter to the top.* **C.** *The third year, prune off all but two or three cane-producing spurs.* **D.** *The fourth year, you will have a permanent framework of 5 to 7 main branches that will look like this before pruning.* **E.** *After pruning, only 5 to 7 spurs, each bearing two buds, will remain. (The buds have been exaggerated for clarity.)* **F.** *The final product of your training—a graceful weeping grapevine.*

How to Train a Weeping Grape

The weeping grape, a beautiful and fruitful interest and accent plant, is best developed from spur-pruned rather than cane-pruned grapes. Most European and California wine grapes, as well as the cultivars 'Muscat,' 'Tokay,' 'Ruby Seedless,' 'Perlette,' and 'Black Monukka,' can be trained to be a weeping grape.

During the first year, do not prune the plant at all, but during the second year be prepared to be ruthless —though with a definite plan. Your guiding principle is to create a clean trunk. Select a central stem to be trained as the central leader or trunk. Stake this stem. This will become the permanent structure or trunk of the vine.

Establish the height of the weeping grape—5–6 feet is recommended—by heading back; that is, taking the top off of the central leader, leaving only two or three lateral branches at the top. Cut *all other* lateral branches off to bring out the tree form (Figure E. 62A). Next, build a supporting structure with brown- or black-painted metal pipes or 4×4-inch wooden posts. On top of this structure attach a hoop of metal tubing 18–24 inches in diameter, or a recycled tricycle wheel (Figure E. 62B).

When pruning the third year, create two or three more main branches (Figure E. 62C) and cut off the rest of the previous year's growth. If any flower buds appear in the spring, remove them. Fruiting diverts energy from the developing vines.

By the fourth year you will have a permanent renewal area at the top of the trunk. Before being pruned it will look like Figure E. 62D; after pruning it will look like Figure E. 62E (the size of the buds has been exaggerated for clarity). Every succeeding winter you will prune off all the long canes and leave the permanent four or five branches, each with two buds. Figure E. 62F shows the final form of the weeping grape.

be grown only with an aggressive fungicide program. However, in wet weather even these measures do not seem to help. In arid climates do not plant grapes near lawns that get overhead watering.

Japanese beetles are sometimes a problem. To control, handpick, use milky-spore disease (see chapter 7), and use bug traps. The larvae of the grape-berry moth are sometimes a problem; they can chew their way through your grapes. See chapter 7 for information on *Bacillus thuriengensis*.

Pierce's disease is a serious problem on grapes in the Southeast. There is no cure. In affected areas, plant muscadine grapes, or one of the few varieties of European grapes that are immune. Choose from 'Blue Lake', 'Lake Emerald', 'Norris', or 'Stover'.

Birds are sometimes a problem—cover plants with netting.

Harvesting

Cut off bunches of grapes when they are fully colored and sweet. Ripe grapes will come off easily in your hand, and their seeds are brown. Grapes will not ripen further once they are picked.

How to Purchase

Forms and Sources

Buy bare-root plants in late winter or plants in containers throughout the year. Both are readily available from local or mail-order nurseries.

Pollinators

Except for muscadine grapes, the great majority of varieties are self-pollinating. Muscadine grapes come in two types—those that are perfect-flowered, that is, self-pollinating, and those that are female only and need a pollinator. The perfect-flower type not only will pollinate themselves but will also pollinate other varieties that are female only. Check carefully when you order to make sure that you have a suitable pollinator.

Varieties

Hundreds of varieties of grapes exist. The following have been chosen for their disease resistance, availability, and quality of fruit. Among them you should find ones suitable for your growing conditions.

AMERICAN GRAPES

American grapes are adaptable to the East, Midwest, and Northwest. These grapes are readily available from local nurseries and mail-order firms. They are usually pruned to the cane method.

'Alden'—reddish, purple-black large grapes; excellent quality; strong and vigorous vines. (46, 57)

'Beta'—blue grapes; heavy producer as hardy as the wild grapes; good for coldest climates. (28)

'Concord'—the standard to which all other American grapes are compared; excellent blue, slip-skin grapes; widely adaptable; will tolerate cool summers; readily available; 'Concord Seedless' also available. (6, 28, 46, 72)

'Delaware'—standard of excellence for its type; pale red grapes with sweet flavor, good for eating fresh or as wine; one of the most ornamental vines but susceptible to mildew. Do not plant in areas where this is a problem. (6, 57, 58, 62, 72)

'Fredonia'—one of the best black grapes; hardy vines; early ripening. (6, 28, 57, 62, 72)

'Himrod'—American hybrid; best of the white seedless for the East; very hardy. (6, 46, 57, 72)

'New York Muscat'—reddish-black grapes; dessert fruit; not very vigorous vines. (46, 57)

'Niagara'—very old variety; white grapes; very vigorous vines; heavy bearer; moderately hardy. (6, 10, 28, 62, 72)

'Schuyler'—American hybrid; blue-black grapes; flavor similar to European; disease resistant; can be trained as spur or cane vine. (46)

'Steuben'—blue-black grapes; hardy vine; disease resistant. (**46, 57, 62**)

EUROPEAN TABLE GRAPES

These table grapes are mostly for warmer parts of the East and West. They are readily available from local nurseries or mail-order firms.

'Black Monukka'—reddish-black seedless grapes; one of the hardiest European grapes; prune to cane or spur. (**10, 60, 71**)
'Muscat of Alexdria'—green to pink grapes; well known for its musky sweet taste; used for wine and raisins; spur-type pruning. (**60, 71**)
'Olivette Blanche' ('Lady Finger')—deep-green grape; prune to cane. (**4, 10, 60, 71**)
'Ruby Seedless' ('King's Ruby')—medium-size, red, seedless sweet grapes; makes good raisins; prune to cane or spur. (**4**)

EUROPEAN WINE GRAPES

These varieties are generally limited to the wine-growing areas of California, Washington, and Oregon.
A good source for many of these grapes is (**71**).

'Cabernet Sauvignon'—red wine grapes for cool climates; needs a long growing season. (**10, 60, 71, 72**)
'French Colombard'—white-wine grapes; very vigorous and productive; needs a long hot growing season. (**10, 71**)
'Grenache'—red-wine grapes; for moderately cool to hot climates. (**10, 71**)
'White Riesling'—white-wine grapes; for cool areas; one of the hardiest of the wine grapes; can produce good wine as far north as Geneva, New York. (**46, 71**)
'Zinfandel'—red-wine grapes; makes good jelly; for areas with mild winters and cool summers. (**10, 60, 71**)

MUSCADINE GRAPES

The muscadine grapes are for the Southeast.
Perfect grapes, identified as such below, do not need a pollinator. A good source is (**23**); this nursery ships plants only between December 1 and March 15.

'Carlos'—medium-size grapes, gold with a pink blush; very vigorous; quite hardy; disease resistant; perfect. (**6, 23, 62**)
'Fry'—very large, bronze grapes with good flavor; high yield; particularly good in Florida; female plant needs a pollinator (a good one is 'Southland'). (**62**)
'Hunt'—black grapes with very good flavor; good for wine or juice; highly recommended; highly disease resistant; female plant needs a pollinator. (**6, 23, 62**)
'Jumbo'—very large, black grapes; good eaten fresh; single grapes, not clusters; disease resistant; female plant needs a pollinator. (**6, 23**)
'Magoon'—medium-size, reddish-black grapes; excellent flavor; highly disease resistant; for northern Florida; perfect. (**23**)
'Scuppernong'—oldest grape variety in the United States; many imitations exist, so make sure you get the real one; this muscadine is *the* muscadine; used as a benchmark, all the others are compared to it; bronze fruits with distinctive flavor and aroma; excellent fresh or for juice or wine; female plant needs a pollinator. (**6, 23, 58, 62**)
'Southland'—black grapes; good eaten fresh or as jelly; for south-eastern part of Gulf Coast; probably the best grape for Florida; perfect. (**23, 28, 62**)

HYBRIDS

The following American-European hybrids are all wine grapes suitable for colder regions. Good sources of many of these grapes are (**46** and **57**).

'Aurora' (Seibel 5279)—white grapes; ripens early; needs sandy soil; resistant to downy mildew, but somewhat susceptible to powdery mildew. (**6, 46, 57, 62**)
'Baco #1' ('Baco noir')—black grapes; very vigorous; resistant to mildew. (**6, 46, 58, 62**)
'Catawba'—purple or bronze-red grapes; a leading wine and juice grape; not for coldest climates. (**6, 57, 62**)
'De Chaunac' (Seibel 9549)—blue grapes; vines vigorous and productive; among the best for home wines. (**6, 46, 58, 62**)
'Missouri Riesling'—American wine grapes; produces semidry wine; very hardy; for protected areas of zone 4; the wine grape most resistant to mildew. (**Locally Available**)
Seibel 9110—yellow, tender-skinned grapes; produces superior wine; vines need protection in coldest areas. (**6, 41, 57**)
Seyve-Villard 12-375—yellow grape; somewhat hardy; resistant to mildews. (**6, 41, 46**)

Preserving

Grapes can be canned whole or as juice. They can be frozen whole or dried to make raisins; seedless grapes are best for these uses. Grapes are also preserved as jelly, jam, and conserves. Finally, they can be pickled or made into vinegar. (For jam directions, see KIWI.)

The most famous way of preserving grapes, of course, is to make them into wine. Choose your varieties carefully if you plan to put your grapes to this use. Home winemaking is becoming a popular hobby; supplies and kits, as well as books on the subject, are available.

Greens

Endive and escarole, *Cichorium Endivia*
Kale and flowering kale, *Brassica oleracea*, Acephala Group
Mustard (India mustard) and spinach mustard, *B. juncea*
New Zealand spinach, *Tetragonia tetragonioides*
Spinach, *Spinacia oleracea*
Swiss chard, *Beta vulgaris* var. *cicla*

Effort Scale

NO. 2
Must be planted annually
Watering, mulching, and fertilizing usually needed
Some weeding necessary

Zones

Annual

Thumbnail Sketch

Annuals, biennials, or perennials planted as annuals

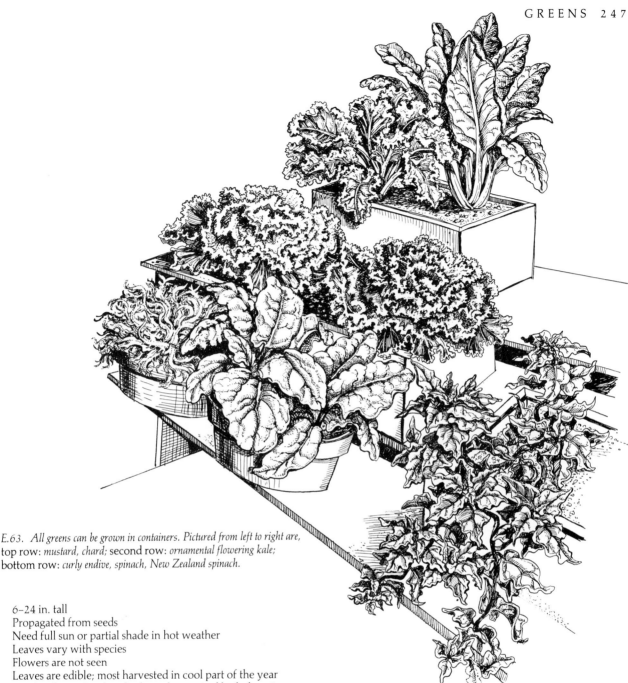

E.63. *All greens can be grown in containers. Pictured from left to right are,* top row: *mustard, chard;* second row: *ornamental flowering kale;* bottom row: *curly endive, spinach, New Zealand spinach.*

6–24 in. tall
Propagated from seeds
Need full sun or partial shade in hot weather
Leaves vary with species
Flowers are not seen
Leaves are edible; most harvested in cool part of the year
Used in flower borders, herb gardens, raised beds, hanging
　baskets, containers.

How to Use

In the Kitchen

What would we do without greens? All species are good steamed, and a pot of fresh greens flavored with butter or pork drippings is a springtime delight. Spinach and New Zealand spinach make savory cream soups. For entrees, spinach soufflé, spinach omelet, and my favorite, spinach or chard feta strudel, are rich and nutritious. All of the greens named here add variety to a tossed green salad, and a spinach salad with raw mushrooms and artichoke hearts is a meal in itself.

In the Landscape

Playing with the varied textures, forms, and colors this plant group offers can be great fun. All shades of green are represented —the light yellow green of endive, the bright green of mustard, the darker bright green of Swiss chard, the deeper green of spinach, and the more sombre gray green of New Zealand spinach. The spectrum of color is matched by a variety of leaf shapes—cut and frothy, curly and ruffled, and smooth. It is possible to create a picture by combining curly blue-green kale or curly lettuce-green mustard with the smooth-leaved 'Bibb' lettuce. All three take the same growing conditions. Another colorful scene might be composed of tall ruby-colored chard, with its bright red stalks, standing upright next to a bed of lush, trailing New Zealand spinach. The possibilities are endless for creating your own patterns, geometric or free form. Try the ornamental kale, which grows into frilly, amethyst-colored bouquets and is also edible, in pots on your patio.

How to Grow and Purchase

Chard, endive, kale, mustard, and spinach are all cool-season crops. New Zealand spinach, while it prefers cool weather, does quite well in the hot summer. During warm weather, these leafy vegetables need partial shade. All greens should be started from seed in early spring and planted in rich fertile loam, and all should be kept fairly moist.

To become tender and succulent, greens should grow quickly and vigorously. To encourage such growth, give supplemental organic matter and an extra source of nitrogen during the growing season.

With the exception of kale, the greens mentioned here are vulnerable to very few pests or diseases, though aphids, flea beetles, and snails are occasional problems. Kale is a member of the cabbage family and is often plagued by the pests that bother head cabbage (see CABBAGE).

These greens can all be enjoyed a few leaves at a time as required. The entire plant need not be harvested, as in commercial production. New Zealand spinach in particular will bear over a very long season, so it is wise to pick the new shoots as they appear.

Wash all greens well to remove grit and dirt before using.

Endive, Curly Endive, and Escarole

Leafy, green endive and its close relatives are popular in fresh salads or cooked as "greens." (Do not confuse this type with the Belgian or French endive, known as witloof chicory, which is actually the blanched sprouts of another species, *Cichorium intybus.*)

In hot weather, endive and escarole become bitter and often go to seed. Plant in early spring or late summer. Before eating, blanch the leaves by shading them from the light for a week after harvesting. Bring them into a garage or cellar in containers, and cover them with a paper bag. Or leave them on the plant, tying outer leaves up around the inner ones, and keep the plant watered.

There are many varieties of endive. Some have smooth leaves and look like lettuces; others, usually called escarole, have finely cut fringy leaves that contrast dramatically with smooth-leaved plants such as basil, chard, and butter lettuce.

Many kinds are readily available.

Kale and Flowering Kale

Curly, blue-green kale is beautiful as well as tasty, but its show-off cousin, flowering kale, puts most flowers to shame (see the photograph in chapter 5). Both can be enjoyed in the early spring or fall, and neither do well in warm weather. Flowering kale will not produce its brilliant red or purple foliage unless it has some frost, and the flavor of both plants is improved by frost.

These kales are usually eaten cooked, but the tender new growth is good raw in salads too. Unlike endive, kale is never bitter. The flowering types add color to a green salad in winter, when your only color choice is often the bland, nearly pink store-bought tomatoes.

Many different kinds of kale are readily available.

Mustard (India Mustard) and Spinach Mustard

These stout-hearted members of the cabbage family are spicy and crisp when eaten raw and superb when cooked with salt pork. All mustards need sufficient water or they will become too hot to eat. The younger the leaf, the less bite it has.

'Ostrich Plume' and 'Fordhook Fancy,' with their curled and frilly edges, are among the most beautiful of the mustard greens. 'Tendergreen' (sometimes called mustard spinach) is a smooth-leaved variety. Its flavor is usually not as "hot" as that of the others, and it is easier to clean.

Many mustard varieties are readily available.

Note: The mustard used on hot dogs comes from the ground-up seeds of plants in this family. The best condiment mustards are made from white mustard, *Brassica alba,* or black mustard, *B. nigra* (the latter is obtainable from **52**). The young leaves of these plants can be used as potherbs. To make condiment mustard, allow these plants to go to seed. Harvest the seeds when the pods turn yellow. Put the seeds in a blender with wine vinegar, black pepper, allspice, salt, and water if needed.

New Zealand Spinach

New Zealand spinach is a trailing plant with succulent, triangular leaves. It is not related to spinach but tastes very similar to it and can be used in any recipe calling for spinach, raw or cooked. Standard spinach cannot tolerate heat and quickly goes to seed after a few warm days, but New Zealand spinach can tolerate great amounts of heat without going to seed. It tastes better in cool weather but if shaded in summer will bear delicious "spinach" for three to four months. Keep harvesting the new growth to stimulate new young shoots. Old leaves are tough and bitter.

New Zealand spinach makes a marvelous temporary ground cover, is good in hanging baskets, and will cascade over the sides of planter boxes. Grow it on the patio so it will be close at hand to add to your morning scrambled eggs along with dill and cheese.

This plant can be damaged by frost but can take oceanside conditions. I have seen it growing wild along the Pacific Ocean on cliffs above the water.

New Zealand spinach is somewhat drought tolerant, but the leaves will taste their best if the plant is kept well watered.

New Zealand spinach seems to have few pest or disease problems.

The seeds are available from (**32, 39, 51, 56**).

Spinach

Just think of spinach soup or spinach soufflé to measure the value of this noble vegetable.

If the weather is cool and the soil rich and filled with humus, spinach is easy to grow. It has few pests and diseases, and the deep-green, smooth leaves contrast nicely with the oak leaf lettuces, nasturtiums, carrots, or blue-green kale. Spinach seed is readily available.

Swiss Chard

Chard grows upright and straight. Its strong supporting midribs are either white or cherry red, and its deep-green leaves are usually ruffled and rich looking. The red chards, often called rhubarb or ruby chards, look handsome when planted with the other greens. Chard's colors and forms are fun to design with. Try ruby chard with red nasturtiums and carrots in a large oak barrel or with strawberries in a flower border around the patio. Chard seed is readily available.

Preserving and Preparing

Greens may be canned or frozen.

Sweet-Sour Sauce for Greens

6 slices bacon, cut into small pieces
½ cup onion, chopped
3 teaspoons sugar
½ teaspoon salt
2 teaspoons flour
¼ cup vinegar
⅓ cup water

Brown bacon lightly and remove from pan. Fry onion in drippings until golden brown, and blend in the dry ingredients. Add vinegar and water, stirring and cooking until thickened and bubbly. Remove from heat, add bacon bits, and pour sauce over your choice of raw spinach, New Zealand spinach, or chard.

GROUNDNUT. See *Peanut.*

GUAVA. See *Pineapple Guava.*

GUMBO. See *Okra.*

HAZELNUT. See *Filbert.*

HEAD LETTUCE. See *Lettuce.*

E.64. Hickories are tall, handsome shade trees. When planted near a south wall they can protect a two-story house from summer sun.

Hickory

Shagbark hickory, *Carya ovata*
Shellbark hickory, (king nut), *C. laciniosa*

Effort Scale

NO. 3
Vulnerable to some pests and diseases
Nuts are hard to shell
Some raking necessary
Fertilizing and mulching necessary
Harvest is time-consuming

Zones

4–9

Thumbnail Sketch

Deciduous trees
100–120 ft. tall
Propagated by budding, grafting, or from seeds
Need full sun
Leaves are compound with 5 or 7 leaflets, 6–9 in. long
Bloom in spring
Flowers are green catkins
Nuts are edible; harvested in fall
Used as a shade tree, street tree, interest tree

How to Use

In the Kitchen

The rich, white hickory nuts have a sweet, distinctive taste and are savored in pies, cakes, breads, and cookies. They can be munched as appetizers with cheese or nibbled alone. The nuts are hard to shell but well worth the effort.

Some people smoke their meat over a fire of hickory prunings to give it a hickory-smoked flavor.

In the Landscape

These dignified trees add a note of grandeur to the landscape. They have an upright pyramid form. With age, both species develop an attractive shaggy bark and a strong branching structure. A hickory can shade a simmering south wall, but the tree's stately form is shown to best advantage as a street tree or in a row lining a driveway, where the outstanding shaggy bark plates can be appreciated at close range.

How to Grow

Climate

The shagbark hickory is one of the hardiest nut trees. Its range extends from southern Quebec south to northern Florida and Texas, and from the East Coast west to Minnesota. The natural range of the shellbark hickory is from southern Ontario, south into Louisiana, and west to Oklahoma from the East Coast. Hickory trees are not being grown in the West at the present time.

Exposure

These trees need full sun.

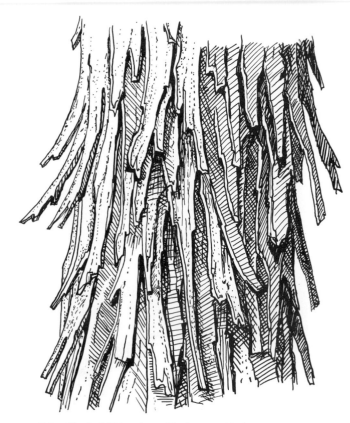

E.65. *Shagbark hickory has strikingly textured bark.*

Planting

Like most nut trees, hickory trees are sometimes difficult to establish if their long taproot has been injured in transplanting or en route from the grower to the planting site. If possible, check the root structure carefully before you buy. To plant your tree, dig a hole deep enough to accommodate the entire length of the taproot. Carefully place the root in the hole without bending it, and just as carefully place the soil around the root. Water the tree well and keep it mulched with organic matter. Staking may be necessary.

Soil

Hickory trees need deep, well-drained soil.

Fertilizing

Hickories respond well to fertilizer and organic mulches.

Watering

The young trees should be kept fairly moist, but usually once the tree is established no supplemental water is needed.

Pruning

New trees should be pruned carefully to establish a strong branching structure. They should be trained to a strong central leader (see Chapter 7), and the branches, where they meet the main trunk, should have wide crotches, with an angle of no less than 45°.

Do not allow major branches to come off the main trunk opposite each other. Once the tree is shaped and established, it will not need regular pruning to produce nuts. Annual shaping and removal of dead growth is sufficient, and will keep you supplied with wood for hickory-smoking meat.

Pests and Diseases

A number of pests—weevils, moth larvae, scale, and aphids—bother the hickories. Also, these trees are susceptible to a number of diseases, namely, scab, anthracnose, leaf blotch, and crown gall. As a rule, these problems do not endanger the life of the tree. Since the trees are grown in their native habitat, the pests are usually in balance with the predators in the areas. But if things seem to be getting out of hand, consult with your local university extension service.

Most hickory trees bear nuts on alternate years. This is normal.

Harvesting

Hickory nuts fall from their husks and are harvested off the ground. Collect the nuts often to prevent the squirrels from getting too many.

How to Purchase

Forms and Sources

Buy grafted hickory trees or seeds from local nurseries or the following mail-order sources: (**6, 26, 29, 55, 58, 68, 72**).

Pollinators

Most authorities recommend at least two trees for cross-pollination. If native trees are close by, they will be sufficient.

Varieties

Much work is being done on the hybridizing of hickory trees. The new varieties have thinner shells and larger nutmeats, both of which make hickory nuts easier to enjoy. Check the mail-order sources and your local nurseries for the latest varieties; new improved varieties are continually being introduced. You will have the most success if you plant varieties that have been developed in your geographical area.

Varieties of shagbark that are often available are 'Davis', 'Fox', 'Glover', 'Neilson', 'Porter', 'Weschcke', and 'Wilcox'. Shellbark varieties are 'Bradley', 'Ross', 'Scholl', and 'Lindauer'. The nursery with the largest selection is (**26**).

Preserving

Hickory nuts can be stored in their shells in a cool, dark place or shelled and frozen.

The shells are very hard. To make shelling easier, soak the nuts in very hot water for 10–15 minutes.

HIGHBUSH BLUEBERRY. See *Blueberry.*

HIMALAYA BERRY. See *Brambleberries.*

Hops

Humulus Lupulus

Effort Scale

NO. 2
Vines need training
Large amounts of water required
Vines need to be cut down annually to control rampant growth

Zones

4–10

Thumbnail Sketch

Deciduous herbaceous perennial
Twining vine 15–25 ft. long
Propagated from seeds or cuttings
Needs full sun
Leaves are light green, lobed, 3–5 in. long
Blooms in summer
Flowers are interesting, small, papery, green cones

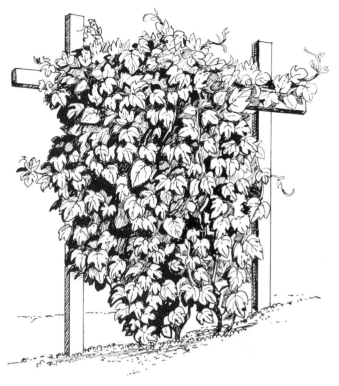

E.67. *Hops are vigorous vines that can be trained over two-by-four supports.*

Flowers are edible, used as seasoning, harvested in fall; shoots
are edible, harvested in spring
Used for trellises, arbors, as accent and interest plants, and in
containers

How to Use

In the Kitchen

The bracts (modified leaves) and flowers of the female hop
plants are used to flavor beer, whether it be commercial or home
brew. If you plan on making beer, this plant could provide you
with the hops you need for the brewing. But the use of hops in beer
has overshadowed the fact that the tender, spring shoots of this
vine are edible and are treated like asparagus. The American colo-
nists used hop shoots in this way, and the dish is still a great favorite
in Belgium and France, where it is known as *jet de houblon*.

In the Landscape

This herbaceous, perennial, fast-growing vine can attain 25 feet
in a season. With its large, light-green, hairy, lobed leaves, it makes
a lovely and quick-forming cover for an arbor, a trellis, or a fence.
The conelike flowers (hops) appear to quake in a manner somewhat similar to that of the seed spikes of rattlesnake grass. The hops
are a delicate green and develop in late summer. They have a
refreshing, pinelike aroma.

A hop vine can be trained on a trellis or with support posts to
become a small weeping tree. In this form the plant is usable in a
container or planter box, or as a small specimen in a yard. In whatever form it is grown, a hop plant will go well with rich-colored
morning glories.

E.66. *The light green seed capsules of hops are decorative on
the vine.*

How to Grow

Hops will grow anywhere except in desert areas. The vines require rich soil, good drainage, and plenty of water after growth starts in the spring. They grow vertically and rampantly (their specific name means "small wolf," and refers to their habit of climbing over other plants—wolfing them, so to speak), so they need a strong support. To train the vines to spread horizontally, you must constantly hand-guide the stem tips.

Every spring, harvest the new shoots to thin them out as soon as they appear. Leave some for further growth, but remove at least half the new shoots so you will not have a tangle of vines. Pick hops in early fall before they shatter and the frost hits.

Mildew, aphids, and mites can sometimes be a problem with hops. Be sure to clean up all litter and compost it in a hot compost heap.

How to Purchase

The plants are commonly grown from root divisions of female plants. Root divisions are available from some local nurseries, but they are hard to find. As for mail-order sources, plants are available from (**28, 42**) and seeds are available from (**40, 51, 54**).

Preserving and Preparing

The hop flowers, used in beer making, are dried out of the sun in warm air until papery.

Hop Shoots

Hop shoots look like thin, branched asparagus. Many shoots are needed for a meal. To prepare them for eating, snap off the top 6 inches of the hop shoot. The whole tender tip is eaten.

Cook as you would asparagus. When boiling hop shoots, add lemon juice to the water to prevent them from discoloring. Serve as you would asparagus too. Hop shoots are particularly good with a cream sauce.

HOT PEPPER. See *Peppers.*

HYACINTH BEAN. See *Beans.*

INDIAN FIG. See *Prickly Pear.*

INDIAN RICE. See *Wild Rice.*

ITALIAN PARSLEY. See *Parsley.*

JAPANESE PLUM. See *Plums.*

JAPANESE ROSE. See *Rose Hip.*

JAPANESE SAND CHERRY. See *Plums, Bush.*

Jerusalem Artichoke (SUN CHOKE)

Helianthus tuberosus

Effort Scale

NO. 1
Stalks must be cut down
Mulching required in coldest climates

Zones

2–9

Thumbnail Sketch

Herbaceous perennial
6–10 ft. tall
Propagated from tubers
Needs full sun
Leaves are dark green, oval, 6–8 in. long
Blooms in early fall
Flowers are medium-size, sunflowerlike, 3–5 in. across
Tubers are edible; harvested in fall after first frost
Used as a quick-growing screen and in the back of flower
  borders

How to Use

In the Kitchen

The crunchiness of Jerusalem artichokes—which neither come from Jerusalem nor taste much like artichokes—makes them a natural addition to a raw-vegetable platter served with a tasty dip. They add an unusual texture to mixed salads, can be served cooked as a vegetable by themselves, or a substitute for potatoes in stews and soups. Their carbohydrate is in the form of inulin rather than starch, which means it is an acceptable carbohydrate in diabetic diets.

In the Landscape

This rangy, stiff, herbaceous perennial, a native to North America, has only a few landscaping uses. Though the sunflowerlike blooms are showy, they are overshadowed by the ranginess of the plant itself. To use Jerusalem artichokes effectively, screen them with a low fence, tall flowers, or shrubs. They grow to a height of 6–10 feet, so they can be used when a quick-growing screen or hedge is needed, and as a tall background to a flower bed. Whether planted with flowers or vegetables, their height should be considered so they do not shade other plants.

How to Grow and Purchase

Jerusalem artichokes are easy to grow in most parts of the country. They require little care and no fertilizer and thrive in both light and heavy soil. Their only pests are gophers. They do equally well with summer rains or with occasional irrigation in arid summers, springing back quickly if wilted. The fact is, these plants are so easy to grow that you should plant them only where you want them to stay. Otherwise, if you decide to move them, one little tuber or even part of one left behind will grow into a plant the next summer, thus becoming a weed. For the same reason, avoid throwing

E.68. *Jerusalem artichokes are fast-growing perennials that die down every winter. They make good screens.*

peelings or discarded chokes into the compost pile, or you may be surprised when new Jerusalem artichoke plants appear among your zinnias. Plant chokes 6 inches deep and 18 inches apart in spring. Keep well mulched.

Jerusalem artichokes can be harvested in the fall, but most people wait until after the first frost because the frost seems to improve the flavor. The artichokes can be harvested all at once and stored. They can also be left in the cold ground if it is heavily mulched and dug up as needed.

Chokes can be purchased from the grocery store or from a few mail-order sources: (**9**, **28**, **35**, and **36**). There is a new variety, 'Stampede' Jerusalem artichoke. It has larger tubers, is shorter (to 6 feet) than the old type, and blooms in July for six to eight weeks. 'Stampede' is obtainable from (**35**).

Preserving and Preparing

Store tubers in plastic bags in the refrigerator or root cellar.

Creamed Jerusalem Artichokes

approximately 1 pound Jerusalem artichokes	¼ cup chopped onions
3 tablespoons butter	1½ cups milk
2 tablespoons flour	Tabasco sauce to taste
dash of salt, pepper, and nutmeg	

Wash, peel, and slice the Jerusalem artichokes. Place them in a saucepan with a small amount of salted water and simmer covered until tender, 10–15 minutes. Lightly brown the onions in 1 tablespoon of the butter.

To make a cream sauce, melt remaining butter in a saucepan and blend in the flour and seasonings. Stir mixture over low heat and cook until frothy, about 2 minutes. While stirring, bring milk to a boil in another pan. Remove the flour mixture from heat, and quickly stir in the boiling milk. Cook until thickened. Add the browned onions and Tabasco sauce.

Pour sauce over the cooked Jerusalem artichokes; reheat if necessary. Garnish with chopped parsley.

Jujube (CHINESE DATE)

Ziziphus Jujuba

Effort Scale

NO. 1
Easy to grow and harvest
Suckers are sometimes a problem
Plants are hard to find

Zones

6–10

Thumbnail Sketch

Deciduous tree
15–30 ft. tall
Propagated from seeds or by grafting
Needs full sun
Leaves are shiny, rich, green, yellow in fall, 2–3 in. long
Blooms in summer
Flowers are insignificant
Fruits are edible; harvested in fall
Used as interest tree, lawn and shade tree, espalier

How to Use

In the Kitchen

The small, round or oval fruits of the jujube tree are reddish brown with a crisp flesh. They have an applelike flavor when barely ripe but become spongy and very sweet when fully ripe. They can be eaten fresh or dried. Dried, they are something like dates. Jujubes are a favored sweet in Asia.

In the Landscape

This handsome, deciduous tree grows to heights of 15–30 feet. It has a graceful, weeping shape and a zigzag branching pattern that makes it dramatic in winter. In the summer it is covered with shiny, green, strongly veined leaves, and thus makes a comforting shade tree, which will grow in a lawn. In fall the leaves turn a rich yellow.

The year-round attractiveness of the jujube makes it an unusual

E.69. *Jujube fruits grow in a zigzag pattern on the branch. The leaves are shiny with three prominent veins.*

accent plant, whether grown to its full size or, by judicious pruning, kept to a size suitable for container growing. It is another tree that can be espaliered against a hot south or west wall.

Note: The one disadvantage of jujubes is that they tend to send out invasive suckers. Deep, infrequent watering helps overcome this tendency. Root pruning or concrete barriers may be necessary to keep the roots from heaving the nearby sidewalks, coming up through asphalt, or coming up in unwanted areas.

How to Grow

Climate

Jujubes are hardy; they tolerate temperatures down to −20°F. But they only fruit well where summers are long, hot, and dry. They dislike humidity.

Exposure

Jujubes require full sun.

Soil

Jujubes are tolerant of heavy clays, alkalinity, and poor drainage, but they prefer good, well-drained garden soil.

Fertilizing

Jujubes grown in average soil seldom need fertilizing. If foliage turns pale, feed with nitrogen.

Watering

These trees need occasional deep watering to reduce suckering and to keep the roots from coming to the surface.

Pruning

Prune only to shape and encourage weeping outline, and to remove dead branches.

Pests and Diseases

Jujubes are free of most pests and disease problems except in desert areas, where Texas root rot can be a problem.

Harvesting

Most people prefer jujubes fresh and crisp, just as they are turning from green to brown. For candying and drying, the fruits must be fully ripe.

How to Purchase

Forms and Sources

Jujubes are hard to find. Purchase them bare root or in containers from local nurseries catering to Oriental clientele, or from mail-order firms. Trees are available at (**4, 71**); seed is available at (**29, 51,**

E.70. *Many varieties of jujube have a weeping shape.*

and **52**). The International Tree Crops Institute also has plants available.

Pollinators

Jujubes need cross-pollination. Plant more than one variety.

Varieties

'Lang' and 'Li' are the only two varieties generally available. Both are the weeping, pendulous forms. (**71**)

KALE. See *Greens.*

KARELI. See *Bitter Melon.*

Kiwi *(CHINESE GOOSEBERRY, KIWIFRUIT)*
Actinidia chinensis

Effort Scale

NO. 2
Some pruning and tying required
Fertilizing and watering necessary

Zones

9, 10

Thumbnail Sketch

Deciduous perennial
Vine to 30 ft. long
Propagated by budding or cuttings
Needs full sun, or light shade in hot climates
Leaves are deep green, 6–8 in. long; new growth is bronzy
Blooms in spring
Flowers are cream-colored, 1–1½ in. across
Fruits are edible; harvested in fall
Used on trellises, arbors, pergolas, fences

How to Use

In the Kitchen

The kiwi's brown fruits are egg-shaped, fuzzy objects three inches long. To some people they look as if they ought to be stepped on. However, one taste of the bright-green, almost transparent flesh beneath the rough exterior quickly alters that opinion. The flavor is sharp but sweet, with overtones of strawberry, melon, and pineapple. It has to be tasted to be believed.

Kiwis are eaten out of hand or in fruit compotes and salads. They make a beautiful garnish for salads and desserts—in Australia, they often top the national dessert, a meringue-like cake called Pavlova. The juice serves as a tenderizing marinade for meats and also makes a bright and zesty jelly.

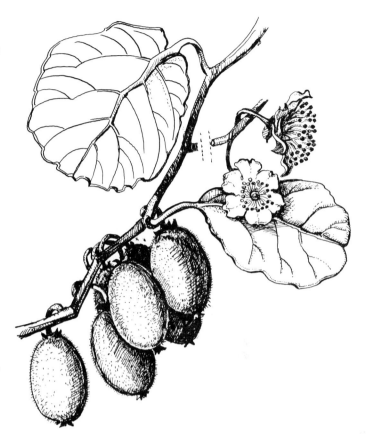

E.71. Kiwi fruits are brown and fuzzy. The cream-colored flowers are large and showy.

In the Landscape

The kiwi is a strong, twining, deciduous vine that needs a firm and sturdy support. When the vines can be properly attached, they are extremely useful for covering arbors, pergolas, fences, and even walls. All elements of the plant contribute to the overall effect: the new growth is covered by a warm, bronzy fuzz; the leaves are big, round, and dark green on top with a lighter underside; and the branches are gnarly, slightly hairy, and light brown. The cream-colored flowers, 1–1½ inches across, bloom in May and are followed by clusters of the brown fruit, which contrast in color and texture with the foliage. Because the fruit is firm, it is not a problem over a patio or deck.

How to Grow

Climate

Kiwis are semihardy. The ripening fruits are not able to withstand the frosts of late October. These plants need approximately 235 days without frost, and protection from wind. They are not good in the desert, and they are still experimental in Florida. Kiwis are being grown commercially in California.

Exposure

In most areas kiwis prefer full sun but can tolerate some shade. In hottest areas give them some afternoon shade.

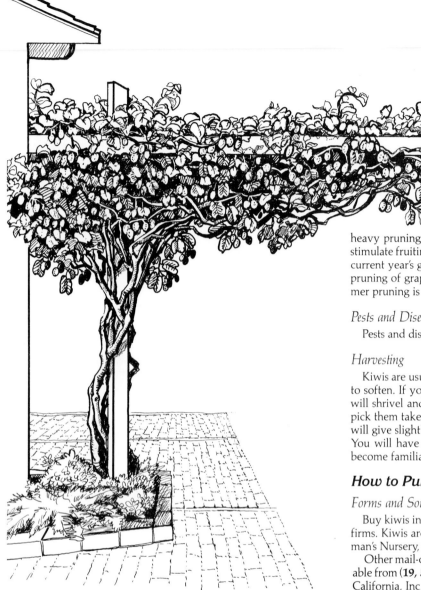

E.72. *Kiwi vines make handsome arbor plants.*

Soil

Kiwis must have good garden loam and excellent drainage.

Fertilizing

These vines require a thick, organic mulch and regular feeding during the growing season.

Watering

Kiwis need constant watering during the growing season in arid climates. They should not be allowed to dry out.

Pruning

Kiwis require pruning twice a year. In the dormant season the heavy pruning is done to cut down excessive "bleeding" and to stimulate fruiting, which occurs on the first three to six buds of the current year's growth. The pruning of kiwis is very similar to the pruning of grapes. Since kiwis are rampant growers, a light summer pruning is necessary to control growth and form.

Pests and Diseases

Pests and diseases are not generally a problem.

Harvesting

Kiwis are usually picked just before they are fully ripe and start to soften. If you pick them when they are not ripe enough, they will shrivel and will taste too tart. Determining the right time to pick them takes some experience. When kiwis are fully ripe they will give slightly, like peaches, to a little pressure of your fingers. You will have to experiment by picking and ripening a few to become familiar with the best time of harvesting for your use.

How to Purchase

Forms and Sources

Buy kiwis in containers from local nurseries or from mail-order firms. Kiwis are available bare root in January only, from Ed Carman's Nursery, 16201 Mozart Avenue, Los Gatos, CA 95030.

Other mail-order sources of plants are (**4, 6, 69, 71**). Seed is available from (**19, 51**). For more information, contact Kiwi Growers of California, Inc., P.O. Box 922, Gridley, CA 95948.

Pollinators

Cross-pollination between a male and female plant is necessary.

Varieties

'Chico' and 'Hayward' are the two fruiting female varieties usually available. (They may be the same variety.)

Note: Kiwis are heavy bearers; therefore, a cookbook on the subject is recommended: Write to Kiwi Growers of California, Inc. (address above) for *Recipes for Kiwifruit Lovers* by Mary Beutel. Include $2.75 plus tax.

Preserving and Preparing

Slightly underripe kiwis can be stored in a refrigerator and brought out a few at a time to ripen.

To freeze kiwis, peel and cut into thick slices. Place in plastic containers, pouring a 40 percent sugar syrup (3 cups sugar to 4 cups water) over them.

To can kiwis, peel and leave whole or cut in small slices. Cover with a 30 percent sugar syrup (2 cups sugar to 4 cups water). Leave ½ inch of space between the mixture and container cover. Seal and process in boiling water—pints for 20 minutes, quarts for 25 minutes.

Kiwi Jam

2 pounds kiwis	1 lemon
1 cup water	3 cups sugar

Peel fruits or cut in half and scoop out the pulp. Put in a large saucepan with the water and lemon juice. Bring mixture to a boil and simmer for 10 minutes. Crush the fruit pulp well and add sugar. Boil, stirring frequently, to the jelly stage.

To determine that your mixture is at the jelly stage, dip a cold spoon into the mixture and hold the spoon over the pan, but out of the steam. Let the mixture drip off the spoon. If it has reached the jelly stage, two streams will flow together, or "sheet," as they fall off the spoon. Take the jam off the stove, pour into hot, sterilized jars, and seal.

These directions may be followed for any fruit recommended for jam or jelly. Proportions of ingredients differ, but the process is the same. The product is called jam when it includes any solid part of the fruits; jelly is made from the juice alone, which is strained through a jelly bag before combining with other ingredients.

KUMQUAT. See *Citrus Fruits.*

LEAF LETTUCE. See *Lettuce.*

LEMON. See *Citrus Fruits.*

LEMON THYME. See *Thyme.*

Lettuce *(HEAD, ROMAINE, AND LEAF LETTUCE)*

Lactuca sativa

Effort Scale

NO. 2
Continuous planting needed
Some weeding, watering, and fertilizing required

E.73. *Lettuce comes in many shapes.* **From left to right:** *two romaine, one iceberg, and one red lettuce are grouped under a young 'Weeping Santa Rosa' plum tree.*

Zones

Annual

Thumbnail Sketch

Annual
6–12 in. tall
Propagated by seed
Needs sun or partial shade
Leaves light to medium green or red, 4–12 in. long
Flowers are not seen
Leaves are edible; harvest season varies
Used in flower beds, herbaceous borders, raised beds,
    containers

How to Use

In the Kitchen

The leaves of the lettuces are a standard salad item—in fact, they are almost indispensable for America's great love affair with salads. Where they are not part of a salad itself, the leaves are often used as serving shells for a salad. In some less common recipes, lettuce is braised or stuffed like cabbage.

In the Landscape

Lettuce comes in a wide variety of forms: firm, round, light-green head lettuce; soft, crinkle-leafed, darker green Boston lettuce; rosette-shaped leaf lettuce in a spectrum of colors and differing leaf shapes; and tall, upright romaine lettuce. All types make formal edges to flower borders. They can be planted near herb gardens, where their form and color will contrast with the smaller leaved herbs. A container planted with Boston lettuce is like a bouquet of green roses. And in a mixed flower bed, these herbaceous annuals are effective in combination with violas, nasturtiums, fibrous begonias, spinach, purple basil, and Alpine strawberries.

How to Grow, Purchase and Preserve

Lettuce is a cool-season annual crop that can be grown in most areas of the country. It will go to seed rapidly when hot weather comes, although leaf lettuce will take more heat than the heading types. Lettuce will grow in considerable shade, and in mild-winter areas can be grown year round. Lettuce is easy to grow when its requirements are met. Its needs are a slightly alkaline, rich loam with humus added; regular moisture; and light feedings of a fish-emulsion-type fertilizer to keep it growing vigorously.

Seeds for all kinds of lettuce are readily available, and nurseries offer seedlings. Whether homegrown or nursery-grown, seedlings can be transplanted into empty spaces left by harvested plants. Another advantage of leaf lettuce is that the outer leaves rather than the whole plant can be picked as needed, so harvesting does not leave gaps in your garden.

The succulent young lettuce leaves are ambrosia to slugs, snails, and cutworms, so protect your seedlings until they lose some of their succulence. 'Oakleaf' seems to have some snail resistance.

There is no way to preserve lettuce.

LIME. See *Citrus Fruits.*

LIMEQUAT. See *Citrus Fruits.*

LOGANBERRY. See *Brambleberries.*

E.74. *More assorted lettuces. In the background, from left to right: 'Ruby' lettuce, romaine, and spiky 'Oakleaf'. In the foreground: 'Buttercrunch' and some young seedlings of Bibb and 'Oakleaf'.*

Loquat

Eriobotrya japonica

Effort Scale

NO. 3
Susceptible to some diseases
Needs moderate fertilizing and mulching
Occasional raking of large leaves needed
Large harvest

Zones

8–10

Thumbnail Sketch

Evergreen tree
15–25 ft. tall
Propagated from seeds and by grafting
Needs full sun; will tolerate partial shade
Leaves are dark green, woolly underneath, 6–10 in. long; new
    growth is bronzy
Blooms in late winter

Flowers are cream-colored, grow in clusters, fragrant, ½ in. across

Fruits are edible; harvested in spring

Used as interest plant, shade tree, screen, large espalier, and in large containers

How to Use

In the Kitchen

Loquats are round, yellow-orange fruits 1–2 inches in length. Their sweet and juicy globes ripen earlier in the spring than other fruits; thus, since they break the winter-long fruit fast, we can overlook their big seeds. Loquats are eaten fresh, made into jelly, and canned. You may have eaten them in commercial cherry pies without knowing it. Before passage of the truth-in-labeling laws, it is reputed that they were sometimes colored and used as cherries.

In the Landscape

This handsome, dramatic evergreen tree grows to 15–25 feet, and its spread can match its height. The tree's botanical name reflects its main characteristic—woolliness—for the *erio* of *eriobotrya* comes from the Greek *erion*, meaning wool. The loquat's huge deeply veined, dark-green leaves are woolly and light-colored on the underside. Its new growth is bronzy and woolly, its new branches are woolly, and its clusters of white, fragrant flowers are woolly. The fruits, which also grow in clusters, contrast nicely with the rich foliage. Thus, the loquat tree is one of those plants that have everything: color, texture, fragrance, and edible fruit.

If the fruits are important to you, try to get a grafted name variety. Ungrafted seedlings are ornamental but their fruits are not guaranteed high quality. You might have to do some searching, since most nurseries only carry seedling loquats.

The loquat tree can be pruned to either a dense, round shape or an open, sculptured appearance. Either way it can make a stunning accent. It looks well as a formal tree near an entrance if kept clear of walks, an espalier on a large wall, or a container plant for close-up enjoyment. Fruit drop can be a problem over patios or decks.

How to Grow

Climate

Loquat trees are semihardy, tolerating temperatures of 15°–20°F. The flowers and fruits that form early in spring are damaged by freezing weather. This limits their fruiting range. The trees do well near the ocean, and they are often used in beach plantings. In borderline areas, they should be grown on a warm south wall.

Exposure

Loquats prefer full sun but will tolerate partial shade.

Soil

These trees prefer a well-drained garden loam but will tolerate fairly sandy or clay soils. They need a soil pH of 5.5–7.5.

Fertilizing

Loquats respond well and produce better fruits when organic mulches and annual fertilizers are applied.

Watering

The trees are quite drought tolerant once established, though fruit size is sometimes reduced by meager watering.

E.75. *Loquats grow in clusters surrounded by dramatically large leaves.*

Pruning

Prune to shape and remove dead or crossing branches. Fruits will be sweeter if the inner leaves are exposed to the sun. Thin fruits to increase their size.

Pests and Diseases

Fireblight is a common problem, particularly in Florida. If leaves and stems turn black at the end of branches—a symptom of fireblight—prune back at least 12 inches into healthy wood. Sterilize pruning shears with a 10-percent bleach solution between cuts and burn diseased prunings.

Harvesting

Fruits are ready when slightly soft and fully colored.

How to Purchase

Forms and Sources

In areas where loquats grow readily you can buy grafted loquat plants in containers from local nurseries. Seeds are available from (**19, 51**). One source, the International Tree Crops Institute (California branch; see Appendix C for address) carries grafted varieties.

Pollinators

Loquats are self-pollinating.

E.76. *Loquat trees make stunning interest plants. This one is trained to a multistemmed form to avoid a "lollipop" look.*

Varieties

'Champagne'—excellent, tart fruits, 1½ in. across with white flesh and yellow skin; April fruiting; best tree for warmest areas.

'Gold Nugget'—good fruits, 1½ in. across, orange; fruits early, often in March; vigorous ornamental tree; widely available.

'Premier'—excellent, sweet fruit, 1 in. across, pale yellow; fruits early; slow-growing tree.

Preserving and Preparing

Loquats are good for canning or making jelly. (See ELDERBERRY or KIWI.)

Loquats in Ginger Syrup

½ cup sugar
1 cup water
3 thin slices fresh ginger
½ teaspoon vanilla
3 tablespoons lemon juice

2 kiwis, peeled and sliced
2 oranges, peeled and sectioned
3 cups fresh loquats (or 1 cup canned, drained), sliced

In a saucepan, combine sugar, water, and ginger, and bring to a boil. Stir until sugar dissolves; then boil for 5 minutes more. Remove from heat and stir in lemon juice and vanilla. Cool. Remove ginger and add fruit. Chill well for at least 3 hours or overnight. Serve fruit covered with the syrup in small bowls. Serves eight.

Lotus *(CHINESE LOTUS, SACRED LOTUS)*

Nelumbo nucifera

Effort Scale

NO. 3
Tubers usually available by mail-order only
Controlling algae sometimes needed
Winter protection and storage required in most zones

Zones

5–10 and Hawaii

Thumbnail Sketch

Herbaceous perennial rhizome
3–5 ft. tall
Propagated from seeds, more usually from rhizomes
Needs full sun
Leaves are silvery blue-green on long stems. 2–3 ft. across
Blooms in summer
Flowers are white, pink, or rose-colored; single or double; showy; 8–12 in. across
Leaves are edible, harvested in spring; seeds and rhizomes ("roots") are edible, harvested in fall
Used in bog gardens, pools, large water containers

E.77. *The lotus is a spectacular cousin of the water lily; its flowers can reach a foot across. Shown here are leaves, flower buds, flowers, and seed pods.*

Planning a Water Garden

"A water garden in my yard?" you might ask. "Too grand!" In this section I want to suggest that water gardens are not only for large estates. Anyone can have one. A dug-out pond is ideal, but half a wine barrel, a washtub, or a preformed plastic pool also serves well for growing several lotus plants and a good supply of water chestnuts. Such a pool can go anywhere except, because of its weight, on a deck.

A barrel might have to be sealed for water retention, a tub might have to be painted to blend into the landscape, and a plastic pool might have to be sunk into the ground and its edges camouflaged with creeping ground plants. A sunken pool will require less water than the other two alternatives. Whatever container you use should be placed in full sun—make sure before you place it that some young tree is not going to become a shade-caster. Although these are containers, their weight when filled will make them stationary features.

To fill the container for planting, place soil in the bottom for the oxygenating underwater plants—the same plants that grow in a home aquarium. Or plant these plants in soil-filled plastic containers and cover the pond bottom with pebbles. These plants help to keep the water clean, help to control algae, and offer a hiding place for fish.

Fish are necessary for eating the insects, especially mosquitoes, that are attracted to the water. Insects that are harmful to your decorative plants are also eaten by the fish. And water snails—not garden variety—are placed in the pool to help keep the water fresh. They scavenge uneaten fish food, rotting vegetation, and algae. Snails cannot vanquish troublesome algae completely, but material is available from water-garden suppliers for treating your water when you first see algae forming.

The final requirement in stocking your water garden, no matter what its size, is a few water lilies other than the lotus. The pads of such plants, which are actually floating leaves, keep oxygen in the water and maintain stable water temperature and underwater animal life. One medium- to large-size water lily is needed for every square yard of surface area in your pond.

Both Chinese lotus plants and water chestnuts are planted in plastic containers before going into the water garden. The receptacle should be round for the lotus and any shape for the chestnuts. These containers should be nearly filled with good soil enriched with a fertilizer recommended by the water-garden supplier. After planting, it is wise to top off the container with rocks, gravel, or sand, to keep the soil from washing out.

The containers are placed on the soil in the pool at the proper water level (see text, here and under WATER CHESTNUTS). Since the water chestnuts should not have as much water over them as the lotus plants, their containers must be raised on bricks, other containers, or flat rocks if both are used.

If your winters are harsh, it is a simple matter to remove the containers from the pool and store your tubers and roots properly for the winter—indoors in damp sand for the lotus and indoors in their containers for the water chestnuts. The storage place should be cool.

Containers, oxygenating plants, fish, snails, special fertilizers, algae reducers, and even the plants themselves—does this all seem like too much to learn about all at once? One big advantage of water gardening is that the suppliers carry everything, are knowledgeable, and are usually willing to instruct beginners. The following is a select list of water-garden suppliers.

Bee Fork Water Gardens
Route 1, Box 115
Bunker, MO 63629
Catalog available for $2.00

Slocum Water Gardens
1101 Cypress Gardens Road
Winter Haven, FL 33880

Taree Springs Fisheries
Lilypons, MD 21717
Catalog available for $1.00

Van Ness Water Gardens
2460 North Euclid Avenue
Upland, CA 91786
Catalog available for 50¢

A good book for people interested in water gardening is *The Lotus Book of Water Gardening*, by Bill Heritage (London: The Hamlyn Publishing Group, 1973).

How to Use

In the Kitchen

The lotus plant is a gem; all its parts are edible. The tuberous roots are probably the most familiar part, since they are used sliced, to show their decorative pattern of holes, in many Oriental dishes. Like the water chestnut, the lotus is used to dress up many vegetables, and it adds elegance to shrimp or meat dishes as well. The root makes an elegant dessert too, when covered with apricot preserves. The flower petals may be floated on a clear soup.

Tender, young lotus leaves are used either raw as part of a green salad or lightly cooked as a hot vegetable. The mature leaves are used as a wrapping to steam meats in; they impart their aroma to the meat inside. But one should only use the leaves in this way if several plants are available, since it is unwise to remove too many leaves from any one plant.

The lotus's flat-topped seed pod is frequently used in dried-flower arrangements. The seeds inside those fascinating pods are edible too. They can be dried, roasted, or pickled, which is how the Japanese use them. The plants known as American lotus and Egyptian lotus are also edible, but the Chinese lotus is considered the most delectable.

In the Landscape

The Chinese lotus is a large, herbaceous, perennial water plant. It must be planted in a water garden (see accompanying section), where it will be among the most spectacular of your water lilies.

The 2-foot-wide, blue-green leaves of the lotus plant rise well above the water, and the many-petalled, fragrant flowers, which can measure 5–12 inches across and which come in a variety of shades of pink, rise above the leaves. The buds take about three days to open fully; as soon as they are open, the seed pod begins to form. The sight of bud, flower, and seed together on the plant occurs often with the lotus and adds to its charm. This show of abundance is yours for a lifetime as long as you do not eat all the tubers or let the tubers freeze.

Neither of the other edible lotus plants are as showy as the Chinese type. The native American one has light yellow blooms, and the Egyptian one has white or pale blue flowers.

How to Grow, Purchase, and Preserve

Lotus roots must be protected from freezing. Usually they are removed from their containers and stored in damp sand in a cool place. In their growing season (April through September) they need full sun. They prefer soil that is rich and fairly heavy. The roots should be planted in April or May in round containers since they grow in a circle and will die if they run into an obstacle.

Lotus tubers are oval and are joined together at narrowed sections. The connections can be broken apart to make separate plants. The growing tips point straight upward out of the tuber. The tips should be about a quarter-inch above the soil when the tubers are planted.

To grow lotus in a water garden, place the container in which the root is planted in water whose level is at least 6 inches but no more than 10 inches above the container line. Add water periodically to counteract evaporation and maintain the correct level. The container for each lotus plant should be at least a 25-gallon size.

Lotus should be fertilized each month during its growing season with a special water-garden fertilizer. For more information on planting, see the section on water gardens. The roots are harvested at the end of September.

The tuber is available from April to June only from water-garden supply houses and a few nurseries. Seeds are hard to find.

The flowers are usable as soon as they are developed. The seeds must be allowed to dry before they are eaten. The skin is peeled and the green embryo usually removed with a toothpick, as it can be bitter.

Lotus root can be canned, frozen, or dried.

LOWBUSH BLUEBERRY. See *Blueberry.*

MANDARIN. See *Citrus Fruits.*

E.78. *Sliced lotus root, its honeycombed pattern shown here in cross-section, is decorative in candied fruit assortments or in stir-fry dishes.*

Mango

Mangifera indica

Effort Scale

NO. 3
Vulnerable to some pests
Some raking needed
Fertilizing needed
Large harvest must be processed

Zones

10 and Hawaii

Thumbnail Sketch

Evergreen tree
40–50 ft. tall with wider spread
Propagated by seed, grafting, or budding

E.79. *Mangoes grow on long stems. The shape of this fruit inspired the traditional paisley pattern.*

Needs full sun
Leaves are large, shiny, green, 8–16 in. long; new growth is
    copper, white, red, or yellow depending on the variety
Blooms in winter
Flowers are red to yellow, fragrant, grow in clusters, not
    particularly showy
Fruits are edible; harvested in summer
Used as shade tree, screen, interest plant, tropical accent

How to Use

In the Kitchen

Mangoes, for those who love them, are indescribably delicious. The flavor of these juicy fruits is quite unlike that of anything else. The flesh is something like that of peaches, but juicier and richer. My praise might seem excessive, but you will understand my enthusiasm if you try them.

Mangoes are relished as a fresh fruit, often serve as the main ingredient in chutney, and make superb sherbets. A jam made from mangoes is a nectar for serving to special friends. Beware, though: mangoes have a slight turpentinelike taste when not quite ripe and some varieties may be fibrous in texture.

In the Landscape

This magnificent tree is limited to hot and fairly dry areas. If you live in a borderline area it may fruit only occasionally for you, but it is worth trying for its beauty alone. The tree is evergreen, and will reach 40–50 feet with an even wider spread. Its large, shiny, dark-green leaves can attain lengths of 8–16 inches and grow in clusters. The new growth is usually coppery red, but can be glossy white, true red, or yellow. The flowers are small, fragrant but inconspicuous, and grow in upright clusters. They are followed on the tree by large fruits—up to 8 inches long—which are slightly flattened and egg-shaped. The fruits range in color from green to yellow, but are usually a blushed crimson. They hang in long clusters and are extremely decorative.

How to Grow

Climate

Mangoes cannot tolerate frost. And because of their need for heat and dryness, they will not fruit in areas that have extremely heavy rains. They are grown successfully only in south Florida, Hawaii, and in the area of San Diego, California. In borderline areas trees should be covered whenever there are frost warnings. Wrap small trees in heavy paper; for larger trees, wrap trunks in fiberglass.

Exposure

Mangoes require full sun.

Soil

These trees are not very fussy about soil but it must be well drained. They prefer a pH of 5.5–6.5.

Fertilizing

In the first year, fertilize new trees once a month during the summer. After that, follow the same program you would for citrus —a citrus fertilizer supplemented with zinc and manganese. Like most fruit trees, mangoes respond to substantial amounts of compost or manure. For information specific to your area, contact your local university extension service.

Watering

Mangoes like to be kept fairly moist.

Pruning

Prune to shape, and remove dead and crossing branches.

Pests and Diseases

The fungus disease anthracnose is the most serious problem. A complicated fungicide program is called for if it gets out of hand. Good hygiene helps control the disease. Rake up the affected leaves and fruits, and destroy them. Call your local extension service if you have a severe problem.

Pests include spider mites, thrips, red scale, mango shield scale, and pyriform scale. An oil emulsion applied in June usually helps control these pests.

Harvesting

Mangoes are ripe when they give slightly if pressed, as with peaches.

E.80. Mangoes are large trees that can be used to shade your house from the hot tropical sun or to screen off the world.

How to Purchase

Forms and Sources

Grafted varieties can be purchased from local nurseries in containers. You can sprout seeds and grow your own mangoes, but fruits from the seedlings will be variable.

Pollinators

Mangoes are self-pollinating.

Varieties

The following may be available locally.

'Carrie'—fiber-free fruit; green skin; ripens early.
'Edward'—large fruits; orange skin; good flavor; ripens midseason.
'Glenn'—excellent flavor; medium-size, midseason fruit.
'Irwin'—good flavor.
'Kent'—red fruits; good flavor; most popular; ripens midseason.
'Pairi'—medium-size fruits; red skin, yellow pulp; fine flavor; freezes well.
'Zill'—small- to medium-size fruits; fine flavor; ripens early.

Preserving and Preparing

Mangoes can be peeled and sliced for freezing, preserved in chutney or jam, and used in many dessert recipes, including delicious sorbets and sherbets.

Maple *(SUGAR MAPLE, ROCK MAPLE)*

Acer saccharum
Acer species

Effort Scale

NO. 3
Some raking required
Syrup making is time-consuming

Zones

3–6

Thumbnail Sketch

Deciduous tree
60–100 ft. tall
Propagated from seeds or by budding
Needs full sun
Leaves are medium green, palmate, 4–6 in. across; turn yellow, red, or orange in the fall
Flowers are insignificant
Sap is edible; harvested in spring
Used as street tree, shade tree, lawn tree, and in woodland gardens

How to Use

In the Kitchen

Maple syrup is probably the most delicious syrup for flapjacks and waffles. Many of us, not fortunate enough to live where maple trees grow, have only enjoyed maple-flavored syrup. Nor have we had the fun of making letter-shaped popsicles by writing our names with hot syrup in the snow and letting it freeze. Maple syrup and maple sugar are used in puddings, pies, frostings, and in an evilly delicious sauce for ice cream. All these confections are sweet, sweet, sweet. In fact the recipe for one dessert, maple walnut tart (*Tarte au Sirop d'Érable*) ends with the suggestion that "if the sweetness of the tart is overpowering, accompany each serving with a wedge of lemon." Another instance of pure gustatory decadence.

In the Landscape

The New England countryside in fall would be anemic without the maple's blazing red, orange, and clear yellow. What glory these trees give to fall! In addition to this spectacle, they provide shade for hammocks and porches on hot, sultry August days.

Instead of planting a half-acre of lawn to mow, consider a grove of maples and a woodland path planted with blueberries, wild strawberries, and wildflowers—an exciting composition requiring much less work. Use maples as screens to block a view or to shade a hot south wall. They also make beautiful street trees for suburban areas.

How to Grow

Maple trees grow in most of the Northeast and Midwest, from New England west to Oklahoma, in sections of Canada, as far south as northern Alabama, and in sections of the Northwest and northern California. But although the tree has a wide growing range, sap production is good only where a wide differential occurs between the day and night temperatures during the spring. In mild-winter areas, tapping the trees for sap is unrewarding.

Maple trees are not fussy about soil as long as it is well drained. However, the largest production and highest quality syrup is produced on loamy soils high in humus. Sugar maples do not take hot, dry conditions or warm winters. They need occasional deep watering in arid climates.

A number of pests and diseases bother these trees, but they are usually not fatal. Natural predators generally keep these problems in balance. Maples generally do not do well under city conditions.

E.81. Raking up maple leaves is an integral part of fall in the Northeast.

How to Purchase

Seed is readily available and a number of selected varieties are available bare-root or in containers from local nurseries and mail-order firms: (**20, 22, 28, 72**).

'Green Mountain'—does better under adverse city conditions and is more drought tolerant than other varieties.
'Newton Sentry'—has a columnar shape.
'Temple's Upright'—has a columnar shape.
'Sweet Shadow'—has a deeply divided leaf.

E.82. *To collect maple sap, a spile is pounded into the trunk of the tree (left). A bucket is then hung on the spile (right) to collect the dripping sap.*

Other Syrup Trees

Besides *Acer saccharum,* other maple species also give good syrup. They include the following:

Acer glabrum (Rocky Mountain maple)
A. macrophyllum (Big-leaf maple)
A. rubrum (Red maple)
A. saccharinum (Silver maple)
A. s. grandidentatum (Big-tooth maple)
A. s. nigrum (Black maple)

Some birch species also are used for syrup. The most common one is *Betula lenta,* black, or sweet, birch. Black birch produces copious amounts of sap, usually in April. It is collected in the same way as maple sap (see below), but because it usually has a lower concentration of sugar it has to be boiled longer. Birch beer is also made from the sap of this tree. Young birch twigs, honey, and yeast are combined with the sap. This mixture is allowed to ferment and is said to be quite a potent beer. Black birches, too, are available in containers from local nurseries or from mail-order firms.

Preserving

Making Maple Syrup

Tapping maple trees for sap to make maple syrup is great as a family activity for an outing in February or March. All you need for a pint of syrup are half a dozen maple trees. Of course, with thirty or forty good-size trees at your disposal you can make enough maple syrup for a year.

You do not need any elaborate equipment for tapping trees. Just gather together some clean glass gallon jugs or make buckets out of shortening cans. Make some spiles—hollow tubes used as spigots (Figure E. 82A)—out of sumac branches, ½–¾-inch dowels, or old broom handles. Drill through the branch or dowel to create a tube, sharpen one end, and notch the other to hold the bucket handle.

Choose a warm, bright day that follows a cold, frosty one. This kind of weather makes the sap "run"—that is, causes the tree to send nutrient-rich sap up from the roots into the branches.

The trees you choose should be at least a foot in diameter at your shoulder. Drill a hole just large enough to accomodate the spile an inch deep into the living tissue just below the bark. A tree that is 15–24 inches in diameter can take up to three holes, and a tree 2 feet (or more) in diameter can take four holes.

Hang the bucket on the spile (Figure E. 82B). Check your buckets every few hours to see how they are filling. A good-size tree can produce as much as 2 or more gallons of sap a day.

Collect all the sap in a large, clean plastic or metal container. Gather firewood, some cinder blocks or large rocks, and a large metal washtub.

The sugar content of maple sap averages 2–3 percent of the whole. To evaporate the excess liquid and concentrate the syrup, you must boil the sap for a long time. This process is best done outside, even for small amounts; otherwise, the steam will deposit sugar on your ceiling. Place the washtub on the cinder blocks and start a fire under it. Pour all the sap into the tub and boil until a candy thermometer registers 219° F at sea level. (The boiling point for the sap decreases 1° F for every 550 feet above sea level.)

Pour the finished syrup into sterilized jars, immediately turning them upside down to sterilize the caps. The syrup will keep indefinitely until opened. Refrigerate after opening.

Marjoram

Sweet marjoram, *Origanum Majorana*

Effort Scale

NO. 1
Easy to grow
Must be taken indoors or planted annually in coldest areas

Zones

All; as an annual in 1–7

Thumbnail Sketch

Herbaceous perennial
1–2 ft. tall
Propagated from seeds or division
Needs full sun
Leaves are gray-green, small
Blooms in summer
Flowers are small, white or lavender, grow in spikes
Leaves are edible; used as seasoning; harvest season varies
Used in herb gardens, flower beds, rock gardens, containers

How to Use

In the Kitchen

The aromatic leaves of marjoram are used, fresh or dried, as a seasoning in soups, stews, omelets, and vinegars. They are a necessary ingredient in spaghetti sauce and herb stuffing for poultry. A pinch improves many vegetables and adds interest to fish and meats.

In the Landscape

This small-leaved, gray-green, herbaceous perennial grows to 2 feet in height. Therefore, it can be used in the middle of a mixed-flower border and is ideal as well in herb and rock gardens. Marjoram's white or light lavender flower spikes and gray foliage combine well with chives, dittany of Crete, lavender, or 'Silver Mound' artemesia.

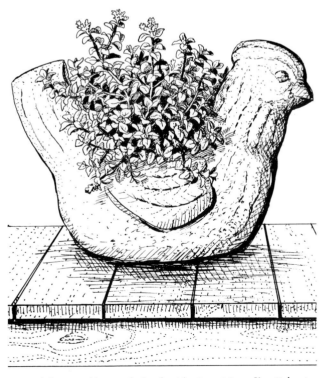

E.83. Marjoram, like many herbs, flourishes in containers. Keep it close to the kitchen on a porch or patio so it is handy for cooking.

How to Grow, Purchase and Preserve

Marjoram grows almost anywhere. It needs medium-rich, well-drained soil, plenty of moisture, and full sun. In harsh-winter areas, plants brought into the house will thrive on a sunny window sill. But wherever they are grown, marjoram plants should be kept pruned back so they will not become woody.

Pick leaves any time for use fresh, but for drying harvest them before the plant has started to flower to insure a good texture and rich flavor.

Marjoram seed or young plants are readily available.

To dry leaves, see the section on drying herbs under BASIL.

MELON. See *Cucumber, Squash,* and *Melon.*

Mint

Peppermint, spearmint, orange bergamont mint, pineapple mint, Corsican mint, *Mentha* species

Effort Scale

NO. 2
Vulnerable to some pests
Pruning needed to keep plant trim and bushy

Zones

4–10 for most species

Thumbnail Sketch

Perennial herb
½–3 ft. tall
Propagated from seeds, cuttings, or divisions
Needs partial shade
Leaves vary from deep green or variegated to light green,
    ¼–2 in. long
Blooms in summer
Flowers are lavender, purple or white, grow in spikes, small
Leaves are edible; used as flavorings; harvest season varies
Used as ground cover, in herb gardens, rock gardens, containers

How to Use

In the Kitchen

The aromatic leaves of all types of mint are eaten fresh as a seasoning in salads, drinks, and jelly. Dried, mint is used in teas.

In the Landscape

These fresh-smelling plants deserve a place in our gardens just so we can pick an occasional leaf and enjoy its pungency. Most types have one common flaw: their underground stems spread—invasively—and therefore must be controlled in containers or by deep header boards.

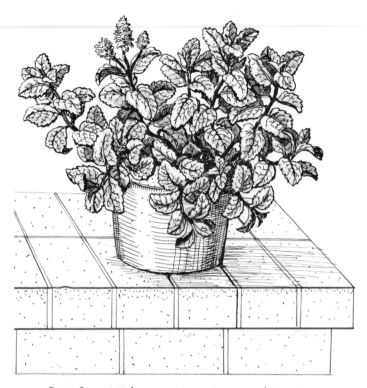

E.84. *Spearmint is best grown in a container to control its invasive roots.*

All but Corsican mint can grow as high as 2–3 feet. All mints have crinkly leaves, but color varies with type. Spearmint and peppermint are dark green, pineapple mint is lighter and somewhat variegated, and orange bergamont mint has purple-edged leaves. All look well together and all combine beautifully with impatiens and begonias. Corsican mint is a tiny-leaved miniature, 1 inch tall, which can be grown between stepping stones in mild climates. It is not as invasive as the other mints.

How to Grow, Purchase, and Preserve

Except for Corsican mint, all the mints are hardy and easily obtainable as seeds or plants from nurseries, seed catalogues, or friends. They all grow best in rich, moist soil, and prefer shade but will grow almost anywhere if they get enough water. Prune the large mints often to keep them bushy. Mint is attractive to whiteflies.

Fresh mint can be picked anytime. The leaves have a better flavor if the flowers are kept picked off.

Pick leaves for drying during a dry spell. They do not dry as easily if they are too succulent. See BASIL for drying information.

Mulberry *(BLACK MULBERRY)*

Morus nigra

Effort Scale

NO. 2
Vulnerable to some diseases and pests, including birds
Harvesting is time-consuming

Zones

5–10

Thumbnail Sketch

Deciduous tree
15–30 ft., depending on variety
Propagated by seed, budding, or from cuttings
Needs full sun
Leaves are medium green, heart-shaped, 6–8 in. across
Blooms in spring or summer
Flowers are insignificant
Fruits are black or red; edible; harvested in summer
Used as background plant, screen, espalier; weeping variety
    used as interest plant

How to Use

In the Kitchen

The mulberry looks like a small blackberry and is juicy and quite seedy. The flavor varies with variety. The best is delicious and relatively seedless; poorer quality berries are best described as insipid. Fruit is commonly eaten off the tree, but it is also used for jams, jellies, and syrup. It is occasionally dried for later use.

In the Landscape

These deciduous trees can attain a height of 15–30 feet and they develop a spreading crown. Their leaves are large, medium green, and heart-shaped. One grafted variety, 'Black Beauty,' develops a beautiful, somewhat pendulous form, and its fruits are more flavorful and less seedy than any of those previously sold. This variety can be used as a handsome accent plant.

The weeping mulberry 'Pendula', the variety most commonly sold as an ornamental, has variable fruits. Someday, when edible ornamentals have become more popular, a true weeping mulberry with superior fruit will probably be available. As it is, you take a chance when you plant one that the quality of the fruits will be poor.

The standard, more readily available mulberry tree is less decorative than the semipendulous and weeping forms. However, it can provide a good background to shrub borders. Several planted close together make a dense screen or hedge. They grow well in a lawn and as shade trees, but at fruiting time sitting under them is hazardous. The fruit drop makes these trees undesirable near patios and sidewalks. The fruit on the ground becomes slippery, and it stains.

Both the standard tree and the semipendulous form can be used as a handsome, fan-shaped espalier on a warm wall, and the trees can also be kept to container size. Mulberry trees are often planted in a yard with cherry trees; birds seem to prefer the mulberries to the cherries.

Note: When buying a mulberry tree for fruit, make sure you do not get one of the most commonly planted, fruitless mulberries.

How to Grow

Climate

Black mulberries are semihardy. They grow as far north as Virginia on the East Coast, and Seattle on the West Coast. They prefer a hot and dry climate in the summer.

Exposure

Mulberry trees need full sun.

Soil

These trees are fairly tolerant of most soils. They prefer good garden loam but will grow on rocky or gravelly soils.

Fertilizing

Mulberries usually do not need fertilizing though they benefit from an organic mulch.

Watering

The trees are somewhat drought tolerant once established.

Pruning

Prune only to shape and to remove dead branches.

E.86. *Mulberries are among the few berries that grow on trees.*

E.85. *Mulberries are a favorite fruit of birds.*

Pests and Diseases

Mulberries are usually free from pests and diseases; however, spruce budworms and tent caterpillars are an occasional problem. Try to remove the colonies by hand.

A bacteria-caused canker is sometimes a problem. Cut into the diseased branch at least a foot below the cankerous tissue. Sterilize the pruning instrument with a 10-percent solution of bleach between cuts.

Birds are the chief pests. Cover trees with netting during harvest season to protect the fruit.

Harvesting

The easiest way to harvest mulberries is to spread a clean, white cloth or a piece of plastic under the tree when most of the fruit is ripe—black and soft—and to shake the tree gently. The berries should be gathered as they fall. Red, not-quite-ripe berries can be picked and are tart and good for jellies and pies.

Note: If you are going to pick mulberries by hand, invest in a package of see-through plastic gloves to protect your hands from staining. They are available from beauty-supply houses, are inexpensive and one package will last for years.

How to Purchase

Forms and Sources

Mulberry trees are available bare root or in containers from local nurseries and from the following mail-order firms: (**4, 24, 26, 28, 46**).

Pollinators

Mulberries are self-pollinating.

Varieties

'Black Beauty'—large, sweet-tart, nearly seedless fruits; semi-pendulous, semidwarf tree; grows to 15 ft. but can be kept shorter. (**4**)

'Hybrid Black'—large, sweet, black fruits; full-size tree grows to 30 ft. (**26**)

'Illinois Everbearing'—large, sweet, black fruits; full-size tree grows to 30 ft. (**26**)

Morus alba 'Pendula'—variable fruit (buy only when in fruit and taste first. Most are insipid; a few are tasty); weeping form; grows to 6–8 ft. (**Locally Available**)

'Wellington'—long, slender fruits with good flavor; large tree, heavy crops; hardy to New York State; might be an old variety known as 'New American.' (**46**)

Preserving

Dry mulberries outdoors by laying them out in a warm, dry place, out of the sun, in a single layer on a screen for four or five days. Protect them from birds. Alternatively, use a food dryer.

To freeze, lay the fruits on a cookie sheet and place it in the freezer. Gather fruits when frozen and put them in freezer bags. Or combine 1 cup sugar with 5 cups fruit. Mix together, put in a container that seals well, and freeze.

MUSCADINE GRAPE. See *Grape.*

MUSTARD. See *Greens.*

NANKING CHERRY. See *Plums, Bush.*

Nasturtium

Dwarf nasturtium, *Tropaeolum minus*
Garden nasturtium, *T. majus*

Effort Scale

NO. 2
Annual planting required
Fairly frequent watering needed

Zones

Annual

Thumbnail Sketch

Herbaceous perennials; grown as annuals in most climates
Vine, to 10 ft; dwarf varieties, to 1 ft. tall
Propagated from seeds or cuttings

E.87. *Nasturtiums make a colorful hanging basket.*

Needs full sun; in hottest areas, prefers partial shade
Leaves are lily-pad shaped, bright to blue-green, 2–3 in. across
Blooms in spring, summer, and fall
Flowers are red, mahogany, yellow, orange, or cream-colored, 2–3 in. across
Flower buds and leaves are edible; harvested in spring, summer, and fall
Used in flower beds, herb gardens, containers; vining types used on trellises, over retaining walls, in hanging baskets

How to Use

In the Kitchen

Nasturtium buds or young seed pods are often pickled and used as a substitute for capers. Tender, young leaves add a peppery flavor to salad, and the flowers can brighten a salad as well.

In the Landscape

These succulent plants are grown as popular annuals in cold climates and as perennials in mild climates. Their large, lily-pad-shaped, bright-green leaves form a good backdrop for the large brilliant flowers, which can be red, orange, yellow, mahogany, or cream-colored. The flowers are gently but spicily fragrant. Some nasturtium varieties have double flowers.

The compact dwarf plants, about 1 foot high, are used in herb gardens and flower borders. Try interplanting them with lettuce, carrots, spinach, chard, or alpine strawberries. The vining kinds, which can trail to 10 feet, are lovely in containers or hanging baskets, flowing over a rock wall, interplanted with vining peas or cucumbers, or climbing up a fence or a post. They are always a bright spot to lift the spirit.

How to Grow, Purchase, and Preserve

Nasturtiums grow so easily that every garden should have some. They grow in any well-drained soil, want moisture but not sogginess, and get along without extra feeding. Aphids are an occasional problem. Nasturtiums often reseed themselves. They are generous in their blooming habits, so you can have bouquets over a long period.

Nasturtium seeds are available in mixed or separate colors on most nursery seed racks. One variety, 'Red Eating Selected,' has been hybridized specifically for eating, and is available from (**63**).

The leaves are delicious as long as you harvest them when they are young. To use the buds as capers, pick them just before they open or use half-grown seed pods.

Nasturtium Seed Capers

1 pint nasturtium seed pods	1 teaspoon salt
¾ cup cider vinegar	1 teaspoon mustard seed
¼ cup water	½ clove garlic, crushed
¼ cup brown sugar	(optional)

Gather the half-grown seed clusters, wash, and pack into sterilized small (½ pint) canning jars. In a stainless steel or enamel saucepan, combine the other ingredients and boil for 10 minutes. Pour over nasturtium seed pods. Seal the jars tightly. Store in a cool place. Do not use for two weeks.

Natal Plum

Carissa grandiflora

Effort Scale

NO. 2
Easy to grow
Some pruning needed
Fruits are usually processed

Zones

10 and Hawaii

Thumbnail Sketch

Evergreen shrub
2–18 ft. tall, depending on variety
Propagated from seeds and cuttings
Needs full sun in coastal areas, partial shade inland
Leaves are round, glossy, deep green, 3 in. long
Blooms in spring, summer, and often all year
Flowers are white, fragrant five-petalled stars, 2 in. across
Fruits are edible; harvested in spring and summer
Used as interest plant, hedge, espalier, foundation plant, barrier plant, ground cover, and in containers

How to Use

In the Kitchen

The beautiful, red fruits of the natal plum plant are 1–2 inches long and are often used for jelly, sauces, and pies. With their combination of sweet and tart flavors, they are delicious fresh in fruit salads or eaten plain as well.

In the Landscape

This handsome evergreen shrub comes in many sizes and shapes and can therefore be used in many situations. Its deep green, leathery leaves, fragrant, white, jasminelike flowers, and green or red fruits which are sometimes on the plant simultaneously with the flowers, are all decorative. A low-growing carissa makes a good ground or bank cover. A tall variety can be trained as a small multistemmed tree that goes well near a doorway or entrance, where its fragrance can be enjoyed. This plant also can be kept small enough for container growing. Most varieties have thorns which make them useful as barriers. Try combining them with citrus, loquats, avocados, and guavas.

How to Grow

Climate

The one disadvantage of this plant for all seasons is that it is hardy only to 24° F. Still, because of its beauty it is often used in

E.88. *Its starlike fragrant flowers and brilliant red fruits make the natal plum an especially ornamental plant.*

E.89. Low-growing varieties of natal plum are suitable for containers.

cooler climates in containers, to be moved to protected areas when the weather turns cold; or planted in zone 9 on a protected south wall and covered when frost threatens. A big advantage of this plant is its tolerance of seacoast conditions, that is, it withstands salt spray. The natal plum grows best in the southern part of California, Hawaii, in Florida, and along the Gulf Coast.

Exposure

The natal plum requires full sun in foggy coastal areas but some shade in hot, desert areas.

Soil

This plant is not fussy about soil type except that it must be well drained.

Fertilizing

Minimal fertilization is required.

Watering

In sandy soil and in hot climates, natal plum should be watered occasionally. Almost no watering is needed under cool, seacoast conditions.

Pruning

It is necessary to shape this plant and to cut out dead or crossing branches. It can be sheared as a hedge but it will not produce as much fruit that way.

Pests and Diseases

The plant has few pests and diseases.

Harvesting

Pick fruits carefully when they become fully colored. Most varieties have thorns at the base of the fruit.

How to Purchase

Forms and Sources

Natal plum plants are available in containers from local nurseries. Seeds are available from (**19**).

Pollinators

To ensure pollinating, plant more than one natal plum.

Varieties

'Fancy'—the best producer of excellent fruits; upright, growth to 6 ft., very thorny; considered self-fertile.
'Tuttle'—fruits are not as good as on 'Fancy'; 2–3 ft. tall with a 3–5 ft. spread; used as a tall ground cover.

Preserving

Natal Plum Jelly

4 cups natal plums   sugar as needed
2 cups water

Wash fruits and slice or crush them. Pour fruit pieces or pulp and water into a kettle. Bring mixture to a boil, and simmer for 20 minutes.

Extract juice, by straining it through a jelly bag; measure it, and mix it with an equal quantity of sugar. In a pot, boil mixture until it reaches the jelly stage. Pour the jelly into hot, sterilized glasses and seal. Each cup of juice yields approximately one 8-ounce glass of jelly. See KIWI for detailed jelly directions.

NECTARINE. See *Peach* and *Nectarine*.

NEW ZEALAND SPINACH. See *Greens*.

Okra *(GUMBO)*

Abelmoschus esculentus [Hibiscus esculentus]

Effort Scale

NO. 2
Annual planting required
Vulnerable to a few minor pests

Zones

Annual

Thumbnail Sketch

Herbaceous annual
Standard, 4–6 ft. tall; dwarf variety 2–4 ft. tall
Propagated from seeds
Needs full sun
Leaves are lobed, 6–10 in. across
Blooms in summer
Flowers are hibiscuslike, yellow or red and yellow, 2–3 in.
  across
Seed pods are edible; harvested in summer and fall
Used in the back of flower beds, or containers

E.90. Most okra plants grow to 4–5 feet. 'Dwarf Long Green Pod', shown here, grows to about 2½ feet.

How to Use

In the Kitchen

Okra, like the olive, is usually an acquired taste. Its best-known use is in seafood or chicken gumbo; the pods are also served as a hot, boiled vegetable or chilled and served vinaigrette as a salad. It can also be fried and is often used in lamb dishes.

In the Landscape

These herbaceous summer annuals are in the same family as hollyhocks and hibiscus. The family resemblance is expressed in their large, creamy yellow blossoms, which usually have red throats. The tall types are 4–6 feet tall and belong in the back of a large flower bed, perhaps in front of your still-taller Jerusalem artichokes. The dwarf varieties, which grow to 2–4 feet tall, can be used in the midst of a flower border or in a container.

The large leaves, 6–10 inches across, the showy flowers, and the green pods that follow give the plant summer-long appeal. One variety, 'Red Okra,' has deep-red stems, yellow and red flowers, and red pods—a real eye-catcher. Try combining it with peppers and large red salvia.

How to Grow

Okra likes heat and will not tolerate cloudy, cool summers. Where corn grows well, okra will usually thrive. Besides heat, it requires well-drained soil that includes plenty of humus. Too much nitrogen fertilizer will make it go to leaf instead of pods. It does not take much water, and it has few pest problems. If caterpillars show up, handpicking is often sufficient since you probably will not be growing very many okra plants (a dozen are usually enough for all but the most ardent okra lovers). *Bacillus thuringiensis* can be used for a serious caterpillar infestation.

Okra pods are best picked before they are 3 inches long. If they are allowed to mature much beyond that, the plant will stop pod production.

How to Purchase

Okra seed is readily available from nurseries or the following mail-order sources: (**8, 9, 16, 20, 28, 29, 32, 48, 51, 59, 62**).

Varieties

'Clemson Spineless'—pods green; good for thickening soup; plant grows 4–4½ ft. tall. (**Readily Available**)
'Dwarf Green Long Pod'—pods green and ribbed; bears early (55 days); plant grows to 2½–3½ ft. (**8, 9, 16, 20, 29, 62**)
'Emerald'—medium green pods; leaves somewhat grayish; plant tall, 6–9 ft. (**16, 29, 48**)
'Park's Candelabra Branching'—green thick pods; bears 4–6 spikes per plant; high yield. (**48**)
'Red Okra'—red tender tasty pods; ornamental plant; tall, to 5 ft., with red stems and leaf veins; flowers yellow with red. (**16, 25, 29, 48**)
'White Velvet'—light green, tender pods; plant grows to 3½ ft. (**16, 62**)

Preserving

Okra can be canned, frozen, or dried.

Olive

Olea europaea

Effort Scale

NO. 4
Very easy to grow
Some pruning needed
Harvesting and preserving are time-consuming

Zones

9, 10

Thumbnail Sketch

Evergreen tree or shrub
25–30 ft. tall
Propagated from cuttings and by grafting and budding
Needs full sun
Leaves are gray-green with whitish undersides, narrow,
  1–3 in. long
Blooms in spring
Flowers are fragrant but insignificant
Fruits are edible if processed; harvested in fall or winter
Used as multistemmed tree, interest plant, screen, large shrub,
  to line a driveway, near an herb garden

How to Use

In the Kitchen

Salad Niçoise, pot roast Provençale, Italian poultry stuffing, Greek olives, Spanish olives—the recipes alone indicate that the Mediterranean area is olive country. The fruits of the olive tree are versatile and add great richness to many dishes. They also are a favorite garnish for salad plates and sandwiches. However, I cannot with good conscience urge you to try preserving olives yourself. The standard procedure for removing the bitterness from the fruits requires that they be soaked in a lye solution. Not only is lye a caustic substance, and so difficult to work with, but also the risk of botulism developing in a non-acid home-canned product is great. All things considered, it is best to purchase canned olives.

However, pickled olives and olive oil are less hazardous to produce. Olive presses are available for making olive oil at home. The flavorful oil of olives improves salads and adds a distinctive flavor to browned meats and poultry, so it is worth preparing fresh and keeping as a staple. Although admittedly olive oil is a chore to produce, the superior product and the resulting money savings for heavy users make the effort worthwhile.

In the Landscape

Olive trees are extremely beautiful—in fact, they are among the loveliest of the edible ornamentals. Their gnarled trunks, graceful branching structures, and soft, gray-green foliage give them the appearance of living sculptures. Nevertheless, these trees are often cursed as a nuisance, since their food crop is exceedingly messy, but they are so beautiful that people put up with the inconvenience to use them as ornamentals. Olive trees are particularly effective in a Spanish- or mission-style landscape; their sculptural qualities are shown to their best advantage against white stucco walls.

E.91. *The olive's glossy fruits are set off by its subtle gray foliage.*

Olive trees should never be planted near patios, sidewalks, or driveways. Their oil, although tasty in salads, is slippery and staining on hard surfaces. Nor should they be planted in a lawn. The ideal location is with ground covers or a mulch.

Note: If your yard is small, I do not recommend that you use up your growing space for edibles with an olive tree. The trees are numerous but very few people process their olives. Whenever I have asked neighbors if I might have some of their olives, naturally expecting to share the resulting olive oil with them, they have readily assented, delighted to know that their olives would be used. If olives have been made available to you, be sure to find out if the trees have been sprayed with pesticides or if herbicides have been applied. Avoid olives that have been so treated.

How to Grow

Climate

Olives need high heat and some winter chill to fruit properly. They are hardy to 13°F. The fruits, which ripen late in fall, need a very long summer to mature. The fruits are injured by temperatures below 27°F.

High humidity inhibits pollination, so these magnificent trees are limited to the warmer parts of the Southwest for fruit production.

Exposure

Olive trees need full sun.

Soil

Olive trees adapt to a wide variety of soils but must have good drainage.

Fertilizer

Occasional applications of nitrogen fertilizer increase fruit production, but trees on normal soils generally produce plenty of fruits without being fed.

Watering

Olive trees are extremely drought tolerant, but deep watering in arid climates once or twice a summer increases fruit production.

Pruning

Prune these trees to shape them. Enjoy accenting their graceful lines. Extreme pruning cuts down on fruit production, but moderate pruning to shape and thin creates a beautiful tree. If you want very large olives, thin the fruits. Olives tend to bear fruits on alternate years. By pruning moderately and thinning the fruits, you can modify this tendency.

Pests and Diseases

Olives are usually unaffected by pests and diseases. You might have some problems with scale or a disease that produces galls (a swelling of plant tissue) on the twigs or branches. Cut those out, and sterilize your tools between cuts.

Do not plant olives where verticillium wilt is a problem, since these trees are quite susceptible. It is not a good idea to plant strawberries as a ground cover under olive trees, as strawberries sometimes carry this disease.

Harvesting

Pick olives green for curing, or green or black for olive oil. To get a very high quality oil, use green olives. You will trade off on amount, however, since fully ripe and black olives produce more oil.

Olives must be processed to remove the bitterness before they are edible.

How to Purchase

Forms and Sources

Buy olive plants in containers at your local nursery or from (**10**).

Pollinators

Most olives are self-pollinating.

Varieties

Make sure you choose a fruiting variety. The "fruitless" varieties usually do produce some fruits, but their crops are poor. The following varieties have good productivity.

'Manzanillo'—large fruits; low growth habit. (**10**)

'Mission'—small fruits with good flavor and high oil content; the most readily available variety. (**Locally Available**)

'Sevillano'—large fruits but low oil content; not recommended for pressing. (**10**)

Preserving

For information about olive curing, order Bulletin Number

E.92. Older olive trees take on gnarled shapes and should be pruned to accent this feature.

HXT-29 from University of California Cooperative Extension Service, 90 University Hall, Berkeley, CA 94720.

Making Olive Oil

Pick the olives when they are still green. Dry them on racks for a week or ten days in a warm place out of the sun, turning the olives a few times a day to ensure even drying. Alternately, use a food dryer and follow the directions.

Press the dried olives in an olive press or a cider press. During pressing, do not squeeze hard enough to crush the pits (the pits contain oil but it is inferior for eating and is used to make soap). Collect the juice as it comes out.

Strain the juice through cheesecloth into glass jars and allow it to separate from remaining solids. Siphon the oil off, using plastic tubing. Now the two- to three-month process of clarifying begins. During that time, as sediment builds up on the bottom of the jar, siphon off the oil again, leaving the sediment on the bottom and again straining the oil through multiple layers of cheesecloth. This can be done every two weeks for as many as five times. When the oil is clear, pour it into sterilized jars and seal. Once the oil is opened, refrigerate it, since it becomes rancid at room temperature.

For more information on making olive oil, send for leaflet Number 2789 from the University of California Cooperative Extension Service (address above).

ORANGE. See *Citrus Fruits.*

ORANGE BERGAMONT MINT. See *Mint.*

E.93. *Oregano's sprawling form lends itself well to hanging containers.*

Oregano (WILD MARJORAM)

Origanum vulgare

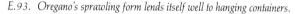

Effort Scale

NO. 1
Very easy to grow
Annual planting required in coldest zones

Zones

All

Thumbnail Sketch

Perennial herb, grown as an annual in cold climates
2–2½ ft. tall
Propagated from seeds, divisions, and cuttings
Needs full sun
Leaves are dull gray-green, small
Blooms in summer

Flowers are pale pink, white, or lavender, grow in spikes, small
Leaves are edible, used as seasoning, harvested year round
Used in herb gardens, to sprawl over a rock wall, in hanging baskets, containers

How to Use

In the Kitchen

Oregano leaves are aromatic and are used as a seasoning in pizza, spaghetti sauce, soups, stews, and salads.

In the Landscape

These herbaceous perennials grow to heights of 2½ feet. They are inclined to be rangy, but their dark gray-green leaves and pale-pink flowers make them a colorful addition to a flower border. You can keep oregano cut back to stay bushy, or you can use the plant's ranginess to advantage, letting it spill over a rock wall. Oregano combines well with the pinks and lavenders of alyssum, garlic chives, ivy geraniums, and marjoram. It is especially showy when planted with any of these in a container. Every herb garden should contain oregano.

How to Grow, Purchase, and Preserve

Oregano can be grown from seed or cuttings and is simple to grow. It needs well-drained, medium-rich soil, plenty of sun, and moderate amounts of water. In winter in the coldest climates, this herb should be brought inside or a new one planted in the spring.

Oregano can be harvested any time during the year for fresh use. However, if you are planning to dry it for the winter, you should harvest the leaves before the plant has started to flower to ensure good texture and rich flavor.

For drying information, see BASIL.

Purchase seed or young plants from local or mail-order nurseries.

ORIENTAL PEAR. See *Pears.*

Parsley

Parsley, *Petroselinum crispum*
Italian parsley, *P. c. neapolitanum*

Effort Scale

NO. 2
Annual planting required
Flower heads must be removed
Must be kept fairly moist

Zones

All

E.94. *The clear green of parsley makes a bright spot in any landscape.*

Thumbnail Sketch

Biennial herbs, usually planted as annuals
6 in.–3 ft. tall, depending on variety
Propagated from seeds
Needs partial shade; full sun in cloudy, cool climates
Leaves are curled, tufted, dark green
Flowers greenish-yellow in umbels; not usually seen
Leaves are edible; used as seasoning; harvested year round
Used in herb gardens, flower borders, raised beds, containers

How to Use

In the Kitchen

Both species have aromatic leaves that are used fresh as a garnish and a seasoning and dried as a seasoning in salad dressings, soups, stews, and sauces. The Italian species has a stronger flavor than common parsley.

In the Landscape

These herbaceous biennials are grown as annuals. Common parsley is a small, curly-leaved herb. The dark-green, stiff, segmented leaves are 6–8 inches long. Italian parsley, with its cut but only slightly curly leaves, grows to 3 feet. The flowers of both species resemble miniature Queen Anne's lace, but they should not be considered landscape material, since they must be picked before opening to stimulate leaf production.

The dark-green of both these plants makes them usable as borders in herb or flower beds. Italian parsley, being taller, can also be grown in the middle of a flower border. I like to combine them in containers with orange violas and alpine strawberries.

How to Grow, Purchase, and Preserve

Parsley is easy to grow and thrives in all areas of the country. In the spring it can be started from seed or from seedlings, available from local nurseries. The seeds take a long time to germinate, so growers are often advised to soak them for twenty-four hours before planting. If you do not follow this advice be patient; the seeds may not sprout for several weeks. The old herbals claimed that parsley seeds had to go to the devil and back seven times before they could sprout.

Parsley prefers partial shade; well-drained, rich, fairly moist soil; and a frost-free climate. In cold-winter areas, plants may be dug up during the winter and brought indoors to a warm windowsill.

Harvest the leaves before the plant has started to flower. The leaves will have a better texture and usually more flavor.

To use parsley fresh, pick leaves as needed. Common parsley does not retain as much of its flavor as most herbs when it is dried, though it is still satisfactory. Italian parsley dries very well. For drying information, see BASIL.

E.95. *Pawpaw fruits, leaves, and flowers.*

Pawpaw

Asimina triloba

Effort Scale

NO. 4
Finding good varieties difficult
Establishing plant difficult
Hand pollination needed occasionally
Pruning and removing suckers usually needed
Fertilizing and mulching necessary

Zones

5–9

Thumbnail Sketch

Deciduous tree or shrub
20–25 ft. tall
Propagated from seeds, by cuttings, and by layering
Needs full sun or light shade
Leaves are oblong, light green, large, 8–12 in. long
Blooms in spring
Flowers are maroon, cup-shaped, 1–2 in. across
Fruits are edible; harvested in fall
Used as interest plant, small tree, in a lawn; as a shrub may be used as accent, screen, or hedge

How to Use

In the Kitchen

The custardlike, yellow-orange flesh of the pawpaw tastes something like that of the banana. Although they are usually eaten fresh, the fruits can be used in custard pies, plum-type puddings, and preserves.

Pawpaw leather is made from the dried fruits. The pawpaw is the American relative of the delicious custard apple, or cherimoya, of Peru and Ecuador.

Note: Some pawpaws have white flesh. These fruits are usually bitter and unpleasant tasting. Always look for the darker-fleshed fruits.

In the Landscape

The pawpaw is native to the United States as far west as Texas, north to Michigan, and south to northern Florida. It is a large deciduous shrub that will grow, slowly, to 25 feet in height. The gracefully drooping, light-green, foot-long, oval leaves help to make this plant useful as a screen or an informal hedge. When trained as a pyramid-shaped tree, the pawpaw contrasts nicely with rounder shapes in the shrub border. Conversely, it can highlight similarly shaped evergreens. The pawpaw grows well in a lawn, and is handsome and dramatic enough to be used as an accent plant. The maroon, cup-shaped flowers and the 5-inch fruits, which turn from green to yellow to brown, are not showy but add interest to the tree.

How to Grow

Note: Despite the fact that pawpaw trees are indigenous, they are sometimes difficult to establish and seem to vary in their need for cross-pollination.

Climate

Pawpaws are hardy to −30°F. They require some winter chilling and hot summers. They star in the Midwest.

Exposure

They need full sun or light shade.

Planting

Pawpaw trees are sometimes tempermental about being transplanted. There is a difference of opinion. Some research has indicated that filling the planting hole with a mixture of half soil, half vermiculite helps the plant to adapt. Other researchers suggest that pawpaws need a symbiotic soil fungus to grow properly, and that soil from around the base of another, successfully growing tree should be added to the planting hole. You are on your own on this

E.96. *Pawpaws are generally grown as shrubs, but the plant can be pruned to a single trunk. Most trees will grow into a pyramid shape.*

one. Consult the 1974 *California Rare Fruit Growers Yearbook* for more details (see Appendix C). Transplanted pawpaws should be handled with care. Get as much of the root system as you can. Do not let the roots dry out. Keep the young trees well watered the first year. Cut the main trunk back to a foot above the graft line at the time of transplanting.

Soil

These trees prefer well-drained, rich garden loam.

Fertilizing

Where pawpaws are not planted in rich bottomland, they respond well to an organic mulch and moderate amounts of fertilizing.

Watering

Pawpaws have high water requirements. They grow best in areas that get at least 30 inches of rain a year. They will grow with irrigation in the arid West.

Pruning

Pawpaws naturally sucker and will form a thicket if not controlled. For a screen or group planting of pawpaws, allow suckers to come up only where you want them, remove all others. To train as a tree, or to maintain the integrity of a grafted plant, remove all suckers as they appear. The plant will sucker less as it ages.

Pests and Diseases

Pawpaws have very few pests and diseases.

Harvesting

Pawpaws are ready to be picked when they are fully colored and slightly soft. Bring them inside to fully ripen.

How to Purchase

Forms and Sources

Pawpaws are available as seeds and as seedlings or grafted varieties in containers. Some nurseries carry them.

Note: Pawpaw is referred to as America's Cinderella fruit. The fruit does not ship well and has therefore received relatively little scientific and commercial attention. But a small group of home gardeners has kept up interest in the plant, and a few mail-order nurseries carry pawpaws for the home grower: (**15, 18, 39, 56, 62, 72**). Seeds are available from (**55**). Source (**15**) is particularly knowledgeable about pawpaws, and puts out a pawpaw bulletin for $1.50. This nursery also carries two grafted varieties: 'Sunflower' and 'Taytwo'.

Pollinators

Usually more than one tree seems to be needed for pollination. For most varieties, hand-pollination can help fruit production but is not always necessary.

Varieties

Some grafted named varieties have been produced, but most of the plants available are ungrafted seedlings with variable fruit.

The most readily available varieties of pawpaw are 'Sunflower', 'Taylor', and 'Taytwo'.

Preserving

Pawpaws can be dried, frozen, and baked into breads.

To freeze, wash, peel, and seed the fruits. Pack the pulp in rigid plastic containers and freeze. The frozen pulp can be stored for four to six months. When thawed, the fruit will be very soft. Eat it promptly.

Peach and Nectarine

Peach, *Prunus Persica*
Nectarine, *P. P.* var. *nucipersica*

Effort Scale

Standard Peach and Nectarine

NO. 5
Vulnerable to many diseases and pests, including birds
Heavy pruning necessary
Fertilizing and mulching usually necessary
Large yield must be harvested quickly
Cleanup of fruit mandatory

Genetic Dwarf Peach and Nectarine

NO. 3
Vulnerable to many pests and diseases
Very little pruning needed
Harvest is pressing but manageable

Zones

5–9

Thumbnail Sketch

Standard Peach and Nectarine

Deciduous trees
15–20 ft. tall
Propagated by budding or from cuttings
Needs full sun
Leaves are narrow, 3–6 in. long
Blooms in spring
Flowers are pink, showy in some varieties; 1–2 in. across
Fruits are edible; harvested in summer
Used as interest trees, espalier, screens

E.97. *Few pleasures approach the taste of sun-ripened peaches right off the tree.*

Genetic Dwarf Peach and Nectarine
    Deciduous small trees or shrubs
    4–10 ft. tall
    Propagated by budding
    Needs full sun
    Leaves are medium green, 6–8 in. long
    Blooms in spring
    Flowers are pink, often double, showy, 1–2 in. across
    Fruits are edible; harvested in summer
    Used as interest plant, hedge, espalier, flowering shrub,
       foundation plant and in containers

How to Use

In the Kitchen

Fresh peaches and nectarines are lusciously juicy and sweet. They bring a real note of midsummer to our menus. Whether served as a salad, a simple dessert consisting of a perfect specimen, sliced and sweetened as a topping for ice cream and shortcake, or as the fruit base in fresh ice cream, the special flavor and color of these fruits enhance our dining pleasure. When cooked or canned, the flavor of both fruits changes but is as delicious and adaptable as that of the fresh fruits. Peach Melba, for example, combines the flavor of cooked peaches with jelly made from currants or raspberries, both of which might originate in your yard. Peach upside-down-cake mixes the flavors of peaches with brown sugar. And who can resist a piece of nectarine pie? Even an unadorned dish of home-canned peaches or nectarines makes a nice end to a meal, and brandied peaches constitute a more dramatic dessert. Both peaches and nectarines result in delicious jams and marmalades, and are excellent as fruit leather.

In the Landscape

Standard peach and nectarine trees are of only limited use in the landscape. If you choose a variety with showy flowers and good form and maintain it with care, the tree will serve as an interest plant or a small tree near a driveway, as long as you plant it back far enough to prevent the fruit from dropping on the concrete. Planting it near the street is tempting fate—and passers-by, who might help themselves.

Genetic dwarf peaches and nectarines are far more versatile and attractive in the landscape. All varieties have beautiful foliage—long, narrow, rich-green leaves that grow in graceful, hanging clusters—and showy, deep-pink flowers.

These graceful plants can be used as informal hedges, foundation plants, or interest plants in a shrub border, in geometric patterns in an herb garden, along paths, in raised beds and in large containers.

Note: Do not plant peach or nectarine trees near windows, because the trees will need to be sprayed.

How to Grow

Climate

Probably no fruit tree elicits more wishful thinking than the peach tree. Everyone wants a peach tree. But no matter what you wish, neither peaches nor their close cousins, nectarines, survive in very cold or very warm winters—period.

Some very hardy peach varieties, such as 'Reliance', are beginning to widen that range, but for all practical purposes, no peaches

or nectarines are successful in the coldest sections of New England or the Northern Plains. In borderline areas, try growing genetic dwarf peaches and nectarines in containers so you can bring them inside for the coldest part of the winter. Cold-weather considerations are discussed in more detail in the subsection headed "Genetic Dwarf Peaches and Nectarines," under "Varieties," below.

Peaches and nectarines do poorly in areas with very warm winters too, since, like most temperate-zone fruit trees, they have a chilling requirement.

Some varieties of peaches and nectarines that have a very low chilling requirement grow in the warmest areas of Florida and the warm deserts, but their fruit is disappointing compared to the real thing.

Exposure

It is extremely important that peaches and nectarines receive full sun.

Soil

Both peaches and nectarines are fussy about soil; they will not grow well in heavy soils and must have good drainage. They prefer well-drained sandy loam.

Fertilizing

A difference of opinion prevails regarding the fertilizing of peaches and nectarines. Some authorities favor feeding them high amounts of nitrogen, and others say that large amounts of nitrogen produce lush, weak growth susceptible to disease and frost.

It is my educated guess that large amounts of nitrogen are called for in commercial growing in fairly warm climates where trees are treated heavily with insecticides and fungicides, and the highest fruit production at whatever cost is the objective. But for growers trying to maintain their landscapes with as few chemicals as possible, I recommend feeding peaches and nectarines in the spring with moderate amounts of nitrogen and keeping the trees mulched with compost or manure during the growing season. The symptoms of nitrogen deficiency are lack of vigor and a pale, light green or slightly yellow leaf color. On trees showing this characteristic, use a supplemental nitrogen fertilizer in early summer. If you live in a cold-winter area, it is critical that this feeding be administered by July 1.

Pruning

Genetic dwarf peach and nectarine trees need pruning only to shape and to remove dead or crossing branches.

Standard and semidwarf trees, however, need heavy pruning to produce good fruit in most climates. Consult local authorities for pruning information if you live in the coldest peach climates. Prune in early spring just as growth is starting so that pruning wounds heal quickly and thus are less apt to become diseased.

Peaches bear on one-year-old wood only. Therefore, new wood must be continually produced to permit fruiting in the following year. To prune standard, semidwarf and regular dwarf trees, thin out a number of branches, particularly in the middle of the tree, to allow sunlight to enter and good air circulation to occur. Prune heavily, removing one third to one half the new growth. Remove any weak growth or crossing branches. Pruning time is a good time to check the crown of the tree for borers.

The crops peaches and nectarines set are usually too heavy and fruit must be thinned when the fruits are about an inch across.

E.98. Nectarines make good dooryard trees, but make sure they are not too near windows or paths.

Leave 6–8 inches between fruits on the early types of peaches and nectarines, 4–5 inches between late-season fruits. If you do not thin your fruits, the tree can be weakened, the peaches will be small, and the branches may break from the weight. Also, the next year's peach crop will probably be small.

Pests and Diseases

It is nearly impossible to grow any size or variety of peach and nectarine without some sort of chemical help. These trees are the weaklings of the fruit world. They are susceptible to many pests and diseases, and must be dormant sprayed in the winter.

Diseases are best controlled by planting resistant varieties when possible, choosing proper exposure with good air circulation, keeping the trees well mulched and pruned, and scrupulous hygiene.

A Bordeaux mixture or lime-sulfur should be applied in late fall and again just before flower buds start to swell in spring to help control peach leaf curl, brown rot, and scale.

With peach leaf curl the foliage develops bumpy, red, swollen areas. This condition slowly defoliates the tree and weakens it.

Brown rot is a common problem for the growers of these trees, particularly nectarines. It makes the fruits turn brown and mushy just before ripening. Clean up all affected fruit and destroy it. If the problem is severe, you will have to spray the fruit with a fungicide just before ripening. See chapter 7.

Powdery mildew is a severe problem in damp climates. On affected trees the leaves, twigs, or fruits become covered with a white, powdery substance.

Peach tree borers are deadly to both peach and nectarine trees. One or two can kill a young tree by girdling the trunk.

San Jose scale and plum curculio are sometimes a problem. Dormant sprays help somewhat on scale. Good hygiene helps also.

See chapter 7 for more information on these pests and diseases.

Peaches and nectarines are short-lived trees; their life expectancy is eight to twenty years. Neglecting them or allowing the diseases that affect them to go uncontrolled will shorten their lives even more. Peach trees are not a good choice for purely organic gardeners or for those who want maintenance-free gardens.

Harvesting

Peaches and nectarines ripen over a fairly short period of time, usually two or three weeks. Try to plan to be at home for the harvest, not off camping, since once ripe, the fruits won't wait.

Peaches and nectarines are ripe when they are fully colored, come off the tree easily in your hand, and give slightly to the touch. You can expect to harvest 2–3 bushels yearly from a mature tree.

How to Purchase

Forms and Sources

Peaches are available bare root from local and mail-order nurseries in late winter to early spring, and in containers throughout the growing season. Nurseries with a particularly good selection are (**6, 14, 24, 46, 57, 58, 60, 71**).

Pollinators

The great majority of peaches and nectarines are self-fruitful. The most commonly grown peaches that need a pollinator are 'J. H. Hale' and 'Indian Free'.

Varieties

Most of the varieties of peaches and nectarines listed have showy flowers, but not all varieties do. Also, most of the varieties listed have some resistance to disease.

Peaches and nectarines come either with a loose pit—freestone—or clingstone, that is, with the pit attached to the flesh. Usually the freestone are easier both to work with in the kitchen and to eat fresh.

STANDARD PEACHES
'Fantastic Elberta'—large freestone fruits; useful for canning, drying, freezing, or just for the beautiful flower show; double pink flowers. (**60, 71**)
'Glohaven'—large, freestone fruits; flowers rose colored, good for freezing and canning. (**Readily Available**)
'Indian Free'—large red-fleshed, freestone, blood peach; needs a pollinator; somewhat resistant to peach leaf curl. (**71**)
'Madison'—medium-size, freestone fruits; very tolerant of frost during blooming. (**1, 6, 30, 68**)
'Monroe'—late-season fruits with fine texture; flowers pink and showy; disease tolerant. (**6, 68**)

'Raritan Rose'—medium-size, freestone fruits; flowers showy; tree hardy. (**1, 30**)

'Reliance'—large, freestone fruits; probably the hardiest of all the peach varieties, good to −20°F; flowers showy. (**Readily Available**)

'Rio Oso Gem'—large, freestone fruits; good peach for freezing; large, showy, light-pink blossoms. (**Readily Available**)

'Washington'—large, freestone fruits; good for Virginia area; flowers showy. (**6, 68**)

STANDARD NECTARINES

'Cavalier'—medium-size, late-season, freestone fruits; flowers showy; highly resistant to brown rot. (**68**)

'Cherokee'—medium-size, midseason, freestone fruits; high resistance to brown rot and frost; flowers showy. (**6, 68**)

'Independence'—medium-size, early-season freestone fruits; flowers showy; will take warm winters. (**24, 71**)

'Red Chief'—medium-size, late-season, freestone, white-fleshed fruits; flowers showy; highly resistant to brown rot. (**6, 68**)

GENETIC DWARF PEACHES AND NECTARINES

In my opinion, genetic, or natural, dwarf peaches and nectarines are much superior to full-size trees for the home landscape. Genetic dwarfs, which differ from regular dwarf fruit trees in that they are naturally small rather than grafted onto dwarfing rootstock, are themselves grafted for propagation purposes and for strong root systems. In the case of peaches and nectarines, the genetic dwarf varieties have many qualities that the standards do not.

1. Genetic dwarf peaches and nectarines are more attractive and have more landscaping uses in the home garden than standard trees.
2. Most varieties need less chilling.
3. They are easier to spray for disease control.
4. Their size makes them easier to use in small yards.
5. Harvesting is easier.
6. Their harvest is smaller. Standard-size peaches and nectarines produce large amounts of very perishable fruits, the processing of which requires large banks of time. Their harvest season is short, meaning that you can only enjoy freshly ripened peaches for a brief period. But three or four mature genetic dwarf trees yield a more manageable harvest of thirty to forty full-size fruits at one time. Furthermore, if you stagger the harvest time by planting different varieties, you can enjoy fresh-ripened peaches for as long as six to eight weeks instead of two or three.
7. Genetic dwarf peaches and nectarines need very little pruning.
8. These miniature trees are not as hardy as some of the standard trees but they can be planted in colder climates because they take readily to container planting, and during the coldest part of the year they can be moved into a garage or a sheltered place. If you have to take this measure while the trees are in bloom, you might have to hand-pollinate them with a pencil eraser—a racy endeavor—since the bees are often not out when the weather is cold.

Many other fruit and nut trees have genetic dwarf varieties available. They include: almonds, apricots, apples, cherries, plums, and pears. Most of these have the same advantages as mentioned above. In addition, most are self-pollinating.

Many varieties of genetic dwarf peaches and nectarines exist,

E.99. Genetic dwarf peaches and nectarines have showy flowers, a beautiful shape, and graceful leaves.

and, because of the increasing demand, many more are being hybridized each year. The following list contains the best currently available, but it is wise to stay informed about new introductions. The flavor of these fruits is generally good, and some of the new introductions are excellent. Except where noted, the trees have a characteristic short, squat form and long leaves.

'Bonanza II'—an improved variety of the best known genetic dwarf peach; medium quality, early-season, freestone, yellow-fleshed fruits; needs moderate amounts of winter chilling to fruit; flowers pink, semidouble, and showy. (**Readily Available**)

'Compact Redhaven'—peach of a different breeding stock than other genetic dwarfs; a mutation of the full-size 'Redhaven'; taller than other dwarfs, to 10 feet, with form and leaf similar to standard peaches; one of the best early peaches; yellow flesh; good for freezing. (**6, 58**)

'Empress'—medium-size, yellow-fleshed, good peaches; ripens in August; beautiful tree with large flowers. (**14**)

'Golden Glory'—large freestone peach; late season; needs 450 hours chilling. (**14**)

'Stark's Sensation'—very good quality freestone peach; needs 850 hours chilling. (**58**)

THE 'GARDEN' SERIES (ZAIGER GENETIC DWARFS)

Floyd Zaiger is a plant breeder of much accomplishment who has produced a number of superior genetic dwarf trees for the home garden. Among them are the following varieties:

'Garden Beauty'—clingstone nectarine; ripens midseason; striking dark pink double-flowered. (**60, 71**)

'Garden Delight'—clingstone nectarine; ripens midseason. (**24, 60, 71**)

'Honey Babe'—freestone peach; ripens early midseason; best-tasting of the Zaiger series. (**71**)

THE 'SOUTHERN' SERIES

This group of genetic dwarf peaches and nectarines is carried by

(**14**). This source is a wholesaler only, supplying retail nurseries with their trees. If you want a tree in the 'Southern' series and cannot find it, contact (**14**) directly. The representative will tell you where these trees are available near you. The 'Southern' series trees are particularly good for the mild-winter areas, as they all have low winter-chilling requirements.

'Southern Belle'—freestone nectarine; ripens late. (**14**)
'Southern Flame'—freestone peach; ripens midseason. (**14**)
'Southern Rose'—freestone peach; ripens midseason. (**14**)
'Southern Sweet'—freestone peach, ripens early midseason. (**14, 24**)

Preserving

Peaches and nectarines can be canned, spiced, pickled, brandied, and made into jams, jellies, fruit leather, chutneys, nectar, and brandy. The fruits can also be frozen.

Peanut (GOOBER, GROUNDNUT)

Arachis hypogaea

Effort Scale

NO. 3
Annual planting necessary
Good soil preparation necessary
Some weeding necessary
Watering usually necessary
Vulnerable to some pests
Harvesting and curing time-consuming

Zones

Annual

Thumbnail Sketch

Herbaceous annual
1–2 ft. tall
Propagated from seeds
Needs full sun
Leaves are bright green, somewhat cloverlike, 1½–2½ in. long
Blooms in summer
Flowers are yellow, small, leguminous
Seeds are edible; harvested in fall
Used in flower borders, raised beds, temporary ground covers, containers

How to Use

In the Kitchen

Eating goober peas, what fun! If only I could stop! Peanut butter toast with pomegranate jelly, peanut brittle, chocolate-covered peanuts, and peanut butter brownies or fudge all make delicious use of the peanut. And then there are "tin roof" sundaes (made with vanilla ice cream, chocolate sauce, and Spanish peanuts) and, of course, peanut butter cookies. All that pleasure, and protein too!

In the Landscape

These annual, perky, green providers are beautiful in flower borders combined with yellow petunias flowing over a sandy bank or planted in a decorative container. They make good temporary ground covers between newly planted trees and shrubs. Their growth habit—developing a "peg" (shootlike structure) from the pollinated flower that enters the soil where the peanut will grow—makes them a good subject for close-up observation near an outdoor living area.

How to Grow

Climate

Peanuts need hot summers at least four months long. They can tolerate no frost.

Exposure

These plants need full sun.

Planting

Carefully shell peanuts—do not scratch the surface or remove the papery skin. Plant shelled peanut seeds 4 inches deep in warm areas of the South and 2 inches deep in the North. Plant them 4 inches apart, and thin to 1 foot apart once they are growing well.

Soil

Peanuts produce their "nuts" (peanuts are actually seeds rather than nuts) on long pegs that descend from the flower. These pegs need to be able to penetrate soft earth before they can produce their peanuts, so the soil must be extremely loose. This quality is achieved by adding large amounts of organic matter or sharp sand.

The seeds will rot if the soil is not well drained. Peanuts prefer a slightly acid soil, with a pH of 5.0–6.0.

Fertilizing

Peanuts are leguminous, which means that nitrogen-fixation bacteria attached to their roots provide them with their own source of nitrogen. But peanuts do need substantial amounts of potassium and calcium. Average garden loam with added humus usually is sufficient, but if your nuts do not fill out their pods well, before planting next year add calcium in the form of gypsum or add as an extra measure eggshells in the compost you work into the soil, and increase potassium by working in extra compost, manure, granite dust, or green sand.

Watering

Keep peanuts well watered during the growing season, particularly when first planted and while they are flowering. Do not water near harvest time or you may stimulate the peanuts to sprout.

Pests and Diseases

Weeds are usually the major pest problem affecting peanuts in home gardens. If you have a long growing season, you will probably have the luxury of preparing your seed bed early and stimulating the weeds to grow with a little extra water. Let the weeds germinate and then chop them out before you plant your crop. Heavy mulches, at least 3–4 inches deep, help considerably; they also keep the soil soft for the pegs and minimize water loss.

Many pests bother commercially grown peanuts, but as a rule

homegrown peanuts are relatively pest free. The most common pests are thrips, cutworms, corn earworms, spider mites and various caterpillars. Try handpicking, or for severe infestation of caterpillars and corn earworm, use *Bacillus thurengiensis.*

Peanuts are susceptible to a few diseases. Leaf spot causes spotting on lower foliage. Southern blight symptoms include dying plant tops and white mold on stems at the soil line. Both can usually be controlled by good plant hygiene and crop rotation.

Harvesting

Digging up peanuts is like going on a treasure hunt. What will the next forkful uncover?

Start testing for ripeness when the foliage starts to turn yellow. Pull up a few plants to see what you have. Do not be too eager to pull all the plants up, as the peanuts still get some food from the dying stems. The peanuts are ripe when they look well formed and the insides of the pods begin to develop dark-colored veins.

In northern gardens, before the yellow leaf stage, check for mature nuts under the central, main part of the plant. This will be your main crop, as the peanuts on the outer pegs probably won't have time to fully ripen. By harvesting when the majority of the central peanuts are ripe you will take no chance of losing your main crop. Cure the nuts for a few weeks in a warm, dry place

before eating them. See cautionary note under "Preserving and Preparing," below.

How to Purchase

Form and Sources

Peanut seed is readily available from southern local nurseries and the following mail-order sources: (**9, 16, 20, 22, 28, 36, 43, 48, 51, 59**).

Varieties

'Jumbo Virginia'—large peanuts; plant is vine-type; growth to 3½ ft. across; for southern areas. (**9, 20**)

'Spanish'—small Spanish-type nuts; plant matures in 100–110 days and will produce mature nuts well into Canada if given light, sandy soil and a southern exposure; must be planted by end of May. (**Readily Available**)

'Tennessee Reds' ('Valencia')—Spanish peanut; small nuts, red skins, two or three nuts per pod; will grow as far north as New York; matures in 120 days; must be planted by end of May. (**16, 48**)

'Virginia Bunch'—large nuts; plant upright; matures in 120 days; for southern areas. (**16, 48, 51**)

Preserving and Preparing

Cure harvested peanuts by leaving the plants in the warm sun for a week or ten days. If it looks like rain, bring them inside. To ensure quality if you wish to cure large amounts, you may want to send for a free brochure: *Peanut Harvesting and Drying, R-19,* available from Alabama Cooperative Extension Service, Auburn, AL 36830.

An alternative method, usually needed in cold climates, is to hang the entire plant from the rafters of the garage or attic. Make sure the room is warm and dry; do not use a basement or cellar floor where the peanuts might stay damp. It is very important to keep the nuts dry, and to allow the moisture in the nuts to evaporate.

Curing and storing peanuts correctly is very important for two reasons. The first is flavor; peanuts have a high oil content and easily become rancid. The second reason is much more important to your health. Moist nuts get moldy. One mold that commonly attacks peanuts produces aflatoxin, a substance dangerous to humans. Aflatoxin is not removed by heat.

Caution: Do not eat moldy peanuts. Throw them away!

To store peanuts for a short period of time, shell them, place them raw in airtight containers, and refrigerate. For longer periods of storage, freeze them.

E.100. *Peanut flowers develop "pegs" that burrow into the ground and become the peanuts. Harvesting them is like a treasure hunt.*

Pear

Common (European) pear, *Pyrus communis*
Oriental pear (sand or pear apple), *P. pyrifolia*

Effort Scale

NO. 3
Vulnerable to many pests and diseases
Large harvest is time-consuming

Zones

4–9, common
5–9, Oriental

Thumbnail Sketch

Deciduous trees
Standard, 30–40 ft. tall; semi-dwarf, 15–20 ft. tall; dwarf
   varieties, to 15 ft. tall
Propagated by budding or grafting
Needs full sun
Leaves are deep green, 1–2½ in. long
Blooms in spring
Flowers are white, grow in clusters, showy, 1–1½ in. across
Fruits are edible; harvested in summer or fall
Used as interest tree, small street tree, espalier, patio tree;
   dwarf types are good for informal hedges, shrub borders,
   and in containers

How to Use

In the Kitchen

An exquisitely ripe European pear, whether it be a late-summer 'Bartlett', a fall 'Comice' or 'Anjou', or a winter 'Bosc', is a delight. Served with Camembert or Brie cheese, it becomes a dessert course that is acceptable in the haughtiest cuisine. The Oriental types offer a different experience. They are smaller and crisper than common pears, and sometimes a little gritty but sweet and juicy. These slightly more exotic types have a flavor all their own and are certainly worth growing.

Pears of all kinds can be canned or used in jams and preserves. As desserts they can be poached and served with flavorful sauces that make use of liqueurs, raspberries, or cranberries. Cooked pears are inclined to blandness; my preference is for fresh ones. Most pears store very well. To my way of thinking, stocking up on several different kinds, properly picked and stored, is much preferable for winter pear eating to making do with cooked ones.

In the Landscape

The shape of most pear trees is strongly vertical, almost like that of a candelabrum. The leaves, medium-dark green, 1–2½ inches long, and glossy, follow a big show of white flower clusters. An advantage of the pear is that the fruit is produced on long-lived spurs, so the flower show does not have to be pruned off. Except for pears such as 'Max-Red Bartlett' and 'Starkrimson', the fruits are not particularly showy, except insofar as any fruit on any tree is an example of nature's skill. The Oriental pear varieties are vigorous trees with shiny, slightly larger deep-green leaves that turn purplish red. The fruits are round and applelike.

E.101. Pear trees characteristically have an upright growth habit.

Full-size pear trees can be used for shade. They do better than most fruit trees in a lawn, and since with most varieties their fruits are picked before they fall, these trees do not cause a fruit-drop problem. Lawn use while never optimum is limited to the East and Midwest, however, because crown rot is a major problem in arid-summer areas. Any size pear tree can be used to line a driveway, can be planted near a patio, and can serve as an entrance accent or a small street tree. Dwarf varieties can be used in containers, as a handsome hedge, and espaliered wherever small trees are needed. The standard tree can be trained into interesting, gnarled shapes. Do not plant disease-prone trees near windows, because they usually need to be sprayed.

How to Grow

Climate

Pear trees are hardy but bloom fairly early. They are more fussy regarding climate than apples, and you must select the variety carefully if you live in a late-frost area or a region where winters are warm. Pears need winter chilling, but the amount required varies from variety to variety. Most varieties of pears flourish in cool-summer areas.

Exposure

These trees need full sun.

Soil

Pears need good garden loam that is on the heavy side. While they prefer good drainage, they can tolerate heavy soil and poor drainage better than other popular fruits. (This is not true of pears grafted on quince rootstock, however.)

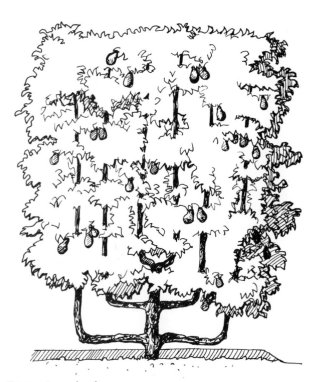

E.102. *An espaliered pear.*

Fertilizing

Pears respond well to a thick organic mulch. Avoid large amounts of nitrogen, because it encourages succulent new growth susceptible to fireblight.

Watering

Pears require moderate amounts of water. In arid summers, deep watering once a month depending on the soil, is usually sufficient. In rainy-summer areas, supplemental watering is usually unnecessary for mature trees.

Pruning

Train young trees to three or four main branches. Like apples, pears bear fruit on long-lived fruiting spurs and need little regular pruning, except to shape and to remove dead or weak growth. Oriental pears need slightly more pruning than common pears. With established trees, thin about 10 percent of the branches and of the fruiting spurs annually. Thin fruit of both species if the tree sets too large a crop.

Pests and Diseases

Pears are plagued with some of the same pests and diseases that bother apples, namely codling moth, San Jose scale, scab, and fireblight. Fireblight is the most serious disease affecting pears. Plant resistant varieties in areas of the country where this condition is a problem.

Follow the dormant-spray schedule recommended in chapter 7 for fruit trees to control scab, scale, and two particularly troublesome pests affecting pears: pear slugs and pear psylla.

Harvesting

Common pears are harvested before they fully ripen. Have you ever eaten a grainy, sawdusty pear that had a brown center? It was probably picked when ripe. Common pears are picked green and firm, at the point when a small tug will separate the stem from the branch. Allow them to ripen at room temperature or store them for later use. Oriental pears are allowed to ripen on the tree, like apples. Standard pear trees produce 3–5 bushels annually when mature. Dwarfs produce ½–1 bushel yearly.

How to Purchase

Forms and Sources

Common pears are readily available bare root or in containers from local nurseries and mail-order sources. (See individual varieties below.) Oriental pears are available in some local nurseries and from mail-order sources. One source (**71**) has a large selection of these pears.

Pollinators

Nearly all varieties need pollinators. Most varieties will cross-pollinate; notable exceptions are 'Seckel' and 'Bartlett' which will not pollinate each other reliably.

Some Oriental varieties will not readily cross-pollinate with common pears. Check with nurseryman before purchasing your Oriental pear trees.

Varieties

COMMON PEARS

'Anjou'—buttery green to yellow, great-tasting, late-ripening fruits; strong grower; somewhat susceptible to fireblight; needs mild weather; for Northwest. (**Readily Available**)

'Bartlett' ('Williams')—most widely known commercially; yellow fruits; ornamental qualities below average; usually sets more fruit with a pollinator other than 'Seckel'; susceptible to fireblight; the following improved varieties are more disease resistant: 'Starkrimson' (**58**), 'Winter Bartlett', 'Sure Crop', 'Spartlett' (**36**), 'Improved Bartlett' (**6**).

'Clapp's Favorite'—large, excellent, early-ripening fruits; hardy but susceptible to fireblight; best in late-spring areas. (**1, 7, 37, 41, 57**)

'Comice'—best eating pear, rich and smooth; stores well; moderately susceptible to fireblight; for mild climate, best in Northwest. (**Readily Available**)

'Golden Spice'—good for pickling and canning; very hardy variety. (**Locally Available**)

'Kieffer'—medium-quality, gritty fruits; Oriental pear hybrid, fireblight resistant; for mild and coldest climates, low chilling requirement. (**6, 41, 58, 68**)

'Little Princess'—large, juicy pears; genetic dwarf tree to 8 ft.; strong tolerance for fireblight; self-fertile, best in zones 5–8. (**6**)

'Moonglow'—yellow, good dessert or canning-type fruits; excellent, fireblight-resistant tree; good for areas with severe fireblight problems; wide climate tolerance. (**Readily Available**)

'Patten'—yellow fruits similar to 'Bartlett', good fresh but not recommended for cooking; tree particularly hardy; good where other pears cannot grow. (**20**)

'Seckel'—small, very tasty, brown fruits, good for canning; resistant to fireblight; a good pollinator but not for 'Bartlett'; good in mild areas; widely adaptable. (**Readily Available**)

'Starking Delicious'—good-quality fruits; fireblight and scab resistant; for mild areas. (**58**)

ORIENTAL PEARS

These crisp pears do well in all pear climates except the very coldest. Sometimes they are listed in catalogues under the name pear apple or Nihon Nashi, which means Japanese pear. They are available from (**6, 7, 24, 57, 62, 68, 71**). (**71**) is particularly interested in these pears and has the largest selection.

'Kikusui'—round green fruits, delicious eating; medium-size tree, spreading and somewhat drooping form; susceptible to fireblight. (**71**)

'Orient'—medium-size, reddish-brown, pear-shaped fruit, cans well; tree large and resistant to fireblight; low chilling requirement. (**6, 62, 68**)

'Shinseiki'—round yellow fruit, keeps well on tree 4–6 weeks; large tree; partially self-pollinating. (**71**)

'Twentieth Century' ('20th Century')—round crisp juicy fruit. Needs a pollinator, either 'Bartlett' or 'Shinseiki' will do. (**71**)

Preserving

Store pears at a temperature as close to 30 °F as possible until you want to use them. Do not let them freeze. Most varieties may be stored this way for four or five months, though they tend to deteriorate slowly in quality after the third month.

Pears can be dried, canned, or made into jam, butter, pickles, or chutney.

PEAR APPLE. See *Pear.*

Pecan

Carya illinoinensis

Effort Scale

NO. 4
Susceptible to many pests and diseases
Fertilizing necessary
Raking necessary
Large harvest is time-consuming

Zones

6–9

Thumbnail Sketch

Deciduous tree
75–100 ft. tall
Propagated from seeds, by grafting, and budding
Needs full sun
Leaves are compound, composed of 11–17 leaflets, medium green
Flowers are catkins, not showy

E.103. *The pecan is an excellent shade tree.*

Nuts are edible; harvested in fall
Used as shade tree, street tree, screen in large yards

How to Use

In the Kitchen

When you have a pecan tree you are a rich person. The nuts, which might as well be flecked with gold in the marketplace, are so versatile that having them in your cupboard ensures good eating. Try them in a tea sandwich, finely chopped with mayonnaise and some tender, young nasturtium leaves, or add them to a mixture of hard-cooked eggs and green olives for a heartier sandwich. Pecans braised in soy sauce are a hot snack that will mark you as an A-1 cook.

It is in desserts that pecans are most commonly used. But pecans also make innovative additions to breads made from bananas, persimmons, and zucchini. Pecan pie is one of the great high-calorie indulgences, of course. Make pralines—brown-sugar and pecan patties—for a truly special treat, and just try to limit the intake. To double the pleasure, crush pralines, blend them with butter creme, and spread the mixture between the layers of that sumptuous French pastry, *génoise*, or between any plain white or yellow cake. Or bake pecan drop cookies or bars and see how quickly they disappear.

In the Landscape

The pecan, like most nut trees, is large and stately. Its cut leaves and graceful, branching pattern provide good shade along with the tree's edible bonus. A few pecans planted in a large backyard can lower the temperature of that yard 5–10 degrees on a hot, sultry day. 'Cheyenne,' a dwarfish variety for the West, is more suitable for small yards. Use pecan trees to line a driveway or street, block a view, or shade a hot south wall.

Pecan trees are large deciduous trees that lose many leaves at one time. This necessitates raking in manicured yards.

How to Grow

Climate

Pecans grow on the Atlantic Coast west to Iowa and Texas, and from Illinois south to the Gulf of Mexico and into Arizona. Some plantings have been successful in the San Joaquin Valley of California. The southern varieties need 270–290 warm growing days, and the northern varieties can produce nuts with as few as 170–190 warm days. Much research is being done to produce hardier cultivars, and the northern range of pecan growing is being extended. At present, though, no pecan varieties exist for the Northeast or the Northwest. Pecans do not do quite as well in areas with high humidity, since their pollen production is inhibited when the relative humidity is 80 percent or more. Pecans are also prone to more diseases in humid conditions.

Exposure

Pecan trees need full sun.

Planting

See HICKORY.

Soil

Pecans need deep, well-drained, rich, alluvial soil. They prefer a soil pH of 5.8–7.0.

Fertilizing

Pecans trees respond well to large amounts of fertilizer, particularly nitrogen. A rule of thumb is that a mature, bearing tree should grow 7–15 inches a year. If growth is less than 6 inches, apply more fertilizer; if it is more than 20 inches, apply less. An annual application of a nitrogen fertilizer plus a mulch of compost or manure is usually sufficient in fairly rich soil. If your pecan tree is in a lawn, it is harder to keep well fertilized. Apply nitrogen fertilizer on the lawn and deep-water it in or, better yet, use a root feeder. Pecans suffer from zinc deficiency in some soils. This condition is indicated by chlorotic leaves and a "rosetting" on the shoots. Where these symptoms appear, application of a foliar spray (a method of fertilizing through the leaves by spraying) with a special-formula fertilizer containing zinc is called for. Follow the directions on the package.

Watering

In sandy soils or in hot climates, pecans usually need supplemental watering. A pecan tree growing in a lawn will require deep-watering beyond that given the lawn.

Pruning

See HICKORY

Pests and Diseases

A number of diseases and pests may attack pecans. They vary with location. The most likely pests are pecan weevils, scale, shuckworm, webworm, and aphids. The most serious and common disease of pecans is scab, a fungus that attacks the leaves and nuts. Dormant spraying helps to control some of these pests and diseases. The average pecan tree needs to be sprayed three or four times during the year to produce high-quality nuts. Consult your university extension service for more information specific to your area.

Pecan trees tend to bear their nuts on alternate years. While this is a normal condition it is exacerbated by a diseased or weakened condition.

Harvesting

In order to beat the squirrels to your harvest, collect nuts off the ground as soon as they fall. Healthy pecan trees produce a large harvest. A ten-year-old tree bears around 10 pounds of nuts, and a mature tree can bear 100 pounds annually.

How to Purchase

Forms and Sources

Buy pecans bare root from local nurseries or mail-order firms in late winter or early spring, or buy in containers spring through fall.

Pollinators

Some varieties will bear a few nuts when planted singly but to insure proper pollination plant more than one variety.

Varieties

It is important to choose a pecan variety suitable for your part of the country. In the list below, pecan varieties with a short growing season have been designated as Northern, those resistant to some of the major fungus diseases as Southeastern, and those with a tolerance for alkaline soils as Western.

The North American Nut Growers Association is offering seed of hardy pecans to its members. If you are interested in growing nut trees, you should join this organization.

One of the ways pecans are judged is by their cracking quality—that is, how easily the shell cracks and whether the nut comes out easily in one piece. The term "papershell" refers to nuts that crack easily, not to a specific variety.

NORTHERN VARIETIES
'Colby'—nuts have good flavor but poor cracking quality; tree retains foliage late into season; very hardy. (6, 26, 58, 62, 68)
'Giles'—high quality nuts; best for southern part of northern zone. (26)
'Major'—good-size nuts with good cracking quality; one of the best for the North. (6, 26, 61, 68)

SOUTHEASTERN VARIETIES
'Caddo'—excellent cracking qualities; scab tolerant. (**Locally Available**)
'Candy'—vigorous tree, scab resistant. (**Locally Available**)
'Cape Fear'—excellent nuts; disease resistant; pollinate with 'Stuart.' (58)
'Desirable'—not good for west Texas; scab resistant. (6, 62)
'Stuart'—one of the old varieties; widely grown; quite disease prone. (6, 24, 58, 62, 68)

WESTERN VARIETIES
'Cheyenne'—excellent cracking quality; small tree, good for small yards. (24, 71)
'Western-Schley'—most commonly grown; vigorous tree. (10, 60, 71)

Preserving

Shell pecans after harvesting and freeze.

Peppers

Capsicum species

Effort Scale

NO. 3
Must be planted annually
Some watering and weeding necessary
Easy only within a fairly narrow temperature range

Zones

Annual
10 as perennial

Thumbnail Sketch

Herbaceous perennial usually treated as an annual; grown as a
  perennial in zone 10
1½–3 ft. tall
Propagated from seeds
Needs full sun, will tolerate some shade
Leaves are deep green, 2–4 in. long
Blooms in summer
Flowers are insignificant
Fruits are edible; harvested in summer
Used in flower borders, raised beds, herb gardens, containers

How to Use

In the Kitchen

The fruits of the pepper, whether from sweet, green, or red bells
or "hot" peppers, are a popular source of seasoning for stews,
salads, and casseroles. Peppers find their way into the cuisines of
many countries. Some recipes call for use of the whole fruit as a
container for a stuffing. Chiles rellenos, using chili peppers, is a
very satisfying dish. Salsas are made from peppers in all degrees of
heat, and pickled peppers vary too in accordance with the species.
Peppers have the further advantage of being a good source of
vitamin C.

In the Landscape

These herbaceous perennials, which are grown as annuals, are all
handsome, bushy, dark-green plants with upright growth. Their
leaves are 2–4 inches long, somewhat glossy, and plentiful, so the
plants are quite lush looking. The flowers are white with yellow
stamens, attractive against the rich, green foliage but insignificant.
The fruits come in all sizes, shapes, and colors: even the green ones
are noticeable on the plant. Some varieties of peppers even display
their yellow or red fruits upright at the top of the plant.

Because these plants are so decorative they are at home in a
flower border, where they might be combined with dwarf zinnias,
red verbena, or portulaca.

All pepper plants are striking in containers. They look especially
nice in a large, old-fashioned clay pot. The colors seem meant for
each other.

How to Grow

Peppers are a warm-weather crop. They cannot tolerate frost

E.104. *All types of peppers are beautiful in containers. Pictured at left is the
sweet green bell pepper, 'Yolo Wonder'; on the right is the hot and colorful
'Holiday Cheer'.*

and they will not set fruit unless the weather is at least 65° F but
does not exceed 80° F. They also need a long growing season, 120
days, and are therefore impractical for many northern gardens.
They prefer full sun (but will tolerate some shade), rich soil, deep
watering, and feeding before the plant starts to bloom. The
fertilizer used should not be too high in nitrogen, since that
element encourages leaf development at the expense of fruit
development.

Tender pepper plants are popular with snails and cutworms.
Keep plants mulched and weeds under control. Otherwise, the
plants are relatively pest free. They are occasionally prone to the
same diseases as afflict tomatoes.

Sweet peppers are picked at the green or red stage. The hot
peppers should be allowed to ripen completely. Both types produce from 1 to 2 pounds per plant.

If you plant peppers that hold their fruits upright, be sure to provide some afternoon shade to protect them from sunburn.

How to Purchase

Seed for peppers is readily available. The mail-order source (**31**)
specializes in peppers and carries 30 varieties.

Varieties

The following peppers are attractive as well as tasty.

'Cherry' (hot)—bright red, round, hot pepper, good for pickling. (**9, 29, 31, 32, 62**)

'Dutch Treat'—yellow and red, conical, sweet fruit; All America Selection; fruits held upright, highly ornamental. (**9, 22, 29, 48**)

'Early Pimento'—red, heart-shaped, delicious sweet peppers, medium-size plant. (**8, 9, 32, 51**)

'Golden Bell'—large, yellow, sweet fruits; compact plant. (**22, 29, 48**)

'Gypsy'—wedge-shaped, yellow, thin-walled, medium-sized, sweet fruits; All America Selection; fruits tender and crunchy; plants 12–20 in. tall. (**Readily Available**)

'Jalapeño'—narrow, medium-size, red, hot pepper, used in traditional Mexican food. (**22, 28, 31, 35, 48, 59, 62**)

'Tequila Sunrise'—golden orange sweet peppers, plant 14 in. tall; peppers held upright on the plant. (**48**)

Preserving and Preparing

Use peppers fresh or preserve them by hanging them up to dry in a warm place. Sweet peppers can be cut up and frozen in plastic bags. See the recipe under CABBAGE for a suggestion for the stuffing for stuffed peppers.

PEPPERMINT. See *Mint.*

PERSIAN WALNUT. See *Walnut.*

Persimmon

American persimmon, *Diospyros virginiana*
Oriental persimmon, *D. kaki*

Effort Scale

NO. 2
Occasional pruning to shape necessary
Sucker growth must be removed in American species
Large harvest

Zones

American Persimmon
5–9

Oriental Persimmon
6–10

Thumbnail Sketch

American Persimmon
Deciduous tree or shrub
30–40 ft. tall
Propagated from seeds, cuttings, by grafting or budding
Needs full sun
Leaves are dark green, shiny, oval, 6 in. long
Blooms in spring

E.105. The fruit of the 'Hachiya' persimmon is large, 4–5 inches long, and usually seedless.

E.106. *Graceful 'Fuyu' persimmon trees frame a formal entrance. The 'Fuyu' tree is smaller than most persimmons, and its fruit can be eaten crisp.*

Flowers are greenish yellow, not showy, ½–2 in. across
Fruits are edible; harvested in fall
Used as interest plant, shade tree, large shrub, screen

Thumbnail Sketch

Oriental Persimmon

Deciduous tree
25–30 ft. tall
Propagated from cuttings, budding, and grafting
Needs full sun
Leaves are heart-shaped, glossy, dark green, red-orange in fall, 5–7 in. across
Blooms in spring
Flowers are yellowish white, not showy, ¾–2 in. across
Fruits are edible; harvested in fall
Used as interest plant, patio tree (some varieties), screen, shade tree, espalier

How to Use

In the Kitchen

Both the American and Oriental persimmon are beautiful orange fruits that can be eaten raw. Though a few wonderful varieties can be eaten firm ripe, like an apple, most varieties must be dead ripe and very soft or they have a puckery, unpleasant quality. You have only to taste an underripe persimmon once in your life; you will never forget it. In contrast, a fully ripe persimmon is velvety and sweet.

Both types are used in desserts. One fabulous pudding, similar to English plum pudding, has become a Thanksgiving tradition at our house (see recipe under "Preserving and Preparing"). You can also enjoy persimmons in cookies and breads. A seedless persimmon may be frozen whole and eaten out of its skin like a kind of sherbet.

In the Landscape

The trees that bear this glorious fruit are deciduous. Both species are slow growing; they may reach 30 feet but can be kept smaller with pruning. The bark is of an interesting checkered pattern that makes the bare tree a handsome sight in the winter landscape. In spring the big leaves, 5–7 inches in length, become shiny and dark green, and in the fall most varieties turn bright yellow-orange or red. As if that is not enough, those orange, decorative fruits add their own kind of beauty. The Oriental types are as big as 5 inches long and heart-shaped. The American types are smaller and rounder. These fruits nestle among the big leaves; when the leaves fall, the fruits stay on the bare tree looking like Christmas tree ornaments.

The bark, handsome foliage, colorful fall leaves, and fruits, make the persimmon tree one of the finest edible ornamentals. These trees are stunning accent plants, small shade trees, and fine espaliers. They are exceptionally well suited to Oriental gardens, and their fall foliage color is breathtaking when backed by pines or other conifers.

Note: Do not plant the trees near a street unless you intend to harvest conscientiously when the fruits are still firm. Fully ripe, juicy persimmons offer a strong temptation to young passers-by. The larger ones, in particular, make a spectacular splat on the pavement.

How to Grow

Climate

Oriental persimmons are hardy to about 0° F. They are limited to areas below the Ohio River and as far south as southern Florida, and are popular on the West Coast. The American species is hardier, growing as far north as Rhode Island and across to the Great Lakes. Hybridizers are improving these hardier plants, making their fruits less seedy, larger, and sweeter, so they will become an item more to be considered in colder climates.

Exposure

Both species require full sun.

Soil

Persimmons prefer a good garden loam, but they will grow in less than optimum conditions. They must have good drainage, and will grow where oak root fungus is a problem.

Fertilizing

Light, organic mulch is beneficial. Avoid large amounts of nitrogen around young trees; it causes the fruit to drop.

Watering

Once established, the trees need very little watering. In arid climates infrequent deep-watering is desirable. Persimmons are quite drought resistant.

Pruning

Young trees should be trained to three to five main limbs. Mature trees need to be pruned only for shape. The American persimmon needs pruning to remove suckers.

Pests and Diseases

The trees in the West have very few pests and diseases. In the deep South, trees are sometimes bothered by anthracnose and scale. Use dormant spray with copper oil. Flat-headed borer occasionally is a problem in the East; remove by hand.

Harvesting

Most varieties are not edible until dead ripe. Pick fruits when firm and fully colored and allow them to ripen indoors. Large-fruited types can be expected to produce 50–75 pounds of persimmons per year, while 'Fuyu' and the American types produce 25–30 pounds.

How to Purchase

Forms and Sources

Purchase persimmons bare root in the spring or in containers in the summer from local nurseries. They are also available from these mail-order firms: (**4, 6, 10, 18, 24, 26, 28, 60, 61, 62, 68, 71, 72**).

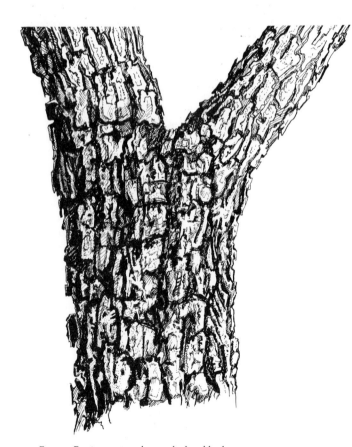

E.107. *Persimmon trees have a checkered bark.*

Pollinators

The Oriental varieties are self-fruitful in the West. Many varieties require a pollinator in the East. 'Gailey' is the usual pollinator for most varieties. Some American varieties need a male and female plant. Some of the newer named varieties are self-pollinating. The International Tree Crops Institute carries a good selection of persimmons. Their Kentucky branch carries American varieties; the California branch carries Oriental varieties.

Varieties

AMERICAN PERSIMMONS

The American persimmons are most readily available as ungrafted seedlings, but for more consistently high fruit quality and fewer seeds, choose a grafted variety such as those listed below. Two nurseries with a sizeable selection of grafted American persimmons are (**26**) and (**61**). Both offer male plants for pollination.

'Early Golden'—very good flavor; ripens in September; most readily available. (**26, 61**)
'Golden Supreme'—extra large fruits; ripens in October. (**26**)
'Meader'—almost seedless; excellent flavor; developed in New Hampshire. (**26**)
'John Rick'—excellent flavor; ripens in September; superior variety. (**26, 61**)

ORIENTAL PERSIMMONS
'Chocolate'—brown-streaked fruits; large tree; available in the West. (**24, 60**)
'Fuyu' ('Fuyugaki')—tomato-shaped fruits, can be eaten firm; one of the best; small tree; finest fall color; needs a pollinator in the East; 'Gailey' is recommended; available in most areas. (**4, 6, 10, 24, 60, 71**)
'Gailey'—inferior red fruits; grown for pollination of other varieties; locally available in the East.
'Hachiya'—large fruits; most shapely tree; heavy bearer; available in the West. (**4, 10, 24, 60, 71**)
'Tanenashi'—large fruits; thick, pasty flesh; tree somewhat weeping; heavy bearer; available in the South. (**6, 18, 24, 62, 68, 71**)

Preserving and Preparing

Persimmons can be dried and frozen. Their pulp can be used as a substitute for applesauce in recipes.

To dry persimmons, thread them onto a string and hang them in the sun.

To freeze, put the pulp of the persimmons in containers. Force out the air at the top by placing plastic wrap directly onto the pulp. Fruit can be frozen for approximately six months.

Eleanor Witherspoon's Persimmon Pudding

1 cup sugar	½ cup ground pecans
½ cup melted butter	1 cup persimmon pulp
1 teaspoon cinnamon	1 cup flour, unbleached
2 teaspoons baking soda dissolved in 2 tablespoons water	2 eggs
2 teaspoons vanilla	¼ teaspoon salt
1 cup seedless raisins	1 teaspoon lemon juice

Mix ingredients together in the above order and pour into a greased plum pudding mold (or substitute a 1-pound coffee can, and use aluminum foil as a cover).

Cover the mold (or coffee can), place in a large pan, and add boiling water until it reaches half way up the mold. Cover the large pan and simmer on the top of the stove 2½ hours. Do not let water level drop; add more if needed. Serves 6–8.

PIE PLANT. See *Rhubarb.*

PIGNOLA. See *Pine Nut.*

Pineapple Guava

Feijoa Sellowiana

Effort Scale

NO. 1
Easy to grow
Fruit drop needs some attention

Zones

9, 10, and Hawaii

Thumbnail Sketch

Evergreen shrub or small tree
15–18 ft. tall
Propagated from seeds, cuttings, or by grafting
Needs full sun; will tolerate partial shade
Leaves are oblong, deep glossy-green above, light woolly gray-green below, 3 in. long
Blooms in spring or summer
Flowers have gray-green fleshy petals and bright dark-red stamens, are showy, 1½ in. across
Fruits and flower petals are edible; fruit harvested in fall
Used as shrub for windbreaks, screens, espaliers, formal or informal hedges, as accent plant, in containers; as a small tree for patios, as accent, multistemmed tree, and in containers

How to Use

In the Kitchen

The gray-green, oblong fruits of the pineapple guava are delicious eaten raw. Their flesh is tangy and sweet, especially when the fruits are allowed to ripen fully—ripe fruits usually fall. A slightly underripe fruit is not unpleasant, but it does not have the full, rich flavor that develops with maturity. When served raw, pineapple guavas are usually cut in half like miniature melons, with the flesh spooned out of the shell. The fruits can be peeled and sliced as an exotic addition to a fruit salad or compote.

Because of the small size of these fruits, peeling them for jelly making is tedious work. The jelly that results, however, has a subtle and delicate flavor, and the color is the palest gold.

E.108. Pineapple guavas are gray-green fruits. The flowers have deep red stamens and the petals are tasty in salads.

In the Landscape

Pineapple guavas are outstanding ornamentals. As small multi-stemmed trees they are effective near a patio. The bark is mottled and checked in interesting patterns and the leaves are ever-changing—deep green one minute and then almost white as the wind causes the undersides to show. In late spring or early summer the flowers are profuse and add a deep red to this color display. Feijoa is in the Myrtaceae family, and, as in the flowers of its relatives, bottlebrush, eucalyptus, and eugenia, the many stamens of these blossoms give them the appearance of little brushes. The fruits are egg-shaped, green and dusted with a white powder, 2–3 in. long.

In its shrub form, pineapple guava is as useful as it is beautiful. It will serve as a windbreak, screen a poor view, accent a yard, or give privacy. If used as a clipped hedge some fruits and flower display will be lost because flowering and fruiting will be forced to the inside branches. It can be used in containers and raised beds, along walks, and as an espalier. This is a truly versatile edible ornamental.

How to Grow

Climate

Pineapple guavas are hardy to about 15–20° F, which limits their growth to the deep South and warmer parts of the Southwest. The fruits are tastiest in cool-summer areas. They will not set fruit in the desert or in the southernmost part of Florida. In parts of Hawaii they grow so well that they can become a weed.

E.109. *The pineapple guava can make a graceful multistemmed tree. Prune carefully to accent its sculptured form.*

Exposure

These plants prefer full sun or partial shade.

Soil

They are adaptable to most soils but need good drainage. They prefer a soil pH of 5.5–7.0. They can tolerate salt fairly well.

Fertilizing

Pineapple guavas prefer a good organic mulch.

Watering

They are drought tolerant but can take a lot of water and can even be planted near a lawn provided the drainage is good.

Pruning

Pineapple guavas can take any amount of shearing, but severe pruning reduces fruit production. Light pruning is usually needed for shaping and removing dead branches. Prune in late spring.

Pests and Diseases

Few serious pests or diseases affect pineapple guava. Dispose of dropped and decaying fruit from under trees.

Harvesting

Pineapple guavas are rarely ripe until they fall from the tree.

How to Purchase

Forms and Sources

Pineapple guavas are available in containers from local nurseries and as seed from (**19**, **51**, and **55**). The International Tree Crops Institute, California branch, carries 'Coolidge' and 'Pineapple Gem.'

Pollinators

Some varieties need a pollinator, but those commonly grown are self-pollinating.

Varieties

Most pineapple guavas sold in local nurseries are seedlings grown for their ornamental qualities whose fruits are sometimes mediocre. To be sure, ask for a grafted name variety, such as 'Coolidge' and 'Pineapple Gem,' both of which are self-pollinating.

Preserving

The pulp of the pineapple guava is preserved by freezing or in jelly and jam. See master jelly recipes under ELDERBERRY and KIWI.

PINEAPPLE MINT. See *Mint.*

PINEAPPLE SAGE. See *Sage.*

Pine Nut (PIGNOLA)

Pinus species

Effort Scale

NO. 2
Easy to grow
Vulnerable to a few pests, including squirrels
Nuts are hard to crack

E.110. *Pine nuts are nestled into the base of the pine cone.*

E.111. *The piñon pine (left foreground) often grows in gnarled, bonsai-type shapes. The Italian stone pine, at right, is a large, graceful tree.*

Zones

3–10

Thumbnail Sketch

10–100 ft., depending on species
Propagated from seed or by grafting
Needs full sun; some varieties will tolerate partial shade
Leaves are needles, vary in length from 3 to 12 in.
Flowers are insignificant
Seeds are edible; harvested in fall
Used as windbreak, accent or interest plant, street tree, shade tree, large shrub, screen, patio tree, and in containers

How to Use

In the Kitchen

Pine nuts are rich and resinous. They are generally eaten roasted and salted, but are also used in pesto, stuffed cabbage, rice dishes, and in the cuisines of Italy and India. They were a staple food of the American Indians. Their price in the market makes them a delicacy.

In the Landscape

I do not generally recommend that people plant pine trees for their nuts. It takes many years, ten to twenty, for most trees to bear, and they do not bear consistently. However, it strikes me as absurd to go down to the store and pay a substantial sum for something you might already be growing in your own backyard.

The information in the table under "Varieties" will allow you to identify pine-nut-bearing trees if you have any or will give you enough information to plant your own if you are patient and love pine nuts.

Pine nuts are produced by several species of pines, particularly in the West. Some, such as the piñons, are short and gnarled. Others, such as the Italian stone pine, are tall and spreading. All of the nut-bearing pines are both beautiful and versatile. The piñon and stone pines make particularly striking accent plants. All the piñons are stunning in containers but do not produce many nuts in that situation. The large species make very effective windbreaks and screens against winter cold and can cut your fuel bill when properly placed.

How to Grow

Climate

Different species have different climatic requirements. The table under "Varieties" will tell you if there is one for your landscaping conditions. Contact local authorities for pest and climate specifics for your area.

Exposure

Pines prefer full sun but some varieties will tolerate partial shade.

Soil

Pines will grow in most soil if it is well drained.

Fertilizing

Pines generally require no supplemental fertilizing.

Watering

The trees require very little watering once established, even in arid climates.

Pruning

Prune only to shape trees and remove dead wood. To control the size of your pine tree, remove half the new growth (called candles) in the spring.

Pests and Diseases

Most pines are damaged by smog. Squirrels are the biggest pest. Worms destroy the nuts in some areas, and I know of no control for this problem. Many of the species are also affected occasionally by scale, mites, or borers; consult local authorities for controls in your area.

Harvesting

Beat the squirrels! Pick the cones when they are ripe but not quite open. Place them in a large paper bag and put in a fairly warm spot indoors. The cones will open, dropping the nuts into the bag. The nuts must then be shelled and lightly roasted.

How to Purchase

Forms and Sources

Buy pines in containers from local nurseries, or buy seed from the following mail-order sources: (**19**, **51**, and **55**).

Varieties

The plants in the following table are all species rather than varieties.

Preserving

Remove the nuts from their shell and put them in airtight containers. If you plan to keep them for more than 4–6 weeks, freeze them.

Producers of Superior Edible Pine Nuts

BOTANICAL NAME	COMMON NAME	HEIGHT	HARDY TO ZONES	NOTES
Pinus cembra	Swiss stone pine	60–75 ft.	3	Bundles of 5 needles, 5 in. long; very slow grower; resistant to white pine blister rust; bears cones regularly after 25 years; very hardy to –35 °F
P. cembroides	Mexican piñon (Mexican stone pine)	10–30 ft.	7	Usually 3 (but sometimes 2, 4, or 5) needles in bundles; drought tolerant, good in deserts; hardy
P. edulis	Piñon (nut pine, Two-leaved pine)	20–30 ft.	5	Bundles of 2 needles, ¾–1½ in. long; horizontal branching; drought tolerant; hardy
P. koraiensis	Korean pine	100 ft.	4	Bundles of 5 needles, 4 in. long; single needles usually ¾–1½ in. long; grows slowly; pyramidal form; hardy
P. monophylla	Single-leaf piñon	10–24 ft.	6	Needles solitary, ¾–1½ in. long; grows very slowly, trunk gnarls with age; for Nevada and Southern California
P. pinea	Italian stone pine (umbrella pine, stone pine)	40–60 ft.	8	Needles in bundles of 2, 6 in. long; broad-topped tree; not for small yards; good near California beaches; semihardy
P. Sabiniana	Digger pine	40–50 ft.	8	Needles in bundles of 3, 8–12 in. long; sparse-looking; lacy, light blue-green needles; drought tolerant

E.112. *Pistachio nuts grow in clusters at the ends of branches.*

Pistachio

Pistacia vera

Effort Scale

NO. 3
Usually obtainable only by mail order
Some pruning necessary
Fertilizing and mulching necessary
Harvesting and shelling are time-consuming

Zones

7–9

Thumbnail Sketch

Deciduous tree
20–30 ft. tall; male plant may grow taller
Propagated from seeds, and by budding
Needs full sun
Leaves are medium green, yellow in fall, oval, grow in
    roundish clusters, 2–4 in. long
Flowers are insignificant
Nuts are edible; harvested in fall
Used as screen, informal hedge, street tree

How to Use

In the Kitchen

One has to work hard to shell a handful of delicious, rich pistachio nuts, but, the reward is worth the effort. Pistachios can be eaten raw or roasted and salted. They are used in ice cream and as an exquisite garnish on other desserts. They are often sprinkled over liver patés as an elegant touch.

In the Landscape

The leaves of these deciduous trees are medium green and are made up of three to five round leaflets. The leaves tend to grow in clusters at the ends of bare branches, so tip pruning and training when the tree is young are necessary to overcome a somewhat scraggly, scarecrowlike appearance. These leaves turn a brilliant yellow in the fall. The flowers are insignificant, but the heavy clusters of yellowish or red fruits can be showy.

Both male and female trees are required for nut production. Male trees generally grow taller than females eventually. Both can be used in the background, as shade or street trees, as screens, or to line a driveway.

How to Grow

Climate

Pistachios can usually be grown where olives are grown. They dislike high humidity but need hot summers as well as some winter chilling; the ideal is 100 days of heat and 30 days of cold. They are not hardy below 10° F. They thrive and are becoming a commercial crop in the Sacramento Valley of California.

Exposure

These trees need full sun.

Soil

Pistachios prefer well-drained, alkaline soil.

Fertilizing

Pistachio trees respond well to an organic mulch and supplemental nitrogen.

E.113. *At left is a large male pistachio tree; at right is the smaller female tree.*

Watering

Once the tree is established, it is drought resistant. However for superior nut production, water as you would an apple tree.

Pruning

Encourage young trees to branch about four feet above the ground. Train to a modified leader with a framework of four or five main branches. For young trees pinch the tips of new growth to keep tree bushy and neat. Prune mature trees to remove dead wood and suckers, and to shape and cut back rank growth.

Pests and Diseases

Pistachios are susceptible to verticillium wilt and to cankers on the shells. Neither condition has a known cure. Sometimes shells do not fill out, usually due to an overly cool summer or incomplete pollination. Pistachios tend to bear nuts in alternate years.

Harvesting

To beat the squirrels to your harvest, pick nuts off the tree. The nuts are ripe when the hulls have turned yellow or reddish, when they separate easily from the tree, and when the hull comes away from the inside shell easily if squeezed. Remove the hulls immediately or they will start to rot within hours. A mature tree (ten years old) should provide 10–20 pounds of nuts annually, older trees much more.

How to Purchase

Forms and Sources

Pistachio trees are not sold bare root. Buy them in containers from a limited number of local California nurseries or by mail-order from (21). Seed is available from (51).

Pollinators

Pistachios must be cross-pollinated, with male and female trees being planted within 50 yards of each other. If space is limited, a piece of male branch can be grafted onto a female tree.

Varieties

The only varieties available at this time are 'Kerman' (female), 'Peters' (male), and 'Red Aleppo' (female).

Preserving

Follow preserving methods under ALMOND.

PITANGA. See *Surinam Cherry*.

PLANTAIN. See *Banana* and *Plaintain*.

E.114. *Plum trees are useful as front-yard accents.*

Plum

Damson plum, *Prunus insititia*
European plum, *P. domestica*
Japanese plum, *P. salicina*
Purple-leaf plum, (flowering plum), *P. cerasifera* 'Atropurpurea,' [*P. pissardi*]

Effort Scale

NO. 3
Vulnerable to pests and diseases
Some pruning necessary
Fertilizing and mulching necessary
Large harvest needs immediate attention

Zones

4–10

Thumbnail Sketch

Deciduous trees
Standard, 20 ft. tall; dwarf varieties 8–12 ft. tall
Propagated by budding or from cuttings
Need full sun

Leaves are medium green or in some varieties wine red above, slightly woolly below, 3–4 in. long

Bloom in spring

Flowers are white or pink, abundant, showy, to 1 in. across

Fruits are edible; harvested in summer

Used as interest tree, screen; dwarf kinds used as large shrub, in containers

How to Use

In the Kitchen

Plums are a delightful fruit with varied uses in the kitchen. All types can be eaten fresh, canned, or made into fruit leather. Most can be used for jams or jellies.

In this encyclopedia entry, I will discuss three types of plums: European, Japanese, and a few varieties of the so-called "flowering plum," some of which bear small, cherry-type fruits. Another type, the American bush plums and their close relatives, will be covered in the next encyclopedia entry, PLUMS, BUSH, which discusses these hardy fruiting bushes.

European plums can be small or large. The small types include Italian and French prune plums, which, with their high sugar content, are ideal for drying. They can also be stewed, used in prune whip, made into a delicious filling for Danish pastry, or combined with other fruits in a pork stuffing. In the cuisines of other countries, prunes are sometimes served as an accompaniment to meat dishes. They can also be eaten raw or, along with some of the jelly made from your currant bushes, can be used as a filling for a Belgian tart (see recipe under "Preserving and Preparing").

The large-fruited plums, both European and Japanese, are all excellent for eating out of hand or for canning. They make good sharp sauces to serve over tapioca or other bland puddings.

The small-fruited cherry-type plums that are a bonus on some varieties of flowering plums are sweet and tasty; they make wonderful eating fresh or in jams or jellies.

In the Landscape

Plum trees are small to medium-size trees with a graceful vase-shaped form. Most varieties are covered with white blooms in early spring. A few types have pink flowers. Their leaves, which follow the blossoms, are 3–4 inches long and usually green, but they are wine red on a few types.

The trees look lovely along a driveway, but they must be far enough away from the pavement to keep fruit drop from being a problem. Plum trees make nice accents in a front or backyard. The dwarf varieties can be espaliered, used as hedges and screens, and grown in containers. One variety, 'Weeping Santa Rosa', is pendulous in form and outstanding in shape, whether espaliered or allowed to grow naturally. Like most fruit trees, plums do not thrive in a lawn.

How to Grow

European plums are the most widely grown of all the plums since they are adapted to most parts of the country. This type, which includes the prune plum and its close relative the Damson, have solid flesh and a wide range of flavors. The fruits should be allowed to ripen on the tree. These trees need moderate amounts of pruning and fruit thinning. They are more resistant to brown rot than other kinds and are grown in zones 5–9.

Japanese plums are primarily grown in the milder plum climates, zones 6–10. The Japanese plum trees bear large, sweet, and juicy fruits, which can be picked when slightly underripe and taken indoors for further ripening. The trees are vigorous growers. They need annual pruning so they will not overbear and lose branches because of the weight. They are also more susceptible to fruit rot.

Climate

Different types of plums need different climatic conditions. For the coldest areas, plant the bush plums covered in the next encyclopedia entry. They are the hardiest. The Damson and European forms are the next hardiest group and can be grown in most of zones 5–9. However, they are primarily grown in the East. Most of the Japanese types are less hardy and are primarily grown on the West Coast.

Plums bloom from one to two weeks earlier than apples, so even in areas that are usually fine for plums, crops occasionally are lost to a late frost. If you can, plant plum trees on the side of a hill so that cold, frosty air will sink away from them.

Plums do poorly in the warmest winter areas because, like most stone fruits, they require some winter chilling. In the warmest parts of zones 9 and 10, be sure to order varieties with a low chilling requirement. Plums cannot be grown in the warmest parts of Florida and Hawaii.

Exposure

Plums need full sun.

Soil

To grow vigorously, plums need a rich soil high in organic matter. The European and Damson type plums grow best on clay or heavy loam; the Japanese types do better on lighter soils. They require good drainage and a pH of 6.0–8.0.

Fertilizing

Plum trees are heavy bearers for their size, so they need large amounts of an organic mulch and fertilizer added yearly to replenish the soil. If your plum tree is not growing consistently and vigorously, or if the leaves get pale in color, add nitrogen. Supplemental nitrogen is particularly beneficial to the Japanese types.

Watering

In the arid parts of the country, plums need occasional deep watering. If the tree has been dry for quite a while and the fruits have started to form, delay watering until after harvest or the fruits will split.

Pruning

The European types are usually trained to a central leader and when mature usually need only slight thinning and shaping annually. They bear only on long-lived spurs. The Japanese types are usually trained to a vase shape and when mature need fairly heavy pruning annually. They bear on both long-lived spurs and one-year-old wood, and they tend to bear too heavily if the branches are not thinned out and some of them shortened. The Japanese types set too much fruit, and the fruit usually has to be thinned in June so that the trees will not become exhausted and the branches will not break.

Pests and Diseases

In most areas of the country, plums need to be dormant sprayed to control scale, borers, mites, aphids, and brown rot. See Chapter 7.

Plum curculio is another pest that occasionally assails plums in the East. This small weevil attacks the fruits, making them rot. Pick up and destroy dropped fruits every day. Malathion might be necessary for a severe infestation.

Harvesting

For cooking, plums are best harvested when somewhat underripe, before they become very soft but after they have developed a whitish "bloom." For juicy, fresh eating, pick plums that are warm from the sun and give slightly to pressure.

Mature standard-size trees will produce 1–2 bushels of plums annually. Dwarf varieties will produce ½–1 bushel.

How to Purchase

Forms and Sources

Plums can be purchased bare root in late winter and early spring and in containers throughout the year from local nurseries and mail-order firms. (See individual varieties, below, for sources.)

Pollinators

Few plums are self-pollinating, but even those that are usually bear more heavily with cross-pollination.

The different plum types rarely cross-pollinate each other. With a few exceptions, European plums pollinate only other European plums, Japanese plums only pollinate Japanese plums. However, many of the small American bush plums covered in the next entry will pollinate all kinds of plums. (See individual varieties, below, for pollinating information.)

Varieties

Scores of varieties of plums exist. Consult local nurseries and university extension services to determine which plums are best for your area. The following lists contain the most popular varieties of each type.

EUROPEAN AND DAMSON PLUMS
'Allred'—medium-size red fruits; striking red foliage and flowers; hardy to zone 4; needs a pollinator; 'Ozark Premier' will do. (**22**)
'Damson'—small blue fruits, great for cooking; improved varieties include 'French Damson' and 'Shropshire'; widely adaptable; self-pollinating. (**Readily Available**)
'French Prune'—small, deep purple, very sweet fruits, good for drying; widely grown in California; large tree; self-pollinating. (**Readily Available**)
'Green Gage'—old-timer, considered one of the best; greenish yellow fruits, good for eating fresh and for cooking; widely adaptable; hardy to zone 4; self-fertile. (**Readily Available**)
'Stanley'—dark blue fruits; prune plum; planted in most areas of the East and Midwest; best for zones 5–7; self-pollinating. (**Readily Available**)

JAPANESE PLUMS
'Cocheco'—small, reddish, tasty fruits; beautiful white flowers and red foliage; quite hardy; needs pollinator, any Japanese variety. (**6**)
'Mariposa'—maroon skin and flesh; needs little winter chill, good for Southern California; needs 'Santa Rosa' for a pollinator. (**Readily Available**)

'Methley'—small reddish purple fruits; low chill requirement; grown in warmer climates including Hawaii; self-pollinating. (**1, 62, 68, 71**)
'Ozark Premier'—large, red, tasty fruits; resistant to brown rot, canker, and bacterial spot; good pollinator for 'Allred'; for zones 5–9; dwarf available; self-pollinating. (**1, 6, 22, 58, 71**)
'Redheart'—large fruits; newly introduced; resistant to brown rot and canker. (**58**)
'Santa Rosa'—crimson-skinned, high quality fruit for eating fresh and cooking; widely grown; stars in the West; tree has upright growth, self-pollinating. (**Readily Available**)
'Satsuma'—wine red skin and flesh; excellent fruits for eating, superb for jelly; great combined with 'Santa Rosa' as pollinator. (**Readily Available**)
'Weeping Santa Rosa'—newly introduced; small tree with graceful form; somewhat more suitable for cold climates than 'Santa Rosa' since it blooms a little later; self-pollinating. (**71**)

ORNAMENTAL FLOWERING AND FRUITING PLUMS
The following are the most popular of this type.
Some of the plants sold as flowering plums in local nurseries bear excellent small cherry-type fruits.

Prunus cerasifera (cherry plum)—green leaves, white flowers; fruits red, 1 in. across; tree 30 ft. tall.
P. c. 'Atropurpurea' [*P. pissardii*] (purple-leaf plum)—red leaves; white flowers, small red plums.
P. c. 'Hollywood'—leaves dark green above, red below; flowers white to light pink; plums red, 2–2½ in. across.

Preserving and Preparing

Plums can be frozen, canned, or made into sauces, jams, and jellies. See master jelly recipes under ELDERBERRY and KIWI.

Prune plums are the best for drying.

To dry, pick ripe fruits. Wash and boil them for one to two minutes until the skins split; this procedure makes the plum skins porous and allows moisture to escape. Another way to do this is to prick the plums all over with a sharp object.

Spread the plums out to dry in a warm, dry place outside in the sun (cover with screening to protect fruit from birds and insects). Or dry them in your oven, spreading them on racks and starting the oven at 130°. Over the course of twenty-four hours, slowly raise the temperature to 165°, turning the plums often. If you raise the temperature too quickly, the outside of the plum will dry too fast and moisture will be sealed in toward the pit causing the prune to eventually rot in storage. If your oven can't be set this low, buy an oven thermometer and turn the oven on for a few minutes every hour during the day to keep the temperature up.

Pack the prunes in airtight containers and refrigerate or freeze.

Belgian Plum Tart

1½ pounds blue plums, cut in half lengthwise and pitted
1 tablespoon sugar
½ cup red currant jelly
3 tablespoons cold water
unbaked, 10-inch pastry shell

Preheat oven to 400°. Arrange plums in circles, cut side up, in the pastry-lined pan. Sprinkle them with sugar.

Bake the tart in lower part of the oven until pastry is lightly browned and plums are tender, 35 to 40 minutes. If crust browns too quickly, cover lightly with aluminum foil. Remove tart from oven.

When tart is cool, heat jelly and water in a small saucepan, stirring until the jelly melts. Cook for a few minutes until mixture is syrupy. Cool slightly and remove any scum. While the jelly mixture is still warm, brush it on the plums. Let the tart stand before serving.

Serve with whipped cream, if you wish. Serves 6–8.

Plum, Bush *(BUSH CHERRY)*

Beach plum, *Prunus maritima*
Japanese bush cherry, *P. japonica*
Nanking cherry, *P. tomentosa*
Western sand cherry, *P. Besseyi*
Bush plum hybrids

Effort Scale

NO. 2
Easy to grow
Processing takes time

Zones

5–7 for beach plum
3–5 for sand cherry, Nanking cherry, Japanese bush cherry, cherry plum hybrids

E.115. *Dark red cherry plums grow in clusters.*

Thumbnail Sketch

Bush Plums (Except Beach Plum)

Deciduous shrubs
4–8 ft. tall, depending on variety
Propagated by budding and from suckers
Need full sun
Leaves deep green, narrow, 1½–3 in. long, some types woolly underneath
Bloom in spring
Flowers are white or pink, small, abundant, showy
Fruits are edible; harvested in summer
Used as foundation plants, hedges, interest plants, and in containers

Beach Plum

Deciduous shrub or small tree
6–10 ft. tall
Propagated from seeds and cuttings
Needs full sun
Leaves deep green, oval, woolly underneath, 1–2½ in. long
Blooms in spring
Flowers are white, small, abundant, showy
Fruits are edible; harvested in summer
Used for beach planting, erosion control, interest plant, large shrub, screen, hedge

How to Use

In the Kitchen

The term bush plum covers a number of small fruits similar in taste to plums and cherries. The fruits are small, generally 1–2 inches in diameter, and are either red, yellow, or purplish black. They can usually be eaten fresh but are most often used in jams, jellies, sauces, pies, and canned.

Many bush plums are native plants and are remembered fondly by those of us who, as children, entertained Raggedy Ann at tea next to a fruiting bush plum hedge and served handfuls of these luscious small fruits.

In the Landscape

The bush type plums, such as the sand cherry, Nanking cherry, Japanese bush cherry, and bush plum hybrids, make beautiful hedgerows that in early spring are completely covered with white or pink blossoms. Often they are among the earliest flowering shrubs. The bushes can serve as flowering accents planted as freestanding shrubs, are pleasant near a patio, and are popular as a foundation plant. Some types of western sand cherries have silvery green foliage that turns red in the fall.

Beach plums can be used as medium to large shrubs and informal flowering hedges. These plants become even more attractive as their dark, shiny bark grows gnarled with age; in a seaside planting, windblown plants take on picturesque forms. Some plants are quite thorny and can be used for a barrier hedge.

How to Grow

Climate

Bush plums are a delicious substitute for cherries and plums in the coldest parts of the country. All varieties are quite hardy.

The native western sand cherry is a star performer in the Mid-

E.116. Beach plum trees get sculptured shapes when exposed to ocean winds.

west, including Wyoming, Minnesota, Colorado, and up into Manitoba.

Beach plums are native to the shores of the East Coast from Maine to Virginia. They are not as cold hardy as the other cherry plums, but have been grown inland successfully in milder areas of the Midwest, New England, and along the shores of the Great Lakes. They can also tolerate seacoast conditions.

All cherry plums need heavy winter chilling, and do poorly in mild-winter areas.

Exposure

Cherry plums need full sun.

Soil

Cherry plums thrive on a wide variety of soils. The small bush types can tolerate fairly poor drainage though they do not prefer it.

Beach plums will grow in poor, sandy soil but need good drainage.

Fertilizing

All bush plums benefit from an annual application of an organic mulch.

Watering

Bush plums are usually grown in areas that receive precipitation the year round, and need no extra watering once established.

Pruning

The sand cherry plums bear fruit along the entire length of their branches; consequently, they can be pruned to form a tailored hedge. Tailored bushes still bear fruit, but their yield is smaller than that of untrimmed plants. All the cherry plums will bear fruit without regular pruning but look better with some care and shaping. Pruning on most types is best done by August. Many of next year's flower buds will be lost if the plants are not pruned until fall.

Beach plums and the taller cherry plums can be trained to be small trees, but they need constant pruning to keep their shape. Their natural form is as a shrub, and they will continue to send up suckers unless pruned carefully.

Pests and Diseases

Bush cherries have few pests and diseases, though birds can sometimes beat you to the goods. To ensure a sufficient harvest, plant extra bushes for the birds. Plum curculio, tent caterpillars, and brown rot are occasional problems.

Harvesting

Pick cherry plums when they are fully colored and give slightly when pressed.

How to Purchase

Forms and Sources

Buy cherry plums in containers from your local nursery or from these mail-order sources: (**18, 20, 22, 28, 37, 43, 57, 72**).

Pollinators

Some types of cherry plums are self-fruitful, but the majority will bear more heavily with cross-pollination, and most types require it.

Varieties

BEACH PLUM

All varieties—fruits are red-purple, usually eaten cooked; 6–10 ft. high and wide; plant becomes gnarled and windblown near the ocean; can be trained to be a small tree; needs a pollinator; varieties are 'Autumn', 'Squibnocket', 'North Neck' (**Available locally** and from **28, 37, 57**).

CHERRY PLUM HYBRIDS

'Black Beauty'—new variety; superior, large, maroon-red fruits, 1 in. in diameter; eaten fresh or cooked. (**22**)

'Compass'—old variety; red fruits eaten cooked or fresh; bush grows to 8 ft.; a very good pollinator for other cherry plums; needs pollinator. (**20, 28**)

'Golden Boy'—yellow fruits; otherwise similar to red cherry plums. (**22**)

'Oka'—dark purple-red fruits, eaten fresh or in jams and jellies; 4–6 ft. tall, treelike form; for heavy crops cross-pollinator, 'Sapa', recommended. (**6, 10, 22, 28**)

'Red Diamond'—large maroon freestone fruits, 1½ in. in diameter; eaten fresh or preserved; bush 6 ft. high; needs cross-pollination, any bush plum. (**20, 28**)

'Sapa'—a widely available hybrid; dark purple-black fruits; sweet and almost freestone; can be pruned to be a small tree; needs pollinator, 'Compass' recommended. (**Readily Available**) An improved 'Sapa' exists, called 'Sapalata'. (**6, 20, 28**)

JAPANESE BUSH CHERRRIES

Red purple fruits used for jams; foliage similar to Nanking cherry; flowers white or pink; bush 5–7 ft. tall. (**20**)

NANKING CHERRIES

All varieties—very hardy, grow in the Great Plains from New Mexico to South Dakota, including high desert regions; many seedlings and improved varieties available; all have white flowers and woolly foliage underneath; excellent hedge plants; fruits bright red, good fresh or cooked; varieties, 'Fields Special Nanking' (**22**), 'Nanking Cherry Orient' (**20**), 'Nanking Hybrid Cherry' (**28**), 'Scarlet Gem' (**6**).

WESTERN SAND CHERRIES

A hardy native of the midwest plains and Rocky Mountains; breeding stock for many improved hybrids; superior dark-red fruits eaten fresh or cooked; generally 4–6 ft. tall; bush can take extreme cold and heat; needs cross-pollination; best-known improved variety is 'Hansens'. (**20, 22, 28, 57**)

Preserving

All cherry plums can be canned or made into sauce or jams.

PLUM, NATAL. See *Natal Plum.*

POLE BEAN. See *Beans.*

Pomegranate

Punica granatum

Effort Scale

NO. 1
Very easy to grow
Occasional pruning to shape needed
Only occasional watering necessary
Fruit processing requires work but is not necessary

Zones

9, 10

Thumbnail Sketch

Deciduous shrub or small tree

10–20 ft. tall
Propagated from seed, cuttings, or by layering
Needs full sun
Leaves are bright green, yellow in fall, 2–3 in. long; new growth is bronzy
Blooms in spring or summer
Flowers are bright red, showy, 1½–2 in. across
Fruits are edible; harvested in fall
Used as small to medium-size multistemmed tree, patio tree, large shrub, screen, interest plant, hedge, espalier, and in containers

How to Use

In the Kitchen

The big, round, red fruits of the pomegranate are filled with seeds covered with a clear, ruby-red, juicy substance. It is this tart-flavored seed covering that gives pomegranates their special quality. The seeds themselves are used raw to decorate salads and desserts. The juice is extracted for use in drinks, for marinating meat and poultry, and as the base for grenadine syrup. The juice also makes good jelly.

In the Landscape

This deciduous, woody plant can be pruned into a large, fountain-shaped shrub or a small, somewhat pendulous tree. No matter how it is trained, this 10–20-foot plant will offer beauty

E. 117. Pomegranate plants bear brilliant red flowers and fruits—sometimes both at once.

over a long period. Its new growth is bronzy, and its long, narrow leaves are a light, bright green that in most climates turn clear yellow in the fall. The extremely showy, orange-red flowers are 1½–2 inches across, many to a branch. The floral display can continue for as long as six weeks in summer. Occasionally one of those clusters contains a flower bud, a fullblown flower, a beginning fruit, and a more mature fruit all at once—a real show-and-tell affair. Some of the fruits remain after the leaves have dropped, looking decorative among the bare branches.

Its size and its continual interest make the pomegranate one of the most ornamental and versatile of the edible plants. It is particularly handsome combined with nandina in a shrub border or against a wall. It may be used as a small interest tree or shrub and as a hedge, a screen, or an espalier on a hot, south wall. This latter use is particularly suitable for colder climates. Pomegranate shrubs can be kept to a proper size for container growing. In this form, their various stages can be appreciated close up.

How to Grow

Climate

Pomegranates generally freeze at around 18–20°F. They prefer hot summers and low humidity. They do poorly on the California coast and in southern Florida. The fruits can tolerate very high summer temperatures. Pomegranates are a good desert plant.

The trees have been grown as far north as Puget Sound on the West Coast, and as far north as Virginia on the East Coast. In these northern zones, they must be grown on a hot south or west wall and given winter protection.

Exposure

Pomegranates need full sun.

Soil

They prefer good garden loam, pH 5.5–7.0, but can tolerate considerable amounts of alkalinity and sodium in the soil. They need good drainage.

Fertilizing

Use a humus mulch. If the foliage is pale apply iron chelate and supplemental nitrogen.

Watering

Pomegranates are drought resistant, but for superior fruits in arid climates or on very light soil, occasional deep watering is usually necessary. Do not deep water after a long dry spell if fruits have formed, or they will split.

Pruning

Pomegranates fruit on new wood and will fruit whether they are pruned heavily or not at all. Young pomegranates can be trained as a bush, or as a single or multistemmed tree. If training as a tree, cut all growth to the ground except one strong branch that will become your trunk for a single tree or three strong branches if you want it to be multistemmed. To keep it in a tree form you will have to cut new sucker growth off for a number of years. In early spring, remove dead growth and shape shrub or tree.

Pests and Diseases

The leaf-footed plant bug is a pest in some desert areas. Mala-

E.118. *In autumn pomegranate trees are usually covered with bright red fruits that hang on the tree for weeks.*

thion in late spring may be needed for severe infestations. Leaf spot occurs in parts of the South. Try dormant oil sprays. Otherwise, few pests and diseases affect the pomegranate.

Harvesting

You can pick a pomegranate once the fruits have turned red. If you leave fully ripe pomegranates on the tree they will often split open.

How to Purchase

Forms and Sources

Pomegranates are available bare root in late winter or in containers from local nurseries. Mail-order sources for plants are (**4, 10, 24, 60,** and **71**). Seed is available at (**19** and **51**).

Pollinators

Pomegranates are self-pollinating.

Varieties

Many varieties of pomegranates only flower but do not set fruit. Be sure you get a fruiting variety. 'Wonderful' is the one most frequently grown. 'Spanish Ruby' is available in Florida.

Preserving and Preparing

If picked before full maturity, pomegranates can be stored for months in a cool, dry place.

Pomegranate juice stains and tends to splatter. The best way to keep clean while using pomegranates is to submerge the fruits in water as you work with them. When you separate the seeds from the pulp, they will sink to the bottom of your container and the waxy fiber and skin will float to the top.

To extract the juice, place seeds in a blender, two cups at a time, and puree for one minute. Put this juicy pulp in a cheesecloth bag and allow it to drip through. This liquid is the base for grenadine, jelly, marinade, and can also be used as is for drinking.

Pomegranate Jelly

3½ cups pomegranate juice, fresh or frozen and thawed
¼ cup lemon juice
1 package (2 ounces) powdered pectin
4½ cups sugar

Follow the standard directions for making jelly that come with the powdered pectin.

Grenadine Syrup

Mix equal parts pomegranate juice and sugar. Let mixture stand for three days. Bring to a boil and simmer for three minutes. Strain the syrup and pour into sterilized jars. Use over ice cream, fruit salad, and cut grapefruit.

POMELO. See *Citrus Fruits.*

POTATO, SWEET. See *Sweet Potato.*

E.119. Prickly pear fruits form at the base of the showy flowers.

Prickly Pear *(INDIAN FIG)*

Opuntia species
Nopalea species

Effort Scale

NO. 2
Very easy to grow
Spines must be removed from most varieties before eating

Zones

5–10 and Hawaii

Thumbnail Sketch

Cactus
3–15 ft. tall
Propagated from joints and seeds
Needs full sun
'Leaves' are padlike with thorns, green or gray-green
Blooms in spring
Flowers are orange or yellow, similar to large portulacas, 3–4 in. across
Pads are edible, harvested in spring; fruits are edible, harvested in fall
Used as interest plant, barrier plant, hedge, on slopes, and in containers

How to Use

In the Kitchen

The prickly pear is a double-barreled plant in the kitchen. The fruits are plum-shaped, 1½–3 inches long; they must be handled carefully and the bristly hairs removed before eating. Their lush red pulp looks like that of watermelon. Some species have orange or yellow flesh. This pulp is sweet, but also extremely seedy, so it has to be eaten with some care. Prickly pear is usually served as a fresh fruit, well chilled. In the Middle East, fruit vendors sell it from trays of shaved ice, and it makes a pleasant, cool treat on a hot day.

The young joints of this cactus, usually referred to as pads, are the other edible part. They also are covered with bristles that must be removed before eating. These pads are cut up, boiled, and served with salt, pepper, and butter. The taste most closely resembles that of string beans, but is unique. It must be experienced to be appreciated. The pads are not too often available in a produce market except those that have a Mexican or Spanish clientele. Nopales, as they are called, are more readily available canned, but the most delicious nopales are fresh and home grown.

In the Landscape

The flat, bristly pads of these evergreen, herbaceous, perennial cacti can be 4–6 inches long. The most commonly grown species will grow to 15 feet in height and are exceptionally dramatic as accent plants, especially with Spanish architecture. Most species have showy, yellow blossoms, similar to large portulaca blooms, and green or red fruit. Both the flower and the fruit are decorative against the green or gray-green pads. The plants add height to desert cacti groupings, can be used on rocky banks, and, because of their prickles, are effective barrier plants. They are dramatic planted against a white stucco wall or in large earthenware containers.

How to Grow

The propagation, planting, and cultivation of cacti are different from those for other kinds of plants. The Sunset book *Cactus and Succulents* is a useful reference. The following section covers some of the basics.

Climate

Some species of prickly pear cacti are hardy to around 20°F. Most are much more tender but are easily grown in containers in colder climates where they can be brought indoors.

Exposure

The plants need full sun.

Planting

If you are able to get a pad from a friend's plant, let the cut portion heal and dry for a few days; then place it right side up in slightly damp sand. If you are using seeds, plant them one-quarter inch deep in good planting mix. Keep barely moist and out of the sun. The germination period is very long; it can last up to six months.

Soil

Prickly pears are not fussy about soil type but must have extremely good drainage.

Fertilizing

These cacti, if grown in the ground, usually do not need fertilizing.

Watering

Prickly pears grown in the ground take care of themselves after the first year, but before that should be watered once a month during the summer if it is dry. The plants are easily overwatered. If you are growing them in containers consult a book on cactus or local authorities.

Pests and Diseases

These cacti have few problems with pests and diseases.

Harvesting

Irritating bristles grow on the fruits and pads of most species. Harvest both with leather gloves. Rub the fruits and pads with rough canvas to remove the bristles and wash to remove the residue. Check carefully, as some bristles are hard to see.

E.120. *A large prickly pear becomes a living sculpture near an adobe-style house.*

How to Purchase

Forms and Sources

Prickly pear cactus is available as seed or plants from local nurseries and some mail-order sources. Seed is available from (**32**). Plants are available from Cactus Gem Nursery, 10092 Mann Drive, Cupertino, CA 95014. Cactus Gem Nursery carries more than 1200 species of cacti. A catalog is available for $1.00.

Varieties

Many edible *Opuntia* and *Nopalea* species are available. Few named varieties are available.

Nopalea cochenillifera—native of Mexico, often called the true 'Nopal'; fruits and pads are edible; flowers are pink to rose; plant grows to 15 ft.

N. dejecta—this cactus has a trunk; flowers and fruits are dark red; plant grows to 6 ft.; from South America.

Opuntia Ficus-indica (Indian fig)—most commonly planted and most commonly eaten; usually considered the best; yellow flowers; plant has variable growth habit, sometimes sprawling, sometimes upright, to 15 ft.; there is a spineless variety, bred by Luther Burbank, and a variety popular in the Middle East that is practically seedless.

O. humifusa (often sold as *O. Opuntia*)—many-branched plant, usually prostrate in habit; yellow flowers; the most hardy prickly pear; grown from Massachusetts to Montana, south to Florida, and east to Texas.

O. leucotricha—treelike; grows to 15 ft.; pads are 4–10 in. long; yellow flowers; from Mexico.

O. phaeacantha (often sold as *O. Engelmannii*)—low-growing, sprawling plant; pads are 4–16 in. long, eaten fried or steamed; yellow flowers; most of these cacti grow in Texas, California, Arizona, New Mexico, and are prized by native Indians and Mexicans.

Preserving and Preparing

The fruits of the prickly pear can be pickled or used to make jelly.

Prickly Pear Dessert

Peel and slice fruits into individual dishes. Sprinkle slices with lime juice and top with sweetened whipped cream to which a small amount of orange liqueur has been added.

PURPLE-LEAF PLUM. See *Plums*.

Quince

Cydonia oblonga

Effort Scale

NO. 3
Vulnerable to some pests
Mulching helpful
Fruits must be processed

Zones

5–9

Thumbnail Sketch

Deciduous tree
15–20 ft. tall
Propagated from cuttings and by budding
Needs full sun
Leaves are oblong, deep green, woolly underneath, yellow in the fall, 4 in. long
Blooms in spring
Flowers are white or pale pink, showy, 2 in. across

E.121. *Quince fruits are usually yellow and quite decorative.*

Fruits are edible; harvested in fall
Used as interest tree or shrub, screen, patio tree, espalier, hedge

How to Use

In the Kitchen

The yellow, orange, or green, woolly, oblong fruit of the quince is too hard and astringent to be eaten raw. Combined with apples, it can be used for sauce or pie. The fruit can be baked like an apple and is often spiced and canned or used in chutney. The Spanish use it in a dessert called *dulce de membrillo*, a molded quince puree. Generally, though, we know quince as the source of an exquisitely colored and flavored jelly. Quince is a good source of pectin and is sometimes used in combination with less pectinous fruits for jelly. Or it can be made into a fruit paste and rolled in sugar.

In the Landscape

The gnarled and twisted form that develops in the quince with age brings an interesting shape to the landscape, whether the tree is used as an accent near a patio or as a container plant. Delicate white or pink flowers sit above the foliage in the spring and colorful fruits in the fall add visual interest, and the fragrance of the fruit enhances the observer's pleasure.

All these advantages make the quice a good espalier subject. As trees or as shrubs, quinces can line a garden walk. The shrubs make a solid screen or hedge.

How to Grow

Climate

Quinces can be grown over a wide area of the country. They are quite hardy but are subject to severe winter injury at −15° F. Since the flowers blossom late in the spring, however, they are not harmed by frost.

Because the quince tree is susceptible to fireblight, it does not do well in the warmest, most humid areas of the country.

Exposure

Quinces require full sun.

Soil

Unlike most fruits, quinces will tolerate somewhat poor drainage, but they prefer well-drained, fairly heavy loam. They will not fruit well in very heavy or very light soils.

Fertilizing

Large amounts of nitrogen should be avoided. Nitrogen encourages succulent new growth, which is particularly susceptible to fireblight. When quince is grown on average soil, an occasional compost mulch or manure is generally all the fertilizer needed.

Watering

Quinces are somewhat drought tolerant, but they bear more reliably with good soil moisture.

Pruning

If you grow quince as a tree, you will have to remove suckers occasionally, since the plant generally grows as a shrub. Keep the tree pruned to shape. You can cut it back quite a bit if you want, because quinces bear on the tips of current growth and pruning will not remove much fruiting wood. Pruning is done in the winter. In areas where fireblight is severe, keep pruning to a minimum, as it encourages the highly susceptible, succulent new growth.

Pests and Diseases

Quinces are susceptible to many of the same problems as apple trees, but seem to be less often affected. Codling moth is the most common pest. Quince curculio, scale, and borers are sometimes problems. Fireblight is the most common disease. See Chapter 7. Leaf blight causes reddish spots on the leaves and occasionally on the fruits. Use lime sulfur for control. Consult local authorities for a spraying schedule.

Harvesting

Pick quinces when they have turned color and are fragrant. Handle them carefully. Quinces are hard, but the skin bruises easily.

How to Purchase

Forms and Sources

Quinces are available from local nurseries bare root in the late winter or early spring or in containers throughout the fall. They are also available from the following mail-order firms throughout the fall: (**10, 24, 28, 37, 57,** and **71**).

Varieties

'Orange'—orange-yellow flesh; matures late August. (**24, 37, 45**)

E.122. *The quince is an attractive small tree. This one is planted near a fence with a recycled spool gate.*

'Pineapple'—white flesh tastes somewhat like pineapple. (**10, 24, 28, 60, 71**)

'Smyrna'—oblong yellow fruits with a strong fragrance; considered the superior variety. (**10, 57, 60, 71**)

Preserving and Preparing

Quinces make a delicious jelly (see below). They can also be used to make a sauce with apples that can be canned. Spicing and canning quinces is another storing technique; use a recipe for spiced pears if you cannot find one for spiced quince.

Quince Jelly

3 pounds fully ripe quinces
4½ cups water
¼ cup lemon juice

7½ cups sugar
½ bottle liquid pectin

Wash the fruits, removing stem and blossom ends and cutting of bruises. Grind or chop very fine the remaining flesh, including skin and cores. Put pieces in a large saucepan, add water, and bring to a boil. Simmer for 15 minutes. Press through a jelly bag or a bag made from double layers of cheesecloth. Keep 4 cups of fruit and combine with the lemon juice and sugar. Follow the directions for making jelly that comes with the liquid pectin. Pour into glass jars and seal.

RABBITEYE BLUEBERRY. See *Blueberry*.

RASPBERRY. See *Brambleberries*.

RED CURRANT. See *Currant* and *Gooseberry*.

RED PEPPER. See *Peppers*.

Rhubarb (GARDEN RHUBARB, PIE PLANT)

Rheum Rhabarbarum

Effort Scale

NO. 1
Mulching necessary
Watering necessary in arid climates

Zones

1–9

Thumbnail Sketch

Perennial herb, treated as annual in high desert areas
3–5 ft. tall
Propagated by divisions or from seeds
Needs full sun; partial shade in desert areas
Leaves are large, deep green, wavy, 1½ ft. wide; stems are red or green.
Blooms in summer

E.123. *Rhubarb's large dramatic leaves look well in containers.*

Flowers are greenish or reddish, in tall spikes
Stalks are edible; harvested in spring
Used as interest plant, in herbaceous borders, flower beds, containers

How to Use

In the Kitchen

In many parts of the country rhubarb is the first "fruit" of spring. The thick, fleshy leaf stalks of the handsome plant are used for sauce and pie. Both dishes are great favorites of those who like them at all, but the world could probably be divided into those who care for rhubarb and those who truly dislike it. Many people make a wine out of the stalks.

Caution: Rhubarb leaves are poisonous.

In the Landscape

A rhubarb plant is a long-lived addition to a yard. It is a herbaceous perennial that can grow to 5 feet tall. Its 18-inch, crinkly, rich-green and red-veined leaves are dramatic atop their rosy red stalks. (One variety, 'Victoria', has green stalks. It does not compare in beauty with the red-stalked varieties; nor does its sauce seem as appealing.) Rhubarb is so handsome that it fits into any herbaceous border or flower bed. It can be an accent in a container or it can fill a corner spot in a garden or yard. It is eye-catching when planted with red geraniums.

The flowers of rhubarb grow on tall stalks, but they should be cut off so the energy used in their development is diverted to the stalks and the leaves.

How to Grow

Rhubarb has some rather definite requirements. It needs cold winters and is not productive in areas with very hot summers, even though it prefers full sun. In the high-desert areas it is planted in the fall as a winter annual and should be given partial shade for coolness.

Its soil requirements are not precise, but it does best in acidic, well-drained, loam rich in organic matter. Mulch annually with manure. If placed correctly and given a modest amount of attention, a plant will last a lifetime.

How to Purchase

Seed or rhizomes of rhubarb are available from local nurseries or mail-order firms. Alternatively, you can be around when your neighbor is dividing a plant.

Do not harvest rhubarb stalks the first year. After that, harvest by pulling the thickest, healthiest stalks off gently. Do not take more than half the stalks of any one plant. Three plants should be adequate for the average family.

Preserving and Preparing

Rhubarb can be made into jam or wine. Stewed rhubarb can be frozen or canned.

Stewed Rhubarb

Cut washed stems into 1–2-inch pieces and place in a saucepan with enough water to prevent sticking. Cover and cook over medium heat until soft. Add sugar to taste.

ROCK MAPLE. See *Maple*.

E.124. Rose hips vary in shape. Rugosa rose hips are usually round.

Rose Hips

Rosa rubrifolia (no common name)
Rugosa rose (Japanese rose), *R. rugosa*
Sweetbriar eglantine, *R. Eglanteria*

Effort Scale

NO. 2
Easy to grow
Processing fruits is time-consuming

Zones

2–9

Thumbnail Sketch

Deciduous shrubs
4–8 ft. tall
Propagated from seeds or by budding
Need full sun or light shade
Leaves are compound, composed of 5–9 leaflets, deep green, crinkled
Bloom in summer
Flowers are white, red, pink, yellow, or lilac, 2–3 in. across
Fruits (hips) are edible; harvested in fall
Used as interest plants, barriers, hedges, and in raised beds, containers

How to Use

In the Kitchen

Rose hips are the small, applelike seed capsules of roses. They are usually red-orange but can be yellow or almost black. Most roses produce hips, but only some of those produced are pleasant tasting. The others are inclined to be astringent. The best rose hips come from the rugosa rose. Rose hips are used to make jelly, tea, and sauces. They can be eaten raw but are seedy. Rose hips contain considerable amounts of vitamin C.

Rose petals can be used raw in salads and omelets, fried in batter, crystallized, or made into jam.

In the Landscape

This vigorous, deciduous shrub, usually 4–8 feet tall, has prickly and thorny branches, so one of its landscape uses is as a barrier plant. Because these species of roses have dense growth and are upright, they serve as good screens and hedges. The deep veining of their lush, dark leaves gives them an almost quilted look. Their gloriously fragrant blooms—single or double, 3–4 inches across, and in colors ranging from white through red and yellow or lilac—are most plentiful in late spring. The 1–inch-long, showy fruits develop in the fall.

One small variety, 'Blanc Double de Coubert', does well in a container.

Note: The plants of rugosa roses are vigorous growers, so they should be restrained by a concrete header or planted in a large container to prevent them from invading the rest of the yard. Do not plant these bushes near open fields or their seeds will be widely dispersed by birds, causing the plants to take over the open spaces.

How to Grow

Climate

Unlike their cousins, the hybrid tea roses, which are grown only for their flowers, the rugosa and other species named here are extremely tolerant of harsh conditions. They are very hardy and take wind, salt air, and drought. They grow everywhere but in the deep South. They need some winter chilling.

Exposure

These roses need full sun or light shade.

Soil

These species of roses are highly tolerant of most soil types, but prefer soil that is neither strongly acidic nor alkaline. Good drainage is essential.

Fertilizing

Very little fertilizer is needed.

Watering

The shrubs are drought tolerant once they are established.

Pruning

For good fruit production, minimize pruning.

Pests and Diseases

Unlike the hybrid tea rose, these roses have very few pests and diseases. Aphids and Japanese beetles are bothersome in some areas.

Caution: Do not use systemic pesticides formulated for roses on plants that will be eaten.

Harvesting

Pick fruits when they are fully colored. Do not allow them to become overripe, that is, soft and wrinkled.

How to Purchase

Forms and Sources

The species of roses mentioned can be purchased bare root or in containers from a few local nurseries or mail-order houses. Some species are available as seed from mail-order firms. Plants: (**13, 28, 53**); seed: (**29**).

The largest selection of plants is available from (**53**). This nursery specializes in old-fashioned roses and has the largest selection in the country. If you are interested in ordering from this source, do so early; the supply is limited and your favorite might be gone by late spring.

Pollinators

Plant more than one variety for good fruit production.

Varieties

ROSA RUGOSA
'Belle Poitevine'—double flowers are lilac pink; flowers repeatedly; plant is 4–8 ft. tall. (**28, 53**)
'Blanc Double de Coubert'—double, white flowers; flowers repeatedly; sweet fragrance; plant is 3–5 ft. tall. (**53**)

E.125. *Rugosa roses are vigorous growers. It is wise to confine the roots in a planter; this one is made from recycled concrete.*

'Delicata'—semidouble flowers are lavender, pink; flowers repeatedly; hips are large; plant is 3–4 ft. tall. (**53**)
'Frau Dagmar Hastrup'—flowers are pink; flowers repeatedly; large, red hips; plant is 2½–3 ft. tall. (**53**)
'Hansa'—violet-red, double flowers; fragrance is clovelike; hips are large, red; plant is 5–6 ft. tall. (**28, 53**)
'Rubra'—reddish-pink flowers; growth less dense than in others; plant is 5 ft. tall. (**28**)
'Will Alderman'—lavender-pink, double flowers; unusual pointed buds; plant is 3–5 ft. tall. (**53**)

OTHER SPECIES
The chief characteristics of the other named species, all of which produce good fruits, are listed below.

Rosa eglanteria—pink flowers; shrub is 10–15 ft. tall. (**53**)
Rosa rubrifolia—pink flowers; shrub is 6 ft. tall. (**53**)

Preserving and Preparing

To dry rose hips, wash the fruits, cut them open and remove the seeds. Spread them on trays, and use a food dryer or a low oven (150°F.) to remove all moisture.

Rose Hip Jelly

4 cups ripe rose hips, halved
1½ cups water
2 cups sugar

Combine the rose hips and water. Cover, and boil gently for 20–25 minutes until tender. Discard the rose hips, and strain the liquid. Add the sugar to the liquid, and boil gently until it reaches the jelly stage. (Follow jelly-making directions under KIWI.)

E.126. *Rosemary comes in many forms. Shown here draped over a retaining wall made of recycled railroad ties, from left to right: common rosemary, upright 'Collingwood Ingram', and 'Prostratus'.*

Rosemary

Rosmarinus officinalis

Effort Scale

NO. 1
Almost grows by itself

Zones

All

Thumbnail Sketch

Evergreen, woody shrub grown as an annual in zones 1–6
2–4 ft. tall
Propagated from seeds or cuttings
Needs full sun
Leaves are needlelike, gray-green, ½–1½ in. long
Blooms in spring
Flowers are blue, small, showy
Leaves are edible; used as seasoning; harvested year round
Used as ground and bank cover and in herb gardens, raised beds, containers

How to Use

In the Kitchen

The aromatic leaves of this herb yield a slight taste of pine. They are commonly used to season lamb, pork, veal, and poultry, as well as casseroles and egg dishes. The leaves can be steeped and added to a fruit punch.

In the Landscape

This woody perennial ranges in height from 2 to 4 feet, depending on the variety. The tall, upright plants make beautiful flowering hedges. Unpruned, they can be used as shrubs or, with their interesting, gnarled shapes, as container or accent plants. The prostrate, trailing varieties are ideal as bank covers or cascading over a retaining wall. Their strong root systems are helpful in controlling erosion. All kinds can be used in herb gardens, and in containers.

All rosemary plants have needlelike leaves with gray undersides. These leaves set off the plentiful blooms, whether they be light blue, lavender, or deep violet-blue. Rosemary is attractive to bees.

How to Grow

Rosemary is semihardy from approximately 0° to 5° F. It is drought tolerant, but in the desert it needs watering three or four times a summer. Its soil requirements are few: alkaline soil and good drainage.

Rosemary can be harvested at any time of the year for use fresh. However, if you are planning to dry it for the winter, harvest the leaves before the plant has started to flower. The leaves will have a better texture and will usually be richer in flavor.

How to Purchase

Forms and Sources

Common rosemary is easily obtained as seed or plants from local nurseries or mail-order firms.

Varieties

The following varieties of rosemary are available as plants from local herb specialists.

'Collingwood Ingram'—shrub type, 2½ ft. tall, 4-ft. spread; bright, deep-blue flowers.
'Lockwood de Forest'—trailing type; bright blue flowers.
'Prostratus'—trailing type, lavender-blue flowers.

Preserving

See BASIL for drying information.

RUGOSA ROSE. See *Rose Hip.*

Saffron

Crocus sativus

Effort Scale

NO. 2
Easy to grow
Harvesting is tedious

Zones

6–9

Thumbnail Sketch

Herbaceous corm
4 in. tall
Propagated from offsets (divisions of corms)
Needs full sun
Leaves are grasslike, 3–4 in. tall
Blooms in fall
Flowers are mauve; 2 in. tall
Flower parts are edible; used as seasoning; harvested in fall
Used in rock gardens, flower beds, containers

How to Use

In the Kitchen

Saffron is the most expensive of all herbs to buy. It is produced from the red-orange stigmas and styles (threadlike female flower parts that receive pollen) of *C. sativus*, also called saffron crocus. Its vivid orange color and strong flavor make it effective in very small amounts. It is an important ingredient in paella, bouillabaisse, and Spanish rice. Saffron is also used in certain breads.

In the Landscape

Saffron is similar to the ordinary spring crocus, but it blooms in the fall. Its grasslike leaves are 3–4 inches tall and its flowers are mauve to purple, not as showy as those of the spring bulbs but lovely nevertheless and a pleasant surprise in the fall landscape. They are used the way spring crocuses are used in landscaping—in rock gardens, in large clusters under high, branching trees, and in containers.

Caution: Do not confuse saffron crocus with autumn crocus, *Colchicum autumnale,* which is poisonous.

How to Grow, Purchase, and Preserve

Like spring crocus, saffron crocus grows in zones 6–9. Plant the bulbs in August, 3–4 inches deep, in rich, well-drained garden loam.

To harvest, remove the stigmas with a tweezer and dry them in a warm place.

These plants are often difficult to obtain. They are sometimes available at local nurseries, and can be ordered from De Jager Bulbs, Inc., 188 Asbury Street, South Hamilton, MA 01982.

You will not have enough to preserve; hundreds of stigmas are needed to make half an ounce. (This is why saffron is so expensive.)

E.127. *Saffron crocuses can be grown in clusters*

Sage

Common sage, *Salvia officinalis*
Pineapple sage, *S. elegans* [*S. rutilans*]

Effort Scale

NO. 1
Very easy to grow
Common sage should be taken inside in coldest winter areas

Zones

Common sage, all
Pineapple sage, 9 and 10

Thumbnail Sketch

Common Sage

Evergreen, woody herb
1–2 ft. tall
Propagated from seeds or divisions
Needs full sun
Leaves are gray-green or variegated, 1–2 in. long
Blooms in summer
Flowers are small, blue or white, on spikes
Leaves are edible, used as seasoning, harvested year round
Used in herb gardens, flower beds, containers

E.128. Sage is a small, versatile plant. The variegated type shown here looks pretty against a background of rocks.

Pineapple Sage

Evergreen woody herb; perennial, often planted as an annual
2–3½ ft. tall
Propagated by cuttings
Needs full sun
Leaves deep green, 2–4 in. long, underside slightly woolly
Blooms in fall
Flowers are red on tall thin spikes
Leaves are edible; used as seasoning; harvest season varies
Used in herb gardens, back of flower beds, containers

How to Use

In the Kitchen

The aromatic leaves of common sage are used as a seasoning for poultry stuffing and homemade sausage. Sage adds a good flavor to soft, mild cheese that is spread on crackers and, because of its congeniality with the chicken flavor, is good in the dressing used on a chicken salad. Pineapple sage has a slight pineapple flavor and is used in jellies and fruit compotes.

In the Landscape

These woody perennials differ sharply from each other in appearance. Common sage grows to 2 feet high and has gray-green, woolly, crinkly leaves and blue or white, spiky flowers. It is used in herb gardens and in containers. The variety 'Tricolor' has purple, red, and white variegated leaves that make a striking accent by itself and combines well with purple alyssum and johnny-jump-ups in the spring and with low, pink dianthus in the summer. It is particularly lovely in a small herb garden, planted in a strawberry jar (one with "pockets" on the outside) along with thyme, parsley, and purple basil.

Pineapple sage grows higher, is more open in appearance, and has deeper green, softer-looking leaves than common sage. Its flowers are bright red and grow in slender spikes. Pineapple sage should not be confused with scarlet sage *(Salvia splendens)*, the strictly ornamental sage. Pineapple sage is a nice addition to any flower bed, toward the back because of its height. Try it with Shasta daisies, green basil, ruby chard, and red zinnias.

How to Grow, Purchase, and Preserve

Garden sage grows in most areas of the country. In the coldest areas grow it as an annual. Pineapple sage is quite tender. Both sages need good drainage, ordinary garden soil, and full sun. Neither needs much watering.

Sage can be harvested at any time of the year for use fresh. However, when you are planning to dry it for the winter, harvest the leaves before the plant has started to flower to ensure good texture and maximum flavor.

Both seeds and plants of common sage are readily available. Pineapple sage plants are sold in small containers in specialty herb nurseries.

See BASIL for information on drying.

Salal

Gaultheria Shallon

Effort Scale

NO. 2
Birds are sometimes a problem
Picking the berries is time-consuming

Zones

6–9

Thumbnail Sketch

Evergreen shrub
2–6 ft. tall, depending on growing conditions
Propagated from seeds, divisions, or cuttings
Grows in sun or shade
Leaves are deep green, 2–4 in. long
Blooms in spring
Flowers resemble lilies of the valley; are white to pink; grow in clusters
Fruits are edible; harvested in fall
Used as informal hedge, shade shrub, border, ground cover, and in rock gardens, containers

How to Use

In the Kitchen

The small, blue-black salal berry makes a delicious jelly and a fragrant wine. It is similar in flavor and use to blueberries.

In the Landscape

This evergreen shrub, a member of the heath family, is a year-round beauty. Its round, leathery, bright-green leaves set off its small blooms, which resemble lily-of-the-valley flowers. The blooms can be either white or pink, and are carried on reddish stems. In the fall the dark, round berries, which grow in clusters, are showy.

In its native woodland, salal will grow to a height of 6, sometimes even 10 feet, but in poor, dry soil and in full sun it will only reach 2–4 feet. Salal is a natural for a woodland garden and is a good companion to other acid lovers—azaleas, rhododendrons, and pieris. In humid, cool areas it can be grown as an informal hedge. When grown in the sun, salal makes a good ground cover, and can be planted on hillsides or in sunny rock gardens.

How to Grow, Purchase, and Preserve

This plant is a native of forests from Santa Barbara, California, to British Columbia. It prefers moist, cool, acid soil, but tolerates poor, dry soil. It will grow in full sun, but will not tolerate desert conditions.

Salal is easy to grow. It needs pruning only to shape; and it has few pests or diseases, although the birds sometimes help themselves to the berries.

The berries are harvested when they are fully colored and the whole cluster is ripe.

Plants are available in containers from local nurseries; seeds are obtainable from (**52, 55**).

To preserve, dry the berries or make jelly.

E.130. *The salal shrub has small- to medium-size, leathery foliage.*

Salal Jelly

Wash berries and cook them gently for several minutes. Do not add water. Strain fruit through a jelly bag and measure the juice. Combine equal amounts of salal juice and tart apple juice. Bring to a boil.

Add 1 cup of sugar for each cup of juice. Follow the procedure described under KIWI for making jelly without pectin.

SAND PEAR. See *Pear.*

SCARLET RUNNER BEAN. See *Beans.*

Sea Grape

Coccoloba Uvifera

Effort Scale

NO. 2
Easy to grow
Vulnerable to some pests
Processing before eating is usual

Zones

10 and Hawaii

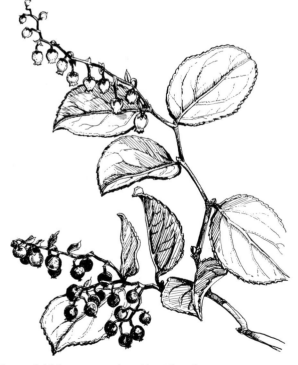

E.129. *Salal flowers are similar to lily-of-the-valley.*

E.131. *The sea grape has large leaves and long fruit clusters.*

The plant is usually grown as a multistemmed, large shrub, but it can be trained and pruned into a dramatic shape and used as an interest plant or a small patio tree. The flowers, though insignificant, are fragrant and the fruits that follow are green to wine-colored, growing in long clusters that are decorative against the foliage. Sea grapes are attractive grown with natal plums.

How to Grow, Purchase, and Preserve

Sea grapes are native to southern Florida and thrive along the ocean. They grow best in moist, well drained, sandy soil. Where winters are frosty, they must be grown in greenhouses. Prune lightly to shape. Occasional pests are aphids, whiteflies, scale, and tip borers. A leaf spot disease is sometimes a problem. Pick fruit when fully colored.

Sea grapes are available in containers from local nurseries only in Florida and Hawaii.

Sea Grape Jelly

3 pounds sea grapes, half ripe	7 cups sugar
½ cup water	½ bottle pectin

Wash, stem, and mash the fruit. Bring to a boil with the water, and simmer for ten minutes. Strain, then measure 4 cups of juice into a large pot. Add sugar and pectin. Follow the procedure described under ELDERBERRY for making jelly with pectin.

If jelly is not flavorful enough, try substituting 3½ cups sea grape juice and adding ½ cup of lemon or lime juice.

Thumbnail Sketch

Evergreen tree or small shrub
15–20 ft. tall
Propagated from seeds and cuttings or by layering
Needs full sun, can tolerate light shade
Leaves are glossy, bluish-green, red-veined, heart-shaped, 8 in. across
Blooms in spring
Flowers are white, grow in long clusters, not showy, small, fragrant
Fruits are edible; harvested in fall
Used for erosion control on seasides, as interest tree, screen, hedge, windbreak, small patio tree, and in containers

How to Use

In the Kitchen

This small, grapelike fruit is eaten raw; made into tasty jelly, syrup, and sauces; and is sometimes used for wine.

In the Landscape

One of the many charms of this evergreen plant is its glossy, 8 inch-wide leaf; it is bluish green, heart-shaped, and veined in red. The bark is light brown and mottled. The combination of texture, shape, and color on this handsome 15–20-foot-high plant makes it an attractive windbreak and screen from salt spray and sand on the Florida seacoast and in Hawaii. The sea grape's ability to grow along the shore is one of its values. Near the ocean it often develops a beautiful gnarled form.

E.132. *Sea grapes grow into rounded shapes after maturing.*

SHAGBARK HICKORY. See *Hickory.*

SHELLBARK HICKORY. See *Hickory.*

E.133. 'Dwarf Gray Sugar' peas have lavender blossoms that contrast with their gray-green foliage.

Snow Pea (CHINESE PEA PODS, SUGAR PEAS)

Pisum sativum var. *macrocarpon*

Effort Scale

NO. 3
Must be planted annually
Pests occasionally a problem
Harvesting is time-consuming

Zones

Annual

Thumbnail Sketch

Herbaceous annual vine
2–6 ft. tall
Propagated from seeds
Needs full sun; tolerates some shade in hot climates
Leaves are blue-green, oval, 1–2 in. long
Blooms in spring or winter
Flowers are leguminous, white or purple, grow in clusters
Pods are edible; harvested in spring
Used in large, herbaceous borders, raised beds, containers, and cascading over retaining walls

How to Use

In the Kitchen

Used fresh, the sweet, crunchy, succulent pods of the snow pea dress up a salad or add sophistication to a raw vegetable platter. They can be steamed briefly and served as a cooked vegetable and are often used in stir-fried Oriental dishes.

Snow peas are extremely expensive in the market, adding to the pleasure of growing your own.

In the Landscape

The snow pea plant is a long climbing vine from 5–6 feet tall. It has bluish-green leaves 1–2 inches long, white legume-type flowers, and some tendrils. Most varieties of snow peas (and their close cousin, the garden pea) have attractive foliage and can be grown on a trellis or fence combined with a flowering vine such as nasturtium.

One variety of snow pea in particular, 'Dwarf Gray Sugar', is quite decorative by itself. 'Dwarf Gray Sugar' peas grow on short vines to 2 feet. This variety is somewhat sprawling and loose in habit and has purple-lavender flowers that bloom in beautiful clusters. The size and shape of the dwarf plants make them pleasant as part of a flower border. 24–36 plants are usually enough for the average family. Try them in a border in front of stock or pink and purple snapdragons. Or grow them in a large hanging basket with alyssum, or by themselves in large, decorative containers. Let your guests pick their own hors d'oeuvres.

Caution: Do not confuse or combine snow peas with sweet peas. Sweet peas are poisonous.

How to Grow

Snow peas are annuals requiring full sun, high humidity, and cool weather. They can tolerate some frost and do poorly in hot

E.134. 'Dwarf Gray Sugar' peas make a fast-growing, sprawling ground cover. They are superb for informal places, such as these railroad-tie steps, but must be replaced with other annuals ('Royalty' bush beans, for example) when the weather warms up.

weather. They are grown in the spring in cold climates, and in the winter and spring in mild winter areas.

The soil should be nonacidic and well drained. These peas need very little fertilizer but respond well to organic mulches.

Pests include the pea weevil. To deter these creatures, try lightly dusting wet or dew-covered foliage with lime. For pea moth, use *Bacillus thurengiensis*. For pea thrip, try a hard spray of water with a nozzle, or sponge foliage with a mild, soapy water solution. To prevent mildew, do not water plants from above in warm weather.

Because the harvest is fairly large and the pods small, harvesting is time consuming. You can expect to pick 2–3 pounds from a 15-foot row over a one-week period. The harvest season lasts from 4–6 weeks. The plants should be pulled out after most of the pods are harvested or they will become scraggly and brown or mildewed.

How to Purchase

Varieties

One mail-order nursery (**67**) has a particularly large selection of peas.

'Dwarf Gray Sugar'—small edible-podded peas; lavender flowers; good disease resistance, short bush vines, 2–2½ ft. tall. (**9, 16, 38, 43, 47, 62, 67**)

'Sugar Snap'—a new vegetable, thick tender pods, eat pods whole or shell like peas. Pods grow on long vines and have white flowers. (**Readily Available**)

Preserving and Preparing

Pea pods can be frozen, but frozen pods lose some of their crispness.

Snow peas add color and texture to many Chinese stir-fry dishes, and are good in a raw vegetable platter with dip.

E.135. Sorrel has distinctive sword-shaped leaves.

Sorrel

French sorrel (oseille), *Rumex scutatus*
Garden sorrel, *R. Acetosa*

Effort Scale

NO. 1
Occasional watering and weeding necessary
Occasional pest problems

Zones

5–9

Thumbnail Sketch

Perennial herbs
18 in.–3 ft. tall
Propagated from seeds or divisions
Needs full sun, will tolerate partial shade
Blooms in summer
Flowers are green or brown, in thin spikes 2–3 ft. tall
Leaves are medium green, shield-shaped, 3–6 in. long
Leaves are edible; harvest time varies
Used in herb gardens, flower beds, woodland paths, raised beds, containers

How to Use

In the Kitchen

Soup lovers claim that cream of sorrel soup is without peer. The slightly sour taste of the leaves in combination with chicken broth, cream, and eggs is delicious and satisfying. The leaves are often used in sauces for salmon or shrimp, and a few can be added to a mixed salad. French sorrel is milder in flavor than the common sorrel. Try them both. Do not confuse garden sorrel with wood sorrel, *Oxalis acetosella*.

In the Landscape

Both species are herbaceous perennials whose rich green foliage differs from that of the more common herb garden plants, so they make a nice change. They are close relatives of dock, a weedy pest. The foliage of garden sorrel is long, to 2 feet, and shield-shaped. The French sorrel has much smaller leaves, to 6 inches long. Both plants drape their leaves and are somewhat sprawling. If not allowed to bloom, they give a soft graceful shape to a flower border. If allowed to bloom, the plants look more upright. Try combining the taller garden sorrel with zinnias or tall marigolds in the background. The shorter French sorrel looks well planted with Alpine strawberries, parsley, and white lobelia. The latter combination is lovely in containers and can be grown in partial shade.

The small green or brown flowers of the sorrel are borne on tall spikes; they are somewhat decorative and can be used fresh or dried in flower arrangements. As is often the case with leafy edibles, however, when you want to use the leaves of a plant you should not allow the flowers to develop.

How to Grow, Purchase, and Preserve

Garden sorrel is native to Europe and Eurasia but has gone wild in North America and can be found in most areas of the country. Its requirements are few, although it does like a moist soil. It will grow in full sun or partial shade. French sorrel is native to central Europe, likes a rather dry soil, and tolerates both full sun and partial shade. Neither species is bothered by cold or heat.

Both plants are prone to minor pest and disease problems, such as black aphids and shot-hole fungus. And, or course, those succulent, green leaves are attractive to snails and slugs.

You should divide sorrel every three years to keep the leaf production at a high level.

Harvesting sorrel is simply a matter of cutting the leaves as you need them. Always allow the plants to regrow and fill in to renew themselves after each harvesting.

Plants are available at local nurseries and some mail-order firms. Seeds are available at (**16, 17, 35, 51,** and **56**). Also look to friends who might be dividing the crowns of their plants.

Sorrel can be frozen like greens, or as sorrel soup. If adding egg yolks or cream to your soup, leave them out when freezing and add them after the soup base is thawed.

SOUR CHERRY. See *Cherry.*

SPEARMINT. See *Mint.*

SPINACH. See *Greens.*

SQUASH. See *Cucumber, Squash,* and *Melon.*

ST. JOHN'S BREAD. See *Carob.*

Strawberry

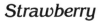

Alpine strawberry (fraise des bois), *Fragaria alpina semperflorens*
Garden strawberry, *F.* x *Ananassa*

Effort Scale

Alpine Strawberry

NO. 2
Fertilizing and weeding are necessary
Watering needed in most areas
Picking fruits is time-consuming
Replanting necessary every three or four years
Winter protection needed in many areas

Garden Strawberry

NO. 4
Susceptible to some pests and diseases, including birds
Replanting necessary every three years
Runners must be controlled
Watering and fertilizing necessary
Weeding necessary
Harvesting the large, perishable yield is time-consuming
Winter protection needed in many areas

Zones

3–10

Thumbnail Sketch

Herbaceous perennials
6–12 in. tall
Propagated from seeds or runners
Garden needs full sun; Alpine prefers partial shade
Leaves are compound; garden species, deep green; Alpine
    species, medium green
Blooms in spring and summer
Flowers are white, small
Fruits are edible; harvested in spring and summer
Used in flower beds, raised beds, to line a woodland path, rock
    gardens, hanging baskets, containers, and for ground covers

How to Use

In the Kitchen

A bowl of garden strawberries served with a little powdered sugar and cream is my idea of the perfect dessert. Close behind are strawberry pie, whether plain, chiffon, or cream, strawberry Bavarian cream, strawberry soufflé, meringues filled with strawberries, and strawberry shortcake, all of which dress up strawberries without spoiling their flavor. Scandinavians use the berries in a wonderful pudding and soup, and Australians often top their meringue-like cake, Pavlova, with fresh berries. If you dress whole, fresh berries with a bit of curaçao about two hours before

E.136. Alpine strawberries lack runners; they bear their berries on stalks that keep them off the ground.

E.137. Hybrid strawberries can be grown in place of many ground covers.

serving, they will have a marvelous fresh look. The curaçao does not draw the juices, but the amount should be small—about 2 tablespoons for 48 berries—so the berry flavor is not covered.

Strawberry jam is such an American traditional it hardly needs mentioning. What a pleasure jam is when it brings the taste and smell of summer to our winter breakfast tables.

If you like garden strawberries, you will love Alpine strawberries (the French call them *fraises des bois*). They are strawberries with the flavor volume turned up. I remember paying $8.00 for a bowl of small, fragrant Alpine berries in France; you can enjoy this delicacy for very little if you choose to grow them.

In the Landscape

Perky, red garden strawberries dangling from hanging baskets or over the side of a strawberry jar are treats for the eyes as well as the tastebuds. These productive ornamentals lend themselves to a number of uses. The deep-green leaves and the small, white flowers contrast nicely with the dark color of wooden tubs or brick walks. The plants form a rich, green ground cover that is nice next to walks or patios, where you can bend down and help yourself to the choicest berry. Strawberries are also good in raised beds or to

line flower borders. Ripe strawberries must be harvested daily to keep the fruits from rotting.

Alpine strawberries are star edible ornamentals. These plants are even more graceful than the garden strawberries. They have the further advantage of having no runners, so they remain neat-looking when planted near a lawn or a walk. The fruits are smaller and are not as pressing to harvest. They dry up and fall off instead of rotting, as the large garden strawberries do. The flowers and fruits sit above light-green foliage in a truly ornamental fashion. They look beautiful combined with sweet woodruff, mint, lettuce, dwarf nasturtiums, and begonias.

How to Grow

Climate

A strawberry variety exists for nearly every area of the United States and Canada. Alpine strawberries are quite hardy and can be grown well into zone 4. In areas with coldest winters, mulching with straw is necessary. In fact, in cold climates all types of strawberries should be covered with a heavy mulch, preferably straw, when heavy frosts are expected, and the mulch should not be removed until hard freezes are over. Alternate freezing and thawing of the soil sometimes heaves the plants out of the soil; the mulch helps keep the soil from freezing.

In desert climates and regions that receive over 300 frost-free days, garden strawberries are usually treated as a winter annual. 'Sequoia' and 'Tioga' are varieties adapted to this method of growing.

Exposure

Plant garden strawberries in full sun. Alpine strawberries prefer morning sun or filtered shade from a high-branching tree. Do not plant Alpines in full sun or in hot, afternoon sun in warm-summer areas.

Planting

Garden strawberries should be grown for only three to four years in one place, because the mother plants stop producing and the runners get too crowded. Diseases are also more of a problem when strawberries are grown in the same place for many years. Plant strawberries in beds that have been well prepared with humus. Plant crowns of the plants at ground level. Strawberry plants that are planted too deep will rot; if they are planted too high they will dry out.

Alpine strawberries are usually started from seeds; follow package directions. For best production divide the plants every three or four years.

Keep the strawberry bed well weeded; mulches help considerably.

Soil

Both types of strawberries need fairly rich, well-drained soil that is high in organic matter. Keep strawberries well mulched. When good drainage cannot be assured, strawberries are often planted in hills. Strawberries prefer a slightly acidic soil pH of 5.0–6.0.

Fertilizing

Both types of strawberries should be kept well mulched with manure or compost. Do not fertilize with large amounts of nitrogen, but watch for symptoms of nitrogen starvation—foliage turns light green or yellowish—and treat by applying small amounts of nitrogen.

Watering

Strawberry plants need to be kept moist. They have a low tolerance for salt, and in areas with high water salinity, as in some high-desert areas, strawberries are difficult to grow.

Pruning

For spring-bearing varieties of garden strawberries, prune off flowers the first year after planting to encourage strong growth. This means you will have no strawberries that year from these plants. Prune off the spring flowers on everbearing varieties, but allow fall flowers to fruit the first year. If you remove most of the runners on your plants you will get more and larger berries. Keep some of the runners intact to provide replacements for the older plants as they decline.

Alpine strawberries need no pruning.

Pests and Diseases

A number of pests bother strawberries but usually chemical controls are unnecessary. Snail and slug problems are an exception. Handpicking helps, but there are so many places for these pests to hide in a lush patch that snail bait is usually necessary. Use it before the fruits form. Japanese beetles are sometimes a problem. To control these pests, handpick and use milky spore disease. A preventive planning measure is to keep strawberry patches away from lawns, where the grubs overwinter. Where weevils are a problem, use spring-bearing berries. Pull up the plants after the second spring and plant something else in their place for the next few years to prevent the weevil population from building up. Aphids, another potential problem, can usually be controlled with a sharp blast of water from the hose nozzle. Nematodes and mites can be a problem in the Southeast. To control the first, use the soil solarization method discussed in chapter 7 before planting; mites require chemical control.

The diseases that affect strawberries—verticillium wilt and red stele (root rot)—can be serious, but are not common with homegrown plants if they have been purchased from a nursery that carries certified disease-free plants. The most important control is crop rotation. Once plants have become diseased, remove them and do not plant strawberries again in the same bed for three or four years. Even if diseases have not affected your fruit, you should alternate strawberries with other plants in succession in the same garden spot. Fungicides are sometimes needed to control leaf spot.

Harvesting

Pick strawberries the day they become ripe—when they are fully colored and slightly soft. Pull them off carefully with the stem and cap still attached. Check the vines daily. Refrigerate berries, but use them quickly, as the quality declines rapidly.

A mature garden strawberry plant should produce about 1 pint of berries each season. Alpine strawberries produce a lighter harvest—plan to grow 4–5 dozen plants for a family of four.

How to Purchase

Forms and Sources

Buy garden strawberries bare root in early spring from local nurseries or mail-order sources, or in containers through the fall.

Varieties

GARDEN STRAWBERRIES

It is very important to choose strawberry varieties appropriate for your climate. The following varieties are disease resistant. Look for them in your local nursery.

'Darrow'—high quality fruits; resistant to red stele and verticillium wilt. (**6, 50**)

'Ft. Laramie'—everbearing, large, aromatic berries; extremely hardy, good for Midwest as well as southern states; nice for hanging baskets. (**8, 20, 22, 28, 36**)

'Guardian'—fruits good for fresh eating or freezing; ripens midseason; resistant to many diseases; for Southeast. (**Readily Available**)

'Ozark Beauty'—large berries; everbearing; very hardy and adaptable to many climates. (**Readily Available**)

'Paris Spectacular'—fruits bear on runners so are particularly attractive in containers; everbearing type; fine flavor; plant good for hanging baskets. (**48**)

'Redchief'—good dessert fruits; resistant to red stele and mildew; for Southeast. (**6, 9, 50**)

'Sequoia'—one of the best-tasting strawberries; resistant to many diseases and somewhat tolerant of soil alkalinity; for West Coast. (**Readily Available**)

'Shasta'—good flavor; ripens midseason; resistant to some virus diseases and mildew; for California. (**Readily Available**)

'Sunrise'—good flavor; ripens early season; resistant to red stele, mildew, and verticillium wilt; for Southeast. (**22, 50, 58, 62, 68**)

'Surecrop'—good quality fruits; ripens early; resistant to most major strawberry diseases and drought; for East Coast. (**9, 22, 50, 58, 62, 68**)

'Tennessee Beauty'—good quality berries; ripens late season; resistant to a number of diseases; for Southeast. (**6, 50, 68**)

ALPINE STRAWBERRIES

Alpine strawberries are sold as seed by the following mail-order sources: (**9, 16, 17, 28, 35, 40, 48, 63, 69**). Some local nurseries sell plants. A number of varieties of Alpine strawberries exist, all quite similar to each other in fruit quality and growth habits.

'Alexandria'—medium-size red fruit; good flavor. (**16, 36, 48, 63**)

'Baron Solemacher'—old favorite variety. (**9, 35, 48, 59**)

'Improved Rugen'—dark red berry; improved quality. (**9, 69**)

'Yellow Fruited'—small yellow fruits, sweet. (**48, 69**)

Preserving

Strawberries can be made into jellies, jams, fruit leather (see CRANBERRY), and wine, or they can be frozen whole with sugar.

SUGAR MAPLE. See *Maple*.

SUGAR PEA. See *Snow Pea*.

SUI MATAI. See *Water Chestnut*.

SUMMER SQUASH. See *Cucumber*, *Squash*, and *Melon*.

SUN CHOKE. See *Jerusalem Artichoke*.

Surinam Cherry (PITANGA)

Eugenia uniflora

Effort Scale

NO. 2
Occasional pruning necessary
Harvesting and processing are time-consuming

Zones

10 and Hawaii

Thumbnail Sketch

Evergreen shrub or small tree

E.138. *The fruit of the Surinam cherry may be yellow, clear red, or a deep red approaching black.*

4–15 ft. tall
Propagated from seeds or cuttings
Needs full sun or light shade
Leaves are waxy, deep green, 2½ in. long
Blooms in spring
Flowers are small, white, fragrant, not showy, ½ in. across
Fruits are edible; harvested in spring and summer
Small tree used as interest plant, screen; shrub used as foundation plant, formal or informal hedge, and in containers

How to Use

In the Kitchen

The small, 1¼-inch Surinam cherries change in color from yellow through dark red as they ripen. (Some varieties even turn black.) It is at the last stage that they become sweetly yet tartly delicious and can be eaten out of hand. Those that are not eaten fresh make tasty pies and jellies. They can also be frozen for future use.

In the Landscape

The Surinam cherry is an evergreen shrub with waxy, deep-green, 2-inch long leaves. Its new growth is bronzy, and its flowers are small, white, brushlike, and fragrant. The unique, eight-grooved globular fruits decorate the shrub at all color stages—green, yellow, red, and dark, dark red—and sometimes all colors are on the bush at one time. The plant can grow as tall as 15 feet but can be kept as low as 3 feet when used as an informal hedge or, clipped, as a formal hedge. Remember, though, that clipping reduces fruit production.

This shrub can be allowed to grow to its full height and be trained as a small, multistemmed tree. In this form it is a delightful accent. Try it in a corner along with a birdbath and a red hibiscus, or in a container on a patio where you can enjoy the fragrant flowers.

How to Grow

These shrubs grow easily in southern Florida, Hawaii, and southern California. They can take no frost and prefer fairly rich, slightly acidic, well-drained soil. Give them a sunny or partially shady spot, keeping the root area quite moist and fertilizing occasionally.

Surinam cherry shrubs are usually pest free, although birds can be a problem.

How to Purchase

The plants are obtainable in containers at local nurseries. There are black-fruited varieties available.

Preserving and Preparing

To freeze Surinam cherries, wash them and cut out the pits and "rabbit ears" (small knobs on some of the berries). Halve fruits and remove seeds. Mix 4–5 pounds of fruit with 1 pound of sugar, or cover the fruit with a 40–50-percent sugar syrup.

Package the prepared cherries and freeze for use in pies. Frozen cherries remain usable for 10–12 months.

Surinam Cherry Jelly

5 pounds Surinam cherries
4 cups sugar

Wash fruit, remove stems and blossom ends, put them in a large saucepan and mash. Barely cover the mashed fruit with water and simmer until soft, about 20 minutes. Transfer to a jelly bag and allow to drip through overnight. Measure 4 cups of cherry juice into a kettle and add sugar. Follow the standard procedure described under KIWI for making jelly without pectin.

E.139. *Surinam cherry bushes sheared to a formal shape.*

SWEET BASIL. See *Basil.*

Sweet Bay and California Bay

Sweet bay (bay laurel), *Laurus nobilis*
California bay, *Umbellularia californica*

Effort Scale

NO. 1, if informal
NO. 2, if sweet bay is clipped into a formal shape or grown in containers
Some watering needed

Zones

8–10

Thumbnail Sketch

Sweet Bay

Evergreen shrub or tree
25–40 ft. tall
Propagated from seeds or cuttings
Needs sun or partial shade
Leaves are deep green, 3–4 in. long
Flowers are insignificant
Leaves are edible; used for seasoning; harvested year round
Used as formal (topiary) shrub, hedge, screen, small tree, and in containers

California Bay

Evergreen tree
25–80 ft. tall
Propagated from seeds
Needs sun or partial shade
Leaves are yellow-green, 3–5 in. long, and narrow
Flowers are insignificant
Leaves are used for seasoning; harvested year round
Used as street tree, shade tree, screen, or windbreak

How to Use

In the Kitchen

Both plants yield aromatic leaves that are similar to each other in taste and are used as seasoning in stews, soups, corned beef, and pickled herring. Some people prefer the taste of sweet bay; California bay is more potent, so must be used with discretion.

In the Landscape

Sweet bay is a slow-growing evergreen shrub or medium-size tree, often multistemmed. Its oval leaves are a deep, shiny green, 2 to 3 inches long. Its flowers are insignificant, but the dark purple berries are a nice addition to the fall scenery. Bay lends itself to pruning and topiary clipping and, with its distinctly formal and

E.140. *Sweet bay grows well in containers; it also takes well to shearing for a formal style.*

classic appearance, is an excellent container plant. In containers, it can make a nice addition to your indoor landscape.

California bay, a native of the redwood forests of California, is a slow-growing evergreen tree that can reach a height of 60–80 feet in the wild. In home gardens it is usually much smaller. It is often multistemmed. Its leaves are a bright yellow-green that can reach 5 inches in length. California bay makes a neat-appearing street or shade tree if properly pruned and is also useful as a screen wind-break, or in a woodland or creekside garden.

How to Grow, Purchase, and Preserve

Both plants are semihardy and can tolerate quite a bit of shade. They can be excellent additions to your landscape plans if they can grow in your climate. In arid climates, water occasionally to keep them looking fresh.

To harvest and preserve, pick leaves in late summer and allow to dry on a screen with good air circulation for 10 days to two weeks. Package in airtight containers.

Sweet bay is usually available at local nurseries. California bay is only obtainable on the West Coast. Seeds of both are available from (**51**). Sweet bay seeds are available from (**32, 51**).

SWEETBRIAR EGLANTINE. See *Rose Hip.*

SWEET CHERRY. See *Cherry.*

SWEET ELDERBERRY. See *Elderberry.*

SWEET FALSE CHAMOMILE. See *Chamomile.*

SWEET MARJORAM. See *Marjoram.*

SWEET PEPPER. See *Peppers.*

Sweet Potato

Ipomoea Batatas

Effort Scale

NO. 4
Must be started from slips
Specific soil, fertilizer, and water requirements
Susceptible to many pests and diseases

Zones

Annual

Thumbnail Sketch

Perennial tuber, planted as an annual
Trailing vine, usually kept to 1½–4 ft.
Propagated from shoots or cuttings
Needs full sun
Leaves vary from oval to lobed, 4–6 in. long
Flowers are sparse, rose to pale pink, 2 in. across
Tubers are edible; harvested in fall
Used in herbaceous borders, containers, and spilling over
  retaining walls

How to Use

In the Kitchen

This sweet, yellow or reddish orange tuber is delicious boiled, fried, or baked.

Sweet potatoes make a pleasant change from the more routinely served white potatoes. They are good both eaten plain and as ingredients in casseroles and pies. A southern favorite, "candied sweets," is a method of cooking baked or boiled sweet potatoes with a sauce of brown sugar and orange juice; it is delicious.

In the Landscape

The sweet potato vine produces lovely, 2–3-inch, lobed leaves that cascade gracefully over the sides of planters and retaining walls. On rare occasions a pink morning-glory-type flower nestles among the leaves. Sweet potato vines are perennials but are used as annuals in most areas. Try them as a ground cover in front of a flower bed combined with low-growing, pink zinnias or around a patio planted with pink petunias.

How to Grow

Sweet potatoes are the most heat-tolerant vegetable grown in the United States. They not only tolerate but must have great amounts of heat to produce a good crop. They need at least 140–150 hot summer days.

Sweet potatoes are planted out in spring by slips, which are sprouts produced by the tubers. To start your own slips, place tubers in a hotbed (a wooden tray with heating coils in the bottom and filled with sand) about 6–8 weeks before the weather warms up. Cover the potatoes with damp sand and maintain a hotbed temperature of 75–85°. Pull, do not cut, the shoots off; they and their roots will pull off easily.

Dig and loosen the planting area very well. The soil should be sandy loam, not clay. Sweet potatoes grown in heavy clay become gnarled and stringy. In planter boxes and containers use a rich, light soil mix. At planting time, use a generous amount of a fertilizer high in potassium and phosphorus. Mix in well. Bury bottoms of slips 4 inches deep and 1 foot apart. Keep the vines fairly moist until they are well established. The plants require less moisture after they are growing vigorously.

A number of pests affect sweet potatoes. Check with your local extension service, since problems differ with region. Choose sweet potato varieties that are resistant to the diseases in your area.

Harvest potatoes in late fall before a frost or when the tops die back. Handle the tubers carefully, because they bruise easily.

How to Purchase

Slips are available in spring from some local nurseries and mail-order houses. Two mail-order nurseries, Fred's Plant Farm, Dresden, TN 38225 and Steele Plant Farm, Box 807, Gleason, TN 38229, offer a large selection of varieties in spring.

Because sweet potatoes are susceptible to many diseases, it is important to choose varieties that are resistant to diseases that affect your area. The following are recommended:

'Allgold'—moist, sweet potatoes; resists viral disease, internal cork, and stem rot; stores well; good in the Midwest. (20, 28, 48)

'Bunch Porto Rico'—compact vines, grow to 18 in.; good for smaller areas and greenhouses. (9, 20, 28, 48)

'Heart-o-gold'—resistant to root-knot nematode.

'Nancy Hall'—moist, sweet potatoes; resistant to soft rot.

Preserving

Store sweet potatoes at temperatures above 50°F or they will rot. Under optimum conditions, they can be stored for four or five months.

Sweet potatoes can be canned or frozen.

SWISS CHARD. See *Greens.*

TANGELO. See *Citrus Fruits.*

E.141. Sweet potatoes can be grown in containers filled with loose, rich soil. Tubers are shown here in cutaway view.

Tea

Camellia sinensis

Effort Scale

NO. 3
Seeds and plants hard to find
Growing is experimental in most areas
Fertilizing and watering necessary
Soil must be kept acid

Zones

8–10

Thumbnail Sketch

Evergreen shrub
4–15 ft. tall, will grow much taller if left untrimmed
Propagated from seeds, cuttings and by grafting
Needs partial shade or, in cool, cloudy climates, full sun
Leaves are deep green, leathery, 3–5 in. long
Blooms in fall
Flowers are white or pink, camellialike, fragrant, 1½–2 in. across
Leaves are edible; used in beverages; harvested spring through fall
Used as interest shrub, formal or informal hedge, and in raised beds, containers

E.142.   *Tea plants have shiny green leaves and handsome white flowers.*

How to Use

In the Kitchen

The young, tender leaves of this plant when dried are the source of spirit-soothing tea. Despite its caffeine content, tea is considered more relaxing than activating. An infusion of tea leaves is often the base for fruit and alcoholic punches.

In the Landscape

This camellia has many of the same landscaping uses as any camellia. The shrub is a dense evergreen with dark-green, leathery leaves up to 5 inches long. Its small flowers, 1½ inches across, are usually white and single, and have prominent yellow stamens. They are fragrant and have the added advantage of blooming in the fall. Because of the flowers' fragrance, the plant is ideal as a doorway plant. Tea plants are slow growers and take many years to reach 4–5 feet. Tea plants can be grown in containers, used as an informal hedge and, clipped, as a formal hedge or screen. Pruning for a formal hedge will not cut down on the production of new growth that provides the tea leaves. Where appearance is a consideration, it is important to prevent them from becoming denuded when you harvest. Plant enough bushes to yield a good supply. Four to six shrubs should be enough for a family of tea lovers.

How to Grow

Climate

Tea can be grown in any area of the country in which camellias grow. The plants are semihardy and can be grown where temperatures rarely go below 24°F. They prefer fairly high humidity. Tea has been grown experimentally as a commercial crop in many areas of the country but has never been economically successful, because, although the plants grow well, the high cost of the hand labor necessary to harvest the leaves makes the endeavor too costly.

Exposure

Tea plants prefer cool summers. In areas that have such summers,

the plants can take full sun. In hot-summer areas they must have shade.

Planting

Instructions for planting generally come with seeds and plants. When planting seeds, remember to place them with the "eye" face down.

Soil

Tea plants will grow in sandy or clayey soil, but they must have plenty of humus and good drainage. An acidic soil with a pH factor of 4.0–6.0 is essential. Tea plants cannot tolerate salty soil. To protect the roots, keep plants well mulched.

Fertilizing

Tea plants prefer cottonseed meal or camellia fertilizer. Avoid overfeeding them.

Watering

Keep young tea plants well watered. Do not allow them to dry out. In arid climates mature tea plants need occasional deep watering during spring and summer.

Pruning

Prune to shape the shrub and to stimulate new growth for harvesting. Clipping is necessary if a formal effect is desired. Extensive clipping provides much new growth for leaf harvesting but cuts down on flower production.

E.143.   *Tea plants used as a hedge.*

Pests and Diseases

Tea suffers from the same pests and diseases as camellias, namely, red spider, weevils, and scale. Most plants are not affected, but in the Southeast leaves may have leaf-spot disease.

Tea planted on neutral or slightly alkaline soils will often become chlorotic. Treat with chelated iron.

Harvesting

Once the shrub is three years old you can start harvesting. After the first flush of growth in spring, pluck two or three of the outer, tender leaves from the top of each shoot. If the plant is growing vigorously, you can harvest three or four times during the summer. Leaves can be plucked from late spring to midfall.

How to Purchase

Forms and Sources

Seeds and plants are hard to find. Plants can be ordered from Java Specialty Growers, 3940 S.W. Halcyon Road, Tualatin, OR 97062. Seeds are available from (**48**) and (**51**).

Varieties

Named varieties of tea are not yet available in the United States. Plan to take what you can find.

Preserving and Preparing

How to Process Tea

There are two primary types of tea for drinking—green and black. Each type has its own curing process. Visit your local tea supplier and try both types to see which you prefer.

PROCESSING BLACK TEA

Place freshly picked leaves in a thin layer on a clean dry surface. Leave them to wilt and get soft, but do not let them become dry or brittle. Within 12–24 hours the leaves will be soft and ready to process. On a clean counter or table, crush a manageable amount (1–2 cups) of the wilted leaves with a rolling pin. Then knead the leaves with your hands as you would knead bread dough, for about 10 minutes. After that time add a rolling and twisting motion to your kneading and gradually increase the pressure. The bruised leaves will take on a twisted appearance and moisture will begin to appear. The tighter the roll of tea leaves is, the more flavor the tea will develop. If the leaves appear dry and no moisture appears, add a few teaspoons of water. Roll the leaves for approximately ½ hour.

After the rolling process is complete squeeze the leaves into a tight ball, cover with plastic wrap or a damp towel and leave to cure in a cool place for 6–8 hours. The processed leaves will have a fruity scent and a coppery color. Spread the processed tea on one or more cookie sheets, and place in a slightly warm oven with the door open. Stir and turn the leaves occasionally until they are completely dry and brittle. Store in an airtight container.

PROCESSING GREEN TEA

Put the freshly picked tea leaves in the top of a double boiler and let the water in the bottom pan boil for 8–10 minutes. The heating process will make the leaves soft and limp. Follow the rolling process described in the black tea directions. As soon as the rolling process is complete omit the curing stage and dry leaves immediately in the oven until brittle.

E.144. Creeping thyme fills in between stepping stones. On the left is common thyme.

Thyme

Caraway-scented thyme, *Thymus Herba-barona*
Common thyme, *T. vulgaris*
Creeping thyme, *T. praecox arcticus*
Lemon thyme, *T. x citriodorus*

Effort Scale

NO. 1
Very easy to grow

Zones

All

Thumbnail Sketch

Evergreen shrub or mat-forming perennial.
4–15 in. tall
Propagated from seeds, cuttings, and divisions, or by layering
Needs full sun

Leaves are gray-green, very small, ¼–½ in. long
Flowers are lavender, white, or pink, grow in small spikes
Leaves are edible; used as seasoning; harvested all year
Used as a ground cover and in herb gardens, as edging plant,
  in flower beds, rock gardens, raised beds, containers

How to Use

In the Kitchen

The aromatic leaves of these shrublets are used to season soups,
omelets, gumbos, poultry stuffing, and sauces for fish. They are
often added to vegetable juice cocktails and bring a subtle interest
to green beans and carrots.

In the Landscape

These evergreen plants vary in form from a matlike growth, as
in creeping thyme, to that of a shrublet up to 15 inches tall, as in
common thyme. Whatever the size of the plant, however, all
thyme leaves are tiny, ranging from ¼ to ½ inch long. The leaves
can be gray-green, dark green, or variegated gold or silver. The
tiny, lavender or pink flowers grow in short spikes and are attractive to bees.

The variations in plant form make thyme useful in several situations. Thyme plants belong both in an herb garden and a flower
border and are handsome in containers, hanging or not. Creeping
thyme is delightful when planted between stepping stones or in
other areas with limited foot traffic.

All the thymes go well with chives, sage, saffron crocus,
alyssum, ageratum, and small, pink zinnias.

How to Grow

Thyme is relatively easy to grow in most climates of the United
States, but ideal growing conditions require a raised bed and rocky
or sandy soil with excellent drainage. It prefers full sun. In areas
with the hottest summers, plants need some watering, but it is easy
to overwater thyme. Foliage should be pruned back in spring to
make it stay compact and lush.

Thyme can be harvested at any time of the year for use fresh.
However, if you are planning to dry it for the winter, harvest the
leaves just as the plant has started to flower to insure good texture
and a rich flavor.

How to Purchase

Plants are available in small pots and as seed from local nurseries
and mail-order firms. The four types are distinguished from one
another by size, scent, and other characteristics noted in the
following list.

Caraway-scented thyme—2–5 in. tall; leaves are dark green;
  flowers are rose-pink; good as ground cover; used as vegetable
  seasoning.
Common thyme—6–12 in. tall; leaves are gray; flowers are
  lavender.
Creeping thyme—2–4 in.; leaves are dark green; flowers are
  purplish-rose, purple, or white; good as ground cover.
Lemon thyme—4–12 in. tall; leaves are green; flowers are
  lavender; variegated silver and gold varieties available.

Preserving

See drying information under Basil.

*E.145. Many of the cherry tomatoes are attractive in containers. Choose a
container whose proportions suit the tall plant.*

Tomato

Lycopersicon Lycopersicum [L. esculentum]

Effort Scale

NO. 3
Must be planted annually
Tying and staking usually needed
Vulnerable to some pests
Harvest is continual

Zones

Annual

Thumbnail Sketch

Perennial, treated as an annual
18 in.–6 ft. tall
Propagated from seeds
Needs full sun
Leaves are compound, medium green
Blooms in summer

Flowers are yellow, not showy, small
Fruits are edible; harvested in summer or fall
Used on fences and in hanging baskets, flower borders,
   containers

How to Use

In the Kitchen

Tomatoes need no introduction. Still, have you ever tried a vine-ripened one, with the heat of the sun still upon it? If you have, you will know why the tomato is the most commonly grown vegetable in the United States. Whether your fruit is a 'Tiny Tim' or a 'Big Boy' does not matter. Once you have tried a fully ripened fruit, store-bought ones will seem a travesty. Enjoy them fresh all through the season—sliced, quartered, stuffed. Their flavor and color can enhance all summer meals.

Canned tomatoes add interest to winter meals in stews, soups, casseroles, and spaghetti sauce. It's hard to imagine cooking without catsup, chili sauce, salsa, tomato paste, and puree.

In the Landscape

When the tomato was first introduced to European gardens from the New World it was thought to be poisonous. Since the plant belongs to the nightshade family, the fruits were suspect, so tomatoes were used only as showy ornamentals. Now the reverse is true: the tomato has been relegated to the vegetable garden. How fickle we are!

The bright-green, lobed, hairy leaves and contrasting red or yellow fruits of the tomato plant are indeed ornamental. Now is the time to let the appearance of this plant increase the tomato's all-round usefulness. Plant tomatoes for beauty and function. The small fruited varieties look nice in hanging baskets or decorative containers. The large vining types can be trained to cover a fence, where they might serve as the background for 'Red Cascade' petunias and green peppers.

When using tomato plants as part of the landscape, try to keep the uses of wire cages to a minimum. Much can be done with less obtrusive stakes. When the plants begin to look spent and yellow, remove them.

How to Grow

Tomatoes like warm summers, rich garden loam, and moderate amounts of fertilizer and water. Start seeds inside in early spring. Set out plants after all threat of frost is over. On most soils they benefit from extra phosphorus, and they seem to bear better with a mulch.

Tie up plants or, where hanging baskets are used, let them trail their cascades of fruits over the sides of the pots.

A few major pests afflict tomatoes, namely, cutworms, tomato horn worms, white fly, and tobacco budworm, but generally pests are not a big problem. See Chapter 7.

Pick tomatoes as they ripen.

How to Purchase

Hundreds of varieties of tomatoes are available. Check with your local nurseries for the plants or seeds that are best for your area.

Large, fruited varieties for planting in the ground are 'Ace', 'Better Boy', 'Big Boy', 'Early Girl', 'Pierce', and 'Ponderosa'. Two yellow varieties, 'Jubilee' and 'Sunray', are sweet and have a low acid content. The 'Peron' tomato (**27**) is reported to be resistant to the tomato horn worm. Heirloom varieties are available from: (**25, 51**).

Small varieties for planting in containers or in the ground are 'Tiny Tim', 'Patio', 'Pixie', 'Small Fry', and 'Toy Boy'.

Good varieties for hanging baskets are 'Red Pear', the best, and 'Yellow Cherry', 'Yellow Pear', 'Red Cherry', and 'Sweet 100'.

Preserving

To preserve tomatoes, freeze or can them as catsup, sauce, paste, puree, juice, or stewed tomatoes.

Green (unripe) tomatoes can be pickled or made into chutney. Tomatoes can also be preserved for 4–8 weeks by harvesting the vines before fruit is fully ripe and hanging them—fruit and all—from the rafters of a cool garage or shed.

Walnut

Black walnut, *Juglans nigra*
Butternut, *J. cinerea*
California black walnut, *J. Hindsii*
Persian (English) walnut, *J. regia*

Effort Scale

NO. 3
Vulnerable to some pests, including squirrels
Mulching is beneficial
Raking is often necessary
Harvest is large

Zones

3–9

Thumbnail Sketch

Deciduous tree
20–80 ft. tall
Propagated from seeds and by grafting
Needs full sun
Leaves are compound, leaflets are 4–5 in. long, medium green
Flowers are in catkins, not showy
Nuts are edible; harvested in fall
Used in very large yards as shade trees, street trees, and screens

How to Use

In the Kitchen

There are two distinct nuts here: Persian (English) walnuts, everyone's favorite; and black walnuts, which, like okra, gooseberries, and rhubarb, are an acquired taste. The latter, which are hard to shell, are used in the same ways Persian walnuts are—in breads, cakes, and frostings—but their flavor is quite strong and they should be used with more discretion.

Persian walnuts can be added to any food that calls for nuts. Their flavor is mild and they get crunchier with baking. These nuts add a richness that we probably do not need but that adds pleasure to the eating. Besides their uses in baked goods, walnuts can be used in place of pine nuts in pesto sauce. A subtly flavored oil made from walnuts, available in foreign and health food stores, provides a nice change from your regular oil on salads and in cooking. Some year when your crop is especially large, you might look into pressing your own.

A delectable hors d'oeuvre is walnut halves sandwiching a layer of softened Roquefort cheese.

In the Landscape

The term walnut comprises a number of closely related deciduous trees of great stature. These stately trees, with their compound leaves and handsome branching structures, are useful for screening an unwanted view or for casting cooling shade in hot weather. Large lots and country lanes are enhanced by their presence. Because of their size and because they are often bothered by aphids, whose secretion is a problem on cars or patios, walnut trees are difficult to use in small yards. Also, the trees drop catkins, leaves, and husks, which is no problem for an informal woodland path or an area with deep ground cover, but is not compatible with a tailored yard. Walnut trees are used as lawn trees in the East.

Note: Black walnuts exude an acid from their roots that inhibits the growth of many plants. Keep them away from vegetable gardens (particularly those containing tomato plants), flower beds, azaleas, and rhododendrons.

How to Grow

Climate

Different types of walnuts grow in different parts of the country.

Butternut is the most hardy. It will grow as far north as zone 3, New Brunswick, Canada; and south to Georgia, west to Minnesota, and in the Midwest, south to Arkansas.

E.146. *Even when bare in winter, the branches of a walnut tree make a handsome pattern.*

Black walnut is also hardy. Its range includes southern Ontario, south to northern Florida, and west from South Dakota to Texas, as well as parts of the West Coast.

Persian walnut grows best in zones 6–9. One strain of Persian walnut, called Carpathian, has proved hardy to −25° F. Persian walnuts do not do well in very hot climates.

California black walnut is grown widely in California and is one of the major rootstocks for commercially grown Persian walnuts.

Exposure

These trees need full sun.

Planting

See HICKORY.

Soil

Walnut trees require well-drained, rich loam. They are at their best in deep alluvial soils. All walnuts have deep root systems. They prefer a soil with a pH of 5.5–7.0. Soils east of the Mississippi usually benefit from liming.

Fertilizing

Do not fertilize the first year. After that, supplemental nitrogen is usually needed. Keep walnut trees mulched but keep the mulch off the crown of the tree. If the trees are in a lawn, apply extra nitrogen to the lawn or use a root feeder.

Watering

In arid climates walnuts need deep-watering occasionally for the best nut production. If a tree is planted in a lawn, keep the grass cleared away from the trunk of the tree. Do not plant anything within 4 feet of a walnut's trunk. This is critical in western yards to prevent crown rot.

Pruning

Do not prune black walnuts from late winter through spring, because they bleed heavily at this time. For further pruning instructions, see HICKORY.

Pests and Diseases

Squirrels and bluejays are usually the pests most seriously affecting home plantings of walnuts. Other possible problems are aphids, walnut husk fly, fall webworm, walnut husk maggot, and walnut caterpillar. To control the latter two pests, try *Bacillus thuringiensis.* Occasionally, malathion may be necessary on the others. Though aphids are seldom severe enough to threaten the tree and to require a spray, they are a nuisance because of the sticky substance they exude, which drips on anything below them. It is for this reason that you should avoid planting walnuts where they will overhang cars or patio furniture.

Harvesting

Harvest the nuts off the ground. Check daily to beat the squirrels. Persian walnuts usually fall from their husks; if the husks are still attached, remove them. In black walnuts the husk is usually still intact over the shell when it falls from the tree. Removing the husks will stain your hands, so use rubber gloves or, wearing heavy shoes, "stomp" the nuts and roll the nuts out of their husks. Some people even drive their cars over black walnuts and let the tires do the job! Cure the nuts in a cool, dry place for two to three weeks before storing.

How to Purchase

Forms and Sources

Buy bare-root trees from local nurseries or from mail-order firms in late winter or early spring, or buy trees in containers through the fall. The largest selection of grafted walnuts is available from (**26**). The International Tree Crops Institute's Kentucky branch carries many varieties of black walnut.

Pollinators

Walnut trees are monoecious—that is, they have male and female flowers on the same tree though often the two genders bloom at different times. Therefore, more than one variety of walnut should be planted for cross-pollination and a heavier yield. Most of the walnut species cross-pollinate.

Note: Some people are allergic to walnut pollen.

Varieties

BLACK WALNUTS

Black walnut can be planted from seed to produce a bearing tree in 4–5 years. 'Baughm No. 25', 'Elmer Myers', and 'Emma K' (all at **26**) have excellent flavor and very good cracking qualities.

BUTTERNUTS

'Kenworthy' and 'Mitchell' (both at **26**) yield good-size nuts of good flavor and good cracking characteristics.

PERSIAN WALNUTS

The Carpathian type of Persian walnut is a hardy type for the coldest Persian walnut climates and the East. A large selection is available from (**26**).

The following Carpathian varieties are very similar to each other in quality; they have good flavor and the nuts crack well: 'Ashworth', 'Colby', 'Fateley', 'Hansen' (a small tree, considered the best), 'Helmle', 'James', 'Lake', 'Merkel', and 'Somers'. Most are available from (**26**).

One of the best Persian walnuts for the colder areas of the West is 'Ambassador,' a smaller than usual walnut, 15–40 ft. and self-pollinating (**71**). 'Chicho', 'Ashley', 'Chandler', and 'Hartley' (the most commonly grown Persian walnut) are good for most areas of California. (**Readily Available**)

For the areas of the West with the mildest winters, plant 'Drummond', 'Payne', and 'Placentia'. (**Readily Available**)

Preserving

Store walnuts in a cool, dark place, or shell and freeze them.

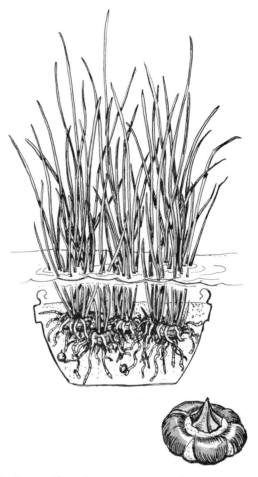

E.147. *For ease of harvesting, water chestnuts are best grown in containers submerged in a pool.*

Water Chestnut

(*CHINESE WATER CHESTNUT, SUI MATAI*)

Eleocharis dulcis

Effort Scale

NO. 2
Necessary to send away for corms
Winter protection and storage necessary

Zones

7–10, and Hawaii

Thumbnail Sketch

Herbaceous corm
1–3 ft. tall
Propagated from offsets
Needs full sun
Leaves are rushlike, tubular, narrow
Flowers are usually not seen; straw-colored spikelet, not showy
Corms are edible; harvested in fall
Used in bog gardens, pools, large water containers

How to Use

In the Kitchen

The corm, or tuber, of the water chestnut plant provides the crisp, crunchy texture enjoyed in many stir-fried Oriental dishes. Fresh water chestnuts are crisper, nuttier, and sweeter than the canned ones most of us know. The difference between a fresh and canned water chestnut is as great as that between fresh and canned orange juice. Besides their use in stir-fried dishes, water chestnuts can be added to salads; they are exceptional in a meat or chicken salad, where their texture is a welcome contrast. They can also be added to sauces, soups, or stews just before serving. And a water chestnut, wrapped in a slice of bacon and broiled, is a favorite hors d'oeuvre.

In the Landscape

The water chestnut is a bog plant, but it can be grown in ornamental pools and freestanding or sunken tubs. The grassy, rushlike stems are stiff and narrow, 1½–3 feet high. They go well with edible lotus, the edible violet-stemmed taro, and water lilies. If you have a bog, or if you are interested in water gardening, consider using this delectable plant.

How to Grow

Water chestnuts are not hardy, but if given winter protection where necessary they can be grown in many areas of the United States. They are planted in large plastic containers filled with ordinary topsoil and submerged in a pond or a shallow pool. A 25-gallon container holds 20–30 chestnuts, a good amount to start with. Make sure the water level in the tub remains at least an inch above soil level. No pruning is necessary. Use a type of fertilizer recommended for water plants or use well-balanced, time-release granules. Water chestnuts have few pests and diseases. They are very easy to grow and mature in six months.

To harvest, lift the containers out of water when foliage dies. Remove whole plants from the container. Wash the mud off and harvest the chestnuts, putting some of them aside for next year's crop. Place these corms back in the container with fresh soil. Keep them moist throughout the winter in a dark, cool place until spring. In areas where corms will not freeze, return them to the garden immediately.

Note: See Lotus for more details on water gardening.

How to Purchase

Water chestnuts are readily available in Chinese grocery stores, but my experience has shown that these corms frequently do not sprout. They probably have been sprayed with a growth-inhibiting hormone. The safest way to get viable corms is to order them in the spring from (**66**).

Preserving

To preserve chestnuts, store them in damp sand for a few months or peel and freeze them.

WATERMELON. See *Cucumber, Squash,* and *Melon.*

WESTERN SAND CHERRY. See *Plums, Bush.*

WILD MARJORAM. See *Oregano.*

Wild Rice (INDIAN RICE)

Zizania aquatica

Effort Scale

NO. 2
Harvesting and hulling are time-consuming
Wildlife compete for harvest

Zones

4–9

Thumbnail Sketch

Large annual aquatic grass
3–10 ft. tall
Propagated from seeds
Needs full sun
Leaves are grasslike, to 10 ft. long
Flowers are spikelets, not showy
Seeds are edible; harvested in fall
Used in streamside gardens

How to Use

In the Kitchen

The exotic flavor of this grain, as well as the cost in the market, makes it a gourmet favorite. It is served as a potato substitute that requires only the lightest seasoning—a little salt and pepper and a dab of butter. Adding mushrooms or snow peas makes wild rice even more elegant, but in a way is like setting diamonds, rubies, and emeralds all in one ring. The hulled seeds can be eaten as a snack raw, but that probably only occurs in Minnesota, where it is chiefly grown and the price is not prohibitive.

In the Landscape

This herbaceous water plant is limited to stream banks or the banks of large ponds and lakes that contain moving water. It grows as a tall grass, 3–10 feet tall, and its seed heads grow to 2 feet in length. Most of us do not have rivers or big lakes on our property, but if you have a likely stream meandering near your house you will enjoy watching this graceful grass and the waterfowl it attracts.

How to Grow

Wild rice will grow in most areas of the United States. It is most common in the northern tier of states, from Maine to Idaho, and along the East Coast as far south as Florida and Louisiana. The main constraint is that it must grow in bodies of moving water that are at least 1 foot but no deeper than 6 feet deep. The water cannot be stagnant, but must have a slow current, and the water level should be constant.

Plant rice in late fall or early spring, and harvest in early fall. Most varieties ripen over a 10-day period. An easy harvest method is to travel by canoe among the plants, letting the seed heads lean over the boat and then striking the seed heads with a stick.

Hull seeds by putting them in a sack and beating it or stepping on it. Shake rice in a basket in front of a fan to remove the hulls from the rice.

How to Purchase

Seeds may be obtained from (**70**) and H. G. Hastings, Box 4088, Atlanta, GA 30302.

Rice reseeds itself each fall. Do not try to sprout store-bought wild rice, as only unhulled rice will sprout.

Preserving

Hulled rice can be stored in airtight containers in a cool place, or frozen.

E.148. Harvesting wild rice from a canoe.

PART THREE

RESOURCES AND REFERENCES

A COMPREHENSIVE CHECKLIST OF EDIBLE SPECIES

Perennials Planted for Food

COMMON NAME	LATIN NAME	SOURCES†	ZONES	EDIBLE PART	LANDSCAPING CONSIDERATIONS
*Almond	*Prunus dulcis* var. *dulcis*	E	6–9	Nut	Medium-size deciduous tree; to 30 ft. White or pink showy flowers. Semi-dwarf and dwarf available. Use for interest and shade.
*Apple	*Malus* species	E	3–9	Fruit	Medium-size deciduous tree; to 30 ft. White to pinkish flowers. Comes in many sizes. Use for interest and shade.
*Apricot	*Prunus Armeniaca*	E	5–9	Fruit	Medium-size deciduous tree; to 25 ft. White or pink flowers; bronzy new growth. Dwarf available. Use for interest and shade.
*Artichoke	*Cynara Scolymus*	E	8, 9	Flower bud	Tall herbaceous perennial; to 5 ft. Striking gray foliage. Flowers are lavender thistles. Use in herbaceous borders.
*Asparagus	*Asparagus officinalis*	E	4–9	Shoot	Herbaceous perennial; to 5 ft. Small, fine-textured foliage. Use as background for herbaceous border.
*Avocado	*Persea americana*	E	10, Hawaii	Fruit	Large evergreen tree; to 40 ft. Dwarf available. Handsome foliage. Good shade tree.
Azarole	*Crataegus Azarolus*	s, 32	7–9	Fruit	Deciduous 30-ft. ornamental tree. Attractive foliage, white flowers, yellow or red fruits.
*Bamboo	*Bambusa* and *Phyllostachys* species	E	7–10, Hawaii	Shoot	Large perennial grasses; to 60 ft.; most smaller. Decorative form. Use as hedge or interest plant.
*Banana	*Musa* species	E	10, Hawaii	Fruit	Tall herbaceous perennial; to 25 ft. Large dramatic leaves. Use as interest plant or in atrium.
*Bitter melon	*Momordica Charantia*	E	5–10	Fruit, leaf	Perennial or annual large vine; to 20 ft. Decorative leaves and fruit. Use on arbors and fences.
*Blueberry and huckleberry	*Vaccinium* species	E	3–9	Fruit	Deciduous shrubs; to 18 ft.; most types shorter. White flowers, colorful fall foliage. Use as hedge, interest plant, and in containers.
*Brambleberry	*Rubus* species	E	3–9	Fruit	Deciduous thorny cane plants; 5–25 ft. Attractive white flowers. Use as barrier and fence plants.

* Starred items are included in the Encyclopedia.
s Indicates available in seed form only; numbers refer to sources listed in Appendix B.
E Sources noted in Encyclopedia.

Perennials (CONTINUED)

COMMON NAME	LATIN NAME	SOURCES†	ZONES	EDIBLE PART	LANDSCAPING CONSIDERATIONS
Breadfruit	*Artocarpus altilis*	Locally available	10, Hawaii	Fruit	Evergreen tree; to 60 ft. Striking cut-leaf foliage. Use for shade, interest.
*Butternut	*Juglans cinerea*	E	3–9	Nut	Deciduous tree; to 80 ft. Use as shade tree.
*Calamondin	*Citrus reticulata* x *Fortunella* sp. *mitis*	E	8–10, Hawaii	Fruit	Small (to 20 ft.) evergreen tree. Handsome foliage, colorful fruits. Use as hedge and interest plant.
Carambola	*Averrhoa Carambola*	Locally available	10, Hawaii	Fruit	Evergreen tropical ornamental tree; to 30 ft. Yellow fruits large and decorative. Use as shade and interest tree.
Cardoon	*Cynara cardunculus*	16, 32	6–9	Stalk	Large herbaceous perennial; to 8 ft. Gray handsome foliage. Blanching process unattractive. Use as background for herbaceous border. Often grown as an annual. Can become a weed in mild winter areas.
*Carob	*Ceratonia Siliqua*	E	9, 10	Pod	Large shrubby evergreen tree; to 40 ft. Handsome foliage and form. Use as screen and interest tree. Roots invasive.
Chayote	*Sechium edule*	Buy fruit from produce market	9, 10	Shoot, seed, and fruit	Large herbaceous vine; to 40 ft. Use to cover large arbors. Plant more than one to ensure pollination.
Cherimoya	*Annona Cherimola*	s, 19	10, Hawaii	Fruit	Medium-size shrubby evergreen tree; to 25 ft. Velvety large leaves. Use as interest plant and screen.
*Cherry, sour	*Prunus Cerasus*	E	4–9	Fruit	Small deciduous tree; to 20 ft. Showy white flowers. Use as interest plant.
*Cherry, sweet	*Prunus avium*	E	5–9	Fruit	Medium-size deciduous tree; to 35 ft. Showy white flowers. Use as interest or shade tree. Dwarf available; use as shrub.
*Chestnut	*Castanea* species	E	5–9	Nut	Large spreading deciduous trees; to 100 ft. White, showy flowers, decorative burrs. Use as shade and interest trees.
Coconut	*Cocos nucifera*	Locally available	10, Hawaii	Nut	Graceful palm tree; to 80 ft. Use as interest tree in areas where falling nuts will not cause damage.
*Crabapple	*Malus* species	E	3–9	Fruit	Medium-size deciduous tree; to 25 ft. Showy white to pinkish flowers. Use as interest and shade tree.
*Cranberry	*Vaccinium macrocarpon*	E	3–8	Fruit	Low-growing evergreen vine; to 1 ft. White flowers, showy red fruit. Use as ground cover.
*Currant	*Ribes sativum*	E	3–8	Fruit	Deciduous shrub; to 5 ft. Showy red fruit. Use as foundation plant and in shrub borders.
Date	*Phoenix dactylifera*	s, 19, 51, 55	10	Fruit	Handsome palm tree; to 100 ft. Use as interest and shade tree.
*Elderberry	*Sambucus* species	E	2–9	Fruit	Deciduous shrubs; to 3 ft. Showy white flower clusters. Use as screen and background shrub. Some species are very weedy.
*Fig	*Ficus carica*	E	8–10, Hawaii	Fruit	Dramatic deciduous tree; to 30 ft.; semidwarf available. Use as shade and interest tree.

Perennials (CONTINUED)

COMMON NAME	LATIN NAME	SOURCES†	ZONES	EDIBLE PART	LANDSCAPING CONSIDERATIONS
*Filbert	*Corylus Avellana*	E	4–8	Nut	Large deciduous shrub or tree; to 25 ft. Handsome foliage and seed covering. Use as hedge, multistemmed interest tree.
*Gooseberry	*Ribes* species	E	3–8	Fruit	Deciduous shrub; to 5 ft. Attractive foliage. Use as foundation plant and in shady shrub borders, pendulous types to drape over retaining walls.
*Grape, American	*Vitis Labrusca*	E	4–9	Fruit	Woody deciduous vine; to 50 ft. Handsome foliage. Use on arbors and fences.
*Grape, European	*Vitis vinifera*	E	5–9	Fruit	Woody deciduous vine; to 50 ft. Handsome foliage. Use on arbors and fences, and as small weeping trees.
*Grape, Muscadine	*Vitis rotundifolia*	E	7–9	Fruit	Woody deciduous vine; to 50 ft. Handsome foliage. Use on arbors and fences.
*Grapefruit	*Citrus x paradisi*	E	10, Hawaii	Fruit	Evergreen tree; to 40 ft.; dwarf available. Use for hedge and interest.
Guava, Chilean	*Ugni Molinae*	s, 51	9, 10	Fruit	Small-leaved ornamental evergreen shrub; to 6 ft. Small lily of the valley–type white flowers, bronzy new growth. Use as foundation shrub, in containers, and in shady shrub borders.
Guava, common	*Psidium Guajava*	s, 19, 32, 51	10, Hawaii	Fruit	Medium-size tree; to 30 ft. Use as shade tree and hedge.
*Guava, pineapple	*Feijoa Sellowiana*	E	9, 10, Hawaii	Fruit	Large evergreen shrub or small tree; to 18 ft. Gray foliage, showy dark red flowers. Use as multistemmed interest tree, screen, and hedge.
Guava, strawberry	*Psidium littorale*	s, 19, 32	10, Hawaii	Fruit	Evergreen shrub or small tree; to 25 ft. White flowers, deep red fruit. Use as hedge or multistemmed tree.
*Hickory	*Carya* species	E	5–9	Nut	Deciduous trees; to 120 ft. Trunk and foliage attractive. Use as shade and interest tree.
*Hops	*Humulus Lupulus*	E	4–10	Flower, shoot	Large (to 25 ft.), deciduous, herbaceous vine. Use on arbors and trellises.
*Jerusalem artichoke	*Helianthus tuberosus*	E	2–9	Tuber	Herbaceous perennial; to 10 ft. Showy yellow flowers. Use as screen and background for large flower borders. Can become a weed.
Jicama (Mexican potato)	*Pachyrhizus tuberosus*	s, 19, 28, 31, 51, 63, or buy tubers in grocery store.	9, 10	Tuber	Large herbaceous perennial vine; to 20 ft. Handsome foliage, white or purple flowers; but should not be allowed to bloom. Use on arbors and fences and in large containers. Seeds are poisonous.
*Jujube	*Ziziphus Jujuba*	E	6–10	Fruit	Deciduous semiweeping tree; to 30 ft. Attractive shiny foliage. Suckering can be a problem. Use as shade and interest tree.
*Kiwi (Kiwifruit)	*Actinidia chinensis*	E	9, 10	Fruit	Deciduous, woody vine; to 30 ft. Attractive foliage; showy, cream-colored flowers. Use on arbors and fences.

Perennials (CONTINUED)

COMMON NAME	LATIN NAME	SOURCES†	ZONES	EDIBLE PART	LANDSCAPING CONSIDERATIONS
*Kumquat	*Fortunella* species	E	9, 10, Hawaii	Fruit	Small evergreen tree; to 25 ft.; dwarf available. Attractive foliage and fruit. Use as hedge, interest tree or shrub.
*Lemon	*Citrus Limon*	E	9, 10, Hawaii	Fruit	Small evergreen tree; to 20 ft.; dwarf available. Attractive foliage and fruit. Use as hedge, interest tree or shrub.
*Lime	*Citrus aurantiifolia*	E	10, Hawaii	Fruit	Small evergreen tree; to 20 ft.; dwarf available. Attractive foliage and fruit. Use as hedge, interest tree or shrub.
*Limequat	*Citrus aurantiifolia* 'Eustis' x *Fortunella margarita*	E	9, 10, Hawaii	Fruit	Small shrublike evergreen tree; dwarf available. Attractive foliage and fruit. Use as hedge, interest tree or shrub.
Lingonberry (mountain cranberry)	*Vaccinium Vitis-idaea* var. *minus*	s, 32	6–9	Fruit	Evergreen shrub; to 1 ft. Dark green leaves, showy red fruits. Use as ground cover.
Litchi	*Litchi chinensis*	Locally available	10, Hawaii	Fruit	Evergreen tree; to 40 ft. Handsome foliage and red fruit clusters. Use as interest and shade tree.
*Loquat	*Eriobotrya japonica*	E	8–10	Fruit	Handsome evergreen tree; to 25 ft. Beautiful woolly foliage and colorful orange fruits. Dramatic form. Use for shade and interest.
*Lotus	*Nelumbo nucifera*	E	5–10, Hawaii	Rhizome, seed, leaf	Large herbaceous water plant. Dramatic leaves to 3 ft. wide; pink flowers 12 in. across. Use in pools and water containers.
Macadamia (Queensland nut)	*Macadamia* species	s, 19, 55	10, Hawaii	Nut	Large spreading evergreen tree with handsome foliage; to 50 ft. Use as shade tree.
*Mandarin orange	*Citrus reticulata*	E	9, 10, Hawaii	Fruit	Small evergreen tree; dwarf available. Attractive foliage and fruit. Use as hedge, screen, interest tree or shrub.
*Mango	*Mangifera indica*	E	10, Hawaii	Fruit	Striking evergreen tree; to 50 ft. Fruits colorful. Use as shade tree, screen, and interest plant.
*Maple	*Acer* species	E	3–6	Sap	Large deciduous, graceful trees; to 100 ft. Dramatic fall foliage. Use as street and shade tree.
Medlar	*Mespilus germanica*	s, 32, 55; plants, 57	6–9	Fruit	Small deciduous tree; to 20 ft. Handsome large foliage, white flowers. Use as shade or interest tree.
*Mulberry, black	*Morus nigra*	E	5–10	Fruit	Medium-size deciduous tree; to 30 ft. Use limited to background plant and screen.
*Mulberry	*Morus* species	E	5–10	Fruit	Medium-size deciduous trees; to 30 ft. Use limited to background plant and screen.
*Mulberry, white	*Morus alba* 'Pendula'	E	5–10	Fruit	Weeping deciduous tree; 6–8 ft. tall. Dramatic form. Variable fruit quality. Use as accent or interest plant.
*Natal plum	*Carissa grandiflora*	E	10, Hawaii	Fruit	Evergreen shrub; to 18 ft. Handsome foliage and white flowers, showy fruits. Use as hedge, interest plant, and ground cover.

Perennials (CONTINUED)

COMMON NAME	LATIN NAME	SOURCES†	ZONES	EDIBLE PART	LANDSCAPING CONSIDERATIONS
*Nectarine	*Prunus Persica* var. *nucipersica*	E	5–9	Fruit	Small deciduous tree; to 20 ft.; dwarf available. Some varieties have showy pink flowers. Use as background tree or interest shrub.
*Olive	*Olea europaea*	E	9, 10	Fruit	Medium-size evergreen tree; to 30 ft. Gray foliage, interesting gnarled shape. Use as interest multistemmed tree, screen, or large shrub.
*Orange	*Citrus sinensis*	E	9, 10, Hawaii	Fruit	Attractive evergreen tree; to 30 ft.; dwarf available. Decorative fruit. Use as hedge, screen, interest tree or shrub.
Papaya	*Carica Papaya*	s, 19, 32, 51	10, Hawaii	Fruit	Evergreen tree; to 25 ft.; dwarf available. Large palmate leaves 2 ft. across. Awkward form. Landscaping use limited to background.
Passion fruit (Granadilla)	*Passiflora* species	s, 19, 32, 51	10, Hawaii	Fruit	Large twining evergreen vine. Attractive foliage and some have showy flowers. Can be used on fences and arbors.
*Pawpaw	*Asimina triloba*	E	4–9	Fruit	Deciduous tree or shrub; to 25 ft. Interesting pyramid shape; attractive foliage. Use as small tree and interest plant.
*Peach	*Prunus Persica*	E	5–9	Fruit	Small deciduous tree; to 20 ft.; dwarf sizes available. Some varieties have showy pink flowers. Use as background tree or interest shrub.
*Pear, common	*Pyrus communis*	E	4–9	Fruit	Medium-size deciduous tree; to 25 ft.; dwarf sizes available. Showy white flowers. Upright form. Use as shade and interest tree or shrub.
*Pear, Oriental	*Pyrus pyrifolia*	E	5–9	Fruit	Medium-size deciduous tree; to 40 ft., with upright growth. Showy white flowers. Use as shade and interest tree.
*Pecan	*Carya illinoinensis*	E	6–9	Nut	Large deciduous tree; to 100 ft. Use as shade or street tree.
*Persimmon, American	*Diospyros virginiana*	E	5–9	Fruit	Deciduous tree or shrub; to 40 ft. Attractive foliage and fruit. Use as shade tree, large shrub, and interest plant.
*Persimmon, Oriental	*Diospyros Kaki*	E	6–10	Fruit	Deciduous tree or shrub; to 40 ft. Attractive red-orange foliage and fruit. Use as shade tree and interest plant.
Pineapple	*Ananas comosus*	39; or start from grocery store fruits	10, Hawaii	Fruit	Herbaceous perennial; 3–4 ft. tall. Leaves in rosettes. Used in hobby gardens clustered with bromeliads. Limited use.
*Pine nut (Pignola or piñon)	*Pinus* species	E	3–10	Seed	Needled evergreen trees; size varies with species from 10–100 ft. Use as interest plants, shade trees, windbreaks.
*Pistachio	*Pistacia vera*	E	7–9	Nut	Deciduous tree; female to 30 ft., male taller. Limited use. Screen or street tree.
*Plantain	*Musa* species	E	10, Hawaii	Fruit	Tall (to 25 ft.), herbaceous perennial. Large dramatic leaves. Use as interest plant or in an atrium.

Perennials (CONTINUED)

COMMON NAME	LATIN NAME	SOURCES†	ZONES	EDIBLE PART	LANDSCAPING CONSIDERATIONS
*Plum, beach	*Prunus maritima*	E	5–7	Fruit	Deciduous shrub or small tree; to 10 ft. Showy white flowers. Use for beach planting, interest plant, hedge.
*Plum, bush (Nanking and Western sand plums)	*Prunus* species	E	3–5	Fruit	Small deciduous shrub; to 6 ft. Showy white flowers. Use as hedge, foundation, and interest plant.
*Plum, European and prune	*Prunus domestica*	E	4–9	Fruit	Medium-size deciduous tree; to 20 ft.; dwarf available. Showy white flowers. Upright form. Use as screen or interest plant.
*Plum, Japanese	*Prunus salicina*	E	6–9	Fruit	Medium-size deciduous tree; to 20 ft.; dwarf available. Upright form. Showy white flowers. Use as screen or interest plant.
*Pomegranate	*Punica granatum*	E	9, 10	Fruit	Deciduous shrub or small tree; to 20 ft. Leaves have bronzy new growth, turn yellow in fall; flowers red and showy. Use as multistemmed tree, large shrub, and interest plant.
*Pomelo (shaddock)	*Citrus maxima*	E	9, 10, Hawaii	Fruit	Rounded evergreen tree; to 30 ft. Attractive foliage and decorative fruit. Use as screen and interest plant.
*Prickly pear	*Opuntia* and *Nopalea* species	E	6–10, Hawaii	Fruit, pad	Large cacti; to 15 ft. Thorny pads. Flowers orange or yellow, showy. Use as interest or barrier plants.
*Quince	*Cydonia oblonga*	E	5–9	Fruit	Small deciduous tree; to 20 ft. Pale pink showy flowers. Use as interest tree or shrub, screen.
*Rhubarb	*Rheum Rhabarbarum*	E	1–9	Stalk	Perennial herb; to 5 ft. tall. Large dramatic leaves and red stems. Use as interest plant in herbaceous borders.
*Rose hips	*Rosa* species	E	2–9	Hips	Deciduous shrub to 8 ft. Lovely crinkled leaves; showy white, red, or pink flowers. Can get invasive. Use as barrier, hedge, and interest plant.
*Salal	*Gaultheria Shallon*	E	6–9	Fruit	Evergreen shrub; to 6 ft. Small leaves, attractive white to pink flowers. Use as hedge or in shrub border.
Sapote	*Casimiroa edulis*	s, 19	10	Fruit	Large evergreen tree; to 50 ft. Use as shade tree and screen.
*Sea grape	*Coccoloba Uvifera*	E	10, Hawaii	Fruit	Small evergreen tree or shrub; to 20 ft. Large decorative leaves and attractive fruit. Use as windbreak, in seaside gardens, as hedge and interest tree.
*Sorrel	*Rumex* species	E	5–9	Leaf	Small herbaceous plant; to 3 ft. Upright growth. Use for herb gardens and perennial borders. Can become a weed.
*Strawberry	*Fragaria* species	E	3–10	Fruit	Herbaceous perennials; most have runners; 9 in. tall. Handsome foliage, decorative fruit. Use in flower beds and as ground cover.
Strawberry tree	*Arbutus Unedo*	s, 19, 32, 52; plants, 39	8, 9	Fruit	Lovely evergreen tree; to 30 ft. Attractive pinkish flowers, showy orange and scarlet fruits of variable quality. Use as screen, multistemmed tree, and interest plant.

Perennials (CONTINUED)

COMMON NAME	LATIN NAME	SOURCES†	ZONES	EDIBLE PART	LANDSCAPING CONSIDERATIONS
*Surinam cherry (pitanga)	Eugenia uniflora	E	10, Hawaii	Fruit	Shrub or small tree; to 15 ft. Showy red or yellow fruits. Use as hedge, screen, multistemmed interest plant.
Tamarind	Tamarindus indica	s, 19, 32	10, Hawaii	Pod	Evergreen tree; to 80 ft. Ornamental pinnate leaves and yellow flowers. Shade tree.
*Tangelo	Citrus paradisi x Citrus reticulata	E	9, 10	Fruit	Evergreen tree or shrub; to 30 ft. Attractive foliage, colorful fruit. Use as screen, hedge, interest plant.
*Tea	Camellia sinensis	E	8–10	Leaf	Variable-size (to 15 ft.) evergreen shrub or tree. Shiny green foliage, showy white flowers. Use as hedge, interest plant.
Tree tomato	Cyphomandra betacea	s, 19, 32	10	Fruit	Evergreen shrub or small tree; to 10 ft. Large leaves, colorful fruits. Awkward form. Landscape use limited.
*Walnut	Juglans species	E	3–9	Nut	Large deciduous tree; to 80 ft. Use as shade and street tree.
*Water chestnut	Eleocharis dulcis	E	7–10, Hawaii	Corm	Herbaceous reed-like water plant; to 3 ft. tall. Use in pools and water containers.

Herbs, Spices, and Condiments—Perennials

COMMON NAME	LATIN NAME	SOURCES†	HARDINESS	EDIBLE PART	LANDSCAPING CONSIDERATIONS
Angelica	Angelica Archangelica	s, 32, 47, 48, 54	Hardy	Stem	Tall, tropical-looking plant; to 6 ft. Compound green leaves, white flowers in large umbels. Biennial or perennial plant. Use as background in herb garden or flower bed.
*Bay, California	Umbellularia californica	E	Tender	Leaf	Large evergreen tree; to 80 ft. Small leaves, bushy form. Use as street or shade tree.
*Bay, sweet	Laurus nobilis	E	Moderately hardy	Leaf	Evergreen tree or shrub; to 40 ft. Glossy green leaves. Use as hedge, shrub, or small tree.
Bee balm	Monarda didyma	s, 32, 47, 51, 54	Hardy	Leaf	Upright, bushy plant; 3–4 ft. tall. Showy red, pink, or lavender flowers. Use in herb and flower gardens.
Burnet	Poterium sanguisorba	s, 32, 47, 51, 54	Hardy	Leaf	Decorative small plant; to 18 in. Leaves grow in a rosette; pinkish flowers. Use in herb and flower gardens. Can become a weed.
*Caper	Capparis spinosa	E	Tender	Flower bud	Sprawling, large shrub; to 5 ft. Roundish leaves; flowers white with showy pink or lavender stamens. Use in large rock gardens and on dry banks.

Perennial Herbs (CONTINUED)

COMMON NAME	LATIN NAME	SOURCES†	HARDINESS	EDIBLE PART	LANDSCAPING CONSIDERATIONS
Catnip	*Nepeta Cataria*	Readily available	Hardy	Leaf	Medium-size, spreading plant; to 3 ft. Gray-green leaves, lavender flowers. Pretty in herb gardens, but attracts neighborhood cats to come roll in your garden.
*Chamomile, Roman	*Chamaemelum nobile*	E	Hardy	Flower	Low-growing, spreading mat; to 12 in. Fine cut leaves; small, buttonlike yellow flowers. Can be used as ground cover and in rock gardens.
Chicory	*Cichorium Intybus*	s, 32, 48, 51, 54	Hardy	Leaf and root	Tall, rangy, gray-green leafed plant; to 4 ft. Blue dandelionlike flowers. Use in back of flower gardens. Can become a weed.
*Chive	*Allium* species	E	Hardy	Leaf	Tubular, grasslike leaves in clumps; to 2 ft. Attractive, cloverlike lavender or white flowers. Use in herb garden or flower border.
Comfrey, Russian	*Symphytum peregrinum*	24, 28, 51	Hardy	Leaf	Large attractive leafed plant; to 3 ft. Use in herb garden.
Costmary	*Chrysanthemum Balsamita*	s, 54	Hardy	Leaf	Straggly plant; to 3 ft. Gray-green leaves, tiny yellow flowers. Keep trimmed; use in herb garden. Will spread.
Geranium	*Pelargonium* species	s, 32, 48	Tender	Leaf	Variable plants—some upright, some vining; some have gray-green leaves, others have variegated ones. Flowers red, pink, or lavender. Use in herb gardens.
Horehound	*Marrubium vulgare*	s, 32, 48, 51, 52, 54	Semi-hardy	Leaf	Small, gray, round, fuzzy-leafed plant; to 18 in. Small white flowers. Can look rangy. Use in herb gardens.
Horseradish	*Armoracia rusticana*	Readily available	Hardy	Root	Stout, wavy-edged, leafed plant; to 15 in. Not particularly attractive; can get weedy. Landscaping use limited.
Lemon balm	*Melissa officinalis*	s, 32, 47, 54	Hardy	Leaf	Erect plant; to 2 ft. Mintlike leaves, flowers insignificant. Use in herb gardens.
Licorice	*Glycyrrhiza glabra*	s, 32	Tender	Root	Medium-size, upright-growing plant; to 3 ft. Attractive small, cut leaves; small light blue, pealike flowers. Use in herb gardens.
Lovage	*Levisticum officinale*	Readily available	Hardy	Leaf	Large, upright plant; to 6 ft. Celerylike leaves, yellow flowers in umbels. Ornamental; good for back of herb gardens.
*Marjoram	*Origanum Majorana*	E	Semi-hardy	Leaf	Short plant; to 2 ft. Tiny gray-green leaves, small white flowers. Use in herb gardens.
*Mint	*Mentha* species	E	Most are hardy	Leaf	Most mints are erect, medium-size plants ½–3 ft. tall, with crinkled leaves, white or lavender flowers. One variety with a creeping mat form is good for ground cover. Use upright forms in herb gardens. Can become invasive.
*Oregano	*Origanum vulgare*	E	Hardy	Leaf	Upright plant; to 2½ ft. Medium-size, gray-green leaves; lavender flowers. Use in herb gardens.
*Rosemary	*Rosmarinus officinalis*	E	Semi-hardy	Leaf	Evergreen shrub with gray-green needlelike leaves. Different varieties have different shapes, from erect, 6 ft. tall to ground hugging. Showy blue flowers on some varieties. Use on dry banks and in herb gardens.

Perennial Herbs (CONTINUED)

COMMON NAME	LATIN NAME	SOURCES†	HARDINESS	EDIBLE PART	LANDSCAPING CONSIDERATIONS
*Saffron	*Crocus sativus*	E	Hardy	Stigma	Small grasslike foliage; to 4 in. Large mauve flowers. Use in rock garden, flower border, and herb garden.
*Sage	*Salvia* species	E	Varied	Leaf	Small, shrubby plants; to 2–3½ ft. Most with gray-green leaves, red or blue flowers. Use in herb garden or flower garden.
Savory, winter	*Satureja montana*	Readily available	Hardy	Leaf	Small, erect, green-leafed shrub; to 12 in. Small white flowers. Use in herb gardens.
Sweet woodruff	*Galium odoratum*	s, 47, 48, 54	Hardy	Leaf	Ornamental low-growing plant; to 12 in. Lovely deep green leaves, clusters of tiny white flowers. Use as ground cover in shady places.
Tarragon, French	*Artemisia dracunculus*	47	Tender	Leaf	Creeping narrow-leafed plant; to 2 ft. Use in herb garden. Preferred French variety only available as cuttings, not seed, from (**47**).
*Thyme	*Thymus* species	E	Hardy	Leaf	A number of very small-leafed plants; to 15 in. Various foliage colors—yellow, variegated, silver, green. Use as ground covers and in herb gardens.
Turmeric	*Curcuma domestica*	Specialty produce markets	Tender	Rhizome	Rhizomatous, tropical-looking plant; to 1½ ft. Attractive leaves. Use in shady borders and containers.
Wintergreen	*Gaultheria procumbens*	s, 55	Hardy	Leaf, berry	Ornamental creeping plant; 6 in. tall. Dark green, shiny leaves; white flowers and scarlet berries. Use as ground cover in shade.

Annuals, and Perennials Commonly Treated as Annuals, Planted for Food

COMMON NAME	LATIN NAME	SOURCES†	EDIBLE PART	LANDSCAPING CONSIDERATIONS
Amaranth (Chinese spinach)	*Amaranthus gangeticus*	s, 32, 48, 51, 64	Leaf	Tall, upright, succulent green- or red-leafed plant; to 3 ft. Cloverlike blossoms. Ornamental plant. Use in the background of perennial borders.
Asparagus bean (Chinese yard-long bean)	*Vigna sinensis sesquipedalis*	s, 28, 38, 51, 64,	Pod	Tall, vining plant with medium green leaves. Insignificant flowers. Very long beans, to 3 ft. Limited landscape use; can be used on trellises.
Asparagus pea (Goa bean or winged bean)	*Lotus tetragonolobus*	s, 48, 63	Pod	Short twining herb; to 1 ft. Beanlike bright red flowers. Attractive plant. Use in hanging baskets and in front of flower beds.
Bean, fava (broad bean)	*Vicia Faba*	s, 32, 35, 51, 63, 67	Leaf, seed	Erect plant; to 6 ft. Gray-green leaves, fragrant white flowers. Dwarf available. Attractive plant, but can get straggly. Use in back of flower borders.

Annuals, and Perennials Commonly Treated as Annuals (CONTINUED)

COMMON NAME	LATIN NAME	SOURCES†	EDIBLE PART	LANDSCAPING CONSIDERATIONS
Bean, garbanzo (chick pea)	*Cicer arietinum*	32	Seed	Bushy plant; to 2 ft. Undistinguished. Limited landscape use.
*Bean, green snap (bush)	*Phaseolus vulgaris humilis*	E	Pod	Small, (to 2 ft.) open, bushy plant. White or purple leguminous flowers. Some varieties are more ornamental than others. Purple varieties are attractive in flower borders.
*Bean, green snap, kidney, pinto, romano, and wax (pole)	*Phaseolus vulgaris*	E	Pod, seed	Vining plant; to 6 ft. Most varieties have small white flowers; some have large white or purple flowers. Some varieties have decorative red, yellow, or purple pods. Use decorative varieties on arbors, fences, and trellises.
*Bean, hyacinth (Bonavista bean)	*Dolichos Lablab*	E	Pod, seed	Large woody climber; to 20 ft. Attractive purple flowers and pods. Use on arbors and trellises.
Bean, lima (bush)	*Phaseolus limensis* var. *limenanus*	Readily available	Seed	Small, bushy plant; to 2 ft. Undistinguished. Use limited in landscape.
Bean, lima (pole)	*Phaseolus limensis*	Readily available	Seed	Vigorous vine; to 6 ft. Undistinguished. Use on trellis or screen for color, interplant with morning glories.
Bean, mung	*Vigna radiata*	s, 20, 32, 35, 43, 63	Seed	Hairy bushy plant; to 3 ft. Small, purplish-yellow flowers. Undistinguished. Limited landscape use.
*Bean, runner	*Phaseolus coccineus*	E	Pod, seed	Tall, twining vine; to 10 ft. Showy red or white leguminous flowers. Decorative on fences, arbors, and trellises.
Bean, soy	*Glycine Max*	Readily available	Seed	Hairy; grows 1–6 ft. Undistinguished. Limited landscape use.
Beet	*Beta vulgaris*	Readily available	Leaf, root	Short (to 18 in.) herbaceous plant with red-veined green leaves. Yellow and white varieties available. Attractive, but hard to use in a landscape. Harvested beets leave empty spaces; try interplanting with flowering annuals to cover the holes after harvest.
Black-eyed pea (cow pea)	*Vigna unguiculata*	Readily available	Seed	Small bushy plant; to 3 ft. Undistinguished. Limited landscape use.
Broccoli	*Brassica oleracea*—Botrytis Group	Readily available	Flower, stem	Short (to 2½ ft.), compact plant with gray-green leaves. Some varieties have purple flower buds. Somewhat decorative, but hard to keep looking neat. Limited landscape use. Use in containers.
Brussels sprouts	*Brassica oleracea*—Gemmifera Group	Readily available	Leaf	Awkward-looking, blue-green leafed plant; to 3 ft. Harvesting sprouts makes plant look scruffy. Limited landscape use.
Buckwheat	*Fagopyrum esculentum*	s, 35	Seed	Triangular-leafed plant; to 3 ft. Small clusters of fragrant white flowers. Landscape use limited. Use in informal yard adjacent to a meadow.
Burdock (gobo)	*Arctium Lappa*	32, 35, 38, 51	Leaf, root	Tall plant; to 8 ft. Leaves 20 in. long. Harvested primarily for its root; use in vegetable garden. Can become a weed.
*Cabbage	*Brassica oleracea*—Capatata Group	E	Leaf	Compact (to 2 ft.), large-leafed plant; grows in tight head. Gray or red foliage. Attractive form. Useful in flower beds and containers.
Cabbage, Chinese (Pe Tsai)	*Brassica Rapa*—Pekinensis Group		Leaf	Compact, glossy green plant; to 20 in. Growth similar to chard. Use in herbaceous borders with other greens.

Annuals, and Perennials Commonly Treated as Annuals (CONTINUED)

COMMON NAME	LATIN NAME	SOURCES†	EDIBLE PART	LANDSCAPING CONSIDERATIONS
*Cantaloupe (melons)	*Cucumis* species	E	Fruit	Trailing vines, 5 ft. long; dwarf available. Attractive ivylike leaves. Dwarf varieties used in flower borders; vining types used on fences. Mildew can make them scruffy looking.
Carrot	*Daucus Carota* var. *sativus*	Readily available	Root	Graceful, ferny foliage; to 1 ft. Plant attractive, but hard to use in landscape. Harvested carrots leave empty spaces. Try in containers or interplant with violas or other flowering annuals.
Cauliflower	*Brassica oleracea—* Botrytis Group	Readily available	Flower	Short (to 2 ft.), compact plant with wide green leaves. Compact flower head forms a ball. Blanching of the head and its tendency to flop over makes its use limited in a landscape. Try in containers.
Celeriac	*Apium graveolens* var. *rapaceum*	Readily available	Swollen crown	Open plant; to 3 ft. Attractive pinnate leaves. Limited landscaping use. Harvesting leaves empty spaces. Use in containers or interplant with nasturtiums.
Celery	*Apium graveolens* var. *dulce*	Readily available	Leaf, stem	Upright plant; to 3 ft. Attractive bright green, pinnate leaves. Blanching and harvesting of individual stalks deforms plant. Use in the background or in containers.
*Chard, Swiss	*Beta vulgaris* var. *cicla*	E	Leaf	Handsome, large, foliage plant; to 18 in. Red-stemmed varieties very attractive. Use in flower beds.
Collard	*Brassica oleracea—* Acephala Group	Readily available	Leaf	Compact foliage plant; to 18 in. Use in landscape combined with other greens in herbaceous borders.
Corn (and popcorn)	*Zea Mays*	Readily available	Seed	Tall, broad-leafed grass; to 15 ft.; dwarf varieties available. Hard to use in a landscape; dwarf types have some possibilities as background plants in informal gardens.
Corn salad (lamb's lettuce)	*Valerianella Locusta*	s, 16, 32, 51, 56	Leaf	Compact foliage plant; to 1½ ft. tall. Use in landscape combined with lettuces in herbaceous borders.
*Cucumber (Armenian, bush, common, Oriental, and pickling)	*Cucumis sativus*	E	Fruit	Trailing vines with ivylike leaves; to 6 ft. Bush varieties available. Trailing types used on trellises and fences; bush types used in flower gardens.
Dandelion	*Taraxacum officinale*	Readily available	Leaf	Compact plant with long leaves; to 1 ft. Can be interplanted with greens in an herbaceous border. If it is to be blanched, it should be relegated to the vegetable garden. Can become a weed (surprise!).
*Eggplant	*Solanum Melongena* var. *esculentum*	E	Fruit	Compact bush to 3 ft. tall with fuzzy gray-green foliage; some varieties have purple stems. Handsome purple flowers and glossy purple or white fruit. Very ornamental. Use in herbaceous borders and herb gardens.
*Endive, chicory, curly, and escarole	*Cichorium* species	E	Leaf	Attractive, compact (to 2 ft. tall), foliage plants with large variety of foliage textures and colors. Use in herbaceous borders with other greens.
Fennel	*Foeniculum vulgare,* var. *azoricum*	Readily available	Leaf	Fernlike foliage; to 5 ft. Rounded clusters of yellow flowers. Use in back of herbaceous borders. Can become a weed.
Ground cherry (dwarf Cape gooseberry)	*Physalis pruinosa*	s, 32	Fruit	Sprawling, bushy plant; to 3 ft. Fruits have papery husks. Limited landscape use.

Annuals, and Perennials Commonly Treated as Annuals (CONTINUED)

COMMON NAME	LATIN NAME	SOURCES†	EDIBLE PART	LANDSCAPING CONSIDERATIONS
Huckleberry, garden	*Solanum melanocerasum*	s, 20, 28	Fruit	Undistinguished plant; to 2½ ft. Small white flowers and black berries. Rangy plant with limited landscaping use. Can become a weed.
Husk tomato (tomatillo)	*Physalis ixocarpa*	s, 19, 32, 51	Fruit	Upright plant; to 4 ft. Weak stemmed and tends to sprawl; needs staking. Landscaping use limited.
*Kale	*Brassica oleracea*— Acephala Group	E	Leaf	Compact (to 20 in.) plant with decorative foliage; pink and white ornamental varieties available. Use in herbaceous borders.
Kohlrabi	*Brassica oleracea*— Gongylodes Group	Readily available	Stem	Low (to 20 in. tall), leafy plant with bulbous stem. Some varieties have purple coloring. Landscaping use limited. Harvesting leaves empty spaces, and the form is awkward.
Leek	*Allium ampeloprasum* var. *porrum*	Readily available	Bulb, leaf	Narrow-leafed plant with handsome fanlike form. Landscaping use limited. Harvesting leaves empty spaces. Try containers or interplant with forget-me-nots or other flowering annuals.
Lentil	*Lens culinaris*	s, 32, 67	Seed	Many-branched open plant; to 1½ ft. tall. Interesting small pinnate foliage. Attractive, but tends to become sprawly. Limited landscaping use.
*Lettuce, curly, head, and romaine	*Lactuca sativa*	E	Leaf	Short, compact (6–12 in. tall), leafy plant; many textures and colors available. Use in herbaceous borders. Keep new plants coming to fill in harvested sections.
*Melon, casaba, honeydew	*Cucumis* species	E	Fruit	Trailing vines; to 5 ft. long; dwarf varieties available. Dwarf varieties used in flower borders; vining types used on fences. Attractive ivylike leaves. Mildew can make them scruffy.
*Mustard, black	*Brassica nigra*	E	Seed	Large, upright plant; to 6 ft. Bright yellow flowers. Attractive in a meadow garden. Can become a weed in confined situations.
*Mustard green	*Brassica juncea*	E	Leaf	Compact (to 18 in. tall), leafy plant with attractive foliage; numerous forms. Combine with greens in an herbaceous border.
Oat	*Avena sativa*	s, 35, health food stores	Seed	Tall grass; to 3 ft. Landscape use limited to informal yards adjacent to meadows.
*Okra (gumbo)	*Abelmoschus esculentus*	E	Pod	Tall, upright plant; to 6 ft.; dwarf varieties available. Large leaves and lovely hibiscus-type cream or yellow flowers. One variety has red stems. Use in herbaceous borders.
Onion, scallion, and shallot	*Allium Cepa*	Readily available	Bulb	Tubular, upright plant; to 18 in. Gray-green leaves. Limited landscaping use. Bulb types must die down before being harvested. Harvesting scallion types leaves empty spaces. Try in containers or interplanting with dwarf nasturtiums or marigolds.
Orach	*Atriplex hortensis*	s, 32, 51	Leaf	Tall, upright, showy plant; to 5 ft. Leaves usually green but can be bright red or yellow. Use in back of herbaceous borders.
Parsnip	*Pastinaca sativa*	Readily available	Root	Short (to 18 in.), clumping plant with cut leaves. Landscaping use limited. Harvesting leaves empty spaces; try containers or interplanting with flowering annuals.
Pea (bush)	*Pisum sativum*	Readily available	Seed	Bushy, sprawling plant; to 2 ft. Gray-green foliage, white flowers. Mildew occasionally disfigures foliage. Landscaping use limited.
Pea (pole)	*Pisum sativum*	Readily available	Seed	Large, twining vine; to 6 ft. Gray-green foliage, white flowers. Landscaping use limited. Mildew occasionally disfigures foliage.

Annuals, and Perennials Commonly Treated as Annuals (CONTINUED)

COMMON NAME	LATIN NAME	SOURCES†	EDIBLE PART	LANDSCAPING CONSIDERATIONS
*Pea, snow (bush) (Chinese pea pod)	*Pisum sativum* var. *macrocarpon*	E	Pod	Bushy, sprawling plant; to 2 ft. Gray-green foliage, white or purple flowers. Mildew occasionally disfigures foliage. Purple-flowered variety attractive in herbaceous borders.
*Pea, snow (pole) (Chinese pea pod)	*Pisum sativum* var. *macrocarpon*	E	Pod	Large, twining vine; to 6 ft. Gray-green foliage, white flowers. Landscaping use limited. Mildew occasionally disfigures foliage.
*Peanut (goober)	*Arachis hypogaea*	E	Seed	Compact plant; to 2 ft. Cut leaves and yellow flowers attractive. Use for temporary ground covers.
*Pepper, sweet, chili, tabasco	*Capsicum* species	E	Fruit	Ornamental, upright plant; to 3 ft. Decorative red or yellow fruits. Use in herbaceous borders and in containers.
Potato	*Solanum tuberosum*	Readily available	Tuber	Ornamental, dark green-leafed, sprawling plant; to 2 ft. Landscape use limited. Vines must turn yellow and die down before harvesting. Try containers.
Radish and daikon	*Raphanus sativus*	Readily available	Root, tuber	Short, clumping plant; to 12 in. Landscaping use limited. Harvesting and very short life leave empty spaces. Try interplanting with sweet allysum.
Rutabaga (swede)	*Brassica Napus—* Napobrassica Group	Readily available	Root	Clumping plant, to 20 in. tall, interesting foliage. Landscape use limited. Harvesting leaves empty spaces; try containers or interplanting with petunias or other flowering annuals.
Rye	*Secale cereale*	s, 35, health food stores	Seed	Tall grass; to 5 ft. Landscape use limited. Try using it in informal yards adjacent to meadows.
Salsify (oyster plant)	*Tragopogon porrifolius*	Readily available	Root	Upright, grasslike leafed plant; to 2 ft. Limited landscaping use. Can become a weed.
Sesame	*Sesamum indicum*	s, 16, 32, 48, 51	Seed	Upright plant; to 3 ft. Pleasant foliage, white or pink flowers. Use in herbaceous borders.
*Spinach, common	*Spinacia oleracea*	E	Leaf	Small foliage plant, to 2 ft., with a rosette form. Use with other greens in an herbaceous border. Spinach has a short growing season. Try interplanting with flowering annuals to prevent holes in the garden.
*Spinach, New Zealand	*Tetragonia tetragonioides*	E	Leaf	Fleshy leafed, sprawling, ornamental plant; to 2 ft. Use in hanging baskets and over walls.
*Squash, summer and zucchini	*Cucurbita Pepo* var. *melopepo*	E	Fruit	Large (to 2 ft.), prickly, deep green leaves. Most varieties are bushlike and have strong, upright growth; to 3 ft. Some varieties have showy yellow flowers. Can become mildewed. Use in herbaceous borders.
Squash, winter, pumpkin	*Cucurbita* species	Readily available	Fruit	Large, sprawling vines; to 12 ft. Some varieties have ornamental flowers and fruits. Plants usually become yellow and withered-looking before harvest. Rampant vines generally unmanageable in the average landscape.
Sunflower	*Helianthus annuus*	Readily available; dwarf available, s, 9	Seed	Tall, upright-growing plant; to 10 ft. Giant yellow flowers. Unwieldy. Dwarf varieties to 5 ft. are available; have limited use for the back of informal flower gardens.

Annuals, and Perennials Commonly Treated as Annuals (CONTINUED)

COMMON NAME	LATIN NAME	SOURCES†	EDIBLE PART	LANDSCAPING CONSIDERATIONS
*Sweet potato (yam)	*Ipomoea Batatas*	E	Tuber	Large, attractive, spreading vines; to 1½ ft. tall. Blooms occasionally, pink flowers. Use to spill over a wall or as temporary ground cover.
*Tomato	*Lycopersicon Lycopersicum*	E	Fruit	Tall, sprawling, upright vine; to 6 ft. Cut leaves, decorative red or yellow fruits. Small varieties available. Use in hanging baskets and on fences.
Turnip	*Brassica Rapa—* Rasifera Group	Readily available	Root, leaf	Short, clumping plant; to 18 in. Limited landscape use. Harvesting leaves empty spaces. Try containers or interplanting with dwarf nasturtiums or pansies.
Watercress	*Nasturtium officinale*	s, 16, 17, 32, 48	Leaf	An aquatic plant to 6 in. with attractive foliage. Landscape use limited to streamsides. Can become a weed.
*Watermelon	*Citrullus lanatus*	E	Fruit	Ivy-leafed, sprawling vines; to 10 ft. Dwarf plants available. Large varieties unwieldy; small varieties ornamental, hanging over retaining walls or trained on a fence.
Wheat, bread	*Triticum aestivum*	s, 35, health food stores	Seed	Tall grass; to 4 ft. Landscape use limited. Try planting in informal yards adjacent to meadows.
*Wild rice	*Zizania aquatica*	E	Seed	Tall aquatic grass; to 10 ft. Landscape use limited to lakes and streamsides.
Winged bean (Goa bean)	*Psophocarpus tetragonolobus*	19	Seed, leaf, tuber	Tall tropical vine; to 10 ft. Experimental in the United States, probably best in Florida. Use on arbor or fence.

Herbs, Spices, and Condiments—Annuals, Perennials Commonly Treated as Annuals, and Biennials

COMMON NAME	LATIN NAME	SOURCES†	EDIBLE PART	LANDSCAPING CONSIDERATIONS
Anise	*Pimpinella Anisum*	Readily available	Seed	Dainty, cut-leaf plant to 2 ft. Flowers white, in small umbels. Use in an herb garden or a flower bed.
*Basil	*Ocimum Basilicum*	E	Leaf	Upright, shiny green-leafed plant; to 2 ft. White flowers. Purple-leafed varieties with pink flowers are available. Use in herb garden or flower bed.
*Borage	*Borago officinalis*	E	Leaf, flower	Large, prickly, gray-green leafed plant; to 2 ft. Bears handsome blue flowers in clusters. Use in herb garden or flower bed. Can become a weed.
Caraway	*Carum Carvi*	Readily available	Seed	Many-branched biennial; to 2 ft. Decorative pinnate leaves, white flowers in umbels. Use in herb garden or flower bed.
*Chamomile, Sweet false (German)	*Matricaria recutita*	E	Flower	Medium-size, ferny, spreading plant; to 2 ½ ft. Small, daisylike flowers. Use in herb garden or flower bed.
Chervil	*Anthriscus Cerefolium*	Readily available	Leaf	Small, parsley-leafed plant; to 2 ft. Ornamental foliage. Use in a shaded herb garden or flower bed.
Chia	*Salvia hispanica*	31, 48, 52	Seed	Small, delicate-looking plant; to 20 in. Small blue flowers stand above leaf clusters. Use for dry rock gardens.
Coriander	*Coriandrum sativum*	Readily available	Leaf, seed	Medium-size, graceful plant; to 3 ft. Compound leaves, small white flowers in umbels. Use in herb garden or flower bed.
Cumin	*Cuminum Cyminum*	Readily available	Seed	Tiny plant with threadlike leaves; height, 6 in. Flowers white or pink in small umbels. Use in front in herb garden or flower bed.
Dill	*Anethum graveolens*	Readily available; dwarf available, s, 48	Seed, leaf	Medium size plant; to 3 ft.; dwarf available. Ferny threadlike foliage, yellow flowers in umbels. Use in herb garden or flower bed.
Garlic	*Allium sativum*	Readily available	Bulb	Tubular, upright plant to 2 ft., gray-green leaves. Awkward-looking plant; becomes unkempt; must die down before harvesting. Limited landscape use.
*Ginger	*Zingiber officinale*	E	Rhizome	Perennial rhizome, usually planted as an annual. Tall, upright stems grow to 4 ft. and have grasslike leaves. Flowers insignificant. Pleasant foliage plant for shady borders.
*Nasturtium	*Tropaeolum* species	E	Flower, bud, leaf	Climbing vine, to 10 ft., with round leaves and bright red, yellow, or orange flowers. Dwarf bush varieties available. Very ornamental. Use in hanging baskets, on fences; bush types in flower gardens.
*Parsley	*Petroselinum crispum*	E	Leaf	Compact, curly-leafed, dark green, biennial plant; 18 in. to 3 ft. Use in herb garden or flower bed.
Savory, summer	*Satureja hortensis*	Readily available	Leaf	Small, upright, bushy, somewhat hairy, green plant; to 18 in. high. Small lavender flowers. Use in herb garden and flower bed.

SOURCES OF PLANTS AND OTHER SUPPLIES

How to Obtain Plant Materials

Plants are available from many sources: a gardening friend or neighbor, horticultural organizations, supermarkets and discount stores, and local and mail-order nurseries. From your friends and horticultural societies the plants will come as seeds, cuttings, or divisions. From commercial sources you can buy them as seeds, started seedlings, tubers, and bare-root or container plants. The information in this section will help you find a wide variety of healthy plants at a reasonable price. Included, in addition to the commonly available edible plants, are old-fashioned vegetables and fruits that are no longer commercially available but that can be found outside the usual channels, and varieties that are commercially available but difficult to obtain. Nearly every plant mentioned in this book is available from at least one of the sources given in this section or in the Encyclopedia section.

Sharing and Saving

One of the great joys of gardening is sharing our bounty with others. Whether we give or receive these edible plants, the plants will be acclimated to our area, will have been proven successful, and sometimes will be a variety that is no longer commercially available. The extra seed from an old-time bean that Aunt Polly grew or budding stock from an out-of-fashion fruit tree can add diversity to a garden. Many edibles are plants that need dividing, so there are many opportunities to pick up an artichoke plant, Jerusalem artichoke tubers, or a creeping rhizome of a banana.

Many edible plants set great quantities of seed that most gardeners enjoy sharing. But remember that no matter how delicious the product or how sturdy the plant, if it is from hybrid seed it is usually not worth saving or giving—that seed will not develop the plant you want next year. Many commercial seeds are now hybrids because of their improved hardiness, a special flavor quality, or a particular growth habit. Plants designated as hybrid or F-1 hybrid on the seed package cannot reliably reproduce themselves. Hybrid seed is produced by crossing parents with different characteristics and this same combination of parents must be continually rebred to produce the hybrid offspring. Another group of plants to avoid when saving seed is the cucurbit family (the cucumbers, melons, pumpkins, gourds, and squashes). Unless planted in complete isolation these plants cross-pollinate with each other and produce strange second generations.

However, many plants do have open-pollinated varieties that will come true from seed. Seeds of plants that can be saved because they will come true from seed are beans, peas, and carrots, as well as select cultivars of many other vegetables. If you have a favorite, share it and cherish it. Some seed companies also make a point of providing a good selection of varieties of seed whose second generation can be saved by the homeowner. They are: (**25, 32, 35, 51, 54**).

To save money, fruit and nut trees can also be grown from seed. These trees take a few years longer to bear and will give a variable product—sometimes better than the parent, sometimes worse, and sometimes the same. Or you can grow your seedling tree and then graft onto it wood from a known cultivar. For information on growing fruit and nut trees from seed and for grafting and budding, see relevant titles in the bibliography. It's also worthwhile to join the fruit and nut societies named in Appendix C, as they are knowledgeable in this area. Sources of seed for fruit and nut trees are: (**19, 32, 51, and 55**).

A pamphlet called *Growing Garden Seeds*, by Robert Johnston, Jr., available from (**35**), is a valuable source of information on seed saving.

Caution: No matter what the form of the shared crop—seeds, cuttings, or divisions—be sure the source is disease free. Virus-infected bean seeds or strawberry roots with nematodes are no bargain. If you save your own seed you must keep only seed that is healthy. Learn to identify virus symptoms in plants (see Chapter 7) and discard seed from plants so affected. Commercial plants are usually pest free because they have been grown under controlled conditions, and have been inspected or handled by people who know how to recognize the problems.

Horticultural Organizations and Seed Exchanges

Horticultural organizations are excellent sources for obtaining antique or unusual edibles. Membership in these organizations is usually required to receive their products, but the dues are minimal and the advantages are many.

Besides offering uncommon seeds, or scion or budwood, they usually publish newsletters and offer cultural and historical material on plants of interest.

A popular way of obtaining seed is through seed exchanges—published lists of gardeners willing to share their seeds. Two of the sources listed at the end of this appendix (**32** and **51**) offer this service, as do some of the gardening magazines and a number of organizations devoted to different aspects of food growing, including:

California Rare Fruit Growers, Inc.,

Home Orchard Society,

North American Fruit Explorers. (See Appendix C for addresses.)

There is one organization devoted solely to the exchange of seeds: Seed Savers Exchange, c/o Kent Whealy, Rural Route 2, Princeton, MO 64673.

State Forestry and Agricultural Departments

Many states have programs to encourage tree planting and provide young trees for reforesting woodland areas and for erosion control at a nominal fee. Inquire at your local extension service office to see if there is such a program in your area. This service is aimed not at homeowners who want to put in one or two trees, but at those who need a number of trees to help control erosion or to establish woodland or windbreak areas.

Cut-Rate Plants

In general, the plants sold at local discount houses, groceries, and hardware stores cannot be considered good buys. These plants usually have been given only sporadic care, with minimal attention to their light requirements and pest problems. The salespeople in these stores usually cannot give you advice on care or suitability.

These stores sometimes carry inferior seeds and occasionally indulge in some questionable practices. For example, they will sell at "bargain" prices rose bushes that were originally used for florist production and have consequently lost their vigor. These discounted plants may also have many health problems. In plants, as in other things, the old adage holds true: you get what you pay for.

A Word about Nurseries

Nurseries, both local and mail-order, reflect the people who run them—some are honorable and well-informed, some are not. Most are run by people who love plants and want you to have a successful garden. They take courses to keep current. Well-informed neighborhood nursery people are aware of local soil, pest, and climate problems and new plant introductions. They often know the best variety for your area—plants resistant to diseases in your area or that have been bred for local soil conditions. They take pride in their knowledge and sell a superior product.

On the other hand, most mail-order houses will not know your area well. You must do your homework diligently to see which species and varieties grow well in your area. If you live in Florida and order a peach variety that has a high chilling requirement, you will probably be sent that variety and it will not do well. Mail-order nurseries seldom have information specific to your area. (Dave Wilson's Nursery is an exception. They can send you a map specific to your area, along with information as to which of their varieties do well there.)

Why do people use mail-order firms? Because they offer a much larger selection of plants than any local nursery could provide. Just remember that you must take the responsibility for learning about a plant's usefulness in your area.

Note: To help control pests and diseases, many states have laws covering the importation of plants. Some plants, such as currants, are banned altogether in a few states. Inspection requirements or agricultural crop protection in a state determine if the mail-order nursery can send you what you want. Read the catalog carefully; it usually tells what can be sent where.

Local Retail Nurseries

The average local nursery is your most valuable plant source because it has information for your area, is handy, and enables you to pick out merchandise yourself. Following are some things to notice in judging a nursery:

Do the plants look healthy?

Do they sell plants for the wrong season? For example, are they selling marigold or pepper plants a month before frost is due? (Seeds do not seem to be sold for a particular season. Seeds for all seasons are often sold at one time, so, again, do your homework.)

Will they order things for you?

Is the person behind the counter able to give you information about the plant you buy?

Do they continually push chemical pesticides and herbicides?

The majority of local nurseries carry deciduous fruit trees and a few perennial vegetables such as asparagus and artichokes in bare-root form during late winter and early spring. Bare root is the least expensive and most beneficial way to buy these plants. Some nurseries will give you a 10–20 percent discount if you order your fruit trees in the fall before they put in their order to the wholesaler.

Many of the retail nurseries I have visited around the country have two shortcomings. The first is their lack of knowledge about edibles, ornamental edibles in particular. This is primarily due to the fact that inedible ornamentals have been stressed by the industry as well as by customers for the last 20 or 30 years. Second, information about garden chemicals (pesticides, fungicides, herbicides, and fertilizers) is not always balanced with information about nonchemical alternatives. The reason for this one-sidedness is that much of the nurseries' knowledge about pest control comes from the companies selling the chemicals. Moreover, money is made when a pesticide is sold to control aphids, whereas an alternative method of control, such as spraying with a heavy jet of water, would entail no sale. The temptation, therefore, is for the nursery to recommend the pesticide.

When you find a good nursery, frequent it and appreciate it. Like a good car mechanic or dentist, it is a valuable resource.

Mail-Order Nurseries

The many mail-order nurseries in the United States are a valuable resource for the home gardener. They are a varied group. There are nurseries like Stark Brothers that specialize in a wide selection of fruit trees, and the grandfather of the mail-order seed business, W. Atlee Burpee, which sells mostly seeds for vegetables and flowers. Most nurseries carry standard edibles, but a few, such as Exotica Seed Co. or Kitazawa Seed Co., carry the unusual. There are even bamboo, pistachio, and bean specialty nurseries. Some, Johnny's Selected Seeds and Nichols Garden Nursery, for example, are particularly interested in organic gardening. Peruse the whole list, and you will find many that interest you.

How to Use a Mail-Order Firm

Write for a catalog; they all have one (some charge a fee that is subject to change). Read it carefully and do your homework. Be leery of "miracle plants." Some mail-order nurseries seem to hire fiction writers to compose their catalogs. There are no climbing strawberries! Zoysia grass is durable and needs little mowing—but it's also almost impossible to get rid of, and it can eat up your flower or vegetable border. The egg tree is really just a white eggplant. I have included some of these imaginative nurseries on my list because they carry some of the plants not carried by any other source, but let the reader beware.

Most mail-order catalogs come out in late winter or early spring. Write for your catalog early so that you can take advantage of bare-root shipping if possible. Send in your order early so you can be assured of the best and most complete selection.

Most seeds and small plants are sent by first class mail; the majority of large plants and trees are sent parcel post.

Sources of Edible Plants

The numbers appearing after plants listed in the Encyclopedia and under "Sources" in Appendix A refer to the numbers assigned to the following nurseries. For example, the number (9) after 'Ambrosia' cantaloupe indicates it is available from Burpee Seed Company.

1
Adams County Nursery & Fruit Farms
Aspers, PA 17304

Fruit specialists. 31-page catalog. They carry a good selection of standard, hardy fruit varieties and offer a large selection of rootstocks.

2
Alexander's Nurseries
1225 Wareham St.
Middleboro, MA 02346
Large selection of lilacs and blueberries.

3
American Bamboo Company
345 W. Second St.
Dayton, OH 45402
Hardy bamboos. They must be ordered in the spring.

4
Armstrong Nurseries
P.O. Box 4060
Ontario, CA 91761
Specialists in fruit trees and roses. 40-page catalog lists genetic dwarf peaches and nectarines, other exotic fruit trees: jujube; four varieties of standard figs; 'Black Jack' dwarf fig; dwarf citrus; 'Littlecado' avocado; kiwis, male and female; 'Black Beauty' mulberry; 'Fuyu' persimmon; pomegranate.

5
Boston Mountain Nurseries
Rte. 2
Highway 71
Winslow, AR 72959
Specialists in berries.

6
Bountiful Ridge Nurseries, Inc.
Princess Anne, MD 21853
Specialists in fruits and nuts. 30-page catalog. They carry a large selection of superior nut and fruit varieties. They have a list of recommended fruits for organic gardeners, including scab-resistant apples. This nursery also sells kiwi, semidwarf 'Bing' cherry, currants, gooseberries, elderberries, hickory, hardy bamboo, and a red-leaf 'Cocheco' plum.

7
Buckley Wholesale Nursery
16819 Vanogles Ford Rd.
Sumner, WA 98390
Many ornamentals and standard fruit and nut trees, including filbert and chestnut. They do not sell retail.

8
Burgess Seed & Plant Company
905 Four Seasons Rd.
Bloomington, IL 61701
32-page catalog of vegetables and fruits. Large selection of common vegetable seeds, dwarf fig, hardy nut trees, common varieties of stone fruits and small fruits, 'Pot Luck' miniature cucumber.

9
Burpee Seed Company
Warminster, PA 18991
180-page general seed catalog, including flowers, vegetables, garden aids, nursery stock; 10 pages on fruit. Of special interest are 'Dwarf Gray Sugar' peas; tampala; 'Bush Porto Rico' sweet potato; miniature watermelons; cucumbers ('Burpee's M & M',

'Bush Champion', and 'Spacemaster'); 'Ambrosia' cantaloupe; Oriental persimmon; genetic dwarf fruit trees; filberts; and bush cherries.

10
California Nursery Company
Niles District
Fremont, CA 94536

Many standard fruit trees plus tender species, including citrus, pomegranate, persimmon, avocado, and some California wine grapes.

11
C & O Nursery
P.O. Box 116
1700 N. Wenatchee Ave.
Wenatchee, WA 98801

Specialists in fruit, including exclusive patented varieties of the major fruits. 40-page catalog. Wholesale and retail.

12
Columbia Basin Nursery
Box 458
Quincy, WA 98848

Colored brochure and price list. Seedling rootstock, dwarfing apple rootstock, dwarf and standard budded fruit trees.

13
Congdon & Weller, Wholesale Nursery, Inc.
Mile Block Rd.
North Collins, NY 14111

A wholesale nursery of mostly ornamentals, but they also carry rugosa roses and many of the small fruits.

14
L. E. Cooke Company
26333 Road 140
Visalia, CA 93277

Wholesale only. Specialists in dwarf and semidwarf fruit trees and genetic dwarf peaches.

15
Corwin Davis Nursery
R.F.D. 1
20865 Junction Rd.
Bellevue, MI 49021

Small nursery particularly interested in pawpaw. Bulletin on pawpaws available for $1.00.

16
DeGiorgi Company, Inc.
1411 Third St.
Council Bluffs, IA 51502

Seed company. Many Italian varieties of vegetables, plus alpine strawberries, red and dwarf okra, sorrel, cardoon, 'Dwarf Gray Sugar' peas, 'Pot Luck' cucumber, 'Ambrosia' cantaloupe, 'Golden Midget' watermelon.

17
J. A. Demonchaux Company
827 North Kansas
Topeka, KS 66608

Importers of French seed, many French varieties of vegetables, including sorrel, cardoon, sweet false chamomile, alpine strawberries, dwarf basil, and other herbs.

18
Emlong Nurseries, Inc.
Stevensville, MI 49127

Mostly ornamentals, but catalog also has 14 pages of common fruit trees, plus Oriental persimmon, pawpaw, cherry plums, and wine grapes.

19
Exotica Seed Company
8033 Sunset Blvd., Suite 125
West Hollywood, CA 90046

Seeds of many unusual edibles, including bamboo, pistachio, piñon, kiwi, pineapple guava, pawpaw, unusual chili peppers, black mulberry, pomegranate, prickly pear, olive, carob, persimmon, loquat, natal plum. Catalog, $2.00.

20
Farmer Seed & Nursery Company
Faribault, MN 55021

76-page general seed catalog. Ornamentals, vegetables, and 8 pages on fruit, including a good selection of cherry plums. Of particular interest are 'Patio-Pik' cucumber, 'Minnesota Midget' cantaloupe, 'Golden Midget' watermelon, 'Porto Rico' sweet potato.

21
Fiddyment Pistachios
2230 Fiddyment Rd.
Roseville, CA 95678

This nursery deals only in pistachios. The only source of pistachio plants known to the author at this time.

22
Henry Field Seed & Nursery Company
Shenandoah, IA 51602

116-page general seed catalog. Ornamentals, vegetables. 16 pages on fruit, including seedling pawpaw, 'Allred' plum, dwarf citrus, hardy nut trees, currants and gooseberries, figs, and a large selection of bush cherries. Of interest are peanuts, 'Kengarden' watermelon; 'New Hampshire Midget' watermelon; and 'Patio-Pik', 'Pot Luck', and climbing cucumbers.

23
Florida's Vineyard & Fruit Garden
P.O. Box 300
Orange Lake, FL 32681

Fruiting plants for the South. A good selection of southern varieties of figs, pears, blueberries, apples, and muscadine grapes.

24
Fowler Nurseries, Inc., and Garden Center
525 Fowler Rd.
Newcastle, CA 95658

Good selection of fruit trees and berries, including 10 varieties of genetic dwarf fruit trees, 7 types of Oriental persimmons. Pomegranates, Oriental pears, and some California wine grapes are available. They carry filberts, western pecans, and walnuts. Free 4-page price list of 200 varieties. 32-page catalog, $1.00.

25
Seeds Blüm
Idaho City Stage
Boise, ID 83707

Carries seeds of ornamental, heirloom, and open-pollinated vegetables. Foodscaping enthusiasts.

26

Louis Gerardi Nursery
R.R. 1
Box 143
O'Fallon, IL 62269

Extensive list of superior grafted nut trees and some fruits. Northern pecans, hicans, hickories, black walnuts, Carpathian walnuts, heart nuts, butter nuts, Chinese chestnuts, and filberts. They also carry pawpaws, American persimmon, and mulberries.

27

Glecklers Seedmen
Metamora, OH 43540

This nursery carries standard vegetable seeds, including the 'Peron' tomato, which is disease and crack resistant and reputed to be immune to hornworms.

28

Gurney Seed & Nursery Company
Yankton, SD 57079

76-page general seed catalog. Flowers, vegetables, and nursery stock; 10 pages on fruit. They carry blueberries, rugosa rose, Jerusalem artichoke, hop plants, red okra, alpine strawberry, ginger root, pawpaw, Chinese chestnut, Nanking cherry, dwarf lemon, orange, lime, grapefruit, banana. In addition, they sell trichogramma wasps, red worms, and organic fertilizers.

29

Herbst Brothers Seedsmen, Inc.
1000 N. Main St.
Brewster, NY 10509

This nursery carries seeds for many species of trees and vegetables for wholesale growers, but they will sell in quarter-pound amounts. Available are seeds for Oriental and American persimmon, olive, sweet bay, walnut, wintergreen, carob, apple, hickory, piñon, rugosa roses, jujube, cardoon, red okra, and a seed mix for wildlife. They also carry a number of biological pesticides and some useful garden tools.

30

Hilltop Orchards & Nurseries, Inc.
Rte. 2
Hartford, MI 49057

Wholesale and retail nursery. Major supplier of standard fruit tree varieties. Large selection of hardy fruits are available, including scab-immune apples.

31

Horticultural Enterprises
P.O. Box 340082
Dallas, TX 75234

Specialist in peppers, this nursery has 30 varieties of sweet and hot peppers. In addition, they have tomatoes and a native Mexican cucumber.

32

J. L. Hudson, Seedsman
P.O. Box 1058
Redwood City, CA 94064

They have a free vegetable seed catalog with a wide selection of different types of vegetables. Their very large general seed catalog is known for its extensive selection of seeds collected from all over the world. Around 4000 varieties of seeds are listed, some of them very unusual, including cacti, succulents, ferns, ornamental grasses, alpines, and wild edibles. This nursery carries seeds for many of the unusual edibles mentioned in Appendix A. A $1.00 charge for this catalog is well worth it. They have a seed exchange.

33

Interstate Nurseries
Hamburg, IA 51644

70-page catalog, including 12 pages on fruits and nuts, 3 pages on vegetables.

34

Jamieson Valley Gardens
Jamieson Rd.
Rte. 3
Spokane, WA 99203

They carry native plants from all over the country, wildflowers, bulbs, ferns, native orchids, plus a few edibles. $1.00 for their catalog.

35

Johnny's Selected Seeds, Organic Seed & Crop Research
Albion, ME 04910

A large selection of organically grown vegetable seeds, with special emphasis on northern gardens. Also available are seeds of Oriental vegetables, including edible chrysanthemum; herbs; chamomile; sorrel; alpine strawberry; white clover; and 'Stampede' Jerusalem artichoke tubers. They carry open-pollinated varieties of vegetables that allow you to save your own seeds. Inquire about "seed swap." 50¢ for the catalog.

36

J. W. Jung Seed Company
Randolph, WI 53956

64-page general seed catalog, with 16 pages on vegetables, 6 pages on fruits. They carry scab-immune apples, peanuts, bush and climbing cucumbers, 'Pot Luck' cucumber, and dwarf cantaloupe.

37

Kelly Bros. Nurseries, Inc.
Dansville, NY 14437

40-page color catalog covering mostly ornamentals, but a good selection of standard fruits, and in addition beach plum and bush plum.

38

Kitazawa Seed Company
356 West Taylor St.
San Jose, CA 95110

Oriental vegetables, including bitter melon, spinach mustard, 'Dwarf Gray Sugar' peas, and edible chrysanthemum.

39

Lakeland Nurseries Sales
Hanover, PA 17331

56-page catalog. Includes common fruits and vegetable seeds and a selection of less common fruit plants, including Manchurian apricot, bamboo, pawpaw, artichoke, 'Everbearing' fig, dwarf citrus, dwarf banana, and New Zealand spinach.

40

Le Jardin du Gourmet
P.O. Box 424
West Danville, VT 05873

Large selection of French vegetables plus seeds for hops and alpine strawberries. 50¢ for catalog.

41

Henry Leuthardt Nurseries, Inc.

East Moriches, Long Island, NY 11940

They specialize in grapes and espaliered hardy fruit trees and ship to most parts of the country. Guidebook on dwarf and espalier-trained fruit trees for $1.00.

42

May Nursery Company

P.O. Box 1312

2115 W. Lincoln Ave.

Yakima, WA 98907

Their catalog includes some of the common edibles. They are one of the few mail-order nurseries that carry hops plants.

43

Earl May Seed & Nursery Company

Shenandoah, IA 51603

80-page general seed catalog including flowers, vegetables, nursery stock, and 10 pages on fruit. Of particular interest are 'Dwarf Gray Sugar' pea, Jerusalem artichoke, 'Patio-Pik' and 'Pot Luck' cucumbers, and 'Golden Midget' and 'New Hampshire Midget' watermelons.

44

Mayo Nurseries

Rte. 14 North

Lyons, NY 14489

Standard fruit varieties.

45

Miller's Nursery, Inc.

Canandaigua, NY 14424

40-page catalog. Large selection of standard fruits and nuts.

46

New York State Fruit Testing Cooperative Association

Geneva, NY 14456

32-page fruit catalog. $5.00 membership fee, refunded on first order. Many new varieties of standard fruits. They have antique varieties of apples, a large selection of rootstock material, dwarf pears, dessert and hardy wine grapes, and 'Wellington' mulberry. A large selection of experimental fruits being tested for disease resistance and hardiness are available.

47

Nichols Garden Nursery

1190 North Pacific Highway

Albany, OR 97321

Extensive list of herbs, including plants as well as seeds; unusual vegetables; miniature flowering kale; 'Pot Luck', Japanese climbing, and Armenian cucumbers; 'Dwarf Gray Sugar' pea.

48

Geo. W. Park Seed Company, Inc.

P.O. Box 31

Greenwood, SC 29647

Park's is one of the major suppliers of vegetables and flower seeds in the United States. They have a 130-page vegetable and flower seed catalog. A small catalog for sunbelt gardeners, which will be available in 1982, includes pomegranate. They have a very large selection of vegetable seeds, including red okra and 'Royal Burgundy' beans. A section for small gardens

includes a bush cantaloupe, a bush cucumber, and dwarf honeydew. They also carry herbs, bitter melon, peanuts, and slips for vineless 'Porto Rico' sweet potatoes.

49

Plants of the Southwest

1570 Pacheco St.

Santa Fe, NM 87501

A good selection of southwestern native plants, plus vegetable varieties for the cool growing seasons of the mountains and high plains of the West.

50

Rayner Bros., Inc.

Salisbury, MD 21801

Specialists in fruits and nuts. Large selection of berries.

51

Redwood City Seed Co.

P.O. Box 361

Redwood City, CA 94064

Seeds of many of the plants mentioned in this book are offered in this company's "Catalogue of Useful Plants." These include carob, chamomile, cranberry, hops, jujube, kiwi, mustard spinach, New Zealand spinach, pineapple guava, piñons, pistachio, pomegranate, sorrel, and sweet bay. They specialize in seeds of vegetables and herbs from Europe, Mexico, and the Orient. They also have a large selection of seeds for fruit and nut trees and berry bushes. Catalog 50¢.

52

Clyde Robin Seed Company, Inc.

P.O. Box 2855

Castro Valley, CA 94546

Collectors of wildflower and wild tree seeds and plants. Seeds for the following edibles: sugar maple, jujube, herbs, California bay, many piñons, black mulberry, sweet bay, salal, and black mustard. Many wildflower seeds, including Matilija poppy, lobelia cardinalis, lupines, native iris, redbud, ceanothus, and manzanita, plus many different wildflower mixes for different areas of the country. $1.00 for catalog.

53

Roses of Yesterday and Today

802 Brown's Valley Rd.

Watsonville, CA 95076

Large selection of old-fashioned and rugosa roses. $1.00 for catalog.

54

Sanctuary Seeds

1913 Yew St.

Vancouver, British Columbia, Canada V6K 3G3

This nursery has a large collection of organically grown seeds for annual vegetables, herbs, and hops.

55

F. W. Schumacher Company

Sandwich, MA 02563

This company carries only seeds. They are primarily a wholesale nursery and sell their seed in bulk. Available are pawpaw, pecan, hickory, natal plum, salal, carob, filbert, Oriental and American persimmon, pineapple guava, walnut, mulberry, olive, piñon, and seeds for common fruits.

56

R. H. Shumway Seedsman, Inc.
628 Cedar St.
Rockford, IL 61105

83-page catalog. Large selection of vegetable seeds offered, including cardoon, sorrel, New Zealand spinach, purple leaf basil, and a good selection of beans. They also carry fruit plants, including dwarf citrus, seedling pawpaw, sugar maple, hardy nuts, and seedling hardy persimmon.

57

Southmeadow Fruit Gardens
2363 Tilbury Place
Birmingham, MI 48009

Probably the largest collection of major fruit varieties, old, new, and rare, in the United States. 112-page illustrated catalog—$6.00, but worth it. 8-page catalog available free. They carry plants of antique apples; numerous varieties of grapes, plums, peaches, pears, cherries; Oriental pears; beach plum; quince; a large selection of gooseberries; medlar; and a selection of hardy native fruits. Order plants from Grootendorst Nurseries (the growers for Southmeadow), Box SM, Lakeside, MI 49116.

58

Stark Brothers Nursery
Louisiana, MO 63353

60-page illustrated catalog and guide. Most of the catalog offers fruit trees, but there are 12 pages of vegetables, ornamentals, and nuts. Stark Brothers is one of the largest growers of fruit trees in the United States. They have many of their own varieties, including 'Sweetheart' apricot and 'Stark Red' apple, plus quince, 'Stella' cherry, hardy nuts, three varieties of scab-resistant apples, and numerous superior varieties of genetic dwarf fruits.

59

Stokes Seeds Inc.
737 Main St.
P.O. Box 548
Buffalo, NY 14240

Seed catalog for vegetables and flowers, with a large selection for northern gardens. They have Bag-a-Bug Japanese beetle traps, Trigagrip garden tools, and Fogg-It nozzles.

60

Willis Stribling Nursery Company
1620 W. 16th St.
Merced, CA 95340

Fruit specialists. 44-page catalog of fruit, nut, and grape varieties, along with tree planting guides and ripening charts. In addition to standard fruits, plants offered include varieties of persimmon; pomegranate; filbert; genetic dwarf peaches; and dwarf and standard size citrus, including kumquat and limequat.

61

Talbott Nursery
R.R. 3
Box 212
Linton, IN 47441

Specialist in nuts and American persimmons, Talbott has the nation's largest selection of named varieties of persimmon. It carries Chinese chestnuts, Carpathian walnuts, and hardy northern pecans.

62

Tennessee Nursery & Seed Company
Tennessee Nursery Rd.
Cleveland, TN 37311

48-page catalog, mostly fruit trees and vegetables. Fruits include pawpaw, American and Oriental persimmon, three varieties of figs, hardy bamboo. Vegetables include 'Dwarf Gray Sugar' pea, 'New Hampshire Midget' watermelon, 'Minnesota Midget' cantaloupe, 'Mini-Midget' cucumber, and 'Royalty' beans.

63

Thompson & Morgan Inc.
P.O. Box 100
Farmingdale, NJ 07727

This seed company specializes in unusual vegetables and flowers. The seed is expensive. They carry seed for 'Violet Podded Stringless' beans, 'Red Eating Selected' nasturtiums, varieties of Chinese and midget vegetables, and 'Spacemaster' cucumbers.

64

Tsang & Ma International
1306 Old County Rd.
Belmont, CA 94002

Large selection of Chinese vegetable seeds, including Chinese chive, bitter melon, and Chinese parsley. They also carry Chinese cooking utensils and seasoning.

65

Upper Bank Nurseries
P.O. Box 486
Media, PA 19063

They specialize in ornamental plants and carry jujube, pomegranate, and bamboo plants.

66

Van Ness Water Gardens
2460 N. Euclid Ave.
Upland, CA 91786

This nursery offers a complete supply of water garden accessories and water plants, including lotus and water chestnuts.

67

The Vermont Bean Seed Company
Garden Lane
Bomoseen, VT 05732

Extensive list of beans and peas, including 'Thomas' Famous White Dutch' runner bean, 'Vermont Cranberry' pole bean, scarlet runner, and 'Royalty'.

68

Waynesboro Nurseries
Waynesboro, VA 22980

Fruit trees and ornamental plants. Large selection of nut trees, including northern pecan, filbert, hickory, and Chinese chestnut.

69

The Wayside Gardens Company
Hodges, SC 29695

Hardy plants, bulbs, shrubs. 145-page color catalog with a large selection of ornamentals and 6 pages of fruits, including kiwi plants, genetic dwarf fruit trees, filbert, fig, and alpine strawberry. Catalog, $1.00 (refunded with first purchase).

70

Wildlife Nurseries
P.O. Box 2724
Oshkosh, WI 54903

This nursery carries seeds for wild rice, American lotus, wildlife food plants.

71
Dave Wilson Nursery
Box 1060
Hughson, CA 95326

This nursery, unlike most, will provide very specific information as to how well their particular fruit varieties will do in your area. They specialize in Zaiger patented fruit trees, including a large and diverse selection of genetic dwarf trees. They also carry wine grapes, plum-cot, low-chill peaches, genetic dwarf cherry, 'Weeping Santa Rosa' plum, 'Sprite' cherry plum, 'Kikusi' Oriental pear, 'Garden Prince' almond, 'Lang' and 'Li' jujube.

72
Zilke Brothers Nursery
Baroda, MI 49101

80-page catalog, including 17 pages of standard fruits; persimmon, mulberry, pawpaw, dwarf fig, hickory, bush plum; and numerous nut varieties.

Additional nurseries that carry edible plants.

Abundant Life Seed Foundation
P.O. Box 772
Port Townsend, WA 98368

An organization dedicated to preserving native species, heirloom vegetables, and self-sufficient living. Specializing in plants for the Northwest. They carry many varieties of vegetable, herb, and wildflower seeds.

The Banana Tree
715 Northampton St.
Easton, PA 18042

This nursery carries a large selection of banana plants as well as seed of many tropical and subtropical edibles.

Epicure Seeds
Box 23568
Rochester, NY 14692

Seeds of gourmet vegetables including red chicory, petite pois, dwarf basil, and French sorrel.

Greek Gardens
2015 North Main
North Logan, UT 84321

This nursery carries a large selection of vegetable seed.

Hastings
434 Marietta St. NW
P.O. Box 4274
Atlanta, GA 30302

Specialists in fruit, nut, and vegetable varieties for the South. Fruits include : rabbiteye blueberries, persimmon, pomegranate, and muscadine grapes.

Hurov's Tropical Seeds
P.O. Box 10387
Honolulu, HI 96816

This company carries over 350 species of tropical and novelty seed including many edibles.

Long Island Seed and Plant
1368 Flanders Rd.
Riverhead, NY 11901

An organization interested in seed-saving, heirloom vegetables, and self-sufficient living. Seed for vegetables and fruit varieties as well as wild rice.

McLaughlin's Seeds
P.O. Box 550
Mead, WA 99021

Very large selection of herb seed.

Pacific Tree Farms
4301 Lynwood Drive
Chula Vista, CA 92010

One of the largest selections of mail-order tropical and subtropical plants including citrus, guavas, pomegranate, sapote, surinam cherry, banana, kiwi, and mango.

Riverside Farm Nursery
Buskirk, NY 12028

Large selection of table and wine grapes, currants and gooseberries.

Unwins
Box 9
Farmingdale, NJ 07727

An old English seed company with an American branch. They carry seed of annual flowers and English and American varieties of vegetables.

The Urban Farmer
22000 Halburton Rd.
Beachwood, OH 44122

Unusual varieties of vegetable seed from Europe and Japan.

Sources of Nonedible Plants

The following nurseries specialize in native wildflowers, plants, or wildlife food.

Dutch Mt. Nursery
Augusta, MI 49012

This nursery specializes in plants that attract birds and wildlife.

Gardens of the Blue Ridge, Edward P. Robbins, proprietor
P.O. Box 10
Pineola, NC 28662

Wildflowers, hardy trees, shrubs, plants, and bulbs. Large selection of native plants.

Jamieson Valley Gardens
Jamieson Road
Rte. 3
Spokane, WA 99203

They carry native plants from all over the country, wildflowers, bulbs, ferns, and native orchids, plus a few edibles. $1.00 for their catalog.

LaFayette Home Nursery
LaFayette, IL 61449

A supplier of prairie plants.

Lamb Nurseries
East 101 Sharp Ave.
Spokane, WA 99202

Specialist in perennials and rock plants, wildflowers, and ground covers.

Midwest Wildflowers
Box 64
Rockton, IL 61072

They specialize in seeds (no plants) of species common to the midwestern United States, including shooting star, columbine, Solomon's seal, wild ginger, jack-in-the-pulpit, mayapple, purple cone flower, Texas bluebonnet. 50¢ for their catalog.

Plants of the Southwest
1570 Pacheco St.
Santa Fe, NM 87501

A good selection of southwestern native plants, plus vegetable varieties for the cool growing seasons of the mountains and high plains of the West.

Clyde Robin Seed Co., Inc.
P.O. Box 2855
Castro Valley, CA 94546

Collectors of wildflower and wild tree seeds and plants. Seeds for the following edibles: sugar maple, jujube, herbs, California bay, many piñons, black mulberry, sweet bay, and black mustard. Many wildflower seeds, including Matilija poppy, lobelia cardinalis, lupines, native iris, redbud, ceanothus, and manzanita, plus many different wildflower mixes for different areas of the country. $1.00 for catalog.

Save The Tallgrass Prairie, Inc.
4101 W. 54th Terr.
Shawnee Mission, KS 66205

A supplier of prairie grass seed.

Springhill Nurseries
P.O. Box 1758
Peoria, IL 61656

84-page color catalog. Ornamentals, some wildflowers, pink lady's slippers, cardinal flowers. 12 pages of fruits, including citrus.

The Theodore Payne Foundation for Wild Flowers and Native Plants, Inc.
10459 Tuxford St.
Sun Valley, CA 91352

A nonprofit organization that offers California wildflower seeds.

Wildlife Nurseries
P.O. Box 2724
Oshkosh, WI 54903

This nursery carries seeds for wild rice, American lotus, wildlife food plants.

Windrift Prairie Shop
R.D. #2
Oregon, IL 61061

A supplier of prairie plants.

Suppliers of Nonplant Materials

Insectaries

The following insectaries provide natural enemies of insect pests.

American Biological Supply Co.
1330 Dillon Heights Ave.
P.O. Box 3149
Baltimore, MD 21228

Carolina Biological Supply Co.
Burlington, NC 27215

Rincon Vitova
Box 45
Oak View, CA 93022

Suppliers of Garden Tools and Equipment

Cumberland General Store
Rte. 3
Crossville, TN 38555

Mail-order source of garden tools.

John Houchins & Sons, Inc.
801 N. Main
Schulenburg, TX 78956

Manufacturer of quality wheelbarrows.

LaMotte Chemical Co.
P.O. Box 329
Chestertown, MD 21620

Supplier of quality soil-test kits.

A. M. Leonard
6665 Spiker Rd.
Piqua, OH 45356

Mail-order supplier of garden tools.

Walter Nicke
19 Columbus Turnpike
Hudson, NY 12534

Supplier of garden tools.

Smith & Hawken Tool Co.
68 Homer
Palo Alto, CA 94301

This mail-order firm carries superior quality garden tools imported from Bulldog Tools Ltd. of Clarington Forge, England, as well as a select group of other garden tools.

Yardman
5389 W. 130th St.
Cleveland, OH 44111

Manufacturer of lawnmowers.

SOURCES OF INFORMATION

Organizations

The following organizations are sources of information on many of the subjects covered in this book. Your county extension service can tell you of local groups such as native plant societies, horticultural societies, and botanic gardens.

Brooklyn Botanic Garden
1000 Washington Ave.
Brooklyn, NY 11225

An organization with a large worldwide membership interested in all aspects of growing plants. Monthly journal published; back issues, available as booklets, contain valuable information for gardeners. See list in the bibliography.

California Rare Fruit Growers, Inc.
The Fullerton Arboretum
California State University, Fullerton
Fullerton, CA 92634

An organization devoted to experimenting with and spreading information about unusual fruits. Has a worldwide membership. Newsletter available.

The Farallones Institute
The Rural Center
15290 Coleman Valley Rd.
Occidental, CA 95465

The Integral Urban House
1516 Fifth St.
Berkeley, CA 94710

An organization devoted to self-sufficiency, the institute gives classes in growing food and, in late winter, offers preordered bare-root trees for sale on the premises. You can tour their Integral Urban House in Berkeley, an old Victorian completely retrofitted for self-reliant city living; phone ahead for times.

Gardens For All
Dept. FG
180 Flynn Ave.
Burlington, VT 05401

This organization is interested in family food gardens. Newsletter available. Annual membership $10.00.

Herb Society of America
300 Massachusetts Ave.
Boston, MA 02115

Organization devoted to promoting the culture of herbs. A pamphlet, *Herb Buyers Guide,* available for 50¢.

Home Orchard Society
2511 S.W. Miles St.
Portland, OR 97219

An organization to promote the culture of fruit-bearing plants and to preserve historic varieties. Newsletter available.

International Association for Education, Development and Distribution of Lesser Known Food Plants and Trees
P.O. Box 599
Lynwood, CA 90262

The association is concerned with introducing new food plants into cultivation to help alleviate world hunger. Newsletter available.

International Tree Crops Institute
California office:
Box 1272
Winters, CA 95695

Kentucky office:
Rte. 1
Gravel Switch, KY 40328

This institute is interested in the research and promotion of multipurpose tree crops for agriculture and conservation.

National Audubon Society
950 Third Ave.
New York, NY 10022

A venerable organization devoted to the study and preservation of birds.

National Wildlife Federation
1412 16th St., N.W.
Washington, DC 20036

This national organization is devoted to the preservation of wildlife.

New York State Fruit Testing Cooperative Association
Geneva, NY 14456

The association provides information about old and new varieties of hardy fruits. It also has trees for sale.

North American Fruit Explorers
c/o Henry Converse
1848 Jennings Dr.
Madisonville, KY 42431

Members of the Fruit Explorers exchange ideas about fruit growing. Newsletter available.

Northern Nut Growers
4518 Holston Hills Rd.
Knoxville, TN 37914

An excellent source of information on nut growing.

Save The Tallgrass Prairie, Inc.
4101 W. 54th Terr.
Shawnee Mission, KS 66205

This organization is interested in reestablishing prairies. It is also a source of prairie seed.

Seed Savers Exchange
c/o Kent Whealy
R.R. 2
Princeton, MO 64673

Seed Savers is dedicated to preserving heirloom vegetable varieties. Newsletter and seeds available.

Sierra Club
530 Bush St.
San Francisco, CA 94108

A national organization devoted to conservation causes.

Publications

The following publications provide up-to-date and in-depth information on food growing.

The Avant Gardener
P.O. Box 489
New York, NY 10028

Marvelous potpourri of gardening information. Published twice monthly. Subscription rate: $15.00 a year. The goal of the magazine is to provide up-to-date gardening information.

Environment
4000 Albemarle St., N.W.
Washington, DC 20016

Published monthly, except bimonthly Jan./Feb. and July/Aug. Subscription rate: $12.50 a year. The magazine explores environmental issues, from nuclear power to pesticides.

The Family Food Garden
1818 Garden Court
Marion, OH 43302

Address Customer Service Dept. for subscription. Rates: $7.95 for one year (10 issues). A marvelous resource for families who want to grow their own food.

Organic Gardening
33 East Minor St.
Emmaus, PA 18049

Published monthly. Subscription rates: one year, $10.00. The publishers of this magazine have been one of the motivating forces behind the organic gardening movement. The monthly magazine carries articles on organic methods of food production and pest control.

Sunset Magazine
Menlo Park, CA 94025

Published monthly. Subscription rates: one year, $10.00 or $14.00 depending on state. This "magazine of western living" emphasizes travel, interior decoration, cooking, and gardening.

GLOSSARY OF TECHNICAL TERMS

Acid soil. A soil with a pH of less than 7.0. Soil bacteria and most plant growth are inhibited in a soil high in acidity. Some plants thrive in it, however; for instance, blueberries and azaleas. Acid soils are usually associated with rainy climates. Acid soils are low in limestone, and limestone is applied to reduce acidity (raise pH). See *pH.*

Alkaline soil. A soil with a pH of more than 7.0. Strongly alkaline soils are harmful to plants. They are associated with arid or desert conditions. Jujube and pomegranate are edibles able to grow in strongly alkaline soils. See *pH.*

Annual. A plant that grows, flowers, sets fruit, makes seeds, then dies—all in one season. Many vegetables are annuals—for example, peas, corn, and squash.

Auxin. A type of plant hormone, natural or synthetic. Auxins affect cell enlargement, branching, root development, fruit development, and fruit set.

Bare root. A term used for plants that are sold without their roots in soil. These trees, shrubs, or perennials are usually deciduous and are dug up while they are dormant. This is the least expensive and usually the healthiest way to buy deciduous fruit trees and shrubs. Most types of stone fruits, cane berries, asparagus, and artichokes are sold this way.

Biennial. A plant that requires two growing seasons to flower. The first year only leaves develop; the second year the plant flowers, makes seed, and dies. Parsley is a biennial.

Biological control. Pest control by natural means, such as parasites, predators, or disease organisms, instead of chemicals. For example, importing lacewing larvae to a yard, instead of spraying malathion, is a biological means of controlling aphids.

Budding. See *Grafting.*

Chelate. An organic agent which, when added to certain plant nutrients such as iron, aids in making these nutrients available to the plant.

Chilling requirement. Many fruit trees, bulbs, and herbaceous perennials need a certain number of hours under 45° F. before they will break dormancy, grow, bloom, and fruit. The number of hours can vary from 400 to 2000 for different plants. Gardeners must choose types and varieties of plants with this requirement in mind. If a plant has a low chilling factor it can be grown in a mild winter climate; a plant with a high chilling factor is used in a location with harsh winters. Local nurseries usually carry the plants for their areas; some research is needed when you order by mail.

Chlorosis. A general term referring to a loss of chlorophyll in plant foliage, resulting in a yellowing of the leaves. Lack of nitrogen or iron can cause this condition. Iron deficiency is usually signified by pale yellow leaves with darker veins. Iron chlorosis is usually treated with chelated iron or iron sulfate applied to the soil, or in some formulations as a foliage spray. Many herbicides restrict the production of chlorophyll and create a chlorotic condition.

Deciduous. Plants that lose their leaves all in one season, every year. Most temperate zone fruit trees are deciduous.

Dethatching. A vertical mowing process for removing thatch from a lawn. It is best done in the fall after the hot weather is over. Good lawn cultural practices eliminate the need for dethatching.

Dormant spray. A chemical applied in late fall, winter, or early spring, when the plants are dormant. It is one of the most effective controls of fungus diseases and some pests. See *Fungicide.*

Drought tolerance. The ability of a plant to survive under water stress conditions. Plants have different mechanisms to help them live through drought conditions: some go dormant; some take up water more efficiently; some, like cacti, adapt to low water supplies, others escape by living only through the rainy season. Pomegranate, olive, and fig are drought-tolerant edibles.

Espalier. The art, dating from medieval times, of training a tree, shrub, or vine in a flat plane. Many plants can be trained in this way, against a wall or a fence or as a free-standing divider. Various forms are shown in Chapter 5.

Evergreen. Plants that retain their leaves or needles for more than one season. Examples of some evergreen edibles are citrus, carob, tea, avocado, and piñon pine.

Fungicide. A chemical used to control fungus diseases, such as mildew and apple scab. Some of the most effective fungicides are applied when the plant is dormant.

Genetic dwarf. A plant that is naturally dwarf; in contrast to induced dwarfs, which are dwarfed by grafting or budding a standard fruit tree on dwarfing rootstock. See *Grafting and budding.*

Grafting and budding. A means of attaching a preferred plant (the scion) to a rootstock (understock) so the resulting plant gives the flower or fruit desired, with the advantage of roots that withstand more types of stress. It is also practiced for dwarfing. Budding is a special kind of grafting.

Groundwater. Water under the surface of the earth. It is in a saturated layer that supplies wells and springs. In some areas the groundwater is near the surface, and in others it is down very deep.

Hardy. Term to describe plants able to winter over without artificial protection. The term is generally used for plants that survive severe winters.

Herbaceous. Soft plants, as contrasted to woody plants. Herbaceous plants are generally annuals but some are perennials. Herbaceous perennials usually die to the ground each year. Examples are artichoke, chives, and rhubarb.

Herbicide. A chemical used to kill weeds. Some herbicides act on contact with the leaf surface; others are taken up through the roots of the weed. Some are selective; others kill most plants.

Humus. The end product of the decomposition of organic materials, best exemplified by forest duff. Composting is a gardener's method of developing humus. Humus is an important soil addition to help keep bacterial and other microorganism activity high, to add to the general fertility of the soil, and to improve soil structure.

Hybrid. Term to describe a plant that results from the crossing of parent plants differing in one or more genes. Plant hybridization aims at increased productivity, flavor, and disease resistance, as well as size and floriferousness of ornamental plants. Seed from hybrid plants will usually not "come true" (be identical to its parents), so it is not saved for another year. Most modern vegetable seeds are hybrids. By law, hybrid seed must be identified as such in catalogs.

IPM (integrated pest management). A process of controlling pest populations by monitoring; timing pest treatment to be most effective and least damaging to natural controls; and using selective, not broad-spectrum, pesticides.

Liming. A process of "sweetening" the soil—that is, reducing its acidity. For most plants, if a soil has a pH below 6, a soil conditioner, usually dolomitic limestone, is added. Sometimes your county agricultural agent can do a soil test to determine if you need it. Soil testing kits are also available. Acidic soils are associated with rainy climates; soils in arid climates rarely need liming. To determine the dosage follow the instructions on the package.

Microclimate. The climate specific to a small local area, such as your yard or a small part of your yard. Your yard may have either a cold or a warm microclimate, depending on sun, wind protection, or position on a slope.

Mulch. A cover that is put over soil to lessen evaporation, maintain even temperature, and keep down weeds. Mulches can be organic—grass, hay, leaves, wood chips, etc.; when decomposed, these can add humus to the soil. Mulches can also be inorganic—aluminum foil or plastic, for example—keeping weeds down but adding nothing to the soil.

Multistemmed. A shrub or tree that is trained to more than one trunk to make it more decorative. A number of young trees can be placed in one prepared hole to achieve the same effect.

Perennial. A plant that lives for an indefinite number of years. The term usually refers to herbaceous plants; strictly speaking it includes all woody plants as well. Examples of edible perennials are artichokes, asparagus, and rhubarb.

pH. An index denoting the acidity or alkalinity of biological systems. The logarithmic scale runs from 0, acid, to 14, alkaline, with 7 being neutral. For gardeners pH is a soil factor to consider when choosing plants. Most plants grow well in a range of 5.5–7.0. The pH of most garden soils falls within this range.

Pollination. A necessary part of the fertilization process, whereby pollen from the stamens, the male flower parts, is transferred to the pistil, the female flower part. Pollination is accomplished naturally by the wind, bees, and other insects. Some plants, instead of having male and female organs on the same plant, have separate female and male plants—kiwi, for instance—so both plants are always necessary for fruit to develop. Other plants, such as 'Bing' cherries, have to be pollinated by another variety of cherry tree, because though the male and female organs are both present, the pollen of the 'Bing' is dissipated before the pistil is ready to receive it.

Self-fertile. A plant able to pollinate itself and produce fruit without another plant of the same species nearby. Also called self-fruitful or self-pollinating.

Self-sterile. A plant unable to pollinate itself; it must have cross-pollination from another plant or another variety. For example, 'Bing' cherry needs another variety, such as 'Van', for pollination and fruit set.

Solar energy. Energy that uses the sun's rays. If you plan to use solar energy for heating and cooling your house, the placement of trees will be a factor in your landscape plan. Solar energy should be used for greenhouse or pool heating.

South wall. A south-facing wall; the warmest wall for plants that need heat and sun.

Spur. Short, specialized twig on which some fruit trees, such as apples and pears, bear their blossoms and fruit.

Stone fruits. A group of commonly grown fruits, known as drupes, that have a stony covering over the seed; includes apricots, cherries, nectarines, peaches and plums.

Sucker. Growth originating from rootstock or underground stems. On a grafted plant the suckers from the root growth will take over the plant if not removed. Some plants sucker more readily than others; pawpaws and jujube sucker heavily and can form new plants in that way.

Taproot. A large central root that grows straight down from the crown. Some plants have a fibrous, spread-out root system, others a strong central taproot. Plants with taproots are usually quite drought resistant, but they transplant poorly. Most nut trees have taproots.

Tender. A term to describe plants unable to withstand low winter temperatures.

Thatch. A spongy-looking intermingled layer of dead and living roots and stems that develop in lawns between the zone of green grass and the soil surface. Excess thatch in a lawn prevents water from penetrating the root zone; is an ideal breeding zone for many lawn diseases; and makes lawn grasses more susceptible to drought, heat, and low-temperature stress. The best biological control of thatch is top dressing with a light soil compost mix and not overstimulating the lawn with nitrogen. Some types of grass are more prone to produce thatch—for instance, 'Merion' bluegrass, 'Tifgreen' bermuda grass, bentgrass, and red fescue.

Thinning. A term with a number of horticultural meanings, including reducing the number of plants in a seed bed so there are not too many of them competing for the available nutrients and moisture. Also, reducing the number of immature fruits on a branch so the remaining fruit will be larger, or removing fruits from trees, such as some peach trees, that are inclined to overbear. In pruning terms, thinning means reducing the number of branches.

Topiary. The practice of shearing and pruning a plant to make unnatural geometric or fanciful shapes.

Windward. The side from which the wind blows.

General Information

American Society of Landscape Architects Foundation. *Landscape Planning for Energy Conservation.* Charles McClenon, ed. Reston, VA.: Environmental Design Press, 1977.

Bailey, L. H., and staff. *Hortus Third.* New York: Macmillan Publishing Co., 1976.

> This 1300-page book is a basic reference for horticulturists. The Latin names and botanical descriptions used in this book are based on *Hortus Third.*

Bienz, Darrel R. *The Why and How of Home Horticulture.* San Francisco: W. H. Freeman and Co., 1980.

> A comprehensive collection of information needed for the average home gardener. The book covers basic botany, plant propagation, and growing techniques. It also includes information on how to preserve harvests and landscape planning. An excellent supplement to this text.

Bottrell, Dale R. *Integrated Pest Management.* Washington, D.C.: Council on Environmental Quality, U.S. Government Printing Office, 1979.

> A comprehensive look at pest control in the United States with an emphasis on the potential for the use of integrated pest management.

Brady, Nyle C. *The Nature and Properties of Soils.* 8th ed. New York: Macmillan Publishing Co., 1974.

> A basic textbook on soils. Valuable for serious gardeners.

Brooklyn Botanic Garden Handbooks. Brooklyn, NY: Brooklyn Botanic Garden.

> Each of the following particularly helpful handbooks discusses one subject thoroughly. They are available for a charge from Brooklyn Botanic Garden, 1000 Washington Ave., Brooklyn, NY 11225.
>
> *Biological Control of Plant Pests,* no. 34.
> *Creative Ideas in Garden Design,* no. 21.
> *Ground Covers and Vines,* no. 34.
> *The Environment and the Home Gardener,* no. 39.
> *Dye Plants and Dyeing.*
> *Natural Plant Dyeing.*

California Fertilizer Association, Soil Improvement Committee. *Western Fertilizer Handbook.* 4th ed. Sacramento, CA: California Fertilizer Association, 1973.

> Very technical, complete information on fertilization of plants, including symptoms of nutrient deficiencies. Emphasis is on agriculture, not home gardens.

Campbell, Stu. *Let It Rot!: The Home Gardener's Guide to Composting.* Charlotte, VT: Garden Way Publishing, 1975.

> Complete book on composting, including ways to compost in a limited space.

Carr, Anna. *Rodale's Color Handbook of Garden Insects.* Emmaus, PA: Rodale Press, 1979.

> 300 color close-ups of insects. Valuable for identifying insects, good and bad.

Creekmore, Hubert. *Daffodils are Dangerous.* New York: Walker & Co., 1966.

> Detailed information on many poisonous garden plants.

Crockett, James. *Crockett's Tool Shed.* Boston: Little, Brown & Co., 1979.

> A comprehensive book on garden tools. Specific brands of tools are discussed.

Debach, Paul. *Biological Control of Natural Enemies.* Cambridge: Cambridge University Press, 1974.

> An in-depth discussion of biological controls—valuable for serious gardeners.

Farallones Institute. *The Integral Urban House.* San Francisco: Sierra Club Books, 1979.

> Extensive information on self-reliant living in the city. It includes suggestions for conserving water and energy, managing household waste, raising food plants and animals, and using solar technology. Rich in practical knowledge.

Hartmann, Hudson T., and Dale E. Kester, *Plant Propagation—Principles and Practices.* Third Edition. Englewood Cliffs, NJ: Prentice-Hall Inc., 1975.

> Detailed information on the propagation of plants from seed, by grafting, layering, and cuttings. 50 pages on specific propagation for edible species.

Janick, Jules. *Horticultural Science.* 2nd ed. San Francisco: W. H. Freeman & Co., 1972.

> Basic horticultural text. Covers the fundamentals of botany.

Jobb, Jamie. *The Complete Book of Community Gardening.* New York: William Morrow & Co., 1979.

> A valuable resource for people interested in community gardening. Information includes how to start and run a community garden.

Logsdon, Gene, and the editors of *Organic Gardening and Farming. The Gardener's Guide to Better Soil.* Emmaus, PA: Rodale Press, 1975.

Very helpful for composting, mulching, soil amendments, and cultivation.

Nehrling, Arlo, and Irene Nehrling. *Easy Gardening With Drought-Resistant Plants.* New York: Dover Publications, Inc., 1975.

Information on gardening with drought-resistant plants.

Organic Gardening Editorial Staff. *Lawn Beauty the Organic Way.* Emmaus, PA: Rodale Books, Inc., 1970.

A commonsense approach to lawn management without synthetic fertilizers and pesticides.

Ortho Books, Chevron Chemical Company Editorial Staff. San Francisco: Ortho Books, Chevron Chemical Co.

All About Fertilizers, Soils, and Water. A. Cort Sinnes, 1979.

A basic illustrated text on the complex subject of soil, fertilizer, and water management in the home yard.

All About Pruning, 1978.

A basic illustrated text on the pruning of ornamental and edible plants.

Garden Construction Know How, 1975.

Excellent basic information on how to build walls, fences, patio covers, decks, and how to lay paving. Excellent section on how to use recycled materials.

Pavel, Margaret Brandstrom. *Gardening with Color—Ideas for Planning and Planting With Annuals, Perennials, and Bulbs,* 1977.

A thorough discussion of the use of color in the garden. Heavily illustrated.

Powell, Thomas, and Betty Powell. *The Avant Gardener.* Boston: Houghton Mifflin Co., 1975.

Marvelous potpourri of gardening information, including suggestions for edible landscaping and native plant use.

Robinette, Gary O. *Plants/People/and Environmental Quality.* Washington, D.C.: U.S. Department of the Interior, National Park Service, and American Society of Landscape Architects Foundation, 1972.

This book provides detailed information for noise, pollution, and glare control in landscaping. Also gives details on placement of trees and vegetation to control heating and cooling in buildings.

Shantz, H. L. *Water Economy of Plants.* Santa Barbara, CA: Santa Barbara Botanic Garden, 1948.

Information on how plants use water, and how to garden under drought conditions.

Smith, J. Russell. *Tree Crops: A Permanent Agriculture.* New York: Harper Colophon Books, Harper & Row, 1978.

A classic in its field (original edition, 1950), providing information on chestnut, mulberry, persimmon, walnut, oak, and carob, among other trees. Permanent agriculture is suggested as an answer to hunger and environmental problems.

Sunset Books Editorial Staff. *New Western Garden Book.* Menlo Park, CA: Lane Publishing Co., 1979.

A comprehensive western plant encyclopedia. Zoned for all western climates. 1200 plant identification drawings; plant selection guide in color. Popularly known as the bible of West Coast gardening. Don't garden without it if you're in the West.

Taylor, Norman, ed. *Taylor's Encyclopedia of Gardening.* 2nd ed. Boston: The American Garden Guild and Houghton Mifflin Co., 1948.

A fine basic encyclopedia of gardening.

Thacker, Christopher. *The History of Gardens.* Berkeley, CA: University of California Press, 1979.

A comprehensive history of landscape gardening.

Ware, George W. *The Pesticide Book.* San Francisco: W. H. Freeman & Co., 1978.

Valuable information on insect control, both chemical and organic.

Landscaping Information

Brookes, John. *Room Outside: A New Approach to Garden Design.* New York: Penguin Books, 1979.

A good basic book on landscape design, with special emphasis on outdoor living space. Well illustrated.

Brooklyn Botanic Garden Handbooks. *Garden Structures,* no. 45. Brooklyn, NY: Brooklyn Botanic Garden.

A thorough discussion of how to use and build garden structures. This handbook is available for a charge from Brooklyn Botanic Garden, 1000 Washington Ave., Brooklyn, NY 11225.

Cotton, Lin. *All About Landscaping.* San Francisco: Ortho Books, 1980.

Highly illustrated information on how to plan and install home landscaping.

Fowler, Ruth S. *Landscaping That Saves Energy Dollars.* New York: David McKay Co., 1978.

Detailed information on how to plan your landscape to help save energy. A valuable addition to your library.

Gothein, Marie Luise. *A History of Garden Art,* Vols. I and II. New York: Hacker Art Books, 1966.

Originally published in German in 1914. This comprehensive study of garden art is considered a classic. It is useful for all students of landscape design.

Ireys, Alice Recknagel. *How to Plan and Plant Your Own Property.* New York: William Morrow & Co., 1975.

Complete plant lists and information for landscaping a small property—including approaches, garden rooms, terraces, paths, hedges, poolside and woodland sites—all practical, with low upkeep. Little or no information on edible plants.

Johnson, Hugh. *The Principles of Gardening.* New York: Simon & Schuster, 1979.

A delightful guide to the art, history, science, and practice of gardening. Very well illustrated.

Kuck, Loraine E., and Richard C. Tongg. *The Modern Tropical Garden.* Honolulu: Tongg Publishing Co., 1960.

A good basic text for Hawaiian gardens.

Lees, Carlton B. *New Budget Landscaping.* New York: Holt, Rinehart and Winston, 1979.

Many good garden plans to make the best use of your outdoor living area.

Nelson, William R. *Landscaping Your Home*. Revised edition. Chicago: University of Illinois Press, 1975.
One of the most detailed and helpful books on home landscape design.

Ortho Books, Chevron Chemical Company Editorial Staff. *Award-Winning Small-Space Gardens*. San Francisco: Ortho Books, 1979.
How to design gardens for balconies, rooftops, narrow side yards, corners, or any other limited space. The best ideas selected by the American Association of Botanical Gardens and Arboreta.

Reader's Digest, eds. *Reader's Digest Practical Guide to Home Landscaping*. Pleasantville, NY: The Reader's Digest Association, 1972.
Answers most common questions about landscaping, from height of benches to laying brick.

Saito, Katsuo. *Japanese Gardening Hints*. Tokyo: Japan Publications, 1969.
Practical information for homeowners who want a Japanese garden. One of the best on the subject.

Smith, Alice Upham. *A Distinctive Setting for Your House*. Garden City, NY: Doubleday & Co., 1973.
Good selection of different styles for landscaping your house.

Smith, Ken. *Western Home Landscaping*. Tucson, AZ: H. P. Books, 1978.
This book describes plants for western gardens, with emphasis on drought-tolerant plants and their culture. It includes excellent information on construction, as well as directions for installing drip irrigation and automatic sprinkler systems.

Sunset Books Editorial Staff. Menlo Park, CA: Lane Publishing Co.
Garden and Patio Building Book. 1973.
Specific construction information for fences, patio covers, decks, paving materials, walls, and pools.
Garden Pools, Fountains and Waterfalls. 1975.
How to install residential pools and fountains.
Homeowner's Guide to Solar Heating. Holly Lyman Antolini, ed., 1978.
Basic information on space heating and cooling, hot water heaters, pools, spas and tubs.
How to Build Fences and Gates. Donald W. Vandervort, ed., 1975.
Basic information on how to build fences and gates.
How to Build Walks, Walls, and Patio Floors. René Klein, ed., 1973.
How to lay brick, concrete, and flagstone; install retaining walls with used concrete, railroad ties, brick, and concrete.
Ideas For Japanese Gardens. Jack McDowell, ed., 1970.
Helpful information for Oriental gardens.
Lawns and Ground Covers. 1979.
Valuable list of lawn substitutes; planting techniques for ground covers; information on sprinkler systems.

Ideas For Small Space Gardens. 1978.
A number of designs for small yards.

Weber, Nelva M., *How to Plan Your Own Home Landscape*. Indianapolis: Bobbs-Merrill, 1976.
A helpful text on home landscaping.

Information on Edible Plants

Baron, Lloyd C., and Robert Stebbins. *Growing Filberts in Oregon*. Extension Bulletin 628, rev. ed. Corvallis, OR: Oregon State University Extension Service, 1978.
A valuable aid for growing filberts. Available for a charge from Oregon State University Extension Service, Oregon State University, Corvallis, OR 97331.

Bianchini, Francesco, Francesco Corbetta, and Marilena Pistoia. *The Complete Book of Fruits and Vegetables*. Translated from the Italian by Italia and Alberto Mancinelli. New York: Crown Publishers, 1976.
Magnificently illustrated book. Gives history of edible plants around the world and some basic botanical information.

Bianchini, Francesco, Francesco Corbetta, and Marilena Pistoia. *Health Plants of the World*. English adaptation (from the Italian) by M. A. Dejey. New York: Newsweek Books, 1979.
Beautifully illustrated book that gives medicinal information on many plants, including some edibles.

Bond, M. D. *Peanut Production Handbook*. Circular P–7. Auburn, AL: Alabama Cooperative Extension Service.
Extensive information on growing peanuts, including insects and diseases. Heavy on pesticides. Available from Alabama Cooperative Extension Service, Auburn University, Auburn, AL 36830.

Brooklyn Botanic Garden Handbooks. Brooklyn, NY: Brooklyn Botanic Garden.
Each handbook discusses one subject thoroughly. All are particularly helpful. Available for a charge from Brooklyn Botanic Garden, 1000 Washington Ave., Brooklyn, NY 11225.
Fruit Trees and Shrubs, no. 67.
Handbook on Herbs, no. 27.
Herbs and Their Ornamental Uses, no. 68.
Japanese Herbs and Their Uses, no. 57.
The Home Vegetable Garden, no. 69.

Bryan, John E., and Coralie Castle. *The Edible Ornamental Garden*. San Francisco: 101 Productions, 1974.
Information on many beautiful edibles. Includes culture and cooking instructions for many plants not usually considered edibles, such as lavender, juniper, calendula, birch, gladiolus, fuchsia, primrose, rose, and violet.

California Rare Fruit Growers. *California Rare Fruit Growers Yearbook*. 12 vols. Bonsall, CA: California Rare Fruit Growers, 1969–1980.
The yearbooks for this organization include valuable research

on many fruits grown in subtropical climates. Back issues are available.

Clark, John C. *The Pecan Tree.* Publication 475, rev. ed. Knoxville, TN: University of Tennessee, Agricultural Extension Service, 1975.

Extensive information on growing pecans in the East. Heavy emphasis on pesticides.

Clark, John C. *Quality Sweet Potato Production.* Publication 420, rev. ed. Knoxville, TN: University of Tennessee, Agricultural Extension Service, 1976.

Extensive information on growing sweet potatoes, including illustrations of disease problems.

Fletcher, W. A. *Growing Chinese Gooseberries.* Bulletin 349. New Zealand Ministry of Agriculture and Fisheries. Wellington, New Zealand: A. R. Shearer, Government Printer, 1976.

Extensive information on growing kiwis, including illustrations of diseases and information on varieties, pollination, pruning, pests, and diseases. For information, write to Ministry of Agriculture and Fisheries, Head Office, P.O. Box 2298, Wellington, New Zealand.

Gibbons, Euell. *Stalking the Wild Asparagus.* New York: David McKay Co., 1962.

Complete guide to edible plants in the wild.

Gilmore, Grant, and Holly Gilmore. *Growing Midget Vegetables at Home.* New York: Lancer Books, 1973.

Marvelous information on small varieties of vegetables. One of the best books on the subject. Good pest and cultural information, including drawings of helpful insects.

Harrington, Geri. *Grow Your Own Chinese Vegetables.* New York: Collier Books, Macmillan Publishing Co., 1978.

Extensive information on 38 Oriental vegetables, including many that are very ornamental, such as garland chrysanthemum, bitter melon, snow peas, Chinese celery cabbage, asparagus pea, Chinese eggplant, Chinese chives, Japanese parsley, day lilies, Chinese lotus, water chestnut, taro, and arrowhead. One of the best books on the subject.

Hill, Lewis. *Fruits and Berries for the Home Garden.* New York: Alfred A. Knopf, 1977.

The best all-around fruit-growing book for the East Coast. It offers extensive cultural information for the major fruits, identifies common diseases and pests, and offers pest controls that are largely organic. A must for eastern and midwestern home fruit gardeners.

Jaynes, Richard A., ed. *Nut Tree Culture in North America.* Hamden, CT: The Northern Nut Growers Association, 1979.

Up-to-date information on nut growing in the United States. A valuable resource for serious nut growers.

Jeavons, John. *How to Grow More Vegetables.* Palo Alto, CA: Ecology Action of the Mid-peninsula, 1974.

A primer on the biodynamic/French intensive method of organic horticulture.

Logsdon, Gene. *Successful Berry Growing.* Emmaus, PA: Rodale Press, 1974.

One of the best books on organic methods for growing small fruits. Primarily for eastern gardens.

Maxwell, Lewis S. *Florida Vegetables.* Tampa, FL: Lewis S. Maxwell, Publisher, 1974.

Valuable book for deep South vegetable gardeners. Many unusual varieties included, as well as descriptions of diseases prevalent in Florida.

Olkowski, Helga, and William Olkowski. *The City People's Book of Raising Food.* Emmaus, PA: Rodale Press, 1975.

All about food raising in the city, from vegetables to chickens. Helpful information on organic pest controls.

Organic Gardening and Farming Editorial Staff. *Unusual Vegetables.* Anne Moyer Halpin, ed. Emmaus, PA: Rodale Press, 1978.

The book discusses how to grow and where to obtain 79 unusual vegetables, including bamboo, prickly pear, jicama, tomatillo, Jerusalem artichoke, sorrel, and peanut. A valuable resource.

Ortho Books, Chevron Chemical Company Editorial Staff. San Francisco: Ortho Books, Chevron Chemical Co.

All About Growing Fruits and Berries, 1976.

Superior information on fruit-producing basics. Separate editions for different sections of the country.

All About Vegetables. Walter L. Doty, ed., 1973.

Excellent book on vegetable garden basics. Editions available for different sections of the country.

The World of Herbs and Spices. James K. McNair, 1978.

How to grow and preserve herbs. One of a series of well-illustrated, helpful books on gardening.

Puls, E. E., Jr. *Louisiana Citrus.* Baton Rouge, LA: Louisiana State University Cooperative Extension Service, 1979.

Extensive information on growing citrus in the South. Covers disease and pest problems in detail. Available from Publications Librarian, Room 192, Knapp Hall, Louisiana State University, Baton Rouge, LA 70803.

Ray, Richard, and Lance Walheim. *Citrus—How to Select, Grow, and Enjoy.* Tucson, AZ: HP Books, 1980.

A beautifully illustrated book covering all aspects of citrus growing.

Riotte, Louise. *The Complete Guide to Growing Berries and Grapes.* Charlotte, VT: Garden Way Publishing, 1974.

Extensive information on all types of berries and grapes. Includes drawings of most berry pests.

——— *Nuts for the Food Gardener.* Charlotte, VT: Garden Way Publishing, 1975.

Extensive information on the major nut varieties grown in the United States, including pecan, walnut, chestnut, filbert, almond, hickory, peanut, and pinon nut.

Seymour, John. *The Self-Sufficient Gardener.* Garden City, NY: Dolphin Books, Doubleday & Co., 1979.

Emphasis on deep-bed method of growing more food in less space. Production, not aesthetics, stressed.

Simmons, Adelma Grenier. *Herb Gardening in Five Seasons.* New York: Hawthorn Books, 1964.
> Extensive information on growing and harvesting herbs in the garden.

Simmons, Alan E. *Growing Unusual Fruit.* New York: Walker & Co., 1972.
> A must for fruit growers. Covers 100 different plants, including alpine strawberry, kiwi, custard apple, guava, jujube, kumquat, loquat, medlar, monstera, pawpaw, and prickly pear.

Southwick, Lawrence. *Dwarf Fruit Trees for the Home Gardener.* Charlotte, VT: Garden Way Publishing, 1973.
> Valuable information on dwarf fruit trees. A good addition to the home library.

Swenson, Allan A. *Landscape You Can Eat.* New York: David McKay Co., 1977.
> Good basic book for easterners in particular. Somewhat heavy on chemicals.

Underhill, J. E. *Wild Berries of the Pacific Northwest.* Seattle: Superior Publishing Co., 1974.
> Helpful information on edible and poisonous berries, including juniper, Oregon grape, gooseberry, service berry, wild strawberry, crabapple, rose hips, blackberry, salmonberry, mountain ash, arbutus, wintergreen, huckleberry, mountain cranberry, elderberry, and salal.

Wheatly, Margaret Tipton. *The Joy of a Home Fruit Garden.* Garden City, NY: Doubleday & Co., 1975.
> Landscaping with some of the Southwest's edible plants.

Wickson, Edward J. *California Vegetables in Garden and Field.* San Francisco: Pacific Rural Press, 1897.
> One of the classic books for California agriculture.

Will, Albert A., Eric V. Golby and Lewis S. Maxwell. *Florida Fruit.* Tampa, FL: Lewis S. Maxwell, Publisher, 1973.
> Filled with excellent information for tropical fruit growing.

Recipes and Food Preserving

Ball Corporation. *Ball Blue Book,* no. 29. New rev. ed. Muncie, IN: Ball Corp., 1974.
> A well-written manual for canning and freezing put out by the makers of Ball canning equipment. It may be ordered for a nominal charge from Ball Blue Book, Dept. PK–2A, Box 2005, Muncie, IN 47302.

California Avocados. *The Avocado Bravo.* Rev. ed. Newport Beach, CA: California Avocados, 1978.
> 50-page recipe book for avocados. May be purchased for a nominal amount from California Avocados, 4533 MacArthur Blvd., Suite B, Newport Beach, CA 92660.

Chandonnet, Ann. *The Complete Fruit Cookbook.* San Francisco: 101 Productions, 1972.
> Recipes for familiar fruits and some exotic ones—beach plums, buffalo berries, citrons, custard apples, gooseberries, guavas, kiwis, mayhaws, passion fruit, persimmons, prickly pears, roselles.

Crowhurst, Adrienne. *The Flower Cookbook.* New York: Lancer Books, 1973.
> An interesting collection of recipes for many different kinds of flowers, including capers, hops, and chamomile.

Hawkes, Alex D. *A World of Vegetable Cookery.* New York: Simon & Schuster, 1968.
> A very rich selection of 188 usual and unusual vegetables, with 500 recipes from Akee to Zucchini.

Lappe, Frances Moore. *Diet for a Small Planet.* New York: Friends of the Earth and Ballantine Books, 1974.
> A must for all cooks. How to feed your family while being less of a burden on the world's resources.

Ortho Books, Chevron Chemical Company Editorial Staff. *All About Pickling.* San Francisco: Ortho Books, Chevron Chemical Co., 1975.
> Extensive information on pickling.

Schuler, Stanley, and Elizabeth Meriwether Schuler. *Preserving the Fruits of the Earth.* New York: Dial Press, 1973.
> How to "put up" almost every food grown in the United States, in almost every way. A must for all foodscapers.

VanAtta, Marian. *Living Off the Land.* Melbourne, FL: Geraventure Corp., 1973.
> Recipes for many unusual vegetables and fruits, such as Surinam cherries, sea grapes, loquats, natal plums.

Wildflower and Native Plant Information

Brooklyn Botanic Garden Handbooks. *Gardening with Wild Flowers,* no. 38. Brooklyn, NY: Brooklyn Botanic Garden.
> How to incorporate wildflowers with your garden. This handbook is available for a charge from Brooklyn Botanic Garden, 1000 Washington Ave., Brooklyn, NY 11225.

Bruce, Hal. *How to Grow Wildflowers and Wild Shrubs and Trees in Your Own Garden.* New York: Alfred A. Knopf, 1976.
> Valuable cultural information, East Coast oriented, from an environmentalist's viewpoint. Includes an encyclopedia of wildflowers and their sources.

DuPont, Elizabeth N. *Landscaping with Native Plants in the Middle-Atlantic Region.* Chadds Ford, PA: Brandywine Conservancy, 1978.
> A good primer for gardening with native plants on the East Coast. Includes information on climate control, birds, and wildlife. Available from Publications, Environmental Management Center, Brandywine Conservancy, Box 141, Chadds Ford, PA 19317.

Lenz, Lee W. *Native Plants for California Gardens.* Pomona, CA: Day Printing Corp., 1973.
> Valuable text for California native gardens.

The New England Wild Flower Society. *A Guide to the Will*

C. *Curtis Garden in the Woods.* Framingham, MA: The New England Wild Flower Society, 1976.

Description of many New England native plants. Available from Garden in the Woods, Hemenway Rd., Framingham, MA 01701.

Santa Barbara Botanic Garden, Santa Barbara, CA.

A series of leaflets that cover a number of subjects about native plants in California. The titles are self-explanatory. Other leaflets are available; the prices vary. For more information, write to the Santa Barbara Botanic Garden, 1212 Mission Canyon Rd., Santa Barbara, CA 93105.

Native California Plants for Ground Covers, no. 9, 1953.
Native Plants for Erosion Control in Southern California, no. 11, 1967.
Native Plants for Southern California Gardens, no. 12, 1969.

Theodore Payne Foundation for Wild Flowers and Native Plants, Inc.: *Colorful California Native Plants.* Edward L. Peterson, ed. Arcadia, CA: California Arboretum Foundation, Inc., 1971.

A booklet available from the Foundation for a small charge. It includes color photographs of California natives, descriptions of landscaping uses, and information on how to plant. Available from Theodore Payne Foundation for Wild Flowers and Native Plants, Inc., 10459 Tuxford St., Sun Valley, CA 91352.

Supplementary Reference Material

All of the books mentioned previously were used in gathering material for this book. The following references are less useful to the individual home landscaper but were valuable resources for the author.

Beard, James B. *Turfgrass: Science and Culture.* Englewood Cliffs, NJ: Prentice-Hall, 1973.

A textbook for turf management. Emphasizes principles, decisions, and methods in turfgrass culture, and deals with environmental factors affecting turfgrasses.

Choudhury, B. *Vegetables: India—The Land and the People.* New Delhi: National Book Trust, India, 1967.

Cultural information on vegetables grown in India.

Council on Environmental Quality. *Environmental Quality—1979.* Washington, D.C.: U.S. Government Printing Office, 1979.

Up-to-date information on pesticides, toxic substances, energy, groundwater problems, conservation. For sale from Superintendent of Documents, U.S. Government Printing Office, Washington, DC 20402.

Harler, C. R. *Tea Growing.* London: Oxford University Press, 1966.

Basic information on tea growing.

Hoyt, Roland S. *Ornamental Plants for Subtropical Regions.* Los Angeles: Livingston Press, 1938.

A basic text for landscape designers. It has detailed lists of landscaping uses for a majority of ornamental plants grown in subtropical regions.

Jackson, Michael, ed. *The World Guide to Beer.* Englewood Cliffs, NJ: Prentice-Hall, 1977.

Comprehensive guide to beer-tasting and brewing.

Masefield, G. B., M. Wallis, S. G. Harrison and B. E. Nicholson. *The Oxford Book of Food Plants.* London: Oxford University Press, 1975.

Background information on a majority of the world's food plants. Superb illustrations.

Nobile, Philip, and John Deedy, eds. *The Complete Ecology Fact Book.* Garden City, NY: Anchor Books, Doubleday & Co., 1972.

Information on pollution, food supply, pesticides, and solid waste.

Pruthi, J. S. *Spices and Condiments: India—The Land and the People.* New Delhi: National Book Trust, India, 1979.

Cultural and usage information on the spices and condiments of India.

Singh, Rnajit. *Fruits: India—The Land and the People.* 2nd ed. New Delhi: National Book Trust, India, 1979.

Cultural information on fruits of India.

Stiles, Winthrop A., III. *A Landscaping Guide to Native and Naturalized Plants.* San Jose, CA: Santa Clara Valley Water District, 1977.

Valuable information on water needs of many landscaping plants. This bulletin is now out of print.

Ukers, William H. *All About Tea.* New York: The Tea & Coffee Trade Journal Co., 1935.

Basic book on tea growing.

University of California, Division of Agricultural Sciences, Berkeley, CA: Agricultural Sciences Publications, University of California.

Plant Growth Regulators: Study Guide for Agricultural Pest Control Advisers, 1978.

Basic information on plant growth regulators in California agriculture. Available from Agricultural Publications, University of California, Berkeley, CA 94720.

Study Guide for Agricultural Pest Control Advisers on Plant Diseases, 1972.

Basic information on plant diseases of agricultural plants in California. Available from Agricultural Publications, University of California, Berkeley, CA 94720.

Wharton, Edith. *Italian Villas and Their Gardens.* New York: Da Capo Press, 1976 (Original edition, 1903).

A classic of interest to garden historians. Helpful information on the history of landscaping.

NOTES

NOTES

NOTES